Legal Aspects of Planetary Defence

Studies in Space Law

VOLUME 17

The titles published in this series are listed at *brill.com/slaw*

Legal Aspects of Planetary Defence

Edited by

Irmgard Marboe

Assistant Editor

Cordula Steinkogler

BRILL
NIJHOFF

LEIDEN | BOSTON

Library of Congress Cataloging-in-Publication Data

Names: Marboe, Irmgard, editor.
Title: Legal aspects of planetary defence / edited by Irmgard Marboe; assistant editor, Cordula Steinkogler.
Other titles: Legal aspects of planetary defense
Description: Leiden; Boston: Brill/Nijhoff, 2021. | Series: Studies in space law, 1871-7659; vol. 17 | Includes index.
Identifiers: LCCN 2021027442 (print) | LCCN 2021027443 (ebook) | ISBN 9789004467590 (hardback) | ISBN 9789004467606 (ebook)
Subjects: LCSH: Hazard mitigation–Law and legislation. | Natural disasters–Law and legislation. | Disaster relief–Law and legislation. | Near-Earth objects. | Asteroids–Collisions with Earth. |
Comets–Collisions with Earth. | Space debris. | Space law–International cooperation.
Classification: LCC K1980 .L44 2021 (print) | LCC K1980 (ebook) | DDC 344.05/349–dc23
LC record available at https://lccn.loc.gov/2021027442
LC ebook record available at https://lccn.loc.gov/2021027443

Typeface for the Latin, Greek, and Cyrillic scripts: "Brill". See and download: brill.com/brill-typeface.

ISSN 1871-7659
ISBN 978-90-04-46759-0 (hardback)
ISBN 978-90-04-46760-6 (e-book)

This book is printed on acid-free paper and produced in a sustainable manner.

Contents

Foreword

Since its formation in the Solar System, 4.54 billion years ago, planet Earth has undergone numerous transformations and geological extreme events. Collisions characterise the Solar System. When Earth was in its earliest stage, a giant impact collision with a planet-sized body is said to have formed the Moon.

Studies often refer to the five main extinctions that the Earth went through. The most recent is the K-Pg extinction. 66 million years ago, a 10 kilometres asteroid struck Earth just off the Yucatán Peninsula and ejected vast quantities of particulate matter and vapour into the air that occluded sunlight, inhibiting photosynthesis. 75 percent of all life, including the dinosaurs, became extinct.

Another event, Tunguska, was a massive explosion that occurred near the Podkamennaya Tunguska River in Russia, on the morning of 30 June 1908. The explosion, generally attributed to the airburst of a stony meteoroid several tens of meters in size over the sparsely populated Eastern Siberian Taiga, flattened about 80 million trees over an area of about 2000 km^2 of forest.

More recently, the explosion of the Chelyabinsk meteoroid, an extra-terrestrial body about 20 metres in diameter that collided with Earth on the morning of 15 February 2013 in the Chelyabinsk region of Russia, produced a shock wave in the air that caused significant material damage in Chelyabinsk and several neighbouring towns, injuring more than 1200 people.

More than 40 impact craters with diameters larger than 20 kilometres have been confirmed on Earth, not to mention many more craters with smaller diameters, in total about 200 impact craters so far, which are evidence for the numerous collisions throughout the history of our planet with other small planetary bodies, all causing destruction on and changes of the Earth surface. Due to the development of sky observation technologies in recent decades and the increase in observation time, we have discovered more and more objects with potential impact on Earth and we have understood the seriousness of the problem.

Studies related to NEOS have intensified, national and international entities have been created to coagulate information, analyse it, and develop planetary defence techniques and technologies that, within a few decades, will be effective in deflecting the dangerous asteroids that threaten planet Earth.

I was a member of the Working Group initiated in 2005 within the Association of Space Explorers (ASE) by astronaut Rusty Schweickart and later on led by astronaut Tom Jones that developed the document 'Asteroid Threats: A Call for Global Response' which was submitted to UNCOPUOS in 2009. As Chairman of UNCOPUOS between 2010 and 2012, I supported and promoted this document, which ultimately led to the creation of IAWN and SMPAG in 2014, as global mechanisms for coordinating action in planetary defence, endorsed by the UN General Assembly.

'Asteroid Day' is a global awareness campaign where people from around the world come together to learn about asteroids and how we can protect our planet. On behalf of ASE, in 2016, I proposed the recognition by the UN General Assembly of 'Asteroid Day' as an international event. It was endorsed in December 2016 by resolution A/RES/71/90.

This book deals with a wide range of issues, which must be considered in the context of the legal aspects of planetary defence. A better understanding of the interaction of scientific and legal expertise is essential for preparing against potential NEO impacts.

Dumitru-Dorin Prunariu, PhD
Cosmonaut,
Former chairman of UNCOPUOS (2010–2012),
Former president of ASE (2011–2014)

Acknowledgements

This book is the result of a cooperative process that started within the Space Mission Planning Advisory Group (SMPAG) under the auspices of the United Nations. Many thanks are due to the longstanding SMPAG Chairman Gerhard Drolshagen (European Space Agency) and the Secretary Romana Kofler (UNOOSA) as well as the coordinators of the SMPAG Ad-hoc Working Group on Legal Issues, Line Drube (then DLR, now Danish Technical University) and Alissa Haddaji (Harvard University). They and many other members of SMPAG and of the Ad-hoc Working Group generously agreed to contribute to the present volume and delve in more detail into the issues raised in the discussions and in the 2020 Report. I am also deeply grateful to the additional authors who accepted the invitation and dedicated a lot of time outside their demanding professional duties to do in-depth research and put forward important additional considerations on legal aspects of planetary defence. All the authors successfully endeavoured to reach the high academic level required for a book published in the prestigious series 'Studies in Space Law' edited by Frans von der Dunk for which the publisher Brill/Nijhoff and its dedicated staff deserve our sincere gratitude.

At the University of Vienna, Cordula Steinkogler provided invaluable input and support in the publication process as assistant editor. She diligently accompanied the dialogue with authors to ensure consistency in structure and contents and to avert potential contradictions and overlaps. Many thanks also go to the research assistants Felicia Schartner and Stephanie Stipsits for their dedication in ensuring complete referencing as well as uniform spelling and writing style. The activities in the area of space law at the University of Vienna have been generously supported by the Austrian Federal Ministry for Climate Action, Environment, Energy, Mobility, Innovation and Technology as well as the Austrian Research Promotion Agency, which enabled the development of expertise and the building up of a team of academics and students to fulfil the tasks of the National Point of Contact for Space Law (NPOC Space Law) in Austria for the European Centre for Space Law (ECSL). This book is one of the results of the long-term engagement in the area of space law at the University of Vienna and is dedicated to the further development of international coordination and cooperation in the peaceful exploration and use of outer space for the benefit of humankind.

Irmgard Marboe (Editor)

Figures and Tables

Figures

Tables

Acronyms and Abbreviations

ADRC	Asteroid Deflection Research Collaboration
AEM	Agencia Espacial Mexicana
AIDA	Asteroid Impact and Deflection Assessment
ASAT	Anti-Satellite Weapons
ASE	Association of Space Explorers
ASI	Agenzia Spaziale Italiana
ATAP	Asteroid Threat Assessment Project
AU	Astronomical Units
Belspo	Belgian Federal Science Policy Office
CAFS	Close-Encounter Fact Sheet
Caltech	California Institute of Technology
CIL	Customary International Law
CNEOS	Center for NEO Studies
CNES	Centre national d'études spatiales
CNSA	China National Space Administration
CS	Canadian Space Agency
CSS	Catalina Sky Survey
DAMIEN	Detecting and Mitigating the Impact of Earth-bound Near-Earth Objects
DART	Double Asteroid Redirection Test
DESTINY+	Demonstration and Experiment of Space Technology for Interplanetary Voyage Phaethon Flyby Dust Science
DLR	Deutsches Zentrum für Luft- und Raumfahrt
DRDC	Defence Research and Development Canada
DSI	Deep Space Industry
EADP	Emergency Asteroid Defence Project
ECHR	European Court of Human Rights
ECSL	European Center for Space Law
ESA	European Space Agency
ESO	European Southern Observatory
FEMA	Federal Emergency Management Agency
FFG	Österreichische Forschungsförderungsgesellschaft
HAIV	Hypervelocity Asteroid Intercept Vehicle
IAA	International Academy of Astronautics
IADC	Inter-Agency Space Debris Coordination Committee
IAEA	International Atomic Energy Agency
IAU	International Astronomical Union
IAWN	International Asteroid Warning Network

ICJ	International Court of Justice
ICISS	International Commission on Intervention and State Sovereignty
IDPAG	Impact Disaster Planning Advisory Group
IEO	Inner Earth orbit Object
IISL	International Institute of Space Law
ILC	International Law Commission
ISA	Israel Space Agency
ISC	International Science Council
ISS	International Space Station
JAXA	Japan Aerospace Exploration Agency
JPL	Jet Propulsion Laboratory
JSGA	Japan Spaceguard Association
KASI	Korea Astronomy and Space Science Institute
LINEAR	Lincoln Near-Earth Asteroid Research
LEO	Low Earth Orbit
LSA	Luxemburg Space Agency
LSC	Legal Subcommittee
LWG	Legal Working Group
MAOG	Mission Authorization and Oversight Group
MOID	Earth Minimum Orbit Intersection Distance
MPC	Minor Planet Center
NASA	National Aeronautics and Space Administration
NATO	North Atlantic Treaty Organization
NEA	Near-Earth Asteroid
NEC	Near-Earth Comet
NED	Nuclear Explosive Device
NEO	Near-Earth Object
NEOMAP	Near-Earth Object Mission Advisory Panel
NEOO	Near-Earth Object Observations
NEOSM	Near-Earth Object Surveillance Mission
NEOSSat	Near Earth Object Surveillance Satellite
NEOWISE	Near-Earth Object Wide-Field Infrared Survey Explorer
NNWS	Non-Nuclear-Weapon State
NOAA	National Oceanic and Atmospheric Administration
NPD	NASA Policy Directive
NITEP	Near-Earth Object Impact Threat Emergency Procedures
NSTC	United States National Science and Technology Council
NWS	Nuclear-Weapon State
OCHA	Office for the Coordination of Humanitarian Affairs

OSIRIS-REx	Origins, Spectral Interpretation, Resource Identification, Security-Regolith Explorer
OSTP	Office of Science and Technology Policy
R2P	Responsibility to Protect
ROSA	Romania Space Agency
ROSCOSMOS	Federal Space Agency of Russia
Pan-STARRS	Panoramic Survey Telescope and Rapid Response System
PDCO	Planetary Defense Coordination Office
PHA	Potentially Hazardous Asteroid
PIERWG	Planetary Impact Emergency Response Working Group
PROCYON	Proximate Object Close flyby with Optical Navigation
PNE	Peaceful Nuclear Explosion
SGAC	Space Generation Advisory Council
SMPAG	Space Mission Planning Advisory Group
SMPAG LWG	SMPAG Ad-Hoc Working Group on Legal Issues
SSAU	State Space Agency of Ukraine
STM	Space Traffic Management
STSC	Scientific and Technical Subcommittee
SUPARCO	Space and Upper Atmosphere Research Commission
SWF	Secure World Foundation
SWSH	Subcommittee on Space Weather, Security, and Hazards
TBT	Test-Bed Telescope
UKSA	UK Space Agency
UN	United Nations
UNCOPUOS	United Nations Committee on the Peaceful Uses of Outer Space
UNDRR	United Nations Office for Disaster Risk Reduction
UNGA	United Nations General Assembly
UNISPACE	UN Conference on the Exploration and Peaceful Uses of Outer Space
UNL	University of Nebraska-Lincoln
UNOOSA	United Nations Office for Outer Space Affairs
UNSC	United Nations Security Council
UNTS	United Nations Treaty Series
UN-SPIDER	United Nations Platform for Space-based Information for Disaster Management and Emergency Response
US GAO	United States Government Accountability Office
VCLT	Vienna Convention on the Law of Treaties
WMD	Weapons of Mass Destruction
WG	Working Group

Legal Documents

Treaties

African Charter on Human and Peoples' Rights (adopted 27 June 1981, entered into force 21 October 1986) 1520 UNTS 217 (Banjul Charter)

Agreement Among the Government of Canada, the Governments of Member States of the European Space Agency, the Government of Japan, the Government of the Russian Federation, and the Government of the United States Concerning Cooperation on the Civil International Space Station (entered into force 27 March 2001) (ISS Intergovernmental Agreement)

Agreement Governing the Activities of States on the Moon and Other Celestial Bodies (adopted 5 December 1979, entered into force 11 July 1984) 1363 UNTS 3 (Moon Agreement)

Agreement on the Rescue of Astronauts, the Return of Astronauts and the Return of Objects Launched into Outer Space (adopted 19 December 1967, entered into force 3 December 1968) 672 UNTS 119 (Rescue Agreement)

American Convention on Human Rights (adopted 22 November 1969, entered into force 18 July 1978) 1144 UNTS 123 (ACHR)

Antarctic Treaty (adopted 1 December 1959, entered into force 23 June 1961) 402 UNTS 71

Charter of the United Nations (adopted 26 June 1945, entered into force 24 October 1945) 1 UNTS 16 (UN Charter)

Comprehensive Nuclear-Test-Ban Treaty (adopted 10 September 1996, not yet in force)

Convention for the Establishment of a European Space Agency (adopted 30 May 1975, entered into force 30 October 1980) CSE/CS (73) 19

Convention on International Civil Aviation (adopted 7 December 1944, entered into force 4 April 1947) 15 UNTS 295 (Chicago Convention)

Convention on International Liability for Damage Caused by Space Objects (adopted 29 November 1971, entered into force 1 September 1972) 961 UNTS 187 (Liability Convention)

Convention on the Prohibition of Military or Any Other Hostile Use of Environmental Modification (adopted 10 December 1976, entered into force 5 October 1978) 1108 UNTS 151 (ENMOD Convention)

Convention on Registration of Objects Launched into Outer Space (adopted 12 November 1974, entered into force 15 September 1976) 1023 UNTS 15 (Registration Convention)

Convention on Third Party Liability in the Field of Nuclear Energy (adopted 29 July 1960, entered into force 1 April 1968) 956 UNTS 251

Convention for the Unification of Certain Rules for International Carriage by Air (adopted 28 May 1999, entered into force 4 November 2003) 2242 UNTS 309

European Convention for the Protection of Human Rights and Fundamental Freedoms (adopted 4 November 1950, entered into force 3 September 1953) 213 UNTS 22 (ECHR)

Hague Convention No. VIII relative to the laying of Automatic Submarine Contact Mines (adopted 18 October 1907, entered into force 26 January 1910), 36 Stat. 2332 TS 541 (Hague Convention VIII)

International Convention on Civil Liability for Oil Pollution Damage (adopted 29 November 1969, entered into force 19 June 1975) 973 UNTS 3

International Convention on the Establishment of an International Fund for Compensation for Oil Pollution Damage (adopted 18 December 1971, entered into force 30 May 2006) 1110 UNTS 57

International Covenant on Civil and Political Rights (adopted 16 December 1966, entered into force 23 March 1976) 999 UNTS 171 (ICCPR)

International Covenant on Economic, Social and Cultural Rights (adopted 19 December 1966, entered into force 3 January 1976) 993 UNTS 3 (ICESCR)

Statute of the International Court of Justice (adopted 26 June 1945, entered into force 24 October 1945) 156 UNTS 77

South Pacific Nuclear Free Zone Treaty (adopted 6 August 1985, entered into force 11 December 1986) 29 ILM 1442 (Rarotonga Treaty)

Tampere Convention on the Provision of Telecommunication Resources for Disaster Mitigation and Relief Operations (adopted 18 June 1998, entered into force 8 January 2005) 2296 UNTS 5

Treaty Banning Nuclear Weapon Tests in the Atmosphere, in Outer Space and Under Water (adopted 5 August 1963, entered into force 10 October 1963) 480 UNTS 43

Treaty Between the United States of America and the Union of Soviet Socialist Republics on the Limitation of Strategic Offensive Arms (signed 18 June 1979)

Treaty for the Prohibition of Nuclear Weapons in Latin America and the Caribbean (adopted 14 February 1967, entered into force 22 April 1968) 634 UNTS 326 (Treaty of Tlatelolco)

Treaty on the Non-Proliferation of Nuclear Weapons (adopted 1 July 1968, entered into force 5 March 1970) 729 UNTS 161

Treaty on Principles Governing the Activities of States in the Exploration and Use of Outer Space, including the Moon and other Celestial Bodies (adopted 19 December 1966, entered into force 10 October 1967) 610 UNTS 205 (Outer Space Treaty)

Treaty on Underground Nuclear Explosions for Peaceful Purposes (adopted 28 May 1976, entered into force 11 December 1990) 1714 UNTS 387

United Nation Convention on the Law of the Sea (adopted 10 December 1982, entered into force 16 November 1994) 1833 UNTS 396 (UNCLOS)

Vienna Convention on Civil Liability for Nuclear Damage (adopted 21 May 1963, entered into force on 12 November 1977) 1063 UNTS 265

Vienna Convention on the Law of Treaties (adopted 23 May 1969, entered in to force 27 January 1980) 1115 UNTS 331 (VCLT)

UN Resolutions

Articles on the International Responsibility of State for Internationally Wrongful Acts, UNGA Res 56/83, Annex (12 December 2001)

Charter of Economic Rights and Duties of States, UNGA Res 3281 (6 November 1974) UN Doc A/RES/3281

Declaration on the Establishment of a New International Economic Order, UNGA Res 3201 (S-VI) (1 May 1974) UN Doc A/RES/3201(S-VI)

Declaration on International Cooperation in the Exploration and Use of Outer Space for the Benefit and in the Interest of All States, Taking into Particular Account the Needs of Developing Countries, UNGA Res 51/122, Annex (13 December 1996) (Space Benefits Declaration)

Declaration of Legal Principles Governing the Activities of States in the Exploration and Use of Outer Space, UNGA Res 1962 (XVIII) (13 December 1963) (Legal Principles Declaration)

Declaration on Principles of International Law concerning Friendly Relations and Co-operation among States in accordance with the Charter of the United Nations, UNGA Res 2625 (XXV), Annex (24 October 1970) (Friendly Relations Declaration)

Declaration of the United Nations Conference on the Human Environment, UNGA Res 2994 (15 December 1972), UN Doc A/RES/2994

Guidelines for the Long-term Sustainability of Outer Space Activities of the Committee on the Peaceful Uses of Outer Space, UNGA Res A/74/20 (20 August 2019)

Principles Governing the Use by States of Artificial Earth Satellites for International Direct Television Broadcasting, UNGA Res 37/92 (10 December 1982)

Principles Relating to Remote Sensing of the Earth from Outer Space, UNGA Res 41/65, Annex (3 December 1986) (Remote Sensing Principles)

Principles Relevant to the Use of Nuclear Power Sources in Outer Space, UNGA Res 47/68 (14 December 1992) UN Doc A/RES/47/68

Recommendations on National Legislation Relevant to the Peaceful Exploration and Use of Outer Space, UNGA Res 68/74 (11 December 2013)

Sendai Declaration, UNGA Res 69/283, Annex I (3 June 2015)

Space Debris Mitigation Guidelines of the Committee on Peaceful Uses of Outer Space, UNGA Res 62/20 (5 December 2007)

Universal Declaration of Human Rights, UNGA Res 217 A (III) (10 December 1948)

UNGA 'Report of the Conference of the Committee on Disarmament' UN GAOR 31st Session Supp No 27 UN Doc A/31/27 (1976)
UNGA Res 377(V) A (3 November 1950) UN Doc A/RES/377
UNGA Res 377(V), GAOR 5th Session Supp 20 (1950) UN Doc A/1775
UNGA Res 1348 (XIII) (13 December 1958)
UNGA Res 1472 (XIV) (12 December 1959) UN Doc A/RES/1472
UNGA Res 1721 (XVII) (21 December 1961) UN Doc A/RES/1721
UNGA Res 1802 (XVII) (14 December 1962) UN Doc A/RES/1802
UNGA Res 1962 (XVIII) (13 December 1963)
UNGA Res 46/182 (19 December 1991)
UNGA Resolution 62/217 (22 December 2007)
UNGA Res 68/75 (16 December 2013)
UNGA Res 71/90 (22 December 2016)
UNSC Res 1368 (12 September 2001) UN Doc S/RES/1368
UNSC Res 2177 (18 September 2014) UN Doc S/RES/2177
UNSC Res 2310 (23 September 2016) UN Doc S/RES/2310
UNGA Res 68/74 (16 December 2016) UN Doc A/RES/68/74
UNSC Res 2397 (22 December 2017) UN Doc S/RES/2397
1992 Rio Declaration on Environment and Development (12 August 1992) UN Doc. A/CONF.151/26 (vol. I), 31 ILM 874
2005 World Summit Outcome, UNGA Res 60/1 (16 September 2005) UN Doc A/RES/60/1

UNCOPUOS Documents

UNCOPUOS, 'Report of the Committee on the Peaceful Uses of Outer Space on its twenty-second session' (18 June–3 July 1979), UN Doc A/34/20
UNCOPUOS, 'Report of the Scientific and Technical Subcommittee on its forty-fourth session' (12–23 February 2007) UN Doc. A/AC.105/890
UNCOPUOS, 'Recommendations of the Action Team on Near-Earth Objects for an international response to the near-Earth object impact threat' (21 December 2012) UN Doc. A/AC.105/C.1/L.329
UNCOPUOS, 'Report of the Scientific and Technical Subcommittee of its fiftieth session' (11–22 Febraury 2013) UN Doc. A/AC.105/1038
UNCOPUOS, 'Report of the Scientific and Technical Subcommittee on its fiftieth session' (7 March 2013) UN Doc A/AC.105/1038
UNCOPUOS, 'Report of the Committee on the Peaceful Uses of Outer Space in its fifty-second session' (16 April 2013) UN Doc A/AC.105/C.2/2013/CRP.24
UNCOPUOS, 'Report of the Committee on the Peaceful Uses of Outer Space Affairs of its fifty-sixth session' (12–21 June 2013) UN Doc. A/68/20

UNCOPUOS, 'Final Report of the Action Team on Near-Earth Objects' (17 December 2013) A/AC.105/C.1/L.330

UNCOPUOS, 'Schematic overview of national regulatory frameworks for space activities' (17 March 2014) UN Doc A/AC.105/C.2/2015/CRP.5

UNCOPUOS, 'Report of the Committee on the Peaceful Uses of Outer Space on its sixty-second session' (12–21 June 2019) UN Doc A/74/20

International Documents

ASEAN Declaration on Mutual Assistance on Natural Disasters of 26 June 1976

Charter on Cooperation to Achieve the Coordinated Use of Space Facilities in the Event of Natural or Technological Disasters, UN Doc Rev.3 (25 April 2000)

Hague (International) Code of Conduct against Ballistic Missile Proliferation (adopted 25 November 2002) UN Doc A/57/724, Enclosure (HCOC)

ILC, Articles on the International Responsibility of State for Internationally Wrongful Acts, with Commentaries, 'Report of the International Law Commission on the Work of its 53rd Session' (23 April–1 June and 2 July–10 August 2001) UN Doc A/56/10

ILC, Draft Articles on the Protection of Persons in the Event of Disasters, with Commentaries, 'Report of the International Law Commission on the Work of its 68th Session' (2 May–10 June and 4 July–12 August 2016) UN Doc A/71/10

ILC, 'Survey on liability regimes relevant to the topic: International liability for injurious consequences arising out of acts not prohibited by international law: study prepared by the Secretariat, Extract from the Yearbook of the International Law Commission, vol II' (23 June 1995), UN Doc A/CN.4/471

ILC, 'Yearbook of the International Law Commission, vol II' (1973) UN Doc A/9010/Rev. 1

UNHCR 'General Comment No 36' (3 September 2019) UN Doc CCPR/C/GC/36 (General Comment No 36)

Notes on Contributors

(As of 12 April 2021)

Victoria P Andrews

is NASA's Deputy Planetary Defense Officer for Interagency Coordination, leading intergovernmental policy, planning, and cooperation efforts for the Planetary Defense Coordination Office (PDCO). Ms Andrews holds a bachelor's degree in anthropology from the University of North Carolina and a master's degree in science and technology policy from the Virginia Polytechnic and State University. She has worked on flight-system and instrument-development projects for NASA's human exploration programme and the Planetary Science Division. After leading an asteroid utilisation study for NASA in 2010, she became passionate about understanding, managing, and explaining the risk posed by near-Earth asteroids. Following stints at National Academies of Science and Engineering, Ms Andrews joined NASA in 2000, leading efforts to address public concerns related to NASA's use of space nuclear power. She currently co-chairs the NASA-FEMA Planetary Impact Emergency Response Working Group and serves as executive secretary of the National Science and Technology Council's Subcommittee on Space Weather, Security, and Hazards.

Setsuko Aoki

is professor of law at Keio University Law School, Tokyo, Japan. She is a specialist in public international law especially in space law, arms control and export control. She obtained a Doctor of Civil Law (D.C.L.) from McGill University, Montreal, Canada in 1993. She is a member of the Committee on National Space Policy (CNSP), Cabinet Office of Japan since July 2012 and chair of its security subcommittee since April 2017. She is also a member of the Japanese delegation to the Legal Subcommittee of the United Nations Committee on the Peaceful Uses of Outer Space (UNCOPUOS) since 2002.

Brent W Barbee

is an aerospace engineer in the Navigation and Mission Design Branch of NASA's Goddard Space Flight Center; he is also adjunct graduate faculty in the Department of Aerospace Engineering at the University of Maryland, where he teaches graduate courses in interplanetary spacecraft navigation and near-Earth object exploration. Mr Barbee supported flight dynamics for launch of the OSIRIS-REx asteroid sample return mission, which launched successfully on 8 September 2016, is the technical lead for NASA's Near-Earth Object

Human Space Flight Accessible Targets Study (NHATS), is managing work on the Double Asteroid Redirect Test (DART) mission at GSFC, conducts research on planetary defense against hazardous near-Earth objects (NEOs), and supports the NASA Headquarters Planetary Defense Coordination Office (PDCO). Mr Barbee is a recipient of NASA's Early Career Achievement Medal and the AIAA National Capital Section 2012–2013 Hal Andrews Young Engineer/ Scientist of the Year Award. He received his Bachelor and Master of Science degrees in Aerospace Engineering from the University of Texas at Austin.

Jack M Beard
is the co-director of the Space, Cyber & Telecommunications Law Program at the University of Nebraska College of Law. His primary fields for teaching and scholarship are public international law and national security law, with a particular emphasis upon space law, cyber capabilities, arms control, and the law of armed conflict. He previously served on the faculty at the UCLA School of Law, as professorial lecturer at the School of Advanced International Studies at The Johns Hopkins University, and as visiting professor in the Political Science Department at the US Naval Academy. He served as the Associate Deputy General Counsel (International Affairs) in the Office of the Secretary of Defense of the United States from 1990 to 2004. He is a graduate of the Georgetown University School of Foreign Service and the University of Michigan Law School and holds an LLM in International and Comparative Law from the Georgetown University Law Center. He is the chair of the Use of Force Committee of the American Branch of the International Law Association (ABILA), a member of the ABILA Board of Directors, and a member of the International Institute of Space Law.

Olavo de Oliveira Bittencourt Neto
is professor at the Catholic University of Santos, Brazil. He holds a bachelor's degree in law, as well as master's and PhD's degrees in international law from the University of São Paulo. He has a listed arbitrator for space related disputes at the Permanent Court of Arbitration (PCA). He was co-vice chair of the Hague International Space Resources Governance Working Group (2016–2019). Professor de Bittencourt Neto is member of the Brazilian delegations to the United Nations Committee on Peaceful Uses of Outer Space (UNCOPUOS), member of the International Institute of Space Law (IISL), having served as a director from 2013 to 2016, member of the Editorial Board of the Journal of Air and Space Law (Kluwer) as well as member of the Brazilian Association of Air and Space Law (SBDA). He served as point of contact for the Latin American Network of Universities and Institutions devoted to Space Technology, Policy

and Law (RELACA), and was guest lecturer and researcher at universities and institutions around the globe. He is the author and co-author of numerous publications in the fields of Space Law, Space Policy, International Law and International Relations. Major accomplishments include Grantee of the Coimbra Group Scholarship Programme for Young Professors and Researchers from Latin American Universities (2011) and of the International Astronautical Federation Emerging Space Leaders Grant Programme (2012), as well as recipient of the IISL Diederiks-Verschoor Award (2012).

Doris Daou
leads strategic and professional communications for NASA's Planetary Defense Coordination Office (PDCO). Ms Daou earned her master's in astronomy from the University of Montreal. She worked at the Space Telescope Science Institute (STScI), the NASA Infrared Processing and Analysis Center (IPAC), the NASA Lunar Science Institute (NLSI), and the NASA Solar System Exploration Research Virtual Institute (SSERVI) before coming to NASA Headquarters in 2012. She has 28 years of experience working on NASA missions. At SSERVI, she served as associate director and also acted as deputy director for international relations, working closely with foreign agencies on cooperation in NASA research and missions. She is an active member of the American Astronomical Society's Planetary Science Division, the International Astronomical Union (IAU), and the Lunar and Planetary Science Conference.

Gerhard Drolshagen
studied physics at the Universities of Giessen and Göttingen. He received his doctoral degree at the University of Göttingen in 1981. He was a post-doc at the Los Alamos National Laboratory in Los Alamos, USA and then a Scientific Assistant at the Max-Planck Institut für Strömungsforschung in Göttingen. In 1987 he joined the European Space Agency (ESA) at its Research Center ESTEC in Noordwijk, The Netherlands, where he worked until end of 2016, when he retired as a senior analyst in the Space Environments & Effects Section. He was involved in many aspects of the space environment, such as the analysis of surface and internal charging effects, ionising radiation, and atomic oxygen in the upper atmosphere. In later years the main emphasis of his work was on the study of meteoroids and space debris fluxes and their effects on orbiting spacecraft. Since 2009 he was co-manager of the Near-Earth Object segment of ESA's Space Situational Awareness Programme. This SSA-NEO programme addresses all NEO related aspects from observations, orbit calculation and predictions of potential impacts with Earth to the assessment of NEO mitigation options. From its creation in 2014 and until 2021 he was chair of

the Space Mission Planning Advisory Group (SMPAG) initiated by the United Nations, which assesses options to prevent the impact of a threatening object from space. Since 2017 he is supporting the new group on Space Environment Studies at the Carl von Ossietzky University of Oldenburg by supervising students and giving a lecture on the space environment. He also provides consultancy to ESA in the NEO field. Asteroid 332733 is named 'Drolshagen' to honour him as a driving force of the European NEO Programme.

Line Drube
was the coordinator of the Ad-hoc Working Group on Legal Issues of the United Nation's Space Mission Planning Advisory Group (SMPAG) on Near Earth Object (NEO) impact hazards from 2016, the year of its establishment, until 2018. She holds a PhD in astrophysics from the University of Copenhagen and was part of the operational science team on NASA's Phoenix Mars Lander during her doctoral research, where she analysed the surface material of Mars. Subsequently, she became interested in the surface of asteroids and planetary defence and took up a position at the German Aerospace Center, DLR, in the Institute of Planetary Research. There she worked in the EU-funded international NEOShield and NEOShield-2 projects researching the surfaces of asteroids and acted as the secondary coordinator of the NEOShield Consortium. She became a member of the German Delegation to SMPAG and assumed the task of the coordinator of the SMPAG's Ad-Hoc Working Group on Legal Issues. Since 2018, she has worked as a project coordinator for ESA's Swarm Mission at the Danish Technical University's Space Department and has helped to launch the Space Safety Institute there.

Steven Freeland
Emeritus Professor, Western Sydney University; Professorial Fellow, Bond University; Visiting Professor, University of Vienna; Permanent Visiting Professor, iCourts Centre of Excellence for International Courts, University of Copenhagen; Visiting Professor, Université Toulouse1 Capitole; Associate Member, Centre for Research in Air and Space Law, McGill University; Adjunct Professor, University of Hong Kong; Senior Fellow, London Institute of Space Policy and Law; External Examiner, Universiti Teknologi MARA (UiTM), Malaysia; Director, International Institute of Space Law; Member of the Space Law Committee, International Law Association; Member of the Space Law Committee, International Bar Association; Member, European Centre of Space Law.

Alissa J. Haddaji
is a faculty researcher and lecturer in Space Law, Policy and Ethics at Harvard University and a lecturer on law at Harvard Law School. She founded and leads the Space Consortium at Harvard & MIT. Since 2018, she is the coordinator of the SMPAG Ad-hoc Working Group on Legal Issues, where she also represents the Committee on Space Research (COSPAR). She is a Planetary Protection and Defense legal and policy consultant for the US Institute for Defense Analysis (IDA) and a guest-lecturer in Space Law, Policy and Space Anthropology at the International Space University (ISU). Dr Haddaji is a UNOOSA Space4Women Mentor, the COSPAR point of contact for the Space Generation Advisory Council (SGAC), a member of the International Astronautical Federation's (IAF) Near-Earth Object Committee and of the International Institute of Space Law (IISL). Prior to her Planetary Defense work, Dr Haddaji held the positions of senior researcher in Space Economics at Harvard Business School, of fellow in Science and Technology Studies at Harvard Kennedy School and of visiting researcher at the GWU's Space Policy Institute in Washington DC. She also served for four years as COSPAR's Planetary Protection Project Officer, where she co-authored and led the coordination of the International Planetary Protection Handbook (IPPH) and its subsequent trainings in America, Europe and Asia. She defended her first PhD dedicated to International Natural Disaster Management applied to Planetary Defense in 2019. She is currently finishing her 2nd PhD (remotely) at École Normale Supérieure (ENS), Paris, on International Space Politics and its social glass ceilings.

Alan Harris
is a senior scientist, retired, at the German Aerospace Center (DLR) Institute of Planetary Research in Berlin, and holds an honorary chair at Queen's University Belfast, UK. Professor Harris has pioneered radiometric data analysis techniques applicable to the study of asteroids. Derivatives of his Near-Earth Asteroid Thermal Model for calculating the sizes and albedos of asteroids have been incorporated into data processing pipelines used by NASA's NEOWISE project, and by researchers using NASA's WISE and Spitzer space telescopes, as well as other facilities. Professor Harris has authored or co-authored many peer-reviewed papers on asteroids and other astronomical research, and is lead-author of chapters in both the Asteroids III and Asteroids IV books published by the University of Arizona. He has served as chair of the European Space Agency (ESA) Near-Earth Object Mission Advisory Panel, as a member of ESA's Solar System Exploration Working Group, and as a member of the US National Academies Committee on Near-Earth Object Observations at Infrared and Visible Wavelengths. He was the coordinator of the European

Commission-funded NEOShield project and currently advises the German delegation to the UN-mandated International Asteroid Warning Network (IAWN) and Space Mission Planning Advisory Group (SMPAG). Professor Harris received his PhD and BSc degrees in physics from the University of Leeds, UK.

Henry Hertzfeld
is a research professor of space policy and international affairs at the Elliott School of International Affairs, Adjunct Professor of Law, and Director of the Space Policy Institute at The George Washington University, Washington, DC. He is both an economist and an attorney and specialises in research and teaching on legal and economic issues of space and high technology industries. He has been at The George Washington University since 1992. Previously Dr Hertzfeld has been an independent consultant and held senior positions at the US National Sciences Foundation and at NASA. He holds a BA in economics from the University of Pennsylvania, an MA in economics from Washington University, and a PhD in economics from Temple University. In addition he holds a JD from George Washington University and is a member of the Bar in both Pennsylvania and the District of Columbia. Dr Hertzfeld has authored numerous articles and monographs on topics that include: property rights and sovereignty in space, space law and the space treaty regime, commercial space, and the use of economic indicators for the space industrial sector. He has been a consultant to international organizations such as the OECD, various US Government Agencies and to private companies on space-related issues. He has also served as a private sector advisor to the United States Delegation to the UNCOPUOS meetings. He is a member of the International Academy of Astronautics, the International Institute for Space Law, the American Institute of Aeronautics and Astronautics, and the American Economic Association.

Rüdiger Jehn
has a degree in mathematics. He joined the European Space Agency (ESA) in 1989 and, until 2017, worked for the European Space Operations Centre in Darmstadt as Space Debris and Mission Analyst. He received his PhD in 1996 for his thesis 'Modelling Debris Clouds'. For more than 10 years he was in charge of running the space debris observations with the German Tracking and Imaging Radar. He was also responsible for the coordination of the observations of objects in the geostationary ring with the ESA 1-m telescope in Tenerife. In his function as mission analyst he designed the complex trajectory of 'BepiColombo' to Mercury. From 2017 to 2020 Rüdiger was head of ESA's Planetary Defence Office.

Lindley N Johnson

is NASA's Planetary Defense Officer and Program Executive of the Planetary Defense Coordination Office (PDCO). Mr Johnson graduated from the University of Kansas in 1980 with a bachelor's degree in astronomy and a commission from the US Air Force Reserve Officers Training Corps. He served 23 years active duty in the Air Force, obtaining the rank of lieutenant colonel and numerous awards and decorations while working on national security space systems. He also earned a master's degree in engineering management from the University of Southern California. After coming to NASA in 2003, he served as Program Executive for NASA's Deep Impact mission. He was then Lead Program Executive for NASA's Discovery Program of mid-class planetary missions for eight years. Mr Johnson became Program Executive for NASA's Near-Earth Object (NEO) Observations Program in 2003. Since then, efforts of the Program have discovered nearly 17000 near-Earth asteroids, about 90 percent of the total known. Mr Johnson has received NASA's Exceptional Achievement Medal. Asteroid 5905 (1989 CJ1) is named 'Johnson' to recognise his efforts in detecting NEOs.

Christian Koeberl

is full professor of geosciences (impact research and planetary geology) at the University of Vienna, Austria, as well as full member of the Austrian Academy of Sciences, and was from 2010 to 2020 director general of the Natural History Museum Vienna. He studied chemistry, physics, and astronomy, obtained his PhD in 1983, and his 'habilitation' in the geosciences in 1990. He had visiting scientist appointments at, among others, the Lunar and Planetary Institute and NASA Johnson Space Center in Houston, and the Carnegie Institution in Washington, and was visiting professor at Dartmouth College (New Hampshire) and the University of the Witwatersrand (South Africa), amongst others. His research deals mostly with impact craters, especially geochemical, mineralogical, and petrographic studies, and the early Earth, meteorites, and planetary geology. His publication record includes about 500 peer-reviewed scientific papers, many of which deal with impact craters; asteroid 15963 is named in his honour 'Koeberl'. Among other awards, he received the Barringer Medal of the Meteoritical Society for his impact research.

Romana Kofler

works as programme officer at the United Nations Office for Outer Space Affairs (UNOOSA), the Committee, Policy and Legal Affairs section. Her work includes supporting intergovernmental negotiations pertaining to space matters in the United Nations Committee on the Peaceful Uses of Outer Space (UNCOPUOS), its Subcommittees and Working Groups, including as the Secretary to the

Working Group on the 'Space2030' Agenda, a policy document negotiated by states for strengthening the use of space for global development. She serves as the Secretariat to the Space Mission Planning Advisory Group (SMPAG) and cooperates with the International Asteroid Warning Network (IAWN) in furthering international efforts to prepare to meet a potential threat to our planet by hazardous Near-Earth Objects (NEOs). She holds a bachelor's degree in International Relations – Political Science from the University of Ljubljana, Faculty of Social Sciences and a master's degree in Asia-Pacific and International Relations from the Hitotsubashi University, Tokyo, Japan. Romana joined the United Nations after successfully passing the Young Professionals Programme Exam. Prior to that, she worked as an Adviser to the parliamentary Committee on the EU Affairs in the Slovenian National Assembly.

David A Koplow

has been a professor of law at the Georgetown University Law Center in Washington, DC since 1981. His primary fields for teaching and scholarship involve public international law and national security law, with particular emphasis upon arms control, non-proliferation, outer space, and counter-terrorism. He has published five books and numerous law review articles regarding treaty negotiation, verification, and implementation, and regarding the intersection between international legal standards and US constitutional law. He has served in government as Attorney-Advisor, and as Special Assistant to the Director, at the US Arms Control and Disarmament Agency from 1978 to 1981; as Deputy General Counsel for International Affairs at the US Department of Defense from 1997 to 1999; as Special Counsel for Arms Control to the General Counsel of the Department of Defense from 2009 to 2011; and as consultant to NASA from 2018 to 2020. He is a graduate of Harvard College and the Yale Law School and was a Rhodes Scholar. He was a member of the Ad-Hoc Legal Working Group established by the Space Mission Planning Advisory Group (SMPAG) to investigate the legal questions associated with planetary defence, and he focused particularly on the issue of the deployment and use of a nuclear explosive device in space.

Detlef Koschny

has a PhD in planetary sciences from the Technical University of Munich, Germany. He has worked in industry and at a Max-Planck Institute in Germany before joining the European Space Agency in 1997. He was involved in many of ESA's planetary missions, mainly working in the field of science operations and the development of the scientific payload. His main focus there are cameras for space applications. Since 2008, he is involved in ESA's activities on Planetary Defence. Since 2020, he has been managing ESA's Planetary Defence Office.

Irmgard Marboe

is professor of international law at the University of Vienna. She is the head of the National Point of Contact for Space Law (NPOC) of the European Centre for Space Law (ECSL) and a member of the Austrian delegation to UNCOPUOS. Between 2008 and 2013, she chaired the Working Group on National Space Legislation of the UNCOPUOS Legal Subcommittee which led to the adoption of General Assembly Resolution 68/74 (Recommendation on national legislation relevant to the peaceful exploration and use of outer space) of 2013. Between 2009 and 2015, she was involved in the development of the Austrian Outer Space Act (2011) and the Austrian Outer Space Regulation (2015) as counsel for the Austrian Ministry for Transport, Innovation and Technology. Her publications on space law include the edited volumes *Soft Law in Outer Space – The Importance of Non-Binding Norms in International Space Law* (Böhlau 2012) and *Small Satellites: Regulatory Challenges and Chances* (Brill/Nijhoff 2016). From September 2014 to March 2015 and in February 2016, she was a visiting scholar at Stanford University (USA). In 2016, she received the Distinguished Service Award of the IISL. Further research interests include international investment law and arbitration, where she focuses on the issue of damages and compensation, and Islamic law.

Sergio Marchisio

is professor of space law at Sapienza University of Rome, General Counsel of the International Astronautical Federation (IAF), Chairman of the European Centre for Space Law (ECSL/ESA), Member of the Advisory Council of the European Space Policy Institute (ESPI). Since 2019, adjunct professor of international law at LUISS University and at UNINT University. Scientific responsible of two international research projects: OSL – Outer Space Law for International Cooperation and Sustainable Development, funded by the Italian Space Agency, 2020–22; HABITABLE – Linking Climate Change, Habitability and Social Tipping Points, funded by the European Commission (Horizon 2020 Programme, 2020–24). Author of over 250 scientific publications. Legal Counsellor at the Italian Ministry of Foreign Affairs and, since 1997, Italian Delegate to the United Nations Committee on the Peaceful Uses of Outer Space (UNCOPUOS); Chairman of the Legal Subcommittee (2004–06), and of Expert Group D of the Working Group on the Long-Term Sustainability of the Outer Space Activities. Member of the EEAS-EU Task Force for an International Code of Conduct on Outer Space Activities (ICoC) and Chair of the multilateral negotiations on an ICoC held in New York (2015). Member of the UN Group of Governmental Experts (GGE) on Outer Space Transparency and Confidence-Building Measures. Member of the UN GGE on Practical Measures for the Prevention of an Arms Race in Outer Space. Member of the Specialized Panel of Arbitrators pursuant to the Optional Rules for Arbitrations of disputes dealing with space matters of the Permanent Court of Arbitration.

Cordula Steinkogler

is senior researcher and lecturer at the Section for Public International Law and International Relations at the Law Faculty of the University of Vienna, where she has been working for the Austrian Point of Contact for Space Law since 2014. Previously, she worked for the Austrian Foreign Ministry, the Vienna School of International Studies and the United Nations Office at Vienna as well as in human rights organisations in Europe and Latin America. She studied law, communication sciences, anthropology, international relations and human rights at universities in Austria, Belgium, Ireland, Italy and Spain and undertook a research stay at McGill University in Canada. She is a member of the SMPAG Ad-hoc Working Group on Legal Issues, the International Institute of Space Law, the European Centre for Space Law and the International Law Association's Committee on Space Law. She is author of several scientific publications on various issues of space law and space policy and has been a member of the Austrian delegation to the United Nations Committee on the Peaceful Uses of Outer Space (UNCOPUOS) and its Subcommittees as well as several working groups since 2014.

Peter Stubbe

is head of the EU Affairs Department of the German Space Agency at DLR. Previously, he has been seconded to the Federal Ministry for Economic Affairs and Energy and was a German delegate to the European Space Agency and to the United Nations Committee on the Peaceful Uses of Outer Space (UNCOPUOS). He holds a master's degree in international relations and a doctoral degree in law. Peter Stubbe's research interests are in international space law, particularly responsibility and sustainability. He is a member of the International Institute of Space Law and the assistant editor of the Cologne Commentary on Space Law. He is also the author of a monography on international accountability for space debris and several international space law articles.

Alexander Soucek

is the head of the Public International Law Division at the European Space Agency (ESA) and ESA's leading expert on space law. Having joined ESA in

2004, he *inter alia* acts as the legal adviser to ESA's International Relations Committee, represents ESA in the United Nations Committee on the Peaceful Uses of Outer Space (UNCOPUOS), is responsible for the negotiation of international agreements and works with governments of ESA member states on national space laws. Alexander earned a master degree in law from Salzburg University, Austria, and a master degree in space studies from the International Space University in Strasbourg, France. He is an alumnus of the Hague Academy of International Law Centre for Studies and Research, and a former visiting researcher at George Washington University. He lectures on international law, space law and the law of international organisations at universities in Europe and beyond, and published books, commentaries and articles on the subject. He *inter alia* received the Social Sciences Book Award of the International Academy of Astronautics and two ESA awards of excellence. He is a corresponding member of the International Academy of Astronautics, a member of the International Institute of Space Law (IISL) and of the European Centre for Space Law (ECSL), and serves as a director of the World Space Week Association. He was a member of the executive board, and president, of the Austrian Space Forum.

Frans von der Dunk

is the Harvey & Susan Perlman Alumni/Othmer Professor of space law at the University of Nebraska-Lincoln's College of Law in the United States, as well as the director of Black Holes B.V., a consultancy company in space law and policy in the Netherlands, and Associate Professor of Research at Lazarski University, Warsaw, Poland. He defended his doctoral thesis in Leiden in 1998 on the subject of the legal frameworks for private space activities and has taught for over thirty years all possible subjects of international and national space law, including such issues as commercialisation and privatisation of space activities, at over two dozen universities across the world. He has published over 200 articles, book chapters and papers, as well as the first *Handbook of Space Law* (2015) and an *Advanced Introduction to Space Law* (2020); and he has spoken at or chaired sessions at hundreds of events world-wide. His public performances include TEDx and PINC talks and a number of TV documentaries and shows, radio shows and podcasts, and he has been interviewed by the media in dozens of countries. He has received *inter alia* the IISL Distinguished Service Award, the IAA Social Science Award and the IAA Social Science Book Award. He currently is member of the board of directors of IISL as well as of numerous other international committees and commissions.

Introduction

Irmgard Marboe

Planetary defence covers a range of scientific and technological activities to address potential impacts of Near-Earth Objects (NEOs) on Earth. NEOs are asteroids or comets that pass relatively close to the Earth's orbit in astronomical terms. While the probability of a large object impacting Earth is small, it could have catastrophic consequences of a global scale. Of the approximately 900000 identified asteroids in our Solar System, about 25000 are NEOs.

In recent years, space agencies and other institutions have increased their efforts in the detection and appraisal of hazardous NEOs and the development of strategies to prevent and mitigate potential impacts. Several missions to explore NEOs and to study technologies for deflecting asteroids are currently prepared and undertaken, such as the international Asteroid Impact Deflection Assessment (AIDA) experiment, which includes NASA's Double Asteroid Redirection Test (DART) Mission and ESA's Hera Mission, or the Japanese Hayabusa 2 Mission.

While these efforts have so far primarily concentrated on scientific research and technical aspects of mitigation measures, several legal questions also need to be answered. Some of the potential mitigation measures may raise concerns with respect to their legality under international law, most notably nuclear explosive devices (NEDs). In addition, states may be liable for the damage caused on Earth or in outer space in the course of a planetary defence mission. Furthermore, states are responsible for national space activities, even when they are carried out by non-governmental entities. Moreover, there are obligations under international law to share information and to take action in the event of potential threats endangering human life.

In view of the potentially global consequences of a NEO impact and the considerable resources required to prevent it, the United Nations Committee on the Peaceful Uses of Outer Space (UNCOPUOS) and the United Nations Office for Outer Space Affairs (UNOOSA) have been involved in awareness raising and in promoting international discourse and global cooperation on the topic of NEOs since the 1990s. The latest achievement in this respect is the establishment of the International Asteroid Warning Network (IAWN)and the Space Mission Planning Advisory Group (SMPAG)in 2013. While the former concentrates on scientific research and exchange of information on NEOs that may pose a hazard to the Earth, the latter is an international forum for proposing options and implementation plans for space mission response activities. In

 | DOI:10.1163/9789004467606_002

2016, an Ad-hoc Working Group on Legal Issues was founded in order to advise SMPAG with regard to legal aspects of planetary defence.

The work of the SMPAG Ad-hoc Legal Working Group has shown that many legal issues need to be taken into consideration in the preparation and development of a mission in response to a NEO threat. In accordance with its mandate, the Working Group concentrated on giving practical guidance to SMPAG. Beyond this particular mandate many issues require more in depth academic analysis, which is the objective of this book. Under current international law and international space law several legal aspects of planetary defence activities are not explicitly regulated so that the existing rules must be interpreted and applied with respect to the new situation of a NEO threat. In the future, more specific rules and guidance for actors may be necessary or useful. This book aims to influence and inspire discussions at the international level on the development and interpretation of the present and future legal regimes applicable to planetary defence activities.

Providing a forum for the discussion of legal aspects of planetary defence from an academic perspective this book puts together views and research results by authors from different disciplines and regions. As an independent scholarly endeavour it includes a broad range of ideas and opinions as well as proposals for solutions to open questions. Some of the authors have been active in SMPAG or in its Ad-hoc Legal Working Group, others have additionally been invited to increase the regional range and diversity of experiences and opinions. Part 1 is dedicated to scientific and technical aspects of planetary defence. Part 2 then delves into the variety of legal issues caused by human activity – or inactivity – in the face of the threat caused by a NEO. It concentrates on the obligations of states under international law in general and international space law in particular.

In Part 1, first, Christian Koeberl and Cordula Steinkogler prepare the ground by introducing definitions, characteristics, and basic terms related to NEOs and their impacts on Earth. They highlight that impacts of extra-terrestrial bodies are among the most spectacular, high-energy geological processes on Earth. While the probability of a large object impacting Earth is small, with an increasing size of the object there is also an increasing likelihood that its impact on Earth produces global effects, including mass casualties and destruction.

Rüdiger Jehn, in chapter 2, addresses the question "what is planetary defence?" at the example of past NEO impacts on Earth and their consequences. Referring to the Chelyabinsk impact of 2013 or the dinosaur killer 66 million years ago he highlights that, in contrast to other natural disasters, such as earthquakes, volcanos or hurricanes, NEO impacts may be averted. Planetary defence activities aim at using available space technology and other technical infrastructure to predict and mitigate them. In addition, the chapter provides a first insight to the classification of NEOs based on their orbits around the Sun. The most difficult to detect from Earth are the Atiras, the so-called Inner Earth orbit Objects (IEOs), because they always remain close to the Sun.

In the subsequent chapter, Alan Harris gives an overview of the various planetary defence technologies and the advantages and disadvantages of their application in different potential NEO impact threat situations. The most important distinction exists between impulsive techniques and slow push/pull techniques. The former aim at applying a strong, short-lived force to the NEO to cause a change in its orbit, or possibly intentionally break it up. The effect can result from a kinetic impactor, such as currently in preparation under NASA's Double Asteroid Redirection Test (DART), or from an explosive charge on or near the NEO that causes material to be ejected. The most powerful effect would come from the explosion of a nuclear explosive device (NED). However, the use of this technique is faced with a number of legal and political challenges, which stand against even the testing of this option. Slow push/pull techniques, such as the gravity tractor, laser ablation or the use of ion-beams, are less problematic in this regard but need a lot more time in advance of the estimated impact in order to ensure an effective result.

The chapter by Gerhard Drolshagen, Romana Kofler and Lindley Johnson is dedicated to international cooperation in planetary defence in the framework of UNCOPUOS, IAWN and SMPAG. It explains the unique role the United Nations and, in particular, the United Nations Committee on the Peaceful Uses of Outer Space (UNCOPUOS) have taken over in the area of space activities since the beginning of the Space Age in the 1950s. First attempts to increase awareness of and discuss the potential impact threats from NEOs date back to 1995, when the United Nations International Conference on Near-Earth Objects was organised in New York. The result from UNISPACE III, held in Vienna in 1999, was the establishment of the Action Team on Near-Earth Objects (Action Team 14), and later, following a recommendation of Action Team 14, the founding of the International Asteroid Warning Network (IWAN) and the Space Mission Planning Advisory Group (SMPAG). The former links together astronomical institutions active in the discovery monitoring and physical characterisation of potentially hazardous NEOs. Its functions include the communication of NEO hazards to political leaders, policy makers, emergency managers, and the general public. SMPAG, by contrast, brings together space agencies and offices of member states to discuss, plan and coordinate projects and techniques for the diversion or disruption of potentially threatening NEOs. The ultimate goal is to build consensus on recommendations for planetary defence measures at the international level.

Chapter 5 written by Frans von der Dunk deals with the enhancement of public awareness regarding planetary defence and the establishment of 'Asteroid Day'. He highlights that the Association of Space Explorers (ASE), the members of which are all former astronauts and cosmonauts, took the initiative to start a global asteroid awareness campaign. The main aim was to disseminate information about the threat and what could be done to protect the Earth and humanity as a whole. They drafted the 'Asteroid Day Declaration', which called for the adoption of an 'Asteroid Day', heightening the awareness of the asteroid hazard and the efforts to prevent impacts, on 30 June. The goal was ultimately achieved by formal endorsement by the United Nations General Assembly in 2016, inspiring numerous events worldwide since.

The United States planetary defence programme and the various missions undertaken in the field of planetary defence are presented in the chapter by Victoria Andrews, Doris Daou, and Lindley N Johnson. The authors provide insightful information on the DART (in collaboration with ESA's Hera mission and the Italian LICIA Cube) and OSIRIS-REx missions (designated to collect and return a sample from asteroid Bennu) as well as the importance of the results coming from space telescopes, such as NEOWISE (Wide-Field Infrared Survey Explorer) and NEOSM (NEO Surveillance Mission). In addition, the chapter addresses the importance of US interagency coordination and national policy development. NASA, in 2016, created the Planetary Defense Coordination Office (PDCO), which amongst others, established the Planetary Impact Emergency Response Working Group (PIERWG) with the Federal Emergency Management Agency (FEMA). At the example of 'table-top' exercises simulating asteroid impact threats and emergency management planning, a number of US agencies are involved, including FEMA, the Coast Guard, the National Oceanic and Atmospheric Administration (NOAA), state emergency response organisations, and the Department of Defense. Finally, the chapter explains the contents and goals of the 2018 US National Near-Earth Object Preparedness Strategy and Action Plan. It addresses the importance of timely international decision-making where there is considerable uncertainty with respect to impact probability and its possible effects. It shows that, in practice, the costs for a deflection mission would need to be weighed against the cost of recovering from the damage of the impact varying greatly with site and location of the impact.

Detlef Koschny gives an overview of the planetary defence work of the European Space Agency undertaken by the ESA Planetary Defence Office under the three pillars, (1) observations, (2) information provision and (3) mitigation. Survey observations aim at covering as large as possible an area in the sky, for which ESA is developing very wide-field telescopes, so-called Flyeye telescopes, one in Sicily, Italy, and one in Chile, hosted by the European Southern Observatory (ESO). To perform follow-up observations, ESA is using a variety of telescopes, such as the Optical Ground Station in Tenerife and the so-called Test-Bed Telescope (TBT). With respect to information provision, Koschny highlights the exchange of data with the Minor Planet Center (MPC), a world-wide clearing house of data on asteroids, funded by the United States. All objects with a probability greater than zero for impacting the Earth are placed on the so-called 'Risk List'. In the area of mitigation, ESA is preparing the Hera mission, cooperating with NASA's DART (Double Asteroid Redirection Test) mission as part of an international asteroid deflection demonstration collaboration, called AIDA (Asteroid Impact Deflection Assessment).

Finally, Brent Barbee introduces activities in the area of planetary defence beyond NASA and ESA, in particular Canadian, Chinese, and Japanese missions. The most recent success was the Hayabusa2 asteroid sample return mission conducted by the Japan Aerospace Exploration Agency (JAXA), which delivered its sample return capsule to Earth on 6 December 2020. The spacecraft is now on an extended mission to perform a high-speed flyby of asteroid 2001 CC21 in July 2026 and then rendezvous with asteroid 1998 KY26 in July 2031. China's Chang'e 2, after having completed its primary mission to collect data of the surface of the Moon for the creation of detailed lunar surface maps in 2010, was directed to proceed to a flyby of the Potentially Hazardous Asteroid (PHA) 4179 Toutatis. In December 2012 it passed within 3.2 kilometres of Toutatis and collected images of the asteroid. With the completion of the Toutatis flyby, China became the fourth spaceflight-capable nation to deploy a successful mission to an asteroid. The approaches of Luxembourg and Russia to planetary defence are also briefly addressed in the chapter.

Part 2 starts with an overview of international space law relevant to planetary defence activities by Steven Freeland. The chapter highlights that several foundational principles of the international law on outer space – for example, the so-called 'common interest', 'freedom' and 'non-appropriation' principles – represent a significant departure from the legal rules relating to air space, which is categorised as constituting part of the 'territory' of the underlying state. Other principles of international space law are also of relevance in the context of planetary defence activities, most importantly the liability of the launching state(s) of a space object for damage caused by that object, the international responsibility of states for national governmental and non-governmental space activities, as well as the principle of cooperation and mutual assistance in the exploration and use of outer space. Having been accepted by states in the early years of spaceflight after the launch of Sputnik 1 in 1957, they quickly became norms of customary international law and were codified in the UN space treaties in the 1960s and 1970s. Subsequently, a set of UN Principles on outer space was agreed upon in UN General Assembly resolutions which, even though not legally binding, also form part of the international framework in which planetary defence activities will have to be planned and implemented. Freeland concludes that it is necessary to develop specific and clear rules and standards that avoid a weaponisation of outer space as well as conflict in outer space in the context of planetary defence. While he doubts that a 'treaty'-approach will come to fruition in medium term, he still underscores the need to develop a regulatory framework for broad and effective measures to ensure that the Earth can be protected from major natural disasters caused by impacts of objects from outer space. Such a framework should strengthen cooperation in outer space and include states, space agencies, and private entities, in order to serve the interests of planetary defence to the benefit of all humankind.

Frans von der Dunk gives an overview of the history of international initiatives dealing with potential NEO threats in chapter 10. The Association of Space Explorers (ASE), consisting of former astronauts and cosmonauts, started the discussion about issues related to threats to humankind and the Earth posed by NEOs at its Annual Congress in 2005. It set up a Panel on NEO Threat Mitigation which produced a report entitled 'Asteroid Threats: A Call for Global Response' in 2008. The report, in its Annex III 'International Legal Framework', contained an overview about legal issues in this context. The University of Nebraska and the Secure World Foundation followed up with a research project on 'Legal Aspects of NEO Threat Response and Related Institutional Issues' which finalised its report and presented it to UNCOPUOS in 2010. The report offered seven recommendations on key issues to the international community. One of these concerned the establishment of a working group by the UNCOPUOS Legal Subcommittee (LSC), which, in close consultation with the Scientific-Technical Subcommittee (STSC), should further investigate, discuss and develop the other six recommendations presented as well as the various options mentioned therein. The author observes that in the decade since the report was presented in UNCOPUOS great progress has been made with respect to a world-wide acknowledgement of the need to address potential NEO threats and undertaking preparatory actions, including the establishment of IAWN and SMPAG now active under the auspices of the United Nations.

Line Drube follows up with a brief account of the final report of the SMPAG Ad-hoc Working Group on Legal Issues in chapter 11. In 2016, SMPAG established this Ad-hoc Working Group in view of its mandate in the subject area 'Legal and policy aspects', namely to identify, for possible detailed review within appropriate forums, any legal and policy issues (such as issues connected to liability) that may arise in undertaking NEO mitigation actions or selecting any likely mitigation options. The Working Group consisted of legal experts nominated by SMPAG members as well as some scientific and technical experts for technical advice. In February 2020, the report of the Working Group entitled 'Planetary Defence Legal Overview and Assessment' was presented to SMPAG, which approved it. Drube summarises the main findings of the report dealt with in the chapters 'Obligations to Inform and to Act', 'Legality of Planetary Defence Methods', 'Responsibility', 'Liability', and 'Considerations for Decision Bodies'. The work of the Working Group showed that a number of international law rules are applicable to the situation of a NEO impact threat, which need to be respected in the event of a planetary defence mission. However, in order to diminish political concerns and to increase international acceptance for such a mission, a number of documents could be developed on beforehand to address important points that should be considered before action is taken. These documents could *inter alia* deal with modalities on the dissemination of information regarding NEO impact threats, a draft agreement by the potentially affected state(s) and the state(s) willing to conduct the planetary defence mission, common procedures and elements of a mandate to undertake the mission, as well as liability considerations and modalities for the compensation of victims on the ground.

The chapter by Irmgard Marboe delves into the question, whether there exists an obligation to share information about potential NEO threats under international law. She highlights that the International Court of Justice in the *Corfu Channel Case* of 1949 pointed out that there was an obligation to warn others from imminent dangers, in the case at hand floating contact mines in the Corfu Channel, even if the coastal state was not the author of such dangers. The Court based its finding on the existence of 'elementary considerations of humanity', even more exacting in peace than in war, which represented a 'general principle of international law'. Furthermore, human rights obligations of states include the obligation to protect the 'right to life' against deprivations caused by persons or entities other than the state itself. The human rights obligations of states therefore entail at least the obligation to share information on NEO threats susceptible to endanger human lives. However, human rights obligations of states only arise with respect to territory and persons under their jurisdiction. The obligation to warn other states and their populations about NEO threats needs to be based on other international legal principles, such as the 'duty to cooperate'. While there is so far no consensus on a general obligation of cooperation in international law, under certain circumstances there exist specific rights and duties of states which do create obligations of cooperation. Examples of such circumstances are natural disasters, or activities which are particularly dangerous or taking place in areas beyond national jurisdiction, such as in outer space. The respective analysis of international disaster law and pertinent principles of outer space law lead the author to the conclusion that these specialised rules and principles contain an obligation of states – and as far as space activities are involved also of non-state entities – to share information about potential NEO threats. To what extent a violation of this obligation leads to state responsibility and the duty to pay compensation depends on a variety of factors, including the question of damage and causation.

Whether there is also an obligation to take action towards the mitigation of a NEO impact threat is addressed by Cordula Steinkogler in chapter 13. At the outset, she highlights the need for a distinction between the obligation of states to protect their own population and the obligation of states to assist and cooperate with other states in the conduct of planetary defence activities. Her analysis begins with international space law, primarily the Outer Space Treaty of 1967, which contains several references to the principle of international cooperation. She continues with the examination of international environmental law and its references to the duty to take preventive measures and to cooperate in order to minimise the risk of transboundary environmental harm. International human rights law and the ensuing obligations of states to protect the 'right to life' bring in additional considerations. States are required to take appropriate measures to safeguard human lives, which may also involve the mitigation of natural hazards. The concept of the 'responsibility to protect' is also analysed as it was developed by the International Commission on Intervention and State Sovereignty (ICISS) in its 2001 Report. However, the 2005 World Summit Outcome document of the United Nations at the level of heads of states and governments, which endorsed the concept of the 'responsibility to protect', reduced its scope to genocide, war crimes, ethnic cleansing and crimes against humanity. More suitable to the situation of a NEO threat therefore seems to be international disaster law, which has been codified by the ILC in its Articles on the Protection of Persons in the Event of Disasters of 2016. The author concludes that states have an obligation to protect their own population from NEO impact threats, which must, however, be assessed in consideration of the circumstances of the specific situation, including the knowledge of the threat and the possibility of its mitigation, the risks involved, and the availability of the necessary resources and capabilities. While the affected state has the primary role in this regard, there exists also a duty of states to cooperate in the mitigation of NEO impact threats. The author notes, however, that there is no obligation of states under international law to assist other states in the conduct of planetary defence measures nor is there an obligation of affected states to accept offers of assistance. Nevertheless, states can fulfil their duty to cooperate in the mitigation of NEO impact threats, for example, by cooperating in the elaboration of internationally agreed procedures and standards for the multilateral development and implementation of planetary defence measures.

Chapter 14 by Setsuko Aoki discusses whether and to what extent international law on the prohibition of the use of force is relevant to various aspects of planetary defence. It analyses, in particular, active mitigation measures, which may be carried out against a NEO threat, except those involving the use of nuclear explosive devices (NED), which are dealt with in the two subsequent chapters of the book. The careful analysis of Article 2(4) of the Charter of the United Nations with its prohibition of the threat or use of force between states reveals that active mitigation measures would not fall under the scope of its application. They would not satisfy the 'purpose element' of the notion of a 'weapon', because an action that causes physical damage to a NEO to change its orbit is not aimed at fighting an enemy in an armed conflict, but at protecting humankind and the Earth. While the use of a kinetic impactor for deflecting a NEO would not be considered as 'use of force' under Article 2(4) of the UN Charter, these actions may, nevertheless, not be permissible under international space law, which contains more specific rules on the use and exploration of outer space. Article IX of the Outer Space Treaty, in particular the requirement to avoid the harmful contamination of outer space and adverse changes in the environment of the Earth, is also related to the obligation of states to use outer space in accordance with international law (Article III), which includes rapidly developing international environmental law. The author points out that active mitigation measures, specifically methods that lead to fragmentation, may therefore be affected by Article IX and may be less preferred. While it is relatively clear that the issue of 'force' used against natural objects, such as asteroids and comets, is not prohibited under Article 2(4) of the UN Charter, the author considers it desirable to address any legal uncertainty with regard to planetary defence activities through international rule-making. This would help to avoid mistrust and tensions at the international level and enhance transparency and confidence building among states.

In the subsequent chapter, David Koplow elaborates on the legal aspects of the use of nuclear explosive devices (NEDs) in planetary defence. He starts by putting the question of what constitutes a 'weapon' under international law, including international space law and space-related arms control treaties. The author observes that the Outer Space Treaty of 1967 and the Limited Test Ban Treaty of 1963, reflecting the drafting style of their era, fail to include the relevant definitions. According to the rules of treaty interpretation contained in the Vienna Convention on the Law of Treaties, the ordinary meaning of the term would typically denote a tool of hostility, wielded for warlike, criminal, or other unfriendly purposes, to injure human beings and to damage or destroy their property for mercenary reasons. A NED for planetary defence, on the other hand, would be beneficial for all of humanity, it would save lives and protect property, not the opposite. In this vein, a NED would not be a nuclear weapon and would not be covered by Article IV of the Outer Space Treaty, which prohibits the placing of nuclear weapons in Earth orbit, installing them on a celestial body, and stationing such weapons in space in any other manner. However, the author disagrees with such an interpretation and points out that a nuclear explosive is inherently a weapon, even if it could be devoted to a non-hostile purpose. This interpretation is supported by the terms of the Limited Test Ban Treaty which prohibits the test of nuclear weapons and 'any other nuclear explosions'. The author points out that this clarification reflects the discussions about the possible uses of so-called 'peaceful nuclear explosives' (PNEs) for the purpose of civil engineering, such as deepening harbours or underground storage chambers. They were ultimately abandoned, mainly due to considerations of cost and environmental safety, and because a PNE would largely be indistinguishable from a nuclear weapon and could generate data equivalent to that of a weapon test. The author compares this result with the use of other devices, including kinetic impactors, which are used in missions targeted at asteroids, such as DART and Hayabusa2. He concludes that nuclear weapons must be treated differently from other types of devices, systems, and activities under the Outer Space Treaty because nuclear weapons themselves are inherently different. They are not only much more powerful but also much more threatening to global peace and security. The treaty drafters were aware of this distinction and created special prohibitions specifically for nuclear weapons and other weapons of mass destruction. The proper reading consistent with the object and purpose of the Outer Space Treaty would therefore lead to a classification of NEDs as weapons, regardless of their avowed peaceful purpose and application.

From a different angle, Jack Beard examines the intended use of NEDs in planetary defence under the rules of nuclear non-proliferation in chapter 16. His analysis is based on the Nuclear Non-Proliferation Treaty (NPT) of 1968 which rests on three mutually reinforcing pillars: non-proliferation (avoiding the spread of nuclear weapons to additional states), disarmament (reducing the nuclear arsenals of the states possessing them), and the peaceful use of nuclear energy (encouraging collaboration regarding the non-weapons applications of nuclear energy). He contends that each of these three pillars is difficult, if not impossible, to reconcile with the manufacture, deployment or use of NEDs for peaceful, planetary defence purposes. With respect to non-proliferation, the treaty's clear distinction between nuclear-weapon states (NWSs) and non-nuclear-weapon state (NNWSs) could be jeopardized if a planetary defence mission were to involve NNWSs. Such an involvement could be regarded as assuming some sort of control over nuclear weapons/NEDs, by NNWSs directly, or indirectly, which would be a violation of their treaty obligations. Regarding the second pillar, disarmament, the author is concerned that planetary defence can be used to delay and defeat the obligations of NWSs to reduce their nuclear arsenals and achieve an agreement on complete disarmament as required under the NPT. The threat posed by NEOs could be used and, as the author worries, is already used to justify the continuing possession of nuclear weapons by NWSs. The third pillar, the peaceful use of nuclear energy, which, according to the NPT, is guaranteed to NNWSs would also be severely affected. The safeguards by the International Atomic Energy Agency (IAEA) could be rendered impossible if a NNWS would be allowed to divert peaceful nuclear programs to the production of highly enriched uranium or plutonium in order to manufacture NEDs for the alleged purpose of planetary defence. The author concludes that the threat of a NEO hitting the Earth may be considered as a threat to international peace and security and trigger the competence of the UN Security Council. A decision taken by it to authorise planetary defence missions would ultimately prevail over contradicting treaty obligations, such as those of the NPT. However, the UN Security Council, in its decision, must balance the competing risks to humanity and take into consideration the threat to international peace and security emanating from the proliferation of nuclear weapons.

The chapter by Alissa Haddaji is dedicated to the social aspects of an asteroid impact threat referring to transdisciplinary lessons learned from planetary protection. Under the premise that both planetary protection and planetary defence deal with the notion of protecting/defending the Earth from an 'existential risk' to humanity, they share a common responsibility: putting in place safety procedures in order to mitigate a potential space threat. The author points out that analysing threat perception is key to understanding planetary defence decision-making processes. As nobody has ever experienced an extinction-wide threat, it is important to develop rigorous and in-depth understanding of the critical sociological issues that policy makers and others would most likely have to contend with during the management of an asteroid threat. The chapter delves into various aspects of the term 'catastrophe' which can be described as a large-scale event entailing major damage, whose social and symbolic consequences are of historical order. It is to be distinguished from 'disaster' by its exceptional nature as well as the scale of its consequences regarding political involvement, the socio-cultural environment, space, and time. Ensuing catastrophes can create a mental blocking of unwanted perceptions called scotomisation, which is also referred to as 'comprehension denial'. At the example of a number of catastrophic events in history, such as eruptions of volcanos, tsunamis and large fires, the chapter discusses some of the social, economic, and cultural challenges by reference to socio-anthropological research. This leads to several conclusions for political decision-making on the international as well as the national and local level. According to the author, the lessons learned could help the planetary defence community to improve its preparedness efforts to design mitigation missions by factoring in the challenges that they may face. Such new examples of transdisciplinary and collaborative efforts with socio-anthropologists could inform planetary defence management of pre-emptive steps that can be taken against the social complexities usually emerging during natural disasters.

The current international space law regime on liability and its applications to planetary defence is presented by Alexander Soucek in chapter 18. He highlights that the liability regime – which is both a benefit and burden, depending on the perspective – forms part of the risk management that needs to be undertaken in the context of planetary defence. Absolute and unlimited liability for damage caused by space objects on the Earth or to aircraft in flight as it exists under current international space law represents a considerable burden for any future planetary defence mission which needs to be addressed. The author takes a closer look at the different elements of liability and shows ways of how it would be possible to adapt them to the situation of a potential NEO threat. The analysis includes considerations about the definition of the 'launching state' or 'launching states', the identification of several distinctive types of 'damage' that may occur, the different dimensions of 'causation', and the role of 'fault' if damage is caused to other space objects. The chapter highlights that, as it is unlikely that any state will engage in carrying out a NEO deflection mission alone, there will be an international dimension to such activity. Questions of risk distribution and liability are therefore likely to be addressed on beforehand by international cooperation and coordination. This may result in some sort of arrangement prior to carrying out a planetary defence mission, which can consist in an international mandate, an international agreement, or waivers of liability between launching states and third parties.

Henry Hertzfeld takes up the idea of liability management on beforehand and offers some ideas for possible future solutions in chapter 19. He highlights that suggestions for workable solutions, which may include waivers, reduction, or exoneration of participating states from liability in similar situations, may be based on existing precedents. Examples include the International Disaster Charter, which protects states providing data for humanitarian purposes from liability, the International Space Station (ISS), which includes cross-waivers of liability among the partner states, as well as oil spills and nuclear accidents, where international treaties limit the maximum amount of liability. With respect to the Antarctic Treaty the author notes that the Protocol on Environmental Protection and its Annexes contain interesting aspects of liability, including a proposed obligation of states to require operators to provide insurance or financial security to cover liability. The chapter concludes by reiterating the importance of adequately planning ahead to face the unique liability issues that a planetary defence mission might involve and that will distinguish it from other developing space activities and capabilities.

The international responsibility of states for planetary defence activities is elaborated by Sergio Marchisio in the subsequent chapter. He points out that planetary defence activities are subject to the law of state responsibility under general international law and also to the special responsibility regime of Article VI of the Outer Space Treaty. The latter encompasses the obligation of states to ensure that national activities in outer space by governmental agencies or non-governmental entities are carried out in conformity with the provisions of the Outer Space Treaty. In particular, it includes the obligation of the appropriate state to authorise and continuously supervise the activities of non-governmental entities, as well as the obligation of reparation in case of wrongful acts or omissions by public or private entities. However, as opposed to liability for damage caused by space objects on Earth, which is absolute, state responsibility for wrongful acts can be precluded in a number of circumstances, which may be relevant in a NEO impact threat scenario. While the author dismisses 'self-defence' as an appropriate reference, because the threat caused by a NEO is not an 'armed attack' as referred to in the UN Charter, other circumstances, such as 'consent', 'distress' or necessity' may become legally relevant in such a scenario. The most appropriate circumstance precluding wrongfulness seems to be 'necessity', which may be invoked, if the act is the only way for the state to safeguard an essential interest against a grave and imminent peril, and does not seriously impair an essential interest of the state or states towards which the obligation exists, or of the international community as a whole. However, the conditions need to be interpreted and applied very strictly. Without an institutional framework to channel issues concerning the responsibility of states, the mere fact of having rules of international law precluding wrongfulness in planetary defence is a weak shield. The author concludes that there is a need for an international mandate in order to avoid any concern and abuse.

Building upon the concept of responsibility of states for non-governmental space activities Peter Stubbe discusses the involvement of private actors in planetary defence missions in chapter 21. He briefly describes the increasing role of private actors in the conduct of space activities in the past decades and throws some light on recent developments in the area of so-called 'New Space'. He identifies many different roles non-state actors can assume in planetary defence. Examples include knowledge creation by the scientific community and awareness raising by non-governmental organisations. With respect to deflection missions, the space industry can have a role in developing parts of the technology or even direct engagement. The author notes that planetary defence *per se* appears not to be suitable for commercialisation as there is no private market for a corresponding full mitigation mission. However, it cannot be ruled out that there is interest by private companies in engaging in a humanitarian mission for philanthropic or marketing purposes. In addition, the relevance of private actors in planetary defence is also considered in view of possible future space resources exploitation activities. Once such activities are being pursued, due consideration should be given to potential situations in which a commercially interesting NEO turns into a threat for the Earth and thus a target for planetary defence. This may lead to a situation that exploitation activities or other commercial interests pose an obstacle to take appropriate measures against a NEO threat. The author concludes that non-governmental entities' involvement needs to be fully reflected in any further legal development related to the requirements for planetary defence, including the development of (safety) standards and the prevalence of humanitarian concerns over commercial interests in the authorisation and supervision of non-governmental space activities.

Chapter 22 by Olavo de Oliveira Bittencourt Neto analyses international bodies and procedures for decision-making regarding planetary defence actions. He discusses the competences and functions as well as decision-making procedures of the UN General Assembly, the UN Committee on the Peaceful Uses of Outer Space (UNCOPUOS), the UN Security Council, the Space Mission Planning Advisory Group (SMPAG) and the International Asteroid Warning Network (IAWN) as well as possible *ad hoc* alternatives. While the UN General Assembly with its representation of all UN member states may be considered as one of the prime international bodies to discuss actions related to planetary defence, particular challenges towards expedited and effective decision-making for planetary defence must be acknowledged in times of urgency. The chapter confirms the assessment made in previous chapters that a NEO impact threat, due to its potentially devastating global effects, may represent a threat to international peace and security. The United Nations could therefore deal with planetary defence initiatives from this perspective. However, practical difficulties of assembling all UN member states on short notice to address complex space-related emergencies such as planetary defence should not be minimised. Furthermore, decisions by the UN General Assembly are generally recommendatory. Nevertheless, the potential role and possibilities of the UN General Assembly, in particular through its permanent subsidiary organ, UNCOPUOS with its two Subcommittees, are duly considered. The author points out that UNCOPUOS continues to serve as an important open forum for space faring and non-space faring nations to discuss relevant aspects of space activities and has been instrumental to the advancement of space law, conceiving some of its most important international instruments. Furthermore, the UN Security Council may have an important role in the context of planetary defence. It functions permanently and was designed to address international crises, especially those requiring urgent consideration. However, its composition of fifteen UN member states, with five permanent members, makes it appearing less representative and subject to critique in academia and practice. Nevertheless, the permanent members are major spacefaring nations with significant technical prowess to carry out or at least contribute meaningfully to any related mission. According to the author, this eventually could prove to be instrumental for planetary defence. The author also mentions that, as some of the few recognised nuclear power states (NPS), the permanent members would have the capability to deploy Nuclear Explosive Devices (NEDs) whenever this would be considered necessary for a planetary defence mission. He points out that UN Security Council decisions taken for the maintenance of peace and security may even prevail over existing treaty obligationsunder Article 103 of the UN Charter. This option is discussed at the example of a possible authorisation to use NEDs in contravention of treaties prohibiting nuclear weapons or nuclear explosions in outer space. Another example is the waiver of the strict liability regime of the UN space treaties for the benefit of states carrying out a planetary defence mission. According to the author, the UN Security Council should take advice from SMPAG, even though it has been established under the competence of the UN General Assembly, as it may lack the specific expertise necessary to make an informed decision and to balance the respective risks. Other potential advisory groups are also discussed. The chapter concludes by underlining that multilateral cooperation is key to develop actions capable of addressing cosmic threats in an effective manner and that discussions and decisions in preparation for a NEO threat need to take place at an early stage.

The last chapter contains conclusions and considerations on the way forward. It is written by the editor of the book and offers a summary of the conclusions presented in the different chapters as well as additional considerations and suggestions for the future. Its aim is to synthesise the numerous contributions and to highlight the most relevant issues and proposals. The present book may therefore not only represent an academic exercise but also assist experts and decision makers involved in the preparation of planetary defence activities with conclusions and ideas for the next steps.

PART 1

Planetary Defence and International Cooperative Efforts

CHAPTER 1

Near-Earth Objects – Basic Terms and Characteristics

Christian Koeberl and Cordula Steinkogler

1 Introduction

Planetary defence covers human activities to address potential impacts of Near-Earth Objects (NEOs) on Earth.[1] NEOs are asteroids and (less commonly) comets with a perihelion[2] distance of 1.3 Astronomical Units (AU)[3] or less.[4] This means that their orbits can bring them relatively close to the Earth in astronomical terms: they can come within 0.3 AU, or approximately 45 million kilometres, of Earth's orbit.[5] The majority of NEOs are asteroids, referred to as

1 Different definitions and descriptions of 'planetary defence' exist. According to the NASA Planetary Defense Coordination Office planetary defence "is 'applied planetary science' to address the NEO impact hazard". It is the term used to "encompass all the capabilities needed to detect the possibility and warn of potential asteroid or comet impacts with Earth, and then either prevent them or mitigate their possible effects". NASA Planetary Defense Coordination Office, 'Overview' (*NASA*) <https://www.nasa.gov/planetarydefense/overview> and 'Planetary Defense Frequently Asked Questions' (*NASA*) <https://www.nasa.gov/planetarydefense/faq> accessed 26 February 2021. The Space Mission Planning Advisory Group (SMPAG) describes planetary defence as "activities and actions to predict and mitigate a potential impact by an asteroid or comet on the Earth". SMPAG, 'Terms of Reference V2.0' (13 September 2019) <https://www.cosmos.esa.int/web/smpag/terms-of-reference-vo> accessed 26 February 2021.

2 The perihelion is an orbit's closest point to the Sun. NASA JPL, 'Glossary' (*NASA JPL Center for Near Earth Object Studies*) <https://cneos.jpl.nasa.gov/glossary/perihelion.html> accessed 26 February 2021.

3 1 Astronomical Unit (AU) is the mean distance from the Earth to the Sun and equal to approximately 150 million kilometres. IAU, 'Near Earth Asteroids (NEAs)' (*International Astronomical Union*) <https://www.iau.org/public/themes/neo/nea2/> accessed 26 February 2021.

4 This means that they can come closer to the Sun than 1.3 times the distance from the Earth to the Sun, or approximately 195 million kilometres. ESA, 'Definitions & Assumptions' (*European Space Agency*) <http://neo.ssa.esa.int/definitions-and-assumptions>; NASA JPL, 'NEO Groups' (*NASA JPL Center for Near Earth Object Studies*) <https://cneos.jpl.nasa.gov/about/neo_groups.html> accessed 26 February 2021.

5 IAU, 'Near Earth Asteroids (NEAs)' (*International Astronomical Union*) <https://www.iau.org/public/themes/neo/nea2/> accessed 26 February 2021.

 | DOI:10.1163/9789004467606_003

Near-Earth Asteroids (NEAs).[6] Most asteroids in the Solar System are found in the so-called asteroid belt, which is between the orbits of Mars and Jupiter.[7] Due to close encounters between asteroids and the ensuing gravity disturbances asteroids from this so-called 'main belt' can enter into orbits that bring them close to the inner planets, including Earth. Near-Earth Comets (NECs) are generally further restricted to include only comets with an orbital period of less than 200 years.[8] Most of the NEOs will either eventually fall into the Sun or collide with one of the terrestrial planets or our Moon. The characteristics of NEOs influence their potential to cause damage on Earth as well as the possibility to mitigate potential impacts. This chapter therefore aims at briefly presenting some of the characteristics, definitions and basic terms related to NEOs and their impacts on Earth.

2 NEO Characteristics and Definitions

Comets are bodies with a nucleus composed of rock and (mostly) ice that orbit the Sun and typically have a size of a few kilometres in diameter.[9] When a cometary nucleus moves closer to the Sun on its orbit, the ice is heated and releases gases that form the so-called coma around the nucleus, and the solar wind 'blows' the neutral and ionized gases away from the Sun, forming a tail.[10] Asteroids are "small and often irregularly shaped celestial bodies".[11] They are rocky remnants of the early formation of the Solar System.[12] Asteroids are

6 NASA JPL, 'NEO Groups' (*NASA JPL Center for Near Earth Object Studies*) <https://cneos.jpl.nasa.gov/about/neo_groups.html> accessed 26 February 2021.

7 IAU 'Near Earth Asteroids (NEAs)' (*International Astronomical Union*) <https://www.iau.org/public/themes/neo/nea2/> accessed 26 February 2021.

8 ESA, 'Definitions & Assumptions' (*European Space Agency*) <http://neo.ssa.esa.int/definitions-and-assumptions>; NASA JPL, 'NEO Groups' (*NASA JPL Center for Near Earth Object Studies*) <https://cneos.jpl.nasa.gov/about/neo_groups.html> accessed 26 February 2021.

9 IAU, 'Naming of Astronomical Objects' (*International Astronomical Union*) <https://www.iau.org/public/themes/naming/> accessed 26 February 2021.

10 ESA, 'Search for Comets' (*European Space Agency*) <neo.ssa.esa.int/comets>; IAU, 'Naming of Astronomical Objects' (*International Astronomical Union*) <https://www.iau.org/public/themes/naming/> accessed 26 February 2021.

11 IAU, 'Near Earth Asteroids (NEAs)' (*International Astronomical Union*) <https://www.iau.org/public/themes/neo/nea2/> accessed 26 February 2021.

12 William Crowe, 'What Are NEOs and the Technical Means and Constraints of Solar System Mapping?' in Nikola Schmidt (ed), *Planetary Defense: Global Collaboration for Defending Earth from Asteroids and Comets* (Springer 2019) 34–35; NASA, 'Asteroids' (*NASA Solar System Exploration*) <https://solarsystem.nasa.gov/asteroids-comets-and-meteors/asteroids/in-depth/> accessed 26 February 2021.

visible through sunlight reflected from their surface. Their brightness can, therefore, provide information on their size.[13] Factors that influence how bright an object appears in the sky from Earth include: diameter, surface composition (stony or metallic), surface properties (roughness), and distance from the Earth. Taking these (and a few other) considerations into account, the brightness of an object in the sky can provide information on, for example, its diameter. In astronomy, the brightness of an object is measured with a quantity called magnitude.[14] Absolute magnitude (denoted by the capital letter H) is a measure of brightness that is independent of distance.[15] The absolute magnitude of an object also depends on the fraction of the sunlight it reflects at visible wavelengths. A measure of this fraction is called albedo.[16]

Comets and most of the Solar System asteroids belong to the category of 'small Solar System bodies' which encompasses all objects orbiting the Sun that do not have sufficient mass for their self-gravity to pull them into a nearly spherical, or round shape (see Figure 1.1) and that are therefore too small to satisfy the definition of planet or dwarf planet.[17] Objects with a mass above

---

13 National Academies of Sciences, Engineering, and Medicine, *Finding Hazardous Asteroids Using Infrared and Visible Wavelength Telescopes* (The National Academies Press 2019) 10; William Crowe, 'What Are NEOs and the Technical Means and Constraints of Solar System Mapping?' in Nikola Schmidt (ed), *Planetary Defense: Global Collaboration for Defending Earth from Asteroids and Comets* (Springer 2019) 38.

14 National Academies of Sciences, Engineering, and Medicine, *Finding Hazardous Asteroids Using Infrared and Visible Wavelength Telescopes* (The National Academies Press 2019) 10; See also IAU, 'International System of Units' (*International Astronomical Union*) <https://www.iau.org/publications/proceedings_rules/units/> accessed 26 February 2021.

15 For Solar System objects, the absolute magnitude is the magnitude the object would appear to have if it were located 1 AU from both, the observer and the Sun, and at a phase angle (Sun-object-observer angle) of 0 degrees. See ESA, 'Definitions & Assumptions' (*European Space Agency*) <http://neo.ssa.esa.int/definitions-and-assumptions> accessed 26 February 2021; National Academies of Sciences, Engineering, and Medicine, *Finding Hazardous Asteroids Using Infrared and Visible Wavelength Telescopes* (The National Academies Press 2019) 10. Note, however, that this is a hypothetical configuration, which is impossible to achieve when observing from Earth.

16 National Academies of Sciences, Engineering, and Medicine, *Finding Hazardous Asteroids Using Infrared and Visible Wavelength Telescopes* (The National Academies Press 2019) 10. Albedo is the ratio of the light received by a body to the light reflected by that body. NASA JPL, 'Glossary' (*NASA JPL Center for Near Earth Object Studies*) <https://cneos.jpl.nasa.gov/glossary/albedo.html> accessed 26 February 2021.

17 IAU, 'Pluto and the Developing Landscape of Our Solar System' (*International Astronomical Union*) <https://www.iau.org/public/themes/pluto/>; IAU, 'Resolution B5 – Definition of a Planet in the Solar System' (*International Astronomical Union*, 2006) <www.iau.org/static/resolutions/Resolution_GA26-5-6.pdf> accessed 26 February 2021. A 'planet' is "a celestial body that (a) is in orbit around the Sun, (b) has sufficient mass for its self-gravity to overcome rigid body forces so that it assumes a hydrostatic equilibrium (nearly

$5x10^{20}$ kilogrammes and a diameter greater than 800 kilometres are normally considered to have a nearly round shape.[18] On the lower size end, meteoroids are defined by the International Astronomical Union (IAU) as "solid natural object of a size roughly between 30 micrometers and 1 meter moving in, or coming from, interplanetary space".[19] Thus, asteroids and comets would generally be larger than meteoroids, i.e. larger than one metre, and smaller than planets and dwarf planets, that is smaller than about 800 kilometres. However, the upper size limit of meteoroids is not always used in a uniform way – some researchers use 10, 20 or even 50 metres as upper limit for meteoroids and accordingly as lower size limit for asteroids.

About 25000 NEOs are known today.[20] Of those, 113 are NECs,[21] with the total number of known comets being approximately

---

round) shape, and (c) has cleared the neighbourhood around its orbit". A 'dwarf planet' is "a celestial body that (a) is in orbit around the Sun, (b) has sufficient mass for its self-gravity to overcome rigid body forces so that it assumes a hydrostatic equilibrium (nearly round) shape, (c) has not cleared the neighbourhood around its orbit, and (d) is not a satellite". IAU, 'Resolution B5 – Definition of a Planet in the Solar System' (*International Astronomical Union*, 2006) <https://www.iau.org/static/resolutions/Resolution_GA26-5-6.pdf> accessed 26 February 2021.

18 IAU, 'General Assembly 2006 Newspaper – Nuncio Sidereo III' (*International Astronomical Union*, 2006) <https://www.iau.org/publications/iau/ga_newspapers/> accessed 26 February 2021.

19 IAU, Commission F1 on Meteors, Meteorites and Interplanetary Dust, 'Definitions of terms in meteor astronomy' (*International Astronomical Union*, 2017) <www.iau.org/static/science/scientific_bodies/commissions/f1/meteordefinitions_approved.pdf> accessed 26 February 2021. Note that neither the 1 metre upper size limit nor the 30 micrometre lower size limit is a physical boundary, rather they are set by agreement. In the context of meteor observations, any object causing a meteor can be termed a meteoroid, irrespective of its size. A 'meteor' is defined as "the light and associated physical phenomena (heat, shock, ionization), which result from the high speed entry of a solid object from space into a gaseous atmosphere". The meteor phenomenon can be caused by meteoroids, asteroids, comets or any solid matter with the appropriate combination of velocity, mass and mean-free-path in a planetary atmosphere. A meteor brighter than absolute visual magnitude (distance of 100 km) −4 is also called a 'bolide' or 'fireball'. A meteor brighter than absolute visual magnitude −17 is also termed a 'superbolide'. A 'meteorite' is defined as "any natural solid object that survived the meteor phase in a gaseous atmosphere without being completely vaporized". A meteoroid in the atmosphere becomes a meteorite after the ablation stops and the object continues on dark flight to the ground. See IAU, Commission F1 on Meteors, Meteorites and Interplanetary Dust, 'Definitions of terms in meteor astronomy' (*International Astronomical Union*, 2017) <www.iau.org/static/science/scientific_bodies/commissions/f1/meteordefinitions_approved.pdf> accessed 26 February 2021.

20 NASA JPL, 'Discovery Statistics' (*NASA JPL Center for Near Earth Object Studies*) <https://cneos.jpl.nasa.gov/stats/totals.html> accessed 25 January 2021.

21 NASA JPL, 'Discovery Statistics' (*NASA JPL Center for Near Earth Object Studies*) <https://cneos.jpl.nasa.gov/stats/totals.html> accessed 25 January 2021.

FIGURE 1.1 Several of the asteroids and comets that have been visited by spacecraft so far. 'Asteroids and comets visited by spacecraft as of June 2018' (*Planetary Society*), montage by Emily Lakdawalla <https://www.planetary.org/space-images/asteroids-and-comets-visited>

3710.[22] Of the almost 920900 asteroids that have been assigned proper orbits until today[23] approximately 24900 are categorised as NEAs.[24] Of those, around 2160 are categorised as Potentially Hazardous Asteroids (PHAs).[25] PHAs are asteroids with an Earth Minimum Orbit Intersection Distance (MOID) of 0.05 AU or less and an absolute magnitude of 22 or less, which means that they can come closer than approximately 7.5 million kilometres to Earth and have a size of roughly 140 metres in diameter or larger.[26] However, the size threshold of

22 ESA, 'Search for Comets' (*European Space Agency*) <neo.ssa.esa.int/comets> accessed 25 January 2021.

23 Current number of known asteroids with good orbital information: ESA, 'Search for Asteroids' (*European Space Agency*) <http://neo.ssa.esa.int/search-for-asteroids> accessed 25 January 2021.

24 NASA JPL, 'Discovery Statistics' (*NASA JPL Center for Near Earth Object Studies*) <https://cneos.jpl.nasa.gov/stats/totals.html>; ESA, 'Search for Asteroids' (*European Space Agency*) <http://neo.ssa.esa.int/search-for-asteroids> accessed 25 January 2021.

25 NASA JPL, 'Discovery Statistics' (*NASA JPL Center for Near Earth Object Studies*) <https://cneos.jpl.nasa.gov/stats/totals.html> accessed 25 January 2021.

26 ESA, 'Definitions & Assumptions' (*European Space Agency*) <http://neo.ssa.esa.int/definitions-and-assumptions>; NASA JPL, 'NEO Groups' (*NASA JPL Center for Near Earth Object Studies*) <https://cneos.jpl.nasa.gov/about/neo_groups.html>; IAU, 'Near Earth

140 metres has been criticised, since smaller objects can also cause significant damage when impacting a populated area.[27] Therefore, the term 'threatening object' has been introduced for all objects that have a probability greater than zero to impact the Earth, independently of their size.[28] Currently, 1111 NEAs are categorised as threatening objects.[29]

3 NEO Impacts

Impacts of extra-terrestrial bodies are among the most spectacular, high-energy geological processes on Earth. Of particular interest are the effects and dangers of typical impact events for the geological and biological evolution of the Earth. For example, a huge impact event, 66 million years ago, marking the transition from the Cretaceous to the Paleogene eras, and resulting in the formation of a 200-kilometres-diameter impact structure, has had a catastrophic influence on the biosphere. Impacts of extra-terrestrial bodies on Earth carry a risk that should not be underestimated.

While the probability of a large object impacting Earth is small, with an increasing size of the object there is also an increasing likelihood that its impact on Earth produces global effects, including mass casualties and destruction.[30] Astronomical studies of small Solar System body orbits, as well as dating of known impact craters, allow deriving the frequency with which impacts of certain sizes occur on Earth. Such research has indicated that, for example, bodies with a diameter of 1–2 kilometres, which would cause craters in the order of 20–40 kilometres in diameter (such as the Ries Crater in southern Germany), hit the Earth on average about once every million years. But smaller impacts, leading to craters of about 1 kilometre in diameter (as for instance the Meteor Crater in Arizona, USA – see Figure 1.2), occur much more often, namely every

Asteroids (NEAs)' (*International Astronomical Union*) <https://www.iau.org/public/themes/neo/nea2/> accessed 26 February 2021.

27 William Crowe, 'What Are NEOs and the Technical Means and Constraints of Solar System Mapping?' in Nikola Schmidt (ed), *Planetary Defense: Global Collaboration for Defending Earth from Asteroids and Comets* (Springer 2019) 35.

28 ESA, 'Definitions & Assumptions' (*European Space Agency*) <http://neo.ssa.esa.int/definitions-and-assumptions> accessed 26 February 2021.

29 ESA, 'Risk Page' (*European Space Agency*) <neo.ssa.esa.int/risk-page> accessed 25 January 2021.

30 David Morrison, 'The Cosmic Impact Hazard' in Nikola Schmidt (ed), *Planetary Defense: Global Collaboration for Defending Earth from Asteroids and Comets* (Springer 2019) 19.

FIGURE 1.2 Meteor Crater (also known as Barringer Crater) in Arizona, about 1.2 kilometres in diameter, formed by the impact of an iron meteorite, about 50000 years ago. 'Aerial view of Meteor Crater, color, Coconino County, Arizona' (*United States Geological Survey*), credit: David John Roddy <https://www.usgs.gov/media/images/aerial-view-meteor-crater-color-coconino-county-arizona>

few thousand years. Very large impacts, which cause craters with diameters of more than 100 kilometres, are fortunately not as common and happen only every 50–100 million years.[31]

Depending on the size and other characteristics of an impacting object and the location of its impact the effects may vary considerably. The most notable are airbursts, surface strikes, earthquakes, radiative heat and tsunamis. Even small airbursts, such as the one near Chelyabinsk in 2013, caused by the explosion of a previously undetected 20-metres-diameter object, released more energy than the Hiroshima atomic bomb, causing severe local devastation.[32]

The formation of a crater by hypervelocity impact is – not only in geological terms – a very rapid process that is customarily divided into three stages: (1) contact/compression stage, (2) excavation stage, and (3) post-impact crater

31 See in more detail chapter 2 'What is Planetary Defence?' in this book.

32 National Academies of Sciences, Engineering, and Medicine, *Finding Hazardous Asteroids Using Infrared and Visible Wavelength Telescopes* (The National Academies Press 2019) 2.

modification stage. The most important aspect of impact cratering concerns the release of large amounts of kinetic energy (equal to $\frac{1}{2}mv^2$, m = mass, v = velocity) when an extra-terrestrial body hits the surface of the Earth with cosmic velocities (ranging from about 11 to 72 km/s). The physical processes that govern the formation of an impact crater are the result of the extremely high amounts of energy that are liberated almost instantaneously when the body hits the ground. For example, a body with a diameter of 250 metres has a kinetic energy that is roughly equivalent to about 1000 mt of TNT, which would lead to the formation of a crater about 5 kilometres in diameter. There is a difference between the behaviour of a stony impactor and an iron one. Due to the difference in mechanical strength, smaller iron impactors can reach the ground intact, in contrast to stony impactors, which may undergo catastrophic disintegration in the atmosphere. The impact energy can be compared to that of 'normal' terrestrial processes, such as volcanic eruptions or earthquakes.

During a small impact event, which may lead to craters of 5–10 kilometres in diameter, about 10^{24-25} ergs (10^{17-18} J) are released, comparable to the about 6.10^{23} ergs (6.10^{16} J) that were released over several months during the 1980 eruption of Mount St. Helens. In the case of an impact, the kinetic energy is concentrated more or less at a point on the Earth's surface, leading to an enormous local energy increase.[33]

4 Conclusions

Planetary defence concerns events that may, on the one hand, have a low probability of occurring but that could, on the other hand, entail large-scale catastrophic consequences. Unlike other natural disasters NEO impacts on Earth may in many cases be prevented and their effects be mitigated. However, this requires the timely detection and continued monitoring of potentially Earth-bound NEOs, a precise knowledge of their orbital parameters and their physical characteristics, such as size, mass, shape and structure, as well as an

33 Bevan M French and Christian Koeberl, 'The Convincing Identification of Terrestrial Meteorite Impact Structures: What Works, What Doesn't, and Why' (2010) 98 Earth-Science Reviews 123–170; Christian Koeberl, 'Asteroid Impact' in Peter T Bobrowsky (ed), *Encyclopedia of Natural Hazards* (Springer 2013) 18–28; Christian Koeberl, 'The Geochemistry and Cosmochemistry of Impacts' in Heinrich D Holland and Karl K Turekian (eds), *Treatise on Geochemistry, Volume 2: Planets, Asteroids, Comets and The Solar System* (2nd edn, Elsevier 2014) 73–118.

accurate prediction of the location, time, probability and effect of their impact on Earth.[34]

Once a NEO that is on an Earth-impacting trajectory is discovered there is generally a range of possible response measures, depending on the characteristics of the object and the parameters of its impact. These measures may include the warning of the affected population, the evacuation of target areas, the deflection of the object by changing its orbit and, in certain cases, the disruption of the object.[35] The decision to undertake a deflection (or disruption) mission will depend on many factors including the scale of the hazard posed by the NEO, the probability of the impact and the magnitude of its effects as well as the feasibility of the mission in terms of accuracy and availability of time, technology and resources. Therefore, for a successful mission a timely detection of potentially impacting asteroids and comets would be necessary to allow for sufficient preparation time, as well as a precise characterisation of the NEO, an accurate assessment of the impact risk and the availability of the necessary technology. Efforts undertaken by states, space agencies and other actors to develop capabilities and technologies for the detection and characterisation of NEOs as well as for the mitigation of their impacts on Earth will be discussed in the following chapters.

34 Describing also the difficulties in determining these parameters: David Morrison, 'The Cosmic Impact Hazard' in Nikola Schmidt (ed), *Planetary Defense: Global Collaboration for Defending Earth from Asteroids and Comets* (Springer 2019) 15–32; William Crowe, 'What Are NEOs and the Technical Means and Constraints of Solar System Mapping?' in Nikola Schmidt (ed), *Planetary Defense: Global Collaboration for Defending Earth from Asteroids and Comets* (Springer 2019) 33–48.

35 See in more detail chapter 3 'Planetary Defence Technologies' in this book.

CHAPTER 2

What Is Planetary Defence?

Rüdiger Jehn

1 Introduction

The UN mandated Space Mission Planning Advisory Group (SMPAG) describes 'planetary defence' as "activities and actions to predict and mitigate a potential impact by an asteroid or comet on the Earth".[1]

Our Earth is constantly bombarded by cosmic particles ranging from millimetre sized dust grains to asteroids up to kilometres in size. Of course, the latter ones are extremely rare, the famous dinosaur killer dates back 66 million years. Smaller objects are called "meteoroids" which the Commission F1 of the International Astronomical Union has defined as "solid natural object of a size roughly between 30 micrometres and 1 metre moving in, or coming from, interplanetary space".[2] Asteroids and comets are therefore larger than one metre. Objects of a few metres in size and anything smaller are not able to create damage on the ground and are therefore not subject of planetary defence.

Objects of 20 metres are already a major concern. On 14 February 2013, an asteroid of this size entered the atmosphere over the Russian city Chelyabinsk and exploded about 30 kilometres above the surface, releasing an energy equivalent to 30 Hiroshima bombs. More than 7000 buildings were damaged and around 1600 people were injured.[3] A typical scenario was that a person saw the fireball brighter than the Sun in the sky, out of curiosity rushed to a window, and a few seconds later the shockwave shattered the window splattering the person with the glass fragments. This is a scenario where planetary defence is needed to reduce damage.

---

1 SMPAG, 'Terms of Reference V2.0' (13 September 2019) <www.cosmos.esa.int/web/smpag/terms_of_reference_v2> accessed 25 February 2021.

2 Commission F1 on Meteors, Meteorites and Interplanetary Dust, 'Definitions of Terms in Meteor Astronomy' (*International Astronomical Union,* 30 April 2017) <www.iau.org/static/science/scientific_bodies/commissions/f1/meteordefinitions_approved.pdf> accessed 25 February 2021. See also Detlef Koschny and Jiří Borovička, 'Definitions of terms in meteor astronomy' (2017) 45 Journal of the International Meteor Organization 91.

3 National Academies of Sciences, Engineering, and Medicine, *Finding Hazardous Asteroids Using Infrared and Visible Wavelength Telescopes* (The National Academies Press 2019) 2.

 | DOI:10.1163/9789004467606_004

On 30 June 1908, an even larger asteroid, estimated to be around 40 metres in size, exploded over the uninhabited Tunguska region in Siberia, flattening the forest of an area of 2000 square kilometres. The energy released in this event was equivalent to about 300 Hiroshima bombs.[4] Models predict this kind of event to happen statistically about every 300 years.

When we go further back in history, we find even larger impacts. 50000 years ago, a 50 metres nickel-iron asteroid impacted in Arizona and created a 1.2 kilometres large impact crater.[5] 15 million years ago, a 1.5 kilometres asteroid created the 25 kilometres crater of the Nördlinger Ries, located in Germany in between Stuttgart, Nuremberg and Munich.[6]

2 Near-Earth Objects – Numbers and Impact Frequencies

Before discussing what humankind can and should do about these threats, the numbers of threating objects and their impact frequencies need to be known. What is important is the number of so-called Near-Earth Objects (NEOs). A NEO is an asteroid or comet that may come close to the Earth or, more precisely, that has its perihelion within 1.3 Astronomical Units (AU), so that it comes, at some point along its orbit, closer to the Sun than 1.3 times the distance Sun-Earth (which is 150 million kilometres).[7] The boundary of 1.3 AU was chosen somewhat arbitrarily, but objects inside this boundary can be deflected onto a collision course with the Earth after a flyby at Jupiter at a distance less than 10 million kilometres. This distance seems a lot, but also the flyby geometry must match and hence the probability for this to happen is quite small.[8]

NEOs are divided into four dynamical classes, named after the first object in the respective class:[9]

4 Christopher F Chyba, Paul J Thomas, and Kevin J Zahnle, 'The 1908 Tunguska explosion: atmospheric disruption of a stony asteroid' (1993) 361 Nature 40.

5 Jay Melosh and Gareth S Collins, 'Meteor Crater formed by low-velocity impact' (2005) 434 Nature 157.

6 Eugene M Shoemaker and Edward C T Chao, 'New evidence for the impact origin of the Ries Basin, Bavaria, Germany' (1961) 66 Journal of Geophysical Research 3371.

7 ESA, 'Definitions & Assumptions' (*European Space Agency*) <http://neo.ssa.esa.int/definitions-assumptions> accessed 25 February 2021.

8 Also a flyby at Mars could throw an asteroid towards an Earth crossing trajectory, but due to the much smaller mass of Mars compared to Jupiter, the flyby distance must be in the order of 1000 kilometres, which happens very seldom.

9 ESA, 'Definitions & Assumptions' (*European Space Agency*) <http://neo.ssa.esa.int/definitions-assumptions> accessed 25 February 2021; NASA JPL, 'NEO Groups' (*NASA JPL*

- Amors: objects having orbits with perihelion distance between 1 AU and 1.3 AU.
- Apollos: objects having orbits with semi-major axis greater than 1 AU and perihelion distance less than 1 AU. Their orbital period is longer than 1 year and their orbits can cross the Earth orbital path.
- Atens: objects having orbits with semi-major axis less than 1 AU and aphelion distance greater than 1 AU. Their orbital period is shorter than 1 year and their orbits can cross the Earth orbital path.
- Atiras: also called Inner Earth orbit Object (IEOs). They have orbits entirely inside that of the Earth. As a consequence, they are extremely difficult to discover because they remain always close to the Sun.

This classification helps to define the planetary defence priorities. For Amors where the perihelion is just outside the Earth orbit, it is important to predict future flybys that could lower the perihelion. For Apollos and Atens the top priority is to improve the orbit determination via additional observations in order to accurately calculate the minimum orbital distance to the Earth orbit. For Atiras a high priority is to eventually deploy a space-based telescope that will improve the detection capabilities for these objects which are difficult to observe from Earth.

Due to planetary perturbations which modify the orbit of a NEO, an object can change its class, as it happened on 31 October 2019, when 2019 UN13 flew by the Earth at a distance of about 6200 kilometres above the surface and changed its semi-major axis from 0.99 AU to 1.45 AU and hence its class from Aten to Apollo.[10]

By the end of 1997, only about 450 NEOs had been detected. In the following year, NASA formally stated the goal of finding and cataloguing, by 2008, 90 percent of all NEOs with diameters of one kilometre or larger that could represent an impact risk to Earth.[11] At that time, the Lincoln Near-Earth Asteroid Research (LINEAR) started to discover new NEOs at Lincoln Laboratory's Experimental Test Site on the White Sands Missile Range near Socorro, New Mexico at a rate of about 200 per year and thus increasing the number of known NEOs

Center for Near Earth Object Studies) <https://cneos.jpl.nasa.gov/about/neo_groups.html> accessed 25 February 2021.

10 See ESA's NEO Coordination Centre Newsletter of December 2019 <http://neo.ssa.esa.int/newsletters> accessed 25 February 2021.

11 NASA, 'Study to Determine the Feasibility of Extending the Search for Near-Earth Objects to Smaller Limiting Diameters – Report of the Near-Earth Object Science Definition Team' (Report 2003).

significantly.[12] In the year 2004, the total discovery rate surpassed the number of 500 per year for the first time. LINEAR became less proficient in 2005 but in the same year the Catalina Sky Survey (CSS) took off.[13] This survey is conducted at the Steward Observatory's Catalina Station, located near Tucson, Arizona using three telescopes with apertures between 68 and 150 centimetres. By the end of 2019, almost half of all known NEOs were detected by the CSS. Since 2011, the Panoramic Survey Telescope and Rapid Response System (Pan-STARRS) complements the NEO search capabilities with currently about 800 discoveries each year.[14] Pan-STARRS consists of two 1.8 metres telescopes with a wide field-of-view of 3 degrees located at Haleakala Observatory in Hawaii. The current total detection rate is about 2000 per year with a Catalina and Pan-STARRS contribution of almost 90 percent.[15] It has to be noted that many of the detected NEOs are lost shortly after their discovery because they become too faint to be permanently monitored.

Figure 2.1 shows the number of detected Near-Earth Asteroids (NEAs) since the year 1985.

The latest NEO population models estimate that there are about 100 million NEOs of a size between one and 30 metres in diameter.[16] However, more than 99.9 percent are yet to be detected. Of course, one metre is too small to create any serious concern, but also of the estimated 2 million NEOs of a size between 30 and 100 metres, only a small fraction has ever been seen by human eye.[17] Models predict that objects of 30 metres in size or larger would impact the Earth every 150 years on average.[18] Of the about 40000 NEOs larger than 100 metres we currently know only about 10000.[19] Objects of 100 metres in size or larger are predicted to impact on average every 3000 years.

12 Grant H Stokes and others, 'Lincoln Near-Earth Asteroid Program (LINEAR)' (2000) 148 Icarus 21.

13 Steve J Larson and others, 'The Catalina Sky Survey for NEOs' (1998) 30 Bulletin of the American Astronomical Society 1037.

14 Nicholas H Kaiser and others, 'Pan-STARRS: A Large Synoptic Survey Telescope Array' (2002) 4836 Proceedings of the Society of Photo-Optical Instrumentation Engineers 154.

15 NASA JPL, 'Discovery Statistics' (*NASA JPL Center for Near Earth Object Studies*) <https://cneos.jpl.nasa.gov/stats/site_all.html> accessed 5 August 2020.

16 NASA, 'Update to Determine the Feasibility of Enhancing the Search and Characterization of NEOs' (Report 2017) Figure 2–8 'Cumulative Near-Earth Object Size-Frequency Distribution in Units of Diameter D and Absolute Magnitude H, with the two Overplotted'.

17 NASA, 'Update to Determine the Feasibility of Enhancing the Search and Characterization of NEOs' (Report 2017) Table 2.1 'NEO Population, Impact Frequency, and Projected Completion'.

18 Ibid, Figure 2-8.

19 NASA JPL, 'Discovery Statistics' (*NASA JPL Center for Near Earth Object Studies*) <https://cneos.jpl.nasa.gov/stats/size.html> accessed 27 December 2019.

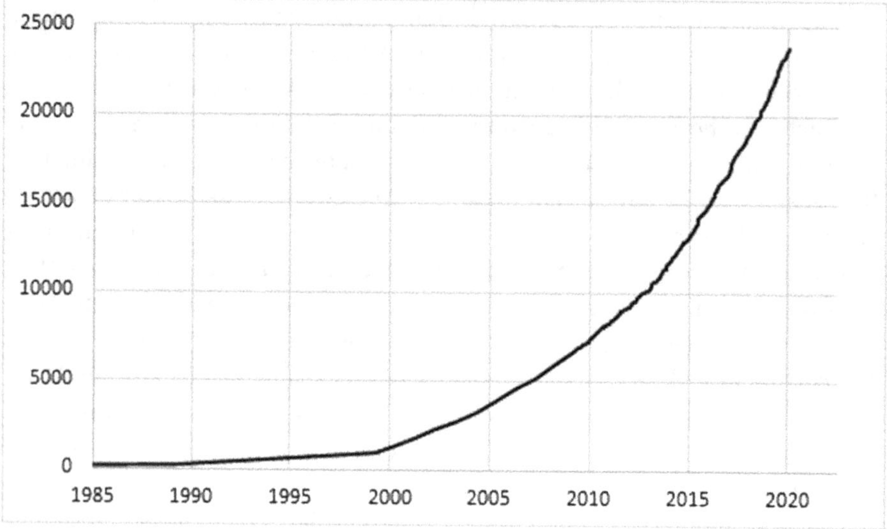

FIGURE 2.1 Number of detected Near-Earth Asteroids
Plot produced based on data from 'Discovery Statistics' (*European Space Agency*) <http://neo.ssa.esa.int/discovery-statistics>

Table 2.1 shows as function of size how many NEOs are estimated to exist according to the latest models, how many of them are already detected and how often they are expected to impact the Earth on average.

TABLE 2.1 Estimated numbers and impact frequencies of NEOs

Size (metres)	1–30	30–100	100–300	300–1000	> 1000
Estimated number	100 million	2 million	30000	5500	930
percent detected	< 0.1 %	0.25 %	15 %	74 %	96 %
Impact frequency for upper size (years)	150	3000	200000	1 million	> 1 million

'Update to Determine the Feasibility of Enhancing the Search and Characterization of NEOs' (NASA *Report 2017*) Figure 2–8

3 Planetary Defence – Prediction and Mitigation of NEO Impacts on Earth

Looking at Table 2.1 gives the impression that a serious threat seems lurking many decades in our future. However, these numbers are statistical probabilities. They do not predict when the next impact will happen. It may happen tomorrow. Research is therefore undertaken and projects are prepared to detect NEOs that may impact Earth. In contrast to other natural disasters, such as earthquakes, volcanos or hurricanes, NEO impacts may be averted. That is where planetary defence comes in. NEO impacts are the only natural disasters where technology is available to prevent them.

If an impacting NEO is below 10 metres in diameter, there is very little damage to be expected, and it will generally be sufficient to inform the population about the event. The International Meteor Organisation maintains a website where everybody can enter and retrieve information about fireballs, a phenomenon that is quite frequent on a global scale.[20]

If the NEO is bigger than 10 metres, but not much bigger than the Chelyabinsk asteroid in 2013, i.e. not bigger than about 30 metres, planetary defence can in general be limited to issue timely and detailed warnings of the affected region (typically a corridor of less than 200 kilometres range) to enable local protection measures, if necessary.[21] NASA and ESA are working on surveillance systems that can detect these threats days or even weeks before the impact.[22]

If the threatening NEO is larger than 30 metres but smaller than 50 metres, planetary defence will in most cases mean the evacuation of the concerned area. However, if feasible, a deflection of the NEO might also be envisaged.

---

20 See the website of the International Meteor Organisation, an international scientific non-profit organization seated in Belgium <www.imo.net> accessed 25 February 2021. Fireballs are meteors brighter than absolute visual magnitude (distance of 100 kilometres) -4. A meteor is the light and associated physical phenomena (heat, shock, ionization), which result from the high-speed entry of a solid object from space into a gaseous atmosphere. See Commission F1 on Meteors, Meteorites and Interplanetary Dust, 'Definitions of Terms in Meteor Astronomy' (*International Astronomical Union*, 30 April 2017) <www.iau.org/static/science/scientific_bodies/commissions/f1/meteordefinitions_approved.pdf> accessed 25 February 2021. See also Detlef Koschny and Jiří Borovička, 'Definitions of terms in meteor astronomy' (2017) 45 Journal of the International Meteor Organization 91.

21 Detlef Koschny and Juan L Cano, 'A Simulated Asteroid Impact over Europe' (2019) Presentation at the third Emergency Response Workshop in Darmstadt, Germany.

22 See the activities by NASA and ESA in chapter 6 'The United States Planetary Defence Programme: NASA and the Planetary Defense Coordination Office' and chapter 7 'ESA Activities in Planetary Defence' in this book.

Depending on whether the NEO will impact in a single piece or whether it explodes a few tens of kilometres in the atmosphere, such as the Tunguska asteroid, a smaller or larger area may suffer catastrophic destruction. For this category of NEOs, warnings should be possible with current detection capabilities at least a few weeks prior to a possible impact, but this is not guaranteed.

Finally, if the NEO is even bigger, the deflection of the asteroid or comet would be the most appropriate, if not the only way of preventing a catastrophe on the entire planet Earth.[23] A prerequisite would be the early detection of the NEO at least a few years before the impact.

4 Conclusion

The goal of planetary defence is generally to localise threats by systematically scanning the sky and by identifying and characterising all potentially impacting asteroids and comets. It also includes a precise orbit determination and impact assessment and, if the need arises, the preparation of a deflection mission. The following chapters will explain in more detail where planetary defence stands today, what the future challenges are and what kind of legal issues arise.

23 This scenario is described in Table 1 of chapter 3 'Planetary Defence Technologies' in this book.

CHAPTER 3

Planetary Defence Technologies

Alan Harris

1 Introduction

The method of choice for the deflection of an Earth-bound Near-Earth Object (NEO) depends on a number of factors, the most important of which are the size and density of the object, its orbit, and the time available before the predicted impact. The size distribution of the asteroid population is very steep, in the sense that there are many more small objects than large ones. Consequently, the first time the decision is made to launch a space mission to deflect a hazardous NEO, the object in question will probably have a diameter near the lower end of the size range that could result in serious damage. The size threshold at which a deflection mission becomes advisable depends on the object's physical characteristics, which may not be well known. An often-quoted diameter is 50 metres, although it should be noted that the Chelyabinsk impactor of 2013, which had a diameter of less than 20 metres before it entered the atmosphere, caused considerable material damage and many injuries, although fortunately no fatalities. If an object with a diameter of 100 metres were to hit the ground it would probably form a crater of 1–2 kilometres diameter and could lead to major loss of life. At that size and larger, a deflection attempt would be morally beyond debate. Table 3.1 provides an overview of NEO sizes, impact frequencies, and mitigation possibilities.

It should be borne in mind that a 'statistical' or 'indicative' interval between impacts (column 3 in Table 3.1) of, for example, 10000 years means that an impact would be expected *on average* every 10000 years. The absence of a 100-metres impact over the past 10000 years would not mean that one is due now. On the other hand, if a 100-metres object had impacted just 100 years ago, the chances of a similar impact in the near future would not be diminished. It is entirely possible, although extremely unlikely, that impacts of two objects with diameters of 100 metres could occur in the same century. In this respect it is notable that the unanticipated Chelyabinsk bolide of 2013 appeared coincidentally *on the very same day* as the anticipated close approach of a 40-metres sized asteroid, now called Duende, at a distance of just 27700 kilometres from the Earth's surface – an event expected only every 40 years for an object of this size.

 | DOI:10.1163/9789004467606_005

The challenge of planetary defence is to be aware of, and make appropriate preparations for, events that have extremely low probabilities of occurring but have the potential to cause large-scale catastrophic destruction. With regard to the statistical nature of impact predictions, the political decision to launch a deflection mission may be taken when the probability of an impact occurring exceeds a certain threshold. If this threshold is, for example, 10 percent, the frequency of deflection missions would exceed that of expected impacts by a factor of 10.

The NEO deflection methods feasible with current technology, or likely to become feasible in the foreseeable future, fall into two categories: impulsive techniques and so-called slow push/pull techniques. An impulsive technique applies a strong but short-lived force to the object to cause a sudden change in its orbit, or possibly intentionally break it up, depending on its size. A slow push/pull technique applies a weak but long-lived force to typically cause a gradual acceleration or deceleration of the object, thereby slowly modifying its orbit. Some examples of such techniques are discussed in the following sections.

2 Impulsive Techniques

2.1 *The Kinetic Impactor*

Theoretical and numerical studies indicate that a promising impulsive technique is to impact a spacecraft on the NEO at high relative velocity, thereby transferring momentum to it and causing a slight but significant change in its orbit around the Sun.[1]

The success of the so-called kinetic-impactor method depends on accurate knowledge of the mass and shape of the NEO, as well as its near-surface structure and the precision of the impact. An impact on a line that does not pass through the centre of mass of the NEO will cause a change in its spin rate and thereby waste energy that would otherwise enhance the change in linear momentum. The impact excavates material from the object's surface and ejects it into space. The greater the mass of ejecta, the greater the resulting change in the orbit of the NEO. The mass of ejecta depends on the near-surface structure of the NEO. A low-density porous surface consisting of a mixture of dust and gravel might simply absorb energy from the impact converting it to

1 ESA NEOMAP, 'Space Mission Priorities for Near-Earth Object Risk Assessment and Reduction' (Report 2004).

TABLE 3.1 Estimated NEO numbers, impact intervals, impact consequences, and mitigation possibilities[a]

Object diameter, D (m)	Estimated total number with diameter ≥ D in the NEO population	Statistical/indicative impact interval (yr) for NEOs with diameter ≥ D	Possible consequences of impact near populated region[b]	Appropriate mitigation/deflection strategy assuming current technology
30	2 million	150	Chelyabinsk/Tunguska-type airburst; crater, depending on composition; some injuries and deaths	Civil defence only
50	300000	2000	Violent Tunguska-type airburst; crater, depending on composition; potentially many injuries and deaths	Slow push/pull or kinetic impactor, if feasible, civil defence if not
100	50000	10000	Crater 1–2 kilometres in diameter; local destruction; tsunami risk from near-shore impacts; many deaths likely	Civil defence; slow push/pull or kinetic impactor – slow push/pull combination
500	3500	140000	Crater some 10 kilometres in diameter; international catastrophe; tsunami risk; potentially millions of deaths	Kinetic impactor – slow push/pull combination if feasible; several kinetic impactors may be necessary. Explosive impulse if no alternative

TABLE 3.1 Estimated NEO numbers, impact intervals, impact consequences (*cont.*)

Object diameter, D (m)	**Estimated total number with diameter ≥ D in the NEO population**	**Statistical/indicative impact interval (yr) for NEOs with diameter ≥ D**	**Possible consequences of impact near populated region[b]**	**Appropriate mitigation/ deflection strategy assuming current technology**
1000	1000	500000	Global effects; partial disruption of civilisation	Series of kinetic impactors or large explosive impulse
10000	4[c]	100 million	End of present civilisation	Series of large explosive impulses; deflection may not be feasible with current technology

[a] This table is based on that in Alan W Harris and others, 'Asteroid Impacts and Modern Civilization: Can We Prevent a Catastrophe?' in Patrick Michel and others (eds), *Asteroids IV* (University of Arizona 2015) 835, 849, with minor updates from NASA, 'Update to Determine the Feasibility of Enhancing the Search and Characterization of NEOs – Report of the Near-Earth Object Science Definition Team' (Report 2017).

[b] The effects listed are rough estimates based on incomplete knowledge of NEO physical characteristics and impact processes in the atmosphere and on the ground. The actual outcome of an impact could differ considerably, depending on parameters such as composition and density of the impactor, impact velocity, impact angle, and the nature of the surface impacted.

[c] The remaining risk is dominated by long-period comets; deflection would not be possible with any foreseeable technology.

heat, thus giving rise to less ejecta than a hard, rocky surface that fragments on impact. Unfortunately, it would be impossible to obtain reliable information on the near-surface structure and other important physical properties of the NEO without a reconnaissance space mission that precedes the deflection attempt, preferably by several years. Therefore, adequate warning time would be an essential prerequisite to a successful deflection campaign. Otherwise it would be necessary to estimate the relevant physical parameters of the NEO on the basis of observations by Earth-based telescopes. Deflection campaign planning may also call for a second reconnaissance mission to assess the outcome of the deflection attempt, which could be designed to double as a gravity tractor (see below) in case the new orbit of the NEO requires fine adjustment.

A kinetic impactor mission to deflect a NEO may partially, or completely, fail as a result of a spacecraft or payload instrument malfunction, or inaccurate knowledge of the properties of the NEO. The consequence of failure may be to cause no change to the trajectory of the NEO, or to change the predicted point of impact to another point on the Earth's surface, rather than to move it off the Earth completely. One advantage of impulsive techniques is that the deflecting energy is delivered all at once so that the success or otherwise of the deflection attempt would be known almost immediately. In the event of failure, there may be time for another attempt.

At the time of writing a mission to test the kinetic impactor concept is under development by NASA. The 'Double Asteroid Redirection Test' (DART) will target the satellite or moon, Dimorphos, of a binary asteroid called Didymos in 2022. The orbit of the moon around the primary asteroid will be slightly altered by the impact of the DART spacecraft. Since the moon eclipses the primary as seen from Earth, even a very small change in the period of the moon's orbit will be measurable with ground-based telescopes.[2] A related reconnaissance mission, Hera, is currently under development, led by the European Space Agency, with a rendezvous with Didymos planned for 2026. Hera will return high-precision data on the size and shape of the impact crater, the mass of Dimorphos, and the dynamics of the binary system after the impact. This is vital information for an accurate assessment of the outcome of the impact experiment.

2 Andrew F Cheng and others, 'The Double Asteroid Redirection Test (DART): New Developments' (50th Lunar and Planetary Science Conference, Texas, 18–22 March 2019) <www.hou.usra.edu/meetings/lpsc2019/pdf/2424.pdf>accessed 26 February 2021.

2.2 *Blast Deflection/Disruption*

An alternative to the kinetic impactor is the use of an explosive charge that causes material to be ejected from the surface of the NEO thereby applying an impulse comparable to a burst from a jet or rocket motor. In principle, any effect that causes material to be ejected from the surface could be used. The most powerful effect available is the explosion of a nuclear device. Due to the presence of the atmosphere and structures on its surface, a nuclear explosion on Earth is a totally different phenomenon to an explosion of a nuclear device in space.[3] The primary effect in space would be the emission of highly energetic radiation, especially x-rays and neutrons, which would cause the temperature of any material nearby to rise dramatically. The resulting sudden vaporisation of surface material and its ejection from the surface would give an impulse to the NEO in the opposite direction.

Blast deflection may be the only realistic method available in the very unlikely event of the late discovery of a relatively large hazardous object. In the case of a diameter of a few hundred metres or more, mission planning would have to ensure that the explosion does not break up the NEO. Fragmentation would act as an energy sink and reduce the magnitude of the deflection. Furthermore, a complete break-up of the target could result in fragments with an overall damage potential similar to that of the original NEO, but more widespread over the Earth's surface. In the case of a small NEO, however, breaking up the object may be an acceptable strategy if the resulting fragments are likely to miss the Earth or be small enough to disperse as bolides[4] in the atmosphere.

A concept currently under study in the United States with funding from NASA is that of a two-body spacecraft capable of destroying an asteroid in the 50–100 metres size category with a short warning time of much less than 10 years (Hypervelocity Asteroid Intercept Vehicle).[5] The fore body hits the asteroid first with a kinetic impact, producing a crater on the object's surface. The aft body then delivers an explosive device into the crater to break up the asteroid into small pieces. Any pieces of the object subsequently entering the

3 See Donald G Korycansky and Catherine S Plesko, 'Effects of Stand-off Bursts on Rubble-pile Targets: Evaluation of a Hazardous Asteroid Mitigation Strategy' (2012) 73 Acta Astronautica 10.

4 Bolides are very bright meteors that can surpass the brightness of the full moon. See for example Michael J S Belton and others (eds), *Mitigation of Hazardous Comets and Asteroids* (Cambridge University Press 2004).

5 Brent W Barbee and others, 'Conceptual Design of a Flight Validation Mission for a Hypervelocity Asteroid Intercept Vehicle' (2015) 106 Acta Astronautica 139.

Earth's atmosphere would largely disintegrate as meteors[6] or bolides, and residual material reaching the ground would be dispersed over a large area. The production of unstable isotopes as a result of neutron bombardment of the surface material of the asteroid is unlikely to be significant,[7] therefore contamination by radioactive material should be a very minor hazard compared to that posed by the approaching object (the destruction of a nuclear power plant as a result of an impact would produce far more radioactive contamination). In another study vehicle designs are investigated that can deliver a kinetic impactor or, alternatively, transport a nuclear explosive to the NEO, in order to deflect it.[8]

A general issue with such studies is that we still have very little idea as to how an asteroid would respond to a nuclear explosion on its surface or in its vicinity. In principle, any deflection technique should undergo testing in realistic circumstances before being deployed in an emergency situation. However, the use of nuclear explosive devices in space for test purposes is legally prohibited.[9]

While blast deflection/disruption is generally considered feasible with current technology, the use of this method would depend on the ability and willingness of spacefaring nations to make a decision in this respect and make suitable nuclear explosive devices available, neither of which can be taken for granted in the current international legal and political landscape.

3 Slow Push/Pull Techniques

3.1 *The Gravity Tractor*

In the case of a predicted impact with high probability of a moderately-sized NEO (i.e. with a diameter of up to a few hundred metres) and warning time measured in decades rather than years, the gravity tractor[10] might provide the

6 Meteors, also known as 'shooting stars', are bright, star-like objects that streak across the sky. See Michael J S Belton and others (eds), *Mitigation of Hazardous Comets and Asteroids* (Cambridge University Press 2004). See also 'Glossary' (*International Meteor Organization*) <www.imo.net/resources/glossary/> accessed 26 February 2021.

7 Catherine S Plesko, 'The Response of Meteoritic and Cometary Materials to Neutron Bombardment' (45th Lunar and Planetary Science Conference, Maryland, 17–21 March 2014).

8 Brent W Barbee and others, 'Options and Uncertainties in Planetary Defense: Mission Planning and Vehicle Design for Flexible Response' (2018) 143 Acta Astronautica 37.

9 See the discussion on the legality of the use of nuclear explosive devices in chapter 15 'Legal Aspects of the Use of Nuclear Explosive Devices in Planetary Defence' in this book.

10 Edward T Lu and Stanley G Love, 'Gravitational Tractor for Towing Asteroids' (2005) 438 Nature 177.

best deflection option. A spacecraft would be brought into close proximity to the NEO so that the very weak mutual gravitational attraction causes the spacecraft to slowly fall towards the object's surface. The spacecraft's engines operate to just oppose the attractive force and cause the spacecraft to maintain a constant distance from the NEO. The net effect is to pull the NEO behind the spacecraft, using the gravitational attraction as a 'tow rope'. Major advantages of this technique are the accurate control of the orbit modification allowed by the long-term operation of the towing spacecraft and the fact that very little knowledge of the NEO's physical properties is required for mission planning. A major disadvantage is the weakness of the gravitational pull, which sets a limit on the rate of change of the NEO's orbit. The weak gravitational pull, which depends on the masses of the NEO and spacecraft, normally leads to the requirement for many years of reliable and largely autonomous operation of the spacecraft. During this time, the potential point of impact on the Earth's surface would be gradually moved across the surface until it misses it entirely. Any failure of the spacecraft's engines during the towing phase could leave the point of impact thousands of kilometres from the original or 'natural' ground zero, but still on the Earth's surface, with potentially serious consequences.

In certain circumstances a NEO that is a potential impactor might make a close approach to the Earth before impacting years later. During the close approach the object is influenced by the Earth's gravitational field so that the later impact is conditional on the NEO passing through a relatively small region of space known as a 'keyhole'. The amount by which the NEO needs to be deflected to miss the keyhole, and therefore the Earth at the later time, is much less than that required to cause it to miss the Earth if the deflection takes place elsewhere in the NEO's orbit. In such circumstances the operational time requirement of a gravity tractor would be much reduced.

In order to speed up the towing process it may be possible for the spacecraft to land on the NEO initially and gather mass from its surface, such as a large boulder. The mass of the towing spacecraft is thereby increased at the expense of that of the NEO, thus increasing the gravitational force between them (the force would be maximum in the case of the two bodies having equal mass). NASA's Asteroid Redirect Mission concept included the option to test the gravity tractor principle after collecting mass from the surface of the target asteroid.[11] In this way the time required to deflect the NEO could be reduced from decades to years.

11 Daniel D Mazanek and others, 'Enhanced Gravity Tractor Derived from the Asteroid Redirect Mission for Deflecting Hypothetical Asteroid 2017 PDC' (5th IAA Planetary Defense Conference, Tokyo, 15–19 May 2017) <https://ntrs.nasa.gov/archive/nasa/casi.ntrs.nasa.gov/20170005468.pdf > accessed 26 February 2021.

However, the development of the Asteroid Redirect Mission was brought to an end in 2017 by White House Space Policy Directive 1 designed to refocus America's space programme on human exploration and discovery.[12]

3.2 *Laser Ablation*

A powerful laser beam, or perhaps several laser beams, directed at close range onto the surface of a NEO would cause material in the beam to vaporise or ablate explosively and be expelled from the surface in a plume, thereby applying a force to the NEO in the opposite direction.[13] The use of lasers in this way has not been as extensively studied as the methods described above but may become a method of choice after further development. A potential problem is that material expelled from the surface may contaminate the optical systems. Laser ablation shares the pros and cons of the gravity tractor: the force applied to the NEO would be relatively weak, so in general the deflection mission would have to operate reliably over a period of years to effect an adequate modification of the object's orbit. On the other hand, the method would allow very accurate manoeuvring of the NEO.

3.3 *The Ion-Beam Shepherd*

High-velocity ions in a quasi-neutral plasma beam emitted from an ion engine could be used to bombard the surface of a hazardous NEO, thereby transferring momentum to it and changing its orbit.[14] The beam could be generated with currently available ion engines from a nearby spacecraft. The spacecraft, hovering typically at a distance of a few asteroid diameters, would need a second propulsion system to compensate for the ion engine reaction and maintain a constant distance to the NEO. As with other slow push/pull techniques the ion-beam shepherd would need to operate reliably over a long period of time but would facilitate accurate deflection of the NEO. As in the case of laser ablation,

12 Executive Office of the White House, 'Space Policy Directive' (11 December 2017) <https://trumpwhitehouse.archives.gov/presidential-actions/presidential-memorandum-reinvigorating-americas-human-space-exploration-program/> accessed 26 February 2021. See also NASA, 'New Space Policy Directive Calls for Human Expansion Across Solar System' (Press Release, 11 December 2017) <www.nasa.gov/press-release/new-space-policy-directive-calls-for-human-expansion-across-solar-system> accessed 26 February 2021.

13 Massimiliano Vasile and others, 'Improved Laser Ablation Model for Asteroid Deflection' (2014) 103 Acta Astronautica 382.

14 Claudio Bombardelli and others, 'The Ion Beam Shepherd: A New Concept for Asteroid Deflection' (2013) 90 Acta Astronautica 98.

further technical development would be necessary before the technique could be considered competitive in terms of effectiveness and reliability.

3.4 *Other Slow Push/Pull Techniques*

Many other slow push/pull techniques have been suggested for deflecting asteroids but have not been developed beyond basic studies of the concept. These include:

- Concentration of solar energy onto the surface of the NEO by means of a large parabolic reflector combined with appropriate lenses or mirrors.[15] The patch of surface beneath the beam of solar radiation is partly vaporised, leading to material being ejected from the surface of the NEO and a commensurate thrust acting in the opposite direction. As in the case of laser ablation,[16] a major issue with the use of mirrors and lenses is the possible contamination of their surfaces with material ejected from the surface of the NEO.
- Ejection of mass from the surface of the NEO using an electromagnetic accelerator to create a thrust in the opposite direction (so-called 'mass driver').[17] Very little is known about the mechanical properties of asteroid surfaces and, therefore, how any thrusting device could be coupled securely to the surface. The rotation of the asteroid would reduce the efficiency of the mass driver, the action of which would have to be synchronised with the asteroid's rotation period to produce thrust in the required direction, or the rotation state of the NEO would have to be modified first.
- Modification of the reflectivity of the NEO's surface by changing its colour. Darkening a light surface would change the thermal emission of the asteroid, causing more emission on the afternoon side, which speeds up or slows down the object in its orbit, depending on its direction of spin (the Yarkovsky effect).[18] However, colouring the surface of an asteroid presents a major technical challenge and the deflection effect would be very weak.
- Attachment of a rocket motor to the surface of an asteroid. This is a deceptively simple idea that becomes much more complicated when the

15 Jay Melosh, 'Asteroid Deflection: The Mirror Ablation Approach' (Planetary Defense Conference, California, 23–26 February 2004).

16 See above.

17 John R Olds and others, 'Multiple Mass Drivers as an Option for Asteroid Deflection Missions' (Planetary Defense Conference, Washington, 5–8 March 2007).

18 David C Hyland and others, 'A Permanently-Acting NEA Damage Mitigation Technique via the Yarkovsky Effect' (2010) 48 Cosmic Research 430.

rotation of the NEO and the mechanical properties of its surface material are taken into account (see the description of the mass driver above).

4 International Collaboration in the Event of Emergency Asteroid Deflection/Disruption

Any attempt to deflect/disrupt a hazardous asteroid would be a major undertaking requiring the skills and ingenuity of many scientists, engineers, and project coordinators, and considerable technological and financial resources. The undertaking would most likely be a deflection 'campaign' involving several missions, for reconnaissance prior to and after the deflection and for back-up in case the primary deflection attempt fails, or one deflection mission alone is inadequate. While some individual nations or agencies may be capable of carrying out such a deflection campaign independently, it would be appropriate for an endeavour of such magnitude and global significance to be undertaken in the framework of international collaboration. The organisation and coordination of such an international project, probably working to a tight schedule, would present a major challenge to administrators and politicians. A group of countries collaborating in an emergency impact-hazard situation would have to tackle many challenging questions, such as:

- Does the seriousness of this particular impact hazard warrant a deflection/disruption mission?
- What type of deflection technique(s) should be chosen? Impulsive or slow push/pull? What experience has been gained from test missions? Should a nuclear explosive device be considered? Who decides?
- Which countries should be members of the project consortium? What scientific and technical resources can they contribute? How should the consortium be managed?
- What launch date should be aimed at and what is the timeline for development/preparation of the component parts of the mission (launcher(s), hardware, software, test facilities)? It is important to take into account that different countries and space agencies have their individual development procedures and 'working cultures'.
- How should the mission be financed?
- In which ways could the deflection mission fail? What are the possible consequences of failure? (For an example, see the section on the gravity tractor above.)
- What arrangements and agreements need to be put in place to deal with a failure scenario?

While there are many examples of successful space missions with international collaboration, these normally take many years or even decades to reach the launch pad. In the case of an emergency impact-hazard scenario, nations and agencies that have little experience of working together might be requested to pool their skills and hardware to work towards a common goal on a very tight schedule. It is therefore necessary to prepare for such international collaboration in times when no emergency situation exists, rather than to wait until we are forced to act 'with our backs to the wall'.

CHAPTER 4

International Cooperation in Planetary Defence – UNCOPUOS, IAWN and SMPAG

*Gerhard Drolshagen, Lindley N Johnson and Romana Kofler**

1 Introduction

Building resilient societies through better coordination and forging of global partnerships is one of the key challenges in the 21st century. Strengthening the use of space for resiliency relates to the ability to depend on space systems to respond to the impact of events, such as natural disasters, space weather and the Near-Earth Object (NEO) impact hazard. Space capabilities can play a crucial role in this regard, ensuring human security through enhanced coordination efforts at the global level.

Since the beginning of the space age, the United Nations (UN) has played a key role in identifying and negotiating matters pertaining to the exploration and use of outer space. In 1959, the United Nations General Assembly established the United Nations Committee on the Peaceful Uses of Outer Space (UNCOPUOS) as the permanent committee mandated to review the scope of international cooperation in the peaceful uses of outer space, devise programmes in this field that would be undertaken under UN-auspices, encourage continued research and disseminate information on the findings, and study legal problems arising from the exploration of outer space.[1]

2 The United Nations and Near-Earth Objects

The interest of the member states in observations, research and information-sharing about NEOs developed along the planetary science indications that impacts of space objects on planets and their moons still constitute a regular occurrence on large time scales. Given a possible global consequence of a NEO

* The views expressed herein are those of the authors and do not necessarily reflect the views of the institutions they are affiliated with.

1 International Co-operation on the Peaceful Use of Outer Space, UNGA Res/1472 (XIV) (12 December 1959).

 DOI:10.1163/9789004467606_006

impact on Earth, UNCOPUOS, with its unique mandate as the only General Assembly's committee dealing exclusively with international cooperation in the peaceful uses of outer space, supported by the United Nations Office for Outer Space Affairs (UNOOSA),[2] acknowledged that the activities in protecting the Earth from the NEO impact hazard is a global issue, demanding a global response. Addressing this hazard, including the identification of those objects that pose a threat of impact and planning a corresponding mitigation campaign, requires cooperative action and could involve diverse and complex scenarios that could be best addressed through international cooperation and improved understanding of the nature of the potential threat posed by NEOs.

One of the first attempts at the international level to increase awareness of and discuss the potential impact hazard from NEOs among the UN member states from a policy perspective was the 1995 United Nations International Conference on Near-Earth Objects, organised by UNOOSA at the UN Headquarters in New York. The Conference focused on the importance of estimations of potential impacts of NEOs as they could have severe consequences on our planet in the case of medium to large-sized asteroids or comets, and proposed an expansion of existing observation campaigns to detect and track NEOs.[3]

A few years later, in 1999, UNCOPUOS convened the Third United Nations Conference on the Exploration and Peaceful Uses of Outer Space (UNISPACE III) that resulted in the Vienna Declaration on Space and Human Development.[4] The Declaration contained 33 recommendations for strengthening the use of space for the benefit of humankind, among them also a recommendation to encourage increased international collaboration to improve understanding of the nature of the potential threat posed by NEOs.

The recommendation resulted in the establishment of the Action Team on Near-Earth Objects (Action Team 14) by UNCOPUOS in 2001. The Action Team was mandated to structure and organise ongoing efforts in the field of NEOs, identify gaps, and propose steps for improvement in the field of international collaboration and coordination between specialised bodies.[5]

---

2 The Office for Outer Space Affairs (UNOOSA) acts as the secretariat to the Committee and is responsible for advancing international cooperation in the peaceful uses of outer space and the use of space science and technology for sustainable development.

3 John L Remo, 'Policy Perspectives from the International Conference on Near-Earth Objects' (1996) 12 Space Policy 13–17.

4 'The Space Millennium: Vienna Declaration on Space and Human Development' Report of the Third United Nations Conference on the Exploration and Peaceful Uses of Outer Space (18 October 1999) A/CONF.184/6.

5 Ibid para (c) (ii).

Based on the proposal by the Action Team to UNCOPUOS, that was approved by the UN General Assembly, the Scientific and Technical Subcommittee (STSC) of UNCOPUOS began considering an agenda item 'Near-Earth Objects' with a multi-year work plan and a dedicated Working Group that would review progress on international cooperation and collaboration on NEO observations, facilitate, for the purpose of NEO threat detection, a more robust international capability for the exchange, processing, archiving and dissemination of data as well draft international procedures for handling the NEO threat and seek agreement on those procedures.[6]

3 The Establishment of IAWN and SMPAG

The Action Team 14 finalised and submitted a set of recommendations for an international response to the NEO impact threat in 2013.[7] These were first considered and agreed upon by the Working Group on Near-Earth Objects of the STSC and then recommended for further endorsement by UNCOPUOS.[8] The recommendations provided for:

1. The establishment of an international asteroid warning network, by linking together the institutions that are already performing many of the proposed functions, including: discovering, monitoring and physically characterising the potentially hazardous NEO population; maintaining an internationally recognised clearing house for the receipt, acknowledgment and processing of all NEO observations; recommending policies regarding criteria and thresholds for notification of an emerging impact threat; and developing a strategy using well-defined communication plans and protocols to assist governments in the analysis of impact consequences and in the planning of mitigation responses;
2. The establishment of a space mission planning advisory group by member states with space agencies, facilitated by the United Nations on behalf

6 UNCOPUOS, 'Report of the Scientific and Technical Subcommittee on its forty-fourth session' (12–23 February 2007) UN Doc. A/AC.105/890, Annex III, para 7.

7 UNCOPUOS, 'Recommendations of the Action Team on Near-Earth Objects for an international response to the near-Earth object impact threat' (21 December 2012) UN Doc. A/AC.105/C.1/L.329; UNCOPUOS, 'Final Report of the Action Team on Near-Earth Objects' (17 December 2013) A/AC.105/C.1/L.330. See also chapter 10 'The 2010 Report on Legal Aspects of NEO Threat Response and Related Institutional Issues' in this book.

8 UNCOPUOS, 'Report of the Committee on the Peaceful Uses of Outer Space Affairs of its fifty-sixth session' (12–21 June 2013) UN Doc. A/68/20, para. 144; UNCOPUOS, 'Report of the Scientific and Technical Subcommittee of its fiftieth session' (11–22 February 2013) UN Doc. A/AC.105/1038, para 198 and Annex III.

> of the international community. The group's responsibilities should include laying out the framework, timeline and options for initiating and executing response activities, informing the civil-defence community about the nature of impact disasters, and incorporating that community into the overall mitigation planning process through an impact disaster planning advisory group.[9]

The recommendations were formally endorsed by UNCOPUOS at its fifty-sixth session in June 2013 and by the UN General Assembly in its resolution 68/75 in December 2013.[10] As a result, two entities, the International Asteroid Warning Network (IAWN) and the Space Mission Planning Advisory Group (SMPAG) were established and had their first meetings in 2014. Following the successful work of the Action Team 14 in fulfilling its mandate it was formally dissolved in 2015. The General Assembly decided in 2016 that UNOOSA should act as the secretariat to SMPAG.[11]

4 Information-Sharing and Awareness-Raising

As an important transparency and information-sharing mechanism in itself, the agenda item 'Near-Earth Objects' of the STSC continues to provide a venue for member states and permanent observers of UNCOPUOS to share latest data on planetary defence-related missions, NEO-observation campaigns and collaborative efforts in that regard.

The goal is to strengthen cooperation and coordination efforts by sharing information on discovering, monitoring and physically characterising potentially hazardous NEOs to ensure that all states, in particular developing countries with limited capacity in predicting and mitigating a NEO impact, are aware of a potential threat.

Both IAWN and SMPAG submit a report annually to UNCOPUOS and its Scientific and Technical Subcommittee under this agenda item (see Figure 4.1). In the event of a credible impact warning by IAWN, SMPAG would propose mitigation options and implementation plans for consideration.

9 The Action Team also recommended that an Impact Disaster Planning Advisory Group (IDPAG) be established. However, at that time, the general consensus was that such roles and responsibilities are already present in other UN groups. As a result, aspects of what the IDPAG would perform were rolled into IAWN responsibilities with respective governmental emergency response entities. The formation of a Mission Authorization and Oversight Group (MAOG) was also discussed by the Action Team. At the time it was considered as premature. The procedure for a 'Decision to Act' is still an open issue to be addressed.

10 UNGA Res 68/75 (16 December 2013) para 8.

11 UNGA Res 71/90 (22 December 2016) para 9.

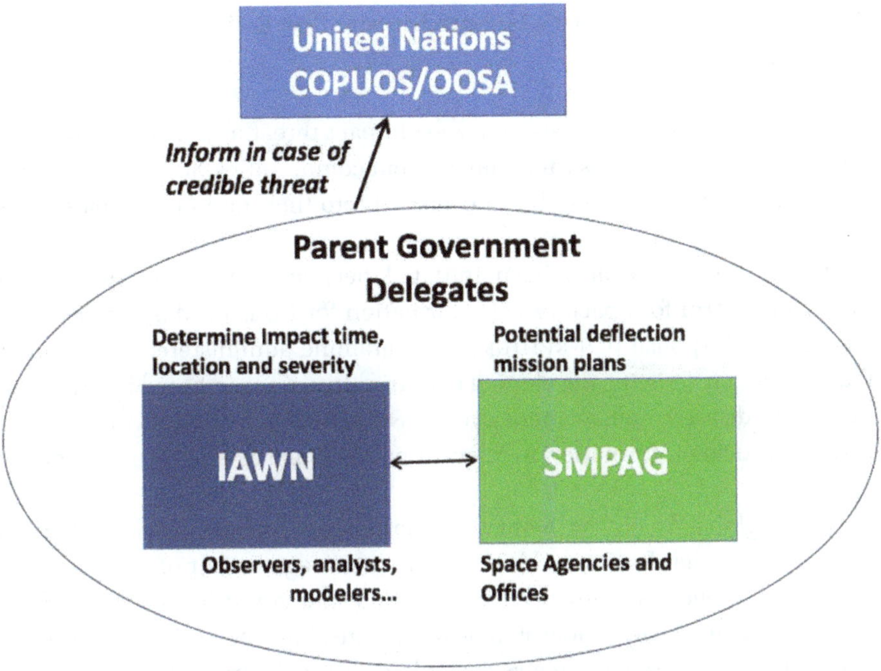

FIGURE 4.1 The relation of IAWN and SMPAG to the United Nations, in particular the Scientific and Technical Subcommittee (STSC) of UNCOPUOS

Another important aspect in information dissemination is reaching out and raising awareness among the general public. With the intention to raise public awareness about the asteroid impact hazard and to inform the public about the crisis communication actions to be taken at the global level in the case of a credible NEO threat, the UN General Assembly in 2016 proclaimed 30 June as the International Asteroid Day. This global observance is held as an annual event for the general public on the anniversary of the Tunguska impact over Siberia on 30 June 1908. It provides an opportunity to sensitise and inform the general public about this subject matter, the work undertaken by SMPAG and IAWN, facilitated by UNOOSA, in preparing for an international response to a potential NEO impact, and the work undertaken in that area by UNCOPUOS and its member states.[12]

12 Ibid para 11. See also chapter 5 'Enhancing Public Awareness: The Establishment of "Asteroid Day"' in this book.

5 Building Resilience – Links to Disaster Risk Reduction Communities

Ensuring preparedness in case of a NEO impact threat also links the work of IAWN and SMPAG with disaster management communities. Several states have already been incorporating the NEO hazard into their national preparedness strategies.[13]

Further links have also been initiated between IAWN and the United Nations Platform for Space-based Information for Disaster Management and Emergency Response (UN-SPIDER), a programme administered by UNOOSA that focuses on assisting developing countries to use space-based information in the full disaster management cycle. UN-SPIDER is related to the work of IAWN to provide information to relevant parties, such as emergency response agencies.[14]

At the global level, the Sendai Framework for Disaster Risk Reduction 2015–2030 (Sendai Framework) is the first major agreement of the post-2015 development agenda, with seven targets and four priorities for action.[15] As a commitment to the Sendai Framework, states have been developing their national preparedness strategies towards disaster risk reduction and emergency response, mainly for hydro-meteorological, geological and man-made disasters as well as disasters emerging due to climate change. Leveraging on the UN-SPIDER programme in connecting the disaster management, risk management and space communities and facilitating capacity-building and institutional strengthening, the goal is to further raise awareness, in particular in developing nations with limited capacity for predicting and mitigating a potential NEO impact, and to share best practices for effective emergency response and disaster management in the event of a NEO impact.

There are also on-going efforts to include NEOs as a natural hazard in the updated glossary of disaster terminology on the Sendai Terminology Review and Classification in post-Sendai frameworks that is currently being done by

---

13 See for example Executive Office of the White House, 'National Near-Earth Objects Preparedness and Strategy and Action Plan' (2018) <https://aerospace.csis.org/wp-content/uploads/2019/02/OSTP-NEO-Strategy-Action-Plan-Jun18.pdf> accessed 26 February 2021.

14 See website of UN-SPIDER <https://un-spider.org/disaster-type/near-earth-objects> accessed 26 February 2021.

15 Sendai Framework for Disaster Risk Reduction 2015–2030, UNGA Res 69/283, Annex II (3 June 2015).

the technical group of the United Nations Office for Disaster Risk Reduction (UNDRR) and the International Science Council (ISC).

6 IAWN and SMPAG – Preparing for an International Response to a Potential NEO Impact at the Global Level

6.1 *IAWN*

The IAWN (pronounced "i-wan") links together the many astronomical institutions that internationally are performing functions such as discovery, monitoring and physically characterising the potentially hazardous NEO population. Its aim is to maintain an internationally recognised clearing house for the receipt, acknowledgment and processing of all NEO observations, to recommend policies regarding criteria and thresholds for notification of an emerging impact threat, and to assist governments in the analysis of impact consequences and in the planning of mitigation responses, using well-defined communication plans and protocols.[16]

The primary functions of IAWN are:

- conduct and coordination of the NEO search effort;
- follow-up and characterisation of NEOs;
- communicating the risks and benefits of NEOs to a wide audience;
- educating the public on NEOs;
- maintaining a clearinghouse for NEO data;
- maintaining a database of potential impact consequences;
- serving as the single international trusted source for information on NEOs.

These functions are further defined in the IAWN Statement of Intent.[17] The signatories to the Statement of Intent recognise the significant importance of being adequately prepared for communications with a variety of audiences about NEOs, their close approaches to Earth, and NEO impact risks. IAWN is the central coordination point to communicate the nature of the NEO hazard and the detection of any specific impact threats with national and international political leaders, policy makers, emergency managers, and the general public. Representatives with core capabilities for IAWN form a Steering Committee, which is coordinated by the NASA Planetary Defense Coordination Office.

---

16 See website of IAWN <www.iawn.net/> accessed 26 February 2021.

17 IAWN, 'Statement of Intent for Participation in the International Asteroid Warning Network' (*International Asteroid Warning Network*, 9 March 2014) <https://iawn.net/documents/iawn_statement_of_intent.pdf> accessed 26 February 2021.

The already existing Minor Planet Center (MPC), sanctioned by the International Astronomical Union for the collection of astrometric observations on all smaller bodies in the Solar System (i.e. asteroids, comets, the irregular moons of the planets and all bodies beyond the orbit of Neptune) by observatories world-wide, has been designated as the central data processing and orbit analysis node of IAWN. All IAWN member institutions send their observations to the MPC for correlation and designation, and for determination and announcement of discovery for a previously undetected body in the solar system. MPC observations and orbital data is also made freely available world-wide for all member state institutions to do their own research, orbit determination and analysis.[18]

IAWN continues to organise observing campaigns as exercises to test the network's real-world capabilities to support planetary defence, involving IAWN signatories and non-signatories alike. The first campaign began with a 2017 NASA campaign to recover the near-Earth asteroid 2012 TC4,[19] which expanded to international and IAWN participation. The orbit of 2012 TC4 was uncertain, and although it was expected to only closely approach and not impact Earth on 12 October 2017, it was an opportunity to test the world's planetary defence capabilities. 2012 TC4 was recovered and its orbit secured, ruling out any potential impacts for the next century. Continued observations collected its physical characteristics to feed into modeling of what its impact effects might have been, including all activities that would happen in the event of an actual detected impact threat.[20]

A second campaign targeted the binary near-Earth asteroid 1999 KW4 during its period of observability that peaked in May 2019 in order to exercise the observing resources and characterisation capabilities that may be applied to a near-Earth object on a reasonably short timescale.[21] A third campaign targets the 2021 observability of 99942 Apophis, utilizing the last good opportunity to physically characterize Apophis before its close approach in 2029 within 40000 kilometres of Earth.[22]

---

18 See website of Minor Planet Center <https://www.minorplanetcenter.net> accessed 26 February 2021.

19 University of Maryland, 'The 2012 TC4 Observing Campaign' (21 June 2019) <https://2012tc4.astro.umd.edu/> accessed 26 February 2021.

20 Vishnu Reddy and others, 'Near-Earth Asteroid 2012 TC4 Observing Campaign: Results from a Global Planetary Defense Exercise' (2019) 326 Icarus 133–150.

21 IAWN, 'NEA (66391) 1999 KW4 Observing Campaign' (*International Asteroid Warning Network*, 21 February 2021) <www.iawn.net/obscamp/1999KW4/> accessed 26 February 2021.

22 IAWN, '99942 Apophis 2021 Observing Campaign' (*International Asteroid Warning Network*, 21 February 2021) <http://iawn.net/obscamp/Apophis/> accessed 26 February 2021.

These campaigns exercise the observing capability and communication channels between IAWN signatories and other observers, and also treat the targets as hypothetical impactors in order to exercise the modelling capabilities for informing decision makers in the event of an actual impact threat.

6.2 *SMPAG*

SMPAG (pronounced "same page") brings together space agencies and offices of member states to discuss and plan collaborative and cooperative projects to develop technologies and test techniques for the diversion or disruption of a potentially threatening NEO while it is still in space.

As per its Terms of Reference, the objectives of SMPAG are to develop cooperative activities among its members and to build consensus on recommendations for planetary defence measures. According to this document, SMPAG shall address the following main areas:[23]

1. *Reference missions, technology roadmaps and collaborative research*
   - Recommend and promote research required for planetary defence. Such investigations can be addressed for example through ground and space-based NEO observations and characterisation, computer simulations, laboratory research, technology development, and space missions.
   - Develop and agree to a set of reference missions addressing a variety of potential NEO impact scenarios and deflection/disruption possibilities, including evaluations of various scenarios. These reference missions will facilitate realistic technical and resource planning.
   - Evaluate the technical maturity and consequences, including failure, of space-based NEO mitigation techniques.
   - Recommend, in collaboration with the IAWN, criteria and thresholds for action (e.g., notification of a significant impact risk, initiation of observation and/or mitigation campaigns). Recommend criteria for deflection targeting, such as a minimum acceptable Earth-miss distance.
   - Develop decision and event timelines for a variety of potential Earth impactors and trajectories identified in the applicable reference missions.

23 SMPAG, 'Terms of Reference V2.0' (13 September 2019) <www.cosmos.esa.int/web/smpag/terms_of_reference_v2> accessed 25 February 2021.

2. *Communication and exchange of information*
   - Identify opportunities for international collaboration on research, technologies and techniques for space-based NEO mitigation. This will help avoid costly duplication of effort, and speed the development of effective capabilities.
   - Keep Members informed about relevant national activities for planetary defence.
   - Communicate its activities to the public following the agreed rules defined [in the SMPAG ToR].
   - Offer a yearly briefing to the Scientific and Technical Subcommittee of UNCOPUOS on the status of these activities.
3. *Legal and policy aspects*
   Identify for possible detailed review within appropriate forums any legal and policy issues (e.g., liabilities) that may arise in undertaking NEO mitigation actions or selecting any likely mitigation options.
4. *Mitigation planning activities*
   - Recommend operational responsibilities for a space-based NEO mitigation campaign.
   - Work in coordination with the relevant actors potentially involved in the implementation of the threat response.
   - In case of a credible threat, recommend viable concepts for a possible mitigation campaign and directly inform those governments that would coordinate and fund space mission activities and request that they in turn inform UNCOPUOS, via the UNOOSA, if necessary.

SMPAG membership is open to all national space agencies or governmental or inter-governmental entities that coordinate and fund space activities and are capable of contributing to or carrying out a space-based NEO mitigation campaign. Each SMPAG member nominates its delegates and a delegation leader. The delegation leaders form the SMPAG Steering Committee.

To fulfil its mandate SMPAG established a work plan with technical issues to be addressed by its members.[24] This document defines specific SMPAG tasks in terms of scope, content and schedule, which have been identified to meet the SMPAG Terms of Reference. It also assigns responsibility for the different work areas to SMPAG members.

This Work Plan defines, at the highest level, the interdependence of the individual tasks. As a 'living document', it includes all on-going, planned and

24 SMPAG, 'Work Plan of the Space Mission Planning Advisory Group' (SMPAG-PL-001, 13 September 2019) <http://smpag.net> accessed 26 February 2021.

completed activities. It also serves as a tool for the SMPAG Steering Committee to check on the progress of the overall efforts, in line with the mandate of SMPAG, for the purpose of reporting to the STSC and SMPAG member agencies.

The work of SMPAG is done on a voluntary basis. Decisions are taken by consensus. Any expenses in connection with SMPAG work or travel has to be borne by the participants' home institutions.

As the name suggests SMPAG is an advisory group only. It prepares mitigation options for different threat and mission scenarios. In case of a real impact threat it will provide advice on potential courses of action to decision makers but has no decision power itself.

7 First Results of IAWN and SMPAG

IAWN and SMPAG work in close cooperation. As a first result, joint criteria were established for warnings and the start of mitigation planning:[25]

1. IAWN shall warn of predicted impacts exceeding a probability of 1 percent for all objects characterised to be greater than 10 metres in size, or roughly equivalent to absolute magnitude of 28 if only brightness data can be collected.
2. Terrestrial preparedness planning should begin when warned of a possible impact:
   - Predicted to be within 20 years,
   - Probability of impact is assessed to be greater than 10 percent, and
   - Object is characterised to be greater than 20 metres in size, or roughly equivalent to absolute magnitude of 27 if only brightness data can be collected.
3. SMPAG should start mission option(s) planning when warned of a possible impact:
   - Predicted to be within 50 years,
   - Probability is assessed to be greater than 1percent, and
   - Object is characterised to be greater than 50 metres in size, or roughly equivalent to absolute magnitude of 26 if only brightness data can be collected.

In the event of a credible impact threat prediction, warnings would be issued by IAWN. If the object is larger than about 50 metres and the impact probability

25 NASA and IAWN, 'Work Plan Item 5.1: Recommended Criteria and Thresholds for Action for Potential NEO Impact Threat' (SMPAG-RP-003, 18 October 2018) <http://smpag.net> accessed 26 February 2021.

is larger than 1 percent within the next 50 years, SMPAG would start to assess mitigation options and implementation plans for consideration of member states. The goal is the global protection of the eco-system, of human beings and their properties on Earth, and of the civilisation of humankind from a devastating asteroid impact.

SMPAG has also issued recommendations to perform a demonstration mission to deflect an asteroid and for a fast NEO reconnaissance mission.[26]

8 The SMPAG Ad-hoc Working Group on Legal Issues

In 2016, SMPAG decided to establish the SMPAG Ad-hoc Working Group on Legal Issues to address possible legal questions related to the work of SMPAG.[27] Scientific and technical advances in the field of planetary defence have reached a stage at which associated legal issues have to be considered. If legal issues are not clarified prior to an emergency situation, valuable time for mitigation planning and the execution of a deflection campaign could be wasted.

The group's work plan consists of the following tasks:

- Describe the existing legal context, in particular in international law, relevant to the work of SMPAG;
- Identify, formulate and prioritise relevant legal questions and issues requiring clarification;
- Where necessary, suggest possible ways forward to deal with legal questions and issues;
- Provide legal advice to SMPAG as required.

As a first result this group produced a report reviewing and assessing existing space law, which could be relevant for space missions aimed to mitigate an impact threat from a NEO.[28]

---

26 SMPAG, 'Statement on Asteroid Orbit Deflection Demonstrations' (6th SMPAG meeting, February 2016) <www.cosmos.esa.int/web/smpag/statement_on_asteroid_orbit_deflection_demonstration> accessed 26 February 2021; SMPAG, 'Recommendation to Perform a Demonstration of a Rapidly Deployable Flyby or Rendezvous Mission to Collect Critical Information on a Threatening Asteroid or Comet' (13th SMPAG meeting, September 2019, Annex).

27 SMPAG, 'Terms of Reference V1.0' (11 October 2017) <www.cosmos.esa.int/documents/336356/336472/ToR_SMPAG_Ad_hoc_Working_Group_on_Legal-Issues_1_0_2017-10-11.pdf/2bb8d5c1-c01c-dca0-2b25-1ffcecb1c270> accessed 26 February 2021.

28 Ad-Hoc Working Group on Legal Issues to SMPAG, 'Planetary Defence Legal Overview and Assessment Report' (SMPAG-RP-004, 8 April 2020); see also chapter 11 'The SMPAG Ad-hoc Working Group on Legal Issues' in this book.

9 Conclusion

Protecting the Earth from the impact hazard of an asteroid or comet is a global issue, demanding a global response. The United Nations, through UNCOPUOS and UNOOSA, recognised that addressing such a hazard, including identifying those objects that pose a threat of impact and planning a corresponding mitigation campaign, requires cooperative action and international coordination. The work under the auspices of UNCOPUOS and its Scientific and Technical Subcommittee under the agenda item 'Near-Earth Objects' led, in 2014, to the establishment of IAWN and SMPAG, which are international entities, whose establishment was endorsed by UNCOPUOS and welcomed by the UN General Assembly.

The work by IAWN and SMPAG is a good example of a successful international coordination and has led to an enhanced exchange of information on issues relevant to planetary defence. Information on NEOs is openly available and freely exchanged. One important aspect of both, IAWN and SMPAG, is the sharing of information and communicating the risks and benefits to a wide audience, including government representatives, as both groups offer a yearly briefing to the STSC on the status of their activities.

Initial results of IAWN and SMPAG include the agreement on thresholds and criteria for warnings and mitigation actions, depending on the impact risk. IAWN organised several successful NEO observation campaigns and agreed on common calculation methods and reporting parameters. SMPAG members studied reference missions for NEO deflection and established a roadmap for NEO mitigation activities. SMPAG also formed an Ad-hoc Working Group on Legal Issues to address legal questions related to the work of SMPAG. This Group produced a report reviewing and assessing legal issues which could be relevant for NEO mitigation space missions.

There is also a need to enhance the capacity for effective emergency response and disaster management in the event of a NEO impact threat. Several states have already been incorporating the NEO hazard into their national preparedness strategies. Important linkages are being made at the global and regional levels with civil protection communities, including through the UN-SPIDER programme and its global network of Regional Support Offices (RSOs).

IAWN and SMPAG will continue their work and consider additional activities. Both groups will closely follow and assess the DART and Hera missions, which will be the first demonstration of an asteroid deflection. In the future more emphasis could be given to specific activities which produce direct and visible results. Examples for IAWN could be regular international observation campaigns of interesting NEOs and the development of a freely available impact risk assessment tool. SMPAG could work towards an interactive tool to assess potential NEO deflection missions and actively support future NEO characterisation space missions, potentially by small, cheap and fast spacecraft. Legal issues relevant for planetary defence will also be addressed as new legal questions arise in relation with the work of SMPAG. Clear communication guidelines in case of a real impact threat also need developing.

With enhanced global observation and mitigation capabilities, early warning and strengthened international cooperation, an asteroid impact is a natural disaster that could be prevented.

CHAPTER 5

Enhancing Public Awareness

The Establishment of 'Asteroid Day'

Frans von der Dunk

1 The Relevance of Public Awareness in the Context of Planetary Defence

The efforts by governments, international organisations, space agencies, scientific organisations and the Association of Space Explorers (ASE) to address possible threats coming from Near-Earth Objects (NEOs) have been given abundant attention.[1] One element within the undertaking of, effectively, humanity to counter such threats, however, has probably been somewhat snowed under in the focus of attention on the scientific, operational, economic, political and legal aspects of planetary defence.

Like any space activity, any proper planetary defence mission costs a major sum of money – in the range of tens of millions of dollars or even magnitudes larger – usually without any direct, 'commercial' benefit in sight which might offset such expenses (or even create a profit). This essentially means those missions will be undertaken by states, at the cost ultimately of the taxpayers.

This in turn means, in democratic societies at least, that the relevant governments in general terms need to convince those taxpayers, read the electorate at large, of the general necessity or desirability for spending huge sums of taxpayer money on such missions, where the benefits for those taxpayers may seem indirect, far off or even unlikely to occur in their lifetime – if at all. Even in authoritarian societies, however, the leadership will take care not to cross the boundaries of its general acceptability to the population at large, so as not to risk profound and long-term widespread opposition which may ultimately result in overthrows or revolutions, and, given the enormous size of sums involved, will thus seek to convince their taxpayers of such necessity

1 They are also presented and assessed in this book. See for instance chapter 4 'International Cooperation in Planetary Defence, UNCOPUOS, IAWN and SMPAG', chapter 6 'The United States Planetary Defence Programme: NASA and the Planetary Defense Coordination Office', chapter 7 'ESA Activities in Planetary Defence' and chapter 11 'The SMPAG Ad-hoc Working Group on Legal Issues' in this book.

 | DOI:10.1163/9789004467606_007

or desirability. Compared to leadership in democratic societies, they just have more leeway in how to frame and enforce the availability of state funds, as well as a larger chance to escape direct accountability as long as they stay away far enough from those boundaries.

This is, of course, where public awareness comes in. Making the general public aware of the relevant risks, the necessity to do something about it, and the capabilities and specific plans of the government to undertake relevant action can go a long way to legitimising the sums that would actually have to be spent from state funds. Planetary defence, from such a perspective, has a probably unique set of tools at its disposal now for such purposes, loosely captured under the heading of 'Asteroid Day' and attendant specific activities such as the 'Asteroid Day Declaration'.

2 The Asteroid Day Declaration

The fundamental role of the ASE as initiator to ensure that planetary defence would be prominently and permanently on the agenda of the international community had reached a culmination point with the handover of the *Asteroid Threats: A Call for Global Response* report in 2009 to the UN Committee on the Peaceful Uses of Outer Space (UNCOPUOS).[2] Since then, UNCOPUOS, as including the main spacefaring nations and effectively hereby involving the main space agencies, has served as the main global forum for discussing and developing relevant strategies, responses and other key elements of planetary defence.[3]

Consequently, the leading ASE members in the above process – notably Rusty Schweickart, Tom Jones, Ed Lu and Dorin Prunariu – then shifted their attention to helping those strategies, responses and other key elements become a reality by initiating a global asteroid awareness campaign.[4] The campaign was tasked to establish and continuously enhance awareness with the general public of the issue of planetary defence, any specific developments in

2 UNCOPUOS, 'Asteroid Threats: A Call for Global Response–Report of Scientific and Technical Subcommittee of its forty-sixth session' (9–20 February 2009) <www.unoosa.org/pdf/pres/stsc2009/tech-30.pdf> accessed 24 February 2021.

3 See further chapter 3 'Planetary Defence Technologies' in this book.

4 Elizabeth Howell, 'What if Earth Was Threatened by an Asteroid Strike? Astronaut Panel Brings up Ideas to Search, Deflect these Threats' (*Universe Today*, 26 October 2013) <www.universetoday.com/105757/what-if-earth-was-under-attack-by-an-asteroid-astronaut-panel-brings-up-ideas-to-search-deflect-these-threats/> accessed 24 February 2021.

that context and what the international community and its major component parts – the spacefaring nations and their space agencies – were planning to do in this respect. To quote Schweickart from a 2014 email, "to learn about asteroids and what we can do to protect our planet, our families, communities, and future generations".[5] The focus was on generating public pressure upon governments in particular to step up the current campaigns to discover potentially hazardous asteroids, and to establish new ones wherever possible, as a precursor to more difficult and more politically sensitive discussions between those governments on how to then handle any actual threat emanating from NEOs.

Thus, in late 2014 the idea was born to have the international community agree on 30 June 2015 to label that day 'Asteroid Day' and celebrate it annually henceforth. Not accidentally, of course, 30 June happened to be the day when back in 1908 the Tunguska event took place, the largest threat to Earth by a NEO in recorded human history, with an asteroid several tens of meters in diameter exploding above the Siberian forests.[6]

In order to make that happen, the 'Asteroid Day Declaration' was drafted. Its text ran as follows:

> As scientists and citizens, we strive to solve humanity's greatest challenges to safeguard our families and quality of life on Earth in the future.
>
> Asteroids impact Earth: such events, without intervention, will cause great harm to our societies, communities and families around the globe. Unlike other natural disasters, we know how to prevent asteroid impacts.
>
> There are a million asteroids in our solar system that have the potential to strike Earth and destroy a city, yet we have discovered less than 10,000 – just one percent – of them. We have the technology to change that situation.
>
> Therefore, we, the undersigned, call for the following action:
>
> 1. Employ available technology to detect and track Near-Earth Asteroids that threaten human populations via governments and private and philanthropic organisations.
> 2. A rapid hundred-fold acceleration of the discovery and tracking of Near-Earth Asteroids to 100,000 per year within the next ten years.
> 3. Global adoption of Asteroid Day, heightening awareness of the asteroid hazard and our efforts to prevent impacts, on June 30.

5 Email from Rusty Schweickart to the author (2014).

6 See chapter 2 'What is Planetary Defence' in this book.

> I declare that I share the concerns of this esteemed community of astronauts, scientists, business leaders, artists and concerned citizens to raise awareness about protecting and preserving life on our planet by preventing future asteroid impacts.[7]

The Asteroid Day Declaration, at the moment of going public on 3 December 2014 by way of simultaneous press conferences in London, United Kingdom, and San Francisco, United States, had already been signed by dozens of leading astronauts (such as the leaders in the ASE efforts), world-famous scientists including a number of Nobel Prize Laureates (such as British Astronomer Royal Martin Rees, Stephen Hawking and Richard Dawkins), science popularisers such as Bill Nye, and other luminaries such as Brian May, a doctor in astrophysics but better known as the guitarist of the legendary rock band Queen, Peter Gabriel (of another legendary rock band, Genesis), Whoopy Goldberg and other famous public personalities.[8] As of now, the Declaration has been signed by more than 22000 citizens worldwide.[9]

3 Asteroid Day

Apart from so profoundly extending the group of signatories, the Asteroid Day Declaration also achieved its main short-term goal: on 6 December 2016 the United Nations General Assembly did proclaim that International Asteroid Day would henceforth be observed globally annually on 30 June.[10] That it took two years to achieve that milestone meanwhile did not keep the Asteroid Day initiative from already organising the first Asteroid Day on 30 June 2015.

Effectively, while Asteroid Day is organised, coordinated and/or supported (depending upon which particular activity one focuses) by a permanent but small organisation, it consists of a series of events across the world annually taking place on, or very close to Asteroid Day. Already the first Asteroid Day, in 2015, by that token consisted of some 90 events scheduled in 33 countries.[11] Five years later, the cumulative tally stands at 2000 events across 78

---

7 See website of the Asteroid Day <https://asteroidday.org/about/asteroid-day-100x-declaration/> accessed 24 February 2021.

8 See for a list of 'notable signatories' <https://asteroidday.org/about/our-team/#hash_filters=100x-signatories> accessed 24 February 2021.

9 See website of the Asteroid Day <https://asteroidday.org/about/asteroid-day-100x-declaration/> accessed 24 February 2021.

10 Ibid.

11 Email from Grig Richters to the author (29 June 2015).

countries.[12]

Those events run, in terms of size and impact, from local initiatives organized by a few enthusiastic amateurs consisting of a single public talk for a few dozen people, sometimes in fairly remote places where one would not expect such an interest at all, to major events raising widespread attention and involving many participants. The events organised in Luxembourg, a leading country in terms of interests in asteroids, both from a scientific and from a commercial perspective,[13] are an outstanding example in terms of visibility. In 2017 the first of these events took place, a multi-day multi-media spectacle with particular highlights being a public 'Meet The Astronauts' event and a full-day TV marathon on RTL Luxembourg widely made available also on YouTube.[14]

4 Concluding Remarks

Repeatedly annually since 2017 due to their enormous success, the Luxembourg events may be considered the backbone of Asteroid Day, but this should not diminish the importance of having hundreds of other events going on simultaneously all around the globe organised and participated in by many thousands of enthusiasts from all walks of life and all generations. Though no serious investigation has been conducted to corroborate this, it would be hard to imagine that those events together with the Asteroid Day Declaration did not at least considerably contribute to the visibility with the public at large and thereby also to the ongoing and ever-increasing interest and involvement of relevant governments and space agencies in planetary defence activities and initiatives. In that sense, the initiative occupies a perhaps peculiar but certainly non-negligible part in the efforts to ensure humanity can escape the fate of the dinosaurs.

12 See 'Asteroid Day Press Release – Events World Wide' (*Asteroid Day*, 12 February 2020) <https://asteroidday.org/resources/asteroid-day-press-release-2020/> accessed 24 February 2021.

13 Luxembourg in 2017 established a specific national law to allow for commercial resource extraction activities on asteroids and invested considerably in several private commercial operators expected to lead the way; the Law on the exploration and utilisation of space resources: Loi du 20 juillet 2017 sur l'exploration et l'utilisation des ressources de l'espace of 20 July 2017 (published 28 July 2017) <http://legilux.public.lu/eli/etat/leg/loi/2017/07/20/a674/jo> accessed 24 February 2021.

14 For the recorded versions, see <www.youtube.com/playlist?list=PLzbX4PGfSjCEal1QhA-lujMZq1pSWM66lo accessed 24 February 2021.

CHAPTER 6

The United States Planetary Defence Programme

NASA and the Planetary Defense Coordination Office

*Victoria P Andrews, Doris Daou and Lindley N Johnson**

1 Introduction

This chapter focuses on United States' activities related to planetary defence, specifically summarising the work of the National Aeronautics and Space Administration (NASA), and the recent instantiation of the Planetary Defense Coordination Office (PDCO).[1]

NASA has studied Near-Earth Objects (NEOs)[2] since the 1970s as small bodies are of interest to both planetary science and cosmology communities. In 1992, NASA began conducting scientific workshops and research into the identification, characterisation, and tracking of NEOs, as well as into potential mitigation strategies.[3] NASA reported that NEOs with a diameter greater than one kilometre (0.62 miles) posed the greatest hazard to life on Earth and predicted that an organised survey could identify most NEOs of this size within a decade.[4] This report was followed in 1998 by a confirmation from the US House of Representatives Committee on Science, Space, and Technology that NASA should develop a plan to discover, characterise and catalogue within ten years (to the extent practicable), the potentially threatening comets and asteroids larger than one kilometre in diameter.[5]

* The views expressed in this chapter are those of the authors in their private capacity and do not necessarily represent those of the institution they are affiliated with, i.e. the US National Aeronautics and Space Administration.

1 Further information regarding NASA's Planetary Defense Coordination Office can be found at <https://nasa.gov/planetarydefense> accessed 21 February 2021.

2 NEOs are asteroids and comets whose orbits periodically bring them within approximately 1.3 Astronomical Units (AU) of the Sun. This implies that they can come within 0.3 AU – about 50 million kilometres, or 30 million miles – of Earth's orbit.

3 David Morrison (ed), 'The Spaceguard Survey – Report of the NASA International Near-Earth Object Detection Workshop' (NASA Technical Memorandum 1992).

4 NASA, 'Asteroid and Comet Impact Hazards – Report of the Near Earth Objects Survey Working Group' (Report 1995).

5 US House of Representatives Subcommittee on Space and Aeronautics of the Committee on Science, 'Hearing on "Asteroids: Perils and Opportunities"' (21 May 1998).

 | DOI:10.1163/9789004467606_008

Therefore, NASA officially established a NEO survey programme, now called the 'Near-Earth Object Observations (NEOO) Program' in 1998. The NEOO Program is responsible for finding, tracking, and characterising NEOs. In the same year, NASA initiated a 'Spaceguard Survey' to search for NEOs that was also sponsored by the multinational Spaceguard Foundation.[6] To date, NASA-sponsored NEO surveys have provided about 98 percent of all NEO discoveries.

In 1998, NASA was also encouraged by Congress to conduct a programme to discover at least 90 percent of one-kilometre-diameter or larger NEOs within ten years.[7] This tasking was accomplished by the end of 2010, according to the best statistical models of the overall population.

The United States Congress' interest in NEOs has continued. The George E. Brown, Jr. Near-Earth Object Survey Act,[8] which was included in NASA's fiscal year 2005 Authorization Act, amended the National Air and Space Act of 1958 to make a clear statement on the importance of NASA's efforts:

> Congress declares that the general welfare and security of the United States require that the unique competence of the Administration be directed to detecting, tracking, cataloguing, and characterizing near-Earth asteroids and comets in order to provide warning and mitigation of the potential hazard of such near-Earth objects to the Earth.[9]

Additionally, NASA was directed to submit an analysis of alternatives of technologies that NASA could employ to divert an object on a likely collision course with Earth.[10] A subsequent report by the National Research Council made recommendations regarding efficient means to complete the Spaceguard Survey and analysed potential mitigation approaches.[11] After nearly a decade of slow, but steady progress with the Survey, the White House updated the United

6 Further information regarding the Spaceguard Foundation can be found at <https://archive.is/20040126185957/http://spaceguard.esa.int/SGF/history.html> accessed 21 February 2021.

7 US House of Representatives Subcommittee on Space and Aeronautics of the Committee on Science, 'Hearing on "Asteroids: Perils and Opportunities"' (21 May 1998).

8 George E Brown, Jr, 'Near-Earth Object Survey Act' (109th Congress Report, US House of Representatives, 2005) <www.congress.gov/congressional-report/109th-congress/house-report/158/1> accessed 21 February 2021.

9 Ibid.

10 NASA, 'Near-Earth Object Survey and Deflection Analysis of Alternatives: Report to Congress' (Report 2007) <www.nasa.gov/pdf/171331main_NEO_report_march07.pdf> accessed 21 February 2021.

11 National Research Council, *Defending Planet Earth: Near-Earth Object Surveys and Hazard Mitigation Strategies Final Report* (National Academies Press 2010).

States National Space Policy in 2010, in which NASA was directed to pursue capabilities, in cooperation with other departments, agencies, and commercial partners, to detect, track, catalogue, and characterise NEOs to reduce the risk of harm to humans from an unexpected impact on our planet and to identify potentially resource-rich planetary objects.[12]

NASA's current congressionally-directed objective is to detect, track, and catalogue at least 90 percent of NEOs equal to or greater than 140 metres in size by 2020, and characterise the physical properties of a subset representative of the entire population. This tasking will not be met given current resources dedicated to the task, however significant progress is being made.[13]

In April 2010, President Barack Obama announced a new goal for NASA: a human mission to an asteroid.[14] Consequently, the President requested, and Congress authorised in 2012, an expanded NASA NEOO Program to augment efforts underway to identify a potential candidate destination for that mission.[15] While the mission was cancelled in 2017 in favour of a human mission to the lunar surface, the NASA planetary defence programme budget was expanded in fiscal year 2014, and again in 2016.

2 Planetary Defence Goals and Organisation

NASA's planetary defence goals include efforts to ensure early detection and warning, and provide accurate characterisation and communications regarding Potentially Hazardous Objects (PHOs).[16] While NASA's planetary defence

12 Office of the Press Secretary of the White House, 'Fact Sheet: The National Space Policy' (2010) <https://obamawhitehouse.archives.gov/the-press-office/fact-sheet-national-space-policy> accessed 21 February 2021.

13 NASA, 'Update to Determine the Feasibility of Enhancing the Search and Characterization of NEOs – Report of the Near-Earth Object Science Definition Team' (Report 2017) <https://cneos.jpl.nasa.gov/doc/2017_neo_sdt_final_e-version.pdf> accessed 21 February 2021.

14 See for example Tariq Malik, 'Obama Aims to Send Astronauts to an Asteroid, then to Mars' (*Space.com*, 15 April 2010) <www.space.com/8222-obama-aims-send-astronauts-asteroid-mars.html> accessed 21 February 2021.

15 The effort was terminated in 2017 when the newly-elected Trump administration shifted focus from sending humans to asteroids in favor of a return to the lunar surface.

16 PHOs are asteroids or comets coming within 0.05 AU of Earth. All comets are considered PHOs when coming this close to Earth because the size cannot be readily determined. Potentially Hazardous Asteroids (PHAs) are additionally defined as being of a size that could survive entry through Earth's atmosphere and could be expected to cause damage at Earth's surface. See also chapter 1 'Near Earth Objects -Basic Terms and Characteristics' in this book.

goals focused on accurate, early detection, characterisation, and communications, development of strategic response capabilities was also needed. To that end, NASA created the Planetary Defense Coordination Office (PDCO) in January 2016 to research potential techniques to mitigate a predicted impact and to serve as a coordination and communications node for the federal government in the event that a close-approaching or potentially impacting object is discovered. The PDCO is managed in the Planetary Science Division of the Science Mission Directorate at NASA Headquarters in Washington, DC.

The NASA PDCO efforts are focused on three areas:

- Ground- and space-based detection and characterisation,
- Interagency coordination including national policy development, and
- Technology and mission concept development.

2.1 *Ground-based Detection and Characterisation*

The PDCO manages the Near-Earth Object Observation (NEOO) Program. The NEOO Program funds applied research conducted at NASA field centres, astronomical observatories, space science institutes, other federal agencies, and other locations around the United States. All NEO search and tracking projects supported by the programme are required to make their data permanently available in a timely manner to the global scientific community. The internationally-recognised public archive for these data is the Minor Planet Center, which is sanctioned by the International Astronomical Union and supported by the NEOO Program as a subnode of NASA's Planetary Data System's Small Bodies Node. NEO observation data worldwide are made available to researchers, and the public. The Minor Planet Center is also tasked with notifying observers worldwide about new discoveries so they can conduct timely follow-up observations critical for confirmation and future orbit determination.[17]

The NEOO Program conducts a sustained and productive campaign to find and track NEOs, collecting data of sufficient precision to allow accurate predictions of the future trajectories of discovered objects.[18] The program also supports efforts to characterise a representative sample of NEOs by measuring their sizes, shapes, and compositions.

17 For further information about the Minor Planet Center, see <www.minorplanetcenter.net> accessed 21 February 2021.

18 An in-depth discussion of the survey programme can be found at the website of CNEOS <https://cneos.jpl.nasa.gov/about/search_program.html> accessed 21 February 2021.

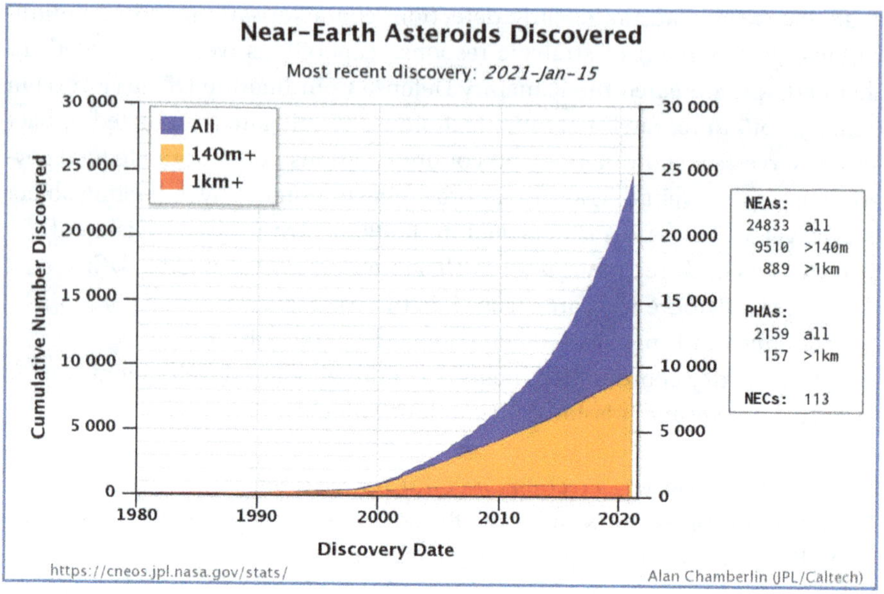

FIGURE 6.1 Cumulative total of Near-Earth Asteroids discovered in three size bins 'Discovery Statistics' (*NASA JPL Center for Near Earth Object Studies*) <https://cneos.jpl.nasa.gov/stats/totals.html>

These NASA-funded survey projects have found about 98 percent of the known catalogue of over 23000 NEOs[19] with the NASA-funded surveys currently finding NEOs at a rate of about 2000 per year. Roughly 40 percent of the known catalogue of NEOs – about 9100 – are objects larger than 140 metres in size.[20] The estimated population of NEOs of this size is about 25000.[21] Current surveys are finding NEOs of this size at a rate of about 500 per year, and roughly two thirds of the population remain to be discovered after almost 20 years of NEO search efforts (see Figure 6.1).

The NEO surveys currently supported by the NEOO Program include the University of Hawaii's Panoramic Survey Telescope & Rapid Response System

19 NASA JPL, 'Discovery Statistics' (*NASA JPL Center for Near Earth Object Studies*) <https://cneos.jpl.nasa.gov/stats/totals.html> accessed 30 May 2020.

20 Ibid.

21 NASA, 'Update to Determine the Feasibility of Enhancing the Search and Characterization of NEOs – Report of the Near-Earth Object Science Definition Team' (Report 2017) <www.nasa.gov/sites/default/files/atoms/files/2017_neo_sdt_final_e-version.pdf> accessed 21 February 2021.

(Pan-STARRS) and the Asteroid Terrestrial-impact Last Alert System (ATLAS), the University of Arizona's Catalina Sky Survey, and the Lincoln Near-Earth Asteroid Research (LINEAR) project on the Space Surveillance Telescope. Additionally, NEO follow-up and physical characterisation efforts are supported at a number of observatories, universities, and space institutes in the United States.

Also funded by the PDCO, the Jet Propulsion Laboratory (JPL) in Pasadena, California, hosts the Center for NEO Studies (CNEOS) for the NASA NEOO Program.[22] The CNEOS maintains up-to-date data and statistics on NEO discoveries. The CNEOS also uses the collected observations to compute high-precision orbits of NEOs, model new orbits for NEO discoveries to determine any impact hazard, perform long-term analyses of future orbits of Potentially Hazardous Asteroids (PHAs), and calculate the impact time, location and other parameters in the event of a predicted impact.

2.2 *Space-Based Activities Related to the Detection and Characterisation of NEOs*

NASA's current flight missions relevant to this topic are NEOWISE, OSIRIS-REx, and NEOSM.

2.2.1 NEOWISE

The Wide-Field Infrared Survey Explorer (WISE) was a successful astrophysics sky mapping space telescope whose continuous images were also used to detect, track and characterise asteroids and comets that operated from 2009 to 2011, when it was decommissioned and put into hibernation.[23] The image processing was enhanced by the NEOO Program to detect and track asteroids and comets moving through its field of view, and archive all the imagery for future research during its original prime mission. In 2013, when the NEOO Program obtained additional budget, the spacecraft was reactivated, renamed NEOWISE, and assigned a full time mission to identify and characterise the population of NEOs.[24] Operating since 2013, NEOWISE has discovered 291 Near-Earth

22 For further information about the CNEOS, see <https://cneos.jpl.nasa.gov> accessed 21 February 2021.

23 Additional information on the NEOWISE mission can be found at <www.nasa.gov/mission_pages/neowise/main/index.html> accessed 21 February 2021.

24 The Principal Investigator for NEOWISE is Dr Amy Mainzer, formerly of the Jet Propulsion Laboratory (JPL). JPL manages NEOWISE for NASA's Science Mission Directorate and carries out mission operations. The Space Dynamics Laboratory, Utah State University provided the science instrument. Ball Aerospace and Technologies Corp. built the spacecraft.

Asteroids (NEAs) and 28 comets, and contributed substantially to characterisation of the populations of asteroids and comets. As of mid-October 2019, NEOWISE is 70 percent of the way through its 12th coverage of the sky since the start of the reactivation mission. Over 860000 infrared measurements have been made of 35277 different Solar System objects, including 1044 NEOs and 179 comets.

2.2.2 OSIRIS-REx

A NASA New Frontiers programme-funded mission, the Origins, Spectral Interpretation, Resource Identification, Security-Regolith Explorer (OSIRIS-REx) is currently preparing to collect and return a sample from the asteroid Bennu.[25] A PHA, Bennu, is of interest scientifically to the small-body science community in general, and to planetary defence in particular. What little is known about asteroids indicates that the population is highly variable, therefore the more detailed information that can be obtained, the better our ability to appropriately respond to an impact threat; to do this in-situ investigations are best suited to obtain required information. OSIRIS-REx contains five instruments to explore Bennu, each of which provides important information for the mission. The suite of instruments is used for remote sensing to scan the surface of the asteroid. Bennu is being mapped in detail and OSIRIS-REx is establishing the composition of the asteroid including the distribution of elements, minerals, and organic material. The mission is mapping the asteroid, documenting the sample site, and will collect, return a sample of Bennu's surface, compare observations at the asteroid to ground-based observations, and measure the orbit deviation caused by solar-induced forces, such as the Yarkovsky effect.[26]

Science operations, data processing and archiving take place at the Infrared Processing and Analysis Center at the California Institute of Technology.

25 Missions in NASA's New Frontiers Program tackle specific solar system exploration goals identified as top priorities by the planetary science community with medium-class spacecraft missions that conduct high-science-return investigations for a roughly USD 1 Billion cost cap. OSIRIS-REx is the third New Frontiers mission for NASA. See <www.nasa.gov/planetarymissions/newfrontiers.html> accessed 21 February 2021.

26 The Yarkovsky Effect may be summarised as the influence of the Sun on the asteroid's trajectory. Exposure to sunlight causes the asteroid's surface to heat. Then, as the object turns, this heat is released from the surface causing small amounts of thrust to be added to the asteroid's velocity. Over time, these small perturbations change the asteroid's orbit. See, for example, explanation of the OSIRIS-REx mission's Yarkovsky Effect investigation: NASA, 'How sunlight pushes asteroids' (*NASA Goddard Media Studios*, 29 July 2015) <https://svs.gsfc.nasa.gov/11964> accessed 21 February 2021.

2.2.3 NEOSM

NASA is currently in initial stages of development of a space-based infrared survey telescope optimised to more quickly meet Congressionally-mandated goals to find and characterise NEOs 140 metres in size and larger. The NEO Surveillance Mission (NEOSM)[27] would deploy the space-based telescope in a gravitationally-stable orbit between the Earth and the Sun and be able to detect NEOs at wavelengths where they are bright, but background stars and galaxies are dim. The instrument will be able to more rapidly detect and characterise objects due to its 'field of regard': the spacecraft will be placed to enable wider and more consistent viewing of the NEO population as it orbits around the Sun, without interference from the Sun.

2.2.4 DART

NASA's planetary defence goals include developing techniques for deflecting or redirecting PHAs, if possible, that are determined to be on an impact trajectory with Earth. The PDCO funds and coordinates mission concept studies across US government agencies and academic space science institutions that explore such techniques.

One such concept, now in development phase of a technology demonstration mission, is the Double Asteroid Redirection Test (DART).[28] DART will demonstrate the kinetic impactor technique on the secondary member of the binary NEA, Didymos, in late September of 2022. While the Didymos primary body (Didymos A) is approximately 780 metres in diameter, its secondary body or 'moonlet' (Didymos B = 'Dimorphos') is about 160 metres in size, which is more typical of the size of asteroids that are most likely to pose a considerable threat to Earth. The goal of the DART mission is to modify the orbital period of the Didymos secondary body by at least 73 seconds from its orbital period of 11.92 hours. This change in the orbital period, caused by the momentum transfer of the impactor and enhanced by the ejecta, will be measured through the use of ground-based telescopic measurements of rotational light curves, augmented if necessary, with planetary radar measurements. The DART mission is currently in Phase D of development.

The kinetic impactor technique is assessed to be the most mature impact mitigation technology. Impacting a planetary body with a mass has been done

27 Further information on NEOSM can be found at <www.lpl.arizona.edu/missions/NEOSM> accessed 21 February 2021.

28 Further information on the DART mission can be found at 'Double Asteroid Redirection Test (DART) Mission' (*NASA*) <www.nasa.gov/planetarydefense/dart> accessed 21 February 2021.

previously for scientific purposes, not actual deflection,[29] but the technology exists to perform the precise navigation required to safely divert an object. A kinetic impactor used to modify the trajectory of an asteroid would leverage existing technologies and extend the technique to planetary defence purposes.

Built by the Johns Hopkins University Applied Physics Laboratory, with support from NASA centres, the DART mission is planned for launch in July 2021 from the Vandenberg Air Force Base in California and will spend one year in cruise phase before it intercepts the Didymos moonlet in late September 2022. Observations by ground-based telescopes and planetary radar will be possible as the impact will occur when the asteroid system is a mere 11 million kilometres from Earth. The energy to be imparted by DART to the moonlet is estimated to be enough to change the orbit of the moonlet but will not change the orbit of the binary asteroid system about the Sun. The mission therefore poses no hazard to Earth.

The 'LICIA Cube' is a CubeSat provided by the Italian Space Agency (ASI) that will be deployed from the DART spacecraft a few hours before impact to photograph the resulting ejecta plume, crater (if visible), and the side of Didymos B opposite the impact, which DART will never see.[30]

Further information about the impact to the Didymos moonlet will be obtained by 'Hera.' Hera is a mission by the European Space Agency (ESA) that will rendezvous with, and explore, the Didymos binary asteroid system approximately four years after the impact of DART, studying both Didymos A and Didymos B in detail and examining the visible after-effects of the impact. DART and Hera will achieve their primary goals independently and will leverage the overall investments by complementing each other synergistically: more can be learned from the combined results from DART, Hera, and LICIA Cube taken together than individually. The international collaboration among planetary defence and asteroid researchers to take advantage of this synergy is known as the Asteroid Impact and Deflection Assessment (AIDA). AIDA is not itself a flight mission; it is the combined, agency-supported collaboration of the DART, LICIA Cube, and Hera teams, along with other researchers worldwide, to extract the best possible information for planetary defence and Solar System science from these groundbreaking space missions.

29 The Deep Impact mission to comet Temple 1 delivered an impactor in order to study the ejecta with instrumentation on a flyby spacecraft.

30 Simone Pirrotta, and others, 'LICIA Cube, the Light Italian CubeSat for Imaging of Asteroid joining NASA DART mission to Didymos binary system' (2019) 21 Geophysical Research Abstracts.

2.3 *Interagency Coordination and National Policy Development*

Should a NEO be discovered that is determined to be on an impact trajectory with Earth, the NASA Policy Directive (NPD) 8740.1 defines a process by which communication would take place from the PDCO to NASA management, to the White House through the Office of Science and Technology Policy (OSTP), and then on to other federal agencies.[31] If an impact is predicted outside of the United States, NASA would coordinate with the US Department of State to communicate the threat to affected countries.

This communications policy was tested in 2017 as part of an exercise of the planetary defence detection and notification system through the recovery and characterisation of 2012 TC4 – an asteroid that had not been observed since its 2012 discovery. It was known that 2012 TC4 would make a close- approach on 12 October 2017 and while it was known it would not impact Earth, there was enough uncertainty in the orbit for the asteroid to make a good test case for a planetary defence exercise by the NEO observation community. Notifications were sent and acknowledged by the White House announcing the exercise itself, the targeted recovery of 2012 TC4, the timing of when existing NEO surveys would have picked up the asteroid via normal operations, and updates in the weeks and days before close-approach.

The PDCO has a long and productive working relationship with the Federal Emergency Management Agency (FEMA) through establishment of the Planetary Impact Emergency Response Working Group (PIERWG). The PIERWG's mission is to inform and coordinate responsibilities and resolve preparedness and operational issues relating to interagency response and recovery activities at the national level. PDCO has held three 'tabletop' exercises with FEMA, the last also including state and local emergency planners, to simulate an asteroid impact threat, and inform emergency management planning.

Interagency exercises such as these enable fast responses and better decision-making by NASA, and other agencies responsible for responding to national emergencies and natural disasters.[32] These exercises educate participating agencies on the unique nature of the threat and also provide insight to NASA on how to best to present information. Participating entities include FEMA, the

---

31 The full text of the NASA Policy Directive can be found at NASA, 'Notification and Communications Regarding Potential Near-Earth Object Threats' (*NASA Policy Directive*, 27 January 2017) <https://nodis3.gsfc.nasa.gov/displayDir.cfm?t=NPD&c=8740&s=1> accessed 21 February 2021.

32 Reports of each of the table top exercises can be found at NASA, 'Supporting Documents' (*NASA*) <www.nasa.gov/planetarydefense/supporting_documents> accessed 21 February 2021.

Coast Guard, the National Oceanic and Atmospheric Administration (NOAA), state emergency response organisations, and the Department of Defense. These exercises involve timeline scenarios developed by NASA that convey how a threatening asteroid might be discovered, the difficulties in acquiring enough information on the asteroid's orbit and characteristics for planning an adequate response, and the evolution of the uncertainty in impact location over time. Modelers at NASA centres and national laboratories calculate impact effects and damage estimates from the theoretical impact. Such scenarios have also been used at the international Planetary Defense Conferences to engage in practical exercises with the international small bodies community. The collaborative exercises led directly to the development of a national strategy under the auspices of the White House.

3 The United States National Near-Earth Object Preparedness Strategy and Action Plan

In 2016, the White House Office of Science and Technology Policy (OSTP), with the NASA PDCO, convened an interagency working group entitled Detecting and Mitigating the Impact of Earth-bound Near-Earth Objects (DAMIEN). Comprised of representatives from agencies across the federal government, the DAMIEN working group developed a set of five goals that, if addressed, would substantially improve the nation's preparedness to detect and respond to a predicted impact. The working group assessed the status of interagency efforts and recommended that NEO impacting events be incorporated into federal emergency preparedness, planning, scenarios, training, and exercises. The White House released the National Near-Earth Object Preparedness Strategy and Action Plan (Action Plan) in June 2018.[33]

With the Action Plan published, and NASA and other agencies initiating work to address the actions, the OSTP created a new subcommittee under the auspices of the United States National Science and Technology Council (NSTC). The Subcommittee on Space Weather, Security, and Hazards (SWSH) is co-chaired by NASA and the National Science Foundation. NASA is to provide regular updates to the Subcommittee on progress in the Action Plan. The

33 National Science and Technology Council Interagency Working Group on Detecting and Mitigating the Impacts of Earth-bound Near-Earth Asteroids (DAMIEN), 'The National Near-Earth Object Preparedness Strategy and Action Plan' (Report 2018) <https://aerospace.csis.org/wp-content/uploads/2019/02/OSTP-NEO-Strategy-Action-Plan-Jun18.pdf> accessed 21 February 2021.

OSTP most recently created the Near-Earth Object Impact Threat Emergency Procedures (NITEP) interagency working group, co-chaired by NASA and OSTP, to strengthen impact emergency response protocols as required by Goal 5 of the Action Plan.[34]

The Action Plan provides a policy framework for improving the United States' overall preparedness to address the hazard of NEO impacts over the next 10 years. The Action Plan's primary goal is to organise and coordinate NEO-related efforts within federal departments and agencies, with a particular focus on leveraging efforts that are already existing and resourced. Fulfilment of the Action Plan will enhance existing assets and capabilities – national and international, public and private – to effectively manage the risks associated with NEOs. The Action Plan is based on existing efforts at NASA, and the Departments of Homeland Security (DHS) and Energy (DOE) to detect and characterise the NEO population, and to prevent and respond to NEO impacts on Earth.

Five strategic goals, each supported by a set of strategic objectives and specific associated actions, underpin the effort to enhance the nation's preparedness for potential NEO impacts:[35]

> *Goal 1: Enhance NEO Detection, Tracking, and Characterization Capabilities*: NASA will lead the development of a roadmap for improving national capabilities for NEO detection, tracking, and characterization. Supporting actions will reduce current levels of uncertainty and aid in more accurate modeling and more effective decision-making.
>
> *Goal 2: Improve NEO Modeling, Prediction, and Information Integration*: Agencies will coordinate the development of validated modeling tools and simulation capabilities that aid in characterizing and mitigating NEO impact risks while streamlining data flows to support effective decision-making.

34 The National Science and Technology Council Committee on Homeland and National Security convened the Subcommittee on Space Weather, Security and Hazards (SWSH) to monitor NASA's progress on fulfilling the Action Plan and is co-chaired by OSTP and NASA PDCO. The Near-Earth Asteroid Impact Threat Emergency Procedures (NITEP) interagency working group collaborates on developing recommendations for the Action Plan; the NITEP is co-chaired by OSTP, NASA, and the National Science Foundation.

35 National Science and Technology Council Interagency Working Group on Detecting and Mitigating the Impacts of Earth-bound Near-Earth Asteroids (DAMIEN), 'The National Near-Earth Object Preparedness Strategy and Action Plan' (Report 2018) <https://aerospace.csis.org/wp-content/uploads/2019/02/OSTP-NEO-Strategy-Action-Plan-Jun18.pdf> accessed 21 February 2021.

Goal 3: Develop Technologies for NEO Deflection and Disruption Missions: NASA will lead development of technologies for fast-response NEO reconnaissance missions and timely missions to deflect or disrupt hazardous NEOs. Developing these technologies before an imminent threat arises will strengthen our ability to prevent NEO impact disasters.

Goal 4: Increase International Cooperation on NEO Preparation: Agencies will work to inform and develop international support for addressing global NEO impact risks. International engagement and cooperation will help the Nation to prepare more effectively for a potential NEO impact.

Goal 5: Strengthen and Routinely Exercise NEO Impact Emergency Procedures and Action Protocols: The United States will strengthen and exercise procedures and protocols for assessing NEO threats, communication regarding threats, and response and recovery activities. Coordinated communications and notifications within the U.S. Government and with foreign governments will improve impact emergency preparedness and reduce the physical and economic harm to the Nation.

The Strategy and Action Plan should inform the policy development process. Any commitment of Federal resources to support the activities outlined in this document will be determined through the budget processes.

In the first year since publication of the Action Plan, NASA has convened several interagency working groups and conducted one impact exercise workshop, in addition to regularly planned activities and projects. The planetary defence workshop was held in April 2019, prior to the International Academy of Astronautics (IAA) Planetary Defense Conference. The purpose of the workshop was to familiarise members of the interagency working groups with the technical issues that would complicate decision-making.

3.1 *Decision-making Under Uncertainty and the United States National Near-Earth Object Preparedness Strategy and Action Plan*

Significant asteroid impacts have happened in Earth's history and will continue to occur in the future. With sufficient asteroid detection and monitoring capabilities, it is possible to predict future impacts and, with adequate lead time, it is even possible to prevent these natural disasters. However, there will be uncertainties in the understanding of the hazard that will need to be identified and reduced, if possible, in order to develop an appropriate successful response. This, ultimately, is the goal of the Action Plan: to ensure that decisions can be quickly made in events where there is considerable uncertainty.

Questions naturally arise related to how an impact threat might be measured against other hazards and how the probability of impact would be modelled. Examples include: How will the uncertainties be measured and managed? What information is required to reduce the uncertainties and can that information be obtained in a timely fashion? And, what is a feasible response? NASA sought answers to some of these questions by convening a 'Science Definition Team' in 2016.[36] The team was asked to address questions and provide a cost-benefit analysis of different types of observation systems for completing the Spaceguard Survey referenced above. The key recommendations were:

- NASA should base its goal for completing the survey on a cost/benefit analysis to identify investments in a way that "eliminates the maximum amount of statistical risk uncertainty per dollar of investment",
- Systems exist that can reduce the global statistical risk from the 140 metre-1 kilometre object population over a period of 25 years, however,
- Space-based search systems will be required to complete the survey in that a space-based system located at Lagrangian point L1 could be expected to achieve the "fastest completion of the objective" while also "providing a substantial warning benefit".[37]

Once a potential impactor has been discovered, the next concern is how large does a threatening asteroid need to be to warrant investment in a reconnaissance and/or deflection mission. The PDCO's working assumption is that the threshold asteroid size for mounting a mission, assuming there is enough time to do so, may lie somewhere in the range of 30 to 60 metres (i.e. significantly larger than the 2013 Chelyabinsk impactor, which was ~20 metres in size). In broad terms, the cost of a deflection mission would need to be weighed against the cost of recovering from the damage of the impact; costs that would vary tremendously with size and the location of the impact. Immediately after detection, the asteroid's size (and therefore the damage potential) would not likely be known with great precision, resulting in a decision that would probably be based on worst-case estimates of the asteroid's likely size. For example, in the 2019 Planetary Defense Conference exercise,[38] the hypothetical asteroid's size was in the range of 100 to 300 metres (capable of causing regional devastation), and large enough to warrant consideration of a deflection mission.

---

36 NASA, 'Update to Determine the Feasibility of Enhancing the Search and Characterization of NEOs' (Report 2017) <https://cneos.jpl.nasa.gov/doc/2017_neo_sdt_final_e-version.pdf> accessed 21 February 2021.

37 Ibid 192.

38 See the Conference exercise summary at <https://cneos.jpl.nasa.gov/pd/cs/pdc19/> accessed 21 February 2021.

But what if the impact is not 100 percent certain? The impact probability estimate will depend on the accuracy of the orbital estimate of the asteroid; the uncertainties would be reduced only through the continued observations of the asteroid over time. It may take months or years before the impact can be predicted with certainty.

However, if decisions are delayed in favour of complete certainty, there may not be enough time remaining to carry out a deflection mission. The asteroid's orbital dynamics will dictate the optimum times for deflection and, although these repeat from orbit to orbit, the physics of the problem indicates that earlier deflection opportunities are almost always more effective and easier to accomplish. Ideally, the deflection should be applied at least one asteroid orbital period (on average, several years) before the predicted impact. This phase would become the basis for estimating the total time required to design and build (18 months to four years) the spacecraft, prepare for launch (a minimum of six months), and the transit time for the spacecraft to reach the asteroid (many months to years). To achieve a successful deflection, it is quite probable that the decision to begin designing and building the mission(s) would need to be made while considerable uncertainties remain regarding the impact probability and potential damage.

NASA has estimated that a warning time of about eight years could provide enough time to carry out deflection missions if decisions to act are expedient. For a robust design, two basic parameters must be known: 1) the magnitude of the velocity change required to make the asteroid's trajectory miss the Earth, and 2) the magnitude of the velocity change possible from the deflection mission. If these parameters are known adequately in advance, a successful campaign could be undertaken even if multiple missions are required to achieve the desired deflection. If these two quantities are poorly known, the deflection campaign may need to be dramatically over-designed to ensure success. The Action Plan's Goal 3 outlines a series of actions that, when completed, will increase the United States' ability to build and deploy rapid reconnaissance and deflection missions.

A reconnaissance mission to a threatening asteroid would provide critically important information that could dramatically increase the chances of a successful deflection. Primarily, the mission would yield accurate trajectory information, confirming whether an impact would occur, and enabling a precise prediction of the impact location. Secondarily, the mission would provide a precise measure of how much the asteroid's trajectory must be moved to make it miss the Earth.

The third major benefit of a reconnaissance mission is that it would provide a much more precise estimate of the size and mass of the asteroid, essential data for sizing the deflection mission(s). The mass of the asteroid, in particular, is key for predicting the amount of force needed for the velocity change required of the deflection, and Earth-based observations can typically only estimate this to within an order of magnitude. A factor of 10 uncertainty in the mass would result in a factor of 10 uncertainty in the velocity change to be imparted to the asteroid. The precise knowledge of the asteroid's physical parameters that a reconnaissance mission could obtain would lead to much more accurate predictions of the asteroid's potential impact effects, again enabling a more informed deflection decision.

While a reconnaissance mission has many benefits, it also must reach the asteroid as early as feasible, in order to inform the design of the follow-on deflection campaign. Rapid response, i.e. the ability to rapidly develop and deploy the reconnaissance spacecraft, is important. One way to reconnoitre the asteroid as early as possible is to use a flyby trajectory, which typically has a much shorter flight time than a rendezvous trajectory. A rendezvous mission has significant advantages in that it could accurately measure the mass of the asteroid through its gravitational attraction over time, remain on station to observe the arrival of the deflection missions (if determination is made that deflection is required) and verify that the velocity change imparted to the asteroid is sufficient to prevent the impact.

Many factors must be considered when deciding whether or not to build and launch a deflection mission. Is the asteroid large enough to pose a significant hazard? How great does the impact probability need to be to justify the resources? Is the data adequate to inform the decision that must be made? Is there enough time to execute the deflection? Even if the mission(s) perform as planned, can decisionmakers be assured the mission(s) will deliver sufficient deflection to make the asteroid miss the Earth? Could attempts at deflection just make matters worse? These questions are likely to be asked by any government reacting to the news that an asteroid is on a trajectory that will likely impact Earth – no matter the predicted impact location. NASA, required by Goal 5 of the Action Plan, co-chairs an interagency working group that is addressing how the United States could effectively respond. This interagency working group is examining what procedures and protocols might already be in place that could be utilised for an impact scenario. The following sections outline NASA's current activities to address Goal 5 of the Action Plan.

3.2 *Modelling and Assessment*

The PDCO's Asteroid Threat Assessment Project (ATAP) develops and refines capabilities to rapidly analyse data from various sources, and then to integrate it with asteroid characterisation data, before applying it to entry simulation and testing, hazard simulations, and probabilistic risk assessment analyses. The Project links asteroid characterisation factors (size or magnitude, orbital trajectory, asteroid class, composition, shape) to impact parameters (diameter, density, strength, efficiency, velocity, entry angle, and coordinates) to produce a probabilistic asteroid impact risk model to show casualties and damage estimates.[39] This capability should improve damage and risk assessments enabling better-informed decisions under uncertainty.

The Action Plan called for establishing an interagency impact modelling working group to evaluate the computational tools and expertise required for accurately and rapidly modelling impact risks.[40] Convened by ATAP in June 2019, this interagency impact-modelling working group will exercise, evaluate, and formulate ways to continually improve modelling and analysis capabilities. The working group's near-term goal is to determine the information required and the timeframe to perform the analysis, as well as to identify gaps in the analysis chain. The assessment will identify the computational tools that would be able to assess the outcome of deflection or disruption techniques, as well as tools for assessing the local, regional, or global risks associated with an impact scenario. Creation of this interagency impact-modelling working group is considered a high priority to ensure that the United States can rapidly respond when the need arises.

With this type of low-probability/high-consequence event, initial discussions would need to focus on time. A short-warning scenario would logically focus on emergency operations planning. With a longer warning time, that might permit space-based mitigation options, decisions for which there is little experience would need to be made. Complicating factors such as the time needed to ready a reconnaissance mission for launch, strategies to optimise the launch date to maximise build/development time while reducing cruise phase, and the time needed to build/develop the deflection/disruption spacecraft would need to be weighed. For example, in the hypothetical scenario discussed at the 2019 Planetary Defense Conference, the decisions to deploy reconnaissance and deflection spacecraft had to be made well before confirmation that

39 Donovan Mathais and others, 'Next Steps in Impact Risk Assessment' (IAA Planetary Defense Conference, Maryland, 29 April – 3 Mai 2019) IAA-PDC-19-06-03 <https://core.ac.uk/download/pdf/227726255.pdf> accessed 21 February 2021.

40 National Science and Technology Council Interagency Working Group on Detecting and Mitigating the Impacts of Earth-bound Near-Earth Asteroids (DAMIEN), 'The National Near-Earth Object Preparedness Strategy and Action Plan 14' (Report 2018) <https://aerospace.csis.org/wp-content/uploads/2019/02/OSTP-NEO-Strategy-Action-Plan-Jun18.pdf> accessed 21 February 2021.

the object had a 100 percent probability of impact.[41] Plans for an effective government response would need to identify the resources (personnel, computing, manufacturing, etc.) that would be required to develop decisions. Routine exercise of the processes to inform decision-making would ensure that the resources (computing tools and personnel) would be available to effectively respond.

3.3 *Technology and Mission Concept Development*

Taking the factors discussed above into consideration, NASA has begun developing mission concepts to identify instrument suites and mission designs to enable rapid development of reconnaissance and mitigation missions. In 2018, the PDCO convened an interagency working group to conduct an assessment of reconnaissance mission concepts to enable a high-fidelity cost-estimate and development path for the required instruments and spacecraft design.

In addition to the DART mission discussed above, NASA PDCO is also investing in technology development to explore techniques that can be used to deflect or disrupt an Earth-approaching asteroid. As required by the Action Plan, NASA is to develop technologies and designs for rapid-response deflection and disruption missions. The interagency working group described above will also assess technologies and mission design for deflection and disruption missions with an ultimate goal of developing flight demonstrations of these designs.

The most mature techniques to deflect or disrupt an asteroid on an Earth-impacting trajectory, determined by the United States National Academy of Sciences, are the kinetic impactor, gravity tractor, or high-energy explosive devices. They require technology demonstration and validation before being implemented for impact mitigation.[42] Kinetic deflection is currently the most mature as the technology already exists (see the discussion of the DART mission above). One of NASA's key goals in planetary defence is to detect asteroids well before a potential impact can occur to give humanity time to prepare for, respond to, and possibly prevent, an impact.

41 A summary of the 2019 Planetary Defense Conference can be found at <www.lpi.usra.edu/sbag/meetings/jun2019/presentations/Barbee.pdf> accessed 21 February 2021.

42 National Research Council, *Defending Planet Earth: Near-Earth Object Surveys and Hazard Mitigation Strategies Final Report* (National Academies Press 2010).

4 International Coordination

The PDCO works closely with the United Nations Office for Outer Space Affairs and the Committee on the Peaceful Uses of Outer Space, initially through its Action Team on Near Earth Objects (also known as Action Team 14). The International Asteroid Warning Network (IAWN) and the Space Missions Planning Advisory Group (SMPAG) are multinational endeavours endorsed by the United Nations for an international response to the NEO impact hazard. NASA currently leads support to IAWN, whose intent is to establish a worldwide effort to detect, track, and physically characterise NEOs to determine those that are potential impact threats to Earth and provide warning of any potential impact threat to the international community. IAWN currently has 25 international signatories that include observatories, national institutes, and space agencies.[43] NASA participates with other space-capable nations in SMPAG, whose objectives are to develop cooperative and collaborative projects and understanding on applicable technologies and techniques among national space agencies and offices and then to build consensus on space mission recommendations for planetary defence measures. In the event of a credible impact warning by IAWN, the SMPAG would propose mitigation options and implementation plans for consideration by the international community.

5 Conclusion

NASA's overarching goals for planetary defence focus on supporting development of an overall understanding of the threat of NEOs, and developing the means to mitigate the risk to Earth. The NASA Planetary Defense Coordination Office (PDCO), detects, tracks and characterises near-Earth asteroids and comets and assesses the potential for harm. The National Near-Earth Object Preparedness Strategy and Action Plan provides a national policy framework for much of the PDCO's activities as the PDCO works domestically and internationally to plan for, and coordinate, actions that may be undertaken to respond to an identified impactor. Furthermore, the PDCO funds development of space-based missions to improve overall understanding of the

43 IAWN, 'Members' (*International Asteroid Warning Network*, 11 December 2020) <http://iawn.net/about/members.shtml> accessed 21 February 2021.

risk and develops new concepts for technologies and systems that could be deployed in response. Finally, the PDCO is working with other United States government agencies to develop the processes and policies that will enable effective responses.

CHAPTER 7

ESA's Activities in Planetary Defence

Detlef Koschny

1 Introduction

The European Space Agency (ESA) is an intergovernmental organisation promoting "cooperation among European States in space research and technology and their space applications, with a view to their being used for scientific purposes and for operational space applications systems".[1] ESA has been officially dealing with Earth-threating asteroids since January 2009. That was when it started its 'Space Situational Awareness' programme. This programme, which has developed into the 'Space Safety' programme, consists of three segments: space weather, space debris, and Near-Earth Objects (NEOs). This chapter will focus on the NEO-related work – now called 'Planetary Defence' – of ESA.

ESA's planetary defence activities are executed within the so-called 'Planetary Defence Office', located in the Space Safety Office in the Directorate of Operations. The goals of the Planetary Defence Office are to:

- Become aware of the current and future position of NEOs relative to our planet,
- Estimate the likelihood of Earth impacts,
- Assess the consequences of any possible impact,
- Inform relevant parties, e.g. national emergency response agencies,
- Develop methods to deflect any risky asteroids.[2]

To achieve this, the work of the Planetary Defence Office is structured in three 'pillars': (1) Observations, (2) Information provision, and (3) Mitigation. They stand on a common basis, called 'ground and data systems support'. In the following, the activities of the three pillars will be explained in more detail. Most of the work is done by the so-called NEO Coordination Centre (NEOCC), which is located at ESA's establishment ESRIN in Frascati, Italy, and was inaugurated in May 2013.

1 Article II, Convention for the Establishment of a European Space Agency (adopted 30 May 1975, entered into force 30 October 1980) CSE/CS(73) 19, rev.7.

2 See the description of the goals of the Planetary Defence Office at the ESA website: <www.esa.int/Safety_Security/Risky_asteroids> accessed 26 February 2021.

 | DOI:10.1163/9789004467606_009

2 Observations

NEO observations are divided in two steps: (a) survey and (b) follow-up. Survey observations aim at covering as large as possible an area in the sky, to discover new objects. To do this, the same field in the sky is typically observed three to four times within 10 to 15 minutes. The stars will be at the same location – asteroids will move in this time period. With special software, these moving objects are detected. Currently, all major NEO surveys are funded by NASA.[3] ESA is testing survey strategies using their TOTAS (Teide Observatory Tenerife Asteroid Survey) system.[4]

To build up European capability to survey the sky, ESA is developing a very wide-field telescope, called the Flyeye telescope.[5] It is designed to cover a large area in the sky by a very large field-of-view of 6.7 x 6.7 deg^2 in the sky. The Moon has an apparent diameter of about 0.5 deg. This means that the Flyeye telescope will image a sky area of about 170 times that of the full Moon in just one image. This is achieved via a novel design, where the image plane is split into 16 smaller field-of-views. These are individually imaged by 16 different digital cameras.

The first Flyeye telescope is fully funded and expected to become operational at its foreseen site in Sicily, Italy, in 2021 to 2022. Software to schedule the telescope and to perform the needed data processing is currently being developed. A separate contract to build up the site infrastructure is in place. The development of a second Flyeye telescope started in 2020. This second telescope is expected to be installed at La Silla in Chile, a site hosted by the European Southern Observatory (ESO).[6]

Besides the activities for discovering new NEOs, ESA is very active in performing so-called follow-up observations of NEOs. Once an object has been discovered, follow-up observations are very important to ensure a good

3 The activities by NASA are explained in more detail further below in this book, see chapter 6 'The United States Planetary Defence Programme: NASA and the Planetary Defense Coordination Office' in this book.

4 Detlef Koschny and Matthias Busch, 'The Teide Observatory Tenerife Asteroid Survey' (2015) 118 Planetary and Space Science 305.

5 Lorenzo Cibin and others, 'The Fly-Eye Telescope, Development and First Factory Tests Results' (1st ESA NEO and Debris Detection Conference, Darmstadt, 22–24 January 2019) <https://conference.sdo.esoc.esa.int/proceedings/neossti/paper/481/NEOSST1-paper481.pdf> accessed 26 February 2021.

6 The European Southern Observatory (ESO) is a European intergovernmental organisation providing astronomical telescopes on several locations in Chile to European researchers. See <www.eso.org> accessed 12 July 2020.

knowledge of its orbit. This knowledge is paramount to reduce errors in the prediction of the orbit, and thus the probability of an impact on our planet.

To perform these follow-up observations, ESA is using its own telescopes, such as the Optical Ground Station in Tenerife and the so-called Test-Bed Telescope (TBT).[7] One TBT is operational in Cebreros, Spain. The second one is being installed in La Silla, Chile. ESA also has a number of contracts to get support from other telescopes.[8] In case of important follow-up observations, an ESA observer gets in touch with the contact points at these telescopes and triggers observations.

In addition, ESA has access to one of the largest telescopes on this planet, operated by ESO. ESA can trigger up to 11 hours of observations per semester to observe NEOs which are too faint to be observed from other telescopes, using the 8 metre Very Large Telescope (VLT).[9]

All position measurements are sent to the Minor Planet Center (MPC). The MPC, funded by the United States, is the world-wide clearing house of data on asteroids.[10]

3 Information Provision

The second pillar of ESA's planetary defence activities is the preparation and distribution of relevant data. Positional data of asteroids is taken from the MPC's database regularly, and precise orbital elements (the parameters describing the objects orbit around the Sun) are determined. In a second step, this orbit is propagated 100 years into the future. A special 'Impact Monitoring' system is checking the probability of any given object to impact on our planet. This work is closely coordinated with the NASA-funded 'Center for NEO Studies' at the Jet

7 The TBT is a telescope with 56 cm aperture which was developed for ESA to develop and test software and operational procedures for the larger Flyeye telescope. See Francisco Ocana and others, 'First results of the Test-Bed Telescopes (TBT) project: Cebreros telescope commissioning' (2016) 9906 Proceedings of the SPIE 9.

8 Examples are the 80 centimetre Calar Alto Schmidt telescope (Spain), the 1 metre Klet telescope (Czech Republic), and the ISON Network (Russia).

9 Marco Micheli and others, 'NEO Follow-up, Recovery, and Precovery Campaigns at the ESA NEO Coordination Centre' (2015) *10 Proceedings of the International Astronomical Union* 274; Marco Micheli and others, 'An ESA NEOCC effort to eliminate high Palermo scale virtual impactors' (2014) 113 Earth, Moon, and Planets 1.

10 See website of the Minor Planet Center <http://www.minorplanetcenter.org> accessed 26 February 2021.

Propulsion Laboratory in the United States.[11] Every critical impact prediction is double-checked between the two systems to avoid false alarms.

All objects for which the Impact Monitoring system computes a probability greater than zero for impacting the Earth are placed on the so-called 'Risk List'.[12] Of the currently known roughly 25000 NEOs, a little over 1000 objects are on this Risk List.[13] These are the ones which are closely monitored. By use of its telescopic assets, ESA attempts to conduct more observations of these objects to reduce the orbital uncertainties.

Besides performing this key task of computing orbits and predicting the impact probability of NEOs, the NEOCC also collects and distributes other relevant information. Most notably, it provides a database with physical properties of NEOs, such as their size, mass, rotational period, and many more. The size can be estimated, assuming an average reflectivity of 14 percent, from measuring the brightness at a given distance. Most of the other parameters can only be determined if additional measurements have been performed. Once available, these parameters can be searched via the NEOCCs technical web portal.[14]

Other information which is being provided includes information on comets, a database with fireballs brighter than -10 magnitudes (about the brightness of the Moon during first or last quarter), information on close approaches, discovery statistics, and historical information on activities related to NEOs.

4 Mitigation

Once a possible NEO impact threat has been identified, there must be a means to communicate this information to the relevant parties, in particular political decision makers and emergency response agencies. An important tool for this is the so-called Close-Encounter Fact Sheet (CAFS). If an object reaches an apparent brightness of 11 mag (visible with a pair of binoculars), the production of the CAFS is triggered. This means that, for larger objects, it will be triggered at larger flyby distances, while smaller objects only trigger the production of

11 The 'Center for NEO Studies' has tasks similar to ESA's NEO Coordination Centre, namely to compute asteroid and comet orbits and their odds of impacting our planet. See <https://cneos.jpl.nasa.gov/> accessed 26 February 2021.

12 ESA, 'Risk page' (*European Space Agency*) <http://neo.ssa.esa.int/risk-page> accessed 26 February 2021.

13 Ibid. See also ESA, 'NEO Coordination Centre' and 'Search for Comets' (*European Space Agency*) <http://neo.ssa.esa.int./web/guest/comets> accessed 26 February 2021.

14 ESA, 'Search for Asteroids' (*European Space Agency*) <http://neo.ssa.esa.int/search-for-asteroids> accessed 26 February 2021.

the CAFS for close flybys. Between August 2017 and September 2019, six CAFSs were produced.[15]

The CAFS contains information on the flyby distance, speed, estimated size and maximum brightness of the object, as well as information on where the object would be visible and on whether it has a chance to impact our planet. If the latter is true, additional information is provided about the possible impact corridor on the ground and the expected damage. This last information, however, will at least in the beginning only be distributed to emergency response agencies. The CAFS is distributed to a list of contact points, e.g. at the German Space Situational Awareness Centre. In addition, ESA also organises training sessions with emergency response agencies.

ESA moreover participates in activities by the International Asteroid Warning Network (IAWN) and the Space Mission Planning Advisory Group (SMPAG). These two groups have been formed under the auspices of the United Nations, but are independent expert bodies.[16] They are the forum where the topic of planetary defence is discussed on a truly international level. ESA supports the work of IAWN by providing observational capabilities, producing software to estimate the effect of a NEO impact, and by the above-mentioned work with the emergency response agencies. As for SMPAG, the main aim of this group is to prepare activities needed by space agencies to mitigate a NEO impact threat. ESA is currently chairing this group.

ESA is also preparing the Hera mission as part of an international asteroid deflection demonstration collaboration, called AIDA (Asteroid Impact Deflection Assessment).[17] Hera complements NASA's DART (Double Asteroid Redirection Test) mission. DART will impact the smaller of the objects in a double asteroid system, called Didymos. It is scheduled to arrive at Didymos in October 2022. The European Hera mission will be an observer spacecraft, which will arrive in 2026 and characterise the surface and mass properties of the asteroid. It will also observe the impact crater produced by DART. These measurements will be crucial in understanding the details of how efficient such an asteroid deflection can be.

15 ESA, 'CAFS' (*European Space Agency*) <http://neo.ssa.esa.int/cafs> accessed 26 February 2021.

16 Romana Kofler and others, 'International Coordination on Planetary Defence: The Work of the IAWN and the SMPAG' (2019) 156 Acta Astronautica 409; see also chapter 4 'International Cooperation in Planetary Defence – UNCOPUOS, IAWN and SMPAG' in this book.

17 ESA, 'Hera' (*European Space Agency*) <https://www.esa.int/Safety_Security/Hera/Hera> accessed 26 February 2021.

5 Ground and Data Systems Support

The 'ground and data systems support' combines all the needed work on telescope- and other hardware, computer and network systems, including common processes for software development and delivery.[18] A single ground segment team and a data systems team support all elements in ESA's Space Safety programme in a synergetic manner.

6 Current Status and Near Future

The NEOCC in Frascati, Italy, is the focal point of ESA's NEO-related work since 2013. Support is provided by experts from other ESA centres, such as ESTEC/Netherlands and ESOC/Germany, all funded via the Space Safety programme of ESA

The first Flyeye telescope is fully funded and is expected to become operational between 2021 and 2022 in Sicily, Italy. The development of a second Flyeye telescope has been approved by the ESA member states at the Council Meeting at Ministerial Level in November 2019 and started in 2020.

The activities related to the Hera space mission, which has originally been prepared in the General Studies Programme of ESA, have become part of the Space Safety programme to ensure a direct link between ground- and space-based activities. The mission is due to launch in 2024.

Other near-term activities are the consolidation of interfaces with emergency response agencies of all member countries of the programme, the upgrading of the web portal to include the possibility of automated access, and an expansion of the software tools and the available personnel to provide better support to the community.

18 Gianpiero di Girolamo and others, 'SSA Data Centres and Data Systems: Evolution towards a Hybrid Architecture' (2018 SpaceOps Conference, Marseille, 28 May–1 June 2018) <https://arc.aiaa.org/doi/pdfplus/10.2514/6.2018-2594> accessed 26 February 2021.

CHAPTER 8

Planetary Defence Activities beyond NASA and ESA

Brent W Barbee

1 Introduction

The collision of a significant asteroid or comet with Earth represents a singular natural disaster for a myriad of reasons, including: its extra-terrestrial origin; the fact that it is perhaps the only natural disaster that is preventable in many cases, given sufficient preparation and warning; its scope, which ranges from damaging a city to an extinction-level event; and the duality of asteroids and comets themselves – they are grave potential threats, but also tantalising scientific clues to our ancient past and resources with which we may one day build a prosperous spacefaring future.

Accordingly, the problems of developing the means to interact with asteroids and comets for purposes of defence, scientific study, exploration, and resource utilisation have grown in importance over the past several decades. Since the 1980s, more and more asteroids and comets (especially the former) have been discovered, radically changing our picture of the Solar System. At the beginning of the year 1980, approximately 9000 asteroids were known to exist. By the beginning of 2001, that number had risen to approximately 125000 thanks to the Earth-based telescopic survey efforts of the era.[1] Today, about 1067500 asteroids have been discovered, with more and more being found every week, month, and year.[2]

The hazards posed to us by asteroids affect people everywhere around the world. As well, the opportunities presented by asteroids may benefit our entire species. Thus, with such a large number of currently known asteroids and so many yet to be discovered, it is not surprising that individuals, organisations,

1 Scott Manley, 'Asteroid Discovery – 1970–2015 – 8K resolution' (YouTube, 24 September 2015) <www.youtube.com/watch?v=BKKg4lZ_0-Y> accessed 26 February 2021.

2 NASA JPL, 'JPL Small-Body Database Search Engine' (*NASA JPL Center for Near Earth Object Studies*) <https://ssd.jpl.nasa.gov/sbdb_query.cgi> accessed 5 March 2021. Of those, approximately 21400 are categorised as Near-Earth asteroids (NEAs), 2000 of which are categorised as Potentially Hazardous Asteroids (PHAs). See NASA JPL, 'Discovery Statistics' (*NASA JPL Center for Near Earth Object Studies*) <https://cneos.jpl.nasa.gov/stats/totals.html> accessed 5 March 2021.

 | DOI:10.1163/9789004467606_010

institutions, and governments all around the world have become interested in the study of asteroids. Indeed, a variety of government space agencies, private organisations, and individuals have worked on developing the means by which to observe, study, and even interact with asteroids and comets for purposes including science, exploration, pioneering, commerce, and planetary defence. This includes significant individual contributions by amateur asteroid astronomers all over the world. International cooperation in planetary defence within the contexts of the United Nations, the Space Mission Planning Advisory Group (SMPAG) and the International Asteroid Warning Network (IAWN) are discussed in Chapter 3, and the activities undertaken by the world's larger space agencies, ESA and NASA, are discussed in Chapters 4 and 5. But, what of the other agencies and institutions around the world who are also working on the problem of defence against hazardous asteroids and comets, or related topics? In this chapter an overview is provided, in alphabetical order, of some of the planetary defence related efforts that have been undertaken around the world beyond the activities at the United Nations, NASA, and ESA.

2 B612 Foundation

The B612 Foundation is a private non-profit foundation whose headquarters is located in Mill Valley, California, USA. B612 was founded in 2002 by Edward Lu, Russell Schweickart, Piet Hut, and Clark Chapman, with the goal of "significantly altering the orbit of an asteroid in a controlled manner".[3] The foundation is named after the asteroid lived on by the main character of the 1943 novella *The Little Prince* by Antoine de Saint-Exupéry. B612 has previously advocated for increased NASA funding to enable completion of the search for potentially hazardous Near-Earth Objects (NEOs) and worked to help motivate and organise international planetary defence preparedness efforts. In 2012, ten years after its founding, B612 began attempting to raise private donation funding to deploy an infrared space-based NEO survey telescope mission named Sentinel.[4] The mission was originally planned to launch in 2017 or 2018, but

3 'Apollo Astronaut to Discuss Asteroid Threats to Earth' (*The Orange County Register*, 13 January 2008) <www.ocregister.com/2008/01/13/apollo-astronaut-to-discuss-asteroid-threats-to-earth/> accessed 26 February 2021.

4 Debra Werner, 'Group Raising Funds for Telescope To Detect Deadly Asteroids' (*SpaceNews*, 9 July 2012) <https://spacenews.com/group-raising-funds-telescope-detect-deadly-asteroids/> accessed 26 February 2021; note that Sentinel was intended to be an infrared space-based NEO survey telescope placed in a 'Venus-trailing' or 'Venus-like' orbit, i.e., an orbit around the Sun similar to Venus' orbit, but with the spacecraft not located near Venus itself.

by 2015 efforts to raise funds for the mission were falling short of the needed funding milestones.[5] As a result, B612 decided to end development of Sentinel.

After discontinuing Sentinel development, B612 began studying the use of the synthetic tracking technique deployed on multiple smaller telescope spacecraft as an alternative concept to the more traditional single, large telescope spacecraft.[6] The foundation's focus then shifted to algorithm development and data analysis, and those efforts continue as of the time of this writing. In 2018, B612 announced the consolidation of their research efforts under the Asteroid Institute, a virtual organisation collaborating with the Data Intensive Research in Astrophysics and Cosmology Center (DIRAC) at the Department of Astronomy of the University of Washington.[7] One of their analysis projects is the Asteroid Decision Analysis Machine (ADAM), the goal of which is to improve abilities to make decisions on potential asteroid threats.[8]

3 Canada

The Canadian Space Agency (CSA) and Defence Research and Development Canada (DRDC) funded the development and launch of a small Canadian spacecraft named NEOSSat (Near Earth Object Surveillance Satellite).[9] NEOSSat was originally scheduled to launch in 2007, but the launch was delayed until February of 2013. The goal of the 74 kilogramme spacecraft was the detection of NEOs, particularly those with orbits largely or entirely interior to Earth's orbit around the Sun.

Various problems that included issues with the electrical system, camera control software, and pointing stability systems degraded the quality of images produced by the spacecraft, which prevented it from being able to carry out its

5 Traci Watson, 'Private Asteroid Hunt Lacks Cash to Spy Threats in Orbit' (2015) 522 Nature 402.
6 Jeff Foust, 'B612 Studying Smallsat Missions to Search for Near Earth Objects' (*Spacenews*, 20 June 2017) <https://spacenews.com/b612-studying-smallsat-missions-to-search-for-near-earth-objects/> accessed 26 February 2021.
7 B612, 'B612 Annual Progress Report 2018: Protecting the Earth from Asteroid Impacts' <https://b612foundation.org/wp-content/uploads/2018/10/2018-B612-Annual-Progress-Report.pdf> accessed 26 February 2021.
8 B612, 'B612's Progress Report, vol 2: Engaging the World in Planetary Defense' <https://b612foundation.org/b612s-progress-report-vol-1-engaging-the-world-in-planetary-defense-2/> accessed 26 February 2021.
9 Canadian Space Agency, 'NEOSSat: Canada's Sentinel in the Sky' (*Canadian Space Agency*, 16 July 2018) <www.asc-csa.gc.ca/eng/satellites/neossat/> accessed 26 February 2021.

planned NEO detection mission.[10] The issues preventing NEOSSat from operating as intended are detailed in the report of an audit conducted by the CSA's Audit and Evaluation Directorate, which was published in early 2014.[11]

However, the NEOSSat team was able to devise means of overcoming the problems with the spacecraft, resulting in NEOSSat becoming able to carry out its mission.[12] Although no longer focused on near-Sun surveying, NEOSSat is currently making follow-up observations of various asteroids and comets, including NEOs,[13] and it participated in the past several IAWN campaigns. The NEOSSat astronomy raw image archive is publicly available on CSA's Open Data Portal[14] and on the Canadian Astronomy Data Centre website of the National Research Council of Canada (NRC).[15]

4 China

4.1 *Chang'e 2 Flyby of Potentially Hazardous Near-Earth Asteroid 4179 Toutatis (1989 AC)*

The China National Space Administration (CNSA) launched the Chang'e 2 spacecraft on 1 October 2010,[16] after which it proceeded to enter orbit around the Moon and begin mapping the lunar surface. The spacecraft's primary

10 Jordan Press, 'Asteroid-tracking Satellite not up to the Job: Review' (*Ottawa Citizen,* 6 July 2014) <https://ottawacitizen.com/news/national/asteroid-tracking-satellite-not-up-to-the-job-review> accessed 26 February 2021.

11 Canadian Space Agency, 'Evaluation of the Near Earth Object Surveillance Satellite (NEOSSat) Project. For the period from February 2005 to December 2013' (*Canadian Space Agency,* February 2014), <www.asc-csa.gc.ca/eng/publications/er-1314-0202.asp> accessed 26 February 2021.

12 Viqar Abbasi and others, 'Resurrecting NEOSSat: How Innovative Flight Software Saved Canada's Space Telescope' in Helen Pasquier and others (eds), *Space Operations: Inspiring Humankind's Future* (Springer 2019).

13 Viqar Abbasi and others, 'The NEOSSat Experience: 5 Years in the Life of Canada's Space Surveillance Telescope' (1st NEO and Debris Detection Conference, Darmstadt, Germany, 22–24 January 2019), published by the ESA Space Safety Programme Office <http://neo-sst-conference.sdo.esoc.esa.int> accessed 26 February 2021.

14 Canadian Space Agency, 'Open Data' (*Canadian Space Agency,* 1 October 2020) <www.asc-csa.gc.ca/eng/open-data/default.asp> accessed 26 February 2021.

15 CADC, 'Near-Earth Object Surveillance Satellite (NEOSSat)' (*Canadian Astronomy Data Centre,* 14 November 2019) <www.cadc-ccda.hia-iha.nrc-cnrc.gc.ca/en/neossat/> accessed 26 February 2021.

16 Stephen Clark, 'China's Second Moon Probe Dispatched from Earth' (*Spaceflight Now,* 1 October 2010) <www.spaceflightnow.com/news/n1010/01change2launch/> accessed 26 February 2021.

mission objectives were completed by November of 2010, and detailed lunar surface maps constructed using data collected by the spacecraft were published during the months and years that followed.[17] Meanwhile, the spacecraft was directed to depart lunar orbit in June 2011 and travel to the Sun-Earth Lagrange point 2 (SEL2).[18] After departing from SEL2, Chang'e 2 was directed to proceed to a flyby of the Potentially Hazardous Asteroid (PHA) 4179 Toutatis (1989 AC) in December 2012,[19] when the asteroid was approximately 7 million kilometres from Earth.

Toutatis[20] is categorised as a PHA due to its Earth minimum orbit intersection distance (MOID) of 0.0064 AU (Astronomical Units).[21] Its absolute magnitude is 15.3 and its albedo (surface reflectivity) is 0.405, which together suggest an approximate diameter of 1800 metres. By contrast, planetary radar observations revealed that Toutatis is rather irregularly shaped, with dynamically equivalent, equal volume ellipsoid dimensions of 1700 metres × 2030 metres × 4260 metres.[22] Thus, Toutatis serves as a good example of how challenging it can be to assess an asteroid's true shape and size without radar imagery and/or close proximity imaging via spacecraft.

The Chang'e 2 spacecraft passed within 3.2 kilometres of Toutatis at a relative velocity of 10.73 kilometres/second and collected images of the asteroid at approximately 10 metre per pixel resolution. The spacecraft imagery was later compared to the radar-derived shape model of Toutatis, revealing some small but interesting differences between the radar-derived shape model and the actual asteroid shape shown in the spacecraft camera images.[23] With the completion of the Toutatis flyby, China became the fourth spaceflight-capable nation to deploy a successful mission to an asteroid, following NASA, ESA, and the Japan Aerospace Exploration Agency (JAXA).

17 Tariq Malik, 'China Unveils Best Moon Map yet from Lunar Orbiter' (*Space.com*, 10 February 2012) <www.space.com/14536-china-moon-map-change-2-images.html> accessed 26 February 2021.

18 The spacecraft arrived at SEL2 in August 2011. In doing so, it became the first spacecraft ever to travel directly from lunar orbit to SEL2.

19 Emily Lakdawalla, 'Chang'E 2 has Departed Earth's Neighborhood for … Asteroid Toutatis!?' (*The Planetary Society*, 14 June 2012) <www.planetary.org/blogs/emily-lakdawalla/2012/20120614-change-2-toutatis.html> accessed 26 February 2021.

20 The asteroid has a heliocentric orbit semi-major axis of 2.543 AU, eccentricity of 0.626, and inclination of 0.44°. Lightcurve observations show its rotation period to be 176 hours.

21 1 AU is the mean distance of Earth from the Sun, 149,597,870.7 km.

22 NASA JPL, '4179 Toutatis (1989 AC)' (*NASA JPL Small-Body Database Browser*) <https://ssd.jpl.nasa.gov/sbdb.cgi?sstr=Toutatis> accessed 5 March 2021.

23 Xiaoduan Zou and others, 'The preliminary analysis of the 4179 Toutatis snapshots of the Chang'E-2 flyby' (2014) 229 Icarus 348.

4.2 *Potential Mission to 469219 Kamo'oalewa (2016 HO_3)*

In April 2019, CNSA announced a concept for a ten-year mission named ZhengHe, which would launch in 2022 or 2024 to collect and return samples of the near-Earth asteroid (NEA) 469219 Kamo'oalewa (2016 HO_3),[24] which is also categorised as an Earth quasi-satellite. Although not captured by the Earth's gravity, the asteroid makes distant repeating loops around the Earth when viewed in a frame of reference that moves with Earth along its orbit around the Sun. The repeating loop-like motion around Earth, which occurs well beyond the Earth's gravitational sphere of influence, is due to the nature of the relative motion between the Earth and the asteroid as they move independently around the Sun.[25]

Kamo'oalewa[26] has an Earth MOID of 0.0333 AU, which meets the PHA Earth MOID criterion of less than or equal to 0.05 AU. However, the asteroid is not technically categorised as a PHA because its absolute magnitude of 24.3 does not meet the PHA criterion of absolute magnitude less than or equal to 22.0.[27] Its absolute magnitude suggests that its approximate size should be between 23 metres and 105 metres, depending on how reflective the asteroid's surface is.[28]

After collecting samples from Kamo'oalewa and returning them to Earth, the ZhengHe spacecraft would then proceed to the main asteroid belt region beyond the orbit of Mars, where it would visit and study the object 7968 Elst-Pizarro, which is categorised as both an asteroid (due to its orbital location within the Solar System) and a comet (due to its display of a cometary dust tail when near perihelion). As with most missions to asteroids or comets, the goals of ZhengHe would include studying the compositions and origins of the Solar System, as well as the origins of life on Earth. As of the time of this writing, the Chinese government has not yet formally approved the ZhengHe mission.[24]

---

24 Elizabeth Gibney, 'China Plans Mission to Earth's Pet Asteroid' (*Nature*, 30 April 2019) <www.nature.com/articles/d41586-019-01390-5> accessed 26 February 2021.

25 NASA JPL, 'Small Asteroid Is Earth's Constant Companion' (*NASA JPL Center for Near-Earth Object Studies*, 15 June 2016) <https://www.jpl.nasa.gov/news/small-asteroid-is-earths-constant-companion> accessed 5 March 2021.

26 The asteroid has a heliocentric orbit semi-major axis of 1.0011 AU, eccentricity of 0.1035, and inclination of 7.78°. Lightcurve observations show its rotation period to be 0.476 hours.

27 An absolute magnitude less than or equal to 22 corresponds to an approximate physical size of 140 metres or larger, assuming an albedo of approximately 14 %.

28 NASA JPL '469219 Kamo`oalewa (2016 HO3)' (*NASA JPL Small-Body Database Browser*) <https://ssd.jpl.nasa.gov/sbdb.cgi?sstr=2016HO3> accessed 5 March 2021.

5 Denmark

A group called the Emergency Asteroid Defence Project (EADP) formed in Denmark circa 2015, with the goal of crowdfunding a standing NEO deflection system based on the Hypervelocity Asteroid Intercept Vehicle (HAIV) concept.[29] The HAIV concept was developed by Professor Bong Wie and his graduate students at the Asteroid Deflection Research Collaboration (ADRC), located in the Department of Aerospace Engineering at Iowa State University. The EADP website is no longer accessible, and there are no indications that the project was able to move forward. Their Indiegogo crowdfunding website for collecting donations indicates that they were able to raise 8834 USD, from 187 donors ('backers'), towards their original goal of 200000 USD.[30]

The EADP concept of collecting private donations to fund a non-governmental planetary defence related initiative is unique thus far, with only the B612 Foundation's attempt to fund a NEO survey telescope using private donations being comparable. The inability of either the EADP or B612 efforts to ultimately fund their missions and bring them to fruition suggests that planetary defence mission activities will remain the province of governments, at least for the time being. However, the fact that some donor funds were able to be raised at all is still significant, demonstrating that some citizens are interested in planetary defence and believe that conducting planetary defence activities is an important and worthwhile use of resources.

6 Japan

6.1 *Hayabusa*

On 9 May 2003, JAXA launched the Hayabusa spacecraft to the PHA 25143 Itokawa (1998 SF_{36}), with the goals of rendezvousing with the asteroid, studying it with onboard instruments, and returning samples of the asteroid material to Earth. The mission was originally designated Mu Space Engineering Spacecraft C (MUSES-C), but its name was subsequently changed to Hayabusa, which means "peregrine falcon" in Japanese.

29 Brent Barbee and others, 'Conceptual design of a flight validation mission for a Hypervelocity Asteroid Intercept Vehicle' (2015) 106 Acta Astronautica 139–159.

30 Henrik Skaksen Jacobsen, 'Help Defend Earth Against Asteroid Threats' (*Indiegogo*) <www.indiegogo.com/projects/help-defend-earth-against-asteroid-threats/> accessed 26 February 2021.

Itokawa[31] is categorised as a PHA due to its Earth MOID of 0.013 AU. The asteroid's orbit also makes it relatively accessible for spacecraft missions. Its absolute magnitude is 19.2, which suggests that its approximate size should be between 250 metres and 1100 metres, depending on how reflective the asteroid's surface is. The Hayabusa mission discovered that Itokawa is somewhat irregularly shaped, with approximate physical dimensions of 535 metres × 294 metres × 209 metres, and that the asteroid has an average density of 1.9 g/cm^3.[32]

Hayabusa's low-thrust solar electric xenon propulsion system brought it to rendezvous with Itokawa in September 2005, after which the spacecraft performed station-keeping approximately 20 kilometres from the asteroid. Hayabusa later moved to the asteroid's surface for sample collection by means of firing small projectiles into the asteroid's surface and then collecting the material kicked up by the impacts of those projectiles. However, the spacecraft experienced a variety of technical problems that impeded the sample collection attempt,[33] and only a few tiny grains of asteroid material were actually collected. Prior to the spacecraft's collection of material from Itokawa, Hayabusa had deployed a small mini-lander (approximately 10 centimetres in size) named MINERVA, which was intended to descend to Itokawa's surface and then utilise an internal flywheel to hop between locations on the asteroid. However, errors in deployment resulted in MINERVA instead tumbling into space, away from Itokawa.[34]

Hayabusa's initiation of its flight back to Earth after asteroid sample collection was delayed due to technical issues with the attitude control and propulsion systems.[33] However, the spacecraft's mission control personnel were able to resolve those issues and the spacecraft began its journey back to Earth in April 2007. Hayabusa reached Earth and deployed its sample return capsule on 13 June 2010, at which time both the spacecraft and sample return capsule entered the Earth's atmosphere. The spacecraft was destroyed by atmospheric entry, as planned, while the sample return capsule performed a parachute

---

31 The asteroid has a heliocentric orbit semi-major axis of 1.324 AU, eccentricity of 0.28, and inclination of 1.62°. Its rotation period is 12.132 hours.

32 NASA JPL, '25143 Itokawa (1998 SF36)' (*NASA JPL Small-Body Database Browser*) <https://ssd.jpl.nasa.gov/sbdb.cgi?sstr=Itokawa> accessed 5 March 2021.

33 Maggie McKee, 'New Data Reveals Mysteries of Asteroid Itokawa' (*NewScientist*, 20 March 2006) <www.newscientist.com/article/dn8868-new-data-reveals-mysteries-of-asteroid-itokawa/> accessed 26 February 2021.

34 James Oberg, 'Asteroid-hopping Robot Misses its Mark' (*NBC News*, 14 November 2005) <www.nbcnews.com/id/10013920> accessed 26 February 2021.

landing within the designated landing zone in the Woomera Prohibited Area in South Australia, after which it was successfully recovered.[35]

Examination of the capsule and its contents revealed that 1500 grains of material, each approximately 10 micrometres in size, had been collected from Itokawa. Although only a tiny amount of material, this would still constitute the first return of asteroid material to Earth. Analyses of those samples suggest that Itokawa was previously part of a larger asteroid, indicate that Itokawa's surface material is approximately 8 million years old, and show that Itokawa's composition matches that of an LL chondrite meteorite (largely comprised of the minerals pyroxene and olivine, with some iron oxide).[36]

6.2 *Hayabusa2*

Following the success of the Hayabusa mission, JAXA developed and deployed the Hayabusa2 spacecraft to visit, study, and return samples from the PHA 162173 Ryugu (1999 JU_3). Ryugu is a dark, primitive carbonaceous asteroid of the rare spectral type Cg (exhibiting characteristics of both C-type and G-type asteroids).[37]

Ryugu is categorised as a PHA due to its Earth MOID of 0.00063 AU. The asteroid is also relatively accessible for spacecraft missions, with heliocentric orbit semi-major axis of 1.189 AU, eccentricity of 0.19, and inclination of 5.88°. Its absolute magnitude is 19.3, which suggests that its approximate size should be between 240 metres and 1070 metres, depending on how reflective the asteroid's surface is.[38] The Hayabusa2 mission discovered that Ryugu has a roundish shape featuring an equatorial bulge, with approximate physical dimensions of 1040 metres × 1020 metres × 880 metres, and that the asteroid has an average density of 1.19 g/cm^3, with >50 % porosity.[39]

---

35 Coober Pedy News and Events, 'Hayabusa Capsule – Parachutes Into Woomera Protected Area Far North SA' (*Coober Pedy Regional Times*, 6 June 2010) <https://cooberpedytimes.com/2010/06/06/hayabusa-capsule-parachutes-from-outer-space-to-coober-pedy-in-far-north-sa/> accessed 26 February 2021.

36 Multiple Authors, 'Hot Topic: Hayabusa – Dust from Itokawa' (*Science*, 26 August 2011) (issue containing seven papers) <www.sciencemag.org/site/feature/data/hottopics/hayabusa2011/> accessed 26 February 2021.

37 Wendy Zuckerman, 'Hayabusa 2 Will Seek the Origins of Life in Space' (*NewScientist*, 18 August 2020) <www.newscientist.com/article/dn19332-hayabusa-2-will-seek-the-origins-of-life-in-space/> accessed 26 February 2021.

38 NASA JPL, '162173 Ryugu (1999 JU3)' (*NASA JPL Small-Body Database Browser*) <https://ssd.jpl.nasa.gov/sbdb.cgi?sstr=Ryugu> accessed 5March 2021.

39 Seiichiro Watanabe and others, 'Hayabusa2 arrives at the carbonaceous asteroid 162173 Ryugu – A spinning top-shaped rubble pile' (2019) 64 Science 268–272.

The Hayabusa2 mission launched in December 2014 and utilised its solar electric ion thruster propulsion system to reach rendezvous with Ryugu on 27 June 2018. The spacecraft spent nearly a year and half surveying Ryugu in close proximity and then collecting surface and subsurface samples. The surface samples were collected using a mechanism based on that of the previous Hayabusa mission. The spacecraft descended to the surface, where the sample collection horn made contact and a 5 gram tantalum bullet was fired into the surface at 300 m/s, creating surface material ejecta that were collected in the top portion of the horn.[40] The subsurface samples were collected by first excavating a 14.5±0.8 metre crater using a more substantial impactor, a 2000 gram copper impactor fired at 2000 m/s.[41] Additionally, the spacecraft deployed three rovers to the asteroid's surface, all of which operated nominally. Hayabusa2 departed Ryugu on 13 November 2019 and delivered its sample return capsule to Earth on 6 December 2020.[42] The sample container was opened on 15 December 2020 and found to contain sampled material from Ryugu, including many black-coloured grains several millimetres in size.[43] The spacecraft is now on an extended mission to perform a high-speed flyby of asteroid 2001 CC_{21} in July 2026 and then rendezvous with asteroid 1998 KY_{26}, which is a small fast-rotating asteroid, in July 2031.[44]

6.3 *PROCYON*

PROCYON (Proximate Object Close flyby with Optical Navigation) was a small, low-cost spacecraft co-launched with Hayabusa2 in December of 2014. PROCYON was planned to perform a flyby of the PHA (185851) 2000 DP_{107} during 2016.[45]

---

40 Paul Rincon, 'Hayabusa-2: Japan spacecraft touches down on asteroid' (*BBC News*, 22 February 2019) <www.bbc.com/news/science-environment-47293317> accessed 26 February 2021.

41 Masahiko Arakawa and others, 'An Artificial Impact on the Asteroid 162173 Ryugu Formed a Crater in the Gravity-dominated Regime' (2020) 368 Science 67.

42 Dennis Normille, 'Japan's Hayabusa2 Capsule Lands with Carbon-rich Asteroid Samples' (*Science*, 7 December 2020) < https://www.sciencemag.org/news/2020/12/japan-s-hayabusa2-capsule-lands-carbon-rich-asteroid-samples> accessed 5 March 2021.

43 JAXA Hayabusa 2 Project, 'Images of the Samples from Ryugu', <https://www.hayabusa2.jaxa.jp/en/topics/20201225_samples/> accessed 5 March 2021.

44 JAXA Hayabusa2 Project, 'Asteroid Explorer, Hayabusa2, Reporter Briefing' <https://www.hayabusa2.jaxa.jp/enjoy/material/press/Hayabusa2_Press_20200915_ver9_en2.pdf> accessed 5 March 2021.

45 Stefano Campagnola and others, 'Low-Thrust Trajectory Design and Operations of PROCYON, the First Deep-Space Micro-Spacecraft' (25th International Symposium on Space Flight Dynamics, Germany, 19–23 October 2015) <https://issfd.org/2015/files/downloads/papers/072_Campagnola.pdf> accessed 26 February 2021.

2000 DP_{107}[46] is categorised as a PHA due to its Earth MOID of 0.0147 AU. Its absolute magnitude is 18.2, which suggests that its approximate size should be between 400 metres and 1800 metres, depending on how reflective the asteroid's surface is. Characterisation via planetary radar revealed that 2000 DP_{107} is a binary asteroid system, where the primary object in the system has dimensions of 992 metres × 938 metres × 964 metres, a bulk density of approximately 1.365 g/cm^3 (with bulk porosity likely in the range of 55–65 %), and a geometric albedo of 0.137.[47] The diameter of the secondary object is approximately 300 metres, and the objects orbit one another with a 1.76-day period at a separation distance of 2600 metres. Remote observations of its spectra indicate that 2000 DP_{107} exhibits both C-type (carbonaceous) and M-type (metallic) characteristics.

PROCYON initiated the use of its ion thruster in February 2015 to begin its journey towards 2000 DP_{107}. However, the ion thruster system failed in March 2015 and contact with the spacecraft was lost in December 2015. Prior to loss of contact, the spacecraft was able to provide observations of the hydrogen coma of comet 67P/Churyumov-Gerasimenko (the destination of ESA's Rosetta mission) and assess the rate at which the comet discharges water. This constituted the first scientific observations collected by such a small spacecraft (~70 kg mass, ~60 cm size).[48] Additionally, the spacecraft was able to collect the first complete observations of Earth's hydrogen corona, enabling the discovery of its north-south symmetry.[49]

6.4 *DESTINY+*

DESTINY+ (Demonstration and Experiment of Space Technology for INterplanetary voYage Phaethon fLyby dUSt science) is a spacecraft mission currently under development at JAXA for a 2022 launch, with the goal of studying and understanding interplanetary dust and its origins.[50] The spacecraft

46 The asteroid's heliocentric orbit semi-major axis is 1.365 AU, its eccentricity is 0.376, and its inclination is 8.67°. Lightcurve data indicates the primary object is rotating with a period of 2.7754 hours.

47 NASA JPL, '185851 (2000 DP107)' (*NASA JPL Small-Body Database Browser*) <https://ssd.jpl.nasa.gov/sbdb.cgi?sstr=2000DP107> accessed 5 March 2021.

48 National Astronomical Observatory of Japan, 'Micro Spacecraft Investigates Cometary Water Mystery' (*NAO*, 24 January 2017) <www.nao.ac.jp/en/news/science/2017/20170124-procyon.html> accessed 26 February 2021.

49 Shingo Kameda and others, 'Ecliptic North-South Symmetry of Hydrogen Geocorona' (2017) 44 Geophysical 11,706–11,712.

50 JAXA, 'DESTINY+' (*Japan Aerospace Exploration Agency*) <https://destiny.isas.jaxa.jp/> accessed 26 February 2021.

design utilises efficient solar electric low-thrust ion engines and demonstrates very lightweight solar panel technology.[51] As part of its mission profile, DESTINY+ would perform a flyby of the PHA 3200 Phaethon (1983 TB), which has been observed to emit dust despite appearing to otherwise display asteroidal, rather than cometary, characteristics.

Phaeton[52] is categorised as a PHA due to its Earth MOID of 0.0195 AU.[53] Its absolute magnitude is 14.6, which suggests that its approximate size should be between 2100 metres and 9200 metres, depending on how reflective the asteroid's surface is. Arecibo radar observations show the object's size to be about 6250 metres.[54] Infrared Astronomical Satellite (IRAS) observations indicate the object's geometric albedo is 0.1066, and combining that with the aforementioned absolute magnitude yields an estimated size of 4890 metres, which is within approximately 20 % of the actual object size as assessed via radar. The 4890 metre size estimate based on the absolute magnitude and albedo is much closer to the results of thermophysical modelling, which estimated the effective diameter of the object to be 5100 +/- 200 metres.[55]

Unusual for an object with asteroidal properties, Phaeton is the parent body of the mid-December Geminids meteor shower.[56] It is categorised as a NEA yet occupies a rather elliptical and inclined orbit that is more reminiscent of a cometary orbit. As well, at times the object has appeared to be ejecting dust and/or exhibiting a dust tail. Thus, Phaeton seems to have a mixture of asteroidal and cometary characteristics, and is, therefore, an interesting object for more detailed study.

---

51 Hiroyuki Toyota and others, 'DESTINY+: Deep Space Exploration Technology Demonstrator and Explorer to Asteroid 3200 Phaethon' (Low-Cost Planetary Missions Conference, Pasadena, 15–17 August 2017).

52 Phaeton occupies a rather elliptical and inclined orbit around the Sun, with heliocentric orbit semi-major axis of 1.271 AU, eccentricity of 0.89, and inclination of 22.26°. Lightcurve observations indicate that it rotates with a period of about 3.6 hours.

53 NASA JPL, '3200 Phaethon (1983 TB)' (*NASA JPL Small-Body Database Browser*) <https://ssd.jpl.nasa.gov/sbdb.cgi?sstr=Phaethon> accessed 5 March 2021.

54 Patrick Taylor and others, 'Arecibo Radar Observations of Near-Earth Asteroid (3200) Phaethon During the 2017 Apparition' (2019) 167 Planetary and Space Science 1–8 <https://doi.org/10.1016/j.pss.2019.01.009>.

55 Josef Hanuš and others, 'Near-Earth Asteroid (3200) Phaethon: Characterization of its Orbit, Spin State, and Thermophysical Parameters' (2016) 592 Astronomy & Astrophysics A34.

56 Fred L Whipple, '1983 TB and the Geminid Meteors' (1983) 3881 International Astronomical Union Circular.

6.5 *The Japan Spaceguard Association*

The Japan Spaceguard Association (JSGA) is a Specified Nonprofit Corporation in Japan whose goal is to observe and study NEOs for the purpose of supporting defence against NEO impacts on Earth. Towards this end, the JSGA operates the Bisei Spaceguard Center (BSGC), which is owned by the Japan Space Forum and located near the town of Bisei (Oda District, Okayama Prefecture) in western Japan.[57]

The BSGC is an observatory facility constructed during 1999–2000 that carries out the Bisei Asteroid Tracking Telescope for Rapid Survey (BATTeRS), which has discovered 440 minor planets as of October 2019.[58] The observatory operates a 1-metre telescope for object search, and a 0.5-metre telescope for follow-up observations.[59]

7 Luxembourg

In 2017, the government of Luxembourg established a national legal framework for the mining of resources in space,[60] which, of course, includes the mining of asteroids. Although asteroid mining is not specifically oriented towards planetary defence, the activities necessary to support and conduct asteroid mining are very synergistic with planetary defence objectives. Asteroid mining activities may include: telescopically searching for asteroids; characterising the orbital and physical properties of asteroids; sending robotic spacecraft to asteroids for resource prospecting (which would collect most, if not all, of the data about the asteroid that would be desired for planetary defence related assessments); designing/testing systems for manipulating asteroid material; and, eventually, sending actual mining missions to asteroids. Such activities would accelerate the discovery of Earth-impacting NEOs before their Earth impact dates, and help advance technologies needed for characterising and interacting with NEOs, all of which is highly relevant to planetary defence.

---

57 See website of the Japan Spaceguard Association <www.spaceguard.or.jp/html/ja/index.html> accessed 26 February 2021.

58 IAU, 'Minor Planet Discoverers' (*Minor Planet Center*, 15 June 2020) <https://minorplanetcenter.net//iau/lists/MPDiscsNum.html> accessed 21 August 2020.

59 Makoto Yoshikawa and others, 'Current status of asteroid observations in Bisei Spaceguard center' (2002) 73 Memorie della Società' Astronomica Italiana 772–775.

60 Law of July 20th 2017 on the exploration and use of space resources (Loi du 20 juillet 2017 sur l'exploration et l'utilisation des ressources de l'espace)' (*Luxembourg Space Agency*, 18 November 2019) <https://space-agency.public.lu/en/agency/legal-framework/law_space_resources_english_translation.html> accessed 26 February 2021.

The Luxembourg Space Agency (LSA) operates its 'SpaceResources.lu Initiative', the goals of which include ensuring that space resources explored under the jurisdiction of Luxembourg "serve a peaceful purpose, are gathered and used in a sustainable manner compatible with international law and for the benefit of humankind".[61] As incentives to commercial entities pursuing related activities, Luxembourg offered financial investments in research and development work, as well as tax credits. An agreement was also made with the US-based company Deep Space Industries, Inc (DSI) whereby Luxembourg would co-fund DSI's development of asteroid rendezvous spacecraft missions, for purposes of asteroid rendezvous technology demonstration as a precursor to resource prospecting and eventual asteroid mining.[62]

However, those missions have yet to be brought to fruition. While LSA maintains its intentions to pursue asteroid resource utilisation efforts, it is worth noting that the US asteroid mining companies DSI[63] and Planetary Resources, Inc[64] have both since been purchased by other companies for purposes other than asteroid mining. As such, while interest in asteroid mining remains, the status and future of such missions is unclear.

8 Russia

Russia has the distinction of being the location of the three most significant asteroid impacts in recent history: the Tunguska event in Siberia in 1908,[65] the Chelyabinsk meteor in 2013,[66] and the Kamchatka meteor in

61 Luxembourg Space Agency, 'Spaceresources.lu initiative' (*Luxembourg Space Agency*) <https://space-agency.public.lu/en/space-resources/the-initiative.html> accessed 26 February 2021.

62 Peter B de Selding, 'Luxembourg Invests to Become the "Silicon Valley of Space Resource Mining"' (*SpaceNews*, 3 June 2016) <https://spacenews.com/luxembourg-invests-to-become-the-silicon-valley-of-space-resource-mining/> accessed 26 February 2021.

63 Jeff Foust, 'Deep Space Industries Acquired by Bradford Space' (*SpaceNews*, 2 January 2019) <https://spacenews.com/deep-space-industries-acquired-by-bradford-space/> accessed 26 February 2021.

64 Jeff Foust, 'Asteroid Mining Company Planetary Resources Acquired by Blockchain Firm' (*SpaceNews*, 31 October 2018) <https://spacenews.com/asteroid-mining-company-planetary-resources-acquired-by-blockchain-firm/> accessed 26 February 2021.

65 Lorien F Wheeler and Donovan Mathias, 'Probabilistic Assessment of Tunguska-scale Asteroid Impacts' (2019) 327 Icarus 83.

66 Olga P Popova and others, 'Chelyabinsk Airburst, Damage Assessment, Meteorite Recovery, and Characterization' (2013) 342 Science 1069.

2018.[67] However, despite this, Russia's involvement in planetary defence and related activities has been limited to date. Thus far, there has been some Russian participation in IAWN and SMPAG, and the Russian Academy of Sciences has expressed intentions to develop national programmes aimed at planetary defence research and development.[68]

9 Conclusion

This chapter has surveyed some of the more notable activities related to planetary defence taking place around the world beyond the efforts at the United Nations, NASA, and ESA. Of these, the most significant are the Hayabusa and Hayabusa2 asteroid sample return missions flown by JAXA, followed by the Chang'e 2 flyby of Toutatis performed by CNSA. Thus, the Japanese and Chinese space agencies are currently the two national space agencies most active in planetary defence related endeavours, besides NASA and ESA. In terms of both flown and planned spacecraft missions, JAXA is the most active overall.

It is clear that planetary defence and related activities are considered to be important by various organisations the world over. Additional missions to asteroids are in development, and research programmes are proceeding apace. Assuming the trend of increasing activity levels continues, we can expect to see planetary defence related activities beyond those at NASA and ESA continue to expand in the years to come. We can also expect to see increasing international collaboration on planetary defence and related topics. These are certainly desirable outcomes, as the opportunities presented by asteroids and comets may benefit our entire species and the hazards presented by such objects pose a threat to all the people and nations of the world.

67 Leonard David, 'Huge Meteor Explosion a Wake-Up Call for Planetary Defense' (*Scientific American*, 21 March 2019) <www.scientificamerican.com/article/huge-meteor-explosion-a-wake-up-call-for-planetary-defense/> accessed 26 February 2021.

68 Sputnik International, 'Russia Kicks Off Work on Countering "Hazards" From Outer Space' (*Sputnik News*, 17 January 2019) <https://sputniknews.com/russia/201901171071548760-russia-space-threats-asteroids-program/> accessed 26 February 2021.

PART 2

Legal Analysis of Different Aspects of Planetary Defence

CHAPTER 9

Overview of Current International Space Law in the Context of Planetary Defence

Steven Freeland

1 Introduction

More than 50 years after the entry into force of the Outer Space Treaty,[1] it is appropriate to continue to reflect on the significance of ensuring that outer space is properly protected from dangers that may ultimately jeopardise future space missions, as well as life on Earth. It is for this good reason that issues relating to the 'safety, security and sustainability' of outer space are frequently raised in multilateral fora such as the United Nations Committee on the Peaceful Uses of Outer Space (UNCOPUOS), and its two Subcommittees.[2]

An overarching theme in these discussions relates to our future ability to utilise space, and the potential benefits that it may offer to humankind. In this sense, the notion of 'planetary defence' represents an important element. As it will be discussed further below,[3] the term 'defence' is not entirely appropriate for describing a mission aiming at the deflection or destruction of a Near-Earth Object (NEO), at least from a public international law perspective. However, most of the methods potentially being applied, in particular the use of kinetic impactors,[4] can be considered as 'weapons' and thus are subject to regulation under public international law and international space law.[5] One very important element of this is to prevent (armed) military conflict from taking place in outer space, as well as to restrict (ideally also to prevent) the proliferation and

1 Treaty on Principles Governing the Activities of States in the Exploration and Use of Outer Space, including the Moon and other Celestial Bodies (adopted 19 December 1966, entered into force 10 October 1967) 610 UNTS 205 (Outer Space Treaty).
2 The Scientific and Technical Subcommittee (STSC) and the Legal Subcommittee (LSC). See chapter 4 'International Cooperation in Planetary Defence – UNCOPUOS, IAWN and SMPAG' in this book.
3 See chapter 14 'The Use of Force and Planetary Defence' in this book.
4 See chapter 3 'Planetary Defence Technologies' in this book.
5 See chapter 15 'Legal Aspects of the Use of Nuclear Explosive Devices in Planetary Defence' in this book.

 | DOI:10.1163/9789004467606_011

placement in orbit of space 'weapons'.[6] Indeed, these threats to the long-term future of our space activities represent significant challenges to the evolution of a regulatory framework regarding planetary defence that will best serve humanity's interests.

The existing legal regime has not prevented the development of military technology capable of utilising outer space. Some restrictions have been included in the UN space treaties[7] and UN General Assembly resolutions,[8] as will be discussed further below. However, these were specified in relatively general terms and were open to divergent interpretation as to what they did (and did not) prohibit. This is not entirely surprising, since the development of space-related technology was, at least initially, inextricably related to military capability – both in reality and to influence the perception of others. It is no coincidence that the space race emerged at the height of the Cold War, when both the United States and the Soviet Union strove to flex their respective technological 'muscles'. The early stages of human space activity coincided with a period of quite considerable tension, with the possibility of large scale and

6 See chapter 16 'Nuclear Non-Proliferation and Planetary Defence: Competing Potential Disasters' in this book.

7 These include, in addition to the Outer Space Treaty, the Agreement on the Rescue of Astronauts, the Return of Astronauts and the Return of Objects Launched into Outer Space (adopted 19 December 1967, entered into force 3 December 1968) 672 UNTS 119 (Rescue and Return Agreement); the Convention on International Liability for Damage Caused by Space Objects (adopted 29 November 1971, entered into force 1 September 1972) 961 UNTS 187 (Liability Convention); the Convention on Registration of Objects Launched into Outer Space (adopted 12 November 1974, entered into force 15 September 1976) 1023 UNTS 15 (Registration Convention); and the Agreement Governing the Activities of States on the Moon and Other Celestial Bodies (adopted 5 December 1979, entered into force 11 July 1984) 1363 UNTS 3 (Moon Agreement).

8 Declaration of Legal Principles Governing the Activities of States in the Exploration and Use of Outer Space, UNGA Res 1962 (XVIII) (13 December 1963); Principles Governing the Use by States of Artificial Earth Satellites for International Direct Television Broadcasting, UNGA Res 37/92 (10 December 1982); Principles Relating to Remote Sensing of the Earth from Outer Space, UNGA Res 41/65 (3 December 1986); Principles Relevant to the Use of Nuclear Power Sources in Outer Space, UNGA Res 47/68 (14 December 1992); Declaration on International Cooperation in the Exploration and Use of Outer Space for the Benefit and in the Interest of All States, Taking into Particular Account the Needs of Developing Countries, UNGA Res 51/122 (13 December 1996). More recent 'guidelines' have also been agreed relating to various other important issues, including the problem of space debris: see Inter-Agency Space Debris Coordination Committee, 'IADC Space Debris Mitigation Guidelines' (IADC-02-01 September 2007) <www.unoosa.org/documents/pdf/spacelaw/sd/IADC-2002-01-IADC-Space_Debris-Guidelines-Revision1.pdf> accessed 25 February 2021, and UNGA Resolution 62/217 (22 December 2007), which (in paragraph 26) endorsed the Space Debris Mitigation Guidelines agreed by UNCOPUOS.

potentially highly destructive military conflict between the (space) superpowers of the time always lurking in the background. Despite the possibilities for humankind that it would present, the successful launch of the first artificial satellite to orbit the Earth, Sputnik 1, in 1957 generated unease in the West, since the technology used was similar to that for ballistic missiles.[9]

The conventional obligations and restrictions that were eventually agreed and codified in the UN space treaties addressed, in part, specific military and weapons-related aspects of space activities. With these developments in mind, this chapter looks at the existing international legal regime with respect to planetary defence activities.

2 Regulating Outer Space – Fundamental Principles of Space Law

The journey of Sputnik immediately gave rise to difficult and controversial legal questions, involving previously undetermined concepts. Although prior scholarship had considered the nature and scope of laws that might apply to the exploration and use of outer space, this was only on a hypothetical basis.[10] All of a sudden, the reality of humankind's aspirations and capabilities with respect to outer space became apparent. The world had to react to an unprecedented event in a largely unregulated legal environment.

Moreover, these embryonic space activities and the rapid development of space technology that followed were, as noted above, largely driven at the time by the prevailing geopolitical situation. The desire for ever-increasing technological prowess was as much motivated by military considerations as a wish to explore and use space for other (scientific) purposes. It was in this context that the international community had to react, as it walked a fine balancing line between the wishes of the then two existing superpowers on the one hand, and a general sense of uncertainty as to where exactly these military-driven achievements involving space might ultimately lead on the other.

It was therefore no surprise that, shortly after the Sputnik launch, the UN established a new committee to take primary responsibility for the development and codification of the fundamental rules relating to outer space – UNCOPUOS. An *ad hoc* Committee on the Peaceful Uses of Outer Space, with

---

9 See NATO, 'Update 1957' (*NATO*) <www.nato.int/docu/update/50-59/1957e.htm> accessed 25 February 2021.

10 For a summary of the main academic theories relating to 'space law' in the period prior to the launch of Sputnik, see for example, Francis Lyall and Paul B Larsen, *Space Law: A Treatise* (2nd edn, Routledge 2018) 3–9.

18 initial member states, was established in 1958,[11] and it subsequently became a permanent body in 1959.[12] It was no coincidence, in the context within which it was created, that the 'P' – *Peaceful* – was included within the name of the Committee. UNCOPUOS is now regarded by many as the principal multilateral body involved in the development of international space law, a sentiment that is frequently repeated during its meetings and those of its two Subcommittees.

As to legal principles, first and foremost, the journey of Sputnik necessitated a clarification as to the legal categorisation of outer space for the purposes of international law. This issue was put to UNCOPUOS early on, but to date, the question of where air space 'ends' and outer space 'begins' has thus far remained unanswered from an international legal viewpoint, with member states having differing perspectives, thus preventing a consensus-based resolution. The question of the 'definition and delimitation of outer space' remains on the agenda of UNCOPUOS meetings.[13]

There was also the question of the 'status' of outer space. Although the Soviet Union had not sought the permission of other states to undertake the Sputnik mission, there were no significant protests that it had infringed on any country's sovereignty as it circled the Earth. This international (in)action confirmed that this new frontier of human activity did not possess the elements of sovereignty that had already been well established under the international law principles regulating land, sea and air space. As was observed by Judge Manfred Lachs of the International Court of Justice:[14]

> [T]he first instruments that men sent into outer space traversed the air space of States and circled above them in outer space, yet the launching States sought no permission, nor did the other States protest. This is how the freedom of movement into outer space, and in it, came to be established and recognised as law within a remarkably short period of time.

---

11 See UNGA Res 1348 (XIII) (13 December 1958).

12 See UNGA Res 1472 (XIV) (12 December 1959). As at the beginning of 2020, UNCOPUOS had 95 Members, which, according to its website, makes it "one of the largest Committees in the United Nations", see United Nations Office for Outer Space Affairs, 'Members of the Committee on the Peaceful Uses of Outer Space' (*UNOOSA*) <www.unoosa.org/oosa/en/members/index.html> accessed 25 February 2021.

13 See UNCOPUOS, 'Report of the Legal Subcommittee on its fifty-eighth session' (1–12 April 2019) UN Doc A/AC.105/1203, item V.

14 *North Sea Continental Shelf Cases* (*Federal Republic of Germany v. Denmark and Federal Republic of Germany v. The Netherlands*) (Judgment) Dissenting Opinion of Judge Lachs, [1969] ICJ Rep 3, 230.

Notwithstanding the lack of a clear definition of outer space, a number of fundamental legal principles relating to the exploration and use of outer space quickly emerged, although their codification into a treaty form took more time. This was due to a number of reasons, including the unique environment with which any legally binding instrument would have to deal, the significant political and strategic factors at play, and the rapid growth of space-related technology that followed almost immediately from the Sputnik success.

Thus, several foundational principles of the international law of outer space were born – in particular, the so-called 'common interest', 'freedom' and 'non-appropriation' principles. These were later incorporated into the terms of the UN space law treaties,[15] with the result that they also constitute binding conventional rules, codifying what had already amounted to principles of customary international law.

As noted, these fundamental rules represent a significant departure from the legal rules relating to air space, which is categorised as constituting part of the 'territory' of the underlying state. The territorial nature of air space is reflected in the principal air law treaties.[16] The International Court of Justice has confirmed that this characteristic of air space also represents customary international law.[17] As a consequence, civil and commercial aircraft have only certain limited rights to enter the air space of another state,[18] in contrast to the freedom principle relating to outer space.[19] Even though, as noted above, the delimitation between air space and outer space has not been definitively

15 See for example Articles I and II, Outer Space Treaty.

16 For example, reaffirming the principle already acknowledged as early as in 1919, Convention on the Regulation of Aerial Navigation (adopted 13 October 1919, entered into force 1 June 1922) 11 LNTS 173 (Paris Convention); Article 1, 1944 Convention on International Civil Aviation (adopted 7 December 1944, entered into force 4 April 1947) 15 UNTS 295 (Chicago Convention) provides that "every state has complete and exclusive sovereignty over the air space above its territory".

17 In *Case Concerning Military and Paramilitary Activities in and against Nicaragua* (*Nicaragua v. United States*) (Merits) (Judgment) [1986] ICJ Rep 14, 128, the International Court of Justice noted that "the principle of respect for territorial sovereignty is also directly infringed by the unauthorized overflight of a State's territory by aircraft belonging to or under the control of the government of another State".

18 See Articles 5 and 6, Chicago Convention.

19 Of course, any space activities requiring a launch from Earth and/or a return to Earth will also involve a 'use' of air space. In this respect, the law of air space may be relevant to the legal position if, for example, the space object of one state travels through the air space of another state. See also Article II, Convention on International Liability for Damage Caused by Space Objects (adopted 29 March 1972, entered into force 1 September 1972) 961 UNTS 187 (Liability Convention), which applies *inter alia* to 'aircraft in flight' (i.e. in air space).

agreed, this has not in practice led to any significant confusion as to 'which law' might apply in particular circumstances.[20]

By contrast to the position regarding airspace, Article II of the Outer Space Treaty encompasses the 'non-appropriation' principle.[21] The provision reads:

> Outer space, including the Moon and other celestial bodies, is not subject to national appropriation by claim of sovereignty, by means of use or occupation, or by any other means.

In general terms, Article II confirms that outer space (which includes the Moon and other celestial bodies) is not subject to ownership rights and prohibits *inter alia* any sovereign or territorial claims to outer space. Outer space therefore is not to be regarded as 'territorial', a principle that was already well accepted in practice. Indeed, by the time that the Outer Space Treaty was finalised, both the United States and the Soviet Union had been engaged in an extensive range of space activities; yet neither had made a claim to sovereignty over any part of outer space, including celestial bodies, notwithstanding the planting by the Apollo 11 astronauts of an American flag on the surface of the Moon.[22]

The codification of this non-appropriation principle immediately follows Article I of the Outer Space Treaty, which elaborates on the 'common interest' and 'freedom' principles and confirms that the exploration and use of outer space is to be undertaken "for the benefit and in the interests of all countries"

---

20 However, as the range of activities in outer space becomes ever broader, the issue will become more important in relation not only to the broad principles of international space law, but also on a practical level – for example, to the regulation of commercial sub-orbital space tourism activities: see Steven Freeland, 'Fly Me to the Moon: How Will International Law Cope with Commercial Space Tourism?' (2010) 11(1) Melbourne Journal of International Law 90.

21 For a detailed analysis of Article II of the Outer Space Treaty, see Steven Freeland and Ram Jakhu, 'Article II' in Stephan Hobe, Bernhard Schmidt-Tedd, and Kai-Uwe Schrogl (eds), *Cologne Commentary on Space Law*, vol I (Carl Heymanns Verlag 2009) 44.

22 This is to be compared with the situation in Antarctica, which had seen a series of sovereign claims by several states in the period leading up to the finalisation in 1959 of the Antarctic Treaty (adopted 1 December 1959, entered into force 23 June 1961) 402 UNTS 71. Article IV of the Antarctic Treaty has the effect of suspending all claims to territorial sovereignty in Antarctica for the duration of that instrument, as well as prohibiting any "new claim, or enlargement of an existing claim". The Protocol on Environmental Protection to the Antarctic Treaty, which came into force in 1998, augments the Antarctic Treaty by protecting Antarctica from commercial mining for a period of 50 years. See Steven Freeland and Anja Pecujlic, 'How Do You Like Your Regulation – Hard or Soft? The Antarctic Treaty and the Outer Space Treaty Compared' (2018) 30(1) National Law School of India Review 11.

and freely "by all States without discrimination of any kind, on a basis of equality and in accordance with international law". These would be important and relevant concepts with respect to any global approach to addressing a NEO threat. In broader terms, however, the primary intent of Article II was to reinforce these important concepts by confirming that principles of territorial sovereignty do not apply to outer space. Not only does this reflect the practice of states from virtually the beginning of the space age,[23] but it was an important proactive step designed to protect outer space from the possibility of conflict driven by territorial or colonising ambitions.

In this regard, the United States delegate to UNCOPUOS, Herbert Reis, reiterated the specific object and purpose of Article II on 31 July 1969, just a matter of days after the Apollo 11 astronauts had landed on the Moon, as follows:[24]

> The negotiating history of the Treaty shows that the purpose of this provision (i.e. article II) was to prohibit a repetition of the race for the acquisition of national sovereignty over overseas territories that developed in the sixteenth, seventeenth, eighteenth and nineteenth centuries. The Treaty makes clear that no user of space may lay claim to, or seek to establish, national sovereignty over outer space.

The sentiments reflected in Article II are therefore fundamental to the regulation of outer space and its exploration and use for peaceful purposes. The binding principle of non-appropriation is an essential element of international space law, to be preserved and followed in the conduct of all activities in outer space.

Other principles of international space law are also of relevance in the context of planetary defence activities. This includes the liability of the launching state(s) of a space object for damage caused by that object,[25] the international responsibility of states for national governmental and non-governmental

23 One notable exception in this regard was the Bogota Declaration. In 1976, a number of equatorial states – including Brazil, Colombia, the Congo, Ecuador, Indonesia, Kenya, Uganda and Zaire – claimed sovereign rights over segments of the geostationary synchronous orbit above their respective territories, principally based upon the lack of an accepted delimitation between air space and outer space.

24 Cited from Erik N Valters, 'Perspectives in the Emerging Law of Satellite Communications' (1970) 5 Stanford Journal of International Studies 53, 66.

25 Provisions on liability are contained in Article VII Outer Space Treaty and in the Liability Convention. See chapter 18 'The Current International Space Law Regime on Liability and Its Application to Planetary Defence' and chapter 19 'Critical Issues and Future Perspectives on Liability in the Context of Planetary Defence' in this book.

space activities,[26] as well as the principle of cooperation and mutual assistance in the exploration and use of outer space,[27] which will be discussed in more detail throughout this book.

Apart from the express fundamental principles specified in the UN space treaties, the degree to which general international law governs outer space is perhaps less straightforward. The Outer Space Treaty affirms that activities in space are to be carried on "in accordance with international law",[28] but the fact that most existing international law at the time was developed for 'terrestrial' purposes meant that it was not readily or directly applicable in many respects to this new paradigm of human endeavour. Moreover, the non-sovereignty aspect of outer space meant that any then existent national law (which, in any event, did not specifically address space-related issues) would not *prima facie* apply to this frontier, though it might apply to the conduct of a state's nationals,[29] or to its space objects,[30] and would not be the appropriate legal basis upon which to establish the initial framework for regulating the conduct of humankind's activities in outer space. It was clear, therefore, that, at the dawn of the development of 'space law', specific international binding rules would be required to address the particular characteristics and legal categorisation of outer space.

As noted, the law of outer space has developed as a body of law embedded within general public international law. There is now a substantial body of law dealing with many aspects of the use and exploration of outer space, mainly codified in and evidenced by UN space treaties,[31] UN General Assembly resolutions,[32] national legislation, decisions of national courts, bilateral arrangements, and determinations by Intergovernmental Organisations.

---

26 The responsibility of states for space activities is addressed in Article VI Outer Space Treaty. See chapter 20 'The International Responsibility of States for Planetary Defence Activities' and chapter 21 'The Involvement of Private Actors in Planetary Defence Missions' in this book.

27 The principle of international cooperation can be found in Articles IX and XI Outer Space Treaty. See chapter 12 'International Law Rules Related to the Sharing of Information About Potential NEO Threats' and chapter 13 'Rules of International Law Regarding an Obligation of States to Undertake Planetary Defence Activities' in this book.

28 Article III, Outer Space Treaty.

29 For a discussion of the possible 'extra-terrestrial' application of national (criminal) law, see Danielle Ireland-Piper and Steven Freeland, 'Star Laws: Criminal Jurisdiction in Outer Space' (2020) 44(1) Journal of Space Law 44. See also Article VIII, Outer Space Treaty.

30 Article VIII, Outer Space Treaty.

31 See above, fn 7.

32 See above, fn 8.

Notwithstanding this quite extensive body of law, it is clear that the existing legal and regulatory regime has not kept pace with the remarkable technological and commercial progress of space activities since 1957. This represents a major challenge in relation to the ongoing development of effective legal principles, all the more in view of the strategic and military potential of outer space in an era of globalisation. The Outer Space Treaty provides a number of general principles that are intended to restrict the military uses of outer space. One of these is the requirement that activities in the exploration and use of outer space shall be carried out "in accordance with international law, including the Charter of the United Nations".[33] A primary reason for the inclusion of this provision was the concern among many states that outer space would become a new arena for international conflict. In December 1958, the UN General Assembly (UNGA) emphasised the need "to avoid the extension of present national rivalries into this new field".[34]

By 1961, the UNGA had recommended that international law, including customary international law,[35] and the UN Charter should apply to "outer space and celestial bodies".[36] This was repeated in UNGA Resolution 1962, which set out a number of important principles that were ultimately incorporated into the Outer Space Treaty.[37] The specific reference to the UN Charter was considered to be important, given that the maintenance of international peace and security is the underlying principle of the system established under that instrument.[38] The prohibition of the use of force contained in Article 2(4) of the UN Charter represents a crucial element in the regulation of international relations and is equally applicable to the use of outer space.[39]

---

33 Article III, Outer Space Treaty. Article 2 of the Moon Agreement extends these sentiments further by referring to "the Declaration on Principles of International Law concerning Friendly Relations and Co-operation among States in accordance with the Charter of the United Nations, adopted by the General Assembly on 25 October 1970".

34 UNGA Res 1348 (XIII) (13 December 1958), Preamble paragraph 3.

35 The sources of international law include treaties, customary international law, and general principles of law. See Art 38(1), Statute of the International Court of Justice (adopted 26 June 1945, entered into force 24 October 1945) 156 UNTS 77.

36 UNGA Res 1721 (XVI) (20 December 1961), paragraph 1(a).

37 UNGA Res 1962 (XVIII) (13 December 1963), paragraph 4.

38 Charter of the United Nations (adopted 26 June 1945, entered into force 24 October 1945) 1 UNTS 16 (UN Charter). The first 'purpose' of the United Nations specified in Article 1(1) of the UN Charter begins with the words: "To maintain international peace and security (...)".

39 Article 2(4), UN Charter provides: "All Members shall refrain in their international relations from the threat or use of force against the territorial integrity or political independence of any state, or in any other manner inconsistent with the Purposes of the United Nations."

The sentiments underlying the UN Charter were strengthened further by the restrictions imposed in relation to nuclear weapons and weapons of mass destruction by Article IV of the Outer Space Treaty, although, as has been well documented, this provision in and of itself does not represent a complete restriction on the placement of weapons in outer space, nor of their use.[40] Article IV provides that "the Moon and other celestial bodies shall be used by all States Parties to the [Outer Space] Treaty *exclusively for peaceful purposes*."[41]

While there were divergent views as to whether the 'peaceful' use of space was to be interpreted as 'non-military' rather than merely 'non-aggressive' activities,[42] the reality has been that, in addition to the many commercial, civilian and scientific uses, outer space has and continues to be used for an expanding array of military activities. Unless concrete steps are taken to arrest this trend – which will require a significant shift in political will, particularly among the major powers – it is likely that space will increasingly be utilised to further the military and strategic aims of specific countries, particularly as military and space technology continues to evolve and develop. However, the current political momentum does, unfortunately, appear to be directed towards a greater incorporation of satellite technology in outer space as part of the course of warfare.[43]

This is particularly relevant given that the use of satellite technology already represents an integral part of the military strategy and the conduct of many armed conflicts. As this technology continues to develop, the armed conflicts of the 21st century and beyond will increasingly involve the utilisation of outer space.

The use of force in the context of planetary defence is dealt with in chapter 14 'The Use of Force and Planetary Defence' in this book.

40 For a detailed analysis of Article IV of the Outer Space Treaty, see Kai-Uwe Schrogl and Julia Neumann, 'Article IV' in Stephan Hobe, Bernhard Schmidt-Tedd and Kai-Uwe Schrogl (eds), *Cologne Commentary on Space Law*, vol I (Carl Heymanns Verlag 2009) 70–93. The use of nuclear explosive devices in the context of planetary defence activities is discussed in detail in chapter 15 'Legal Aspects of the Use of Nuclear Explosive Devices in Planetary Defence' and in chapter 16 'Nuclear Non-Proliferation and Planetary Defence: Competing Potential Disasters' in this book.

41 Emphasis added. See also Article 3(1), Moon Agreement.

42 For a discussion of the differing interpretations that arose even prior to the conclusion of the Outer Space Treaty see Bin Cheng, 'The Legal Status of Outer Space and Relevant Issues: Delimitation of Outer Space and Definition of Peaceful Use' (1983) 11(1) Journal of Space Law 89, 98–101.

43 See for example, 'France follows US to set up Military Space Command' *Financial Times* (London, 14 July 2019) <www.ft.com/content/a479bcb6-a628-11e9-984c-fac8325aaa04> accessed 25 February 2021.

This is highly troubling and flies in the face of the principles of the Outer Space Treaty. Yet, it would be naive to ignore the realities – rather it is important to determine what needs to be done to provide, at least from a regulatory perspective, an appropriate framework to protect humankind in the future from the threats of NEOs while avoiding a further militarisation and weaponisation of outer space.

3 The Way Forward

If we are to provide a framework which strengthens cooperation in outer space and serves the interests of planetary defence to the benefit of all stakeholders, it is necessary to develop specific and clear rules and standards that avoid a weaponisation of outer space, as well as conflict in the region of outer space in the context of planetary defence. Whilst the object and purpose of the Outer Space Treaty, as well as the practice of states have (thus far) helped to avoid conflict in outer space, without a clearer understanding of the serious consequences that will flow from irresponsible behaviour in space, ambitious efforts to protect our planet from the threat of a NEO impact might be compromised.

Ideally, binding treaty norms should be negotiated, to be adhered to in good faith by all relevant states. However, a 'treaty' approach to dealing with NEO threat mitigation is unlikely to come to fruition in the medium term, if at all, and any additional regulation that does emerge will thus only take the form of a voluntary non-binding basis. Indeed, a 'softly, softly' approach seems to be the preferred strategy amongst many states, but this brings with it more uncertainty, a lack of formal enforcement capability and enforcement mechanisms, and the possibility of undue flexibility of approach by the main stakeholders.

We thus find ourselves somewhat at a crossroad. We need to develop a regulatory framework for broad and effective measures to ensure that the Earth can be protected from major natural disasters caused by impacts of objects from outer space. Such an effort should encourage and support cooperative space activities carried out by states, space agencies, or private entities that are clearly 'in the interest of all countries' and as a function of the 'province of humankind'.

CHAPTER 10

The 2010 Report on Legal Aspects of NEO Threat Response and Related Institutional Issues

Frans von der Dunk

1 Introduction

While the threat posed by Near-Earth Objects (NEOs) had been recognised for some time, it was only in the early 2000s that a substantial and concerted effort was initiated to address the question of what to do if such a threat materialises. Several research initiatives by authoritative international bodies of scientists and academics, such as the International Academy of Astronautics (IAA)[1] the Planetary Society,[2] the B612 Foundation,[3] the Secure World Foundation (SWF)[4] and the Space Generation Advisory Council (SGAC)[5] had already given rise to a more general awareness of the issue, but it was the involvement of the Association of Space Explorers (ASE) which drove the issue to be addressed in the political and operational domains.

2 From the Association of Space Explorers to the University of Nebraska-Lincoln

More precisely, upon the initiative of Rusty Schweickart, Apollo-9 astronaut, the ASE at its Annual Congress in Salt Lake City in 2005 discussed the issue of potential threats to humankind and the Earth posed by NEOs in some detail. Three main conclusions were drawn: (1) developments in space science and

1 Ivan Bekey (ed), 'Dealing with the Threat to Earth from Asteroids and Comets' (IAA Study 2009).

2 See website of the Planetary Society <www.planetary.org/defend-earth> accessed 20 February 2021.

3 See website of the B612 Foundation <www.b612foundation.org/> accessed 20 February 2021.

4 Brian Weeden, 'The NEO Primer: A Tool for Collaboration, Communication and Outreach' (1st IAA Planetary Defense Conference, Granada, 27–30 April 2009), <https://swfound.org/media/205434/neo_primer.pdf >accessed 20 February 2021.

5 See website of the Space Generation Advisory Council <https://spacegeneration.org/projects/near-earth-object> accessed 20 February 2021.

 | DOI:10.1163/9789004467606_012

space technology had by then made it possible to predict with some accuracy, and sometimes decades in advance, whether a particular NEO might present a serious threat of colliding with Earth; (2) developments had also made it possible to, at least in many cases, undertake successful efforts to minimise the chance of such a collision actually occurring; but (3) a, preferably international, framework for dealing with such threats was conspicuously missing, resulting in unnecessary risks of NEO threats causing potentially catastrophic damage.[6]

The ASE consequently established a NEO Committee, originally chaired by Rusty Schweickart, now led by US Shuttle astronaut Tom Jones, with Sergei Avdeev (Russia), Franklin Chang-Diaz (USA/Costa Rica), Pedro Duque (Spain), Chris Hadfield (Canada), Edward Lu (USA), Soichi Noguchi (Japan), Dumitru Prunariu (Romania), Viktor Savinykh (Russia) and Gerhard Thiele (Germany) as further members, which picked up the task of "bringing to the attention of world leaders and key international institutions the threat of asteroid impacts to life on Earth".[7] In order to help achieve that goal, also a Panel on NEO Threat Mitigation was established.[8]

The ASE NEO Committee and Panel on NEO Threat Mitigation organised four workshops in 2007 and 2008, in Strasbourg (France), Sibiu (Romania), Guácimo (Costa Rica) and San Francisco (United States), giving rise to the Report on *Asteroid Threats: A Call for Global Response.*[9] The Report came up with the recommendation to establish an international decision-making framework, which resulted in 2014 in the establishment, under United Nations (UN) auspices, of an International Asteroid Warning Network (IAWN) and a Space Mission Planning Advisory Group (SMPAG).[10] The former maintains an internationally recognised clearing house for the receipt, acknowledgement

6 See further 'Open Letter of the Association of Space Explorers' (19th Annual Congress, Salt Lake City, 14 October 2005) <http://spaceref.com/news/viewsr.html?pid=18404> accessed 20 February 2021.

7 See website of the Association of Space Explorers <https://aose26.wildapricot.org/page-18104> accessed 20 February 2021.

8 The Panel consisted of Adigun Ade Abiodun (Nigeria), Vallampadugai Arunachalam (India), Roger- Maurice Bonnet (Switzerland), Sergio Camacho-Lara (Mexico), James George (Canada), Tomifumi Godai (Japan), Peter Jankowitsch (Austria), Sergey Kapitza (Russia), Paul Kovacs (Canada), Walther Lichem (Austria), Gordon McBean (Canada), Lord Martin Rees (United Kingdom), Karlene Roberts (United States), Michael Simpson (United States), Sir Crispin Tickell (United Kingdom), Richard Tremayne-Smith (United Kingdom), Frans G von der Dunk (Netherlands), and James Zimmerman (United States).

9 International Panel on Asteroid Threat Mitigation, 'Asteroid Threats: A Call for Global Response' (Association of Space Explorers 2008).

10 UNOOSA, 'Near-Earth Objects and Planetary Defence' (United Nations 2018) 2.

and processing of all NEO observations collected from observatories worldwide, by facilitating the dissemination of information related to NEOs to UN member states; whereas the latter, consisting of major space agencies and offices around the world, is tasked to develop potential deflection mission plans.[11]

The 2008 Report on *Asteroid Threats: A Call for Global Response* also represented the first instance where substantial and coherent attention was paid to some of the major legal issues involved in addressing NEO threats; it contained an Appendix III 'International Legal Framework', which *inter alia* assessed some of the NEO threat response scenarios from the perspective of international liability for damage caused by space objects as per the 1967 Outer Space Treaty[12] (notably Article VII) and the 1972 Liability Convention.[13]

The Report then gave rise to the international 'Conference on Near-Earth Objects: Risks, Responses and Opportunities – Legal Aspects', hosted in April 2009 at the College of Law of the University of Nebraska-Lincoln (UNL).[14] The conference provided for a broad discussion of those legal and institutional issues; the main conclusion was that some key legal and institutional issues should be resolved at an early stage, while at the same time more research would be required in order to arrive at consolidated and feasible conclusions and recommendations.

---

11 See chapter 4 'International Cooperation in Planetary Defence – UNCOPUOS, IAWN and SMPAG' in this book.

12 Treaty on Principles Governing the Activities of States in the Exploration and Use of Outer Space, including the Moon and Other Celestial Bodies (adopted 19 December 1966, entered into force 10 October 1967) 610 UNTS 205 (Outer Space Treaty).

13 Convention on International Liability for Damage Caused by Space Objects (adopted 29 November 1971, entered into force 1 September 1972) 961 UNTS 187 (Liability Convention).

14 The Conference comprised seven substantive sessions, respectively 'Setting the Scene', 'Legal and Policy Aspects of NEO Threat Mitigation', 'Institutional Aspects of NEO Threat Mitigation', 'International Legal Aspects of Exploring and Exploiting NEOs', 'US Domestic Aspects of Exploiting NEOs', an 'Intergovernmental Panel on Legal and Policy Aspects of NEO Response Activities' and 'The Role of the Military in Addressing National and International Responses to NEO Impact Scenarios'. A summary report on the conference can be found at <www.black-holes.eu/resources/Granada-2009-PDC.pdf> accessed 20 February 2021.

3 The Research Project on Legal Aspects of NEO Threat Response and Related Institutional Issues

The need for more comprehensive and in-depth analysis of the key legal and institutional issues involved in future international activities of NEO threat mitigation, preferably prior to the first occasion of an actual serious NEO threat arising, had thus become clear. In order to address this need, in 2009 the present author, with the support of the UNL College of Law and the Secure World Foundation (SWF) took the initiative to undertake a Research Project on 'Legal Aspects of NEO Threat Response and Related Institutional Issues', himself acting as rapporteur in this context.

An International Advisory Board was constituted, consisting of the following eminent international space law experts from various corners of the world, members of the International Institute of Space Law (IISL) and the International Academy of Astronautics (IAA):[15]

- Steven Freeland, University of Western Sydney, Australia;
- Joanne Gabrynowicz, Director, National Center for Remote Sensing, Air & Space Law, University of Mississippi, United States;
- Stephan Hobe, Director of the Institute of Air and Space Law, University of Cologne, Germany;
- Mahulena Hofmann, University of Giessen, Germany;
- Ram Jakhu, Institute of Air and Space Law, McGill University, Montreal, Canada;
- Sergio Marchisio, University of Rome 'La Sapienza', Italy;
- Matthew Schaefer, University of Nebraska-Lincoln, United States; and
- Maureen Williams, University of Buenos Aires / Conicet, Argentina.

The Research Project stated as its overriding goal the intention to support the international community of states and the relevant decision-makers at the level of states, space agencies and international organisations in their efforts to arrive at a proper, fair, transparent, comprehensive, workable, politically, institutionally and legally sound and feasible framework for international decision-making in the face of future NEO threats, notably by analysing some of the key legal and institutional issues involved and by offering, where appropriate, recommendations on how to further develop the legal and institutional framework for NEO threat response.

The Final Report resulting from the Research Project was to be made available in particular to the international community of states, as the constituency

15 Note, that the affiliations are given as they were at the time of the Research Project.

ultimately responsible for and capable of taking action in the event of a major NEO threat, notably for the purposes of discussion in the United Nations Committee on the Peaceful Uses of Outer Space (UNCOPUOS) as the most readily available international body in this context.[16]

The research, analysis and conclusions undertaken in the context of the Research Project, while acknowledging this approach not to be exhaustive, focused on five interlocking major clusters of legal/institutional issues which were seen to present the most important and pressing issues to be dealt with in this context:

1. General state responsibilities and obligations;
2. Specific liabilities for damage;
3. The use of physical force, possibly even nuclear devices, in outer space;
4. The institutional structure; and
5. The proper role of commercial interests, in particular those of private enterprise.

The methodology of the Research Project for each of the clusters was to first formulate the relevant key question, followed by an analysis of the current status of international law, using Article 38(1) of the Statute of the International Court of Justice (ICJ) as determining applicable international law,[17] and the interpretation of treaty law following the customary international law rules for interpretation as codified in Articles 31 and 32 of the Vienna Convention on the Law of Treaties.[18] Next, it was to outline where further research, analysis

16 See Frans G von der Dunk and others, 'Legal Aspects of NEO Threat Response and Related Institutional Issues' (Final Report 2010).

17 Article 38(1), Statute of the International Court of Justice (adopted 26 June 1945, entered into force 24 October 1945) 156 UNTS 77, provides in full: "The Court, whose function is to decide in accordance with international law such disputes as are submitted to it, shall apply: a. international conventions, whether general or particular, establishing rules expressly recognized by the contesting states; b. international custom, as evidence of a general practice accepted as law; c. the general principles of law recognized by civilized nations; d. subject to the provisions of Article 59, judicial decisions and the teachings of the most highly qualified publicists of the various nations, as subsidiary means for the determination of rules of law." This clause is generally recognised as representing the most authoritative statement on the sources of public international law generally speaking; see Rüdiger Wolfrum, 'Sources of International Law' in Rüdiger Wolfrum (ed), *Max Planck Encyclopedia of Public International Law* (Oxford University Press 2012) vol IX 299–313; James Crawford, *Brownlie's Principles of Public International Law* (8th edn, Oxford University Press 2012) 20–47; Malcolm N Shaw, *International Law* (6th edn, Cambridge University Press 2008) 69–128.

18 Article 31, Vienna Convention on the Law of Treaties (adopted 23 May 1969, entered into force 27 January 1980) 1155 UNTS 331, entitled 'General rule of interpretation', provides in

and/or discussion would be required, to come up with conclusions as to where gaps, overlaps, inconsistencies or lack of clarity exist, and finally to offer some recommendations on how such flaws in the current legal framework could be addressed.

4 Cluster One: General State Responsibilities and Obligations

The key question in this realm was formulated as: to what extent is there, under current international law, including as relevant general principles of national law, a general responsibility of individual states, perhaps regional groupings of states (where mid-size NEO threat scenarios might only directly involve one or a few regions of the world), alternatively the international community as a whole, to address serious threats to humankind or major parts thereof, including natural disasters, which could apply in the specific context of NEO threats?

The Project undertook an in-depth analysis of such concepts as the 'interest of (hu)mankind', 'international peace and security' and 'international cooperation', such as *inter alia* enshrined in the Outer Space Treaty,[19] in conjunction with the (at the time) emerging concept of a 'responsibility to protect' which was initially developed in 2001 in a report by the Canadian Government's International Commission on Intervention and State Sovereignty[20] and then

full: "1. A treaty shall be interpreted in good faith in accordance with the ordinary meaning to be given to the terms of the treaty in their context and in the light of its object and purpose. 2. The context for the purpose of the interpretation of a treaty shall comprise, in addition to the text, including its preamble and annexes: (a) any agreement relating to the treaty which was made between all the parties in connection with the conclusion of the treaty; (b) any instrument which was made by one or more parties in connection with the conclusion of the treaty and accepted by the other parties as an instrument related to the treaty. 3. There shall be taken into account, together with the context: (a) any subsequent agreement between the parties regarding the interpretation of the treaty or the application of its provisions; (b) any subsequent practice in the application of the treaty which establishes the agreement of the parties regarding its interpretation; (c) any relevant rules of international law applicable in the relations between the parties. 4. A special meaning shall be given to a term if it is established that the parties so intended."

Article 32, entitled 'Supplementary means of interpretation', provides in full: "Recourse may be had to supplementary means of interpretation, including the preparatory work of the treaty and the circumstances of its conclusion, in order to confirm the meaning resulting from the application of article 31, or to determine the meaning when the interpretation according to article 31: (a) leaves the meaning ambiguous or obscure; or (b) leads to a result which is manifestly absurd or unreasonable."

19 Articles I, III, Outer Space Treaty.

20 ICISS, *The Responsibility to Protect: Report of the International Commission on Intervention and State Sovereignty* (International Development Research Centre 2001); Michael Clough,

included in the 2005 World Summit Declaration.[21] It interpreted in this context rules of pertinent international law, such as the UN Charter, including self-defence,[22] and the responsibility of states to protect fundamental human rights of their respective populations as enshrined in several international human rights conventions,[23] or even the 1968 Rescue Agreement.[24] It analysed further concepts such as the "obligation not to allow knowingly its territory to be used for acts contrary to the rights of other states"[25] and the existence of *erga omnes* obligations in the international community,[26] as well as the UN Principles on Remote Sensing[27] and the International Charter for Space and Major Disasters.[28]

The Project concluded on this issue that, beyond very specific contexts, recognition of a responsibility to protect as of yet arises in a rather vague manner only. This even applies to a certain extent to an obligation to share relevant information on NEO threats, as the necessary point of departure for any NEO response action.[29] Thus, any application to the NEO context of such a principle

---

'Darfur: Whose Responsibility to Protect?' (*Human Rights Watch*, January 2005) <http://hrw.org/wr2k5/darfur/index.htm> accessed 20 February 2021.

21 2005 World Summit Outcome, UNGA Res 60/1 (16 September 2005) UN Doc A/RES/60/1; see also Evan R Seamone, 'The Duty to "Expect the Unexpected": Mitigating Extreme Natural Threats to the Global Commons such as Asteroid and Comet Impacts with the Earth' (2003) 41 Columbia Journal of Transnational Law 735.

22 Article 51, Charter of the United Nations (adopted 26 June 1945, entered into force 24 October 1945) 1 UNTS 16 (UN Charter); Article III, Outer Space Treaty.

23 Cf also *The Responsibility to Protect*, §§ 1.3, 2.15, 2.21, on the related concept of 'human security'. Further, Nancy D. Arnison, 'International Law and Non-Intervention: When Humanitarian Concerns Supersede Sovereignty' (1993) 17–2 The Fletcher Forum of World Affairs 199–200.

24 Articles 1 – 4, Agreement on the Rescue of Astronauts, the Return of Astronauts and the Return of Objects Launched into Outer Space (adopted 19 December 1967, entered into force 3 December 1968) 672 UNTS 119 (Rescue Agreement).

25 *Corfu Channel Case* (*United Kingdom v Albania*) (Merits) [1949] ICJ Rep 4, 22; see also *Trail Smelter Arbitration* (*US v Canada*) [1941] R.I.A.A. No.3 at 1905.

26 See *Barcelona Traction, Light and Power Company, Limited* (*Belgium v Spain*) [1970] ICJ Rep 3 at 33.

27 Principles Relating to Remote Sensing of the Earth from Outer Space (hereafter UN Principles on Remote Sensing), UNGA Res 41/65 (3 December 1986) UN Doc A/AC.105/572/Rev.1, 43.

28 Charter On Cooperation To Achieve The Coordinated Use Of Space Facilities In The Event Of Natural Or Technological Disasters, UN Doc 25/4/2000 Rev. 3.2 (hereafter International Charter for Space and Major Disasters), see <https://disasterscharter.org/web/guest/home> accessed 20 February 2021.

29 See Principles X, XI, UN Principles on Remote Sensing; Sergio Marchisio, 'Legal Aspects of Disaster Management: European Efforts Including GMES' (Space Law Symposium, Vienna, 3 April 2006) 6 <http://esamultimedia.esa.int/docs/ECSL/symposium/sym-03.pdf>

would require considerable elaboration in order to provide guidance on specific obligations to undertake, or contribute to, mitigation activities against NEO threats. Here, analogies with principles found elsewhere in international law (like the ones referred to stemming from international human rights law, the UN Principles on Remote Sensing and the International Charter on Space and Major Disasters) may be used if some form of legal codification of an obligation to act in defence of the interests of other states and their citizens in the context of NEO threats would be undertaken in order to provide appropriate and generally acknowledged standards for such obligations.

At present, the more appropriate and effective approach would be to develop the international decision-making framework called for *inter alia* by the ASE Report along the lines of the UN Charter's construct for collective action: the powers of the UN Security Council under Chapters VI (on peaceful solution of disputes)[30] and VII (on forceful action)[31] of the UN Charter in principle are certainly broad enough to encompass such a NEO threat-related decision-making framework. That construct may have been developed in the context of the 'traditional' threats to international peace and security,[32] where 'traditional' use of force against a state might be necessary to restore peace and security; it would be rather appropriate – and at the same time politically much less problematic – to extend its scope to threats to humankind's peace, safety and security presented by natural disasters as stemming from NEOs not *ipso facto* harming (an)other state(s), in the present case.[33]

Establishment of the international decision-making framework along those lines might result in the combination of a legal right, even mandate, to act and a political and moral obligation to act. Such a combination should be sufficiently strong to guarantee one or more of the key states would indeed act if a relevant NEO threat arises, and, whilst itself currently much more realistic

accessed 20 February 2021; Maureen Williams, 'The UN Principles on Remote Sensing Today' in IISL (ed), *Proceedings of the Forty-Eighth Colloquium on the Law of Outer Space* (AIAA 2006) 4; Frans G von der Dunk, 'Legal Aspects of Geospatial Data-gathering in Space' (2005) 19–8 GIM International 69; Sylvia Ospina, 'SOS – Is Anyone Getting This Message' in IISL (ed), *Proceedings of the Forty-Ninth Colloquium on the Law of Outer Space* (AIAA 2007) 82.

30 Articles 33 – 38, UN Charter.

31 Articles 39 – 51, UN Charter.

32 UNGA Res 377(V), GAOR 5th Session Supp 20 (1950) UN Doc A/1775; also *Reparation for Injuries Suffered in the Service of the United Nations* (Advisory Opinion) [1949] ICJ Rep 174.

33 Tyra R Saechao, 'Natural Disasters and the Responsibility to Protect: From Chaos to Clarity' (2007) 32 Brooklyn Journal of International Law 663.

than any straightforward legal obligation to act, could also lead to such an obligation arising in the future as a matter of customary international law.

5 Cluster Two: Specific Liabilities for Damage

Here, the key question concerned the existence of specific liabilities for damage that would arise in the context of NEO response activities. Such damage could, in theory, follow from (1) the lack or refusal of distribution of relevant knowledge about asteroid threats (or on the contrary the distribution of incorrect or incomplete information); (2) the absence of appropriate action; (3) actions taken but not being entirely successful; or (4) actions inadvertently resulting in greater damage than would otherwise have been the case; whether such actions are those of individual states or undertaken jointly, perhaps even globally.

The Project analysed these four different liability scenarios from the perspective of the Liability Convention[34] and its focus on damage being caused by a space object,[35] the unsuccessful claims by several foreign entities against the US National Oceanic and Atmospheric Administration (NOAA) for failure to issue appropriate warnings on the 2004 Indian Ocean tsunami[36] and the International Charter on Space and Major Disasters.[37] Also, an assessment of relevant aspects of general international law was undertaken, such as the International Law Commission (ILC) Draft Articles on State Responsibility[38] (notably Article 28 on the duty of reparation) and the *Chorzów Factory Case*,[39]

34 Articles I – III, Liability Convention.

35 Noting that asteroids as such do not qualify as 'space objects'; see Frans G von der Dunk, 'Defining Subject Matter Under Space Law: Near Earth Objects Versus Space Objects' in IISL (ed), *Proceedings of the International Institute of Space Law 2008* (AIAA 2009) 293; Fabio Tronchetti, 'Space Treaties and Disaster Management' in IISL (ed), *Proceedings of the Fiftieth Colloquium on the Law of Outer Space* (AIAA 2008) 679; Bruce A Hurwitz, *State Liability for Outer Space Activities* (Martinus Nijhoff 1992) 12–19.

36 William C Nicholson, *Legal Issues: Warning Systems* (Public Entity Risk Institute 2005).

37 Article 5(4), International Charter for Space and Major Disasters.

38 ILC, Articles on the International Responsibility of States for Internationally Wrongful Acts, with Commentaries, 'Report of the International Law Commission on the Work of its 53rd Session' (23 April–1 June and 2 July–10 August 2001) UN Doc A/56/10.

39 *Case Concerning the Factory at Chorzów* (*Germany v Poland*) (Merits) 1928 PCIJ Rep Series A No 17; Malcom N Shaw, *International Law* (6th edn, Cambridge University Press 2008) 800–808, esp. 801; Ian Brownlie, *Principles of Public International Law* (7th edn, Oxford University Press 2008) 434–440, esp. 435.

as well as even more general principles of tort liability and the 'Good Samaritan' principle[40] as elaborated in a number of national jurisdictions.

On this set of issues, the Project concluded that the considerable variety in application of tort liability-concepts and versions of the 'Good Samaritan' principle allowing for waivers of liability in appropriate cases, as set against the global character of most relevant NEO threats and the need to respond to them at a principally global level, would still make application of either concept at the international level rather complicated, if not impossible without further ado. In consequence, codification by means of some treaty-version of the principle for this purpose would be recommended.

To that end, further research might be able to provide a common denominator in those concepts. This might be particularly helpful in the context of drafting an alternative to the current regime of the Liability Convention as applicable under the most acceptable interpretation, even if by way of a protocol to the Liability Convention which would take into account the specific NEO threat mitigation context as described above, as one interesting possible solution on this issue.

Such a new liability framework specifically designed for dealing with NEO issues, where necessary and appropriate deviating from the default application of the Liability Convention, may make use to a certain extent of the International Charter as a model, for example regarding the way the latter deals with who would be authorised to activate a response. Also, it would logically take the approach of waiving international liability for damage caused by or in the course of a *bona fide* effort at NEO threat mitigation along the lines of the 'Good Samaritan' principle.

Finally, development of such a regime should be given high priority in the context of the development of a global framework for decision-making in the context of NEO threats and required mitigation efforts. Liability issues are evidently amongst the most immediate concerns in any potentially risky undertaking.

40 See also Rajapakse MRB Nawinne, 'The Principles of State Responsibility and Humanitarian Assistance in the Context of Disaster Management', in IISL (ed), *Proceedings of the Fiftieth Colloquium on the Law of Outer Space* (AIAA 2008) 742.

6 Cluster Three: The Use of Physical Force, Possibly even Nuclear Devices, in Outer Space

This cluster addressed the specific legal issues involved when NEO response efforts would require the use of physical force in outer space (for instance through 'kinetic impactors'), in view of the general prohibition on the use of force under international law and the general impossibility of building a device which is only capable of exercising force against a NEO and not against another space object, or indeed against a target on Earth. After all, "targeting an asteroid involves many of the same technical issues as targeting a satellite".[41]

A specific situation would furthermore arise where the possibility of the use of nuclear devices, an option in any event to be considered only as a last-resort measure where humankind is confronted with too short a time and too large a NEO for any other option to feasibly work, would be contemplated.

The discussion undertaken in the context of the Project focused on the definition of weapons of mass-destruction, notably as per the Outer Space Treaty[42] and domestic US law,[43] and the related prohibitions pursuant to, in particular, the 1963 Partial Test Ban Treaty[44] and the 1996 Legality of the Threat or Use of Nuclear Weapons Advisory Opinion.[45] Finally, the Nuclear Power Source Principles[46] were briefly assessed from this perspective as well.

The conclusion of the Project was that, whilst existing international rules on these issues implicitly or explicitly allow for the use of conventional force as part of a relevant NEO response action, further parameters should be developed for such a use of force. This is certainly the case for the use of nuclear

---

41 Joan Johnson-Freese, *The Viability Of U.S. Antisatellite Policy: Moving Toward Space Control* (USAF Academy, USAF Institute for National Security Studies, January 2000) 21; see also John C Kunich, 'Planetary Defense: The Legality of Global Survival' (1997) 41 Air Force Law Review 119.

42 Article IV, Outer Space Treaty; also David P Fidler, 'Weapons of Mass Destruction and International Law' (2004) 14 Duke Journal of Comparative & International Law 39.

43 18 U.S.C. 2332a (2), Sec. 921(4).

44 See Article I(1.a), Treaty Banning Nuclear Weapon Tests in the Atmosphere, in Outer Space and Under Water (adopted 5 August 1963, entered into force 10 October 1963) 480 UNTS 43 (Partial Test Ban Treaty); further e.g. David S Jonas, 'The Comprehensive Nuclear Test Ban Treaty: Current Legal Status in the United States and the Implications of a Nuclear Test Explosion' (2007) 39 Journal of International Law and Politics 1008–1019, 1029–1040.

45 *Legality of the Threat or Use of Nuclear Weapons* (Advisory Opinion) [1996] ICJ Rep 1996, 226.

46 Principles Relevant to the Use of Nuclear Power Sources in Outer Space, UNGA Res 47/68 (14 December 1992) UN Doc A/AC.105/572/Rev.1 (UN Principles on Nuclear Power Sources) 47.

force, not permitted as such in outer space under international law except perhaps in the most extreme circumstances related to a state's survival – at least under standard textual interpretations. If such use of nuclear force is to be permitted, in a last-resort effort to save humankind and the Earth, it is adamant that at the very least a proper international decision-making framework providing for a set of fundamental parameters be developed.

7 Cluster Four: The Institutional Structure

The key question to be tackled here concerned the extent to which an institutional structure ultimately established could limit or distribute the responsibilities and liabilities of individual states. It was suggested in this respect to take note of international efforts to address other major 'threats' – for example, the threats posed by climate change. In that context, the world is attempting to put into place a workable and efficient institutional structure and attendant rules to deal with the problems at stake. Of course, it is not clear whether or not this will ultimately be successful (or even if the underlying framework will meet with widespread agreement of states) – yet it would be interesting to at least gauge what lessons the NEO threat mitigation approach discussion could learn from those other international efforts and why (or why not) those examples might be useful 'models' to follow in the case of threats posed by NEOs.

The discussions in the framework of the Project very much focused on the United Nations, as either the actual institution most appropriate to at least coordinate, and perhaps lead NEO threat mitigation efforts, involving in any event the Security Council[47] and at a secondary level also the General Assembly,[48] or the best model for a new entity specifically charged to do so.

The conclusions resulting from the Project were that, without prejudicing the outcome of any international discussions on the establishment of an international framework for decision-making, both the UN General Assembly[49] and the UN Security Council would have to play a role in this context, generally

47 2005 World Summit Outcome, UNGA Res 60/1 (16 September 2005) UN Doc A/RES/60/1, 79–80; cf. also Articles 2(2), 2(5), 24, 25, 39–43, 48, UN Charter; UNSC Res 1373 (28 September 2001) UN Doc S/RES/1373 <www.unhcr.org/refworld/docid/3c4e94552a.html> accessed 20 February 2021.

48 Articles 10 – 11, UN Charter, under which the General Assembly may call the attention of the Security Council to situations which are likely to endanger international peace and security.

49 See further, *The Responsibility to Protect*, § 6.29.

comparable to their respective roles in the context of threats against international peace and security in the classical sense. At the same time, the specifics of space activities and NEO response actions in particular should, at least ultimately, lead to a Security Council-like body much more congruent with the community of the main spacefaring nations, which should probably consult and cooperate with the actual Security Council on all aspects which may threaten international peace and security in a more classical vein, and could well refer to the General Assembly as the main representative of those states without mature NEO response capabilities.

Ideally, therefore, the general parameters for such decision-making should be outlined by a UN General Assembly Resolution, basing itself fundamentally on the contributions of UNCOPUOS on this issue and learning the lessons from the climate change process up to what many have described as a failure in Copenhagen, whilst specific NEO threats might then be subject to more detailed and focused Resolutions by a Security Council-like body providing for the necessary mandate and guidance for the NEO response efforts themselves with regard to a particular NEO threat-related event.

Such a baseline approach should both allow for long-term planning and coordination and for (sometimes urgent) action in case of a concrete threat situation. It would also allow coordination with other UN agencies which may need to be involved in global disasters, such as the UNHCR, the UN Refugee Agency.

In case the United Nations is not to be charged with such a role in the NEO threat mitigation context, the structure to be chosen, elaborated or established should at least in general terms mirror the UN construct, in particular as regards the relationship between the Security Council and the General Assembly with reference to tackling threats to international peace and security, whilst keeping in mind the different constituency of the Security Council respectively the NEO-response capable community.

8 Cluster Five: The Proper Role of Commercial, Including Private, Activities

The key question regarding this cluster concerned the proper role of commercial activities in such endeavours, and the legal parameters for and consequences of such a role. Under no circumstance should commercial interests, whether private, governmental, or of yet another nature, be allowed to lead to deviations from the main goals of NEO threat response actions. In particular with commercial activities conducted by private entities, this raises key issues such as state responsibility and state liability for those activities[50] which should be guiding the development of any legal framework on the issue.

At a second level, therefore, the legal differences between public and private parties should be taken into consideration. For example, sovereign immunity issues could affect the former but not the latter. Any role of private enterprise in particular should be limited by the understanding that NEO response actions should be first and foremost a public, (inter)governmental affair. Thus, much will depend upon the role that a commercial private entity will play, leading to different legal ramifications: as subcontractor to a state manufacturing hardware or providing a service, as partner in a public-private partnership, or as a stand-alone profit-generating venture.

Cost being a major aspect of any space activity including NEO mitigation campaigns, interesting opportunities may exist to draw commercial interests into contributing to NEO threat mitigation in all cases short of a nuclear explosion (which should explicitly be considered a last-resort option in any event). Such opportunities might arise if missions using technologies like a 'gravity tractor' or 'kinetic impactor' would have the potential to yield valuable (information on) mineral or energy resources.

If such an approach of trying to defray costs by getting commercial interests to join relevant efforts is to be effective, obviously the *bona fide* interests of private operators have to be taken into consideration,[51] if not indeed positively supported and underpinned by legal arrangements as much as necessary and possible.

The Project addressed the issue primarily from the perspective of a possible international regime arising for commercial exploitation of celestial bodies' resources, which could incentivise the private sector to (co-) fund missions to celestial bodies that might also be of value in the context of NEO threat mitigation.[52] Here, the focus was mainly on the Outer Space

50 With reference to Articles VI, VI, Outer Space Treaty; see further Michael Gerhard, 'Article VI' in Stephan Hobe, Bernhard Schmidt-Tedd and Kai-Uwe Schrogl (eds), *Cologne Commentary on Space Law,* vol I (Carl Heymanns Verlag 2009) 114, 117–122; Armel Kerrest de Rozavel & Leslie Jane Smith, 'Article VII' in Stephan Hobe, Bernhard Schmidt-Tedd and Kai-Uwe Schrogl (eds), *Cologne Commentary on Space Law,* vol I (Carl Heymanns Verlag 2009) 129–130, 134–139; Frans G von der Dunk, *Private Enterprise and Public Interest in the European 'Spacescape'* (International Institute of Air and Space Law 1998) 17–22, 48–51.

51 See also Henry R Hertzfeld and Frans G von der Dunk, 'Bringing Space Law into the Commercial World: Property Rights without Sovereignty' (2005) 6 Chicago Journal of International Law 81.

52 See already Declan J. O'Donnell, 'A New Institution is Proposed to Manage Space Resources: The Metanation in Space' in IISL (ed), *Proceedings of the Forty-First Colloquium on the Law of Outer Space* (AIAA 1999) 28–29; JoAnn Clayton-Townsend, 'Property Rights

Treaty,[53] the Rescue Agreement[54] and the Moon Agreement,[55] noting of course that the latter did not enjoy widespread support in the international community of states.

The Project came to the conclusion that to the extent that – and only to the extent that – commercial interests, in particular those of private enterprise, may play a beneficial and contributory role to NEO threat mitigation activities, their proper interests and rights, likely focused on the exploitation of resources of NEOs, should be at the least taken into account and perhaps formally be incorporated in the legal/institutional framework for decision-making to be established.

While it is perhaps too early to speculate on the precise form and extent of such commercial exploitation interests, and in particular on any role of private parties in that context, as the ongoing discussions on these issues tend to show the desirability of a proper and fair regime for exploitation, including commercial exploitation, of celestial bodies, including NEOs, and their resources is difficult to deny.[56] They should, from the perspective of NEO response, ensure that any involvement of entities in NEO response activities for commercial

and Future Space Commercialization' in IISL (ed), *Proceedings of the Forty- Second Colloquium on the Law of Outer Space* (AIAA 2000) 159.

53 See esp. Article II Outer Space Treaty and the non-appropriation principle; further on this Frans G von der Dunk, Elisabeth Back-Impallomeni, Stephan Hobe and Rosa-Maria Ramirez de Arellano, 'Surreal Estate: Addressing the Issue of 'Immovable Property Rights on the Moon'' (2004) 20 Space Policy 149.

54 Articles 1–4, Rescue Agreement: the execution of a rescue pursuant to the Rescue Agreement renders no property right in the *in situ* space resources at the rescue site, and applying such a concept to NEO response would be a legal novelty at least to be further studied thoroughly before allowing it to become international law.

55 Article 1(3), Agreement Governing the Activities of States on the Moon and Other Celestial Bodies (adopted 5 December 1979, entered into force 11 July 1984) 1363 UNTS 3 (Moon Agreement). As the Moon Agreement was drafted essentially to allow exploitation of natural resources of the moon and other celestial bodies only within the framework of a regime under a heading of 'common heritage of mankind', this clause provides that the Agreement "does not apply to extraterrestrial materials which reach the surface of the earth by natural means". This phrase suggests both that celestial bodies below a certain size would qualify merely as 'materials' rather than as full-blown 'celestial bodies', and that the provisions regarding the 'common heritage of mankind', often perceived to considerably constrain or even completely rule out private commercial exploitation, are not automatically applicable to such small-size celestial bodies even under the Moon Agreement.

56 See further on this Frans G von der Dunk, 'Private Property Rights and the Public Interest in Exploration of Outer Space' (2018) 13(2) Biological Theory – Integrating Development, Evolution and Cognition 142.

gain (whether private or public) is only to be allowed if the overarching goal of such missions is not threatened or compromised thereby.

9 The Main Conclusions and Recommendations Offered by the Research Project

Summarising the various analyses and discussions, the Project concluded that with regard to most of the aspects of legal issues analysed above, problems arise in terms of application of existing international law to solve the potentially dangerous and divisive, in worst cases catastrophic, threats NEOs could come to pose.

In some cases, there exists no international law of much substance and at best some general principles that could be distilled from national law, such as on tort liability and the 'Good Samaritan' principle – and even these principles are not completely uniform across the various national jurisdictions. In other cases, such international law has just started to develop and is still subject to considerable debate as to its precise ramifications; this is the case for instance with the 'responsibility to protect' and the ramifications of the International Charter on Space and Major Disasters in this specific context. In still other cases, moreover, there may perhaps not be such an absence of relevant international norms in general terms, but application thereof to the NEO threat response issue in particular may result in considerable, likely counter-productive complications, such as with the Liability Convention and (arguably) the use of nuclear force.

A first crucial step towards solving such issues in the most generic fashion would be to establish a proper international framework for decision-making. Such a framework would, firstly, where necessary, carve out from existing, more international and more general responsibilities and liabilities in the specific context of NEO threat response actions and provide for adequate specific versions thereof. Secondly, alongside existing principles and customary law applicable to the subject, it would result in – or at least provide a starting point for developing – customary international (and at a later stage perhaps treaty) law where no relevant international legal rules or principles exist, using as appropriate concepts and principles of national law. And thirdly, perhaps most important of all, it would underpin the development of a level of transparency and trust that would help to prevent divisive political tensions where the legal rules would not (yet) be clear.

Key to the success of such a framework would be a proper and workable balance between the interests and sovereign competencies of the (relatively few) states capable of actually undertaking successful NEO response missions and the rights and interests of all other states and humanity as a whole in being protected against threats posed by NEOs.

Under the current circumstances, a construction *mutatis mutandis* analogous to the roles of the UN Security Council, the UN General Assembly and individual sovereign states in the context of the UN role in preserving international peace and security, whether actually involving these UN bodies or not, provides the shortest and most effective route to such a balanced framework.

Under such a framework:

– any acknowledged responsibility to protect would be given a realistic chance of being complied with against a NEO threat by means of a balanced mandate on behalf of all states and humankind to be implemented according to certain guidelines and standards;
– liabilities for damage caused in spite of a mission taking place within the terms of the mandate concerned may be properly arranged, waived or otherwise dealt with as the case may be;
– the use of force, including even nuclear force as a measure of last resort, will not be prohibited if genuinely required in the defence of humankind – whilst allowing as little room for abuse as possible; and
– where necessary commercial interests, including those of private enterprise, can be harnessed for the cause by the states undertaking missions related to NEO threat responses, as long as remaining within the mandate.

The Report consequently offered the following seven key Recommendations to the international community:

1. It is important to soon start discussions within the UN framework as to whether and how to develop an international decision-making framework along the lines sketched above within the present structure of the UN, notably as regards the roles of the UN Security Council and the UN General Assembly.
2. A form of the 'responsibility to protect' should also be recognised in the NEO context as specifically requiring from states that have the capacity to generate relevant information and/or to respond to NEO threats to undertake such actions, after proper international coordination – preferably within a decision-making framework as recommended above in recommendation 1 – and without interfering with their sovereign powers to determine the details of any such mission.
3. It should be recognised that if damage occurs in spite of a NEO response mission, or as a consequence of such a mission being not (completely) successful, the state(s) responsible for such mission should not be held liable for such damage as long as the mission was undertaken within the

parameters set by a proper mandate by the international community – preferably through a decision-making framework as recommended above in recommendation 1 – as well as by specific agreements with the state(s) responsible for such a mission, as appropriate and applicable.

4. In the international discussions on the use of force in outer space care should be taken that the result of such discussions will not unduly obstruct the use of force that might be required under some scenarios of NEO threats.
5. As to the use of nuclear force in particular, this should be expressly recognised to be acceptable only as a last resort option, whilst ways should be explored to carve out very limited exceptions for NEO response purposes from the existing legal regime, which clearly prohibits any nuclear explosions in outer space, and which are consistent to the maximum degree possible with the UN Principles on Nuclear Power Sources.
6. A proper legal regime for handling possible commercial interests, including those of private enterprise, in the exploitation of natural resources in outer space without threatening the clear-cut interests of all states and humankind at large in the proper conduct of such activities should be developed to ensure that any involvement in NEO response activities for commercial gain is only to be allowed if the overarching goal of such missions is not threatened or compromised thereby.
7. A working group should be instituted by UNCOPUOS, notably by the Legal Subcommittee in close consultation with the Scientific-Technical Subcommittee, to further investigate, discuss and develop the recommendations 1-6 offered by the present Report, as well as the various options available in this regard.

More than a decade has now passed since the Final Report of the Research Project was presented, and great progress has been made in terms of a worldwide acknowledgement of the need to address potential NEO threats and undertaking preparatory actions, such as per the IAWN and SMPAG now active under UN auspices. Other aspects have been addressed by other contributors to this book; at this stage the present author wants to limit himself in this respect to the ongoing growth of annual Asteroid Day activities and events, which are literally covering almost the entire globe.[57] In that sense at least, there is no question that this particular area of "exploration and use of outer

57 See Asteroid Day website <https://asteroidday.org> accessed 20 February 2021. See also chapter 5 'Enhancing Public Awareness: The Establishment of "Asteroid Day"' in this book.

space, including the Moon and other celestial bodies" is "carried out for the benefit and in the interests of all countries".[58]

58 Article 1, Outer Space Treaty.

CHAPTER 11

The SMPAG Ad-hoc Working Group on Legal Issues

Line Drube

1 Introduction

If an asteroid is heading towards Earth, what would happen if a deflection campaign is considered necessary from a legal point of view? Who could authorise the campaign? Who would be liable for (unintended) damage? Can nuclear explosive devices be used in the deflection campaign? Does a nation have a legal obligation to participate in a deflection campaign to protect its own population or the population of other states? Questions such as these prompted the Space Mission Planning Advisory Group (SMPAG) to establish an Ad-hoc Working Group on Legal Issues, the purpose of which is to look into the existing international legal framework relevant to planetary defence. If such questions are not clarified before an emergency situation arises, precious time for planning a deflection campaign could be wasted.

2 Formation of the Ad-hoc Working Group on Legal Issues

In accordance with the recommendations of the Action Team on Near-Earth Objects,[1] the Scientific and Technical Subcommittee (STSC) of the United Nations Committee on the Peaceful Uses of Outer Space (UNCOPUOS) established the International Asteroid Warning Network (IAWN) and the Space Mission Planning Advisory Group (SMPAG) in 2014.[2] SMPAG members are space agencies or governmental or inter-governmental entities that coordinate and fund space activities and are capable of contributing to or carrying out a space-based NEO mitigation campaign.[3]

1 See chapter 4 'International Cooperation in Planetary Defence – UNCOPUOS, IAWN and SMPAG' in this book.

2 Romana Kofler and others, 'International Coordination on Planetary Defence: The Work of the IAWN and the SMPAG' (2019) 156 Acta Astronautica 409. See also chapter 4 'International Cooperation in Planetary Defence – UNCOPUOS, IAWN and SMPAG' in this book.

3 See chapter 4 'International Cooperation in Planetary Defence – UNCOPUOS, IAWN and SMPAG' in this book.

 | DOI:10.1163/9789004467606_013

The primary purpose of SMPAG is "to prepare for an international response to a NEO impact threat through the exchange of information, development of options for collaborative research and mission opportunities, and NEO threat mitigation planning activities".[4] SMPAG serves as a source of authoritative advice for decision makers on planetary defence methods in the case of an impact threat. Of its four subject areas,[5] the tasks connected to 'Legal and policy aspects' are described in the following way:

> Identify for possible detailed review within appropriate forums any legal and policy issues (e.g. liabilities) that may arise in undertaking NEO mitigation actions or selecting any likely mitigation options.[6]

At the 5th SMPAG meeting in November 2015, the SMPAG Steering Committee discussed the legal and policy issues and invited the present author to expand on the subject and develop her idea of creating a working group on legal issues by the next meeting.[7] The working group should consist of experts in space law, which were not represented in the existing SMPAG membership, together with scientific and technical advisors.

At the 6th SMPAG meeting in February 2016, after two presentations were given on legal issues related to planetary defence,[8] SMPAG unanimously agreed to establish a working group entitled 'Ad-Hoc Working Group on Legal Issues', abbreviated to 'SMPAG Legal WG'.[9] It was agreed that the mandate of

4 SMPAG, 'Terms of Reference V2.0' (13 September 2019) <www.cosmos.esa.int/web/smpag/terms_of_reference_v2> accessed 25 February 2021.

5 The four subject areas include (1) Reference missions, technology roadmaps and collaborative research, (2) Communication and exchange of information, (3) Legal and policy aspects, and (4) Mitigation planning activities. See also chapter 4 'International Cooperation in Planetary Defence – UNCOPUOS, IAWN and SMPAG' in this book.

6 See ibid.

7 SMPAG, 'Summary of the 5th Meeting (Steering Committee Only) of the Space Mission Planning Advisory Group' (10 November 2015) <www.cosmos.esa.int/web/smpag/meeting_05_-_nov_2015> accessed 25 February 2021.

8 See Line Drube and Alan Harris, 'Legal issues in planetary defence' (15 February 2016) <www.cosmos.esa.int/documents/336356/932894/Drube_Legal_issues_2016-02-15.pdf/a7172448-a58a-4c2e-b89a-5c505fc42b02> accessed 25 February 2021; Peter Stubbe, 'Overview of Existing Space Laws Relevant for SMPAG' (16 February 2016) <www.cosmos.esa.int/documents/336356/932894/Existing_relevant_space_laws_Stubbe_2016-02-16.pdf/33a50ef0-6cda-4d8c-bc65-30ca123098de> accessed 25 February 2021.

9 SMPAG, 'Summary of the 6th Meeting of the Space Mission Planning Advisory Group, 16–17 February 2016' (2016) <www.cosmos.esa.int/web/smpag/meeting_06_-_feb_2016> accessed 25 February 2021.

the SMPAG Legal WG should be confined to legal issues and not be extended to include economic, moral, or political issues.

The first teleconference of the Working Group was held in November 2016 and the first physical meeting in February 2017. The Terms of Reference of the SMPAG Legal WG were drawn up by SMPAG with advice from the SMPAG Legal WG. They were approved by SMPAG during its meeting in October 2017 and included the following tasks:

- Describe the existing legal context, in particular international law, relevant to the work of SMPAG.
- Identify, formulate and prioritize relevant legal questions and issues requiring clarification.
- Where necessary, suggest possible ways forward to deal with legal questions and issues.
- Provide legal advice to SMPAG as required.[10]

3 Members of the Ad-hoc Working Group on Legal Issues

SMPAG decided that the membership of the group should include scientific and technical experts from SMPAG, in addition to legal experts. The scientific and technical experts are responsible for ensuring that the work of the SMPAG Legal WG is technically sound and for clarifying technical questions. It was decided that SMPAG Legal WG members should be nominated by SMPAG members on behalf of their organisations and would be appointed upon consensus by SMPAG. In line with the conditions for membership of SMPAG itself, the Legal WG members' organisations should provide the funding and resources to facilitate the members' participation in the Working Group. No funding was provided by the United Nations. The membership of the group was limited to 15 legal experts and five technical experts, although exceptions could be authorised by SMPAG. Supporting experts or observers could also be invited by SMPAG to participate in meetings.[11]

By the time of the first teleconference of the Working Group, ten legal experts had been nominated by delegates from seven countries and ESA, and SMPAG had nominated four members as technical experts. The present author

10 SMPAG, 'Terms of Reference for the Space Mission Planning Advisory Group's Ad-Hoc Working Group on Legal Issues, Ver. 1.0' (11 October 2017) <www.cosmos.esa.int/documents/336356/336472/ToR_SMPAG_Ad_hoc_Working_Group_on_Legal-Issues_1_0_2017-10-11.pdf> accessed 25 February 2021.

11 Ibid.

was appointed as the coordinator of the Working Group[12] with Alissa J Haddaji supporting the coordination. Over time more legal experts were added and a couple of experts substituted. The following have contributed to the work to date:

Coordinators:

- Line Drube, Institute of Planetary Research, German Aerospace Center (DLR) (primary coordinator 2016 – October 2018);
- Alissa J Haddaji, Planetary Protection and Defense Projects, Committee on Space Research (COSPAR) (primary coordinator from November 2018).

Legal experts:

- Teresa Castillo, Director for International Affairs, Mexican Space Agency;
- Frans G von der Dunk, College of Law, University of Nebraska-Lincoln;
- Robin J Frank, Associate General Counsel for International Law, Office of the General Counsel, National Aeronautics and Space Administration NASA HQ;
- David A Koplow, Consultant to NASA Planetary Science Division and the Office of the General Counsel, Professor at Georgetown University Law Center;
- David Lopez, International Law Practice Group, The General Counsel, NASA HQ;
- Irmgard Marboe, Department of European, International and Comparative Law, University of Vienna;
- Sergio Marchisio, Legal Sciences Department, Sapienza University of Rome, member of the ASI Board of Directors;
- Jean-François Mayence, Legal Unit of Belgian Federal Office for Science Policy (BELSPO);
- Nicholas Fernandes, Government Legal Department, UK;
- Rosa Ma Ramírez de Arellano, General Deputy Director for International Affairs and Space Security, Mexican Space Agency;
- Michael Schlabs, International Law Practice Group, The General Counsel, NASA HQ;
- Alexander Soucek, International Law Division, European Space Agency (ESA);
- Cordula Steinkogler, Department of European, International and Comparative Law, University of Vienna;
- Peter Stubbe, Department of ESA-Affairs, DLR.

---

12 SMPAG, 'Summary of the 7th Meeting of the SMPAG' (14 October 2016) <www.cosmos.esa.int/web/smpag/meeting_07_-_oct_2016> accessed 25 February 2021.

Technical and scientific experts:

- Gerhard Drolshagen, SSA Programme Office, ESA;
- Line Drube, Institute of Planetary Research, DLR;
- Alan Harris, Institute of Planetary Research, DLR;
- Lindley N Johnson, Planetary Science Division, Science Mission Directorate, NASA HQ;
- Daniel Mazanek, NASA Langley Research Center.

4 The Work of the Ad-hoc Working Group on Legal Issues

Before the start of the SMPAG Legal WG few law experts had looked into the legal aspects of planetary defence. The main literature on the subject was a report published in 2010 by Professor Frans von der Dunk from the University of Nebraska-Lincoln's Programme on Space and Telecommunications Law, entitled 'Legal Aspects of NEO Threat Response and Related Institutional Issues'.[13] The report was presented in February 2010 to the UNCOPUOS STSC recommending that a working group should be instituted by UNCOPUOS, notably by its Legal Subcommittee in close consultation with the Scientific-Technical Subcommittee, to further investigate, discuss and develop the recommendations offered by the Report, as well as the various options available in this regard. Such a working group should consult closely with the various space agencies and non-governmental expert bodies involved to ensure input from all relevant perspectives. It should work in an interdisciplinary mode, since the precise facts needed to be known and understood as much as possible in order to elaborate realistic proposals.[14]

While this was not the reason for establishing the SMPAG Legal WG some five years later, the recommendation was very much in line with the same idea, and the Report was initially an inspiration to structuring the issue. Frans von der Dunk was invited to participate in the SMPAG Legal WG and provided input at various stages of the work.

An important goal of the SMPAG Legal WG was to have first findings ready to present to SMPAG after two years. In the first year, the legal expert members of the group examined all the relevant issues to provide material for discussion.

---

13 See Frans G von der Dunk and others, 'Legal Aspects of NEO Threat Response and Related Institutional Issues' (Final Report 2010). See also chapter 10 'The 2010 Report on Legal Aspects of NEO Threat Response and Related Institutional Issues' in this book.

14 See Frans G von der Dunk and others, 'Legal Aspects of NEO Threat Response and Related Institutional Issues' (Final Report 2010) 43.

In the second year, the issues were broken down into several subject areas with one or two lead authors, although all legal experts were encouraged to comment on all subjects. These subjects evolved into chapters of a report, designed to be a practical guide to SMPAG members on the existing legal framework relevant to the work of SMPAG. In October 2018, an advanced version of the report, entitled 'Planetary Defence Legal Overview and Assessment', was presented to SMPAG. During the following year, SMPAG members and legal experts reviewed the report and their comments were taken into account in the final version of the report, which was approved by SMPAG in February 2020. SMPAG decided to upload the report to SMPAG's website[15] and to make the executive summary available as a conference room paper for the 58th session of the Scientific and Technical Subcommittee.[16] In the following, some of the main findings, listed by chapter in the report, will be presented.

4.1 *Obligations to Inform and to Act*

This chapter addresses two questions:

1) Are states obligated to inform others about a potential NEO impact threat? The conclusion in the Report was that this type of information should be made available in line with elementary considerations of humanity[17] and the Outer Space Treaty,[18] in particular Article XI, which requires states parties to inform others about the results of space activities to the greatest extent feasible and practicable.

2) Do states have an obligation to respond to a NEO impact threat and participate in planetary defence efforts? It was concluded that, in particular in accordance with international human rights, a state has the right and obligation to attempt to protect its own territory and population against harm, taking into account the available technological and economic capabilities, but that there appears to be no clear legal obligation for a state to help other states in any particular way or to any particular degree.

---

15 Ad-Hoc Working Group on Legal Issues to SMPAG, 'Planetary Defence Legal Overview and Assessment' (SMPAG-RP-004, 8 April 2020) <https://www.cosmos.esa.int/web/smpag/documents_and_presentations> accessed 21 June 2021.

16 Information by the Space Mission Planning Advisory Group (SMPAG): Summary of the Report by the SMPAG Ad-Hoc Working Group on Legal Issues to SMPAG – Planetary Defence: Legal Overview and Assessment (22 April 2021), UN Doc A/AC.105/C.1/2021/CRP 10.

17 *Corfu Channel Case* (*United Kingdom v Albania*) (Merits) [1949] ICJ Rep 4, 22.

18 Treaty on Principles Governing the Activities of States in the Exploration and Use of Outer Space, including the Moon and Other Celestial Bodies (adopted 19 December 1966, entered into force 10 October 1967) 610 UNTS 205 (Outer Space Treaty).

4.2 *Legality of Planetary Defence Methods*

This chapter looks at the legality of planetary defence methods, focusing on methods that have reached a sufficient level of technological maturity. The conclusion was that, while there were no special legal issues under public international law relevant to slow push/pull methods and different kinetic energy methods, the use of Nuclear Explosive Devices (NEDs), which are by far the most powerful of the existing methods, would raise serious legal questions. Placing or exploding NEDs in space, irrespective of the purpose, is prohibited by several international treaties, such as the Limited Test Ban Treaty, in which the states parties undertake to prohibit, to prevent, and not to carry out any nuclear explosion in the atmosphere, in outer space or underwater,[19] as well as the Outer Space Treaty, which in Article IV prohibits the placement of nuclear weapons in orbit around Earth, installing them on celestial bodies, or stationing them in outer space in any other manner.[20] Furthermore, obligations on nuclear non-proliferation which restrict the spread of nuclear devices and materials, in particular the Nuclear Non-Proliferation Treaty, would tightly circumscribe the use of NEDs for planetary defence and inhibit possible forms of collaboration between states in this regard.[21] It was therefore concluded by the SMPAG Legal WG that the use of a NED for the purposes of planetary defence would be in conflict with existing treaties. In addition, the SMPAG Legal WG concluded that planetary defence devices could have some applicability also against other targets, which could raise political concerns at the international level. International cooperation and information sharing with regard to the conduct of planetary defence missions could enhance transparency and confidence among states.

4.3 *Responsibility*

This chapter addresses state responsibility, referring to the consequences of an action in non-conformity with international obligations. Any violation of an international obligation in the course of a planetary defence mission, such as the use of NEDs, entails the international responsibility of the state(s) involved and may provide the basis for claims for compensation. However, state responsibility law includes rules for the rare cases in which non-compliance with a

19 Treaty Banning Nuclear Weapon Tests in the Atmosphere, in Outer Space and Under Water (adopted 5 August 1963, entered into force 10 October 1963) 480 UNTS 6964 (Limited Test Ban Treaty).

20 Article IV, Outer Space Treaty.

21 Treaty on the Non-Proliferation of Nuclear Weapons (adopted 1 July 1968, entered into force 5 March 1970) 729 UNTS 169 (Nuclear Non-Proliferation Treaty).

state's international obligations can be justified and excused.[22] The SMPAG Legal WG considered in particular the circumstances precluding wrongfulness 'consent', 'distress' and 'necessity' which are the most relevant in the context of planetary defence. It was concluded that utmost care should be applied when invoking such circumstances and that in practice it might be difficult to conduct a comprehensive evaluation of whether in a concrete case the specific conditions for invoking circumstances precluding wrongfulness are met.[23]

The SMPAG Legal WG also considered what would happen if a planetary defence mission is undertaken by, or in collaboration with, non-governmental entities and concluded that this variation is consistent with international law. Under Article VI of the Outer Space Treaty, each state is internationally responsible for national space activities carried out by governmental agencies or non-governmental entities and is required to authorise and continuously supervise non-governmental activities.

4.4 *Liability*

This chapter deals with liability for damage caused in the context of a planetary defence mission, including damage on the ground, or to space assets caused by a planetary defence spacecraft, or other damage caused by a NEO as a result of the mission.

In this context, the Working Group analysed in particular Article VII of the Outer Space Treaty and the Liability Convention,[24] which have been drafted to protect the victims of damage from space activities. They establish the duty of the launching state(s) to compensate for damage when a causal link between the space activity and the damage can be shown. If the damage occurs in outer space, then fault has to be proven, but if the damage is caused on the ground or to an aircraft in flight, the liability is absolute. The SMPAG Legal WG therefore considered that as much as liability secures protection on the side of the victim, it also represents a risk on the side of launching state(s). This might reduce the willingness of states to assist others in a NEO threat situation by carrying out a planetary defence mission, since their good intention would not

22 International Law Commission, Draft Articles on Responsibility of States for Internationally Wrongful Acts, 'Report of the International Law Commission on the Work of its fifty-third Session' (23 April–1 June and 2 July–10 August 2001) UN Doc A/56/10, para 76.

23 See Ad-Hoc Working Group on Legal Issues to SMAPG, 'Planetary Defence Legal Overview and Assessment' (SMPAG-RP-004, 8 April 2020) 37–41; see also chapter 20 'The International Responsibility of States for Planetary Defence Activities' in this book.

24 Convention on International Liability for Damage Caused by Space Objects (adopted 29 November 1971, entered into force 1 September 1972) 961 UNTS 187 (Liability Convention).

reduce their liability. The SMPAG Legal WG concluded that the liability issue could be resolved through the establishment of an appropriate international understanding by means of legal instruments.

4.5 *Considerations for Decision Bodies*

This chapter deals with the issue of international decision-making bodies appropriate for international coordination and cooperation among states in the context of planetary defence. The decision-making bodies considered in more detail by the SMPAG Legal WG are the UN Security Council, the UN General Assembly, the United Nations Committee on the Peaceful Uses of Outer Space (UNCOPUOS), and the creation of an ad-hoc group. The SMPAG Legal WG considered that, from a legal point of view, the UN Security Council is unique in that it has the authority to issue binding decisions for all UN member states, which prevail over existing international obligations, whereas the UN General Assembly could allow a more representative and inclusive deliberation, but its recommendations are not binding upon states and cannot overrule contradicting international law obligations. The SMPAG Legal WG also found that SMPAG and IAWN represented important mechanisms at the international level for increased coordination in the area of planetary defence. It was concluded that international organisations, including UN bodies like UNCOPUOS, could contribute to establish broad political support, international cooperation and expertise in the context of a planetary defence mission, but only the UN Security Council has the authority to permit actions that are as such contrary to international law. The SMPAG Legal WG highlighted that, when it comes to choosing which one of these decision-making procedures to use, this choice is based on both legal and political considerations and will be made by political actors. Moreover, the choice will likely depend heavily on the facts and circumstances of the specific situation at the time. Each of the possible options has advantages and disadvantages but the decision-making bodies are not mutually exclusive of one another. It may be possible to employ more than one of them simultaneously or sequentially.

5 Conclusion

The work of the SMPAG Legal WG showed that a number of international law rules are applicable to the situation of a NEO impact threat, which need to be respected in the event of a planetary defence mission. In order to diminish political concerns and to increase international acceptance for such a mission, additional steps could be taken by states in advance.

For example, the Working Group suggested that, since in the case of a NEO impact threat emergency situation time will be limited, a number of documents could be developed on beforehand to address important points that should be considered before action is taken. These documents could *inter alia* deal with modalities on the dissemination of information regarding NEO impact threats, a draft agreement by the potentially affected state(s) and the state(s) willing to conduct the planetary defence mission, common procedures and elements of a mandate to undertake the mission, as well as liability considerations and modalities for the compensation of victims on the ground. In addition, the SMPAG Legal WG highlighted the need for the development of criteria and standards, such as for the selection of planetary defence methods.

The Working Group also found that many of the decisions, which may be taken in the context of a planetary defence operation, are political rather than legal. While legal factors frame the choices, the ultimate decisions are taken by political actors. In the case of a NEO impact threat emergency situation, there will be limited time to take decisions. The Working Group therefore concluded that it is important to increase awareness among the international community about the possibility of a NEO impact threat as well as about the legal questions involved.

The members of the Working Group have presented results of their work at several conferences and public events, they have participated in workshops, meetings, and discussions on the subject of legal issues in planetary defence and have undertaken publications related to this topic. It is hoped that the SMPAG Legal WG activities help to advance the field and encourage more experts to take an interest in the subject, as exemplified by this book.

CHAPTER 12

International Law Rules Related to the Sharing of Information about Potential NEO Threats

Irmgard Marboe

1 Introduction

The collection of information about potential NEO threats is currently the most important task governments, space agencies, and other actors are pursuing in the area of planetary defence. They have increased their efforts, raised money, developed technology, and engaged in the observation of outer space and celestial bodies to gain knowledge about existing asteroids and comets and their potential danger to the Earth. As other chapters in this book have shown, information is collected, processed, and stored in large quantities.[1]

An important question in this context is, whether and to what extent there is an obligation to share the respective information with others, in particular if the information indicates that a potential NEO threat becomes imminent. While one would readily assume that there exists some moral or ethical duty to share such important information, the crucial question is whether there is a legal obligation to this effect and – as a consequence – its omission would lead to responsibility and the obligation to pay compensation.

The legal framework of space activities is largely determined by rights and obligations of states as the primary – and originally the only – actors carrying out space activities. These rights and obligations are codified in the United Nations treaties and principles on outer space, but are also contained in other instruments of international law not directly related to space.[2] This legal framework is also relevant for the activities of non-state actors, because states are responsible for national space activities, irrespective of whether they are

1 See in particular chapter 6 'The United States Planetary Defence Programme: NASA and the Planetary Defense Coordination Office', chapter 7 'ESA Activities in Planetary Defence', and chapter 8 'Planetary Defence Activities Beyond NASA and ESA' in this book.

2 See chapter 9 'Overview of Current International Space Law in the Context of Planetary Defence' in this book.

 | DOI:10.1163/9789004467606_014

carried on by governmental agencies or by non-governmental entities under Article VI of the Outer Space Treaty.[3]

Obligations of states with respect to information exchange on potential NEO threats can be identified from various angles. If one considers a NEO impact primarily as a natural disaster, existing international obligations may be analysed from this perspective. The International Law Commission (ILC) has codified obligations of states with respect to the protection of persons in the event of disasters and published a set of pertinent Draft Articles with commentaries in 2016.[4] A NEO threat can also be regarded as a threat to human life and human rights so that existing international principles and treaties in this respect are applicable. With its devastating consequences a NEO threat could also be seen as a threat to international peace and security which could trigger the application of the UN Charter and raise the question of the duty of international cooperation. Finally, specific rules contained in the UN treaties on outer space may be applicable and prescribe the duty to share information.

The most important aspects with respect to the obligation of states to inform others about a potential NEO impact threat were highlighted in the Report of the SMPAG Ad-hoc Working Group on Legal Issues of 2020.[5] The ideas put forward therein will be followed-up and complemented by some more in-depth considerations.

2 The Obligation to Warn

Sharing information about NEO threats can be equated to the question whether there exists an obligation of states to warn about existing dangers to human life and property under international law. It involves humanitarian considerations and raises the question of the extent of state obligations under

3 Treaty on Principles Governing the Activities of States in the Exploration and Use of Outer Space, including the Moon and other Celestial Bodies (adopted 19 December 1966, entered into force 10 October 1967) 610 UNTS 205 (Outer Space Treaty); see also Frans G von der Dunk, 'International Space Law' in Frans G von der Dunk and Fabio Tronchetti (eds), *Handbook of Space Law* (Edward Elgar 2015) 29, 45–46; and chapter 21 'The Involvement of Private Actors in Planetary Defence Missions' in this book.

4 Article 7, ILC, Draft Articles on the Protection of Persons in the Event of Disasters, with Commentaries, 'Report of the International Law Commission on the Work of its 68th Session' (2 May–10 June and 4 July–12 August 2016) UN Doc A/71/10.

5 Ad-Hoc Working Group on Legal Issues, 'Planetary Defence Legal Overview and Assessment' (SMPAG-RP-004, 8 April 2020) 18–21. See also chapter 11 'The SMPAG Ad-hoc Working Group on Legal Issues' in this book.

international human rights law. These two aspects of the obligation to warn will be addressed in the following.

2.1 *Elementary Considerations of Humanity*

The obligation to warn was the subject matter of the first case brought before the International Court of Justice after its creation in 1945, namely the *Corfu Channel Case* (*United Kingdom v Albania*) which was decided on the merits in 1949.[6] Two British warships were severely damaged by anchored automatic mines when they attempted to pass the Corfu Channel off the coast of Albania on 22 October 1946. This resulted in the death and injuries of almost 90 British soldiers.

While it remained disputed and unclear who the authors of the minelaying were,[7] the Court was convinced that the laying of the minefield in the territorial waters of Albania could not have been accomplished without at least the knowledge of the Albanian government.[8] From this knowledge – which according to the Court was proven by means of indirect evidence and left no room for reasonable doubt[9] – emanated the obligation to warn ships approaching the Corfu Channel about the imminent danger.

The Court pointed out that the obligation to warn, when a state has knowledge about a dangerous situation, was not disputed between the parties. It highlighted that the Albanian government itself had expressly recognised that duty:

> The obligations resulting for Albania from this knowledge are not disputed between the Parties. Counsel for the Albanian Government expressly recognised that [*translation*] "if Albania had been informed of the operation before the incidents of October 22nd, and in time to warn the British vessels and shipping in general of the existence of mines in the Corfu Channel, her responsibility would be involved ..."[10]

The obligation to warn was therefore pre-existing to the dispute between the United Kingdom and Albania, even though, in legal scholarship, the *Corfu*

---

6 *Corfu Channel Case* (*UK v Albania*) (Merits) [1949] ICJ Rep 4.
7 Ibid, 17.
8 Ibid, 22.
9 Ibid, 18.
10 Ibid, 22.

Channel Case is often referred to as evidence of the existence of such an obligation.[11]

The legal source of this obligation is indeed interesting. The British government argued that the obligation to notify was enshrined in the Hague Convention No VIII relative to the laying of Automatic Submarine Contact Mines of 1907[12] in accordance with the general principles of international law and humanity.[13] However, the Hague Convention No VIII represents an instrument designed to restrict and regulate the employment of automatic submarine contact mines in order to mitigate the severity of war and to ensure, as far as possible, the security of peaceful navigation, in spite of the existence of war.[14] It is therefore an instrument of so-called 'humanitarian international law' which is only applicable in times of war and armed conflict. The incident, however, occurred, in October 1946, thus after the official ending of World War II.

The Court therefore rejected the applicability of the Hague Convention No VIII, but held that the obligation to notify existing dangers in order to safe human life and property was based on 'elementary considerations of humanity':

> Such obligations are based, not on the Hague Convention of 1907, No. VIII, which is applicable in time of war, but on certain general and well-recognised principles, namely: elementary considerations of humanity, even more exacting in peace than in war;[15]

These 'elementary consideration of humanity', as the International Court of Justice put it, have been taken up in legal scholarship and have since then been

---

11 While, of course, it is generally recognised that a judgment of the International Court of Justice can never be a source of international law, but only a "subsidiary means for the determination of the rules of law", in accordance with Art 38(1)(d), Statute of the International Court of Justice (adopted 26 June 1945, entered into force 24 October 1945) 156 UNTS 77. See also Michael Waibel, 'Corfu Channel Case', *Max Planck Encyclopedia of Public International Law* (Oxford University Press 2013) paras 10, 28.

12 Hague Convention No. VIII relative to the laying of Automatic Submarine Contact Mines (adopted 18 October 1907, entered into force 26 January 1910), 36 Stat. 2332 TS 541 (Hague Convention VIII). Articles 3 and 4 of that Convention provide that states must take every possible precaution for the security of peaceful shipping and notify in advance where automatic contact mines have been laid. This notice must be communicated to ship owners and to the governments through diplomatic channels.

13 *Corfu Channel Case* (*UK v Albania*) (Merits) [1949] ICJ Rep 4, 22.

14 See the preamble of the Hague Convention VIII.

15 *Corfu Channel Case* (*UK v Albania*) (Merits) [1949] ICJ Rep 4, 22.

repeatedly referred to and generally accepted as 'general principle of public international law'.[16]

What is the concrete content of the obligation to warn? The Court, in the *Corfu Channel Case,* referred to the 'imminent danger' the minefield represented to the approaching British warships, but also to shipping in general:

> The obligations incumbent upon the Albanian authorities consisted in notifying, for the benefit of shipping in general, the existence of a minefield in Albanian territorial waters and in warning the approaching British warships of the imminent danger to which the minefield exposed them.[17]

There are significant similarities between the facts of the *Corfu Channel Case* and a potential NEO threat. In parallel to the case before the International Court of Justice, the origin of the danger is unknown and/or cannot be attributed to any particular state. Nevertheless, the mere knowledge about the danger triggers the obligation to share this information. In the *Corfu Channel Case,* the obligation to share the information was even extended to a state which did not concede that it had that information but – given the indirect evidence available to the Court – must have known about it.

The difference of the *Corfu Channel Case* and the situation of a NEO threat is that the imminent danger existed in the territorial waters of Albania, which is considered to be part of the territory of the coastal state, while a NEO is a danger coming from outer space, an area which is not subject to territorial sovereignty of any state. However, the International Court of Justice did not specifically link the obligation to warn to the rights and obligations of coastal states under the law of the sea, but rather on 'elementary considerations of humanity' which it referred to as representing a 'general principle of international law'. Moreover, also the law of the sea, as codified in the UN Convention on the Law of the Sea (UNCLOS), contains the obligation to save human life in danger on the High Seas,[18] an area not subject to territorial sovereignty of any state, similar to outer space.

16 Malcolm N Shaw, *International Law* (8th edn, Cambridge University Press 2017) 909; James Crawford, *Brownlie's Principles of Public International Law* (9th edn, Oxford University Press 2019) 41; Michael Waibel, 'Corfu Channel Case', *Max Planck Encyclopedia of Public International Law* (Oxford University Press 2013) paras 10, 28.

17 *Corfu Channel Case (UK v Albania)* (Merits) [1949] ICJ Rep 4, 22.

18 Article 98, United Nation Convention on the Law of the Sea (adopted 10 December 1982, entered into force 16 November 1994) 1833 UNTS 396 (UNCLOS).

In the area of planetary defence, the evidence that a state 'must have seen' a NEO will probably not be feasible or at least be very difficult. However, when it can be proven that a state in fact had knowledge and sufficient information about a potential NEO threat, the clear message of the *Corfu Channel Case* is that the state is obliged to share this information with representatives of the potentially affected states, which may include all states on the Earth.

2.2 *The Right to Life*

In addition to considerations of 'humanity', the existence of 'human rights' – whose international codifications gradually appeared during and after the times of the *Corfu Channel Case* – also indicates that states have an obligation to share information about a potential NEO threat. The most important human right in this context is the 'right to life' which is codified in Article 3 of the Universal Declaration of Human Rights,[19] Article 6 of the International Covenant on Civil and Political Rights,[20] Article 2 of the European Convention for the Protection of Human Rights and Fundamental Freedoms,[21] Article 4 of the American Convention on Human Rights,[22] and Article 4 of the African Charter on Human and Peoples' Rights.[23] The right to life is most precious for its own sake as a right that inheres in every human being, but it also constitutes a fundamental right, the effective protection of which is the prerequisite for the enjoyment of all other human rights.[24]

The right to live entails a number of obligations of states, not only 'to respect' the right, but also 'to ensure' it,[25] which means that states must exercise due

19 Article 3, Universal Declaration of Human Rights (adopted 10 December 1948), UNGA Res 217 A(III) (UDHR).

20 Article 6, International Covenant on Civil and Political Rights (adopted 16 December 1966, entered into force 23 March 1976) 999 UNTS 171 (ICCPR).

21 Convention for the Protection of Human Rights and Fundamental Freedoms (adopted 4 November 1950, entered into force 3 September 1953, as amended) 213 UNTS 22 (ECHR).

22 American Convention on Human Rights (adopted 22 November 1969, entered into force 18 July 1978) 1144 UNTS 123 (ACHR).

23 African Charter on Human and Peoples' Rights (adopted 27 June 1981, entered into force 21 October 1986) 1520 UNTS 217 (Banjul Charter).

24 UNCHR 'General Comment No 36' (3 September 2019) UN Doc CCPR/C/GC/36 (General Comment No 36) para 2.

25 Niels Petersen, 'Life, Right to, International Protection', *Max Planck Encyclopedia of Public International Law* (Oxford University Press 2019) paras 2, 32; Philip Alston and Ryan Goodman, *International Human Rights*, (Oxford University Press 2013) 181–185; Richard White and Clare Ovey, *Jacobs, White, and Ovey: The European Convention on Human Rights* (5th edn, Oxford University Press 2010) 152–156; Malcolm N Shaw, *International Law* (8th edn, Cambridge University Press 2017) 256–257; James Crawford, *Brownlie's Principles of Public International Law* (9th edn, Oxford University Press 2019) 614.

diligence to protect the lives of individuals against deprivations caused by persons or entities other than the state itself.[26] The obligation of states parties to respect and ensure the right to life extends to reasonably foreseeable threats and life-threatening situations that can result in loss of life.[27] States may be in violation of the right to life, even if such threats and situations do not result in loss of life.[28] States are also called to develop, when necessary, plans designed to increase preparedness and address natural and manmade disasters that may adversely affect enjoyment of the right to life, such as hurricanes, tsunamis, earthquakes, radioactive accidents and massive cyberattacks resulting in disruption of essential services.[29] It can therefore be concluded that states are obliged to share information on imminent NEO threats on the basis of their obligations emanating from the 'right to life'.

However, the states' obligations under human rights treaties are limited in two respects: firstly, and as a matter of principle, they are only binding upon states parties to the respective treaties. While certain aspects of the right to life may have acquired the status of customary international law – creating obligations to states regardless of their respective treaty obligations[30] – the exact extent of the obligations may be subject to dispute.[31] Moreover, and this represents the second limitation, the right to life generally creates obligations of states only vis-à-vis subjects under their jurisdiction. This means that an obligation to ensure the lives of humans living outside of their jurisdiction – residing outside their territory or not having their nationality – cannot be readily assumed. Circumstances creating a specific link between the individuals to be protected and the respective state would have to be identified.[32]

---

26 General Comment No 36, para 7.

27 General Comment No 36, para 7.

28 General Comment No 36, para 7.

29 General Comment No 36, para 26.

30 The various sources of international law are enumerated in Art 38(1), Statute of the International Court of Justice (adopted 26 June 1945, entered into force 24 October 1945) 156 UNTS 77. See also chapter 9 'Overview of Current International Space Law in the Context of Planetary Defence' in this book.

31 Niels Petersen, 'Life, Right to, International Protection', *Max Planck Encyclopedia of Public International Law* (Oxford University Press 2019) para 22; James Crawford, *Brownlie's Principles of Public International Law* (9th edn, Oxford University Press 2019) 618; Malcolm N Shaw, *International Law* (8th edn, Cambridge University Press 2017) 216.

32 For example, states must refrain from deporting, extraditing or otherwise transferring individuals to countries in which there are substantial grounds for believing that a real threat exists that their right to life would be violated. See General Comment No 36, para 30.

In the present context it is important to note that the states' obligations with respect to the human right to life entail an obligation to share information about a potential NEO threat with respect to a state's own population and areas under its jurisdiction. The obligation to share this information with other states and their populations needs some further linkage or may be readily based on 'elementary considerations of humanity', as highlighted in the *Corfu Channel Case* above. In respect of the exchange of information between states, the 'duty to cooperate' may provide an additional basis, as will be discussed in the following.

3 Duty to Cooperate

In the area of space activities, the disparity between space faring and non-space faring countries is characteristic. Since the beginning of the space age, only technologically advanced states have been in the position to carry out space activities. Starting with the 'Space Race' in the 1950s and 1960s between only two states, the United States and the Soviet Union, the number of space faring nations has increased but is still limited to a rather small circle of technologically highly developed countries. Within the framework of the United Nations, the inequality of states with respect to their level of development is one of the recurring themes, exemplified by the initiatives to establish the so-called New International Economic Order (NIEO) in the 1970s[33] and various subsequent initiatives and programmes by the United Nations to support developing countries. In the present context the duty to cooperate will only be analysed to the extent to which it requires the sharing of information about a potential NEO threat.[34] Such information will generally be available only to technologically advanced countries which have the means to observe outer space by using sophisticated space technology or from the ground with the help of highly specialised telescopes. The question is to what extent these countries have a legal duty to share this information with other countries, in particular with developing countries, in light of the principle of cooperation.

33 See Declaration on the Establishment of a New International Economic Order, UNGA Res 3201 (S-VI) (1 May 1974) UN Doc A/RES/3201(S-VI) and Charter of Economic Rights and Duties of States, UNGA Res 3281 (6 November 1974) UN Doc A/RES/3281.

34 The further reaching duty to actively contribute to a NEO threat mitigation measure will be analysed in chapter 13 'Rules of International Law Regarding an Obligation of States to Undertake Planetary Defence Activities' in this book.

3.1 *The UN Charter and the Principle of Cooperation*

Already the founders of the United Nations have recognised that the unequal distribution of wealth represents one of the most important reasons for threats to international peace and security so that Article 1(3) of the UN Charter identifies "international co-operation in solving international problems of an economic, social, cultural, or humanitarian character" as one of its principle purposes.[35]

Nevertheless, it has remained a rather unsettled question whether and to what extent this principle establishes a legally binding 'duty to cooperate' under international law. The Friendly Relations Declaration of 1970 addressed the topic and attempted to offer further clarifications:

> States have the duty to co-operate with one another, irrespective of the differences in their political, economic and social systems, in the various spheres of international relations, in order to maintain international peace and security and to promote international economic stability and progress, the general welfare of nations and international co-operation free from discrimination based on such differences.
>
> To this end:
>
> (a) States shall co-operate with other States in the maintenance of international peace and security; (…)
>
> (c) States shall conduct their international relations in the economic, social, cultural, technical and trade fields in accordance with the principles of sovereign equality and non-intervention; (…)
>
> States should co-operate in the economic, social and cultural fields as well as in the field of science and technology and for the promotion of international cultural and educational progress. States should co-operate in the promotion of economic growth throughout the world, especially that of the developing countries.[36]

35 See also Articles 11 and 13 which define the competence and mandate of the UN General Assembly in this respect as well as Articles 55 and 56 addressing specific goals and means of international cooperation within the additional competence of the Economic and Social Council (ECOSOC).

36 Declaration on Principles of International Law concerning Friendly Relations and Co-operation among States in accordance with the Charter of the United Nations, UNGA Res 2625 (XXV), Annex (24 October 1970) UN Doc A/RES/2625(XXV) (Friendly Relations Declaration).

The formulation of these paragraphs shows the compromise which had to be reached, at the time, between the developing and the Socialist countries on the one hand and the Western countries on the other. While the former advanced the opinion of the existence of a general legal obligation of cooperation, the latter denied it. This divergence of opinions is evident in the use of the word 'shall' in some paragraphs, and the word 'should' and the mentioning of the principles of 'sovereign equality and non-intervention' in others. Western countries considered the principle of cooperation only as a moral duty in the conduct of international relation, but not as a binding norm and enforceable legal obligation. According to them, it was only of a declaratory nature and, to the extent it was written in the UN Charter, represented not more than a general statement on the competences of the United Nations in that regard.[37]

Until today, the nature and content of the principle of cooperation have remained unclear and are still subject to intensive debates among scholars and in practice.[38] The debate is also relevant in the context of international environmental law, where the principle of cooperation has been codified in the Stockholm Declaration[39] and the Rio Declaration.[40]

While there is so far no consensus on a general legal obligation of cooperation, in certain areas of international law there exist specific rights and duties of states which do create obligations of cooperation. Such obligations may arise under certain circumstances, for example in the event of natural disasters, or for activities which are particularly dangerous or taking place in areas beyond national jurisdiction, such as in outer space. As these situations are relevant in the present context, they will be addressed in the following.

---

37 Rüdiger Wolfrum, 'Cooperation, International Law of', in Rüdiger Wolfrum (ed), *Max Planck Encyclopedia of Public International Law* (Oxford University Press 2012) vol II 783, para 16.

38 See Jost Delbrück, 'The International Obligation to Cooperate – An Empty Shell or a Hard Law Principle of International Law? – A Critical Look at a Much Debated Paradigm of Modern International Law', in Jost Delbrück (ed), *Coexistence, Cooperation and Solidarity* (Brill 2012) vol I 1, 15 f., as well as the numerous other contributions in the two volumes and more than 2000 pages in this *Liber Amicorum Rüdiger Wolfrum.*

39 Principle 22, Declaration of the United Nations Conference on the Human Environment, UNGA Res 2994 (15 December 1972), UN Doc A/RES/2994.

40 Principle 7, 9, 27 Rio Declaration on Environment and Development, UN Doc A/CONF.151/26 (14 June 1992); 31 ILM 874. See also Chukeat Noichim, 'International Cooperation for Sustainable Space Development' (2005) 315 Journal of Space Law 319; Tamar Meshel, 'Unmasking the Substance Behind the Process: Why the Duty to Cooperate in International Water Law is Really a Substantive Principle' (2020) 29 Denver Journal of International Law 31; Malcolm N Shaw, *International Law* (8th edn, Cambridge University Press 2017) 653–655.

3.2 *Cooperation in the Event of Disasters*

In the event of natural disasters, governments need to act in order to mitigate damage and injuries as far as possible. The ILC in its Draft Articles on the Protection of Persons in the Event of Disasters[41] has highlighted the pertinent obligations of states under international law. The overall aim is to protect human life. While primarily focusing on the obligations of states to protect their own populations, they also address rules and conditions of cooperation among states and with other actors, including international organisations and non-governmental organisations. As a NEO impact may certainly be classified as natural disaster, the ILC Draft Articles are of interest in the context of planetary defence. With respect to the question addressed in the present chapter, it suffices to throw light on the obligation to share information about a potential NEO threat, that is *before* a natural disaster actually occurs. It will be examined to what extent states are obliged to prevent or mitigate a potential NEO impact by information sharing and early warning.

Article 7 of the ILC Draft Articles deals with the duty to cooperate, as its title indicates. This provision enumerates various potential partners of cooperation, such as the states amongst themselves, the United Nations, the components of the Red Cross and Red Crescent Movement, and other assisting actors, with which state shall cooperate "as appropriate". This qualification, however, does not envisage the level of cooperation but rather the actors with whom the cooperation should take place, depending on the actor and the context in which assistance in being sought and offered.[42]

The United Nations are explicitly mentioned as a potential partner to cooperate with in view of the central role of the Office for the Coordination of Humanitarian Affairs (OCHA) and the Emergency Relief Coordinator.[43] This United Nations focal point for complex emergencies is interesting in the present context, because it is supposed to assist affected countries by the provision of consolidated information, including early warning on emergencies.[44]

With respect to the forms of cooperation in the response to disasters Article 8 of the ILC Draft Articles enumerates "humanitarian assistance, coordination

---

41 See above, n 4.

42 See Article 7, ILC, Draft Articles on the Protection of Persons in the Event of Disasters, with Commentaries, 'Report of the International Law Commission on the Work of its 68th Session' (2 May–10 June and 4 July–12 August 2016) UN Doc A/71/10, para 6.

43 See UNGA Res 46/182 (19 December 1991).

44 See Commentary to Article 7, ILC, Draft Articles on the Protection of Persons in the Event of Disasters, with Commentaries, 'Report of the International Law Commission on the Work of its 68th Session' (2 May–10 June and 4 July–12 August 2016) UN Doc A/71/10, para 7.

of international relief actions and communications, and making available relief personnel, equipment and goods, and scientific, medical and technical resources". While this formulation only loosely includes communications, the Commentary makes clear that the list is not exclusive and in particular includes information-sharing.[45] It explains that the text was tailored to appropriately reflect the context and purpose of the Draft Articles taking into account the major areas of cooperation dealt with in international instruments addressing disaster response, such as the ASEAN Declaration on Mutual Assistance on Natural Disasters of 1976, which refers to disaster warnings and exchange of information and documents.[46]

Concerning the reduction of the risk of disasters Article 9(2) of the Draft Articles explicitly mentions "dissemination of risk and past loss information" as well as "the installation and operation of early warning systems" as disaster risk reduction measures. The Commentary refers to the Global Platform for Disaster Risk Reduction which, in 2013, drew attention to the "growing recognition that the prevention and reduction of disaster risk is a legal obligation, encompassing risk assessments, the establishment of *early warning systems,* and the *right to access risk information*".[47] At the Third United Nations World Conference on Disaster Risk Reduction, states reiterated their commitment to address disaster risk reduction and the building of resilience to disasters with a renewed sense of urgency.[48] The ensuing Sendai Framework indicated that "it is urgent and critical to anticipate, plan for and reduce disaster risk in order to more effectively protect persons, communities and countries" and called for "accountability for disaster risk creation (...) at all levels."[49] In particular, it is the task of government coordination forums to

> identify sectoral and multisectoral disaster risk, build awareness and knowledge of disaster risk through sharing and dissemination of non-sensitive disaster risk information and data, contribute to and coordinate reports on local and national disaster risk, coordinate public awareness campaigns on disaster risk, facilitate and support local multisectoral cooperation (e.g. among local governments) and contribute to the

45 Ibid, Article 8, para 4.
46 Ibid, Article 8, para 2.
47 Ibid, Article 9, para 3 (emphasis added).
48 Ibid, referring to the Sendai Framework for Disaster Risk Reduction 2015–2030, UNGA Res 69/283, Annex II (3 June 2015).
49 Ibid, referring to the Sendai Framework (Guiding Principles), para. 19(a).

determination of and reporting on national and local disaster risk management plans and all policies relevant for disaster risk management.[50]

Subsequent practice in the wake of the Sendai Framework confirms that numerous states have implemented such schemes in their national disaster risk reduction and management laws and frameworks.[51]

It can therefore be concluded that states have a legal obligation to share information about a potential NEO threat under existing norms of international law based on their obligations in the context of the protection of human lives in the event of natural disasters.

3.3 *UN Treaties and Principles on the Use of Outer Space*

The detection of a NEO threat may be the result of the use of specialised instruments placed on a satellite or of data gathered by telescopes placed on the surface of the Earth, or a combination of both. The rules of international space law, as codified in the UN treaties and principles on the use of outer space, are only relevant for the first alternative, namely the conduct of activities in outer space. The use of telescopes on Earth does not fall under the scope of application of the UN treaties on outer space.

Nevertheless, it is appropriate to look at the norms of international space law because they entail a specialised body of law acknowledging the different levels of development and technical capacities between countries. In the area of outer space this appears as the dichotomy of space faring and non-space faring countries. As a consequence the question of the existence of a duty of international cooperation is of particular significance. In the context of the present chapter this duty shall be analysed with respect to the sharing of information about a potential NEO threat. When such information at least in part stems from the operation of a space object, international space law is undoubtedly applicable.

The Outer Space Treaty represents the most important legal source in this respect. In its Articles I, III, IX, X, and IX the duty to cooperate is explicitly mentioned. According to Article I, "[t]he exploration and use of outer space, including the Moon and other celestial bodies, shall be carried out *for the benefit* and *in the interests of all countries*, irrespective of their degree of economic or scientific development [emphasis added]". This principle reflects the formulation of Principle 4 of the Legal Principles Declaration of 1963.[52] Its

50 Ibid, Art 9, para 6, referring to the Sendai Framework, para 27(g).

51 Ibid, Art 9, para 6, listing numerous examples of relevant state practice.

52 Declaration of Legal Principles Governing the Activities of States in the Exploration and Use of Outer Space, UNGA Res 1962 (XVIII) (13 December 2963) (Legal Principles

particular focus is on non-space faring countries, in the sense that they shall participate in the benefits without being themselves capable of actively participating in the exploration and use of outer space.[53] While the exact scope of this duty remains unclear, it is undisputed that Article I of the Outer Space Treaty responds to the existing differences of economic and scientific development and underlines that the non-space faring members of the international community should also benefit from the results of space activities to a certain degree.[54] This reflects also the object and purpose of the Outer Space Treaty laid down in its preamble, namely that the exploration and use of outer space should be carried on for the benefit of all peoples irrespective of the degree of their economic or scientific development. Considering the question analysed in this chapter it can therefore be concluded that Article I of the Outer Space Treaty requires that states that have gained information about a potential NEO threat by the use of technology in outer space, with or without the help of terrestrial telescopes, must share this information with all other states, in particular with developing countries.

Article III of the Outer Space Treaty reaffirms that states shall carry on activities in the exploration and use of outer space "in accordance with international law, including the Charter of the United Nations, in the interest of maintaining international peace and security and promoting international co-operation and understanding."[55] In addition to the explicit reference to the principle of international cooperation the Article points out that the existing body of international law is applicable in the conduct of space activities. Even though, as mentioned above, the duty of international cooperation is rather undefined under the UN Charter and in general international law, Article III provides the basis for adding the principles of humanity and the obligations under human rights treaties to the legal framework of outer space activities.

Declaration); see Karin Traunmüller, 'The "Declaration of Legal Principles Governing the Activities of States in the Exploration of Outer Space"' in Irmgard Marboe (ed), *Soft Law in Outer Space – The Function on Non-binding Norms in International Space Law* (Böhlau 2012) 145, 159.

53 See Stephan Hobe, 'Article I', in Stephan Hobe, Bernhard Schmidt-Tedd and Kai-Uwe Schrogl (eds), *Cologne Commentary on Space Law*, vol I (Carl Heymanns Verlag 2009) 38, para 51.

54 Ibid.

55 This rule is also contained as Principle 6 in the Legal Principles Declaration. See in more detail to the importance of Article III of the Outer Space Treaty chapter 9 'Overview of Current International Space Law in the Context of Planetary Defence', chapter 14 'The Use of Force and Planetary Defence' and chapter 20 'The International Responsibility of States for Planetary Defence Activities' in this book.

The duty of international cooperation is furthermore contained in Article IX which provides that "[i]n the exploration and use of outer space, including the Moon and other celestial bodies, States Parties to the Treaty shall be guided by the principle of co-operation and mutual assistance." While Article IX primarily focuses on the promotion and fostering of international cooperation in the actual conduct of outer space activities[56] and less on the sharing of results, it can nevertheless be referred to as an additional confirmation of the general duty of space faring countries to consider the interests of other countries, in particular developing countries, in their space programmes and projects. However, the exact contents and scope of such involvement is not clear and needs to be based on other, more concrete rules.[57] In the present context, one may think of Article XI, which will be discussed in more detail below.

The Space Benefits Declaration of 1996[58] which is specifically dedicated to the principle of international cooperation reiterates that the exploration and use of outer space should be carried out for the benefit and in the interest of all states irrespective of their degree of development.[59] It confirms Article I of the Outer Space Treaty, but goes further and adds disparities in 'social' and 'technological' development between countries as a matter of concern. It highlights that states with relevant space capabilities should contribute to promoting and fostering international cooperation. However, the duty to cooperate is qualified in many respects, including that states are "free to determine all aspects of their participation" and that everything has to be carried out on an "equitable and mutually acceptable basis".[60]

56 Sergio Marchisio, 'Article IX', in Stephan Hobe, Bernhard Schmidt-Tedd and Kai-Uwe Schrogl (eds), *Cologne Commentary on Space Law*, vol I (Carl Heymanns Verlag 2009) 169, paras 19–20.

57 Ibid, para 21.

58 Declaration on International Cooperation in the Exploration and Use of Outer Space for the Benefit and in the Interest of All States, Taking into Particular Account the Needs of Developing Countries, UNGA Res 51/122 (13 December 1996) (Space Benefits Declaration).

59 Principle 1, Space Benefits Declaration. See also Stephan Hobe et al, 'Space Benefits Declaration' in Stephan Hobe, Bernhard Schmidt-Tedd and Kai-Uwe Schrogl (eds), *Cologne Commentary on Space Law*, vol III (Carl Heymanns Verlag 2015) 299, para 67.

60 Principles 2 and 3, Space Benefits Declaration. See also Stephan Hobe et al, 'Space Benefits Declaration', in Stephan Hobe, Bernhard Schmidt-Tedd and Kai-Uwe Schrogl (eds), *Cologne Commentary on Space Law*, vol III (Carl Heymanns Verlag 2015) 299, paras 69–85; Gerhard Hafner, 'The Declaration on International Cooperation in the Exploration and Use of Outer Space for the Benefit and in the Interest of All States' in Irmgard Marboe (ed), *Soft Law in Outer Space – The Function of Non-Binding Norms in International Space Law* (Böhlau 2012) 267, 272–279; Stephan Hobe, *Space Law* (Nomos 2019) 63–64.

Nevertheless, despite the vague language and the unclear scope of Article IX and the Space Benefits Declaration with respect to the fostering of international cooperation in the conduct of outer space activities, the obligations enshrined in Article I and Article III leave little doubt that states are obliged to share information about potential NEO threats gained from activities in outer space with other countries, in particular with developing countries.

4 Principle of Due Regard

A principle specific to the law regulating areas beyond national jurisdiction is the principle of 'due regard'. It is prominently present in the law of the sea where Article 87(2) UNCLOS provides that the freedoms of the High Seas shall be exercised by all states, coastal or landlocked, with 'due regard' for the interests of other states in their exercise of the freedom of the High Seas.[61] Similarly, in international air law, the principle of 'due regard' is contained in Article 3 of the Chicago Convention which requires military and other state aircraft to fly with "due regard for the safety of civil aviation".[62]

In the law of outer space, the principle of 'due regard' is enshrined in Article IX of the Outer Space Treaty which provides that states, "in the exploration and use of outer space (…) shall conduct all their activities in outer space, including the Moon and other celestial bodies, with due regard to the corresponding interests of all other States Parties to the Treaty."

Generally, the principle of 'due regard' is to be understood as a limitation of the freedom to use outer space. It means that outer space must be explored and used with due diligence, taking into account the interests and rights of other states with respect to their respective use of outer space.[63] The provision primarily envisages the situation that the space activities of one state may interfere with the space activities of another state, which should be avoided. It can be described as the duty to act with a certain standard of care, attention,

61 United Nations Convention on the Law of the Sea (adopted 10 December 1982, entered into force 16 November 1994) 1833 UNTS 396 (UNCLOS).

62 Convention on International Civil Aviation (adopted 7 December 1944, entered into force 4 April 1947) 15 UNTS 295 (Chicago Convention). See also Sergio Marchisio, 'Article IX', in Stephan Hobe, Bernhard Schmidt-Tedd and Kai-Uwe Schrogl (eds), *Cologne Commentary on Space Law*, vol I (Carl Heymanns Verlag 2009) 169, para 24.

63 Sergio Marchisio, 'Article IX', in Stephan Hobe, Bernhard Schmidt-Tedd and Kai-Uwe Schrogl (eds), *Cologne Commentary on Space Law*, vol I (Carl Heymanns Verlag 2009) 169, para 23; Stephan Hobe, *Space Law* (Nomos 2019) 60, 89.

or observance, so that a state must prove that everything possible was undertaken to prevent a harmful act from occurring.[64]

Even though Article IX does not primarily address situations of planetary defence, a potential NEO impact may also be regarded as a 'harmful act' in this context. Depending on the particular facts and circumstances of the case, the principle of 'due regard' would then require to do everything possible to prevent the harmful act from occurring, including at least to share information about the NEO threat with other countries.

5 The Obligation to Share the Results of Space Activities

The obligation to share information is another key feature of legal frameworks governing areas beyond national jurisdiction. It shall ensure transparency and cooperation in the preservation and protection of those areas as well as their exploration and use for the benefit of humankind.[65]

In the law of the sea, an obligation of exchange of information and data is stipulated for the protection and preservation of the marine environment as well as in the context of marine scientific research.[66] The International Seabed Authority has the task to coordinate and disseminate the results of research and analysis of marine scientific research in the Area, the deep seabed beyond the continental shelf.[67] Similarly, the Antarctic Treaty provides that information regarding scientific observations and results shall be exchanged and made freely available to the greatest extent feasible and practicable.[68]

In the context of outer space activities, the obligation to share information is contained in Article XI of the Outer Space Treaty, which provides:

> In order to promote international co-operation in the peaceful exploration and use of outer space, States Parties to the Treaty conducting

---

64 Sergio Marchisio, 'Article IX', in Stephan Hobe, Bernhard Schmidt-Tedd and Kai-Uwe Schrogl (eds), *Cologne Commentary on Space Law,* vol I (Carl Heymanns Verlag 2009) 169, para 25; Francis Lyall and Paul B Larsen, *Space Law. A Treatise* (2 edn, Routledge 2018) 267.

65 Jean-François Mayence and Thomas Reuter, 'Article XI', in Stephan Hobe, Bernhard Schmidt-Tedd and Kai-Uwe Schrogl (eds), *Cologne Commentary on Space Law,* vol I (Carl Heymanns Verlag 2009) 194, para 22; Francis Lyall and Paul B Larsen, *Space Law. A Treatise* (2 edn, Routledge 2018) 62–63.

66 Articles 200, 244, 248 and 250, UNCLOS.

67 Article 143, UNCLOS.

68 Article III(1)(c), The Antarctic Treaty (adopted 1 December 1959, entered into force 23 June 1961) 402 UNTS 71.

> activities in outer space, including the Moon and other celestial bodies, agree to inform the Secretary-General of the United Nations as well as the public and the international scientific community, to the greatest extent feasible and practicable, of the nature, conduct, locations and results of such activities. On receiving the said information, the Secretary-General of the United Nations should be prepared to disseminate it immediately and effectively.

Article XI of the Outer Space Treaty clearly requests from states the sharing of information about the 'results' of their space activities. Obviously, information about a potential NEO impact gained from a dedicated satellite represents such a 'result'. However, the obligation to share information is qualified, namely that it must be done to the "greatest extent feasible and practicable". While this may be understood as an exhortation to undertake maximum efforts in information sharing, it can also easily be used as a limitation of the obligation to share.

It is not clear which criteria can be applied to identify what "feasible and practicable" means in a particular situation. Possible reasons advanced by states for non-disclosure of information include strategic interests, military secrets, the protection of intellectual property rights, and commercial interests.[69] While there may be legitimate interests of states not to disseminate certain information, Article XI nevertheless requests sharing of information to the greatest extent feasible and practical. It follows that efforts need to be undertaken to balance the interest of states to keep certain information confidential with the overall duty to share.[70]

In view of the obligation to explore and use outer space for the benefit and in the interest of all countries contained in Article I, it can be concluded that Article XI does not only contain an obligation of space faring countries to share the results of their space activities but even an entitlement for non-space faring countries to receive certain data, in particular with respect to data regarding environmental conditions and the prevention and handling of natural disasters.[71]

69 Jean-François Mayence and Thomas Reuter, 'Article XI', in Stephan Hobe, Bernhard Schmidt-Tedd and Kai-Uwe Schrogl (eds), *Cologne Commentary on Space Law*, vol I (Carl Heymanns Verlag 2009) 197–198, paras 47–51.

70 Ibid.

71 Ibid, para 52; see also Fabio Tronchetti, 'Legal Aspects of Satellite Remote Sensing', in Frans G von der Dunk, Fabio Tronchetti (eds), *Handbook of Space Law* (Edward Elgar Publishing 2015) 501, 524.

Explicit provisions to this effect are contained in the Remote Sensing Principles of 1986,[72] which stipulate that remote sensing shall "promote the protection of humankind form disasters". Principle XI explains the ensuing principle as follows:

> To this end, States participating in remote sensing activities that have identified processed data and analysed information in their possession that may be useful to States affected by natural disasters, or likely to be affected by impending natural disasters, shall transmit such data and information to States concerned as promptly as possible.[73]

The principle of information sharing in Principle XI is formulated more directly and less contingent than in Article XI of the Outer Space Treaty. The limitation "to the greatest extent feasibly and practicable" is replaced by the notion of "as promptly as possible" with the aim to ensure expeditious transmission of data and information.[74] The purpose of the duty is clearly identified, namely the prevention or mitigation of natural disasters, which a NEO impact would certainly represent. This has an influence on the balancing of the interests of states involved. The interests of the state in possession of the respective information not to disclose it for various reasons – strategic, military, protection of intellectual property, commercial – almost inevitably will be outweighed by the interests of the other states in being protected form a natural disaster.

However, the Remote Sensing Principles do not address remote sensing activities in general, but only "sensing of the Earth's surface from space".[75] They technically do not include remote sensing activities which observe outer space or celestial bodies. Strictly speaking the Remote Sensing Principles are therefore not relevant for planetary defence activities. On the other hand, the Remote Sensing Principles are not applicable in a legal sense to any space activities anyway, as they only represent non-binding recommendations adopted by the UN General Assembly. Their value lies in the interpretation and application of the Outer Space Treaty to newly developed space activities.[76] As

---

72 Principles Relating to Remote Sensing of the Earth from Outer Space, UNGA Res 41/65, Annex (3 December 1986) UN Doc A/AC.105/572/Rev. (Remote Sensing Principles).

73 Ibid, Principle XI.

74 See Joanne Gabrynowicz and others, 'Remote Sensing Principles', in Stephan Hobe, Bernhard Schmidt-Tedd and Kai-Uwe Schrogl (eds), *Cologne Commentary on Space Law*, vol III (Carl Heymanns Verlag 2015) 81, para 198.

75 Principle I(a), Remote Sensing Principles.

76 See Setsuko Aoki, 'The Function of 'Soft Law' in the Development of International Space Law' in Irmgard Marboe, *Soft Law in Outer Space – The Function of Non-Binding Norms in International Space Law* (Böhlau 2021) 57, 66–68; Joanne Gabrynowicz and others,

such they can be taken into consideration in the application of space activities which are similar and serve the same purpose as remote sensing activities of the Earth, namely the protection against and prevention, if possible, of natural disasters.

Finally it should be mentioned that also the Moon Agreement contains an obligation to share the results of space activities, requiring states parties to "promptly inform the Secretary-General, as well as the public and the international scientific community, of any phenomena they discover in outer space, including the Moon, which could endanger human life or health, as well as of any indication of organic life."[77] This formulation reflects the situation of a potential NEO impact quite aptly, and the urgency of the obligation to share is reflected by use of the term 'promptly'. However, the Moon Agreement has been ratified only by a limited number of countries,[78] not including major space faring nations, so that its relevance in practice is likely to remain limited in the context of planetary defence.

It can therefore be concluded that the body of international space law with its specialised rules and principles regulating activities of states in outer space undoubtfully contains an obligation to share information about potential NEO threats. While such an obligation stems from a variety of rules and principles of international space law, the most prominent is Article XI of the Outer Space Treaty. Other articles of the Outer Space Treaty, such as Article I, III, and IX, as well as the Remote Sensing Principles, provide an additional basis to support and explain the rationale and the extent of this obligation. In addition, Article VI of the Outer Space Treaty makes clear that also information about a potential NEO threat collected by non-governmental entities must be shared.

6 State Responsibility for Omissions

The violation of an international obligation entails the state's international responsibility. It triggers the application of so-called 'secondary norms of

'Remote Sensing Principles', in Stephan Hobe, Bernhard Schmidt-Tedd and Kai-Uwe Schrogl (eds), *Cologne Commentary on Space Law*, vol III (Carl Heymanns Verlag 2015) 81, paras 1–2.

77 Article 5(3), Agreement Governing the Activities of States on the Moon and Other Celestial Bodies, UNGA Res 34/68 (adopted 5 December 1979, entered into force 11 July 1984) 1363 UNTS 3 (Moon Agreement).

78 Only 18 countries have ratified the Moon Agreement as of 2021.

international law',[79] which were codified by the International Law Commission in its Articles on the International Responsibility of States for Internationally Wrongful Acts[80] and taken note of by the UN General Assembly in 2001.[81] The responsibility of a state becomes engaged when an act that is attributable to the state consists in an act or an omission that constitutes a breach of an international obligation of that state.[82] A breach of an international obligation exists, when an act of that state – or an omission – is not in conformity with what is required of it by that obligation, regardless of its origin or character.[83]

A state can therefore be internationally responsible when it fails to share information about a potential NEO threat. It would be the consequence of the omission of an obligation – namely the obligation to share information – required under international law. The consequences of such a failure include most importantly the obligation to make full reparation for the injury.[84] Injury includes any damage – whether material or moral – caused by the internationally wrongful act.[85] Full reparation for the injury shall take the form of restitution, compensation and satisfaction, either singly or in combination.[86] Compensation for the damage caused shall cover any financially assessable damages including loss of profits insofar as it is established.[87]

With respect to compensation for an omission it is important to identify the damage that actually was caused by the omission. To establish a causal link between the unlawful act and the damage is more complicated in this case than it is for an active behaviour of a state. Causation does not automatically follow from the factual chain of events but is qualified by the extent to which the unlawful act was the proximate cause of the damage.[88] If other

79 See Eric David, 'Primary and Secondary Rules', in James Crawford, Alain Pellet, Simon Olleson, Kate Parlett (eds), *The Law of International Responsibility* (Oxford University Press 2010) 27 f.

80 ILC, Articles on the International Responsibility of State for Internationally Wrongful Acts, with Commentaries, 'Report of the International Law Commission on the Work of its 53rd Session' (23 April–1 June and 2 July–10 August 2001) UN Doc A/56/10.

81 Articles on the International Responsibility of State for Internationally Wrongful Acts, UNGA Res 56/83, Annex (12 December 2001) (Articles on State Responsibility).

82 Article 2, Articles on State Responsibility. See in more detail the discussion of state responsibility in the area of planetary defence in chapter 20 'The International Responsibility of States for Planetary Defence Activities' in this book.

83 Article 12, Articles on State Responsibility.

84 Article 31, Articles on State Responsibility.

85 Ibid.

86 Article 34, Articles on State Responsibility.

87 Article 36, Articles on State Responsibility.

88 ILC, Articles on the International Responsibility of State for Internationally Wrongful Acts, with Commentaries, 'Report of the International Law Commission on the Work of

events intervene, the chain of causation may be broken and the damage be considered as too remote and thus not compensable.[89] On the other hand, if it is obvious that, absent the omission, damage would not have occurred, the responsible state must pay compensation. In case of a failure to warn about an imminent danger, it depends on whether the warning alone could have prevented the injury or whether further actions would have been needed to prevent the damage.

In the *Corfu Channel Case*, the International Court of Justice came to the conclusion that the damage could have been readily avoided, if the United Kingdom had received the warning about the mines anchored in the Corfu Channel. Albania was therefore responsible under international law for the loss of life and damage to property that was caused by the explosion of the mines. The Court held:

> In fact, nothing was attempted by the Albanian authorities to prevent the disaster. These grave omissions involve the international responsibility of Albania. The Court therefore reaches the conclusion that Albania is responsible under international law for the explosions which occurred on October 22nd, 1946, in Albanian waters, and for the damage and loss of human life which resulted from them, and that there is a duty upon Albania to pay compensation to the United Kingdom.[90]

In the context of planetary defence causation between the failure to warn and the avoidance of damage may not be so clear. It would be necessary to consider a 'but for'-scenario in order to identify the causes for the damage that occurred. The entailing assumptions necessarily involve a certain degree of judgment. As the Permanent Court of International Justice put it in the *Chorzów Factory Case*:

> The essential principle contained in the actual notion of an illegal act – a principle which seems to established by international practice and in

its 53rd Session' (23 April–1 June and 2 July–10 August 2001) UN Doc A/56/10, Article 36, para 10.

89 Ibid, with references to Herbert L A Hart and Anthony M Honoré, *Causation in the Law*, 2nd ed. (Clarendon Press 1985); Anthony M Honoré, 'Causation and remoteness of damage', André Tunc (ed), *International Encyclopedia of Comparative Law* (Mohr/Nijhoff 1983) vol XI part I chap 7.

90 *Corfu Channel Case* (*UK v Albania*) (Merits) [1949] ICJ Rep 4, 23; see also Michael Waibel, 'Corfu Channel Case', *Max Planck Encyclopedia of Public International Law* (Oxford University Press 2013) paras 17–20.

> particular by the decisions of arbitral tribunals – is that reparation must, as far as possible, wipe out all the consequences of the illegal act and re-establish the situation which would, *in all probability*, have existed if that act had not been committed. Restitution in kind, or, if this is not possible, payment of a sum corresponding to the value which a restitution in kind would bear; the award, if need be, of damages for loss sustained which would not be covered by restitution in kind or payment in place of it.[91]

If a state does not share information about a potential NEO threat it would be necessary to examine, for example, whether the affected states could have initiated mitigation measures against the NEO or whether evacuation of the respective territory would have been feasible and sufficient to avoid damage and destruction. This counterfactual must be taken into account in the evaluation of compensation which the responsible state would have to pay.

If the examination reveals that the damage could not have been prevented, or if no damage actually occurs because the NEO threat does not materialise, the responsible state still remains under the duty to make reparation. Financial compensation is only one of the three forms of reparation, the other two being restitution and satisfaction.[92] Satisfaction is the remedy for injuries which are not financially assessable. They arise from the very fact of the breach of the obligation, irrespective of its material consequences for the state concerned.[93] Satisfaction may consist in an acknowledgement of the breach, an expression of regret, a formal apology, or another appropriate modality.[94] It does not have a punitive character but intends to repair non-material injury caused to the state by non-compliance with an international obligation owed to it.[95] At the same time the acknowledgement of the breach helps to confirm the continuing existence of the norm in question.[96]

---

91 *Case Concerning the Factory at Chorzów (Germany v Poland)* (Merits) [1928] PCIJ Ser A No 17, para 47 (emphasis added).

92 Article 34, Articles on State Responsibility.

93 ILC, Articles on the International Responsibility of State for Internationally Wrongful Acts, with Commentaries, 'Report of the International Law Commission on the Work of its 53rd Session' (23 April–1 June and 2 July–10 August 2001) UN Doc A/56/10, Article 37, para 3.

94 Article 37(2), Articles on State Responsibility.

95 ILC, Articles on the International Responsibility of State for Internationally Wrongful Acts, with Commentaries, 'Report of the International Law Commission on the Work of its 53rd Session' (23 April–1 June and 2 July–10 August 2001) UN Doc A/56/10, Article 37, para 4.

96 Deviation from existing norms, even of treaty norms, if consistent and extensive, can lead to a change of the respective norms, if accompanied by the belief of the states that there

It follows from the above that the omission of sharing information about a potential NEO threat may lead to state responsibility, but not necessarily to the payment of compensation. Compensation is not required when material damage does not occur because the NEO threat does not materialise, or when damage occurs but is not directly caused by the omission because it could not have been mitigated anyway. It depends on the circumstance to what extent there exists a causal link between the omission and the damage. Nevertheless, states – and those for whom they are responsible – which do not share information about potential NEO threats commit an internationally wrongful act with all its negative – at least – reputational consequences.

7 Conclusion

The present chapter has shown that there exist various legal bases for the international obligation of states to share information about a potential NEO threat. Starting from early jurisprudence of the International Court of Justice, which confirmed the legal significance of humanitarian principles in international law, human rights and other obligations require actions from states in the face of a potential NEO impact. These include at least the sharing of the respective information. The principle of international cooperation, which is enshrined in the UN Charter and several UN General Assembly resolutions, adds to this the goal to maintain friendly relations among countries and equalise the disparities between highly industrialised countries and developing countries which lack the respective economic and technological means. That disparity is particularly pertinent in the area of space activities where the dichotomy between space faring and non-space faring countries is characteristic. For this reason the law governing the activities of states in the exploration and use of outer space is highly relevant in the present context.

Information about potential NEO threats is gathered by the use of outer space technology in combination with highly specialised infrastructure on Earth, such as telescopes. The UN treaties and principles governing outer space activities are only applicable to the former. Nevertheless, the acquired information about NEOs must still be regarded as a result, even if only in part, of a space activity, so that the Outer Space Treaty is applicable. One of its most important principles is that the exploration and use of outer space must be

---

exists a new rule of law requiring it. See Tullio Treves, 'Customary International Law', in Rüdiger Wolfrum (ed), *Max Planck Encyclopedia of Public International Law* (Oxford University Press 2012) vol II 937 paras 85–88.

carried on for the benefit of all peoples irrespective of the degree of their economic or scientific development. In that sense Article XI provides that states must share the results of their space activities with the United Nations, the public and the scientific community to the greatest extent feasible and practicable. The latter qualification may safeguard strategic, military, intellectual property, and commercial interests of the respective space faring states, which will, however, in most cases be outweighed by the interests of states to be warned about a potential NEO impact.

The omission of the obligation to share information about a potential NEO impact entails the responsibility of the state. This does not necessarily mean that the state has to pay compensation, for example, when the NEO threat does not materialise, or when damage occurs but is not caused by the omission. It needs to be examined whether the affected state would have had the possibility to initiate mitigation or evacuation measures in order to avoid the damage. The obligation to pay compensation depends on the causal relation between the failure of information sharing and the damage.

While the obligation to share information is based on international law which is only binding upon states, also space agencies and non-governmental actors must comply with it. Under Article VI of the Outer Space Treaty states bear responsibility for national space activities irrespective of whether they are carried out by governmental agencies or non-governmental entities. How and to whom and which information is to be shared would be governed by the national law of the respective state which is under an obligation to ensure that its national space activities are carried out in accordance with the UN space treaties and other pertinent obligations under international law.

CHAPTER 13

Rules of International Law regarding an Obligation of States to Undertake Planetary Defence Activities

Cordula Steinkogler

1 Introduction

A core issue from a legal point of view in the context of planetary defence is whether an obligation of states exists under international law to take action to mitigate the threat of a Near-Earth Object (NEO) impact on Earth. As discussed in other chapters of this book, a range of missions and projects related to planetary defence are currently planned or carried out by states, space agencies and other actors.[1] The question this chapter tries to shed light on is whether states are obliged under international law to undertake planetary defence measures in order to prevent or mitigate potential NEO impact threats.

This question has two dimensions: first, whether an international law obligation exists for states to conduct planetary defence activities in order to protect their own population and second, whether states are obliged under international law to assist and cooperate with other states in the mitigation of NEO impact threats.[2] While currently no instrument of international law specifically addresses planetary defence and explicitly establishes obligations in this regard, this chapter aims at analysing whether existing international legal instruments may nevertheless provide a basis for a duty of states to take action towards the mitigation or prevention of a NEO impact threat.

In case a planetary defence measure includes a space mission, international space law will be applicable. Therefore, the second part of this chapter will

1 See chapter 6 'The United States Planetary Defence Programme', chapter 7 'ESA's Activities in Planetary Defence' and chapter 8 'Planetary Defence Activities Beyond NASA and ESA' in this book on the various planetary defence activities.

2 While there is no definition under international law of the term 'cooperation', it has been described as "the voluntary co-ordinated action of two or more States which takes place under a legal regime and serves a specific objective (…) it marks the effort of States to accomplish an objective by joint action, where the activity of a single State cannot achieve the same result". See Rüdiger Wolfrum, 'Cooperation, International Law of' in Rüdiger Wolfrum (ed), *Max Planck Encyclopedia of Public International Law* (Oxford University Press 2012) vol II, 783, para 2.

 | DOI:10.1163/9789004467606_015

address provisions of space law that may be relevant in the context of planetary defence. The mitigation of threats of NEO impacts on Earth can also be regarded from an environmental and human rights perspective. The third and fourth part of the chapter will thus discuss international environmental law and international human rights law of relevance to planetary defence. The fifth part of the chapter will be dedicated to analysing the applicability of the concept of the responsibility to protect to planetary defence activities. Finally, in the sixth part of the chapter, the question of an obligation to undertake planetary defence activities will be addressed from the angle of international disaster law.[3]

2 International Space Law

The Outer Space Treaty of 1967 provides the basic framework for the international regulation of space activities and sets forth the main principles that govern the exploration and use of outer space.[4] It establishes rights and obligations of states for the conduct of space activities and therefore also covers planetary defence space missions aimed at deflecting (or disrupting) a NEO that is on an Earth-bound trajectory. It contains a number of principles that can be of relevance with regard to the question whether an obligation exists under international law to carry out or cooperate in planetary defence activities.

Article I, Paragraph 2 of the Outer Space Treaty is of particular importance in this respect. It stipulates that outer space, including celestial bodies, "shall be free for exploration and use by all States without discrimination of any kind, on a basis of equality and in accordance with international law, and there shall be free access to all areas of celestial bodies".[5] The explicit non-discrimination

---

3 The question of an international obligation of states to undertake planetary defence measures was addressed in the Report of the Space Mission Planning Advisory Group (SMPAG) Ad-Hoc Working Group on Legal Issues. In this chapter the ideas put forward in the Report are discussed in more detail. See Ad-Hoc Working Group on Legal Issues, 'Planetary Defence Legal Overview and Assessment' (SMPAG-RP-004, 8 April 2020) 18–26. See also chapter 11 'The SMPAG Ad-hoc Working Group on Legal Issues' in this book.

4 Treaty on Principles Governing the Activities of States in the Exploration and Use of Outer Space, including the Moon and Other Celestial Bodies (adopted 19 December 1966, entered into force 10 October 1967) 610 UNTS 205 (Outer Space Treaty).

5 The term 'freedom' in this context is interpreted as meaning that every state may access, use and explore outer space and celestial bodies without the need to seek permission. Stephan Hobe, 'Article I' in Stephan Hobe, Bernhard Schmidt-Tedd and Kai-Uwe Schrogl (eds), *Cologne Commentary on Space Law*, vol I (Carl Heymanns Verlag 2009) 33–36. The right to use and explore outer space is regarded as a right of all states and not only a right

language "without discrimination of any kind" and "on a basis of equality" was included during the negotiation of the Treaty to assure cooperation among states in space activities.[6] The provision can nevertheless not be interpreted as establishing a specific obligation of states to carry out or to cooperate in planetary defence activities. Yet, the freedoms enshrined in Article 1, Paragraph 2 of the Outer Space Treaty are of importance in allowing states to do so. However, limitations to these freedoms that can be found in the Outer Space Treaty are also relevant in the context of planetary defence.

In this regard, the requirement contained in Article 1, Paragraph 1 of the Outer Space Treaty that the exploration and use of outer space, including celestial bodies, "shall be carried out for the benefit and in the interests of all countries, irrespective of their degree of economic or scientific development, and shall be the province of all mankind" is of importance. This limitation to the above-mentioned freedoms is "an attempt to facilitate and encourage international co-operation"[7] and highlights the community aspects of space activities, including to take particular account of those states that are technologically less advanced.[8] However, due to the general wording of Article I it is difficult to determine its exact scope with regard to a duty to cooperate and to carry out space activities for the benefit of all countries.[9] In order to give guidance in this regard, the Space Benefits Declaration was elaborated in the framework of UNCOPUOS and adopted in 1996.[10] The Declaration calls for international

mutually recognized by parties to the Outer Space Treaty. See Francis Lyall and Paul B Larsen, *Space Law: A Treatise* (2nd edn, Routledge 2018) 54. See also Frans G von der Dunk, 'International Space Law' in Frans G von der Dunk and Fabio Tronchetti (eds), *Handbook of Space Law* (Edward Elgar Publishing 2015) 55–60, arguing that as a consequence of elevating outer space to the status of a 'global commons' the Outer Space Treaty does not only constitute an agreement between a group of states but rather establishes a legal framework for the entire area of outer space.

6 Paul G Dembling, 'Treaty on Principles Governing the Activities of States in the Exploration and Use of Outer Space, including the Moon and Other Celestial Bodies' in Nandasiri Jasentuliyana and Roy S K Lee (eds), *Manual on Space Law* (Oceana Publications 1979) vol I, 10.

7 Stephan Hobe, 'Article I' in Stephan Hobe, Bernhard Schmidt-Tedd and Kai-Uwe Schrogl (eds), *Cologne Commentary on Space Law*, vol 1 (Carl Heymanns Verlag 2009) 40.

8 Stephan Hobe, 'Article I' in Stephan Hobe, Bernhard Schmidt-Tedd and Kai-Uwe Schrogl (eds), *Cologne Commentary on Space Law*, vol 1 (Carl Heymanns Verlag 2009) 40–41; Bess C M Reijnen, *The United Nations Space Treaties Analysed* (Edition Frontieres 1992) 88–89; Francis Lyall and Paul B Larsen, *Space Law: A Treatise* (2nd edn, Routledge 2018) 57–59.

9 A core question in this regard is whether there must be a sharing of benefits in a practical sense or whether it is sufficient that an activity is beneficial in a general way, which may also include to merely not be harmful. Francis Lyall and Paul B Larsen, *Space Law: A Treatise* (2nd edn, Routledge 2018) 57–59.

10 Declaration on International Cooperation in the Exploration and Use of Outer Space for the Benefit and in the Interest of All States, Taking into Particular Account the Needs of

cooperation in the exploration and use of outer space and recommends that particularly states possessing space capabilities should contribute to promoting and fostering international cooperation. Yet, it also specifies that states are free to determine all aspects of their participation in international cooperation in space activities.[11] Therefore, while a specific obligation to assist other states cannot be drawn from Article I, it does establish a general call for cooperation in space activities, whereby the interests of other states, in particular those that are technologically and economically less advanced and are lacking space faring capabilities, need to be taken into account.

International cooperation in space activities is furthermore addressed in Article IX Outer Space Treaty which stipulates that states parties "shall be guided by the principle of cooperation and mutual assistance" in the exploration and use of outer space and conduct their space activities with "due regard to the corresponding interests" of other states.[12] The principle of cooperation and mutual assistance enshrined in Article IX also highlights the disparity between space faring and non-space faring countries regarding the availability of economic and technological means, due to which many states are not able to participate in space activities without resorting to international cooperation.[13] Yet, the exact scope of Article IX in this regard remains unclear. It is considered as establishing a general principle that provides guidance for states' activities and that needs to be concretised by more specific rules and instruments dealing with international cooperation in space activities.[14] Such a concretisation can for instance be found in Article III Outer Space Treaty, which requires states to carry out space activities in the interest of promoting

---

Developing Countries, UNGA Res 51/122 (13 December 1996) (Space Benefits Declaration). See generally Stephan Hobe, VS Mani, Haifeng Zhao and Fabio Tronchetti, 'The 1996 Declaration on International Cooperation in the Exploration and Use of Outer Space for the Benefit and in the Interest of All States, Taking into Particular Account the Needs of Developing Countries' in Stephan Hobe, Bernhard Schmidt-Tedd and Kai-Uwe Schrogl (eds), *Cologne Commentary on Space Law,* vol III (Carl Heymanns Verlag 2015) 299–362. For an analysis of the historical development and political context of the Declaration see: Marietta Benkö and Kai-Uwe Schrogl, 'Article I of the Outer Space Treaty Reconsidered After 30 Years' in Gabriel Lafferranderie and Daphné Crowther (eds), *Outlook on Space Law Over the Next 30 Years* (Kluwer Law International 1997) 67–79.

11 Paragraphs 1, 2 and 3, Space Benefits Declaration.

12 Article IX, Sentence 1, Outer Space Treaty.

13 Sergio Marchisio, 'Article IX' in Stephan Hobe, Bernhard Schmidt-Tedd and Kai-Uwe Schrogl (eds), *Cologne Commentary on Space Law,* vol I (Carl Heymanns Verlag 2009) 174.

14 Sergio Marchisio, 'Article IX' in Stephan Hobe, Bernhard Schmidt-Tedd and Kai-Uwe Schrogl (eds), *Cologne Commentary on Space Law,* vol I (Carl Heymanns Verlag 2009) 174–175.

international cooperation,[15] as well as in other space law provisions referring to international cooperation.[16] Besides establishing a general principle of cooperation and mutual assistance, Article IX Outer Space Treaty requires states to exercise their rights and freedoms in the conduct of space activities with a certain standard of care, taking into account the rights and interests of other states and avoiding interference with or jeopardy to the safety of their activities.[17]

In addition, Article IX establishes a consultation mechanism regarding the avoidance of harmful interference in space activities. It requires states to undertake appropriate international consultations before proceeding with any space activity that they have reason to believe would potentially cause harmful interference with activities of other states.[18] Furthermore, a state that has reason to believe that an activity planned by another state would cause potentially harmful interference with its space activities may request consultation concerning that activity.[19] This would also be applicable in the context of planetary defence activities. In case there is reason to believe that a NEO impact threat mitigation measure would cause potentially harmful interference with the space activities of other states, the state or states undertaking the measure would be under the obligation to carry out consultations with the likely affected state or states. While this provision does not provide a possibility for affected

15 For an analysis of Article III see Olivier Ribbelink, 'Article III' in Stephan Hobe, Bernhard Schmidt-Tedd and Kai-Uwe Schrogl (eds), *Cologne Commentary on Space Law,* vol I (Carl Heymanns Verlag 2009) 64–69.

16 This includes for instance Article XI Outer Space Treaty stipulating that states should inform the UN Secretary-General, the public and the scientific community of the nature, conduct, locations and results of space activities in order to promote international cooperation in the peaceful exploration and use of outer space. Obligations with regard to international cooperation and mutual assistance can also be found in Article V Outer Space Treaty requiring states to render astronauts all possible assistance in the event of accident, distress, or emergency landing, which is further detailed in the Agreement on the Rescue of Astronauts, the Return of Astronauts and the Return of Objects Launched into Outer Space (adopted 19 December 1967, entered into force 3 December 1968) 672 UNTS 119 (Rescue Agreement). Moreover, Article VI Convention on Registration of Objects Launched into Outer Space (adopted 12 November 1974, entered into force 15 September 1976) 1023 UNTS 15 (Registration Convention) requires states to assist in the identification of space objects which have caused damage or may be of a hazardous nature.

17 Lotta Viikari, *The Environmental Element in Space Law. Assessing the Present and Charting the Future* (Martinus Nijhoff Publishers 2008) 59–61; Sergio Marchisio, 'Article IX' in Stephan Hobe, Bernhard Schmidt-Tedd and Kai-Uwe Schrogl (eds), *Cologne Commentary on Space Law,* vol I (Carl Heymanns Verlag 2009) 175–176.

18 Article IX, Sentence 3, Outer Space Treaty.

19 Article IX, Sentence 4, Outer Space Treaty.

states to object to or inhibit the planned activity, the consultation required under Article IX is not just a mere formality that states need to undertake with no real intention of reaching a solution acceptable to concerned states, since "it would be unfair to other States to allow activities that would cause harmful interference to be conducted without consulting them and taking appropriate preventive measures to avoid such harm".[20]

Article IX also contains environmental considerations, requiring states to carry out the exploration of outer space and celestial bodies so as to avoid their "harmful contamination" as well as "adverse changes in the environment of the Earth resulting from the introduction of extraterrestrial matter".[21] The obligation to prevent harmful contamination is a broad concept that covers all possible forms and instances of harmful interference, whether deliberate or unintentional, and implies a duty of states to take all appropriate measures to prevent harm and minimise the risk thereof.[22] While not establishing an obligation to take action for the mitigation of a NEO impact threat, this provision could nevertheless affect the conduct of planetary defence activities, in particular in cases where the deflection or disruption of an asteroid or comet in the course of a planetary defence mission could result in collisions and the creation of fragments.[23]

It can be concluded that these provisions do not establish a concrete obligation of states to carry out planetary defence activities or to assist other states in the conduct of such activities. Yet, they do include a general duty to cooperate and to take into account the interests of other states in the course of such activities, as well as an obligation to avoid harmful contamination and interference and to conduct consultations, in particular if the activities in question bear the risk of causing harm to other states. In this regard, it is therefore also of importance to take proper account of the risks and uncertainties that may be involved in planetary defence space activities which may make international cooperation and consultation all the more important.

20 Sergio Marchisio, 'Article IX' in Stephan Hobe, Bernhard Schmidt-Tedd and Kai-Uwe Schrogl (eds), *Cologne Commentary on Space Law*, vol I (Carl Heymanns Verlag 2009) 180.

21 Article IX, Sentence 2, Outer Space Treaty.

22 Sergio Marchisio, 'Article IX' in Stephan Hobe, Bernhard Schmidt-Tedd and Kai-Uwe Schrogl (eds), *Cologne Commentary on Space Law*, vol I (Carl Heymanns Verlag 2009) 176–177.

23 Francis Lyall and Paul B Larsen, *Space Law: A Treatise* (2nd edn, Routledge 2018) 236.

3 International Environmental Law

International environmental law can also be of relevance regarding planetary defence activities, in particular provisions relating to activities of states that may be capable of causing environmental harm on the territory of other states or in areas beyond national jurisdiction, which includes outer space. Principle 21 of the Stockholm Declaration on the Human Environment sets out the responsibility of states to "ensure that activities within their jurisdiction or control do not cause damage to the environment of other States or of areas beyond the limits of national jurisdiction".[24] This principle has also been included in the Rio Declaration on Environment and Development[25] and has widely been considered as reflecting customary international law.[26] Furthermore, the International Court of Justice in its advisory opinion on the Legality of the Threat or Use of Nuclear Weapons confirmed that the "existence of the general obligation of States to ensure that activities within their jurisdiction and control respect the environment of other States or of areas beyond national control is now part of the corpus of international law".[27]

Moreover, the Stockholm Declaration regards cooperation as "essential to effectively control, prevent, reduce and eliminate adverse environmental effects resulting from activities conducted in all spheres" and provides that "international matters concerning the protection and improvement of the environment should be handled in a cooperative spirit by all countries".[28] In this connection, the Declaration also determines that states "shall ensure that international organizations play a coordinated, efficient and dynamic role" for the protection of the environment.[29] In addition, the Rio Declaration on

---

24 Principle 21, Declaration of the United Nations Conference on the Human Environment (16 June 1972).

25 Principle 2, Rio Declaration on Environment and Development (14 June 1992).

26 See for instance Philippe Sands and Jacqueline Peel, *Principles of International Environmental Law* (3rd edn, Cambridge University Press 2012) 190–200; Patricia Birnie, Alan Boyle and Catherine Redgwell, *International Law and the Environment* (3rd edn, Oxford University Press 2009) 137–152.

27 *Legality of the Threat or Use of Nuclear Weapons* (Advisory Opinion) [1996] ICJ Rep 226, 29. See also *Pulp Mills on the River Uruguay* (*Argentina v Uruguay*) (Judgment) [2010] ICJ Rep 14, 101; *The Environment and Human Rights*, Advisory Opinion OC-23/17, Inter-American Court of Human Rights (15 November 2017) 128-129. See similarly already *Corfu Channel Case* (*UK v Albania*) (Merits) [1949] ICJ Rep 4, 22.

28 Principle 24, Stockholm Declaration of the United Nations Conference on the Human Environment.

29 Principle 25, Stockholm Declaration of the United Nations Conference on the Human Environment.

Environment and Development contains several references to cooperation among states on diverse aspects of environmental protection.[30] The duty of states to cooperate in mitigating transboundary environmental risks, in particular through notification, consultation and negotiation, is also considered to form part of customary international law.[31]

In addition, the Articles on the Prevention of Transboundary Harm from Hazardous Activities, which have been adopted by the International Law Commission (ILC) in 2001, are also of relevance.[32] In essence, they codify existing obligations concerning consultation, prevention and diligent control regarding activities likely to cause transboundary harm.[33] While acknowledging the freedom of states to carry on or permit activities under their jurisdiction, the Articles also make it clear that this freedom is not unlimited.[34] States have to ensure that such activities are carried out taking into account the interests of other states.[35] According to the Articles, states are obliged to "take all appropriate measures to prevent significant transboundary harm or at any event to minimize the risk thereof".[36] This includes the assessment of the risk of possible transboundary harm, emergency preparedness and the notification of emergencies.[37] The obligation to take preventive measures is one of due

30 See for instance Principles 7, 9, 12, 13, 14, 18, 19 and 27, Rio Declaration on Environment and Development.

31 Patricia Birnie, Alan Boyle and Catherine Redgwell, *International Law and the Environment* (3rd edn, Oxford University Press 2009) 137, 175–184.

32 ILC, Draft Articles on Prevention of Transboundary Harm from Hazardous Activities, with Commentaries, 'Report of the International Law Commission on the Work of its 53rd Session' (23 April-1 June and 2 July–10 August 2001) UN Doc A/56/10 (ILC Articles on Prevention of Transboundary Harm). The Articles apply to activities not prohibited by international law which involve a risk of causing significant transboundary harm through their physical consequences. Article 1, ILC Articles on Prevention of Transboundary Harm.

33 See Patricia Birnie, Alan Boyle and Catherine Redgwell, *International Law and the Environment* (3rd edn, Oxford University Press 2009) 141–142, demonstrating that the Articles are based on existing precedents, draw on case law and treaties, and have been cited by parties to international environmental litigation.

34 Preamble, ILC Articles on Prevention of Transboundary Harm.

35 Preamble, ILC Articles on Prevention of Transboundary Harm, Commentary, para 1.

36 Article 3, ILC Articles on Prevention of Transboundary Harm. 'Harm' in the context of the Articles means "harm caused to persons, property or the environment". 'Transboundary harm' means "harm caused in the territory of or in other places under the jurisdiction or control of a State other than the State of origin". Article 2(b) and (c), ILC Articles on Prevention of Transboundary Harm.

37 In addition, notification of affected states, regular exchange of information among concerned states, and information to the public are required. Articles 7, 8, 12, 13, 16 and 17, ILC Articles on Prevention of Transboundary Harm.

diligence. The required degree of care is "that expected of a good Government" and depends on the specific circumstances of the case, in particular, it is proportional to the degree of risk involved and contingent on the availability of resources and capabilities.[38]

Moreover, the Articles require concerned states to cooperate in preventing transboundary harm and in minimising the risk thereof as well as to seek, as necessary, the assistance of competent international organisations in this context.[39] The requirement of cooperation extends to all phases of planning and implementation and envisages the participation of states that are likely to be affected in any preventive action.[40] In addition, the states concerned are required to enter into consultations to achieve acceptable solutions regarding the prevention of transboundary harm, based on an equitable balance of interests.[41] In order to achieve an equitable balance of interests all relevant factors and circumstances must be taken into account, including the degree of risk of transboundary harm, the availability of means of preventing or repairing such harm, and the importance of the activity, taking into account its overall advantages of a social, economic and technical character.[42]

While the existence of an obligation of states to carry out NEO impact threat mitigation measures or to assist other states in the conduct of such measures cannot be deduced from the analysis above, it is nevertheless of relevance to planetary defence activities, as such activities may pose a risk of causing harm in outer space as well as on Earth. The analysis shows that states are under the obligation to prevent the risk of significant transboundary harm as well as environmental damage that could be caused by their activities to the territory of other states or to areas beyond national jurisdiction. It can also be concluded that a duty of sates to cooperate exists in this regard, which includes

38 Article 3, ILC Articles on Prevention of Transboundary Harm, Commentary, paras 11, 17 and 18. Even in states with limited resources a minimum of infrastructure and monitoring is expected. The Articles define the concept of "risk of causing significant transboundary harm" as encompassing a high probability of causing significant transboundary harm or a low probability of causing disastrous transboundary harm, thus referring to the "combined effect of the probability of occurrence of an accident and the magnitude of its injurious impact". The harm must lead to real detrimental effects on matters such as human health, property or environment, which must be "susceptible of being measured by factual and objective standards". Article 2, ILC Articles on Prevention of Transboundary Harm, Commentary, paras 1, 2 and 4.

39 Article 4, ILC Articles on Prevention of Transboundary Harm.

40 Article 4, ILC Articles on Prevention of Transboundary Harm, Commentary, para 1.

41 Article 9, ILC Articles on Prevention of Transboundary Harm.

42 Article 10, ILC Articles on Prevention of Transboundary Harm.

in particular consultation, negotiation and the participation of states that are likely to be affected. However, these obligations need to be assessed on the basis of the specific circumstances, in particular the risks involved and the resources and capabilities available.

4 International Human Rights Law

International human rights law is also of relevance for the question whether a duty of states exists under international law to undertake planetary defence activities. In this context, the right to life is of particular importance. The right to life is often described as one of the most important human rights, since violations cannot be remedied and life is the precondition for the exercise of all other human rights.[43] No derogation is permitted from the right to life, even in situations of public emergencies that threaten the life of a nation.[44] The right to life is enshrined in international and regional human rights instruments such as Article 3 of the Universal Declaration of Human Rights,[45] Article 6 of the International Covenant on Civil and Political Rights,[46] Article 4 of the

43 Niels Petersen, 'Life, Right to, International Protection', *Max Planck Encyclopedia of Public International Law* (Oxford University Press 2019) para 1; Rhona K M Smith, *International Human Rights Law* (8th edn, Oxford University Press 2018) 219; Manfred Nowak, 'Right to Life' in Manfred Nowak, Karolina M Januszewski and Tina Hofstätter (eds), *All Human Rights for All* (Neuer Wissenschaftlicher Verlag 2012) 311; Human Rights Committee, 'General Comment No. 36, Article 6: Right to Life' (3 September 2019) CCPR/C/GC/36, para 2; *Case of the Pueblo Bello Massacre v Colombia,* Inter-American Court of Human Rights (31 January 2006) 120; African Commission on Human and Peoples' Rights, 'The Social and Economic Rights Action Center and the Center for Economic and Social Rights v Nigeria' (27 May 2002) Communication 155/96, para 67.

44 Article 4(2) International Covenant on Civil and Political Rights (adopted 16 December 1966, entered into force 23 March 1976) 999 UNTS 171; Article 27(2) American Convention on Human Rights (adopted 22 November 1969, entered into force 18 July 1978) 1144 UNTS 123; Article 15(2) European Convention for the Protection of Human Rights and Fundamental Freedoms (adopted 4 November 1950, entered into force 3 September 1953) 213 UNTS 221; Human Rights Committee, 'General Comment No. 36, Article 6: Right to Life' (3 September 2019) CCPR/C/GC/36, para 2; Olivier De Schutter, *International Human Rights Law* (3rd edn, Cambridge University Press 2019) 607–654; Malcolm N Shaw, *International Law* (8th edn, Cambridge University Press 2017) 216–217.

45 Article 3, Universal Declaration of Human Rights, UNGA Res 217 A (III) (10 December 1948): "Everyone has the right to life, liberty and the security of person".

46 Article 6(1), International Covenant on Civil and Political Rights: "Every human being has the inherent right to life. This right shall be protected by law. No one shall be arbitrarily deprived of his life". On the International Covenant on Civil and Political Rights and the Human Rights Committee see: Sarah Joseph and Melissa Castan, *The International*

African Charter on Human and Peoples' Rights,[47] Article 4 of the American Convention on Human Rights,[48] and Article 2 of the European Convention for the Protection of Human Rights and Fundamental Freedoms.[49] The convergence of international instruments in this regard has been described as "significant", it "indicates that the right to life is an inalienable attribute of human beings and forms the supreme value in the hierarchy of human rights".[50] In addition to being included in all major general human rights conventions, the right to life also forms part of customary international law.[51]

The right to life contains a negative and a positive dimension. On the one hand, it establishes a negative obligation of states to refrain from interfering with the enjoyment of the right to life and from unlawfully and intentionally depriving individuals of life. On the other hand, it also contains a positive

Covenant on Civil and Political Rights (3rd edn, Oxford University Press 2013) 166–214; Philip Alston and Ryan Goodman, *International Human Rights* (Oxford University Press 2013) 157–166 and 762–838; Malcolm N Shaw, *International Law* (8th edn, Cambridge University Press 2017) 238–244; Olivier De Schutter, *International Human Rights Law* (3rd edn, Cambridge University Press 2019) 869–942.

47 Article 4, African Charter on Human and Peoples' Rights (adopted 27 June 1981, entered into force 21 October 1986) 1520 UNTS 217: "Human beings are inviolable. Every human being shall be entitled to respect for his life and the integrity of his person. No one may be arbitrarily deprived of this right". On the African human rights system see: Philip Alston and Ryan Goodman, *International Human Rights* (Oxford University Press 2013) 1025–1044; Olivier De Schutter, *International Human Rights Law* (3rd edn, Cambridge University Press 2019) 1048–1060.

48 Article 4(1), American Convention on Human Rights: "Every person has the right to have his life respected. This right shall be protected by law and, in general, from the moment of conception. No one shall be arbitrarily deprived of his life". On the Inter-American human rights system see: Philip Alston and Ryan Goodman, *International Human Rights* (Oxford University Press 2013) 978–1025; Olivier De Schutter, *International Human Rights Law* (3rd edn, Cambridge University Press 2019) 1020–1047.

49 Article 2(1), European Convention for the Protection of Human Rights and Fundamental Freedoms: "Everyone's right to life shall be protected by law. No one shall be deprived of his life intentionally save in the execution of a sentence of a court following his conviction of a crime for which this penalty is provided by law". See for example William A Schabas, *The European Convention on Human Rights – A Commentary* (Oxford University Press 2015) 117–163; Bernadette Rainey, Elizabeth Wicks, and Clare Ovey, *Jacobs, White, and Ovey: The European Convention on Human Rights* (7th edn, Oxford University Press 2017) 205–236; David Harris, Michael O'Boyle, Ed Bates and Carla Buckley, *Harris, O'Boyle and Warbrick: Law of the European Convention of Human Rights* (4th edn, Oxford University Press 2018) 205–236.

50 European Court of Human Rights, *Streletz, Kessler and Krenz v Germany* (35532/97, 34044/96 and 44801/98) Judgment of 22 March 2001, 94.

51 Niels Petersen, 'Life, Right to, International Protection', *Max Planck Encyclopedia of Public International Law* (Oxford University Press 2019) para 1.

obligation of states to protect and ensure the right to life of those under their jurisdiction, which includes the duty to adopt appropriate measures to safeguard human lives.[52] States must thus do the necessary to ensure the right to life, which may also involve the expenditure of public funds by the state to meet its duties.[53] The obligation to safeguard life is extensive, it applies to situations and activities in which the right to life is at risk and which can result in the loss of life, whereby it may go beyond the protection of identified individuals and expand to the protection of the public at large.[54] It may also

---

52 Niels Petersen, 'Life, Right to, International Protection', *Max Planck Encyclopedia of Public International Law* (Oxford University Press 2019) paras 2–4; Philip Alston and Ryan Goodman, *International Human Rights* (Oxford University Press 2013) 181–185; Rhona K M Smith, *International Human Rights Law* (8th edn, Oxford University Press 2018) 220–222; Manfred Nowak, 'Right to Life' in Manfred Nowak, Karolina M Januszewski and Tina Hofstätter (eds), *All Human Rights for All* (Neuer Wissenschaftlicher Verlag 2012) 312–313; Olivier De Schutter, *International Human Rights Law* (3rd edn, Cambridge University Press 2019) 448–464; Sarah Joseph and Melissa Castan, *The International Covenant on Civil and Political Rights* (3rd edn, Oxford University Press 2013) 167–206; Human Rights Committee, 'General Comment No. 36, Article 6: Right to Life' (3 September 2019) CCPR/C/GC/36, paras 7, 21–26; David Harris, Michael O'Boyle, Ed Bates and Carla Buckley, *Harris, O'Boyle and Warbrick: Law of the European Convention of Human Rights* (4th edn, Oxford University Press 2018) 205–223; Bernadette Rainey, Elizabeth Wicks, and Clare Ovey, *Jacobs, White, and Ovey: The European Convention on Human Rights* (7th edn, Oxford University Press 2017) 161–167; William A Schabas, *The European Convention on Human Rights – A Commentary* (Oxford University Press 2015) 122–139; Franz C Ebert and Romina I Sijniensky, 'Preventing Violations of the Right to Life in the European and the Inter-American Human Rights Systems: From the Osman Test to a Coherent Doctrine on Risk Prevention' (2015) 15 Human Rights Law Review 343, 343–344. The Inter-American Court of Human Rights has stated: "in light of the State's obligation to guarantee the full and free exercise of human rights, it requires States to adopt all the appropriate measures to protect and preserve the right to life (positive obligation)". See *Case of the Pueblo Bello Massacre v Colombia,* Inter-American Court of Human Rights (31 January 2006) 120. See very similarly *Case of the Sawhoyamaxa Indigenous Community v Paraguay,* Inter-American Court of Human Rights (29 March 2006) 152. See also already *Case of Velásquez Rodríguez v Honduras,* Inter-American Court of Human Rights (29 July 1988) 174–175. The European Court of Human Rights has stated that Article 2 of the European Convention for the Protection of Human Rights and Fundamental Freedoms "enjoins the State not only to refrain from the intentional and unlawful taking of life, but also to take appropriate steps to safeguard the lives of those within its jurisdiction". See European Court of Human Rights, *Case of LCB v the United Kingdom* (14/1997/798/1001) Judgment of 9 June 1998, 36; European Court of Human Rights, *Case of Osman v the United Kingdom* (87/1997/871/1083) Judgement of 28 October 1998, 115.

53 Philip Alston and Ryan Goodman, *International Human Rights* (Oxford University Press 2013) 181–185.

54 States may be in violation of the right to life even if such threats and situations do not result in loss of life. Human Rights Committee, 'General Comment No. 36, Article

require states to take necessary and appropriate steps to mitigate natural hazards and prevent harm from impending disasters, including in particular the development of "contingency plans and disaster management plans designed to increase preparedness and address natural and manmade disasters that may adversely affect enjoyment of the right to life".[55]

However, states cannot be held responsible for all situations in which the right to life is at risk, rather they can only be held accountable if they fail to take measures that can reasonably be expected from them to ensure the right to life of those under their jurisdiction. Again, the due diligence principle applies.[56]

6: Right to Life' (3 September 2019) CCPR/C/GC/36, paras 7, 21–26. See also European Court of Human Rights, *Case of Öneryildiz v Turkey* (48939/99) Judgment of 30 November 2004, 71; Manfred Nowak, 'Right to Life' in Manfred Nowak, Karolina M Januszewski and Tina Hofstätter (eds), *All Human Rights for All* (Neuer Wissenschaftlicher Verlag 2012) 312–313; David Harris, Michael O'Boyle, Ed Bates and Carla Buckley, *Harris, O'Boyle and Warbrick: Law of the European Convention of Human Rights* (4th edn, Oxford University Press 2018) 206–207, 213–214; William A Schabas, *The European Convention on Human Rights – A Commentary* (Oxford University Press 2015) 126–127; Bernadette Rainey, Elizabeth Wicks, and Clare Ovey, *Jacobs, White, and Ovey: The European Convention on Human Rights* (7th edn, Oxford University Press 2017) 161–162.

55 Human Rights Committee, 'General Comment No. 36, Article 6: Right to Life' (3 September 2019) CCPR/C/GC/36, para 26. See also Article 9, ILC, Draft Articles on the Protection of Persons in the Event of Disasters, with Commentaries, 'Report of the International Law Commission on the Work of its 68th Session' (2 May–10 June and 4 July–12 August 2016) UN Doc A/71/10 (ILC Articles on the Protection of Persons in the Event of Disasters), Commentary, para 4; David Harris, Michael O'Boyle, Ed Bates and Carla Buckley, *Harris, O'Boyle and Warbrick: Law of the European Convention of Human Rights* (4th edn, Oxford University Press 2018) 206; Bernadette Rainey, Elizabeth Wicks, and Clare Ovey, *Jacobs, White, and Ovey: The European Convention on Human Rights* (7th edn, Oxford University Press 2017) 167. The European Court of Human Rights found a violation of Article 2 of the European Convention for the Protection of Human Rights and Fundamental Freedoms because the state in question failed to take appropriate measures to protect the population from a mudslide (Budayeva case) and from a landslide caused by a methane explosion at a rubbish tip (Öneryildiz case). European Court of Human Rights, *Case of Öneryildiz v Turkey* (48939/99) Judgment of 30 November 2004; European Court of Human Rights, *Case of Budayeva and Others v Russia* (15339/02, 21166/02, 20058/02, 11673/02, 15343/02) Judgment of 20 March 2008.

56 Manfred Nowak, 'Right to Life' in Manfred Nowak, Karolina M Januszewski and Tina Hofstätter (eds), *All Human Rights for All* (Neuer Wissenschaftlicher Verlag 2012) 313; Olivier De Schutter, *International Human Rights Law* (3rd edn, Cambridge University Press 2019) 465–467; Franz C Ebert and Romina I Sijniensky, 'Preventing Violations of the Right to Life in the European and the Inter-American Human Rights Systems: From the Osman Test to a Coherent Doctrine on Risk Prevention' (2015) 15 Human Rights Law Review 343, 345–352; Article 9, ILC Articles on the Protection of Persons in the Event of Disasters, Commentary, para 10.

In the assessment of the positive obligation of states to protect the right to life consideration must be given to the context of the case and the operational and policy choices states must take in terms of priorities, resources and existing capacity. No impossible or disproportionate burden should be imposed on states in this respect.[57] An important aspect in this regard is that the state authorities knew, or could according to the circumstances be expected to have known, about the existence of a situation posing a real and immediate risk to life, and that they failed to take the necessary measures which could reasonably be expected to prevent or avoid that risk.[58] Concerning the sphere of disaster response, where states are directly involved in the protection of human lives through the mitigation of natural hazards, the European Court of Human Rights has specified that the scope of the positive obligation imputable to a state in the particular circumstances would depend not only on the clear identification and imminence of the natural hazard, but also on "the origin of the threat and the extent to which one or the other risk is susceptible to

57 *Case of the Sawhoyamaxa Indigenous Community v Paraguay,* Inter-American Court of Human Rights (29 March 2006) 155; *Case of the Pueblo Bello Massacre v Colombia,* Inter-American Court of Human Rights (31 January 2006) 123; European Court of Human Rights, *Case of Budayeva and Others v Russia* (15339/02, 21166/02, 20058/02, 11673/02, 15343/02) Judgment of 20 March 2008, 135; European Court of Human Rights, *Case of Osman v the United Kingdom* (87/1997/871/1083) Judgement of 28 October 1998, 116. See also Article 9, ILC Articles on the Protection of Persons in the Event of Disasters, Commentary, paras 9 and 11; David Harris, Michael O'Boyle, Ed Bates and Carla Buckley, *Harris, O'Boyle and Warbrick: Law of the European Convention of Human Rights* (4th edn, Oxford University Press 2018) 208–211; Bernadette Rainey, Elizabeth Wicks, and Clare Ovey, *Jacobs, White, and Ovey: The European Convention on Human Rights* (7th edn, Oxford University Press 2017) 167.

58 *Case of the Sawhoyamaxa Indigenous Community v Paraguay,* Inter-American Court of Human Rights (29 March 2006) 155; European Court of Human Rights, *Case of Osman v the United Kingdom* (87/1997/871/1083) Judgement of 28 October 1998, 116. See also Manfred Nowak, 'Right to Life' in Manfred Nowak, Karolina M Januszewski and Tina Hofstätter (eds), *All Human Rights for All* (Neuer Wissenschaftlicher Verlag 2012) 313; Olivier De Schutter, *International Human Rights Law* (3rd edn, Cambridge University Press 2019) 481–494; David Harris, Michael O'Boyle, Ed Bates and Carla Buckley, *Harris, O'Boyle and Warbrick: Law of the European Convention of Human Rights* (4th edn, Oxford University Press 2018) 208–211; Bernadette Rainey, Elizabeth Wicks, and Clare Ovey, *Jacobs, White, and Ovey: The European Convention on Human Rights* (7th edn, Oxford University Press 2017) 162–167; Franz C Ebert and Romina I Sijniensky, 'Preventing Violations of the Right to Life in the European and the Inter-American Human Rights Systems: From the Osman Test to a Coherent Doctrine on Risk Prevention' (2015) 15 Human Rights Law Review 343, 345–362 (demonstrating that the criteria of the immediacy of the risk and the knowledge of the state authorities was often applied broadly by the European and the Inter-American Human Rights Courts).

mitigation".[59] The duty to prevent, mitigate and prepare for disasters in order to reduce the risk to life is thus one of conduct, not of result.[60] Nevertheless, the fundamental importance of the right to life requires that the scope of the positive obligation "includes a duty to do everything within the authorities' power in the sphere of disaster relief for the protection of that right".[61]

In the case of a NEO impact threat, the obligation to adopt the reasonable and appropriate measures necessary to protect the right to life could require states to carry out planetary defence measures in order to save the lives of those under their jurisdiction. However, this is subject not only to the knowledge of the threat and the extent to which it is susceptible to mitigation but also to the availability of national resources and capabilities. While the awareness of the risk posed by potential NEO impacts on Earth is increasing and such impacts may be averted and their effects mitigated, this requires the building up of capabilities for detection, observation and characterisation of NEOs as well as for impact prediction and mitigation, including the development of suitable technologies for NEO deflection, already before an actual impact threat is detected. The available resources and existing capabilities may therefore play an important role for states when fulfilling the obligation to protect the right to life in the context of NEO impact threats.

Nevertheless, the positive obligation to protect the right to life concerns only the state having jurisdiction over the individuals whose life is at risk. It does not per se oblige other states to assist or cooperate in planetary defence endeavours. A basic duty to cooperate in the area of human rights can however be found in the UN Charter.[62] Cooperation with respect to human rights is enshrined in Article 1(3) of the UN Charter which lists among the purposes of the United Nations to "achieve international co-operation in solving international problems of an economic, social, cultural, or humanitarian character, and in promoting and encouraging respect for human rights and for fundamental freedoms for all without distinction as to race, sex, language, or religion".[63] This is complemented by Article 55(c) of the Charter according to

59 European Court of Human Rights, *Case of Budayeva and Others v Russia*, (15339/02, 21166/02, 20058/02, 11673/02, 15343/02) Judgment of 20 March 2008, 137.

60 Article 9, ILC Articles on the Protection of Persons in the Event of Disasters, Commentary, para 10.

61 European Court of Human Rights, *Case of Budayeva and Others v Russia*, (15339/02, 21166/02, 20058/02, 11673/02, 15343/02) Judgment of 20 March 2008, 175.

62 Rüdiger Wolfrum, 'Cooperation, International Law of' in Rüdiger Wolfrum (ed), *Max Planck Encyclopedia of Public International Law* (Oxford University Press 2012) vol II, 783, para 32.

63 Article 1(3), Charter of the United Nations and Statute of the International Court of Justice (adopted 26 June 1945, entered into force 24 October 1945) USTS 993 (UN Charter).

which the United Nations shall promote "universal respect for, and observance of, human rights and fundamental freedoms" and Article 56 which stipulates that all member states "pledge themselves to take joint and separate action in co-operation with the Organization for the achievement of the purposes set forth in Article 55".[64] In addition, the 1970 Friendly Relations Declaration also addresses cooperation in the area of human rights stating that "States shall co-operate in the promotion of universal respect for, and observance of, human rights and fundamental freedoms for all".[65] It can therefore be concluded that "the obligation to cooperate for the protection of human rights today possesses a firm legal basis in international law".[66] Thus, besides the obligation of states to protect the right to life of those under their jurisdiction, including, depending on the circumstances, through the mitigation of NEO impact threats, there also exists a duty of states to cooperate. However, there is no obligation of states to assist other states in this regard.

5 The Responsibility to Protect

An important concept regarding the question whether a duty of states exists to protect not only their own population but also that of other states is the 'responsibility to protect'. The concept was first coined by the International Commission on Intervention and State Sovereignty (ICISS) in its 2001 Report

---

In addition, according to Article 2(5), in pursuit of the purposes stated in Article 1, all members "shall give the United Nations every assistance in any action it takes in accordance with the present Charter".

64 For a detailed analysis see Rüdiger Wolfrum and Eibe H Riedel, 'Chapter IX International Economic and Social Co-operation, Article 55(c)' in Bruno Simma and others (eds), *The Charter of the United Nations: A Commentary* (3rd edn, Oxford University Press 2012) vol II, 1565–1602; Tobias Stoll, 'Chapter IX International Economic and Social Co-operation, Article 56' in Bruno Simma and others (eds), *The Charter of the United Nations: A Commentary* (3rd edn, Oxford University Press 2012) vol II, 1603–1610.

65 Declaration on Principles of International Law concerning Friendly Relations and Co-operation among States in accordance with the Charter of the United Nations, UNGA Res 2625 (XXV), Annex (24 October 1970). For a more detailed analysis see chapter 12 'International Law Rules Related to the Sharing of Information About Potential NEO Threats' in this book.

66 Jost Delbrück, 'The International Obligation to Cooperate – An Empty Shell or a Hard Law Principle of International Law? – A Critical Look at a Much Debated Paradigm of Modern International Law' in Holger P Hestermeyer, Doris König, Nele Matz-Lück, Volker Röben, Anja Seibert-Fohr, Peter-Tobias Stoll and Silja Vöneky (eds), *Coexistence, Cooperation and Solidarity – Liber Amicorum Rüdiger Wolfrum* (Brill/Nijhoff 2012) 7.

entitled "The Responsibility to Protect".[67] The ICISS Report defines two core principles which form the basis of this concept: First, state sovereignty implies responsibility, and each state has the primary responsibility for the protection of its population. Second, if the state in question is unwilling or unable to fulfil this responsibility the international community has a residual responsibility to protect populations that are under serious threat.[68]

The concept of the responsibility to protect aims at bridging the divide between intervention for human protection purposes on the one hand and sovereignty on the other hand by establishing the circumstances and standards under which the international community should act.[69] State sovereignty is a general principle of international law and forms part of customary international law.[70] The territorial sovereignty of states is an essential foundation of international relations between independent, equal states and most of the other institutions and principles of international law rely directly or indirectly on state sovereignty.[71] The principle of sovereign equality of states is guaranteed in Article 2(1) of the UN Charter. Principal corollaries of the sovereignty

67 The independent Commission was established by the Canadian government in 2000 and was composed of 12 Commissioners from a wide range of backgrounds. ICISS, *The Responsibility to Protect: Report of the International Commission on Intervention and State Sovereignty* (International Development Research Centre 2001) Appendix A and Appendix B. See also Janina Barkholdt and Ingo Winkelmann, 'Responsibility to Protect', *Max Planck Encyclopedia of Public International Law* (Oxford University Press 2019) para 5; Alex J Bellamy, 'The Responsibility to Protect: A Wide or Narrow Conception?' in Peter Hilpold (ed), *Responsibility to Protect: A New Paradigm of International Law?* (Brill/Nijhoff 2015) 42; Alex J Bellamy and Tim Dunne, 'R2P in Theory and Practice' in Alex J Bellamy and Tim Dunne (eds), *Oxford Handbook of the Responsibility to Protect* (Oxford University Press 2016) 6.

68 ICISS, *The Responsibility to Protect*, XI, 17–18.

69 ICISS, *The Responsibility to Protect*, XI, 2, 11, 17–18. See also Janina Barkholdt and Ingo Winkelmann, 'Responsibility to Protect', *Max Planck Encyclopedia of Public International Law* (Oxford University Press 2019) para 2.

70 Samantha Besson, 'Sovereignty' in Rüdiger Wolfrum (ed), *Max Planck Encyclopedia of Public International Law* (Oxford University Press 2012) vol IX, 366, paras 86–87; *Military and Paramilitary Activities in and against Nicaragua* (*Nicaragua v United States of America*) (Merits) [1986] ICJ Rep 14, 212.

71 Malcolm N Shaw, *International Law* (8th edn, Cambridge University Press 2017) 166–169, 874; Ian Brownlie, *Principles of Public International Law* (7th edn, Oxford University Press 2008) 289–290; Samantha Besson, 'Sovereignty' in Rüdiger Wolfrum (ed), *Max Planck Encyclopedia of Public International Law* (Oxford University Press 2012) vol IX, 366, para 2; *Military and Paramilitary Activities in and against Nicaragua* (*Nicaragua v United States of America*) (Merits) [1986] ICJ Rep 14, 202.

and equality of states under international law are the jurisdiction[72] of states over their territory and population as well as the duty of non-intervention[73] in internal affairs of other states.[74] The UN Charter protects the 'domaine réservé' of sovereign states and prohibits interventions on their territory through Article 2(4), which forbids "the threat or use of force against the territorial integrity or political independence of any state", and Article 2(7), which determines that the UN may not "intervene in matters which are essentially within the domestic jurisdiction of any state".[75]

The recommendations made by the ICISS are based on the reconceptualisation of sovereignty as responsibility and the acknowledgement that sovereignty implies a dual responsibility with an external dimension that comprises the respect of the sovereignty of other states and an internal dimension that encompasses the respect of the basic rights of the population of a state.[76] This is founded on the understanding that new expectations for action and

---

72 The term 'jurisdiction' describes "the power of the state under international law to regulate or otherwise impact upon people, property and circumstances". Malcolm N Shaw, *International Law* (8th edn, Cambridge University Press 2017) 483. Under international law the two main bases of jurisdiction are territoriality and nationality. Christopher Staker, 'Jurisdiction' in Malcolm D Evans (ed), *International Law* (4th edn, Oxford University Press 2014) 309–335; Malcolm N Shaw, *International Law* (8th edn, Cambridge University Press 2017) 483–522.

73 The principle of non-intervention is one of the fundamental duties of states and forms part of customary international law. It prohibits the interference in the internal affairs of a sovereign state by use of methods of coercion and with the aim of imposing a certain conduct. See Philip Kunig, 'Intervention, Prohibition of' in Rüdiger Wolfrum (ed), *Max Planck Encyclopedia of Public International Law* (Oxford University Press 2012) vol VI, 289, paras 1–3, 7–8; *Military and Paramilitary Activities in and against Nicaragua* (*Nicaragua v United States of America*) (Merits) [1986] ICJ Rep 14, 202 and 205.

74 Malcolm N Shaw, *International Law* (8th edn, Cambridge University Press 2017) 166–169, 874; Ian Brownlie, *Principles of Public International Law* (7th edn, Oxford University Press 2008) 289–290; Samantha Besson, 'Sovereignty' in Rüdiger Wolfrum (ed), *Max Planck Encyclopedia of Public International Law* (Oxford University Press 2012) vol IX, 366, para 2; *Military and Paramilitary Activities in and against Nicaragua* (*Nicaragua v United States of America*) (Merits) [1986] ICJ Rep 14, 202.

75 Samantha Besson, 'Sovereignty' in Rüdiger Wolfrum (ed), *Max Planck Encyclopedia of Public International Law* (Oxford University Press 2012) vol IX, 366, para 88.

76 ICISS, *The Responsibility to Protect*, 7–8, 13. The concept of 'sovereignty as responsibility', which underpins the responsibility to protect but is a distinct, wider and more flexible concept, rests on the foundation that the sovereignty of states is derived from human rights and that states have the primary responsibility for protecting these rights, but where they fail to protect them, the international community has a responsibility to assure their fulfilment. See for instance Alex J Bellamy, 'The Responsibility to Protect: A Wide or Narrow Conception?' in Peter Hilpold (ed), *Responsibility to Protect: A New Paradigm of International Law?* (Brill/Nijhoff 2015) 38–59.

new standards of conduct have emerged over the past decades, including the development of stronger norms and mechanisms for the protection of human rights[77] and the evolution of the concept of human security,[78] which have changed the conditions under which sovereignty is exercised and create new constraints and demands concerning the way states treat their own population.[79] Yet, the responsibility to protect "is not to be seen as an antithesis to the defence of state sovereignty, nor is R2P the successor concept to sovereignty" it is "rather an integral part of sovereignty, and today one of its foremost elements".[80]

According to the ICISS Report, the responsibility to protect has three interrelated components: the responsibility to prevent, the responsibility to react, and the responsibility to rebuild. Thus, action in support of the responsibility to

77 This includes for instance the Universal Declaration of Human Rights, the four Geneva Conventions and additional Protocols on international humanitarian law, the Convention on the Prevention and Punishment of the Crime of Genocide, the two Covenants on civil, political, social, economic and cultural rights, and the Rome Statute of the International Criminal Court.

78 During the post-Cold War era the traditional concept of national security based on state sovereignty and territorial integrity seemed increasingly inapt to encompass the multiple dimensions of a newly emerging perception of security. The broader concept of human security goes beyond purely military issues and places the individual at the centre of security concerns. A comprehensive description and analysis of the concept of human security was presented in the 1994 Human Development Report published by the UN Development Programme (UNDP) according to which the concept encompasses economic, food, health, environmental, personal, community and political security. Human security thus includes not only the physical safety of individuals, but also the respect of their dignity and fundamental freedoms, as well as their economic and social well-being, endangered by 'soft threats' such as diseases, poverty, economic deprivation, environmental degradation, or lack of social cohesion. See for instance Ramesh Thakur, *The United Nations, Peace and Security: From Collective Security to the Responsibility to Protect* (2nd edn, Cambridge University Press 2017) 81–89; Martin Wählisch, 'Human Security', *Max Planck Encyclopedia of Public International Law* (Oxford University Press 2016); Roland Paris, 'Human Security: Paradigm Shift or Hot Air?' (2001) 26 International Security 87, 88–91; United Nations Development Programme, 'Human Development Report 1994' (Oxford University Press 1994) 22–33.

79 ICISS, *The Responsibility to Protect*, 6–8, 14–16. For an analysis of the development of the principle of state sovereignty see for instance Peter Hilpold, 'From Humanitarian Intervention to the Responsibility to Protect' in Peter Hilpold (ed), *Responsibility to Protect: A New Paradigm of International Law?* (Brill/Nijhoff 2015) 1–37; Hans-Georg Dederer, "Responsibility to Protect' and 'Functional Sovereignty'' in Peter Hilpold (ed), *Responsibility to Protect: A New Paradigm of International Law?* (Brill/Nijhoff 2015) 156–183.

80 Peter Hilpold, 'From Humanitarian Intervention to the Responsibility to Protect' in Peter Hilpold (ed), *Responsibility to Protect: A New Paradigm of International Law?* (Brill/Nijhoff 2015) 9.

protect may involve a wide range of long- and short-term assistance, response and rebuilding measures aimed at preventing human security-threatening situations from occurring, intensifying or recurring.[81] The ICISS identifies prevention as the most important dimension of the responsibility to protect and considers that for successful prevention strong support from the international community is often needed, whereby early warning, the comprehensive knowledge of the situation and the risks associated with it, is essential.[82]

In addition to proposing non-military measures, the ICISS also determines six basic criteria for military intervention as an exceptional and extraordinary measure in extreme cases to protect civilians from harm. These include: right intention (the primary purpose of the intervention must be to halt or avert human suffering), last resort (all non-military avenues should have been explored and there must be reasonable grounds to believe that non-military measures would not succeed), proportional means (the scale, duration and intensity of the military intervention should be the minimum necessary to secure the humanitarian objective in question), reasonable prospects (there must be a reasonable chance of success in halting or averting the atrocities or suffering that triggered the intervention and the consequences of the intervention must not be worse than if there is no action), right authority and just cause.[83]

The just cause threshold determines that military intervention for human protection purposes is justified only if there is "serious and irreparable harm occurring to human beings, or imminently likely to occur", either in the form of large scale loss of life, which is the product of deliberate state action or the inability to act, or large scale ethnic cleansing.[84] According to the ICISS these two conditions would in particular include: actions defined in the Genocide Convention that involve large scale loss of life; manifestations of ethnic cleansing, including the systematic killing or physical removal of members of a particular group; crimes against humanity and violations of the laws of war which involve large scale killing or ethnic cleansing; as well as "overwhelming natural or environmental catastrophes", where the concerned state is unwilling or unable to cope and significant loss of life is occurring or threatened.[85]

As regards the criterion of the right authority the Report finds that "there is no better or more appropriate body than the Security Council to deal with

81 ICISS, *The Responsibility to Protect*, 17–18, 19–27, 29–37, 39–45.

82 ICISS, *The Responsibility to Protect*, XI, 19–22.

83 ICISS, *The Responsibility to Protect*, 32–37.

84 ICISS, *The Responsibility to Protect*, 32.

85 ICISS, *The Responsibility to Protect*, 32–33.

military intervention issues for human protection purposes" and its authorisation should be sought in all cases prior to military intervention.[86] In case the Security Council fails to act, the ICISS proposes the consideration of the situation in question by the General Assembly under the 'Uniting for Peace' procedure or by regional or sub-regional organisations as alternative options.[87] Yet, it also warns of the consequences of inaction by the Security Council noting that "if the Security Council fails to discharge its responsibility in conscience-shocking situations crying out for action, then it is unrealistic to expect that concerned states will rule out other means and forms of action to meet the gravity and urgency of these situations".[88]

The Report also highlights that accurate information from an internationally respected and impartial source is essential for determining if the events on the ground meet the proposed criteria and warrant an intervention. It moreover stresses that multilateral intervention is preferred to intervention by a single country.[89] In addition, the ICISS Report defines operational principles, including *inter alia*: a precisely defined objective, a clear mandate and matching resources, precise rules of engagement, and a common approach among involved actors with clear communication mechanisms and the protection of the population as primary goal.[90] By establishing these criteria, conditions and principles, the concept of the responsibility to protect as proposed by the ICISS aimed to reconcile the protection of state sovereignty with humanitarian ideals and the protection of individuals, while preventing unilateral use of force for self-interested purposes.[91]

In the 2005 World Summit Outcome document adopted by the General Assembly at the level of heads of state and government the concept of the responsibility to protect was endorsed and two paragraphs were dedicated to it:

> 138. Each individual State has the responsibility to protect its populations from genocide, war crimes, ethnic cleansing and crimes against humanity.

86 ICISS, *The Responsibility to Protect*, 49–50.

87 ICISS, *The Responsibility to Protect*, 53–54. For a detailed discussion of the different decision-making bodies in the context of planetary defence see the chapter 22 'International Bodies and Procedures for Decision-Making Regarding Planetary Defence Actions' in this book.

88 ICISS, *The Responsibility to Protect*, 55.

89 ICISS, *The Responsibility to Protect*, 34–36.

90 ICISS, *The Responsibility to Protect*, 58–67.

91 Ramesh Thakur, *The United Nations, Peace and Security: From Collective Security to the Responsibility to Protect* (2nd edn, Cambridge University Press 2017) 407–408; Janina Barkholdt and Ingo Winkelmann, 'Responsibility to Protect', *Max Planck Encyclopedia of Public International Law* (Oxford University Press 2019) para 7.

This responsibility entails the prevention of such crimes, including their incitement, through appropriate and necessary means. We accept that responsibility and will act in accordance with it. The international community should, as appropriate, encourage and help States to exercise this responsibility and support the United Nations in establishing an early warning capability.

139. The international community, through the United Nations, also has the responsibility to use appropriate diplomatic, humanitarian and other peaceful means, in accordance with Chapters VI and VIII of the Charter, to help to protect populations from genocide, war crimes, ethnic cleansing and crimes against humanity. In this context, we are prepared to take collective action, in a timely and decisive manner, through the Security Council, in accordance with the Charter, including Chapter VII, on a case-by-case basis and in cooperation with relevant regional organizations as appropriate, should peaceful means be inadequate and national authorities are manifestly failing to protect their populations from genocide, war crimes, ethnic cleansing and crimes against humanity. We stress the need for the General Assembly to continue consideration of the responsibility to protect populations from genocide, war crimes, ethnic cleansing and crimes against humanity and its implications, bearing in mind the principles of the Charter and international law. We also intend to commit ourselves, as necessary and appropriate, to helping States build capacity to protect their populations from genocide, war crimes, ethnic cleansing and crimes against humanity and to assisting those which are under stress before crises and conflicts break out. [92]

92 2005 World Summit Outcome, UNGA Res 60/1(16 September 2005) UN Doc A/RES/60/1, paras 138–139. Note that the concept of the responsibility to protect was also taken up by the High-level Panel on Threats, Challenges and Change in its 2004 Report entitled 'A More Secure World: Our Shared Responsibility', which defines five basic criteria of legitimacy the Security Council should address when considering the authorization or endorsement of the use of military force in the event of genocide and other large-scale killing, ethnic cleansing or serious violations of international humanitarian law which the state in question is unwilling or unable to prevent. These include seriousness of threat (Is the threatened harm sufficiently clear and serious to justify the use of military force?), proper purpose (Is the primary purpose of the military action to halt or avert the threat in question?), last resort (Are there reasonable grounds for believing that non-military measures would not succeed?), proportional means (Are the scale, duration and intensity of the military action the minimum necessary to meet the threat in question?) and balance of consequences (Is there a reasonable chance of the military action being successful in meeting the threat?). See UNGA, 'Report of the High-level Panel on Threats,

This important expression of the recognition of the responsibility to protect by states has significantly shaped the development of the concept and has in particular reduced its scope.[93] It has *inter alia* been clarified that the concept covers only genocide, war crimes, ethnic cleansing and crimes against humanity, rather than including also other situations, such as natural or environmental catastrophes, as proposed by the ICISS Report.[94]

Based on the World Summit Outcome document the responsibility to protect can be divided into three pillars. Pillar one: the primary responsibility of each state to protect its population from genocide, war crimes, ethnic cleansing and crimes against humanity; Pillar two: the responsibility of the international community to assist states in fulfilling their responsibility under pillar one; Pillar three: the subsidiary responsibility of the international community, in case a state is failing to protect its population, to take timely and decisive collective action through peaceful diplomatic and humanitarian means or, if these prove inadequate, through enforcement measures, in accordance with Chapters VI, VII and VIII of the UN Charter.[95]

Challenges and Change – A More Secure World: Our Shared Responsibility' (2 December 2004) UN Doc A/59/565, 57–58.

93 The formula 'R2P lite' has evolved in this context. See Peter Hilpold, 'From Humanitarian Intervention to the Responsibility to Protect' in Peter Hilpold (ed), *Responsibility to Protect: A New Paradigm of International Law?* (Brill/Nijhoff 2015) 15; Alex J Bellamy, 'The Responsibility to Protect: A Wide or Narrow Conception?' in Peter Hilpold (ed), *Responsibility to Protect: A New Paradigm of International Law?* (Brill/Nijhoff 2015) 40–43.

94 Of particular relevance with regard to the definition of these four crimes is the Rome Statute of the International Criminal Court which refers to crimes against humanity, war crimes and genocide (as well as aggression). In addition to these crimes contained in the Rome Statute, the World Summit Outcome document also mentions 'ethnic cleansing', which does not constitute a specific crime under the Rome Statute but is regarded as being closely connected to and covered by the crimes within the jurisdiction of the International Criminal Court. See Peter Hilpold, 'From Humanitarian Intervention to the Responsibility to Protect' in Peter Hilpold (ed), *Responsibility to Protect: A New Paradigm of International Law?* (Brill/Nijhoff 2015) 15–19; Sir Nigel Rodley, 'R2P and International Law' in Alex J Bellamy and Tim Dunne (eds), *Oxford Handbook of the Responsibility to Protect* (Oxford University Press 2016) 195–197. For a detailed discussion of ethnic cleansing see Robin Geiß, 'Ethnic Cleansing', *Max Planck Encyclopedia of Public International Law* (Oxford University Press 2013).

95 UNGA, 'Report of the Secretary-General – Implementing the Responsibility to Protect' (12 January 2009) UN Doc A/63/677; Alex J Bellamy, 'The Responsibility to Protect: A Wide or Narrow Conception?' in Peter Hilpold (ed), *Responsibility to Protect: A New Paradigm of International Law?* (Brill/Nijhoff 2015) 40–41; Irmgard Marboe, 'The Responsibility to Protect' in Manfred Nowak, Karolina M Januszewski and Tina Hofstätter (eds), *All Human Rights for All* (Neuer Wissenschaftlicher Verlag 2012) 503; Sir Nigel Rodley, 'R2P and International Law' in Alex J Bellamy and Tim Dunne (eds), *Oxford Handbook of the Responsibility to Protect* (Oxford University Press 2016) 186–205.

With regard to the legal nature of the responsibility to protect diverse views have been advanced. The concept has been understood as "an emerging norm",[96] as "soft law",[97] as a "political concept",[98] as not yet having attained the status of an international legal norm,[99] as "the most dramatic normative development of our time",[100] as an "established international norm",[101] as a "set of principles and norms",[102] as an "authoritative and effective norm of international law",[103] and as a "new paradigm".[104]

Concerning the first pillar of the responsibility to protect, the legal bindingness can be derived from existing obligations in human rights instruments, the system of international humanitarian law and international criminal law.[105] Regarding the second pillar, it appears to be difficult to find obligations of states under international law to provide assistance to other states in building up protection and prevention capacities.[106] Such assistance may only be provided on

96 UNGA, 'Report of the High-level Panel on Threats, Challenges and Change – A More Secure World: Our Shared Responsibility' (2 December 2004) UN Doc A/59/565, 57.

97 Jennifer Welsh and Maria Banda, 'International Law and the Responsibility to Protect: Clarifying or Expanding States' Responsibilities?' (2010) 2 Global Responsibility to Protect 213, 230–231.

98 Thilo Marauhn, 'Der Beitrag der internationalen Schutzverantwortung zu einer Ethik des gerechten Friedens' in Ines-Jacqueline Werkner and Thilo Marauhn (eds), *Die internationale Schutzverantwortung im Lichte des gerechten Friedens* (Springer 2019) 145.

99 Peter-Tobias Stoll, 'The Responsibility to Protect – One-time Incentive or Lasting Advancement of International Law?' in Peter Hilpold (ed), *Responsibility to Protect: A New Paradigm of International Law?* (Brill/Nijhoff 2015) 147.

100 Ramesh Thakur and Thomas Weiss, 'R2P: From Idea to Norm – and Action?' (2009) 1 Global Responsibility to Protect 22, 23.

101 Alex J Bellamy, 'The Responsibility to Protect Turns Ten' (2015) 29 Ethics & International Affairs 161, 163.

102 Melissa Labonte, 'R2P's Status as a Norm' in Alex J Bellamy and Tim Dunne (eds), *Oxford Handbook of the Responsibility to Protect* (Oxford University Press 2016) 133.

103 Peter Hilpold, 'From Humanitarian Intervention to the Responsibility to Protect' in Peter Hilpold (ed), *Responsibility to Protect: A New Paradigm of International Law?* (Brill/Nijhoff 2015) 30.

104 Sir Nigel Rodley, 'R2P and International Law' in Alex J Bellamy and Tim Dunne (eds), *Oxford Handbook of the Responsibility to Protect* (Oxford University Press 2016) 202.

105 Peter Hilpold, 'From Humanitarian Intervention to the Responsibility to Protect' in Peter Hilpold (ed), *Responsibility to Protect: A New Paradigm of International Law?* (Brill/Nijhoff 2015) 26; Janina Barkholdt and Ingo Winkelmann, 'Responsibility to Protect', *Max Planck Encyclopedia of Public International Law* (Oxford University Press 2019) para 35. See similarly Melissa Labonte, 'R2P's Status as a Norm' in Alex J Bellamy and Tim Dunne (eds), *Oxford Handbook of the Responsibility to Protect* (Oxford University Press 2016) 136.

106 Peter Hilpold, 'From Humanitarian Intervention to the Responsibility to Protect' in Peter Hilpold (ed), *Responsibility to Protect: A New Paradigm of International Law?* (Brill/Nijhoff

a voluntary basis at the request or with the consent of the state concerned.[107] As to the third pillar, a legal basis can be found in the law of state responsibility as reflected in the ILC Articles on State Responsibility.[108] According to Articles 40 and 41 states "shall cooperate to bring to an end through lawful means any serious breach" by a state "of an obligation arising under a peremptory norm of general international law".[109] This is the case for the Genocide Convention.[110] The obligation to prevent and punish genocide established in Article I of the Convention has been interpreted as extending beyond a state's territorial jurisdiction.[111] This however seems less clear with regard to the other crimes referred to in the World Summit Outcome document.[112]

Due not only to the unclear legal status of the concept of the responsibility to protect but also to its focus on military intervention for protection purposes and its limitation to the crimes of genocide, war crimes, ethnic cleansing and

---

2015) 27; Janina Barkholdt and Ingo Winkelmann, 'Responsibility to Protect', *Max Planck Encyclopedia of Public International Law* (Oxford University Press 2019) para 36.

107 Sir Nigel Rodley, 'R2P and International Law' in Alex J Bellamy and Tim Dunne (eds), *Oxford Handbook of the Responsibility to Protect* (Oxford University Press 2016) 191; Alex J Bellamy, 'The Responsibility to Protect: A Wide or Narrow Conception?' in Peter Hilpold (ed), *Responsibility to Protect: A New Paradigm of International Law?* (Brill/Nijhoff 2015) 41.

108 Peter Hilpold, 'From Humanitarian Intervention to the Responsibility to Protect' in Peter Hilpold (ed), *Responsibility to Protect: A New Paradigm of International Law?* (Brill/Nijhoff 2015) 28; Janina Barkholdt and Ingo Winkelmann, 'Responsibility to Protect', *Max Planck Encyclopedia of Public International Law* (Oxford University Press 2019) para 38.

109 Articles 40 and 41(1), ILC, Draft Articles on Responsibility of States for Internationally Wrongful Acts, with Commentaries, 'Report of the International Law Commission on the Work of its 53rd Session' (23 April–1 June and 2 July–10 August 2001) UN Doc A/56/10 (ILC Articles on State Responsibility). See also Jochen A Frowein, 'Ius Cogens', *Max Planck Encyclopedia of Public International Law* (Oxford University Press 2013).

110 Convention on the Prevention and Punishment of the Crime of Genocide (adopted 9 December 1948, entered into force 12 January 1951) 78 UNTS 277.

111 *Application of the Convention on the Prevention and Punishment of the Crime of Genocide* (*Bosnia and Herzegovina v Serbia and Montenegro*) (Merits) [2007] ICJ Rep 43, 430, 438. Peter Hilpold, 'From Humanitarian Intervention to the Responsibility to Protect' in Peter Hilpold (ed), *Responsibility to Protect: A New Paradigm of International Law?* (Brill/Nijhoff 2015) 27–28; Janina Barkholdt and Ingo Winkelmann, 'Responsibility to Protect', *Max Planck Encyclopedia of Public International Law* (Oxford University Press 2019) para 38. The obligation of states in this regard is one of due diligence "to employ all means reasonably available to them, so as to prevent genocide so far as possible". *Application of the Convention on the Prevention and Punishment of the Crime of Genocide* (*Bosnia and Herzegovina v Serbia and Montenegro*) (Merits) [2007] ICJ Rep 43, 430.

112 Peter Hilpold, 'From Humanitarian Intervention to the Responsibility to Protect' in Peter Hilpold (ed), *Responsibility to Protect: A New Paradigm of International Law?* (Brill/Nijhoff 2015) 28–29; Janina Barkholdt and Ingo Winkelmann, 'Responsibility to Protect', *Max Planck Encyclopedia of Public International Law* (Oxford University Press 2019) para 38.

crimes against humanity, the concept is not directly applicable to planetary defence. Nevertheless, several of the considerations with respect to the responsibility to protect, in particular regarding state sovereignty, can also be of relevance in the context of planetary defence. This includes firstly, that states have the primary responsibility to protect their own population, secondly, that assistance can only be provided on a voluntary basis, and thirdly, that actions which would infringe the sovereignty of a state would be contrary to international law and prohibited according to the principle of non-intervention.[113]

In this context, some of the conditions, criteria and principles developed in the framework of the responsibility to protect could, while not directly transferable, give guidance in preparing for and taking decisions on planetary defence actions, in particular if the use of a nuclear explosive device is contemplated. This may for instance include the criteria of right intention, last resort, proportional means, reasonable prospects, right authority and just cause, as well as some of the operational principles, such as a precisely defined objective, a clear mandate and matching resources, precise rules of engagement and a common approach among involved actors with clear communication strategies, and several other ideas, including the importance of accurate information from an internationally respected and impartial source, the focus on multilateral rather than single country action, and the significance of early warning and prevention. Such considerations could inform the debate, cooperation and decision-making in the context of planetary defence which could not only enhance the transparency of planetary defence missions but could also increase international support for them.

6 International Disaster Law

Since NEO impacts can be qualified as a type of natural disaster, international disaster law is also applicable to situations of NEO impact threats. In this regard the ILC Articles on the Protection of Persons in the Event of Disastersare of particular relevance. Central to the Articles is not only the response to natural disasters, but also the reduction of the risk of disasters.[114] Article 9 contains

113 Unless authorized by a decision of the UN Security Council or justified by a circumstance precluding wrongfulness such as consent. See Articles 20–25, ILC Articles on State Responsibility. This is discussed in detail in chapter 20 'International Responsibility of States for Planetary Defence Activities' and chapter 22 'International Bodies and Procedures for Decision-Making Regarding Planetary Defence Actions' in this book.

114 Article 2, ILC Articles on the Protection of Persons in the Event of Disasters. 'Disaster' is defined as "a calamitous event or series of events resulting in widespread loss of life,

an obligation of states in this regard, determining that each state "shall reduce the risk of disasters by taking appropriate measures (…) to prevent, mitigate, and prepare for disasters".[115] The concept of disaster risk reduction has its origins in several General Assembly resolutions as well as the "Yokohama Strategy for a Safer World: Guidelines for Natural Disaster Prevention", the "Hyogo Framework for Action: Building the Resilience of Nations and Communities to Disasters", and most recently the "Sendai Framework for Disaster Risk Reduction".[116] The Sendai Framework contains the comprehensive goal to prevent and reduce disaster risk through the implementation of "integrated and inclusive economic, structural, legal, social, health, cultural, educational, environmental, technological, political and institutional measures" that reduce the exposure and vulnerability to disasters, increase preparedness for disaster response and recovery, and thus strengthen resilience.[117]

A legal basis for the obligation to reduce disaster risk can be found not only in the principle of state sovereignty and in international human rights law, including in particular the protection of the right to life, but also in the widespread practice of states reflected in the adoption of multilateral, regional and bilateral instruments concerned with reducing the risk of disasters.[118] The focus of the obligation of states to reduce the risk of disasters is placed on the reduction of the risk of harm potentially caused by a disaster, rather than the prevention of the disaster itself. The duty envisaged is therefore one of conduct

great human suffering and distress, mass displacement, or large-scale material or environmental damage, thereby seriously disrupting the functioning of society". Article 3(a), ILC Articles on the Protection of Persons in the Event of Disasters.

115 Article 9(1), ILC Articles on the Protection of Persons in the Event of Disasters.

116 Article 9, ILC Articles on the Protection of Persons in the Event of Disasters, Commentary, para 2. For a detailed analysis see Arnold N Pronto, 'The ILC's Articles on the Protection of Persons in the Event of Disasters and Disaster Risk Reduction: A Legislative History' in Katja L H Samuel, Marie Aronsson-Storrier and Kirsten Nakjavani Bookmiller (eds), *The Cambridge Handbook of Disaster Risk Reduction and International Law* (Cambridge University Press 2019) 71–86; Hugo Cahueñas Muñoz, 'Disaster Risk Reduction Cooperation for the Protection of Persons in the Event of Disasters' in Katja L H Samuel, Marie Aronsson-Storrier and Kirsten Nakjavani Bookmiller (eds), *The Cambridge Handbook of Disaster Risk Reduction and International Law* (Cambridge University Press 2019) 87–106.

117 Sendai Framework for Disaster Risk Reduction 2015–2030, UNGA Res 69/283, Annex II (3 June 2015) para 17.

118 Article 9, ILC Articles on the Protection of Persons in the Event of Disasters, Commentary, paras 4 and 5. See also Carlo Focarelli, 'Duty to Protect in Cases of Natural Disasters', *Max Planck Encyclopedia of Public International Law* (Oxford University Press 2013) para 20.

and not of result.[119] This is achieved by "taking appropriate measures" to "prevent, mitigate and prepare for" disasters. In this context, 'prevention' means the complete avoidance of potential adverse impacts of hazardous events; 'mitigation' is defined as "lessening or minimizing of the adverse impacts of a hazardous event"; and 'preparedness' denotes the knowledge and capacities "to effectively anticipate, respond to and recover from the impacts of likely, imminent or current disasters".[120] The reference to 'appropriate measures' means that concrete and specific measures aimed at prevention, mitigation and preparedness, rather than just any general measures, are required. When evaluating what might be considered as 'appropriate' in a particular situation, the capacity and resources of the respective state need to be taken into account. The use of the word 'appropriate' therefore also indicates the relative nature of the obligation. At the same time, it implies the requirement of due diligence and the effectiveness of the measures taken to prevent, mitigate and prepare for disasters.[121]

Measures for disaster risk reductionlisted in Article 9 include the conduct of risk assessments, the collection and dissemination of risk information and the installation and operation of early warning systems.[122] The first measure, conduct of risk assessments, includes generating knowledge concerning hazards, exposure and vulnerabilities. A solid understanding of the circumstances and factors that drive disaster risk is regarded as essential to define effective measures to reduce the risk of disasters. The second measure, the collection and dissemination of risk information, enhances transparency and allows involved actors to make a risk-informed determination of planning priorities. The third measure, the installation and operation of early warning systems, is instrumental in developing and implementing contingency plans and thus a prerequisite for effective disaster preparedness and response.[123] This list is, however, non-exhaustive, the "practical structural and non-structural measures that can

119 Article 9, ILC Articles on the Protection of Persons in the Event of Disasters, Commentary, para 10.

120 United Nations Office for Disaster Risk Reduction, 'Online Glossary' <www.undrr.org/terminology> accessed 26 February 2021; Article 9, ILC Articles on the Protection of Persons in the Event of Disasters, Commentary, para 16.

121 Article 9, ILC Articles on the Protection of Persons in the Event of Disasters, Commentary, para 11.

122 Article 9(2), ILC Articles on the Protection of Persons in the Event of Disasters.

123 Article 9, ILC Articles on the Protection of Persons in the Event of Disasters, Commentary, paras 20–22.

be adopted are innumerable and depend on the social, environmental, financial, cultural and other relevant circumstances".[124]

The Articles also contain a duty to cooperate enshrined in Article 7, which includes not only cooperation among states but also cooperation with the United Nations, components of the Red Cross and Red Crescent Movement, as well as other assisting actors.[125] The United Nations are explicitly referenced due to the central role of the Office for the Coordination of Humanitarian Affairs (OCHA), which is mandated to assist in the coordination of international assistance, and the Emergency Relief Coordinator, who is the United Nations focal point for complex emergencies and natural disasters and processes requests from states for emergency assistance requiring a coordinated response.[126] Forms of cooperation in the response to disasters, which are enumerated in Article 8, include humanitarian assistance, coordination of international relief actions and communications, making available relief personnel, equipment and goods, as well as providing scientific, medical and technical resources.

The ILC regards the duty to cooperate as a well-established principle of international law which can be found in numerous international instruments, including the UN Charter, the Friendly Relations Declaration and international human rights instruments.[127] Regarding cooperation in the area of disaster relief, the General Assembly also recognised that the "magnitude and duration of many emergencies may be beyond the response capacity of many affected countries. International cooperation to address emergency situations and to strengthen the response capacity of affected countries is thus of great importance".[128] In addition, a large number of multi- and bilateral instruments exists

124 Article 9, ILC Articles on the Protection of Persons in the Event of Disasters, Commentary, para 18.

125 'Other assisting actor' in this context means "a competent intergovernmental organization, or a relevant non-governmental organization or entity, providing assistance to an affected State with its consent". Article 3(d), ILC Articles on the Protection of Persons in the Event of Disasters.

126 Article 7, ILC Articles on the Protection of Persons in the Event of Disasters, Commentary, para 7; Strengthening of the coordination of humanitarian emergency assistance of the United Nations, UNGA Res 46/182 (19 December 1991) Annex.

127 Article 7, ILC Articles on the Protection of Persons in the Event of Disasters, Commentary, paras 1–2. See also Carlo Focarelli, 'Duty to Protect in Cases of Natural Disasters', *Max Planck Encyclopedia of Public International Law* (Oxford University Press 2013) para 24; Hans-Joachim Heintze, 'Responsibility to Protect and the Protection of Persons in the Event of Disasters' in Peter Hilpold (ed), *Responsibility to Protect: A New Paradigm of International Law?* (Brill/Nijhoff 2015) 323–324.

128 Strengthening of the coordination of humanitarian emergency assistance of the United Nations, UNGA Res 46/182 (19 December 1991) Annex, para 5.

that reflect the importance of cooperation in tackling the effects of disasters.[129] Article 7 acknowledges the importance of international cooperation in the areas of international disaster relief assistance and disaster risk reduction and contains a legal obligation to cooperate for the various parties concerned. Yet, the nature of this obligation "may vary, depending on the actor and the context in which assistance is being sought and offered".[130]

The duty of cooperation "should not be interpreted as diminishing the primary role of the affected State" as provided for in Article 10, according to which the affected state "has the duty to ensure the protection of persons and provision of disaster relief assistance in its territory" and "has the primary role in the direction, control, coordination and supervision of such relief assistance".[131] This obligation and primary role of the affected state regarding the protection of persons and the provision of disaster relief stems from its sovereignty, which includes not only rights but also obligations.[132]

Article 10 is premised on the understanding that the affected state is in the best position to determine the appropriate disaster response measures. It should therefore hold the primary role in the cooperative relationships with assisting actors and should exercise control over the implementation of disaster response activities. However, the use of the word 'role' instead of 'responsibility' in this context allows for some flexibility if a state prefers to play a more limited role in the coordination of disaster response, for instance due to a limitation of resources.[133]

129 Article 7, ILC Articles on the Protection of Persons in the Event of Disasters, Commentary, para 3.

130 Article 7, ILC Articles on the Protection of Persons in the Event of Disasters, Commentary, para 6.

131 Article 7, ILC Articles on the Protection of Persons in the Event of Disasters, Commentary, para 4; Article 10, ILC Articles on the Protection of Persons in the Event of Disasters. 'Affected state' means a state "in whose territory, or in territory under whose jurisdiction or control, a disaster takes place". Article 3(b), ILC Articles on the Protection of Persons in the Event of Disasters.

132 Article 10, ILC Articles on the Protection of Persons in the Event of Disasters, Commentary, paras 2-4. See also Carlo Focarelli, 'Duty to Protect in Cases of Natural Disasters', *Max Planck Encyclopedia of Public International Law* (Oxford University Press 2013) para 17; Hans-Joachim Heintze, 'Responsibility to Protect and the Protection of Persons in the Event of Disasters' in Peter Hilpold (ed), *Responsibility to Protect: A New Paradigm of International Law?* (Brill/Nijhoff 2015) 325–326.

133 Article 10, ILC Articles on the Protection of Persons in the Event of Disasters, Commentary, paras 6–8.

In case a disaster manifestly exceeds the national response capacity of the affected state, it has the duty to seek external assistance.[134] This obligation is contained in Article 11 which lists not only other states, but also the United Nations and other potential assisting actors as addressees of such requests for assistance. This does however not imply that the affected state is obliged to seek assistance from every source mentioned in Article 11, rather it may choose the assistance that it views most appropriate to match its disaster response needs.[135] The duty of the affected state to seek assistance is based on international human rights law and customary international law, whereby the recourse to external assistance may be a necessary element in complying with the state's international obligations towards individuals in case its resources are insufficient to fulfil their protection needs.[136]

Yet, the duty to seek external assistance in case the national capacity of the affected state is exceeded does not mean that states should not seek assistance in disaster situations of lesser intensity. Rather, the ILC generally regards "cooperation in the provision of assistance at all stages of disaster relief to be central to the facilitation of an adequate and effective response to disasters" and considers that even in situations where the affected state is capable of providing the necessary protection and assistance to its population, "cooperation and assistance by international actors will in many cases ensure a more adequate, rapid and extensive response to disasters and an enhanced protection of affected persons".[137]

---

134 'External assistance' means "relief personnel, equipment and goods, and services provided to an affected State by an assisting State or other assisting actor for disaster relief assistance". Article 3(e), ILC Articles on the Protection of Persons in the Event of Disasters.

135 This also reinforces the primary role of the affected state in the direction, control, coordination and supervision of disaster relief assistance, as expounded in Article 10. Moreover, Article 11 is a specification of Articles 7 and 10 in that it affirms on the one hand the obligation of the affected state to do its utmost to protect and provide disaster relief assistance to persons in its territory and on the other hand that the duty to cooperate is not only incumbent upon assisting states or other assisting actors, but also upon the affected state to the extent that a disaster exceeds its response capacity. Article 11, ILC Articles on the Protection of Persons in the Event of Disasters, Commentary, paras 1 and 8.

136 Article 11, ILC Articles on the Protection of Persons in the Event of Disasters, Commentary, para 3. See also Carlo Focarelli, 'Duty to Protect in Cases of Natural Disasters', *Max Planck Encyclopedia of Public International Law* (Oxford University Press 2013) para 19; Hans-Joachim Heintze, 'Responsibility to Protect and the Protection of Persons in the Event of Disasters' in Peter Hilpold (ed), *Responsibility to Protect: A New Paradigm of International Law?* (Brill/Nijhoff 2015) 326–327.

137 Article 11, ILC Articles on the Protection of Persons in the Event of Disasters, Commentary, para 9.

The ILC Articles also address offers of external assistance. In this regard, Article 12 provides that in the event of disasters, "States, the United Nations, and other potential assisting actors may offer assistance to the affected State".[138] However, this Article "should not be construed as recognition of the existence of a legal duty to assist", rather offers of assistance "are essentially voluntary".[139] Such offers cannot be regarded as interference in the internal affairs of the affected state nor as an infringement on its sovereignty. In this regard it is important to distinguish the offer of assistance from its concrete delivery. Article 12 only deals with offers of assistance, not with the provision thereof. Offers of assistance do not create a corresponding obligation of the affected state to accept them. In conformity with the principle of sovereignty an affected state may accept in whole or in part, or not accept, offers of assistance in accordance with Article 13.[140]

According to Article 13(1) the "provision of external assistance requires the consent of the affected State". This reflects "the core principle that implementation of international relief assistance is contingent upon the consent of the affected State" which the ILC regards as "fundamental to international law" and which is rooted in the affected state's sovereignty and the principle of non-intervention.[141]

However, the right of the affected state to refuse an offer is not unlimited. Article 13(2) stipulates that consent by the affected state to external assistance "shall not be withheld arbitrarily". This is based on "the dual nature of sovereignty as entailing both rights and obligations" and is also reflected in the duty of the affected state contained in Article 10 to ensure the protection of persons and the provision of disaster relief assistance in its territory.[142] This duty

138 Article 12(1), ILC Articles on the Protection of Persons in the Event of Disasters. The Article reflects the interest of the international community in the protection of persons in the event of disasters which the ILC views as an expression of the principles of solidarity and cooperation. Article 12, ILC Articles on the Protection of Persons in the Event of Disasters, Commentary, para 1.

139 Article 12, ILC Articles on the Protection of Persons in the Event of Disasters, Commentary, para 2.

140 Article 12, ILC Articles on the Protection of Persons in the Event of Disasters, Commentary, para 3. See also Carlo Focarelli, 'Duty to Protect in Cases of Natural Disasters', *Max Planck Encyclopedia of Public International Law* (Oxford University Press 2013) para 22.

141 Article 13, ILC Articles on the Protection of Persons in the Event of Disasters, Commentary, paras 1–2. See also Strengthening of the coordination of humanitarian emergency assistance of the United Nations, UNGA Res 46/182 (19 December 1991) Annex, para 3; Carlo Focarelli, 'Duty to Protect in Cases of Natural Disasters', *Max Planck Encyclopedia of Public International Law* (Oxford University Press 2013) para 21.

142 Article 13, ILC Articles on the Protection of Persons in the Event of Disasters, Commentary, para 3.

is central to the protection of the right to life of those within the territory of an affected state. "An offer of assistance that is met with refusal might thus under certain conditions constitute a violation of the right to life."[143] The determination of whether consent is withheld arbitrarily must be made on a case-by-case basis. The withholding of consent to external assistance is not considered as arbitrary, if the affected state is capable and willing to provide an adequate disaster response on the basis of its own resources or if the affected state has accepted appropriate and sufficient assistance from elsewhere.[144]

When the affected state receives an offer of external assistance it "shall, whenever possible, make known its decision regarding the offer in a timely manner".[145] In addition, the affected state is under the duty to "facilitate the prompt and effective provision of external assistance".[146] At the same time, the affected state may also establish conditions on the provision of external assistance which take into account the identified needs of the persons affected by disasters and the quality of the assistance.[147]

It can be concluded from the analysis of the ILC Articles on the Protection of Persons in the Event of Disasters that states have an obligation to reduce the risk of disasters by taking prevention, mitigation and preparation measures. This may, depending on the specific circumstances and available resources, also include the carrying out of planetary defence activities. While the affected state has the primary role in this regard, there exists also a duty of states to cooperate. However, there is no obligation of states under international law to assist affected states. Nor is there an obligation of affected states to accept offers of assistance, rather their consent to the provision of external assistance is required.

---

143 Article 13, ILC Articles on the Protection of Persons in the Event of Disasters, Commentary, para 4. See also Hans-Joachim Heintze, 'Responsibility to Protect and the Protection of Persons in the Event of Disasters' in Peter Hilpold (ed), *Responsibility to Protect: A New Paradigm of International Law?* (Brill/Nijhoff 2015) 327.

144 Article 13, ILC Articles on the Protection of Persons in the Event of Disasters, Commentary, para 8. In this regard, it has been criticised that it remains unclear who should determine whether a refusal is arbitrary. See Carlo Focarelli, 'Duty to Protect in Cases of Natural Disasters', *Max Planck Encyclopedia of Public International Law* (Oxford University Press 2013) para 23. For a detailed discussion see Craig Allan and Therese O'Donnell, 'An Offer You Cannot Refuse? Natural Disasters, the Politics of Aid Refusal and Potential Legal Implications' (2013) 5 Amsterdam Law Forum 36, 54–57.

145 Article 13(3), ILC Articles on the Protection of Persons in the Event of Disasters.

146 Article 15(1), ILC Articles on the Protection of Persons in the Event of Disasters.

147 Article 14, ILC Articles on the Protection of Persons in the Event of Disasters.

7 Conclusion

The analysis in this chapter shows that while there is no international legal instrument that specifically addresses planetary defence, international law nevertheless provides a basis for an obligation of states to take action towards the mitigation and prevention of NEO impact threats.

It can be concluded that there exists an obligation of states under international law to protect their population from NEO impact threats, which is mainly based on international human rights law, the principle of sovereignty, and international disaster law. However, this obligation is one of conduct, not of result and must be assessed in consideration of the circumstances of the specific situation, including the knowledge of the threat and the possibility of its mitigation, the risks involved and the availability of the necessary resources and capabilities. In addition, the focus not only on response mechanisms but also on risk reduction, planning, prevention, preparedness, risk assessment and early warning in the instruments and concepts discussed above is of particular relevance in the context of planetary defence, since an efficient response to a NEO impact threat situation is dependent on the existence of capabilities for the detection, observation and characterisation of NEOs as well as on the development of mitigation strategies and deflection technologies already before an impact threat is detected. The state affected by a potential NEO impact has the primary role in fulfilling this obligation. This might also include the duty to seek external assistance in case the NEO impact threat exceeds the response capacity of the affected state.

However, an international law obligation of states to assist other states in the mitigation of NEO impact threats cannot be identified, rather states may offer assistance on a voluntary basis. In conformity with the principle of sovereignty such offers of assistance do not create a corresponding obligation on the part of the affected state to accept them. However, sovereignty is not unlimited and also includes responsibilities and obligations. It is therefore to be exercised in a way that best ensures the protection of persons under the jurisdiction of the state affected by a potential NEO impact, which may also include that consent to the provision of assistance is not withheld arbitrarily.

In addition, states have a duty under international law to cooperate in the mitigation of NEO impact threats. A duty to cooperate can be found in international space law, environmental law, human rights law and disaster law. While the exact scope and nature of this obligation may vary depending on the context, a wide range of possibilities and forms of cooperation can be inferred from the instruments analysed above. International cooperation in NEO impact threat mitigation may for instance include the provision of assistance, the coordination of international planetary defence actions, and the supply of financial, scientific and technical resources. The above analysis also shows that international organisations, and in particular the United Nations, have a central role in international cooperation in areas relevant to planetary defence. In a NEO impact threat situation, it is therefore important to ensure that the cooperation through and with relevant international bodies is well coordinated.

International cooperation is of particular relevance in the context of planetary defence. This is on the one hand, due to the fact that many states lack the necessary economic and technological means to undertake planetary defence measures, and on the other hand, to the large number of countries that may potentially be affected by a NEO impact on Earth, depending on the specific circumstances of the case, in particular the size of the NEO and the location of its impact. Moreover, the risks and uncertainties that may characterise NEO impact threat situations and mitigation measures, regarding for instance the knowledge of the precise characteristics of the NEO and the probability, location and effects of its impact as well as the feasibility and success of the envisaged mitigation measures, may make international cooperation in planetary defence not only desirable but also necessary. Cooperation may therefore in many cases be essential for the provision of an effective response to NEO impact threats and for the comprehensive protection of affected persons.

In order to enhance the efficiency of cooperation in the field of planetary defence and to facilitate a comprehensive fulfilment of the duty to cooperate in the mitigation of NEO impact threats, the elaboration of internationally agreed procedures and standards for the multilateral development and implementation of planetary defence measures could be a useful step. This may include common consultation and coordination mechanisms, modalities for cooperation in the framework of planetary defence measures, the main features of a mandate to undertake joint NEO impact threat mitigation activities, parameters for the selection of planetary defence measures and technologies as well as operational principles and procedures. The various concepts and areas of law analysed above may provide useful guidance with regard to the development of such common international standards and procedures. Such common standards and procedures could enhance the transparency and objectivity of decision-making in the response to NEO impact threats as well as of the implementation of planetary defence measures and could therefore maximise international support and acceptance of such measures and strengthen international cooperation. They could form part of a broader international framework or agreement that addresses legal questions related to planetary defence such as liability, responsibility, authorisation and decision-making, which are dealt with in the following chapters.

CHAPTER 14

The Use of Force and Planetary Defence

Setsuko Aoki

1 Introduction: the Scope of the Study

This chapter studies whether and to what extent international law on the prohibition of the use of force is relevant to various aspects of planetary defence.

Planetary defence comprises prediction and mitigation.[1] Mitigation measures presently studied can roughly be grouped into evacuation and active response to a foreseeable impact.[2] Since evacuation is effective only against a small Near-Earth Object (NEO), the major mitigation responses are expected to be deflection and disruption missions. In addition, the fragmentation method has also been taken into consideration by scientists although as a less preferred option due to the less secure outcome.[3]

The scope of the objects in this chapter includes: i) prediction, ii) evacuation and iii) active mitigation measures except those by the use of nuclear explosive device (NED) as this issue is dealt with in the later chapters of this book.[4] While admitting that deflection and disruption methods are the central point of discussion, this chapter does not exclude the fragmentation option in considering if some of the planetary defence activities and actions could amount to the prohibited use of force or otherwise violate certain rules of international law. Without touching further upon the technological details, for the purposes of this chapter, the term 'active mitigation measures' is used as long as the distinction between deflection, disruption and fragmentation technologies is not necessary for the precise legal analysis.

---

1 Planetary defence is defined as "activities and actions to predict and mitigate a potential impact by an asteroid or comet on the Earth" by the Space Mission Planning Advisory Group (SMPAG). See SMPAG, 'Terms of Reference V2.0' <www.cosmos.esa.int/web/smpag/terms_of_reference_v2> accessed 25 February 2021.

2 See e.g. Nikola Schmidt (ed), *Planetary Defense: Global Collaboration for Defending Earth from Asteroids and Comets* (Springer 2019).

3 Thomas J Ahrens and Alan W Harris, 'Deflection and Fragmentation of Near-Earth Asteroids' (1992) 360 Nature 429.

4 The issues of the nuclear disarmamentand non-proliferation are discussed in chapters 15 'Legal Aspects of the Use of Nuclear Explosive Devices in Planetary Defence' and 16 'Nuclear Non-Proliferation and Planetary Defence: Competing Potential Disasters' in this book.

 | DOI:10.1163/9789004467606_016

This chapter consists of four sections including the introduction and concluding remarks. In the next section, it is studied how planetary defence would be evaluated in regard to the principle of the non-use of force. As this principle under general international law consists of the 'prohibition of the use of force' and the 'prohibition of the threat of force', the next section addresses both aspects in order. In section three, possible treaty restrictions on the military use of outer space are considered from the point of view of planetary defence. That is followed by the concluding remarks which underline the significance of an international mechanism for planetary defence as well as robust transparency and confidence building measures among states.

2 The Scope of the Prohibition of the Threat or Use of Force under International Law

2.1 *Article 2(4) of the UN Charter as Reflection of Customary International Law*

The International Court of Justice (ICJ) has acknowledged on several occasions that Article 2(4) of the United Nations (UN) Charter[5] and a rule of customary international law on the prohibition of the threat or use of force have an identical content.[6] Thus, independent study is not needed on the rule of non-use of force under customary international law. Analysis of Article 2(4) of the UN Charter suffices.

Article 2(4) of the UN Charter provides:

> All Members shall refrain in their international relations from the threat or use of force against the territorial integrity or political independence of any state, or in any other manner inconsistent with the Purposes of the United Nations.

To evaluate planetary defence in the context of the prohibition of the threat or use of force, first, the prohibition of the use of force is studied. Two points have to be clarified in this regard. These are the meaning of 'force' and the

5 Charter of the United Nations (adopted 26 June 1945, entered into force 24 October 1945) 1 UNTS 16 (UN Charter).

6 *Military and Paramilitary Activities in and against Nicaragua* (*Nicaragua v USA*) (Merits) [1986] ICJ Rep 14, 187–190; *Legal Consequences of the Construction of a Wall in the Occupied Palestinian Territory* (Advisory Opinion) [2004] ICJ Rep 136, 87.

'circumstances' in which such use of force is prohibited. Both points are considered in order.

2.2 *First Criterion: the Notion of 'Force'*

First, the notion of 'force' is to be clarified. It is duly confirmed that 'force' means 'armed force' or 'military force' used directly (e.g. the incursion of regular military troops into the territory of another state) or indirectly (e.g. arming and training of a private rebel group in the territory of another state) and that political or economic force/coercion is not included in the notion of 'force' in Article 2(4) of the UN Charter.[7] The use of physical force of a non-military form/nature (e.g. cross-border spreading of fire; cross-frontier expulsion of populations) is also not on the whole included in the notion of 'force'.[8] Therefore, to be recognised as 'force' in the meaning of Article 2(4), two criteria need to be met. That is: i) actor: armed forces, and ii) means: a 'weapon', "designed or used for inflicting bodily harm or physical damage; a means of gaining advantage or defending oneself".[9] This definition of a 'weapon' shows that for a device/instrument to be a 'weapon', both a) capability and b) purpose are required. Further, it is confirmed that weapons or weapon systems include non-kinetic systems, such as those used in electronic warfare and a cyber attack,[10] and thus, the use of force may be committed by a cyber operation "when its scale and effects are comparable to non-cyber operations rising to the level of a use of force".[11] This is important as some of the active mitigation measures would be carried on by cyber capabilities.

---

7 Oliver Dörr and Albrecht Randelzhofer, 'Ch.I Purposes and Principles, Article 2 (4)' in Bruno Simma and others (eds), *The Charter of the United Nations: A Commentary* (3rd edn, Oxford University Press 2012) vol I 207–213; James Crawford, *Brownlie's Principles of Public International Law* (9th edn, Oxford University Press 2019) 720; Malcom N Shaw, *International Law* (8th edn, Cambridge University Press 2017) 855–856.

8 Oliver Dörr and Albrecht Randelzhofer, 'Ch.I Purposes and Principles, Article 2 (4)' in Bruno Simma and others (eds), *The Charter of the United Nations: A Commentary* (3rd edn, Oxford University Press 2012) vol I 210; Oliver Dörr, 'Use of Force, Prohibition of' in Rüdiger Wolfrum (ed) *The Max Planck Encyclopedia of Public International Law* (Oxford University Press 2012) vol X 607, 609–610.

9 Concise Oxford English Dictionary (11th edn, Oxford University Press 2006), cited in William Boothby, 'Weapons, Prohibited' in Rüdiger Wolfrum (ed) *Max Planck Encyclopedia of Public International Law* (Oxford University Press 2012) vol X 839, 840.

10 Program on Humanitarian Policy and Conflict Research at Harvard University (ed), *Commentary on the HPCR Manual on International Law Applicable to Air and Missile Warfare* (HPCR 2010) 41–42 (Section A 1(t)).

11 Michael N Schmitt (ed), *Tallinn Manual 2.0 on the International Law Applicable to Cyber Operations* (Cambridge University Press 2017) 330.

From the above analysis, it seems that the cross-frontier evacuation of population as a part of planetary defence mitigation measures would not fall under the 'use of force', even if this operation could fit into a different category of an internationally wrongful act. Noting that it is difficult to reach a conclusion without considering concrete possible scenarios, it may be said that the possible wrongfulness of the cross-frontier evacuation of the population of a certain state could well be precluded by certain rules under the international law of state responsibility, e.g. distress or necessity.[12] However, addressing this issue primarily by the international law of state responsibility seems less pertinent than by different fields of international law such as human rights including refugee issues, natural disasters, human security and international cooperation.[13] This seems to be the exact field in which the UN and its family organisations can play a critical role.[14]

In addition, it can be said that active mitigation measures would not satisfy the 'purpose element' of the notion of a 'weapon', because an action that causes physical damage to a NEO to change its orbit is not aimed at fighting an enemy in an armed conflict, but at protecting humankind and the Earth.

2.3 *Second Criterion: 'Circumstances'*

Next, the aspect of the 'circumstances' in which the 'force' is used has to be considered. This criterion relates to the phrases "in their international relations", "against the territorial integrity or political independence of any state", and "in any other manner inconsistent with the Purposes of the United Nations".

The wording 'threat or use of force' was newly introduced to the UN Charter so as to ban not only traditional 'war' but also any 'international armed conflicts', which was not accomplished by the 1928 General Treaty for the

---

12 Articles 24 and 25, Articles on the International Responsibility of States for Internationally Wrongful Acts, UNGA Res 56/83, Annex (12 December 2001).

13 The international law of disaster responses has developed to a certain degree, but cross-frontier evacuation as a preventive measure of a massive natural disaster remains explored. See e.g. David D Caron, Michael J Kelly, and Anastasia Telesetsky (eds), *The International Law of Disaster Relief* (Cambridge University Press 2014); IFRC, 'International Disaster Response Laws, Rules and Principles' (IDRL) <www.ifrc.org/en/what-we-do/disaster-law/about-disaster-law/international-disaster-response-laws-rules-and-principles/> accessed 25 February 2021.

14 See e.g. Kentaro Nishimoto, 'The Role of International Organizations in Disaster Response: A Case Study of Recent Earthquakes in Japan' in David D Caron, Michael J Kelly, and Anastasia Telesetsky (eds) *The International Law of Disaster Relief* (Cambridge University Press 2014) 295–313. For instance, the UN Office for the Coordination of Human Affairs (OCHA) coordinates the global emergency response to save lives and protect people in humanitarian crises. See <www.unocha.org/> accessed 25 February 2021.

Renunciation of War (the Kellogg-Briand Pact).[15] Thus, naturally, the prohibition of the threat or use of force is the obligation between sovereign states, as the phrase "international relations" in Article 2(4) explicitly demonstrates. Accordingly, the prohibition of the use of force does not regulate domestic situations such as a rebellion.[16] Nor does it regulate the situation of the use of 'force' against natural objects in outer space, since in this situation 'force' is not used "against the territorial integrity or political independence" of a state. As an activity to protect humankind and the Earth, mitigation measures would generally also not be "in any other manner inconsistent with the Purposes of the United Nations".[17] Rather, such an activity would be fully consistent with those purposes (Article 1(1)).

In conclusion, neither the cross-frontier evacuation of population nor active planetary defence mitigation measures qualify as the 'use of force' under Article 2(4) of the UN Charter, because they do not meet the 'force' or the 'circumstances' criterion.

2.4 *How to Justify the 'Force' Used in Active Mitigation Measures?*

Since active planetary defence mitigation measures are not within the scope of Article 2(4) of the UN Charter, they do not need to be justified by either of the two exceptions foreseen in the Charter, i.e. an authorisation under the system

15 Oliver Dörr and Albrecht Randelzhofer, 'Ch.I Purposes and Principles, Article 2 (4)' in Bruno Simma and others (eds), *The Charter of the United Nations: A Commentary* (3rd edn, Oxford University Press 2012) vol I 206–207; James Crawford, *Brownlie's Principles of Public International Law* (9th edn, Oxford University Press 2019) 718–719; Malcom N Shaw, *International Law* (8th edn, Cambridge University Press 2017) 853–854.

16 Oliver Dörr and Albrecht Randelzhofer, 'Ch.I Purposes and Principles, Article 2 (4)' in Bruno Simma and others (eds), *The Charter of the United Nations: A Commentary* (3rd edn, Oxford University Press 2012) vol I 215–217; James Crawford, *Brownlie's Principles of Public International Law* (9th edn, Oxford University Press 2019) 720; Malcom N Shaw, *International Law* (8th edn, Cambridge University Press 2017) 856–857, 874–876.

17 It is sometimes claimed that not all threat or use of force is prohibited, but only the force "against the territorial integrity or political independence of any state" is prohibited. This interpretation may enable a state to exercise military operations in the territory of another state to save its nationals therein and engage in unilateral humanitarian intervention involving the use of force. Not undisputed, but the prevailing view is that the use of force is comprehensively prohibited between sovereign states except in the cases qualified by the UN Charter as collective security (Chapter VII) or self-defence (Article 51). James Crawford, *Brownlie's Principles of Public International Law* (9th edn, Oxford University Press 2019) 720; Malcom N Shaw, *International Law* (8th edn, Cambridge University Press 2017) 857–858; Oliver Dörr, 'Use of Force, Prohibition of' in Rüdiger Wolfrum (ed), *Max Planck Encyclopedia of Public International Law* (Oxford University Press 2012) vol X 607, 610.

of collective security according to Chapter VII or self-defence in accordance with Article 51.[18] Likewise, an individual state cannot resort to the use of 'force' in the context of planetary defence as self-defence due to the non-existence of the preceding 'armed attack' within the meaning of Article 51 of the UN Charter.[19] As far as the rule of the prohibition of the use of force as well as the rules of collective security and self-defence in general international law are concerned, active mitigation measures are neither prohibited nor qualified.

When an active mitigation measure is taken, kinetic or otherwise, the 'use of force' as a mere fact in a general sense still exists, while it is not within the meaning of that prohibited in Article 2(4) of the UN Charter.[20] Therefore, further consideration is needed before a conclusion regarding the legal implications of planetary defence measures can be drawn. Since an action whose external appearance is tantamount to the 'use of force' might be prohibited or otherwise restricted by special rules, other relevant rules of international law, including especially international space law, will be analysed in section three of this chapter.

2.5 *The Issue of 'the Threat of Force'*

Before inquiring into the special rules concerning planetary defence, there is yet another issue to be addressed. That is the question if a certain planetary defence activity or action could in some cases be assessed as a 'threat of force' prohibited under Article 2(4) of the UN Charter. While it is difficult to formulate criteria to satisfy the 'threat of force', due, in part, to the scant precedents in the context of Article 2(4),[21] the important prerequisite is that the prohibition of the 'threat of force' is symmetrical to the prohibition of the 'use of force'.[22] The ICJ confirmed this relationship:

---

18 Jinyuan Su, 'Measures Proposed for Planetary Defence: Obstacles in Existing International Law and Implication for Space Arms Control' (2015) 34 Space Policy 1, 3.

19 The first sentence of Article 51 UN Charter states: "Nothing in the present Charter shall impair the inherent right of individual or collective self-defence if an armed attack occurs against a Member of the United Nations, until the Security Council has taken the measures necessary to maintain international peace and security." On Article 51 UN Charter see e.g.: James Crawford, *Brownlie's Principles of Public International Law* (9th edn, Oxford University Press 2019) 720–725; Malcom N Shaw, *International Law* (8th edn, Cambridge University Press 2017) 861–874.

20 Jinyuan Su, 'Measures Proposed for Planetary Defence: Obstacles in Existing International Law and Implication for Space Arms Control' (2015) 34 Space Policy 1, 3.

21 Oliver Dörr and Albrecht Randelzhofer, 'Ch.I Purposes and Principles, Article 2 (4)' in Bruno Simma and others (eds), *The Charter of the United Nations: A Commentary* (3rd edn, Oxford University Press 2012) vol I 217–218.

22 See e.g. François Dubuisson and Anne Lagerwall, 'The Threat of the Use of Force and Ultimata' in Marc Weller (ed), *The Oxford Handbook of the Use of Force in International Law* (Oxford University Press 2015) 910, 915.

> The notions of "threat" and "use" of force under Article 2, paragraph 4, of the Charter stand together in the sense that if the use of force itself in a given case is illegal – for whatever reason – the threat to use such force will likewise be illegal. In short, if it is to be lawful, the declared readiness of a State to use force must be a use of force that is in conformity with the Charter.[23]

This applies to the case when different perceptions of 'force' are resorted to by a state. Even if a certain use of 'force' is purported to be a legitimate law enforcement by the implementing state, it may be concluded it is "more akin to a threat of military action rather than a mere law enforcement activity" and it "constituted a threat of the use of force" in contravention to the UN Charter and general international law.[24]

Based on the above, at first glance, the issue of the 'threat of force' in respect of planetary defence seems relatively simple. As no use of force was recognised with regard to evacuation or active mitigation measures in the sense of Article 2(4) of the UN Charter, it would follow that no 'threat of force' could exist pursuant to the symmetrical logic. However, the point below should also be taken into consideration.

Even if a planetary defence measure is not recognised as a use of force in the sense of Article 2(4) of the UN Charter, it may be claimed that there might be the case that such action itself may be a proof of the willingness of a state to subsequently resort to force, for instance, the taking over of the control of a spacecraft of another state.

Considering the prevalent view that 'threat' should be formulated in a precise and concrete way,[25] it seems unlikely that even a fragmentation action taken by an individual state in the context of planetary defence would itself be regarded as a 'threat' under the meaning of Article 2(4). One definition of the 'threat of force' is "an express or implied promise by a government of a resort to force conditional on non-acceptance of certain demands of that government".[26] Only an action does not suffice. For instance, a military exercise or an

---

23 *The Legality of the Threat or Use of Nuclear Weapons* (Advisory Opinion) [1996] ICJ Rep 226, 47.

24 Arbitral Tribunal Constituted Pursuant to Article 287, and in accordance with Annex VII of the United Nations Convention on the Law of the Sea (*Guyana v Suriname*) [2007] 30 RIAA 1, 445 <https://legal.un.org/riaa/cases/vol_XXX/1-144.pdf> accessed 25 February 2021.

25 François Dubuisson and Anne Lagerwall, 'The Threat of the Use of Force and Ultimata' in Marc Weller (ed), *The Oxford Handbook of the Use of Force in International Law* (Oxford University Press 2015) 910, 913.

26 Ian Brownlie, *International Law and the Use of Force by States* (Clarendon Press 1963) 364.

arms acquisition are by themselves not traditionally considered as a 'threat of force'. Such an action needs to be accompanied by a signalled intention or declaration demonstrating the aims of a state towards a targeted state to use force unless the latter state does not act pursuant to the direction of the former.[27]

Even if a state which conducts fragmentation measures as part of a planetary defence operation makes a bellicose declaration to another state to accomplish its goal and this may be construed as a threat of force, that does not yet make the active mitigation measure *per se* a threat of force. However, this may lead to the shared perception that a unilateral activity of planetary defence is much less desirable than an activity that is carried out through international cooperation. Similar situations may be pointed out for the different stages of planetary defence, including detection and evacuation. Individual activities are referred to in the next section, which deals with possible restrictions to the use of outer space by special treaties.

3 The Permissible Scope of the Use of Outer Space

3.1 *The Outer Space Treaty as* Lex Specialis

It was concluded in the previous section that active mitigation measures, such as the use of a kinetic impactor for deflecting a NEO, would not be considered as 'use of force' under Article 2(4) of the UN Charter. These actions, however, may not be permissible under the international space law regime, which constitutes a *lex specialis* against general international law. This will be addressed in this section.

It is doubtless that Article IV of the Outer Space Treaty[28] is by far the most important provision concerning the military use of outer space. This was the case in 1967 when the treaty entered into force and is still the case today. Article IV reads:

> States Parties to the Treaty undertake not to place in orbit around the Earth any objects carrying nuclear weapons or any other kinds of

27 *The Legality of the Threat or Use of Nuclear Weapons* (Advisory Opinion) [1996] ICJ Rep 226, 48.

28 Treaty on Principles Governing the Activities of States in the Exploration and Use of Outer Space, including the Moon and Other Celestial Bodies (adopted 19 December 1966, entered into force 10 October 1967) 610 UNTS 205 (Outer Space Treaty).

> weapons of mass destruction, install such weapons on celestial bodies, or station such weapons in outer space in any other manner.
>
> The Moon and other celestial bodies shall be used by all States Parties to the Treaty exclusively for peaceful purposes. The establishment of military bases, installations and fortifications, the testing of any type of weapons and the conduct of military manoeuvres on celestial bodies shall be forbidden. The use of military personnel for scientific research or for any other peaceful purposes shall not be prohibited. The use of any equipment or facility necessary for peaceful exploration of the Moon and other celestial bodies shall also not be prohibited.

Active mitigation measures, such as deflection or disruption methods, would be expected to be taken from Earth today and in the foreseeable future. However, it cannot be excluded that in a more distant future active mitigation measures could be taken from the Moon and other celestial bodies. Thus, both cases will be studied in this chapter. First focusing on mitigation activities taken from Earth and then activities taken from celestial bodies other than the Earth.

Concerning outer void space, i.e. outer space other than the celestial bodies, it is only weapons of mass destruction (WMD) that are prohibited to be placed in orbit around the Earth or otherwise stationed in outer space. No prohibition is stipulated on conventional weapons in outer void space and on objects carrying WMD to navigate ballistic trajectories.[29] This chapter does not address the legal status of NEDs and other nuclear related instruments. Nor would other WMD such as biological or chemical weapons be studied.

3.2 *The Permissible Scope of Active Mitigation Measures from Earth*

What is the permissible scope of the use of mitigation measures in outer void space if undertaken from Earth? Two questions have to be answered to clarify this: i) if outer void space shall be used 'exclusively for peaceful purposes' as is the case for celestial bodies where such use is explicitly obligated (Article IV(2)); and ii) how 'peaceful purposes' shall be interpreted. A subset of the second question is if the adverb 'exclusively' would change the meaning of 'for peaceful purposes'. There have been three interpretations for questions i) and ii).

---

29 This reflected the US-USSR nuclear strategies already strongly embedded at the time of drafting the Outer Space Treaty. See e.g. United States Senate Committee on Aeronautical and Space Sciences, 'Outer Space Treaty Analysis and Background Data Staff Report' (1967) 26.

The first is that 'peaceful' shall be interpreted as 'non-military' and the obligation of non-military use is extended to outer void space, as Article I(1) of the Outer Space Treaty stipulates that the exploration and use of outer space "shall be carried out for the benefit and in the interests of all countries".[30] Commentators supporting this position claimed that any armed forces or military activities could serve only one state or a group of states but never all countries, and that any military use would contradict Article I(1) of the Outer Space Treaty. If this interpretation is applied, military satellites placed in orbit around the Earth[31] as well as ballistic missiles manoeuvred through outer space shall be prohibited. Such interpretation contradicts the ordinary meaning of the text in Article IV(1)[32] and state practice.[33]

The second interpretation is that 'peaceful' equates 'non-aggressive' and the obligation of the use for "exclusively peaceful purposes" is also imposed on outer void space because of the purposes of the Treaty (Article I) and the drafting history. Under this interpretation, states are free to use outer void space for military purposes as long as this does not constitute the prohibited threat or use of force under Article 2(4) of the UN Charter.[34]

The third interpretation is that 'exclusively for peaceful purposes' is not applied to the outer void space because this is not explicitly stipulated in the Outer Space Treaty. Rather only the banning of WMD and the prohibition of the threat or use of force according to Article 2(4) of the UN Charter is obligatory

30 See e.g. Marko G Markoff, 'Disarmament and 'Peaceful Purposes' Provisions in the 1967 Outer Space Treaty' (1976) 4 Journal of Space Law 11; Gennady P Zhukov, 'On the Question of Interpretation of the Term 'Peaceful Use of Outer Space' Contained in the Space Treaty' in IISL (ed), *Proceedings of the Eleventh Colloquium on the Law of Outer Space* (AIAA 1969) 36.

31 One database shows, as of 30 September 2019, 231 military satellites and 466 dual-use satellites were operating among the total number of 2218 satellites. Union of the Concerned Scientists, Satellite Database <www.ucsusa.org/resources/satellite-database> accessed 20 November 2019.

32 Vienna Convention on the Law of Treaties (adopted 23 May 1969, entered in to force 27 January 1980) 1155 UNTS 331; Article 31(1) provides that "a treaty shall be interpreted in good faith in accordance with the ordinary meaning to be given to the terms of the treaty in their context and in the light of its object and purpose".

33 Kai-Uwe Schrogl and Julia Neumann, 'Article IV' in Stephan Hobe, Bernhard Schmidt-Tedd and Kai-Uwe Schrogl (eds), *Cologne Commentary on Space Law* (Carl Heymanns Verlag 2009) vol I 87-93.

34 Martin Menter, 'Peaceful Uses of Outer Space and National Security' (1983) 17 International Lawyer 584; Bin Cheng, *Studies in International Space Law* (Clarendon Press 1997) 515–522.

in the outer void space.[35] The second and third interpretation lead to the identical conclusion on the permissible scope of the use of outer space. Under either interpretation, military use is permissible to the extent that it falls short of the threat or use of force under Article 2(4) of the UN Charter.

Other than Article IV, Articles I, III, IX and X of the Outer Space Treaty regulate how outer void space has to be utilised. The contents of these regulations are: Article I(1) (the obligation to explore and use outer space "for the benefit and in the interests of all countries"); Article III (the observance of international law in the conduct of space activities); Article IX (the principle of cooperation and mutual assistance as well as due regard to corresponding interests of other states; the avoidance of harmful contamination of outer space and of adverse changes in the environment of the Earth; the obligation of international consultations in case of a potentially harmful interference of a national space activity with the activities of other states); and Article X (the voluntary granting of an opportunity to other states to observe the flight of space objects launched).

Among these provisions, special attention has to be paid to Article IX, because an individual state engaging in an active mitigation measure may cause "potentially harmful interference with activities of other States Parties" and be placed under the obligation of consultation with that likely affected state (Article IX, sentence 3). Article IX, in particular the requirement to avoid the harmful contamination of outer space and adverse changes in the environment of the Earth, is also related to the obligation of states to use outer void space in accordance with international law (Article III), which includes rapidly developing international environmental law. Active mitigation measures, including in particular methods that lead to a fragmentation, may therefore be affected by Article IX and may be less preferred.

While the Outer Space Treaty, in particular Article IX, could present potential restrictions in connection with the conduct of planetary defence activities, from the point of view of the use of force, it can be concluded that except for the stationing of WMD in outer space there is no additional direct or categorical prohibition under the Outer Space Treaty on the use of outer void space.

35 See e.g. Istvan Herczeg, 'Problems of Interpretation of the Space Treaty of 27 January 1967: Introductory Report' (as a view of Eileen Galloway) in IISL (ed), *Proceedings of the Tenth Colloquium on the Law of Outer Space* (AIAA 1968) 105; Carl Q Christol, *The Modern International Law of Outer Space* (Pergamon Press 1982) 20–30.

3.3 *Prediction Activities in Conformity with International Space Law*

As already mentioned, planetary defence consists of prediction and mitigation. As regards prediction, ground- and space-based observations for NEO detection, tracking and remote characterisation have been conducted.[36] Increased use of space-based observation systems such as space telescopes and NEO surveillance satellites already in operation is expected.[37]

The purpose of the space-based observation of NEOs is certainly "for the benefit and in the interests of all countries" (Article I(1) of the Outer Space Treaty) and fully in line with the goal of international cooperation as the basis of the Outer Space Treaty and the UN Charter.[38] The UN's strong involvement with the topic of planetary defence reinforces the value of the detection aspect of planetary defence.[39]

Space telescopes and space-to-space detection satellites tend to have diverse observation purposes,[40] among which NEO observation is only one and it may be possible that such spacecraft for NEO detection also have a military surveillance purpose. Military surveillance from Earth falls within the legitimate activities in accordance with the prevalent interpretation of Article IV(1) of the Outer Space Treaty and state practice since the advent of the space age (see 3.2 of this chapter). Even if space-based observation would be found a 'threat of force' at all under the UN Charter, for instance, due to accompanying demands, declarations, and certain additional military activities of a state, yet detection, tracking and remote characterisation of NEOs *per se* is nothing but lawful for it is in conformity with the purposes and provisions of the UN Charter and the Outer Space Treaty. However, it must be pointed out that the spacecraft in

---

36 See e.g. US National Science and Technology Council, 'The National Near-Earth Object Preparedness Strategy and Action Plan' (2018) 7–8.

37 Peter Vereš, 'Technical Architecture to Deepen Our Solar System Awareness' in Nikola Schmidt (ed), *Planetary Defense: Global Collaboration for Defending Earth from Asteroids and Comets* (Springer 2019) 71, 83–87.

38 International cooperation in solving international problems of humanitarian character is one of the purposes of the UN (Article 1(3) of the UN Charter). Likewise, throughout the provisions of the Outer Space Treaty, especially preamble, Articles I and IX, provide the essential obligations of international cooperation in the exploration and use of outer space.

39 See e.g. UNOOSA, 'Near-Earth Objects and Planetary Defense' (June 2018) ST/SPACE/73.

40 Peter Vereš, 'Technical Architecture to Deepen Our Solar System Awareness' in Nikola Schmidt (ed), *Planetary Defense: Global Collaboration for Defending Earth from Asteroids and Comets* (Springer 2019) 71, 83–87, 91.

question may lose the status of civilian object by such dual-use employment in the context of the laws of armed conflict.[41]

3.4 *The Moon Agreement and Planetary Defence*

The disarmament provision in Article 3 of the Moon Agreement[42] basically reiterates Article IV(2) of the Outer Space Treaty.[43] Therefore, at first glance, it regulates only activities on celestial bodies and is not relevant to the outer void space. However, since the reference to the 'Moon' in the Moon Agreement shall include "orbits around or other trajectories to or around it" (Article 1(2)), it may impose additional restrictions on planetary defence activities.

The clarification process regarding Article 1(2) of the Moon Agreement in the United Nations Committee on the Peaceful Uses of Outer Space (UNCOPUOS) in 1979 confirmed that trajectories and orbits mentioned in Article 1(2) do not include "trajectories and orbits of space objects in earth orbits only and trajectories of space objects between the earth and such orbits".[44] Therefore, it may be said that the establishment of military bases, installations and fortifications, the testing of any type of weapons or any conduct of military manoeuvres would be prohibited in the residual orbits and trajectories within the Solar System.[45] Granting that this interpretation is applied, could an active mitigation measure amount to the testing of a weapon if it is conducted in the orbits and trajectories of the various celestial bodies other than the Earth? The answer will be in the negative because the purpose element of 'weapon' would not be met even if the capability of the device used for that active mitigation measure might amount to that of a weapon (see 2.2 of this chapter). But since the use of 'force' in a general sense could still exist in resorting to an active mitigation measure, planetary defence activities undertaken through

---

41 Michael N Schmitt, 'International Law and Military Operations in Space' (2006) 10 Max Planck Yearbook of United Nations Law 89, 117; Michael Bourbonnière, 'Law of Armed Conflict (LOAC) and the Neutralisation of Satellites or *IUS in Bello Satellitis*' (2004) 9 Journal of Conflict and Security Law 43, 59–61.

42 Agreement Governing the Activities of States on the Moon and Other Celestial Bodies (adopted 5 December 1979, entered into force 11 July 1984) 1363 UNTS 3 (Moon Agreement).

43 While the Moon Agreement provides further limitations to those in Article IV(2) of the Outer Space Treaty, the added provision "any threat or use of force or any other hostile act or threat of hostile act on the Moon" (Article 3(2)) does not substantially add any restrictions on the states' activities conducted on the Moon and other celestial bodies.

44 UNCOPUOS, 'Report of the Committee on the Peaceful Uses of Outer Space on its twenty-second session' (18 June–3 July 1979), UN Doc A/34/20, para 63.

45 Canada supported this interpretation as shown CD/618 and CD/OS/WP.6 (23 July 1985) 32. China and Russia are of the view that 'on the Moon' does not cover activities in any outer void space, see CD/1780 (22 May 2006) 11.

an international mechanism would be more appropriate to avoid unnecessary suspicion among states. With the increase of the states parties to the Moon Agreement, this may be a relatively serious point of discussion.[46]

3.5 *The Restrictions on Environmental Modification*

The Convention on the Prohibition of Military or Any Other Hostile Use of Environmental Modification Techniques (ENMOD Convention)[47] obligates each state party not "to engage in military or any other hostile use of environmental modification techniques having widespread, long-lasting or severe effects as the means of destruction, damage or injury to any other State Party" (Article I). The term 'environmental modification techniques' is defined as any technique for changing the dynamics, composition or structure of the Earth or of outer space through the deliberate manipulation of natural processes (Article II). Not incorporated in the ENMOD Convention itself, the Understandings Regarding the Convention adopted at the same time with the ENMOD Convention provide the interpretation of key terms to determine if prohibited environmental modification has been resorted to:

(a) 'widespread': encompassing an area on the scale of several hundred square kilometres;
(b) 'long-lasting': lasting for a period of months, or approximately a season;
(c) 'severe': involving serious or significant disruption or harm to human life, natural and economic resources or other assets.[48]

Active mitigation measures, especially the fragmentation method and in particular in case of failure, could bring about an 'environmental modification' in outer space or of the Earth tantamount to the criteria shown in the above-mentioned interpretation. The external criterion of an 'environmental modification' may be satisfied by a certain active mitigation measure, but the 'purpose' criterion would not be met since, if applied for the purpose of planetary defence, the mitigation measure would not be a case of "military or any other hostile use of environmental modification techniques" (Article I (1)). Thus, in conclusion, the ENMOD Convention does not add additional restrictions on planetary defence activities as this Convention is irrelevant to these activities.

---

46 As of 1 January 2020, 18 states are parties to the Moon Agreement.

47 The Convention on the Prohibition of Military or Any Other Hostile Use of Environmental Modification (adopted 10 December 1976, entered into force 5 October 1978) 1108 UNTS 151.

48 UNGA 'Report of the Conference of the Committee on Disarmament' UN GAOR 31st Session Supp No 27 UN Doc A/31/27 (1976) vol I 91.

Nevertheless, the protection and preservation of the outer space environment should be respected especially because the rapidly developing international environmental law will apply to active mitigation measuresin the context of planetary defence.

3.6 *The Permissible Scope of Active Mitigation Measures from the Moon and other Celestial Bodies*

Article IV(2) of the Outer Space Treaty explicitly imposes the obligation to use celestial bodies other than the Earth "exclusively for peaceful purposes". Depending on the interpretation of 'peaceful' as equating 'non-military' or 'non-aggressive', the legitimate scope of planetary defence may be different. There are differing views regarding whether the term 'exclusively' adds a certain meaning to the notion of 'peaceful' or not: one interpretation is that 'exclusively' changes the meaning of 'peaceful' from otherwise 'non-aggressive' to 'non-military'; the second is that with or without the addition 'exclusively', 'peaceful' means 'non-military'; and the third is that with or without 'exclusively', 'peaceful' means 'non-aggressive'. The latter two do not attach any importance to the term 'exclusively'.[49] Therefore, while the possibility is slim today due to technological limitations, military uses on celestial bodies other than those concretely prohibited could be conducted in the future, if the third interpretation allowing the 'non-aggressive' use of celestial bodies is applied.

The question is if the legal categorisation of active mitigation measures-would be affected depending on the interpretation of the phrase "exclusively for peaceful purposes". From only the external action, some active mitigation measures could be interpreted as military activity on celestial bodies, but nature and purpose of planetary defence could not conceptually place this activity under the category of military use. Likewise, even fragmentation methods used from celestial bodies could not be regarded as a military activity due to the purposes and nature of the activities.

In addition, even the interpretation prohibiting military uses would not necessarily make planetary defence activities conducted from celestial bodies unlawful, even if they might be regarded as being of a military nature, since the use of military personal, equipment and facilities for peaceful purposes are explicitly not forbidden under Article IV(2). Therefore, as long as mitigation

49 See e.g. Professor Vladimir Kopal's statement in 'Summary of Discussions' in IISL (ed), *Proceedings of the Tenth Colloquium on the Law of Outer Space* (AIAA 1968) 114; Bin Cheng, *Studies in International Space Law* (Clarendon Press 1997) 518–519; Alex Meyer, 'Interpretation of the Term "Peaceful" in the Light of the Space Treaty' in IISL (ed), *Proceedings of the Eleventh Colloquium on the Law of Outer Space* (AIAA 1969) 24–29.

measures do not involve the establishment of military bases, installations and fortifications, the testing of any type of weapons or the conduct of military manoeuvres they would not be prohibited under Article IV(2). Nevertheless, if planetary defence activities involve military personal and facilities as well as devices that could be used for belligerent purposes as much as they could be used for the purpose of planetary defence, this could lead to mistrust and tensions at the international level. This shows again that a multilateral approach to planetary defence would be preferred over a unilateral conduct of active mitigation measures.

4 Concluding Remarks

The findings of this chapter are as follows:

i) Any aspects of planetary defence activities and actions including active mitigation measures will not be in contravention of the prohibition of the threat or use of force under general international law embodied in Article 2(4) of the UN Charter.

ii) Article IV of the Outer Space Treaty, the Moon Agreement or the ENMOD Convention would not impose further restrictions on the conduct of planetary defence activities in addition to those in Article 2(4) of the UN Charter regarding the use of force, except for the prohibition of nuclear weapons or any other kinds of WMD in outer space. The issues of nuclear disarmament and non-proliferation are discussed in other chapters of this book.[50]

iii) Article III (observance of international law) and Article IX (cooperation and mutual assistance, due regard to the space activities of other states, avoidance of harmful contamination of outer space and of adverse changes in the environment of the Earth, and the obligation of international consultations in case of potentially harmful interference) of the Outer Space Treaty, however, may impose some restrictions on states concerning how to engage in planetary defence activities and actions. Rapidly developing international environmental law should be especially taken into consideration in this regard.

iv) Established rules of international law prohibit the 'threat or use of force' between sovereign states. However, the issue of a 'force' in a general

---

50 See chapters 15 'Legal Aspects of the Use of Nuclear Explosive Devices in Planetary Defence' and 16 'Nuclear Non-Proliferation and Planetary Defence: Competing Potential Disasters' in this book.

sense used against natural objects such as asteroids and periodic comets has not duly been addressed by international law.

v) It seems desirable that any legal lacunae found with regard to planetary defence activities and actions are remedied through rule-making for that purpose with special consideration for the building of an international mechanism for active mitigation measures as well as for enhancing transparency and confidence building measures among states. This will substantially lessen the potential problems pointed out in this chapter, which mostly stem from unilateral action.

Finally, it has to be added that issues of planetary defence should be dealt with in the framework of international law of disaster relief rather than international law of the use of force.

CHAPTER 15

Legal Aspects of the Use of Nuclear Explosive Devices in Planetary Defence

*David A Koplow**

1 Introduction

This chapter poses an arcane but important riddle for planetary defence: When is a 'weapon' not a 'weapon'? In particular, should a nuclear explosive device (NED) be legally characterised as a weapon when it is employed in space to attempt to alter the trajectory of an incoming asteroid? This question looms over the international law analysis of planetary defence, because critical space-related arms control treaties tightly regulate nuclear 'weapons' – and they routinely use, but maddeningly fail to define, the key terms that are essential for valid application of those provisions.

In the effort to provide greater clarity, this chapter first presents the legal context surrounding the possible application of a NED in space, focusing on the two treaties of greatest relevance: the 1967 Outer Space Treaty[1] and the 1963 Limited Test Ban Treaty.[2] It explains why those treaties' ambiguous use of terms like 'weapon' in their central prohibitions could become so problematic for planetary defence.

Next, the chapter analyses the question whether the treaties are best understood as applying fully to any exoatmospheric application of NEDs, regardless of the nomenclature or the participants' benign or legitimate motivations. It asserts, in short, that for purposes of these treaties, a nuclear weapon is always

* Professor of law at the Georgetown University Law Center, Washington DC. Previously, he also worked for and acted as consultant for the US Arms Control and Disarmament Agency, for the US Department of Defense, and for NASA. This chapter expresses his views exclusively in his private capacity.

1 Treaty on Principles Governing the Activities of States in the Exploration and Use of Outer Space, Including the Moon and Other Celestial Bodies (adopted 19 December 1966, entered into force 10 October 1967) 610 UNTS 205 (Outer Space Treaty).

2 Treaty Banning Nuclear Weapon Tests in the Atmosphere, in Outer Space and Under Water (adopted 5 August 1963, entered into force 10 October 1963) 480 UNTS 6964 (Limited Test Ban Treaty). This treaty is also known as the Partial Test Ban Treaty.

 | DOI:10.1163/9789004467606_017

a nuclear weapon, based upon its inherent nature, regardless of the specific, peaceful purpose to which advocates may apply it on any particular occasion.

After that initial assertion, however, the chapter proceeds to challenge that bottom line, by discussing other cognate situations in which the appropriate legal focus is not solely upon the inherent nature of a multi-capable space device, but in which a more deft interpretation also considers the intended or actual use. If we routinely use a 'purpose' analysis in construing these other types of possibly weapons-related activities under these treaties, why should we exclusively privilege the 'inherent nature' analysis when it comes to understanding NEDs in space?

Finally, the chapter concludes by sustaining the original, restrictive interpretation – although not with quite as much certainty as asserted in the initial appraisal. A NED must be characterised as a 'weapon' in order to preserve the object and purpose, and the sheer strategic and logical integrity, of space law and arms control law, even when the NED is being appropriately wielded for planetary defence. But upon mature reflection, it is a bit harder to justify the rigidity of that bottom line.

2 Space Law and Nuclear Weapons

As discussed elsewhere in this volume, a nuclear explosion would not be anyone's preferred tactic for dealing with an incoming asteroid.[3] Numerous other candidate devices and methodologies would very likely provide definitive advantages in terms of cost, safety, precision, and politics. But many of those other hypothetical contenders are unproven, and most would take a very long time to operate, becoming plausible only if we have decades of advance warning before an asteroid's impact. In many scenarios, especially if time is short and the threat is large, a NED would likely provide the most mature, tested technology, capable of efficiently applying enormous energy to quickly disrupt the target's trajectory.[4]

3 See, in particular, chapter 3 'Planetary Defence Technologies' in this book.

4 It might be something of an exaggeration to consider a NED to constitute a 'mature' technology in this application, since none has ever been used or tested as a device for modifying the flight path of an asteroid. However, in contrast to most of the other potential planetary defence concepts, nuclear explosions have been frequently undertaken; countries have conducted 2056 test explosions of nuclear devices in a variety of environments, including 20 detonations in the upper atmosphere or in outer space. Comprehensive Nuclear-Test-Ban Treaty Organization, 'Nuclear Testing: World Overview' (*CTBTO*) <www.ctbto.org/nuclear-testing/history-of-nuclear-testing/world-overview/> accessed 25 February 2021.

But uniquely among the contemplated planetary defence techniques, NEDs have been the subject of dedicated international law-making, restricting states' access to these awesome implements and confining the circumstances and locations in which they may be deployed and exercised. The two treaties identified above are discussed here; a third, the 1968 Nuclear Non-Proliferation Treaty,[5] is analysed in the next chapter.

The Outer Space Treaty is frequently characterised as a comprehensive prophylactic against the weaponisation of space, but in truth its actual scope is considerably narrower. The agreement's key military-related provisions are succinctly contained in just the five sentences of Article IV:

> States Parties to the Treaty undertake not to place in orbit around the Earth any objects carrying nuclear weapons or any other kinds of weapons of mass destruction, install such weapons on celestial bodies, or station such weapons in outer space in any other manner.
>
> The Moon and other celestial bodies shall be used by all States Parties to the Treaty exclusively for peaceful purposes. The establishment of military bases, installations and fortifications, the testing of any type of weapons and the conduct of military manoeuvres on celestial bodies shall be forbidden. The use of military personnel for scientific research or for any other peaceful purposes shall not be prohibited. The use of any equipment or facility necessary for peaceful exploration of the Moon and other celestial bodies shall also not be prohibited.

The Limited Test Ban Treaty is even more parsimonious; for present purposes, it is sufficient to quote only a portion of its Article I:

> Each of the Parties to this Treaty undertakes to prohibit, to prevent, and not to carry out any nuclear weapon test explosion, or any other nuclear explosion, at any place under its jurisdiction or control:
>
> (a) in the atmosphere; beyond its limits, including outer space; or under water, including territorial waters or high seas;

Both of these treaties are of critical importance to global security. President Lyndon Johnson rightly referred to the Outer Space Treaty as among the most

5 Treaty on the Non-Proliferation of Nuclear Weapons (adopted 1 July 1968, entered into force 5 March 1970) 729 UNTS 169 (Nuclear Non-Proliferation Treaty).

important arms control instruments concluded during the Cold War.[6] The Limited Test Ban Treaty is similarly prized as an enduring triumph in the hard-fought struggle for international peace and stability. Each treaty has attracted widespread adherence, being joined by the vast majority of countries in the world.[7]

At the same time, each treaty, reflecting the drafting style of its original era, is brief and fails to include any definitions of its key terms. Succeeding iterations of arms control agreements, in contrast, usually append copious definitions to assist (or to further confound) subsequent efforts to construe and apply their meanings.

Under the 1969 Vienna Convention on the Law of Treaties (the most widely-accepted authoritative source on treaty negotiation, drafting, implementation, and construction), "[a] treaty shall be interpreted in good faith in accordance with the ordinary meaning to be given to the terms of the treaty in their context and in the light of its object and purpose".[8] Unfortunately, as we shall see, that spare guidance offers little practical assistance in delving into the intended meaning of the crucial passages in the Outer Space Treaty and the Limited Test Ban Treaty.[9]

Moreover, the application of these pregnant passages to the possible future practice of planetary defence would be a question of first impression, not yet addressed in depth by courts, practitioners, or academics. The leading contemporary analysis comes from the 2020 report of the international Ad-Hoc Working Group on Legal Issues,[10] established, as discussed in other chapters,

---

6 Lyndon B Johnson, 'Public Papers of the Presidents of the United States, Lyndon B. Johnson' (GPO 1967) 1441.

7 The Limited Test Ban Treatyhas been joined by 125 parties and the Outer Space Treaty has been joined by 111 parties (as of January 2021). UN Office for Disarmament Affairs, 'Disarmament Treaties Database' <http://disarmament.un.org/treaties/>.

8 Article 31(1), Vienna Convention on the Law of Treaties (adopted 23 May 1969, entered into force 27 January 1980) 1155 UNTS 331. The Vienna Convention on the Law of Treaties also specifies that '[a] special meaning shall be given to a term if it is established that the parties so intended' (Article 31(4)). See Michael C Mineiro, 'FY-1C and USA-193 ASAT Intercepts: An Assessment of Legal Obligations under Article IX of the Outer Space Treaty' (2008) 34 Journal of Space Law 321 (discussing interpretation of the Outer Space Treaty).

9 ILC, 'Draft Articles on the Law of Treaties with Commentaries' (1966) UN Doc A/6309/Rev. 1, 217–23; Francis G Jacobs, 'Varieties of Approach to Treaty Interpretation: With Special Reference to the Draft Convention on the Law of Treaties Before the Vienna Diplomatic Conference' (1969) 18 International & Comparative Law Quarterly 318; Kenneth J Vandevelde, 'Treaty Interpretation from a Negotiator's Perspective' (1988) 21 Vanderbilt Journal of Transnational Law 281; American Law Institute, *Restatement of the Foreign Relations Law of the United States* (4th edn, American Law Institute Publishers 2018) 55–69.

10 Ad-Hoc Working Group on Legal Issues, 'Planetary Defence Legal Overview and Assessment' (SMPAG-RP-004, 8 April 2020).

to advise the Space Mission Planning Advisory Group (SMPAG) concerning the legal implications of planetary defence options.

A careful parsing of the first sentence of Article IV Outer Space Treaty reveals that the treaty bans three specific activities, each of which might potentially be relevant for planetary defence:

a) placing in Earth orbit a nuclear weapon (or other weapons of mass destruction (WMD));
b) installing such a weapon on a celestial body; and
c) stationing such a weapon in space in any other manner.

Placing in Earth orbit. Regarding the first element, placement in Earth orbit, most schemes for planetary defence would not rely upon this strategy; the preferred concept would usually be to try to intercept the incoming asteroid much further away from our home planet. While there might be, in some scenarios, a tactical benefit to temporarily locating the NED in Earth orbit, such as while assembling all the other elements of a large and lengthy space mission, that approach does not confer major advantages, and would not be essential.

In contrast, this proscription against orbital weapons does not prohibit a non-orbital 'transit' of space by a nuclear weapon. For example, a traditional intercontinental ballistic missile (ICBM) that carried its nuclear warfighting payload temporarily through space *en route* to its terrestrial target would not be barred, nor would a planetary defence mission that carried a nuclear explosive directly upward to the asteroid and detonated it there without achieving Earth orbit.[11]

Installing on a celestial body. The second element, the proscription against 'installing' a nuclear weapon on a celestial body, poses some interesting interpretive questions. At present, the leading planetary defence nuclear concepts contemplate a standoff explosion, detonating the device at some short distance from the asteroid.[12] The resulting deposit of energy would excite volatile molecules on the asteroid's surface; as they evaporate or sublimate, they

11 A NED contained in a system that achieved a 'partial' orbit of the Earth – going less than one full revolution of the planet – would not be covered by this provision of the Outer Space Treaty. The SALT II Treaty would have banned such fractional orbital weapon systems, but it never entered into force. Article IX 1(c), Treaty Between the United States of America and the Union of Soviet Socialist Republics on the Limitation of Strategic Offensive Arms (signed 18 June 1979). But see Kai-Uwe Schrogl and Julia Neumann, 'Article IV' in Stephan Hobe, Bernhard Schmidt-Tedd and Kai-Uwe Schrogl (eds), *Cologne Commentary on Space Law,* vol I (Carl Heymanns Verlag 2009) 79 (arguing that the Outer Space Treaty applies to a NED even on a partial orbit).

12 See chapter 3 'Planetary Defence Technologies' in this book.

would impart momentum to nudge the asteroid in the opposite direction. On the other hand, some alternative concepts could involve attempting to fracture the asteroid, by placing the nuclear device onto the asteroid's surface or even drilling it somewhat into the body's interior, where the explosive energy would be more efficiently coupled. If the device comes into direct and sustained contact with the asteroid (and especially if it is lowered into a borehole beneath the surface), it would seem to be 'installed', in contravention of the Outer Space Treaty.[13]

Stationing in space. Finally, the term 'station' in Article IV is particularly ambiguous, and the uncertainty is only magnified by the appended phrase "in any other manner". The concept of 'stationing' seems to imply a degree of permanence at a fixed place, rather than being transitory or temporary. However, in space, nothing is truly 'fixed' in location, except in relationship to other objects – everything is always travelling through space at high velocity.

A reasonable interpretation of this text would probably bar the placement of a NED in orbit around the Sun; perhaps it would also apply to any hypothesis for using, even temporarily, a Lagrange point (the specific locations where the gravitational pulls from two celestial bodies are in equipoise, allowing an object to linger indefinitely between them, with little expenditure of energy). Even more challenging would be a scenario in which a spacecraft transporting a NED were sent to rendezvous with a hazardous asteroid, and then to fly alongside it for a period of time, before detonating. (This might be the case, for example, if the concept of the operation was first to attempt to employ the spacecraft as a 'gravity tractor',[14] with the nuclear detonation being a fallback option in case that initial ploy failed.) There, the NED could be said to be 'stationed' in the corridor of the asteroid's flight path; it could be considered 'stationary' with respect to the asteroid, even while both were flying through space at enormous speed.

Each of these three passages thus poses its ambiguities as well as its prohibitions. A reasonably confident assessment could be that the Outer Space Treaty prohibits the carriage of a nuclear weapon in certain trajectories (i.e. in Earth orbit or perhaps on a sustained parallel flight path with the asteroid) or in certain applications (installation on the asteroid). But what is probably the most likely planetary defence scenario – a direct ascent of the nuclear

13 We could also ask whether the placement of a nuclear device onto the surface of the asteroid would constitute the establishment of a military 'installation' there, in contravention of the second paragraph of Article IV Outer Space Treaty.

14 See chapter 3 'Planetary Defence Technologies' in this book.

explosive, with a prompt detonation when it intersects the asteroid – would not be barred by Article IV.[15]

The Limited Test Ban Treaty, in contrast, incorporates a very different linguistic formula. That treaty directs its attention to the *use* of the nuclear device (prohibiting an 'explosion'), rather than to its deployment trajectory or its placement in any particular physical location. The Limited Test Ban Treaty is quite categorical in this respect, outlawing not only a nuclear weapon test explosion but also "any other nuclear explosion" in specified environments "including outer space".[16] For the Limited Test Ban Treaty's 125 parties (notably not including France, China, or North Korea),[17] the conduct of a nuclear detonation in space, even for a salutary planetary defence mission, is categorically ruled out.[18]

15 Note, however, as discussed below, that the second paragraph of Article IV prohibits "testing" any type of weapon on a celestial body. Therefore, while the employment of a NED in the direct ascent mode would be permissible in an *operational* planetary defence mission, ironically the experimental *testing* of that mission concept, in order to develop and improve the operational capacity, would be banned.

16 If a NED were emplaced deep inside the asteroid for a planetary defence mission, it would still be considered to be 'in space', rather than underground, and thereby banned under the Limited Test Ban Treaty. Even if such a detonation were somehow deemed to be legally 'underground', it would still be prohibited by the Limited Test Ban Treaty because it 'causes radioactive debris to be present outside the territorial limits of the State under whose jurisdiction or control such explosion is conducted' (Article I 1(b), Limited Test Ban Treaty).

17 It may be possible to argue that the key provisions of the Limited Test Ban Treaty have become customary international law, thereby binding even on non-parties to the treaty, but that inquiry is beyond the scope of this chapter.

18 The Comprehensive Nuclear-Test-Ban Treaty (adopted 10 September 1996, not yet in force) 35 ILM 1439, would prohibit all nuclear explosions anywhere, including in space. It has been signed by 185 countries, but has not yet entered into force, because it requires the ratification by forty-four designated states, eight of which have not done so, see CTBTO, 'Status of Signature and Ratification' <www.ctbto.org/the-treaty/status-of-signature-and-ratification/> accessed 25 February 2021. Under the Vienna Convention on the Law of Treaties, signatories of the Comprehensive Nuclear-Test-Ban Treaty are nonetheless already prohibited from undertaking activities that "would defeat the object and purpose of a treaty" prior to its entry into force (Article 18, Vienna Convention on the Law of Treaties). The UN Security Council has asserted that a nuclear explosion by a signatory would do so, and is therefore already banned, see UNSC Res 2310 (23 September 2016) UN Doc S/Res/2310.

3 Definition of a 'Weapon'

Returning now to the text of the Outer Space Treaty, it is crucial to recall that the key passage of Article IV applies the prohibitions to "nuclear weapons or any other kinds of weapons of mass destruction". Does that phrase embrace a NED[19] that would be a component of a planetary defence mission? Or is it possible to argue that where the device is intended and actually used for a peaceful, non-military, non-aggressive mission, it no longer fits the description of a 'weapon', so the Outer Space Treaty is simply irrelevant?

This is a plausible stance. In common parlance, the term 'weapon' is typically understood as a tool of hostility, wielded for warlike, criminal, or other unfriendly purposes, to injure human beings and to damage or destroy their property for mercenary reasons.[20] A NED for planetary defence, on the other hand, would be beneficial for all of humanity; it would save lives and protect property, not the opposite. It would be applied against a force of nature, not against humans and their artifacts, and would be motivated by generosity and safety, not by a desire for conquest.[21] The planetary defence mission might be undertaken by one leading state or by several in concert, but it would not be aimed against any state or population; there is no 'enemy' in its application.

In this connection, we can observe that many implements are susceptible of multiple applications – a particular tool might sometimes be characterised

19 In the effort to avoid prematurely prejudicing the debate, this chapter refers to these instruments with the neutral term 'nuclear explosive devices'. As discussed below, however, many authorities would reject that euphemism and insist on calling them nuclear 'weapons' or 'bombs', based upon the lack of inherent physical differences between items intended for different types of purposes.

20 Dictionary definitions sometimes emphasise the actual or intended use of the item for specified purposes, but sometimes focus on the item's inherent capability for being applied in those ways. Oxford English Dictionary, 'Weapon' ("An instrument of any kind used in warfare or in combat to attack and overcome an enemy") www.oed.com/view/Entry/226597 accessed 25 February 2021; Merriam-Webster, 'Weapon' ("something (such as a club, knife, or gun) used to injure, defeat, or destroy") <www.merriam-webster.com/dictionary/weapon> accessed 25 February 2021; US Legal Dictionary, 'Weapon Law and Legal Definition' ("A weapon is generally something used to injure, defeat, or destroy and may cover many types of instruments [including when] used or intended to be used in a club") <https://definitions.uslegal.com/w/weapon/> accessed 25 February 2021; The Law Dictionary, 'Weapon' ("An instrument used in fighting; an instrument of offensive or defensive combat") <https://thelawdictionary.org/weapon/> accessed 25 February 2021.

21 Some might suggest that the better analogy here would be to a barrier system, such as a trench, moat, or wall that was constructed in order to protect a site or a community from an enemy attack (or from a natural disaster, such as a flood). Even if the device served a military function, we do not commonly think of these as 'weapons'.

as a weapon and sometimes not, depending upon its immediate application. A knife is properly conceived as a weapon when it is used to stab someone, but not when it is used to slice an apple. A hammer is most often not a weapon, but it can certainly become a weapon when a miscreant brandishes it while making malevolent threats. An explosive such as dynamite can be used by an army to destroy an enemy facility (weapon) or by a mining company to excavate coal (non-weapon).[22]

In the same vein, perhaps a NED is a weapon, and is properly subject to the restrictions in Article IV Outer Space Treaty, only when it is employed to threaten or damage another state or population, but the same NED is not a weapon, and escapes the treaty's regulation, when it is used exclusively for the peaceful, humanity-protecting mission of planetary defence.[23]

The SMPAG Ad-Hoc Working Group on Legal Issues concluded, however, that any such interpretation is inadmissible, and I have elsewhere agreed.[24] The proper reading of the Outer Space Treaty – the rendering most consistent with the object and purpose of the treaty – would be to apply Article IV to all nuclear explosive devices, regardless of their avowed peaceful purpose and application. A nuclear explosive is inherently a weapon, even if it could be devoted to a non-hostile purpose; this treaty should be understood to apply permanently to all such devices in the regulated environments.

Any looser, more permissive interpretation of Article IV would allow facile circumvention of the treaty. A party could proclaim that it was placing a NED in Earth orbit not as a weapon to threaten or damage its adversaries in war, but merely for a planetary defence contingency. Even if no threatening asteroid

---

22 Even closer to the concerns of this volume, there is an indelible crossover between the technology and hardware necessary for a space launch (including for a planetary defence operation) and that of a long-range ballistic missile.

23 Note that international authorities have differentiated between a nuclear weapon and the use of nuclear fission for generating power, including for satellites. A nuclear chain reaction that is controlled is not a weapon. Principles Relevant to the Use of Nuclear Power Sources in Space, UNGA Res 47/68 (14 December 1992); Kai-Uwe Schrogl and Julia Neumann, 'Article IV' in Stephan Hobe, Bernhard Schmidt-Tedd and Kai-Uwe Schrogl (eds) *Cologne Commentary on Space Law,* vol I (Carl Heymanns Verlag 2009) 76.

24 Ad-Hoc Working Group on Legal Issues to SMAPG, 'Planetary Defence Legal Overview and Assessment' (SMPAG-RP-004, 8 April 2020) 27–34; David A Koplow, 'Exoatmospheric Plowshares: Using a Nuclear Explosive Device for Planetary Defense Against an Incoming Asteroid' (2019) 23 UCLA Journal of International Law and Foreign Affairs 76. See also Kai-Uwe Schrogl and Julia Neumann, 'Article IV' in Stephan Hobe, Bernhard Schmidt-Tedd and Kai-Uwe Schrogl (eds) *Cologne Commentary on Space Law,* vol I (Carl Heymanns Verlag 2009) 76–77; Bryce G Poole, 'Against the Nuclear Option: Planetary Defence Under International Law' (2020) 45 Air & Space Law 1, 55–80.

were presently on the horizon, the cynical state might argue that we need to be prepared, including by pre-positioning the NED (or several of them) in space where they could be quickly dispatched to intercept a sudden incoming hazard. Any such deployment, however, would wreck the Outer Space Treaty; it would lead to a cascade of nuclear weapons in space, all masquerading as planetary defence devices, until some state suddenly decided to use them for war. At a time when the security and stability of the space regime are already imperilled in new and more dangerous ways, it is vital that legal analysis avoid providing yet another excuse for churning the next cycle in the space arms race.[25]

Unfortunately, the negotiating record (*travaux préparatoires*) and the contemporaneous public statements by participating states offer little illumination here. They assert, unambiguously, that the Outer Space Treaty was designed to foreclose an arms race in space and to preserve space as a region free from the spectre of nuclear competition – 'no bombs in orbit' was the mantra.[26] But citation to those materials mostly just begs the question: was the treaty designed to prohibit all nuclear explosive devices from space, or only those that were intended for use as weapons?[27]

The International Court of Justice has noted that "nuclear weapons are explosive devices whose energy results from the fusion or fission of the atom".[28]

---

25 US Defense Intelligence Agency, 'Challenges to Security in Space' (2019) 7; Brian Weeden and Victoria Samson (eds), *Global Counterspace Capabilities: An Open Source Assessment* (Secure World Foundation 2020); Todd Harrison and others, 'Space Threat Assessment 2020' (Center for Strategic and International Studies 2020) 19; Steve Lambakis, 'Foreign Space Capabilities: Implications for US National Security' (National Institute for Public Policy 2017) 75; Russ Read, 'Pentagon official: Threats to US space systems "at an all-time high" ' *Washington Examiner* (Washington D.C. 26 April 2019) para 6.

26 US Senate Committee on Foreign Relations, 'Treaty on Outer Space, Hearings before the Senate Committee on Foreign Relations, March 7, 13, and April 12, 1967' (GPO 1967) 8, 22, 34, 79–84, 90–91, 114 (emphasising the Outer Space Treaty principle of 'no bombs in orbit' and the goal of avoiding an arms race in space).

27 The second paragraph of Article IV Outer Space Treaty specifies that the Moon and other celestial bodies shall be used 'exclusively for peaceful purposes'. But that provision is not helpful here as an additional interpretive guide, because: a) it applies only to the use of celestial bodies, not to activities undertaken in the void of space, even if aimed at a celestial body; and b) the leading interpretation of the term 'peaceful' is that it prohibits only 'aggressive' activities, while allowing non-aggressive military behaviour. Kai-Uwe Schrogl and Julia Neumann, 'Article IV' in Stephan Hobe, Bernhard Schmidt-Tedd and Kai-Uwe Schrogl (eds) *Cologne Commentary on Space Law,* vol I (Carl Heymanns Verlag 2009) 82–84; Francis Lyall and Paul B Larsen, *Space Law: A Treatise* (2nd edn, Routledge 2018) 468–69.

28 *The Legality of the Threat or Use of Nuclear Weapons* (Advisory Opinion) [1996] ICJ Rep 226, 35.

This commentary, from the court's famous 1996 Advisory Opinion regarding the legality of the threat or use of nuclear weapons, does not mention the purpose or application of the device, nor does it quite assert that every device meeting those criteria automatically qualifies as a weapon – so perhaps this passage should not be read in context as a definitive judgment that a nuclear bomb is permanently a bomb.

Definition of 'Weapon' in Other Treaties. Perhaps some traction could be gained here by comparing other arms control treaties' usage of the vocabulary of weaponry; unfortunately, that research, too, provides little illumination. Probably the most pointed contribution comes from the 1967 Treaty of Tlatelolco, which created the Latin American nuclear weapons free zone. Article 5 there defines a nuclear weapon as "any device which is capable of releasing nuclear energy in an uncontrolled manner and which has a group of characteristics that are appropriate for use for warlike purposes".[29] That formulation would seem to capture a NED used for planetary defence, unless perhaps the device's 'group of characteristics' were somehow significantly modified to make it inappropriate for use in hostilities.

Another point of comparison comes from the draft treaty proposed over the past several years by Russia and China to prohibit the placement of weapons in space. This enterprise has not commanded wide international support, but it does suggest a definition of the to-be-banned devices, applying to any "outer space object or its component produced or converted to eliminate, damage or disrupt normal functioning of objects in outer space, on the Earth's surface or in the air, as well as to eliminate population, components of biosphere important to human existence, or to inflict damage to them by using any principles of physics".[30]

Under customary usage, an 'object' in space usually denotes something human-made, in contrast to a naturally-occurring 'celestial body', so the key part of this definition would seem not to characterise a planetary defence device as a 'weapon', since it would be aimed at an asteroid. The rest of the definition simply re-frames our central question, whether a NED that was 'produced' to damage objects or populations on the surface of the Earth (as all

29 Article 5, Treaty for the Prohibition of Nuclear Weapons in Latin America and the Caribbean (adopted 14 February 1967, entered into force 22 April 1968) 634 UNTS 326 (Treaty of Tlatelolco).

30 Article 1(b), Draft Treaty on the Prevention of the Placement of Weapons in Outer Space and of the Threat or Use of Force Against Outer Space Objects (submitted 10 June 2014) CD/1985.

nuclear weapons were) can be recharacterised if it is 'converted' to a different application.

Other instruments of international law and commentary may likewise be regarded as suggestive, but hardly dispositive, in their specification of weapons (or of related concepts such as means or methods of warfare).[31] Overall, international legal authorities have observed that neither space law nor the law of armed conflict provides an authoritative, all-purpose definition of weapon sufficient to guide our understanding of a planetary defence NED under the Outer Space Treaty.[32]

---

31 Jeffrey T Biller and Michael N Schmitt, 'Classification of Cyber Capabilities and Operations as Weapons, Means, or Methods of Warfare' (2019) 95 International Law Studies 179, 195–202 (analysing the definition of 'weapon' under several international legal instruments, for possible application to cyber activities); David P Fidler, 'Cyber Capabilities Are Not Weapons of War? A Closer Look at the Analogy to Biological Weapons' (*Council of Foreign Relations Blog*, 23 July 2019) <www.cfr.org/blog/cyber-capabilities-weapons-war-closer-look-biological-weapons> accessed 25 February 2021.

32 Numerous authorities provide their own definitions of weapon, which may be useful in the abstract or in the particular context of a specified instrument, but do not shed much light on the particular context of Article IV Outer Space Treaty.

The Weapons Law Encyclopedia, produced by the Geneva Academy of International Humanitarian Law and Human Rights, concluded that "[t]here is no definition of a weapon under international law", but provided a "working definition" of a "device that is constructed, adapted, or used to kill, injure, disorient, or threaten a person or to inflict damage on a physical object", see Geneva Academy of International Humanitarian Law and Human Rights, 'Weapon' (*Weapons Law Encyclopedia*, 30 November 2013) <www.weaponslaw.org/glossary/weapon> accessed 25 February 2021. Note that by totally omitting any reference to the purpose of the device, this definition ('inflict damage on a physical object') would include clearly non-weapons such as a trash compactor, a surgeon's scalpel, or a fireplace.

The 2013 HPCR Manual on International Law Applicable to Air and Missile Warfare defines a weapon as "a means of warfare used in combat operations (…) that is capable of causing either (i) injury to, or death of, persons; or (ii) damage to, or destruction of, objects". The accompanying Commentary asserts that the "essence of a weapon is that it is an object used to cause" those effects – i.e. focusing on the actual use of the item, rather than its capabilities. But the Commentary also concludes "[w]hile it is true that almost any object can constitute a weapon in particular circumstances (…) as used in this Manual, the term weapon refers to those objects which are designed to be used as a means of attack" – i.e. focusing on the 'design' of the item. Program on Humanitarian Policy and Conflict Research at Harvard University, *HPCR Manual on International Law Applicable to Air and Missile Warfare* (Cambridge University Press 2013) 49–50.

US Air Force Instruction 51–401 defines weapon as "a device designed to kill, injure, disable or temporarily incapacitate people or destroy, damage, disable or temporarily incapacitate property or materiel", see US Air Force, 'Air Force Instruction 51–401, The Law of War' (3 August 2018) 13. This definition focuses on the original design of the item, rather than its ultimate application.

Peaceful Nuclear Explosives. It is instructive to recall here that at the time of negotiation of the Outer Space Treaty and the Limited Test Ban Treaty there was considerable international enthusiasm for the notion of 'peaceful nuclear explosions' (PNEs). These programs would employ the fierce power of nuclear detonations for civil engineering, such as to deepen a harbour, stimulate oil and gas production, or excavate an underground storage chamber. There was sustained international interest in these applications, but they were ultimately abandoned, largely due to considerations of cost and environmental safety.[33] In addition, the crossover between peaceful and weapons applications was manifest, too – a PNE device would be largely indistinguishable from a nuclear weapon, and any use of a PNE could generate data equivalent to that of a weapon test. Any treaties that undertook to restrict nuclear weapons testing, therefore, also had to impose parallel restrictions on PNEs, lest states evade the prohibitions via tests conducted in the guise of benign explosions.[34] For example, this is a large part of the reason why the Limited Test Ban Treaty

33 Comprehensive Nuclear-Test-Ban Treaty Organization 'Peaceful Nuclear Explosions' <www.ctbto.org/nuclear-testing/history-of-nuclear-testing/peaceful-nuclear-explosions/> accessed 25 February 2021 (noting that approximately seven percent of the world's nuclear explosions were conducted for peaceful purposes); World Nuclear Association, 'Peaceful Nuclear Explosions' (December 2018) <www.world-nuclear.org/information-library/non-power-nuclear-applications/industry/peaceful-nuclear-explosions.aspx> accessed 25 February 2021; Thomas Gaulkin, 'Things You Shouldn't Nuke' (*Bulletin of the Atomic Scientists*, 27 August 2019) <https://thebulletin.org/2019/08/things-you-shouldnt-nuke/> accessed 25 February 2021.

34 In the 1970s, the United States and the Soviet Union concluded two treaties to regulate the size of their underground nuclear explosions: one dealt with tests of nuclear weapons and the other imposed comparable restrictions on the use of PNEs. Treaty on the Limitation of Underground Nuclear Weapon Tests (adopted 3 July 1974, entered into force 11 December 1990) 1714 UNTS 217; Treaty on Underground Nuclear Explosions for Peaceful Purposes (adopted 28 May 1976, entered into force 11 December 1990) 1714 UNTS 387. See also US Department of State, 'Treaty Between the United States of America and the Union of Soviet Socialist Republics on Underground Nuclear Explosions for Peaceful Purposes (and Protocol Thereto)' <https://1997-2001.state.gov/www/global/arms/treaties/pne1.html> accessed 25 February 2021 (observing that "there is no essential distinction between the technology of a nuclear explosive device which would be used as a weapon and the technology of a nuclear explosive device used for a peaceful purpose"). The Comprehensive Nuclear-Test-Ban Treaty, like the Limited Test Ban Treaty, governs both nuclear weapon test explosions and "any other nuclear explosion", thereby effectively banning PNEs. The Comprehensive Nuclear-Test-Ban Treaty does contemplate the possibility that an amendment could be implemented in the future in order to allow nuclear explosions for peaceful purposes – but only underground, and only if a way could somehow be found to preclude any military benefits (Article I, VIII.1, Comprehensive Nuclear-Test-Ban Treaty).

punctiliously addresses both the category of "nuclear weapon test explosion" and also "any other nuclear explosion".

In any event, there is no record of consideration in the 1960s and 1970s of any possible use of PNEs in space, and certainly no discussion about how the Outer Space Treaty might apply to them in a planetary defence scenario. Today, the crossover problem is even more pronounced, because any NED that might be used for a planetary defence mission would, in fact, be a nuclear weapon that would have to be withdrawn from a national weapon stockpile (or from an inventory of previously retired weapons).[35] There are no true, dedicated PNE devices available to be used for planetary defence, even if there could be some characteristics that might in principle differentiate a PNE device from a weapon. Moreover, in each relevant country, there is only a small number of facilities that design, test and construct nuclear devices, so those activities would, once again, be indistinguishable as between weapons and PNE devices.

Finally, it should be noted that the drafters of the Limited Test Ban Treaty were notably more successful in foreclosing non-weapons applications than were the drafters of the Outer Space Treaty. The Limited Test Ban Treaty comprehensively addresses both weapon tests and 'any other' nuclear explosions. In contrast, the Outer Space Treaty could have, but did not, extend its prohibitions to embrace "nuclear weapons, any other kinds of weapons of mass destruction, *and any other nuclear explosive devices*". The negotiators of the Outer Space Treaty should certainly have been aware of the tighter formula in the Limited Test Ban Treaty, which was concluded only a few years previously; perhaps their failure to incorporate mirroring language could be construed as a deliberate choice to keep the door ajar for spaceborne PNEs.[36]

---

35 See US Government Accountability Office, 'Actions Needed by NNSA to Clarify Dismantlement Performance Goal' (GAO 14-449, GAO 2014) 40–41 (reporting that the US government is delaying the dismantlement of excess nuclear weapons, in order to retain some for possible use in planetary defence); Patrick E Tyler, 'Chinese Seek Atom Option to Fend Off Asteroids' *New York Times* (New York, 27 April 1996) 4 (reporting Chinese resistance to joining the Comprehensive Nuclear-Test-Ban Treaty, due to a desire to retain the option of using a NED as a PNE device for planetary defence).

36 Note that some might argue that Article IV Outer Space Treaty applies only to a nuclear weapon that is simultaneously a weapon of mass destruction, thereby omitting a nuclear explosive device that caused only small, localised effects, or that was not employed as a weapon. But that interpretation is inconsistent with the syntax of the Article as well as with the negotiators' intentions. Kai-Uwe Schrogl and Julia Neumann, 'Article IV' in Stephan Hobe, Bernhard Schmidt-Tedd and Kai-Uwe Schrogl (eds) *Cologne Commentary on Space Law*, vol I (Carl Heymanns Verlag 2009) 76.

4 Why Should We Emphasise Inherent Nature rather than Intended Application?

As noted, the report of the SMPAG Ad-Hoc Working Group on Legal Issues determined that a nuclear weapon is inherently and permanently a weapon, regardless of the nobler applications to which it might be put – for purposes of the Outer Space Treaty, it is the object's nature, rather than its intended application, that is dispositive. This section asks anew why that should be so – especially since in other instances regarding heralded space activities, we do look to the actual or intended purpose of an item or activity in order to assess its legal status.

Three instances, all drawn from widely celebrated current, recent, or proposed space operations, illustrate the conundrum. In each, a dual-capable activity or device that looks and sounds a lot like a weapon has been (or will be) applied for welcomed scientific purposes. And in each, compatibility with Article IV Outer Space Treaty has never been seriously challenged.

We begin by noting that the first sentence of Article IV Outer Space Treaty does not apply to non-nuclear, non-WMD weapons; they may lawfully be placed into orbit, installed on celestial bodies, and stationed in space. But the third sentence does impose restrictions, specifically prohibiting "the testing of any type of weapons" on a celestial body. Do the following prominent, peaceful activities escape that coverage?[37]

A standard maxim of legal interpretation holds that, when a particular word (such as 'weapon') is used at multiple places in a document, it should carry the same meaning in each instance, unless a contrary intention is manifest. Here, the second paragraph of Article IV Outer Space Treaty is, if anything, even more inclusive than the first paragraph, because the second paragraph includes the intensifying phrase 'any type of'. We might further suggest that the repeated usage of the same word should naturally invoke the same style of interpretation in each paragraph of the treaty – but that consistency does not seem to be applied in the following three instances.

DART. The first example to consider arises from NASA's forthcoming Double Asteroid Redirection Test (DART) mission, slated to be launched in 2021. There, an advanced spacecraft will intercept the large near-Earth asteroid Didymos and the smaller moonlet asteroid (about 160 meters across) that orbits approximately 1 km around it. The spacecraft will then crash into the moonlet at 6,6

37 The term 'test' includes both activities undertaken to assess the functioning of the weapon and activities designed to gauge the weapon's effects on a target. All of the activities described in this section are therefore properly characterised as tests.

km/sec, providing the first operational test of the kinetic impactor concept for planetary defence. It is anticipated that the collision will alter the speed of the moonlet by less than one percent, but that effect will measurably perturb its trajectory around Didymos.[38]

DART is appropriately heralded as an essential trial for the development of a critical planetary defence methodology, but how do we know that it is not also "the testing of any type of weapons … on celestial bodies", forbidden by Article IV? A kinetic impact, after all, is a well-considered weapon technique in space; it is the favoured testing algorithm for attacking satellites in orbit as well as for destroying incoming ballistic missile warheads. Under current and evolving technology, the leading concept for defeating an enemy's space object is simply to ram your own space object into it at high speed – four countries have successfully tested weapons for accomplishing precisely that.[39]

DART is surely a 'test', and it occurs on a celestial body. The crucial difference has to lie in the *purpose* of the activity: DART is a scientific exploration of a planetary defence technique, not undertaken for weapons applications. While the physical manifestations are similar to weapons, and some of the applied technologies might be suitable for crossover into military functions, it is the purpose, not the inherent nature of the activity, that is deemed dispositive here.

Hayabusa2. A second illustration would come from the ongoing Hayabusa2 mission, launched by Japan in 2014, to rendezvous with and explore the asteroid Ryugu. A key aspect of this engagement is to gather samples from on and beneath the surface of the asteroid, for return to Earth in late 2020. To facilitate the retrieval of surface samples, Hayabusa2 fired a 5-gram tantalum projectile (widely characterised in media accounts as a 'bullet') at 300 m/sec into the surface, to kick up particles that were then collected by a lander. To generate the desired buried samples, on 5 April 2019, Hayabusa2 released an impactor that fired a 2.5 kg copper slug (popularly called a 'bomb'), powered by the

38 NASA Planetary Defense Coordination Office, 'Double Asteroid Redirection Test (DART) Mission' (29 June 2020) <www.nasa.gov/planetarydefense/dart> accessed 25 February 2021; NASA, 'NASA's First Planetary Defense Technology Demonstration to Collide with Asteroid in 2022' (6 May 2019) <www.nasa.gov/feature/nasa-s-first-planetary-defense-technology-demonstration-to-collide-with-asteroid-in-2022> accessed 25 February 2021.

39 Brian Weeden and Victoria Samson (eds), *Global Counterspace Capabilities: An Open Source Assessment* (Secure World Foundation 2020); Todd Harrison and others, *Space Threat Assessment 2020* (Center for Strategic and International Studies, 30 March 2020); Ajey Lele, 'The Implications of India's ASAT Test' (*The Space Review*, 1 April 2019) <www.thespacereview.com/article/3686/1> accessed 25 February 2021.

detonation of 4.5 kg of shaped plastic explosive, suddenly excavating a crater 10 metres in diameter.[40]

Obviously, these Hayabusa2 activities, undertaken in other circumstances, would easily be characterised as weapons, and their testing on a celestial body would be barred.[41] Shooting projectiles at targets, detonating explosives, and blowing up terrain are familiar military functions. Again, however, the world community has readily, albeit implicitly, categorised these programs as scientific experiments, undertaken for valid research purposes, and consistent with the Outer Space Treaty.[42]

---

40 Mike Wall, 'Pow! Japan's Hayabusa2 Bombs Asteroid Ryugu to Make a Crater' (*Space.com*, 5 April 2019) <www.space.com/hayabusa2-bombs-asteroid-ryugu-photo.html> accessed 25 February 2021; Meghan Bartels, 'Touchdown! Incredible Photos Show 2nd Asteroid Landing by Japan's Hayabusa2' (*Space.com*, 11 July 2019) <www.space.com/incredible-asteroid-ryugu-landing-photos-japan-hayabusa2.html> accessed 25 February 2021.

41 Article 9 of the Japanese Constitution imposes stark limits on the country's military activities, including a renunciation of the recourse to war, and restrictions upon the possession of offensive weapons and the conduct of extraterritorial military operations. The interpretation and implementation of these limits have been quite controversial, but have not impeded the Hayabusa2 activities.

42 Several other space missions have adopted similar profiles. The 2005 NASA Deep Impact mission fired a 370 kg copper slug into the comet Tempel 1 at 10 ks/sec, with a force equivalent to five tons of TNT, blasting a 150 metre crater. NASA JPL, 'Mission to Comet Tempel 1, Deep Impact' (*NASA JPL Center for Near Earth Object Studies*, 18 October 2016) <www.jpl.nasa.gov/missions/deep-impact/> accessed 25 February 2021. Similarly, the 2009 Lunar Crater Observation and Sensing Satellite (LCROSS) slammed two large masses into a crater near the moon's south pole, in order to kick up plumes of ejecta that might reveal the presence of water. These impacts (often cited in the media as 'bombing the moon') carried a force equivalent to tons of TNT and created craters several meters across. Pete Spotts, 'NASA Moon bombing: Did NASA Really Drop a Bomb on the Moon?' *Christian Science Monitor* (Massachusetts, 9 October 2009); John Matson, 'Collateral Data: NASA's Planned Moon Crash Churned Up Water, Lots of Mercury and More' (*Scientific American*, 22 October 2010) <www.scientificamerican.com/article/lcross-mission-results/> accessed 25 February 2021. Employing other types of weapon-related technologies, NASA's OSIRIS-REx mission (launched in 2016) is intended to shoot nitrogen gas onto the surface of the asteroid Bennu, to spray samples into a collector for return to Earth. That technology could perhaps be regarded as not too different from that involved in dispersing a chemical weapon, but again, the purpose is very different. NASA, 'NASA's OSIRIS-REx Asteroid Sample Return Mission' <www.nasa.gov/sites/default/files/atoms/files/osiris_rex_factsheet5-9.pdf> accessed 25 February 2021. The Mars 2020 Rover is equipped with a high powered laser (with obvious weapons applications) to blast rocks from a safe distance in order to assess their chemical composition. NASA JPL, 'Mars 2020 Rover Gets a Super Instrument' (*NASA JPL Center for Near Earth Object Studies*, 2 July 2019) <www.jpl.nasa.gov/news/news.php?feature=7443> accessed 25 February 2021.

ARM. Finally, a third enterprise was NASA's 2013 proposed Asteroid Redirect Mission (ARM), which would have landed on some large near-Earth asteroid, employed anchoring grippers to grasp a 4-metre multi-ton boulder from its surface, and then transported the rock intact into a stable lunar orbit for more leisurely study and exploitation. The mission was cancelled in 2017, but other conceits persist for someday capturing an asteroid and relocating it for commercial mining.[43]

Again, the similarity with space weapons programs is evident: US security experts have sounded alarms about possible emerging hostile Russian anti-satellite weapons (ASAT) capabilities featuring an ability to rendezvous with another state's satellite, inspect it in proximity, and damage or capture it.[44] ARM would resemble some of those functions; the key distinction is the legitimate scientific purpose of the test mission, as contrasted with a military operation.

In sum, it is principally the intended purpose or the actual application of the technology that differentiates these peaceful scientific and planetary defence experiments from hostile weapons-related tests banned under Article IV Outer Space Treaty. Pursuit of the ability to crash into a target, to fire projectiles at it, or to seize and relocate it is equivocal – such capacities could be turned to either planetary defence or ASAT applications. Indeed, at the most general level, observers such as Carl Sagan have long apprehended that the capacity to divert an incoming asteroid away from Earth could also be bent in a malevolent direction, to deliberately steer a celestial body toward Earth, to inflict unprecedented damage on an enemy state.[45]

---

43 NASA JPL, 'Asteroid Redirect Robotic Mission' (*NASA JPL Center for Near Earth Object Studies*, 18 December 2018) <www.jpl.nasa.gov/missions/asteroid-redirect-robotic-mission-arrm/> accessed 25 February 2021; John Brophy and others, 'Asteroid Retrieval Feasibility Study' (Keck Institute for Space Studies, 2 April 2012) <https://kiss.caltech.edu/final_reports/Asteroid_final_report.pdf> accessed 25 February 2021; Jeff Foust, 'Planetary Resources Believes Asteroid Mining Has Come of Age' (*The Space Review*, 30 April 2012) <www.thespacereview.com/article/2074/1> accessed 25 February 2021.

44 Brian Weeden and Victoria Samson (eds), *Global Counterspace Capabilities: An Open Source Assessment* (Secure World Foundation 2020) 2.1-2.30; Todd Harrison and others, 'Space Threat Assessment 2019' (Center for Strategic and International Studies, March 2020) 19–28; Theresa Hitchens, 'The Stellar Dance: US, Russia Satellites Make Potentially Risky Close Approaches' (*Breaking Defense*, 10 April 2019) <https://breakingdefense.com/2019/04/the-stellar-dance-us-russia-satellites-make-potentially-risky-close-approaches/> accessed 25 February 2021 (discussing the danger of highly manoeuvrable ASAT weapons that could approach, inspect, damage, or seize another state's satellite).

45 Carl Sagan, *Pale Blue Dot: A Vision of the Human Future in Space* (Random House 1994) 318–26. An effort to commandeer an asteroid in order to attack an enemy would convert the putative planetary defence mission into a hostile military operation, and

What distinguishes the forbidden from the permitted space technologies under the tenets of space law and arms control law is therefore not always something inherent in the device or activity itself – any of these examples could be characterised as weapons or otherwise, depending upon their purpose. Why, then, should we treat NEDs differently – why do we say that in that instance, it is the inherent nature of the mechanism that exclusively governs?

5 Bottom Line: Preserving the Outer Space Treaty

As noted, the touchstone for treaty interpretation under the Vienna Convention on the Law of Treaties is the commitment to preserving and promoting the 'object and purpose' of the treaty. Unfortunately, the text of the Outer Space Treaty itself provides too little guidance here; the treaty-makers simply did not contemplate anything like the concept that a NED might someday be necessary for planetary defence, even while they strove to guard against the imminent weaponisation of space. The SMPAG Ad-Hoc Working Group on Legal Issues concluded that the better reading of Article IV is to ban NEDs (at least in the three modes of orbiting Earth, installing on a celestial body, or stationing in space), and this chapter concurs.

The bottom line is that nuclear weapons (and other WMD) must be treated differently from other types of devices, systems, and activities under the Outer Space Treaty because nuclear weapons themselves are inherently different – they are so much more powerful, and so much more threatening to global peace and security. The treaty drafters were seized with those distinctions and legislated a special regime for nuclear weapons in response to the existential hazard. The object and purpose of the Outer Space Treaty therefore justifies employing an 'inherent nature' test to permanently classify NEDs as weapons, even while the treaty's interpretation can also turn on the 'purpose' or 'function' of other categories of space devices and activities to escape their prohibition as 'weapons'.[46]

In the event that a nuclear planetary defence mission becomes necessary someday, it should be possible to organise the operation or test in a manner that makes perfectly manifest its benign, non-hostile purpose. There could be great transparency regarding the mission profile and the role of NEDs within

---

the captured asteroid would likely qualify as a new type of 'weapon of mass destruction' under Article IV Outer Space Treaty.

46 Note in this connection that the second paragraph of Article IV twice refers to the 'purpose' of an activity, while the first paragraph does not use that word at all.

it, including plenty of advance notice, participation by multiple stake-holding countries, and the availability of independent inspections (consistent with the need to preserve secrecy regarding the operational aspects of nuclear weapons design).[47] Those features do not go directly to the terminology of Article IV Outer Space Treaty, but they may help reassure nervous onlookers about the *bona fides* of the NED function. Under the last two sentences of Article IV, even the participation of military personnel and equipment is expressly contemplated for a peaceful space mission.

Some might prefer simply to defer this whole question, kicking it down the road until such time as the world actually needs to decide whether a NED is the most technically sound vehicle for planetary defence, and avoiding any premature legal judgments that might tie our hands. But the argument here favours rendering a solid legal judgment now, and not allowing the uncertainty to linger. States are already beginning to test some of the evolving planetary defence concepts, and that is surely the responsible path, incrementally exploring gravity tractors, kinetic interceptors and other approaches – but explosive testing of a NED in space is, and should remain, illegal.

The legal judgment that the Outer Space Treaty and the Limited Test Ban Treaty prohibit the use of NEDs for planetary defence is not, of course, the end of the story. As noted elsewhere in this volume, there are suitable mechanisms for addressing the potential political/legal conundrum and circumventing the operation of even the most rigid international legal provisions. Treaties can be amended, replaced, or withdrawn from, and the UN Security Council, in the exercise of its Chapter VII powers under the United Nations Charter, has the authority to supersede contrary law, in order to protect international peace and security. But the starting point for any such remedies is to recognise squarely that there is a problem: existing international law is best understood as prohibiting the use of NEDs for planetary defence.

47 Those undertaking this type of mission could also provide the advance notification and opportunity for consultation specified in Article IX Outer Space Treaty, regarding space activities that "would cause potentially harmful interference with the activities of other States Parties in the peaceful exploration and use of outer space".

CHAPTER 16

Nuclear Non-Proliferation and Planetary Defence

Competing Potential Disasters

Jack M Beard

1 Introduction

This chapter addresses a dilemma created by the prospect of competing potential disasters. One of them, detailed throughout this volume, is presented by a possible (but very unlikely to be imminent) catastrophic impact of an asteroid on Earth. The other involves the very real and existential threat to humanity posed by nuclear weapons. This latter threat takes place at a time when the fragile nuclear weapons non-proliferation and arms control framework is eroding and many experts believe that the risk of nuclear war is greater than it has been in generations.[1] This threat of nuclear disaster comes not only from the direct actions of states, but also from terrorists or other non-state actors who are more able to acquire nuclear weapons as states pursue or permit the proliferation of these weapons.[2] It is in this context that a profound dilemma arises when the choice of means for protecting Earth from asteroids is made dependent on the use of nuclear explosive devices (NEDs). As the prospect of nuclear conflict grows and the eroding nuclear non-proliferation legal regime is in crisis,[3] using some facile legal excuses to pursue the nuclear option for

1 Rob Waugh, 'Prospect of Nuclear War 'Higher Than It's Been for Generations', U.N. warns' *Metro* (London, 3 April 2019) <https://metro.co.uk/2019/04/03/prospect-nuclear-war-higher-generations-un-warns-9105319/?ito=cbshare> accessed 25 February 2021 ("The disarmament and arms control framework upon which the gains of the post-Cold War era were made is eroding, but we have nothing else yet with which to replace it (…) As a result, the prospect of the use of nuclear weapons is higher than it has been in generations").

2 See Graham Allison, 'Nuclear Terrorism Fact Sheet' (*Belfer Center for Science and International Affairs*, April 2010) <www.belfercenter.org/index.php/publication/nuclear-terrorism-fact-sheet> accessed 25 February 2021 (quoting Mohamed ElBaradei, former director of the IAEA and winner of the 2005 Nobel Peace Prize, as saying "nuclear terrorism is the most serious danger the world is facing" and quoting former US President Barack Obama as saying "nuclear terrorism is the most immediate and extreme threat to global security").

3 Alicia Sanders-Zakre and Kelsey Davenport, 'Arms Control Association Report – Assessing Progress on Nuclear Non-proliferation and Disarmament: 2016–2019 Report Card' (Arms Control Association 2019) <www.armscontrol.org/sites/default/files/files/Reports/Report_2019July_ReportCard_1.pdf> accessed 25 February 2021, v ("These findings raise concerns

 | DOI:10.1163/9789004467606_018

planetary defence could further undermine that fragile legal framework, while at the same time encouraging nuclear weapons proliferation itself.

This chapter examines the relationship between planetary defence measures involving NEDs and the international legal framework addressing the threat posed by nuclear weapons proliferation. This legal framework, which centres on the 1968 Nuclear Non-Proliferation Treaty,[4] appears to be fundamentally incompatible with the use of NEDs for planetary defence purposes. Key arms control agreements, which are examined elsewhere in this volume and are briefly discussed here, also stand as legal impediments to the nuclear planetary defence option. Circumvention of these key agreements for planetary defence purposes could instigate new arms races and lead to the unravelling of the Nuclear Non-Proliferation Treaty itself, with unfavourable consequences for nuclear weapons proliferation. Among the planetary defence techniques contemplated in this volume, NEDs pose a unique threat to international peace and security, and unlike other possible technological solutions, have justifiably been the subject of intense international negotiations and legal restrictions.

2 The Nuclear Non-Proliferation Treaty

Although the Nuclear Non-Proliferation Treaty is under increasing stress, it remains the 'cornerstone' of the international nuclear non-proliferation regime.[5] The 'grand bargain' achieved by the states that negotiated the Nuclear Non-Proliferation Treaty rests on three mutually reinforcing

that the risk of nuclear use is increasing and that critical non-proliferation and disarmament norms are eroding"); Council on Foreign Relations, 'The Global Nuclear Non-proliferation Regime' (21 May 2012) <www.cfr.org/report/global-nuclear-nonproliferation-regime> accessed 25 February 2021 ("Recent trends have brought the nuclear non-proliferation regime to a moment of grave crisis. The regime is under siege from both rogue states and nonstate actors, and its core bargain between the nuclear haves and have-nots continues to erode").

4 Treaty on the Non-Proliferation of Nuclear Weapons (adopted 1 July 1968, entered into force 5 March 1970) 729 UNTS 169 (Nuclear Non-Proliferation Treaty). This legal framework is supplemented by five reinforcing, regional, nuclear free zone agreements, discussed below.

5 See US Department of State, 'Treaty on the Non-Proliferation of Nuclear Weapons' (2010) <www.state.gov/wp-content/uploads/2019/03/228-Nuclear-Nonproliferation-Treaty-508.pdf> accessed 25 February 2021; Daniel H Joyner, *International Law and the Proliferation of Weapons of Mass Destruction* (Oxford University Press 2009) 8; Winston Nagan and Erin Slemmens, 'National Security Policy and Ratification of the Comprehensive-Test-Ban Treaty' (2009–2010) 32 Houston Journal of International Law 1, 40.

pillars: non-proliferation (avoiding the spread of nuclear weapons to additional states); disarmament (reducing the nuclear arsenals of the states possessing them); and, the peaceful use of nuclear energy (encouraging collaboration regarding the non-weapons applications of nuclear energy).[6] Each of these three 'pillars' is difficult, if not impossible, to reconcile with the manufacture, deployment or use of NEDs for peaceful, planetary defence purposes.

2.1 *Nuclear Non-Proliferation Treaty Pillar 1: Non-Proliferation*

Under the Nuclear Non-Proliferation Treaty's 'non-proliferation pillar,' nuclear-weapon states (NWSs) are obligated not to transfer nuclear weapons/NEDs to any recipient or in any way assist, encourage or induce any non-nuclear-weapon state (NNWS) in the manufacture or acquisition of a nuclear weapon.[7] However, major proliferation problems that continue to haunt the international community and strain non-proliferation efforts are linked to transfers of nuclear weapons technology between states that occurred outside (and in some cases, likely within) the Nuclear Non-Proliferation Treaty regime. For example, although the People's Republic of China acceded to the Nuclear Non-Proliferation Treaty in 1992, it is widely understood that it previously transferred design information and fissile material to Pakistan (still a non-party to the Nuclear Non-Proliferation Treaty), facilitating Pakistan's development of a nuclear weapon and helping to make Pakistan its own proliferation concern.[8] Some of these transfers are likely to have continued even after China became a party to the Nuclear Non-Proliferation Treaty.[9]

6 US Delegation to the 2010 Nuclear Non-Proliferation Treaty Review Conference, 'Treaty on the Non-Proliferation of Nuclear Weapons' (2010) <https://2009-2017.state.gov/documents/organization/141503.pdf> accessed 25 February 2021; Toby Dalton and others, 'Toward a Nuclear Firewall: Bridging the NPT's Three Pillars' (*Carnegie Endowment*, 20 March 2017) <https://carnegieendowment.org/2017/03/20/toward-nuclear-firewall-bridging-npt-s-three-pillars-pub-68300> accessed 25 February 2021.

7 Article I, Nuclear Non-Proliferation Treaty.

8 Nuclear Threat Initiative, 'China' (*NTI*, April 2020) <www.nti.org/learn/countries/china/> accessed 25 February 2021; Thomas C Reed and Danny B Stillman, *The Nuclear Express: A Political History of the Bomb and its Proliferation* (Voyageur Press 2009) 247–58.

9 See Thazha V Paul, 'Chinese-Pakistani Nuclear/Missile Ties and the Balance of Power' (2003) 10(2) The Nonproliferation Review <www.nonproliferation.org/wp-content/uploads/npr/102paul.pdf> accessed 25 February 2021, 1, 4 (noting that China supplied critical components to Pakistan for its nuclear weapons program in 1994 to 1995, including 500 specialised ring magnets to be used in gas centrifuges for making weapons-grade enriched uranium in 1994–95); Jeffrey Smith, 'China Aids Pakistan Nuclear Program' *Washington Post* (Washington D.C., 7 February 1996) <www.washingtonpost.com/archive/politics/1996/02/07/china-aids-pakistan-nuclear-program/63ce5997-a2f0-4131-aeee-76a033233bc3>

Notwithstanding the duties of NWSs, NNWSs have their own non-proliferation obligations under the Nuclear Non-Proliferation Treaty, particularly not to acquire or manufacture nuclear weapons/NEDs, not to receive the transfer of nuclear weapons/NEDs or of control over such devices and not to seek or receive assistance in the manufacture of such devices.[10] Although the obligation not to acquire nuclear weapons is clear and widely recognised, if a planetary defence mission were to involve any NNWSs, an even more significant problem could be presented by the obligation not to receive the transfer of *control* over nuclear weapons/NEDs, directly, or indirectly.

The potentially problematic 'control' prohibition in the Nuclear Non-Proliferation Treaty forms the basis for continuing charges that some NNWSs in the North Atlantic Treaty Organization (NATO) are essentially serving as "surrogate nuclear-weapon states by equipping their military forces with the necessary tools to deliver US nuclear weapons in times of war".[11] In addition to the storage of US nuclear weapons on the territory of NNWSs, the training of NNWS pilots and other personal in NATO's shared nuclear mission has prompted harsh criticism by the Russian Minister of Foreign Affairs, who argued that such a "joint nuclear mission" is a "serious violation of Articles I and II of the NPT."[12] Since the contours of the shared NATO nuclear mission are shrouded in secrecy, the precise allocation of national responsibilities in this mission is unknown. Questions about compliance with the Nuclear Non-Proliferation Treaty are raised by some possible NATO nuclear arrangements, such as German or other NNWS pilots flying their country's planes on future

---

accessed 25 February 2021 (reporting that "U.S. intelligence officials have concluded that China sold sensitive nuclear weapons-related equipment to Pakistan last year").

10 Article II, Nuclear Non-Proliferation Treaty.

11 Hans M Kristensen, 'Nuclear Weapons Modernization: A Threat to the NPT?' (*Arms Control Association*) <www.armscontrol.org/act/2014-05/nuclear-weapons-modernization-threat-npt> accessed 25 February 2021 (reporting that "[s]lightly more than 180 B61 [nuclear] bombs are currently deployed in underground vaults inside 87 protective aircraft shelters at six bases in five NATO countries (Belgium, Germany, Italy, the Netherlands, and Turkey)" and that these arrangements have given rise to the criticism that "[m]any non-nuclear-weapon states that publicly call for nuclear disarmament continue to call on nuclear armed allies to protect them with nuclear weapons").

12 Holly Ellyatt, 'Russia's Lavrov Says the U.S. is Training Europe to Use Nuclear Weapons Against It' *CNBC* (New Jersey, 28 February 2018) (quoting the Russian Foreign Minister as saying that "as we all know, these nuclear missions violate the Nuclear Non-Proliferation Treaty and non-nuclear states plan and take part in the U.S. exercises and learn how to use the nuclear weapons").

war-time missions with the authority to drop US nuclear weapons – in planes that are specifically configured to carry and drop nuclear weapons.[13]

To the extent that a planetary defence mission involves the cooperation of NNWSs, actions that assist in the deployment of NEDs would be likely to raise questions about the proliferation obligations of the Nuclear Non-Proliferation Treaty. For example, what precisely constitutes prohibited 'control' of a NED in helping to deploy such a device for planetary defence? If a NNWS, such as Canada, manufactured and had their astronauts operate a manoeuvrable arm on a spacecraft (such as on the space shuttle) and use that arm to place a NED onto an asteroid, would that be too much 'control'?

2.2 *Supplemental Non-Proliferation Agreements that Reinforce Pillar I of the Nuclear Non-Proliferation Treaty*

Other concerns about NNWSs participating in collaborative planetary defence missions would be raised if the NNWSs in question are parties to one of the five regional treaties establishing 'nuclear-weapon-free zones'.[14] These treaties contain obligations which supplement and reinforce the Nuclear Non-Proliferation Treaty by imposing even more comprehensive, regional restrictions on activities related to nuclear weapons. For example, the Latin American agreement (the Tlatelolco Treaty) requires parties to refrain from "engaging in, encouraging or authorizing, directly or indirectly, or in any other way participating in the testing, use, manufacture, production, possession or control of any nuclear weapon".[15] Like the Nuclear Non-Proliferation Treaty, regional 'nuclear free zones' raise questions about exactly what a NNWS could not do in support of a planetary defence mission involving NEDs. Here, a state party to the Tlatelolco Treaty could not 'encourage' the 'use' of a nuclear weapon – which may mean that such a state could not 'request' that a NWS use a NED for planetary defence, and could not vote in favour of a resolution (in the UN

13 See Reuters, 'Germany Wants to Know If the US Will Let It Carry Nuclear Weapons on Its New Fighter Jets' (20 June 2018) (noting that Germany operates Tornado warplanes that can deliver nuclear weapons and that "Germany is pressing Washington to clarify whether it would let the Eurofighter Typhoon carry nuclear bombs as part of shared Western defences, an issue that could help decide whether Berlin orders more of the jets").

14 United Nations, 'Nuclear-Weapon-Free Zones' <www.un.org/disarmament/wmd/nuclear/nwfz/> accessed 25 February 2021.

15 Article 1(2), Treaty for the Prohibition of Nuclear Weapons in Latin America and the Caribbean (adopted 14 February 1967, entered into force 22 April 1968) 634 UNTS 326 (Tlateloco Treaty).

General Assembly or the UN Security Council) that would authorise such a mission.

The South Pacific Agreement similarly requires states not to manufacture or otherwise acquire, possess or have control over any NED anywhere inside or outside the zone.[16] It further requires each party to prevent the stationing of any NED in its territory and broadly defines stationing as "emplantation, emplacement, transportation on land or inland waters, stockpiling, storage, installation and deployment."[17]

The 2017 Treaty on the Prohibition of Nuclear Weapons, which entered into force in 2021,[18] would present additional legal obstacles blocking NNWSs from participating in nuclear planetary defence activities. The treaty prohibits parties from possessing, transferring, or using nuclear weapons and from allowing any stationing, installation or deployment of any nuclear weapons/NEDs on their territory.[19] Each party further commits "never under any circumstances" to assist, encourage or induce, in any way, anyone to engage in any activity prohibited to a party under the treaty.[20] Here, too, it would appear that the 'encourage or induce' language means the state could not voice support for a nuclear planetary defence mission.

The prohibitions in the Treaty on the Prohibition of Nuclear Weapons are sweeping and even more exacting than those in the Nuclear Non-Proliferation Treaty, as evidenced by the explanatory comments and vote against the adoption of the treaty by the Netherlands, an NNWS. The Netherlands argued that restrictions in the Treaty on the Prohibition of Nuclear Weapons are so all-encompassing that they are inconsistent with its obligations as a member of NATO.[21]

States that have ratified the Treaty on the Prohibition of Nuclear Weapons and are subject to its comprehensive ban on the possession of nuclear

16 Article 3(a), South Pacific Nuclear Free Zone Treaty (adopted 6 August 1985, entered into force 11 December 1986) 29 ILM 1442 (Rarotonga Treaty).

17 Article 1(d), South Pacific Nuclear Free Zone Treaty.

18 Treaty on the Prohibition of Nuclear Weapons (adopted 7 July 2017, entered into force 21 January 2021).

19 Ibid, Article 1(1)(a),(b),(d).

20 Ibid, Article 1(1)(e).

21 Explanation of vote of the Netherlands on text of Nuclear Ban Treaty (7 June 2017) see e.g. at <https://s3.amazonaws.com/unoda-web/wp-content/uploads/2017/07/Netherlands-EoV-Nuclear-Ban-Treaty.pdf> accessed 25 February 2021 (stating that "the Netherlands could not support the draft that was put before us. We have signaled at the beginning of this session that we would be unable to sign up to any instrument that is incompatible with our NATO obligations, that contains inadequate verification provisions or that undermines the Non-Proliferation Treaty").

weapons and related activities (including assisting, encouraging or inducing the use of a nuclear device) will certainly be excluded from, or greatly restricted in, participation in joint nuclear planetary defence operations. Most space-faring NNWSs are not currently signatories to the Treaty on the Prohibition of Nuclear Weapons, but some are, and others may be soon. For example, Kazakhstan, which hosts the world's oldest and largest space launch facility through its lease of part of its territory to Russia, is a NNWS under the Nuclear Non-Proliferation Treaty, a party to the Central Asia Nuclear Weapon Free Zone Treaty, and a signatory and enthusiastic supporter of Treaty on the Prohibition of Nuclear Weapons.

To the extent planetary defence programs involve various types of collaboration between NNWSs and NWSs related to NEDs, serious legal obstacles will be presented by the Nuclear Non-Proliferation Treaty, applicable nuclear weapons free zone agreements, and the Treaty on the Prohibition of Nuclear Weapons (state parties and signatories, which are obliged not to defeat the object and purpose of the treaty under the Vienna Convention on the Law of Treaties).[22] Allowing NNWSs to ignore, avoid or re-interpret key provisions in these agreements, or to develop other convenient methods of circumvention for purposes of planetary defence, risks undermining and destroying the Nuclear Non-Proliferation Treaty regime.

2.3 *Nuclear Non-Proliferation Treaty Pillar II: Disarmament*

In fulfilling their obligations under the disarmament pillar of the Nuclear Non-Proliferation Treaty, and as part of the grand bargain that they made with NNWSs, each NWS "undertakes to pursue negotiations in good faith on effective measures relating to cessation of the nuclear arms race at an early date and to nuclear disarmament," and "on a treaty on general and complete disarmament under strict and effective international control".[23] In 2002, at a Nuclear Non-Proliferation Treaty Review Conference, all states parties further pledged to implement "thirteen practical steps for the systematic and progressive efforts to implement Article VI", which included "an unequivocal undertaking by the nuclear-weapon states to accomplish the total elimination of their nuclear

22 Article 18, Vienna Convention on the Law of Treaties (adopted 23 May 1969, entered into force 27 January 1980) 1155 UNTS 331 (applicable to those states parties who have signed the Treaty on the Prohibition of Nuclear Weapons subject to its ratification, acceptance or approval until they have made their intention clear not to become a party or those states that have expressed their consent to be bound by the treaty, pending its entry into force).

23 Article VI, Nuclear Non-Proliferation Treaty.

arsenals leading to nuclear disarmament to which all States parties are committed under Article VI".[24] The agreed practical steps also included a pledge to undertake "further efforts by the nuclear-weapon states to reduce their nuclear arsenals unilaterally".[25]

The lack of progress by NWSs in the Nuclear Non-Proliferation Treaty's step-by-step approach to nuclear disarmament has been strongly criticised by many NNWSs.[26] This lack of progress has created even more stress on the Nuclear Non-Proliferation Treaty, recently prompting over two-thirds of the NNWSs parties to the treaty to seek to establish a new international agreement (the Treaty on the Prohibition of Nuclear Weapons), completely banning all nuclear weapons.[27] According to some commentators, this action by the NNWSs has opened a 'fissure' regarding the right course of action for the international community to pursue in realising the Nuclear Non-Proliferation Treaty's goals and may have put the treaty in 'mortal peril'.[28] It is in this context of the Nuclear Non-Proliferation Treaty under severe stress, that new burdens presented by the manufacture, deployment or use of NEDs for planetary defence missions could easily threaten the very existence of the Nuclear Non-Proliferation Treaty regime.

Whatever constitutes the 'further efforts' pledged by the NWSs to reduce their nuclear arsenals unilaterally, these efforts would clearly not be advanced by the creation of new motives or excuses to develop more nuclear weapons or postpone their scheduled elimination. Yet this seems to be precisely what the concept of planetary defence is already doing. For example, in a 2014 report, the US Government Accountability Office (GAO) found that some nuclear warhead components that were scheduled to be disassembled soon "are being

24 Arms Control Association, '2000 NPT Review Conference Final Document' <www.armscontrol.org/act/2000-06/2000-npt-review-conference-final-document> accessed 25 February 2021.

25 Ibid.

26 See Jacek Durkalec, 'The Nuclear Non-proliferation Treaty at fifty: A Midlife Crisis' *NATO Review* (29 June 2018) <www.nato.int/docu/review/2018/Also-in-2018/the-nuclear-non-proliferation-treaty-at-fifty-a-midlife-crisis/EN/index.htm> accessed 25 February 2021 (noting that "Progress toward nuclear disarmament remains, however, the most serious bone of contention within the NPT. (...) [N]on-nuclear-weapon states criticise nuclear possessors for slow progress and for not fulfilling their promise").

27 See discussion *supra* regarding the Treaty on the Prohibition of Nuclear Weapons.

28 Paul Meyer, 'The Nuclear Non-proliferation Treaty: Fin de Regime?' (*Arms Control Today*, April 2017) <www.armscontrol.org/act/2017-04/features/nuclear-non-proliferation-treaty-fin-de-regime> accessed 25 February 2021.

retained in an indeterminate state pending a senior-level government evaluation of their use in planetary defence against earthbound asteroids".[29]

The 2014 GAO Report focuses attention on the very real possibility that planetary defence can be used as an excuse for keeping at least some part of the nuclear arsenal together, thus undermining related disarmament activities.[30] Moreover, commentators have suggested that both Russian and US nuclear weapons experts have long welcomed the prospect of working on nuclear planetary defence in the face of reductions in their nuclear weapons arsenal under new arms control agreements.[31]

Planetary defence and the threat posed by asteroids can thus unfortunately be used to clothe the continuing possession of nuclear weapons by NWSs 'in the robes of altruism' or otherwise serve as a 'convenient narrative' for their need to retain nuclear weapons.[32] This convenient narrative – which clearly does not advance the fulfilment of the disarmament obligations of the Nuclear Non-Proliferation Treaty – has also played out with respect to the testing of nuclear weapons by NWSs. For example, in 1996 China refused to join a comprehensive ban on nuclear testing because it insisted on continuing "peaceful nuclear explosions" to combat the "asteroid threat".[33]

---

29 US Government Accountability Office, 'Nuclear Weapons: Actions Needed by NNSA to Clarify Dismantlement Performance Goal' (GAO 14-449, GAO 2014) 40–41. Even more threatening to the Nuclear Non-Proliferation Treaty regime than the retention of nuclear weapons for planetary defence applications is the possibility of developing (and testing) new types of NEDs to make sure they are optimally suited for a future planetary defence mission. As discussed in the next section, such activities by NNWSs could fatally undermine the Nuclear Non-Proliferation Treaty regime in the name of planetary defence.

30 John R Emshwiller, 'U.S. Takes Asteroid Threat Seriously, Some Nuclear Warheads Once Set for Disassembly, are kept in Reserve' *Wall Street Journal* (New York, 30 September 2014) (noting that "in an era when the size of the atomic-weapons stockpile has been shrinking as a result of arms-control treaties and other factors", asteroid defence, may be, in the words of a professor of earth, atmospheric and planetary sciences, "an excuse for keeping the nuclear arsenal together").

31 Douglas Birch, 'A Real Nuclear Deterrent: US, Russia May Team Up to Use Weapons Against Asteroids' *NBC News* (New York, 16 October 2013) <www.nbcnews.com/news/world/real-nuclear-deterrent-us-russia-may-team-use-weapons-against-flna8C11402729> accessed 25 February 2021 (noting that "U.S. nuclear weapons labs appear to be itching to work with their Russian colleagues on the problem [of planetary defence]" and that "weaponeers in both countries are citing the asteroid threat as a reason to hold onto – or to build – very large yield nuclear explosives, which have declining terrestrial justification").

32 James A Green, 'Planetary Defense: Near-Earth Objects, Nuclear Weapons, and International Law' (2019) 42 Hastings International and Comparative Law Review 1, 29.

33 Patrick E Tyler, 'Chinese Seek Atom Option to Fend Off Asteroids' *New York Times* (New York, 27 April 1996) <www.nytimes.com/1996/04/27/world/chinese-seek-atom-option-to-fend-off-asteroids.html> accessed 25 February 2021; William J Broad, 'For

Although the terms of the Nuclear Non-Proliferation Treatyenvision that any potential benefits from "the peaceful applications of nuclear explosions will be made available by NWSs to NNWSs",[34] the concept of 'peaceful nuclear explosions' (PNEs) has proven to be an erroneous proposition. In practical terms, the technology supporting PNEs is indistinguishable from the technology supporting the testing or use of nuclear weapons.[35] This reality was illustrated by India's Pokhran-I tests in 1974, which India described as PNEs, but were widely regarded as nuclear weapons tests.[36] The risk that states might thus pursue the development of nuclear capabilities "behind the guise of an interest of

Killer Asteroids, Respect at Last' *New York Times* (New York, 14 May 1996) <www.nytimes.com/1996/05/14/science/for-killer-asteroids-respect-at-last.html> accessed 25 February 2021 (noting that "China recently became the focus of international disdain for saying it wanted to keep testing nuclear arms underground to prepare a possible defense in which rocket interceptors and nuclear blasts would nudge doomsday rocks off course").

34 Article V, Nuclear Non-Proliferation Treaty.

35 See Statement by Ambassador Goldberg to the First Committee of the General Assembly, 'Non-proliferation of Nuclear Weapons' (26 April 1968) in United States Arms Control and Disarmament Agency, *Documents on Disarmament* (1968) 225, 229, see also at <http://unoda-web.s3-accelerate.amazonaws.com/wp-content/uploads/assets/publications/documents_on_disarmament/1968/DoD_1968.pdf229> accessed 25 February 2021 ("there is no essential difference between the technology of peaceful nuclear explosive devices and that of nuclear weapons); Paper by the Rapporteur, 'The Peaceful Uses of Nuclear Energy in the Context of Measures to Prevent the Spread of Nuclear Weapons' (12 September 1967) A/CONF.35/PC/L.15, 6 (noting that the US contention that "the technology of nuclear explosions for peaceful purposes was inseparable from that of nuclear weapons" was "explicitly supported by seven other countries ..."); Robert D Bartels, 'The Non-proliferation Treaty and Peaceful Applications of Nuclear Explosions' (1968) 20 Stanford Law Review 1030, 1030–31, 1041–43.

36 Nuclear Threat Initiative, 'India' (November 2019) <www.nti.org/learn/countries/india/nuclear/> accessed 25 February 2021 ("India's 1974 nuclear test was condemned by many countries as a violation of the peaceful-use agreements underlying U.S. and Canadian-supplied nuclear technology and material transfers"); Bernard Weinraub, 'India Becomes 6th Nation To Set Off Nuclear Device' *New York Times* (New York, 19 May 1974) <www.nytimes.com/1974/05/19/archives/india-becomes-6th-nation-to-set-off-nuclear-device-india-signed.html> accessed 25 February 2021 (noting that sources at the disarmament conference in Geneva "viewed the Indian, explosion as a setback to efforts to restrict the spread of nuclear weapons"); Federation of American Scientists, Factsheet on Indian Nuclear Explosions <https://fas.org/nuke/guide/pakistan/doctrine/000513-factsheetindian_nuclear_explosio.htm> accessed 25 February 2021 ("In May 1974, India carried out its first nuclear test, while claiming it to be a Peaceful Nuclear Experiment – which, as proved later, was not actually the case").

peaceful nuclear explosions", along with concerns over environmental harms, generally led to the termination of PNEs in the 1970s and 1980s.[37]

2.4 *Nuclear Non-Proliferation Treaty Pillar III: Peaceful Use of Nuclear Energy*

While enjoying their acknowledged 'inalienable right' under the third pillar of the Nuclear Non-Proliferation Treaty to develop nuclear energy for peaceful purposes, NNWSs are obligated to accept International Atomic Energy Agency (IAEA) safeguards to verify that their nuclear activities serve only peaceful purposes.[38] There has always been considerable difficulty in drawing the lines under the Nuclear Non-Proliferation Treaty to clearly separate prohibited nuclear activities from those which are purportedly undertaken for peaceful purposes.[39] Unfortunately, the nuclear fuel cycle itself raises dual purpose concerns, since that process can produce low enriched uranium for peaceful use in nuclear power plants or highly enriched uranium /weapons-grade uranium for non-peaceful purposes.[40] The inherent proliferation risk associated with peaceful nuclear power programs has long been recognised by states, along with the impossibility of distinguishing a 'PNE device' from a nuclear weapon.[41] For this

---

37 Jozef Goldblat, *Arms Control: The New Guide to Negotiations and Agreements* (2nd edn, Sage Publications 2002) 55. The use of PNEs declined in this period, with no such declared or verified explosions having occurred since the last Soviet PNE in 1989.

38 Articles III and IV, Nuclear Non-Proliferation Treaty. Article IV acknowledges this inalienable right of all Parties to develop nuclear energy for peaceful purposes and to benefit from international cooperation in this area, in conformity with their non-proliferation obligations.

39 Charles D Ferguson, 'Proliferation Risks of Nuclear Power Programs' (*Nuclear Threat Initiative*, 1 December 2007) <www.nti.org/analysis/articles/risks-nuclear-power-programs/> accessed 25 February 2021; Toby Dalton and others, 'Toward a Nuclear Firewall: Bridging the NPT's Three Pillars' (*Carnegie Endowment*, 20 March 2017) <https://carnegieendowment.org/2017/03/20/toward-nuclear-firewall-bridging-npt-s-three-pillars-pub-68300> accessed 25 February 2021 ("There is no clear, internationally accepted definition of what activities or technologies constitute a nuclear weapons program. This lack of definition encumbers nuclear energy cooperation and complicates peaceful resolution of proliferation disputes").

40 Charles D Ferguson, 'Proliferation Risks of Nuclear Power Programs' (*Nuclear Threat Initiative*, 1 December 2007) <www.nti.org/analysis/articles/risks-nuclear-power-programs/> accessed 19 March 2021; Pierre Goldschmidt, 'The Proliferation Challenge of the Nuclear Fuel Cycle in Non-Nuclear Weapon States, International Atomic Energy Agency' (26 April 2004) <www.iaea.org/newscenter/statements/proliferation-challenge-nuclear-fuel-cycle-non-nuclear-weapon-states> accessed 25 February 2021.

41 Statement by ACDA Deputy Director Fisher to the Eighteen Nation Disarmament Committee, 'Nuclear Explosions for Peaceful Purposes' (25 January 1968), in United States Arms Control and Disarmament Agency, 'Documents on Disarmament' (1968) 23, see

reason, any effort by a NNWS to build a new type of NED for a future planetary defence missions is fundamentally incompatible with the safeguards of the Nuclear Non-Proliferation Treaty, undermining both non-proliferation goals and the support of peaceful uses of nuclear energy. The issue of NNWSs manufacturing NEDs for planetary defence purposes is particularly problematic in light of the continuing stress being placed on the Nuclear Non-Proliferation Treaty's third pillar as a result of states having previously used peaceful nuclear power as a pretext for acquiring nuclear weapons.[42]

While the IAEA must nonetheless endeavour to establish precise criteria for what constitutes peaceful purposes and which activities lay beyond the civilian realm, it has been somewhat easier and more practical to develop examples and criteria which identify what clearly is *not* a 'peaceful purpose'. Any indication that a country's nuclear enrichment program is oriented around the production of highly enriched, weapons-grade, uranium would generally qualify as a 'warning sign' that it has "a nuclear program with little (or no) coherence for peaceful purposes, but great coherence for weapons purposes".[43]

Such a simple and reasonable standard (concluding that a programme producing weapons-grade fissile materials has no genuine coherence for peaceful purposes) would be dramatically undermined if NNWSs could use planetary

---

also at <http://unoda-web.s3-accelerate.amazonaws.com/wp-content/uploads/assets/publications/documents_on_disarmament/1968/DoD_1968.pdf> accessed 19 March 2021 ("[I]t is an indisputable technological fact that the development and manufacture of nuclear explosive devices intended for peaceful uses is indistinguishable from the development and manufacture of nuclear weapons"). See Additional Protocol II to the Treaty of Tlatelolco (12 May 1971) ("The United States wishes to point out again the fact that the technology of making nuclear explosive devices for peaceful purposes is indistinguishable from the technology of making nuclear weapons and the fact that nuclear weapons and nuclear explosive devices for peaceful purposes").

42 Alexei Arbatov, 'An Unnoticed Crisis: The End of History for Nuclear Arms Control?' (*Carnegie Endowment,* June 2015) <https://carnegieendowment.org/files/CP_Arbatov2015_n_web_Eng.pdf> accessed 25 February 2021, 20 (noting how the Nuclear Non-Proliferation Treaty principle of peaceful use of nuclear energy is "now frequently inverted: for some countries, peaceful atomic energy projects are a channel or pretext for acquiring either nuclear weapons or the technological means to develop them rapidly. North Korea set the example for such behaviour, and Iran has been suspected of following suit. It is possible that other African, Asian, and Latin American countries, many of which suffer from internal instability and regional threats, will adopt a similar approach").

43 US Department of State, 'Adherence to and Compliance with Arms U.S. Department of State, Non-Proliferation and Disarmament Agreements and Commitments' (2005) <https://2009-2017.state.gov/t/avc/rls/rpt/51977.htm> accessed 25 February 2021 (noting that US officials have publicly outlined some of the "warning signs" that may indicate a "prohibited nuclear weapons purpose").

defence as a pretext for enriching uranium beyond the levels needed for peaceful nuclear power purposes. In IAEA investigations, a NNWS with uranium enrichment facilities and any evidence of the production of highly enriched uranium is always a cause of concern.[44] Identical concerns are raised by the manufacture of plutonium (the isotope Pu-239) which can serve as the fissile material necessary to build a nuclear weapon and is produced in special reactors ('breeder' and 'heavy water' reactors).[45] The construction of such reactors presents a very real proliferation threat and thus serves as another 'warning sign' of a country's potential pursuit of nuclear weapons instead of peaceful civilian nuclear activities.[46]

The sole purpose of the IAEA inspection process is to ensure the verification of a state's fulfilment of its obligations under the Nuclear Non-Proliferation Treatywith "a view to preventing diversion of nuclear energy from peaceful uses to nuclear weapons or other nuclear explosive devices".[47] Allowing a NNWS to divert peaceful nuclear programs to the production of highly enriched uranium or plutonium in order to manufacture NEDs for the alleged purpose of planetary defence would create an unmanageable, illogical and dangerous exception. Such a programme would be fundamentally incompatible with

44 David Albright and Jacqueline Shire, 'A Witches' Brew? Evaluating Iran's Uranium-Enrichment Progress' (*Arms Control Association*, 27 September 2007) <www.armscontrol.org/act/2007-11/iran-nuclear-briefs/witches'-brew-evaluating-iran's-uranium-enrichment-progress> accessed 25 February 2021 (noting that "[a] key milestone will be reached when Iran accumulates enough LEU to break out and relatively quickly produce weapons-grade uranium"); IAEA Board of Governors, 'Implementation of the NPT Safeguards Agreement in the Islamic Republic of Iran' (15 November 2004) <www.iaea.org/sites/default/files/gov2005-67.pdf> accessed 25 February 2021 (raising "important issues relevant to the Agency's investigation in order to provide assurance that there are no undeclared enrichment activities in Iran" including "the origin of LEU and HEU particle contamination found at various locations in Iran").

45 The Nuclear Weapon Archive, 'Plutonium Manufacture and Fabrication' <https://nuclearweaponarchive.org/Library/Plutonium/index.html> accessed 25 February 2021.

46 US Department of State, 'Adherence to and Compliance with Arms U.S. Department of State, Non-Proliferation and Disarmament Agreements and Commitments' (2005) <https://2009-2017.state.gov/t/avc/rls/rpt/51977.htm> accessed 25 February 2021, 64 (listing "heavy water production" as a possible warning sign that "may indicate a prohibited nuclear weapons purpose"); see also UNSC Res 1737 (27 December 2006) S/RES/1737 (citing outstanding issues and concerns regarding Iran's nuclear programme, "including topics which could have a military nuclear dimension" and deciding that "Iran shall without further delay suspend the following proliferation sensitive nuclear activities: (…) work on all heavy water-related projects, including the construction the construction of a research reactor moderated by heavy water").

47 Article III(1), Nuclear Non-Proliferation Treaty.

the Nuclear Non-Proliferation Treaty regime, its regulation of the nuclear fuel cycle, and the IAEA inspection process itself.

3 The Role of Key Arms Control Agreements

Nuclear weapons non-proliferation objectives are clearly not advanced by undercutting any of the few, historic, hard-won, existing arms control agreements, which limit the use or deployment of nuclear weapons. Planetary defence nuclear options that provide an excuse for evading these agreements may contribute to conditions that instigate or aggravate dangerous arms races, particularly in the volatile outer space domain where threats to space systems and counterspace capabilities continue to grow.[48]

As noted in the previous chapter, two key Cold War Era arms control agreements stand as barriers to the deployment and use of NEDs in planetary defence: the 1963 Limited Test Ban Treaty[49] and the foundational document of space law, the 1967 Outer Space Treaty.[50] Both are important parts of the legal framework controlling nuclear weapons, but that fragile framework is under severe stress and needs no additional burdens placed on it – including the convenient circumvention of its prohibitions for planetary defence or for any other purpose.[51]

---

48 See Todd Harrison, Kaitlyn Johnson, and Thomas G Roberts, 'Space Threat Assessment 2018' (Center for Strategic and International Studies 2018); Brian Weeden and Victoria Samson (eds), *Global Counterspace Capabilities: An Open Source Assessment* (Secure World Foundation 2018); National Academies of Sciences, Engineering, and Medicine, *National Security Space Defense and Protection, Public Report* (The National Academic Press 2016).

49 Treaty Banning Nuclear Weapon Tests in the Atmosphere, in Outer Space and Under Water (adopted 5 August 1963, entered into force 10 October 1963) 480 UNTS 6964 (Limited Test Ban Treaty). This treaty is also known as the Partial Test Ban Treaty. The treaty has attracted widespread adherence, although the 126 states parties do not include China, France and North Korea.

50 Treaty on Principles Governing the Activities of States in the Exploration and Use of Outer Space, Including the Moon and Other Celestial Bodies (adopted 27 January 1967, entered into force 10 October 1967) 610 UNTS 205 (Outer Space Treaty).

51 Alexei Arbatov, 'An Unnoticed Crisis: The End of History for Nuclear Arms Control?' (*Carnegie Endowment,* June 2015) <https://carnegieendowment.org/files/CP_Arbatov2015_n_web_Eng.pdf> accessed 25 February 2021, 3 (noting that "[f]or over fifty years, starting with the signing of the Partial Nuclear Test Ban Treaty in 1963, the world has had in place a legally binding framework for controlling the most devastating weapon ever invented by mankind", but that now there is "a real and unprecedented possibility that this framework will disintegrate").

The Limited Test Ban Treaty addresses the detonation of NEDs while the Outer Space Treaty addresses the placement or deployment of such devices. The Limited Test Ban Treaty includes an express and unambiguous prohibition against nuclear explosions of any sort in Earth's atmosphere or outer space.[52] Nuclear explosions for purposes of planetary defence, or for any other purpose, are categorically outlawed.[53] Weakening these restrictions under the pretext of planetary defence would be a costly mistake, considering the crucial importance of the Limited Test Ban Treaty and the catastrophic effects of a nuclear war on Earth.

The Limited Test Ban Treaty would be augmented by the 1996 Comprehensive Nuclear-Test-Ban Treaty, which would extend prohibitions contained in the Limited Test Ban Treaty to cover all nuclear explosions (including PNEs) "in any environment".[54] Although the Comprehensive Nuclear-Test-Ban Treaty has been signed by 184 countries and ratified by 168, it has not yet entered into force.[55] Unfortunately, the treaty faces a daunting challenge in achieving this goal, since it requires forty-four specific countries to ratify the treaty before it enters into force and the specified countries that have *not* ratified the treaty to date include some that are unlikely to join the regime.[56] However, it is important to note that those signatory states of the Comprehensive Nuclear-Test-Ban Treaty that are also parties to the Vienna Convention on the Law of Treaties are obligated to refrain from acts that would defeat the treaty's object and purpose pending its entry into force.[57]

---

52 Article I of the Limited Test Ban Treaty specifies: "Each of the Parties to this Treaty undertakes to prohibit, to prevent, and not to carry out any nuclear weapon test explosion, or any other nuclear explosion, at any place under its jurisdiction or control: (a) in the atmosphere; beyond its limits, including outer space".

53 The pending Comprehensive Nuclear-Test-Ban, which has not yet entered into force, constitutes an all-encompassing prohibition against all nuclear explosions in any environment. Article I(1), Comprehensive Nuclear-Test-Ban Treaty, (adopted 10 September 1996, not yet in force) 35 ILM 1439.

54 Article I(1), Comprehensive Nuclear-Test-Ban Treaty; Comprehensive Nuclear-Test-Ban Treaty parties are also subject to the sweeping requirement "to refrain from causing, encouraging, or in any way participating in the carrying out of any nuclear weapon test explosion or any other nuclear explosion"; ibid Article I(2).

55 UN Office of Disarmament Affairs <http://disarmament.un.org/treaties/t/ctbt> accessed 25 February 2021.

56 Article XIV(1), Comprehensive Nuclear-Test-Ban Treaty . Thirty-six of the forty-four countries named in Annex II have ratified the treaty. Those countries that have not ratified it to date are: China, the Democratic People's Republic of Korea (North Korea), Egypt, India, Iran, Israel, Pakistan, and the United States of America. See UN Office of Disarmament Affairs, <www.un.org/disarmament/wmd/nuclear/ctbt/> accessed 25 February 2021.

57 Article 18, Vienna Convention on the Law of Treaties. On September 15, 2016, the members of the UN Security Council declared that a nuclear test by any country would defeat

There is precious little arms control to be found in space, making the restrictions on nuclear weapons in the Outer Space Treaty a particularly significant achievement. Although the Outer Space Treaty is the foundational document of space law, it also includes limited provisions advancing efforts to prevent a nuclear arms race in space. States are prohibited from 'placing' nuclear weapons and other weapons of mass destruction (WMD) in orbit around the Earth, 'installing' them on celestial bodies, or 'stationing' them in outer space 'in any other manner'.[58]

While the Limited Test Ban Treaty covers any type of nuclear explosion in space and the Nuclear Non-Proliferation Treaty explicitly covers both nuclear weapons and NEDs, the Outer Space Treaty refers only to nuclear *weapons*. However, as eloquently addressed in the preceding chapter, nuclear weapons themselves are: inherently different from other systems, devices, and activities; cannot realistically be distinguished from devices intended for peaceful nuclear explosions;[59] and constitute a profound threat to global peace and security. As articulated, the best reading of the Outer Space Treaty makes its prohibitions applicable to both nuclear weapons and PNE devices.[60] It is not hard to imagine how a lax, permissive interpretation of the Outer Space Treaty allowing the stationing of PNE devices could easily circumvent the nuclear weapons prohibition in Article IV and sabotage the Outer Space Treaty, as well as the Nuclear Non-Proliferation Treaty.

The negotiating record of the Outer Space Treaty sometimes leaves the objectives of the negotiating states unclear, but that is not the case with respect to efforts to ban nuclear weapons in space. The Outer Space Treaty negotiators were clearly focused on the menace of nuclear weapons proliferation and

---

the object and purpose of the Comprehensive Nuclear-Test-Ban Treaty, see UNSC Res 2310 (23 September 2016) UN Doc S/Res/2310.

58 Article IV, Outer Space Treaty.

59 The United States, along with other countries, has long emphasised the indistinguishable nature of nuclear weapons and PNEs. See US Statement on Signature of Protocol II to the Latin American Denuclearization Treaty, United States Arms Control and Disarmament Agency, *Disarmament Documents* (1968) 205 ("The United States wishes to point out again the fact that the technology of making nuclear explosive devices for peaceful purposes is indistinguishable from the technology of making nuclear weapons and the fact that nuclear weapons and nuclear explosive devices for peaceful purposes are both capable of releasing nuclear energy in an uncontrolled manner and have the common group of characteristics of large amounts of energy generated instantaneously from a compact source").

60 This prohibition does not, however, extend to nuclear power sources in space. See Principles Relevant to the Use of Nuclear Power Sources in Outer Space, UNGA Res 47/68 (14 December 1992) UN Doc A/RES/47/68.

an arms race in space.[61] While the possible use of PNE devices for planetary defence was not addressed by the negotiating states, contemporaneous international arms control and disarmament discussions left no doubt about the danger of failing to include PNEs within the definition of nuclear weapons. For example, the US Secretary of State reported to the President in 1968 that "a nuclear explosive device intended for peaceful purposes can be used as a weapon or can be easily adapted for such use" and that "the technology for making such [PNE] devices is essentially indistinguishable from that of making nuclear weapons."[62] Similarly, the Soviet First Deputy Foreign Minister Kuznetsov, speaking to the First Committee of the General Assembly in 1968, said that "technically speaking, there is absolutely no difference between nuclear weapons and those devices which are used for peaceful explosions."[63]

The Limited Test Ban Treaty and the Outer Space Treaty thus offer no special exceptions for the use of NEDs in the peaceful cause of defending the Earth from asteroids. Given the threat to humanity posed by arms races which can provoke or escalate nuclear weapons proliferation, undermining these two key agreements with assorted excuses for avoiding their obligations would be a reckless course of action for the planet, regardless of noble aims such as protecting Earth from asteroids. A retrograde movement allowing the permissive interpretation of key terms in the Limited Test Ban Treaty and the Outer Space Treaty would be disastrous for the Nuclear Non-Proliferation Treaty and nuclear non-proliferation efforts generally, particularly since it could jeopardise remaining support for the fragile Nuclear Non-Proliferation Treaty regime by already disgruntled NNWSs.

4 The Way Forward

The nuclear weapons non-proliferation and arms control legal regime clearly imposes constraints on the ability of states to employ NEDs for planetary defence. Identifying possible legal solutions to this problem is a critical part of prudent planning and preparations for defending the Earth from a future

61 Paul G Dembling, 'The Evolution of the Outer Space Treaty' (1967) 33 Journal of Air Law and Commerce 421, 427 (noting the general agreement of all the states negotiating the Outer Space Treaty "that a critical need existed to include a provision banning nuclear weapons and other weapons of mass destruction from outer space").

62 United States Arms Control and Disarmament Agency, 'Disarmament Documents' (1968) 473.

63 Ibid 375.

catastrophic asteroid impact. States might at first be tempted to argue that an incoming asteroid in the future constitutes 'circumstances precluding the wrongfulness' which would allow them to invoke the principles of distress, necessity, or consent to overcome prohibitions in non-proliferation and arms control agreements.[64] States might also turn to the treaties in question and seek to amend them, suspend them by consent, withdraw from them, replace them, or excuse their non-performance. Unfortunately, all these options face serious challenges, which may include: stringent criteria; cumbersome consensus requirements; limitations on the individual discretion of states to invoke or employ some mechanisms; time-consuming formal processes; exceptional, unavailable conditions: or extremely limited circumstances involving imminent – not merely possible – danger.[65]

If an asteroid threatens to cause imminent, existential damage to Earth, states may be inclined to take hasty action by whatever means necessary – and without much regard for the finer points of law. But if a more remote, distant possibility of an asteroid impact is envisioned, using various imperfect work-arounds or short cuts to circumvent or ignore key agreements in the nuclear non-proliferation and arms control legal regime would undercut those agreements, undermine international security, and risk increasing the exposure of humanity to a different but very real, existential threat – a nuclear one.

The threat to humanity posed by nuclear weapons and other WMD has been the focus of numerous important decisions by the UN Security Council. Invoking its powers under Chapter VII of the UN Charter, the Security Council has found and frequently affirmed that the proliferation of WMD, particularly nuclear weapons, constitutes a 'threat to international peace and security'.[66]

---

64 Articles on the International Responsibility of States for Internationally Wrongful Acts, UNGA Res 56/83, Annex (12 December 2001) Chapter V, Circumstance Precluding Wrongfulness.

65 See David A Koplow, 'Exoatmospheric Plowshares: Using a Nuclear Explosive Device for Planetary Defense against an Incoming Asteroid' (Spring 2019) Journal of International Law and Foreign Affairs 1, 53–61 (discussing the shortcomings of various legal solutions or "work-arounds" enabling states to employ a nuclear explosive device for planetary defence); James A Green, 'Planetary Defense: Near-Earth Objects, Nuclear Weapons, and International Law' (2019) 42 Hastings International and Comparative Law Review 1, 48–52 (discussing several "promising" possibilities for precluding the apparent unlawfulness of nuclear planetary defence, but concluding that they remain reactive and ad hoc, that treaty withdrawal may be problematic, and that treaty suspension by consent may be a difficult option to implement successfully because of the need for universal agreement).

66 See e.g. UNSC Res 2397 (22 December 2017) UN Doc S/RES/2397 (reaffirming that "proliferation of nuclear, chemical and biological weapons, as well as their means of delivery, constitutes a threat to international peace and security").

The Security Council has wide discretion in making such determinations and in recent years has dramatically expanded the boundaries of 'threats to the peace' far beyond acts of aggression and military confrontations between states, setting the stage for such a finding also in the case of the natural threat posed by asteroids.

A finding of a 'threat to the peace' empowers the Security Council, at its discretion, to impose mandatory measures in the form of enforcement actions on states to restore international peace and security.[67] The legally binding nature of Security Council decisions has particular significance with respect to the treaties discussed in this chapter, which potentially block the employment of NEDs against asteroids. The UN Charter provides that "in the event of a conflict between the obligations of the Members of the United Nations under the present Charter and their obligations under any other international agreement, their obligations under the present Charter shall prevail".[68]

The Security Council, which has the 'primary responsibility for the maintenance of international peace and security', offers a recognised international forum for legitimate decision making by states as they balance competing risks as they discuss, plan and prepare for future actions to protect Earth from asteroids.[69] Under the UN Charter, all member states are legally obligated to comply with the decisions of the UN Security Council.[70] If there is a conflict between states' obligations under the UN Charter and their obligations under any other international agreement (including all the agreements discussed in this chapter), the obligations under the Charter shall prevail.[71] A Security Council decision would thus effectively displace the obligations in these other agreements.

5 Conclusion

The prospect of an asteroid causing catastrophic damage to Earth is a complex technical and political challenge for the international community, but it is also one in which international law must play a significant role. This is particularly

67 Articles 41 and 42, Charter of the United Nations (adopted 26 June 1945, entered into force 24 October 1945) 1 UNTS XVI (UN Charter).

68 Ibid Article 103.

69 Ibid Article 24. For a detailed discussion of the various options for decision-making at the international level see chapter 22 'International Bodies and Procedures for Decision-Making Regarding Planetary Defence Actions' in this book.

70 Article 25, UN Charter.

71 Article 103, UN Charter.

true if NEDs are to be utilised in any way for planetary defence purposes. If a nuclear option is considered, the fragile non-proliferation and international arms control legal framework must be a central concern.

There is no shortage of calculations about the probability of an asteroid or other near-Earth object hitting Earth and causing serious damage or, in less likely circumstances, catastrophic effects. But whatever the exact risks presented by asteroids, it is indisputable that the threat to Earth posed by nuclear weapons is real, growing and perhaps greater than it has been in generations. This stark (and terrifying) fact is accompanied by the reality that the international legal regime designed to control nuclear weapons proliferation and nuclear arms racesis already under stress and should not be further weakened by hasty, ill-conceived, or unnecessary actions undertaken for any reason, including planetary defence. In these circumstances, some commentators have argued that the threat posed by asteroids is overstated when compared to the threat posed to humanity by nuclear weapons.[72]

A theoretical contest between competing possible disasters and risks must give way to, at a minimum, respect for law and avoidance of unnecessary risks. Thus, this situation demands (1) that as much planning and preparation for planetary defence as possible occur before a moment of crisis in order to avoid hasty, careless or lawless actions that cause unnecessary damage to the critical nuclear non-proliferation and arms control legal framework and (2) that the UN Security Councilbe charged with ultimate responsibility for managing this important issue, since it is the only international body with the ability to operate with full legal sanction and at the same time it is charged with the primary responsibility to address threats to international peace and security – particularly those emanating from the proliferation of nuclear weapons.

72 See e.g. Thomas Graham Jr and Russell L Schweickart, 'NASA's Flimsy Argument for Nuclear Weapons' (2008) 298 Scientific American 3.

CHAPTER 17

Understanding the Social Aspects of an Asteroid Impact Threat from Socio-Anthropological Lessons Learned in Natural Disaster Management

Alissa J. Haddaji

1 Introduction

This chapter will aim to explore the lessons learned from socio-anthropology of natural disaster management and how they can be applied to the newly developed field of planetary defence management. To do so, three axes will be presented: (1) concepts, definitions and theoretical background of space threat management, which will establish a state-of-the art of the field, (2) understanding the societal aspects of an asteroid impact threat and the lessons learned from natural disaster management, and (3) making sense of disasters, catastrophes and perceptions through socio-anthropology. The goal will ultimately be to explain how social sciences such as socio-anthropology can inform scientific space threat management structures such as those of planetary defence by shedding light on key specificities to take into account in order to best support the populations they aim to protect.

2 Distinguishing Planetary Defence from Planetary Protection

Planetary defence and planetary protection are often confused as they misleadingly sound synonymous.[1] The confusion is so common that the distinction between the two needs routinely to be explained in the first five minutes of most presentations given by planetary protection experts.[2] As both fields

1 European Space Agency and NASA Planetary Protection Officers (PPOs) commonly teach the difference existing between planetary protection and planetary defence during planetary protection training programmes.

2 Cf. first slide of the presentation by ESA PPO Gerhard Kminek on 'What Planetary Protection is Not' (2 March 2017) <http://pposs.org/wp-content/uploads/2017/03/2.-PPOSS-Planetary-Protection-Basics-G.-Kminek.pdf> accessed 21 December 2020. Observations on COSPAR planetary protection trainings were made while the present author worked as the

 | DOI:10.1163/9789004467606_019

cover completely different areas of expertise, precise definitions are of utmost importance in that matter: as explored in this book, planetary defence is a scientific field which focuses on Near-Earth Objects that are potential threats to Earth. The purpose of planetary protection, on the other hand, is to prevent contamination between Earth and other bodies in the context of space exploration missions, including sample-return missions.[3] Planetary protection has a twofold goal: avoiding as little contamination as possible in places where human-brought particles/spores could grow and spread (such as in the under-ice oceans of Enceladus)[4] while ensuring that scientific investment in space exploration is not compromised by cross-contamination.[5] Planetary protection was developed with the start of modern space exploration in the 1960s. Theoretical concerns were raised as early as 1956 at the International Astronautical Federation 7th Congress in Rome before the Committee on Space Research (COSPAR)'s first recommendations in 1958. As planetary protection takes into consideration the environment in which the experiment is conducted (on the Moon, Mars, icy moons of Jupiter and Saturn, or asteroids), its guidelines will vary.

Though distinct, both PP (planetary protection) and PD (planetary defence) share a common responsibility: putting in place safety procedures in order to mitigate a potential space threat. For example, the practice of voluntarily extracting and bringing samples back from asteroids, moons or planets of our Solar System to Earth is a human activity which follows strict international planetary protection protocols and guidelines in order to avoid any risk of threatening the Earth with an unknown contaminant. Likewise, planetary defence officers need to make sure to carry mitigation missions that would, to the best of their ability, push a threatening asteroid away from Earth. Both planetary protection and planetary defence deal with the notion of protecting/defending the Earth from an 'existential risk' to humanity. While the former refers to contaminants, the latter refers to an impact threat, both planetary protection and planetary defence operate on a global scale. To better understand their common reach in managing 'existential threats', one first needs to accurately understand the lexicon of threat management.

Planetary Protection of Outer Solar System (PPOSS) project officer from September 2015 to February 2019.

3 Missions bringing samples back to Earth from asteroids, moons or planets such as Mars.

4 Enceladus is one of Saturn's natural satellites and is believed to have a liquid ocean under its iced surface.

5 See the website of the Planetary Protection of Outer Solar System <http://pposs.org/pp-101/> accessed 21 December 2020.

3 Concepts, Definitions and Theoretical Background of Space Threat Management

3.1 *What is an Existential Space Risk?*

The meaning of the very word 'risk' will depend on who defines it as there are as many perceptions as there are cultures, social practices, and individuals. It will also depend on the set of social circumstances and judgments considered, as well as how such a risk will be communicated to a set population. Thus, it is to be understood that space risk acceptability will greatly vary in range, depending on the population possibly impacted.

3.2 *Space Risk Perception*

Examining and analysing threat perception is key to understanding planetary protection and planetary defence decision-making processes. But as in its history humankind has never faced an extinction-wide threat coming from either an asteroid impact to Earth nor a wide-spread unknown space contaminant, no one has ever experienced how the decision-makers, the planetary protection and planetary defence experts, and the general population as a whole, would rise to such challenges. It is thus imperative to develop rigorous and in-depth understanding of the critical sociological issues that policy makers and others would most likely have to contend with during the management of any future space hazard events.

3.3 *Geographic and Temporal Scales*

Depending on the asteroid's characteristics (size, composition, velocity, angle on entry), an impact on Earth could either be local (such as what happened in Chelyabinsk), national, regional, or global. NEO detection has greatly improved over the past twenty-five years: it is now possible for an asteroid predicted to come near the Earth to be detected several decades in advance (such as *Apophis* which was detected in 2004 to come back close to the Earth in 2029).

3.4 *Definitions of Risk, Threat and Hazard*

After distinguishing planetary defence from planetary protection, the words most often affiliated with them such as 'risk', 'threat', 'hazard' and 'catastrophe' need all the more to be precisely defined and differentiated as their common usage differs from the meaning they have in the specific context of disaster management.

A 'risk' is defined as a probability a hazard will be happening. The Global Economic Forum Report calls an 'existential risk' a risk that could either annihilate intelligent life or permanently and drastically curtail its potential.[6] In that sense, the risk of an asteroid impact larger than 10 kilometres in diameter[7] may be classified as an existential risk. On the other hand, when discussing the potential for Earth to be impacted by an asteroid, the US Planetary Defence Office refers to the NEO impact 'hazard'.[8] As for the word 'threat', the same Planetary Defence Office advises to use it only when a specific object has been identified on a potential impact course towards Earth. It will coordinate US government planning in response to an 'actual impact threat'. The distinction between hazard and threat helps us, therefore, to distinguish when we are talking hypothetically about an impact, as opposed to when we have determined there is potential for an actual impact.[9] In other words, a threat is a hazard that has become certain. Moreover, the term 'threat' also carries the significance that one has become aware of the danger posed by a hazard and wants to be protected from it.[10]

Making the distinction between the term 'threat' from that of 'disaster' is equally important. While a natural disaster suggests that the event has occurred and exceeds the capacities of local management,[11] a threat characterises an event that has not yet taken place and involve local and/or international decision-making structures. For example, if/when an asteroid is on its route to impact Earth, the term asteroid 'threat' will be used. After the impact, the term 'disaster' will be used. Notwithstanding references to the 1883 comet that nearly missed Earth, a major asteroid impact is something unprecedented in human experience. Consequently, when talking about NEO research and detection, the terms 'threat' and 'disaster' are incorrect and should not be used for 'hazard'.

6 World Economic Forum, *Global Risks 2014* (9th ed, World Economic Forum 2014).

7 Based on the 10 kilometres Chicxulub Asteroid which impacted the Earth 65000 years ago and is commonly referred to as the 'dinosaur killer', Charles Q Choi, 'Chicxulub Asteroid Impact: The Dino-Killer That Scientists Laughed At' (*Space.com*, 7 February 2013) <www.space.com/19681-dinosaur-killing-asteroid-chicxulub-crater.html> accessed 21 December 2020.

8 See website of NASA on planetary defense <www.nasa.gov/planetarydefense/overview> accessed 21 December 2020.

9 American Chemistry Council, 'Risk vs Hazards' (*Campaign For Accuracy In Public Health Research*) <https://campaignforaccuracyinpublichealthresearch.com/risk-vs-hazard/> accessed 21 December 2020.

10 Yves Dupont, *Dictionnaire des risques* (Armand Colin 2003).

11 Patrick Pigeon and Julien Rebotier, *Les Politiques de Prévention des Désastres, Penser et Agir dans L'imperfection* (ISTE 2017).

3.5 *Not a First in Human History*

If a large asteroid impacted the Earth, it would not be the first time the world would face a mass extinction. Such information can be found in pandemics literature. For instance, during the four years of the 1347 – 1351 pandemic, 20 percent to 60 percent of the western world population – depending on sources in a context with few statistics – was killed by the Black Plague. In other circumstances, entire cities were erased due to a natural disaster. Such was the case of the eruption of Vesuvius that destroyed Pompeii in 79 AD. However, these events are so rare that the means to fight them and adapt to them tend to fade over the centuries.[12] That timescale defies generational memory and is one of the challenges facing planetary defence. The scope and magnitude of these events is another challenge.

3.6 *More than a Disaster: A "Catastrophe", an Unthinkable Event*

Taking upon socio-anthropologist Yves Dupont's definition of '*catastrophe*', the term refers to a "large-scale event entailing major damage, whose social and symbolic consequences are of historical order"; it etymologically means, in the context of Greek tragedy, "the writing of the last stanza (*cata-strophein*)". The word also implies a difficulty in thinking the unthinkable, the unimaginable, and preparing for it or even protecting oneself from it.[13] Accordingly, an asteroid impact or the world-wide spread of an extra-terrestrial contaminant would rightfully be a 'catastrophe', an unthinkable turn of events. The fact that it is 'unthinkable' is one of the specific characteristics of a space risk. This is unthinkable in a unique way because of its magnitude, the scope of its consequences, the rapidity and brutality of the event. A nuclear holocaust may not compare in size, and climate change may span much longer time periods. The science fiction genre, through literature, movies and television series, has visited these risks but they remain nonetheless difficult to comprehend

---

12 Rene Favier and Anne-Marie Granet-Abisset, *History and Memory of Natural Risks* (MSH-Alpes 2000).

13 Yves Dupont, *Dictionnaire des Risques* (Armand Colin 2003), "Catastrophe: A large-scale event entailing major damage, whose social and symbolic consequences are of historical order (...) Etymologically, it suggests a reversal and the writing of the last stanza of a Greek tragedy (cata-strophein)(...) It implies a difficulty in thinking, preparing for and finding protection from the unthinkable and the unimaginable", translated from French: "Catastrophe: Evènement causant un sinistre d'ampleur majeure, dont les conséquences sociales et symboliques sont d'ordre historique. (..) Elle désigne étymologiquement l'idée d'un renversement et l'écriture de la dernière strophe de la tragédie grecque (cata-strophein). Elle Implique une difficulté de penser et de se préparer à l'impensable, l'inimaginable (voire de s'en protéger)".

due to the fact that they are not part of humankind's historical consciousness. There is no record of an asteroid impact devastating a large part of the human population nor is there any record of a foreign pathogen brought from outer space. Such is not the case when thinking about other earthly natural disasters. Erupting volcanoes or tsunamis are nowadays better known as they are both experienced and studied on a regular basis. The surreal and exceptionally rare nature of a NEO threat finds a more tangible reference in Pompeian civilians, taken by surprise and unable to protect themselves from a natural but devastating event. Thinking the unthinkable and trying to prepare for it, with very little data available, is one of the biggest challenges when considering such low probability risks. In that context, learning from natural disaster management agencies is essential as they are the most knowledgeable structures on how to deal with potentially devastating and previously unknown phenomena.

Bearing all these elements in mind, asteroid hazards should therefore be categorised as 'natural disastrous/catastrophic hazards' (depending on the size and amount of damage they may cause) as they have not been experienced by humans but have been somewhat partially recognised as a possible danger requiring further investigation so as to know better how to protect populations from it.

What distinguishes a 'catastrophe' from a 'disaster' is thus the exceptional nature of the event as well as the scale of its consequences regarding political involvement, the socio-cultural environment, space and time, and last but not least, the way it is perceived: whereas disasters are politically dealt with locally, sociologist Enrico Quarantelli explains that catastrophes mobilise governments at both a national and an international level as that kind of event impacts a plurality of countries and requires international assistance.[14] Quarantelli also suggests it is harder to recover from a catastrophe than a disaster: as the destruction level is much bigger, populations as well as emergency organisations have no resources, no facilities to turn to:

> The distinction we draw between catastrophes and disasters is not just an academic exercise (although the distinction is also important for research purposes not discussed here). What is crucial is that catastrophes require some different kinds of planning and managing than do

14 Enrico Quarantelli, 'Catastrophes are different from disasters: some implications for crisis planning and managing drawn from Katrina' (*The Social Science Research Council*, 11 June 2006) <https://items.ssrc.org/understanding-katrina/catastrophes-are-different-from-disasters-some-implications-for-crisis-planning-and-managing-drawn-from-katrina/> accessed 21 December 2020.

> even major disasters. This is true whether the focus is on the planning for mitigation, preparedness, response or recovery.[15]

Moreover, a catastrophe, by its very magnitude, represents a higher scale threat not only to material structures but also to the social and cultural order of the zone impacted.[16] An asteroid with the capacity to destroy an entire region (shared by one or more countries) and creating a large-scale impact on the planet would be considered a catastrophe rather than a disaster. Differences in the time scale of impact also separates a disaster from a catastrophe. The consequences of an asteroid impact could last several hundreds or even thousands of years and may have irreversible effects. They could entail global imbalances since some species might completely vanish from our global ecosystem. Finally, the distinction between disaster and catastrophe will not only depend on the scale of the event but also on the way it is perceived. On the scale of the event Quarantelli says:

> In a disaster there is usually only one major target for the convergence after a disaster. In a catastrophe, many nearby communities not only cannot contribute to the inflow, but they themselves can become competing sources for an eventual unequal inflow of goods, personnel, supplies and communication.[17]

15 Ibid.

16 Jaque Berlioz and Grégory Quenet, 'Catastrophes: Definitions and Documentation' in Rene Favier and Anne-Marie Granet-Abisset (eds), *History and Memory of Natural Risks* (MSH-Alpes 2000) 61: "In the strong sense of the word a catastrophe radically threatens the very existence and meaning of the socio-cultural order (…) What sets a catastrophe apart is its exceptional character (…) Catastrophes are characterized by strong political involvement. In disasters only local authorities are involved whereas catastrophes mobilize both the government and all the higher political instances.", translated from the French: "Au sens fort, la catastrophe est une menace radicale contre l'ordre culturel et social, à la fois dans son existence et dans sa signification. (…) La distinction se situe dans le caractère exceptionnel d'une catastrophe. (…) Une catastrophe se caractérise par une forte implication politique. Lors d'un désastre, l'implication politique se limite au niveau local. Une catastrophe mobilise le gouvernement et toutes les instances politiques supérieures".

17 Enrico Quarantelli, 'Catastrophes are Different from Disasters: Some Implications for Crisis Planning and Managing Drawn from Katrina' (*The Social Science Research Council*, 11 June 2006) <https://items.ssrc.org/understanding-katrina/catastrophes-are-different-from-disasters-some-implications-for-crisis-planning-and-managing-drawn-from-katrina/> accessed 21 December 2020.

The distinction between disaster and catastrophe entailed by an asteroid impact threat or a space contaminant brings us to the notion of risk perception theorised by essayist Nassim Taleb, which he named 'black swan'.

3.7 *"Black Swan" Catastrophe and Scotomisation*

In his *Black Swan* essay,[18] Taleb defines a *black swan* as a low probability, unpredictable event (a so-called 'rare event' in probability theory) which, should it occur, would have exceptionally far-reaching consequences. Such catastrophes can create a mental blocking of unwanted perceptions called scotomisation. Anthropologists Susanna Hoffman and Anthony Oliver-Smith explain that rather than reveal real ignorance of the phenomena or a lack of adequate education, this can be interpreted as 'comprehension denial'. That characteristic was identified by Oliver-Smith according to whom, "many natural hazards are not common enough or do not entail frequent enough catastrophes, so that they are often not identified as threats."[19] A scotomisation is a psychological and cultural defence mechanism consisting of automatic or unwilling denial meant as a 'blind spot' to avoid any possible anxiety.[20] Some space events such as the scientifically established eventual death of our Sun 4 to 5 billion years from now can go unrecognised simply because their reference scales do not make much sense to humankind. Nobody worries about the fate of humans after that because, as human life expectancy does not typically exceed a hundred years, this ultra-generational dimension totally excludes human beings from the phenomenon. They cannot feel either touched or affected by it, nor can they comprehend the stakes concerning such a distant future. Similarly,

18 Nassim N Taleb, 'The Black Swan: The Impact of the Highly Improbable' *The New York Times* (New York, 22 April 2007) <www.nytimes.com/2007/04/22/books/chapters/0422-1st-tale.html> accessed 21 December 2020.

19 Anthony Oliver-Smith, 'Theorizing Disasters' in Susanne Hoffman and Anthony Oliver-Smith (eds), *Catastrophes & Culture: The Anthropology of Disaster* (School of American Research Press 2002) 142 : "Many natural hazards are not common enough or do not entail frequent enough catastrophes, so that quite often they are not identified as threats", translated from French: "De nombreux risques naturels ne sont pas suffisamment fréquents ou ne produisent pas de catastrophes assez fréquentes, de sorte qu'ils peuvent souvent ne pas être perçus comme des menaces".

20 Anthony Oliver-Smith, 'Theorizing Disasters' in Susanne Hoffman and Anthony Oliver-Smith (eds), *Catastrophes & Culture: The Anthropology of Disaster* (School of American Research Press 2002) 136 : "A scotomization (…) is a psychological and cultural defence mechanism consisting of automatically or unwillingly turning a blind eye on something so as to block a possible source of anxiety", translated from French: "Scotomisation (…) c'est-à-dire un dispositif psychologique et culturel de défense qui, à travers une occultation, automatique ou involontaire, vise à ne pas voir un possible élément d'anxiété".

the risk of an asteroid eradicating the human race can hardly be acknowledged, first due to its low probability rate but also because nothing in human history, except the knowledge accumulated on the extinction of dinosaurs, can prepare humanity to grasp the broad, unfamiliar and somewhat unnatural idea that the entire human race or even the whole planet could be wiped-out in an instant.

This psychological inability to grasp the 'unthinkable' also arouses among decision-makers the fear of grand scale panics among populations. In order to face that particular risk, scientists and politicians need to further research and develop adequate answers. The analysis of disaster as an interface may serve that purpose.

3.8 *Disaster as an Interface*

A natural disaster is an interface, a place of interaction between man and nature, a dialogue between a social system and its natural environment.[21] Anthropologist Douglas identified three main attitudes towards a disaster: optimism, pessimism, and fatalism. In the case of an asteroid impact or of a contamination, all the parties involved (scientists, decision-makers as well as the populations) could adopt any of the following attitudes:

- an optimistic attitude: in the case of an asteroid impact threat, the reaction will be to consider that the asteroid is actually going to miss the Earth or that a mitigation mission will be successful,
- a pessimistic attitude which may result in mass panic and attempts to evacuate the zone of potential impact and,
- a fatalistic approach, with people believing that it is their fate to die from the asteroid impact. The latter could be explained by religious and/or spiritual beliefs that this impact is an 'act of God' and/or of the Universe and is consequently not meant to be prevented.

These three attitudes will entail radically different reactions and will thus impact risk management. Risk management definitions enable one to understand natural disaster management literature and may thus enable lessons learned transfers towards the new field of space threat management. More importantly, risk vocabulary informs us on a key concept: that risk perception will vary depending on the local population observed, thus rendering even

21 Yves Dupont, *Dictionnaire des Risques* (Armand Colin 2003) 63: "A natural disaster is an interface phenomenon, a dialectical exchange between man and nature, a dialogue between a social system and its ecosystem", translated from French: "La catastrophe naturelle est un phénomène d'interface, car elle implique la dialectique entre l'homme et la nature, le dialogue entre un système social et un écosystème".

more complex its management in times of crisis. It is now time to explore how best to plan on communicating an 'existential space threat' to the world population.

4 Understanding Societal Aspects of an Asteroid Impact Threat: Lessons Learned from Natural Disaster Management

4.1 *Keeping Track of Rare Recurring Events through Decades and Centuries*

Much like asteroids and comets coming close to the Earth periodically, some natural disasters are cyclical, as are those related to biennial natural phenomena like El Niño, or prone to happen regularly as the eruptions of Colombian volcano Nevado del Ruiz. The latter is an example of a large-scale recurring disaster[22] spanning such long periods of time that they outdo human memory (see Figure 17.1). Because Nevado del Ruiz's 1985 eruption was only preceded by two others in 1595 and in 1623, it was difficult for many to accept the danger presented by the volcano; locals called it 'the Sleeping Lion'.[23] Yet worse than the actual eruption was what turned out to be the worst volcanic mudflow disaster in historic time and the second worst volcanic disaster of the 20th and 21st centuries.[24]

Its death toll ranks fourth in history, behind only Tambora in 1815 (92000) and Krakatoa in 1883 (36000) both in Indonesia, and Mount Pelée, Martinique,

---

22 The volcano erupted in the years 1595, 1623, 1805, 1826, 1829, 1831, 1845, 1916, 1984–1985, and 1987–1991 according to the United Nations Disaster Risk Reduction (UNDRR) website, see <www.unisdr.org> accessed 21 December 2020.

23 'Volcano kills thousands in Colombia' (*BBC*, 13 November 1985) <http://news.bbc.co.uk/onthisday/hi/dates/stories/november/13/newsid_2539000/2539731.stm> accessed 21 December 2020.

24 Barry Voight, *The 1985 Nevado del Ruiz Volcano Catastrophe: Anatomy and Retrospection* (Penn State University Press 1989). The flows of lava coalesced and entrained debris, vegetation and ponded water to form lahars, the Javanese word used internationally to mean a mud or debris flow of volcanic origin. These successive lahar waves obliterated Armero (population 29000), the prime regional agricultural center. About five vertical kilometres below the summit of Ruiz, Armero became a crypt sealed in lahar mud. Over 20000 were entombed and 5000 more were injured. In the vicinity of the volcano, all roads, bridges, telephone lines, power grids and aqueducts were damaged or destroyed. Sixty percent of the region's livestock, thirty percent of its grain sorghum and rice crops, and half a million bags of coffee were lost. Lahars buried 3400 hectares of the agricultural land, damaged or eradicated fifty schools and two hospitals, destroyed 5092 homes, 58 industrial plants and 343 commercial establishments, and damaged the National Coffee Research Center. About 7700 were rendered homeless. Total damage exceeded a billion dollars.

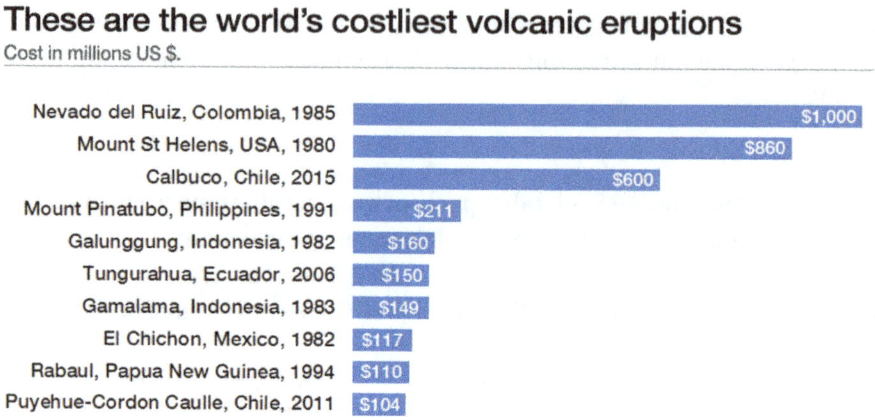

FIGURE 17.1 World's costliest volcanic eruptions
Website of the Centre for Research on the Epidemiology of Disasters <www.emdat.be/>

in 1902 (28000).[25] Nevado del Ruiz may consequently also serve as an example of a recurring disaster whose secondary effects are worse than the eruption itself. Studying such natural disasters may help the planetary defence community prepare for major secondary effects resulting from an asteroid impact. Finally, lessons may be extracted from the local knowledge and resilience developed from Colombians in this region, having had to face throughout multiple generations the same recurring natural disaster. Such knowledge may be useful when designing planetary defence policies meant to be resilient and adaptable to an impact detected several decades in advance.

4.2 *Population Displacements*

An asteroid impact may also have indirect social effects which would be hard to predict and be spread out over long periods of time. The planetary defence community may learn from socio-anthropologists who have worked on cases of costly and long-lasting natural disasters such as the ones which impacted the Japanese city of Fukushima on 11 March 2011. The earthquake and tsunami which impacted Fukushima are considered the costliest natural disaster in human history, with a cost estimated at USD 235 billion. Together, they resulted in almost 16000 deaths, as well as 6000 people injured and 2500 still missing.

---

25 See website of United Nations Office of Disaster Risk Reduction <www.unisdr.org> accessed 21 December 2020.

More than 470000 people were ordered to leave their homes and about 174000 were still displaced in March 2016.[26] Such a problem of population displacement is one that would have to be tackled in case an asteroid impact threat necessitated the evacuation of a populated area. The United Nations Refugee Agency estimated that out of the 70.8 million people forcibly displaced worldwide, 80 percent live in countries neighbouring their countries of origin. When rehearsing an asteroid impact scenario such data should be taken into account to inform countries sharing borders with the impacted country, considering the high probability of refugees they may have to accommodate.[27]

4.3 *Economic Damage*

The World Economic Forum studied and classified the natural disasters that inflict the most economic damage.[28] Floods and tsunamis – which may occur if an asteroid was to fall into an ocean – have been the most common natural disasters over the last twenty years. They account for 43 percent of all recorded natural disasters and have been evaluated as the third costliest ones, especially if they were to impact the Americas or Asia. Such data may be considered when training for an asteroid impact in an Earth's ocean.

4.4 *Loss of World Heritage*

Finally, an asteroid impact may result in great cultural loss which previous disasters may inform the planetary defence community on. For example, such was the case when Latin America's oldest and most important historical and scientific museum was consumed by fire in Brazil on 3 September 2018.[29] Much of its archive of 20 million items covering two centuries of work, research and knowledge is believed to have been destroyed. The loss to Brazilian science, history and culture was incalculable. The collection included Egyptian and Greco-Roman artefacts, 'Luzia', a 12000-year-old skeleton and the oldest in the Americas, fossils, dinosaurs, and a meteorite found in 1784. The fire of Alexandria's library is also considered a common example of cultural loss. Built in 334 BC, the library burnt in 48 BC and with it the largest collection

26 According to the Reconstruction Agency, set up by the Japanese government to oversee the reconstruction of the country's infrastructure, industry and livelihood.

27 See website of the United Nations High Commissioner for Refugees <www.unhcr.org/> accessed 21 December 2020regarding displaced populations worldwide

28 See website of the World Economic Forum <www.weforum.org/agenda/archive/davos-2016/> accessed 21 December 2020.

29 Dom Phillips, 'Brazil Museum Fire: "Incalculable" Loss 200-year-old Rio Institution Gutted' (*The Guardian*, 2 September 2018) <www.theguardian.com/world/2018/sep/03/fire-engulfs-brazil-national-museum-rio> accessed 21 December 2020.

of classical antiquity and Egyptian literature estimated to more than 100000 pieces of literature.

An asteroid impact would raise local cultural and political challenges that socio-anthropology commonly addresses. It is now time to explore the key takeaways from the field of socio-anthropology of natural disaster management.

5 Making Sense of Disasters, Catastrophes and Perceptions through Socio-Anthropology

5.1 *The Input of Socio-Anthropology*

Disaster, as previously explored, is an interface between humankind and its environment.[30] The way an astronomical event can be perceived as a disaster or a catastrophe depends on the sets of beliefs and on the cultural background through which such an event is being perceived.

Socio-anthropology enables the analysis of local cultural knowledge, especially useful in emergency relief situations; it helps contextualise and understand key socio-cultural elements in disaster management.[31] A disaster will disrupt a pre-established social order that one must get acquainted with in order to better assist that social order. During emergency relief situations for example, if the culture of the impacted populations is not taken into account, the survivors will have an even harder time recovering from the event.[32] When thinking about an asteroid impact, resorting to anthropologic knowledge

30 Yves Dupont, *Dictionnaire des Risques* (Armand Colin 2003) 63: "A natural disaster is an interface phenomenon, a dialectical exchange between man and nature, a dialogue between a social system and its ecosystem", translated from French: "La catastrophe naturelle est un phénomène d'interface, car elle implique la dialectique entre l'homme et la nature, le dialogue entre un système social et son écosystème."

31 Anthropologist Sandrine Revet explored in 2007 the idea that, in order to help prepare populations for a disaster situation, the notion of natural hazard needs to be contextualised, put in perspective and compared to everyday risks related to socio-economic hardship, and thus, to be taken into account in disaster management.

32 Gaelle Clavandier, *La Mort Collective: Pour une Sociologie des Catastrophes* (CNRS Éditions 2004): "A catastrophe will disrupt a pre-established social order that one must get acquainted with in order to better assist that social order. During emergency relief situations for example, if the culture of the impacted populations is not taken into account, the survivors will have an even harder time recovering from the event", translated from French: "La catastrophe naturelle vient rompre un ordre social préétabli qu'il se faut de connaître afin de l'assister au mieux. Lors de ces situations d'aide d'urgence, une ignorance de la culture des populations impactées contribue à renforcer les difficultés que les rescapés de la catastrophe auront à se remettre de l'évènement".

and methods serves to better know and see the population that stands to be impacted, and to better understand that each place on Earth has a local identity. It is also to be noted that it might be counterproductive to use a rhetoric that would tend to impose a single global approach over an overly generalised and uniformly perceived category of 'victims' for that would fail to pay enough attention to contextual and cultural differences.

5.2 *Socio-Economic Vulnerability and Inequalities in Coping with Natural Disaster*

The vulnerability of the populations needs to be taken into account through the acknowledgment of not only physical vulnerability (which pertains to the nature of buildings and land use – namely resistance of materials and structures in various places) but also social vulnerability and inequalities. Social factors induce the probability that some social categories will suffer more significant damage than others, which will affect their capacity to recover after a disaster. Also, all populations have to face various socio-economic struggles and, on most occasions, these socio-economic problems will be perceived as more important than the natural threat itself. The risk of an asteroid colliding with Earth may seem quite abstract and not of immediate importance to populations facing life-threatening struggles such as famines, war, economic hardship or lack of health care coverage.

Economic inequalities will also impact the way disasters are dealt with and will amplify their magnitude. As environmental researcher Pauline Texier explains:

> Vulnerability to natural events is closely related to socio-economic conditions. Even though a natural phenomenon does not, upon occurring, distinguish "the rich" from "the poor", inequalities between these two groups are noticeable from the very moment of the impact through the aftermath and its consequences. Disasters are the result of an interaction between a particularly vulnerable human population and a potentially destructive agent, among which are found natural events.[33]

---

33 Pauline Textier and others, 'Risk Management Stakes in Informal Urban Districts, Two Case Studies: Jakarta (Indonesia) and Angeles City (the Philippines)' in Sylvia Becerra and Anne Peltier (eds), *Risks and Environment: Interdisciplinary Research on the Vulnerability of Societies* (L'Harmattan 2009) 46.

5.3 *Resistance to Displacement*

As anthropologists, such as Boscoboinik have explained, despite seismic shocks or tsunami warnings, human communities over the ages have consistently avoided being displaced and have refused to leave certain sites or have returned to them.[34] This can be explained by a variety of reasons among which cultural attachment to their land, or a fatalistic belief that it is 'their fate' to be killed by the disaster in question. Economic reasons can also play an important part in their refusal to be displaced. Indeed, they may not have anywhere else to go and/or may not have the economic resources necessary to leave. Decision makers dealing with asteroid threat management will therefore have to consider that some populations will decide to remain in the zone of impact.

5.4 *Mass Death Management*

Additionally, should an asteroid impact happen, planetary defence officials and emergency responders would also have to face mass death management challenges. This domain of research has been explored by the sociologists of natural disaster. One of their main findings comes from the observation that local populations can be deeply disturbed by the lack of cultural care during mass burials. Death management is indeed a highly important cultural and social matter dealt with primarily by the local populations, rather than by national and international decision-makers.[35] Different cultures and sets of beliefs will create different behaviours when facing a disaster. For instance, in some countries special units are created to face mass death disasters.[36] But in such a situation, corpses may not be identifiable and the authorities may find it impossible to take into account the socio-cultural rites of the living regarding death management as they are acting in a state of emergency.[37]

---

34 Andrea Boscoboinik, 'Le Processus Catastrophe: Vulnérabilités, Discours, Réponses' (PhD thesis, Université de Fribourg 2007) 204: "Despite seismic shocks or tsunami warnings, human communities over the ages have consistently avoided being displaced and have refused to leave certain sites or have returned to them", translated from French: "Malgré les secousses sismiques, les groupes humains ont de tout temps évité les déplacements, ont refusé d'abandonner certains sites ou les ont réintégrés".

35 Andre Corbet, 'Death and the Dead in Haiti after the January 12, 2010 Earthquake, A Report Commissioned by the French Strategic Defence Department' (Department of Strategic Affairs 2011) 100.

36 France has, for example, a Disaster Victim Identification National Unit (l'Unité Nationale d'Identification des Victimes de Catastrophes (UNIVIC)) dedicated to organising searches to recover French citizens' corpses in the case of a natural disaster. Ibid 99.

37 Ibid.

In this context, populations can perceive death rituals as necessary to try to make sense and somehow 'normalise' the disaster. A disregard for death rituals can deeply disturb sets of population and enhance their traumas. For example, the literature indicates how important it is to follow death rituals especially for violent deaths as was the case in Guede Nibo in Haiti.[38] An asteroid impact would entail a collective trauma where "the living sleep along the dead"[39] with mass graves, cities eradicated, saturated cemeteries, local cultures being entirely wiped out, populations being displaced by thousands if not by millions, and mass panic.[40] Another example is to be found in some indigenous Central and Latin American cultures which strongly believe in afterlife. Populations suffering mass deaths due to an asteroid impact may be terrified of the possible retaliation of spirits blocked in limbo between two worlds, not having been buried properly or having been cast into mass graves. Consequently, when dealing with mass death management, experts recommend that collective graves endeavour to respect people's individualities, religious beliefs and rights.[41]

However, it can also be envisaged that an asteroid impact may deprive some people of their faith. Such was the case after the earthquake that shook Lisbon, Portugal, in 1755, killing in an instant a hundred thousand people. Philosophers from all over Western Europe came then to challenge the concept of divine justice, the existence of God itself and precipitated the belief of a 'secular catastrophe'.[42]

This secular positioning is similar to the scientific fact-based one displayed by IAWN and SMPAG scientists who endorse the matter-of-factness of the law in their planetary defence management planning.

---

38 Ibid.

39 Fabrizio Scapin and Pieter Van Eecke, *Goudougoudou* (Polymorfilm 2012).

40 Pan American Health Organization and World Health Organization, 'Management of Dead Bodies in Disaster Situations' (2004) 5 Disaster Manuals and Guidelines Series.

41 The Inter-American Court of Human Rights recognised in the Blake case "The need for preserving the cultural value of respecting the dead as breaching that need results in intensified grief and suffering of the family members." See *Blake Case Reparations* (1999) Inter-American Court of Human Rights, Series C no 48, para 11.

42 David Le Breton, *Sociologie du Risqué* (Que Sais-Je 2017) 40: "In 1755, the earthquake that shook Lisbon, Portugal, and killed in an instant a hundred thousand people, ruined the concept of divine justice in the eyes of philosophers, and precipitated a secular view of catastrophe", translated from French: "Le tremblement de terre de Lisbonne (1755), qui tue en un instant cent mille personnes, ruine aux yeux des philosophes toute idée de justice divine et précipite une vision laïque de la catastrophe".

5.5 *Legal Aspects of Natural Disasters*

Various countries have passed a series of laws dealing with disaster management. For example, in France, the law passed on 13 July 1982 and, entitled "The natural disaster compensation law",[43] defines insurance requirements and the victims' compensation rights. This law acknowledges the complexity of the consequences of natural disasters and the fact that all the parties involved will enter unchartered territory given the intrinsic uncertainties of that kind of events. It acknowledges that the cost of such highly complex and unpredictable events is hard to assess, both because of the possible concatenation of events and because of the limits of standard statistical methods. Insurance premiums rarely prove to be adapted to situations characterised by such great uncertainties and where the financial reserves required for compensation go beyond the scope of insurance standards. The stakes related to territorial and urban vulnerability are linked to human presence (people, houses, economic activities, infrastructures etc.) which is hard to price and should therefore be researched further.[44]

5.6 *Political Structures*

The efficiency of an international humanitarian governance endeavour may be challenged if that governance ignores the specificities either of the culture or local resources.[45] Historically, collective risk has been managed by the state.[46] But it remains to be seen how a trans-border catastrophe as that of a large asteroid impact could be managed. Such a collective global threat could be managed by the United Nations or by a transnational system yet to be developed. However, in order to be efficient and resilient, any intervention would need to also be locally rooted. Top/down-only systems should be avoided as they are eventually poorly adapted to local needs or do not know or take into consideration local practices.[47] Moreover, such transnational catastrophes might occur in places with differing political models/regimes: in democratic or totalitarian countries; complying or not with UN conventions/treaties, etc. This would force or block the implementation of top/down systems and would create one more hurdle that would have to be taken into consideration and

---

43 French law of 13 July 1982, "The natural disaster compensation law" or "Loi d'indemnisation des catastrophes naturelles".

44 Patrick Pigeon and Julien Rebotier, *Les Politiques de Prévention des Désastres, Penser et Agir dans l'Imperfection* (ISTE 2017).

45 Ibid 27.

46 Ibid 64.

47 Such as the way a local population will deal with its dead.

overcome. Detailed knowledge of international relations and local regimes are consequently quite important to set up cross-border space risk management systems.

6 Conclusion

The planetary defence and planetary protection scientific communities must take into account the social, cultural and psychological aspects of the populations they will be trying to help and protect. In order to manage the challenging existential space threats that are asteroid impact threats and microbial and organic contamination. It will also be important to properly assess the social, cultural, and psychological impact a space catastrophe could create. It will be necessary to provide psychological assistance to the populations in order to help them deal with shock/possible scotomisation effect, loss, massive disappearances of friends and family and the emergence of both rational and irrational fears while respecting their cultural specificities. To prepare addressing the psychological hardships the populations are likely to experience, this chapter concurs with James's and Friedman's recommendation to invite anthropologists and religious experts in the design phase of crisis management planning and would extend it to future planetary defence conferences and similar venues.[48] The objective will be to build awareness among policy makers of a given population's needs so that the emergency responders operating under their authority may provide adequate help in a way that will be best received locally, rather than follow political plans designed in a way that may be dismissive of the local specificities of a country or a territory.[49] This may also help alleviate other possible political difficulties: as humankind has had so far, no direct experience of the consequences of a large asteroid impact, it relies for argumentation's sake on what it knows, namely natural disasters. Be they earthquakes, hurricanes, landslides, volcanic eruptions, tsunamis or wildfires, natural disasters are generally considered a-political, 'nature' possibly being the one to blame. We can, however, note that natural disasters linked to issues such as climate change and human industrial activity may be more politically charged. Moreover, in two other instances natural disasters can be linked to political responsibility: disaster prevention and ways governments deal with

48 John W James and Russell Friedman, *The Grief Recovery Handbook* (Harper Perennial 1998) 62.

49 Ibid.

the aftermath.[50] Natural disaster-related relief and assistance efforts can create substantial tensions among populations, international organisations and government institutions. These conflicts can reveal different visions of, and assumptions about, relief and assistance as well as the often-unquestioned representations of risk and vulnerability that each group supports.[51]

A transdisciplinary approach will, one hopes, lessen these conflicts. This is why it is important to tackle natural disaster literature through the social science lens to better apprehend, reflect and make forecasts on the human impact space disasters might have. 'Natural' phenomena are not natural per se but are rather the result of an interaction between a natural hazard and the conditions of physical and social vulnerability prevailing among given social categories.[52] The lessons learned could help the planetary defence community improve their preparedness efforts to design mitigation missions by factoring in the challenges that it may face, as a scientifically-led structure, when it will interact with impacted and non-impacted populations before, during and after an asteroid impact. Such new examples of transdisciplinary and collaborative efforts with socio-anthropologists could inform planetary defence management of pre-emptive steps that can be taken against the social complexities usually emerging during natural disasters. This chapter's main recommendation would consequently be that space science experts connect with sociologists, anthropologists and psychologists who have an expertise in natural disaster management, so as to discuss jointly what possible academic research could be conducted to reflect on and plan the most adequate ways to interact with populations under a potential asteroid impact threat. Some needs will have to be defined in socio-cultural contexts that will be changing and evolving over unknown stretches of time, namely from the time policies are written to the time the disaster occurs. This could span decades or more, and such lengths of time will be a challenge as they imply a large number of unknown parameters and is out of step with political time. This will also imply the necessity of putting into place evolving policies and decision-making structures, resilient and adaptable to the long-term approach required by emergency systems.

Consequently, in addition to coordinating with the US Federal Emergency Management Agency (FEMA) and other governmental emergency response

---

50 Ibid.

51 Jörn Birkmann, *Measuring Vulnerability to Natural Hazards Towards Disaster Resilient Societies* (United Nations University Press 2006).

52 Georg Danhoundo, *La Gestion des Catastrophes "Naturelles": Vers une Analyse des Fondements de la Prise en Charge Internationale du "Risque"* (Editions Universitaires Européennes 2011).

teams, SMPAG, the US Planetary Defence Coordination Office, ESA's Planetary Defence Office or any other planetary defence managerial structures could seek the help of anthropologists and sociologists, expert urban planners and geographers in addressing movements of population and supporting populations 'at risk' in order to plan adapted assistance to the various communities.

Planetary defence management must continue being developed in a way that enables it to be passed down to the next generations so as to help them face a hazard potentially beyond the scope of typical human lifetimes. Additionally, planetary defence management must also ensure the trust of the populations so that their warnings be heard and listened to, should such warnings be sent out. To that end, communication campaigns should be started to get these institutions to be better known from the general public. Such communication campaigns could be extended through educational exercises, organising in-classroom planetary defence exercises. Moving forward in a prospective way, one might also imagine that other space threats such as solar flares, coronal mass ejections or cosmic radiation could also be considered new forms of natural catastrophes yet to be linked to the domain of natural disaster management.

CHAPTER 18

The Current International Space Law Regime on Liability and Its Application to Planetary Defence

*Alexander Soucek**

1 Introduction: From Risk to Liability in Spaceflight

Modern society has embraced the belief that 'unthinkable' does not equal 'impossible'.[1] While the idea of planetary defence, of interfering with a celestial body's natural course, may lend itself as an epitome of human hubris, the idea of humans walking on the Moon was once considered unthinkable, too. Sixty years after the dawn of the space age, the ratio between science and fiction in planetary defence may still convey a clear message. However, planetary defence has become the subject of research and international cooperation.[2] While it remains, for the time being, theoretical in nature, one of its characteristics is evident: its inherent risk.

There is no single accepted standard definition of 'risk'.[3] For the purpose of this chapter, it will be described as the potentiality of an undesired consequence materialising. In order to identify and handle risk in spaceflight, various approaches are used, including methods of risk assessment and risk analysis. Space mission planning and development will aim at reducing identified risk (*risk mitigation*) and, to the extent this cannot be done, managing it

* The views expressed in this chapter are made exclusively in private capacity.

1 US President Kennedy, 'We chose to go to the Moon' (Speech, 12 September1962): "If this capsule history of our progress teaches us anything, it is that man, in his quest for knowledge and progress, is determined and cannot be deterred. (…) We choose to go to the moon in this decade and do the other things, not because they are easy, but because they are hard, because that goal will serve to organize and measure the best of our energies and skills, because that challenge is one that we are willing to accept, one we are unwilling to postpone, and one which we intend to win (…)." Transcript at <https://er.jsc.nasa.gov/seh/ricetalk.htm> accessed 1 March 2021.

2 See chapters 1–8 in this book.

3 Lawrence Gratt 'The Definition of Risk and Associated Termonoligy for Risk Analysis' in James J Bonin and others (eds), *Risk Assessment in Setting National Priorities* (Plenum Press 1989) 675–680.

DOI:10.1163/9789004467606_020

(*risk management*). In recent years, risk assessment has also found its way into national space laws, where risk assessments have become part of the authorisation process for non-governmental space activities.[4]

Law forms part of risk management at large. This includes the element of liability: managing the expectation that those taking a risk and imposing it on others shall be obliged to compensate for ensuing damage suffered by others. In doing so, the very notion of 'liability' appeals to the inner sense of justice; it is a central factor in the societal equation of risk management.

This chapter first presents the international legal framework for state liability established by the Outer Space Treaty[5] and the Liability Convention.[6] It is applicable to any space activity, regardless of its nature, including planetary defence activities. The application of this framework to planetary defence is discussed in the second part of the chapter. Future planetary defence missions will be comparatively complex and entail risks that are beyond the horizon of experience of 'classic' spaceflight. A legal discussion of liability in the context of planetary defence must, therefore, take stock of the specific circumstances and tolerate a certain level of uncertainty owed to missing practice, both technically, operationally, and in legal terms.

2 The Janus-faced Character of Liability: Benefit and Burden

Liability implies both an element of protection, or benefit, and an element of 'burden'.[7] The weighting factor of both depends on the relative point of view.

2.1 *Benefit*

Liability protects those who suffer damage resulting from another one's action (or omission). It cannot prevent such consequence from happening, but it creates the legal ground for compensation. It unfolds its effect *ex post* to

4 Risk assessments in national space legislation may refer to technical and operational risks, financial and business risks, and environmental risks including the risk of environemtal harm or pollution, and space debris.

5 Treaty on Principles Governing the Activities of States in the Exploration and Use of Outer Space, including the Moon and Other Celestial Bodies (adopted 27 January 1967, entered into force 10 October 1967) 610 UNTS 205 (Outer Space Treaty).

6 Convention on International Liability for Damage Caused by Space Objects (adopted 29 March 1972, entered into force 1 September 1972) 961 UNTS 187 (Liability Convention).

7 Ad-Hoc Working Group on Legal Issues to SMPAG, 'Planetary Defence Legal Overview and Assessment' (SMPAG-RP-004, 8 April 2020) (SMPAG LWG Report). Besides, liability entails also an element of order, or regulation.

relief those having suffered damage. Arguably, liability also yields preventive effects: its mere existence as a legal consequence forces those under its obligation to plan and undertake actions with more caution and care. Liability is therefore not only a consequence to be factored in risk management; it influences the approach to risk mitigation, too.

This is evident, and appears rational, in the sphere of civil law for experiences of everyday life, such as driving a car and causing an accident. The same is true for less ordinary yet common activities, such as launching rockets or operating spacecraft. But whether or not liability is, as a legal concept, suitable to manage the consequences of intercepting, diverting or destroying a celestial body to save Earth, may be an entirely different question.

2.2 *Burden*

While the purpose of liability is to protect the victim, it is also a burden for the actor. For the one who will be the subject of attribution of liability, the potentiality to be held liable is a risk in itself; a sword of Damocles. The higher the possible consequences for being held liable, the more attention must be given to mitigate and manage this risk. This is particularly true for space law and its institute of absolute, or strict, liability for damagecaused by space objects on the surface of Earth or to aircraft in flight. Liability for such damage is unlimited in time and in financial terms. This represents a potential burden that cannot be ignored, neither by state actors nor by private operators who may carry part of the financial consequences of liability incurred by states under international law.[8]

The idea of a protective, victim-oriented approach is particularly important in international space law. As will be shown below, both Article VII Outer Space Treaty and the Liability Convention have been drafted based on the understanding that the freedom of states to carry out space activities shall not be to the detriment of others.

3 Liability in Public International Law

Liability, i.e. the duty to compensate for damage, is an established concept in civil law. In public international law, it continues to stand back behind the

8 Non-governmental actors may be required to compensate a State, in part, for liability incurred by the latter on the international level. Consequently, they may be obliged to take out insurance.

notion of 'responsibility', i.e. the duty to make reparation for the injury caused by an internationally wrongful act.[9]

Liability and responsibility are consequences of an act or omission. Responsibility necessitates a foregoing breach of international law (an 'internationally wrongful act'),[10] whereas liability requires a causal, material damage which may not necessarily follow from a breach of international law. The difference lies in the nature of an action's or omission's result: 'breach of law' versus 'damage'.[11] States may act internationally wrongfully without causing material damage, and they may cause material damage without having breached a rule of international law, i.e. without having acted internationally wrongfully.[12] It is, therefore, important to distinguish both concepts *ab initio* and *in principio*, even though they are related and intertwined in international legal theory and practice.

The International Law Commission (ILC) refers to this dialectic relation when it underlines that the Draft Articles on State Responsibility:

> (...) deal only with the responsibility for conduct which is internationally wrongful. There may be cases where States incur obligations to compensate for the injurious consequences of conduct which is not prohibited, and may even be expressly permitted, by international law (...).[13]

---

9 For a critical discussion of the concepts of 'responsibility' and 'liability' in international law, see Julio Barboza, *The Environment, Risk and Liability in International Law* (Martinus Nijhoff 2011) in particular chapter III, 'Responsibility and Liability in International Law' 21–29.

10 Every internationally wrongful act of a State entails the international responsibility of that State. Such act must be attributable to the State under international law and constitute a breach of an international obligation of the State, see ILC, Articles on the International Responsibility of States for Internationally Wrongful Acts, with Commentaries, 'Report of the International Law Commission on the Work of its 53rd Session' (23 April–1 June and 2 July–10 August 2001) UN Doc A/56/10. For a detailed discussion of international responsibility in the context of planetary defence, see chapter 20 'The International Responsibility of States for Planetary Defence Activities' in this book.

11 International responsibility can only take full effect where, and to the extent that, international legal norms exist which prescribe and define the scope of State action. Where such norms are rudimentary, or in a *status nascendi* (such as in international environmental law; to a certain degree also in space law), the possibility to evoke international responsibility is limited; see Jutta Brunnée, 'Of Sense and Sensibility: Reflections on International Liability Regimes as Tools for Environmental Protection' (2004) 53 The International and Comparative Law Quarterly 351–367: „Since State responsibility is contingent upon a violation of a rule of international law, the limitations of relevant international (...) norms also impact on the role that State responsibility can play" (354).

12 See also SMPAG LWG Report, section 4.2.2, 37.

13 ILC, Articles on the International Responsibility of States for Internationally Wrongful Acts, with Commentaries, 'Report of the International Law Commission on the Work of

Space activities, including the exploration and use of outer space and free access to all areas of celestial bodies, are expressly permitted.[14] But they entail considerable risks and are prone to injurious consequences.[15] Liability, therefore, protects from "harmful consequences of lawful but risk-intensive activities".[16]

However, the dividing line between responsibility and liability in international law is blurred. The terms are not firmly and dogmatically separated from one another.[17] Ultimately, the central difference comes down to the element of wrongfulness. If wrongfulness is absent or precluded, state responsibility cannot be invoked, whereas state liability may still be invoked conditional on objective factors (damage; causation)and, at times, subjective factors (fault).[18]

The dominance of state responsibility as a fundamental principle of international law[19] may overshadow the more practical notion of state liability, but this is not true for international space law, where their role can be considered as equally important.[20]

---

its 53rd Session' (23 April–1 June and 2 July–10 August 2001) UN Doc A/56/10, General Commentary, section 4(c) 31.

14 Article I(2), Outer SpaceTreaty: "Outer space, including the Moon and other celestial bodies, shall be free for exploration and use by all States without discrimination of any kind, on a basis of equality and in accordance with international law, and there shall be free access to all areas of celestial bodies."

15 This includes risk both for those carrying out an activity (i.e. the actors) and for third parties.

16 Jutta Brunnée, 'Of Sense and Sensibility: Reflections on International Liability Regimes as Tools for Environmental Protection' (2004) 53 The International and Comparative Law Quarterly 352.

17 On the use of the terms 'responsibility' and 'liability' in international law, see Julio Barboza, *The Environment, Risk and Liability in International Law* (Martinus Nijhoff 2011) 22–24: "Rivers of ink have flowed to point out the subtle differences between such words within the Anglo–American legal system, as if those differences could automatically be transferred to international law. We might as well have called them 'Accountability I" and "Accountability II". (...) Be that as it may, the fact is that "responsibility" in United Nations legal parlance has become shorthand for "State responsibility for wrongful acts," and "liability" for "international liability for acts not prohibited by international law." For a discussion of both terms within the space law context, see e.g. Frans G von der Dunk, 'Liability versus Responsibility in Space Law: Misconception or Misconstruction?' in IISL (ed), *Proceedings of the Thirty-Fourth Colloquium on the Law of Outer Space* (AIAA 1992) 363–71.

18 There are contending theories whether international responsibility is strict or requires a subjective element, too; see Malcolm N Shaw, *International Law* (7th edn, Cambridge University Press 2010) 783.

19 Ibid, 778.

20 Responsibility under Article VI Outer Space Treaty has an exceptionally wide notion. See chapter 20 'The International Responsibility of States for Planetary Defence Activities' in this book.

4 The International Space Law Regime on Liability

4.1 *Preliminary Remarks*

Liability for damage caused by carrying out space activities has been inscribed in the space law canon at an early stage. Once it had been established that all states enjoyed the freedom to explore and to use outer space without discrimination of any kind, to carry out scientific investigations and to access all areas celestial bodies,[21] the question of how to deal with potential damage in the 'ultra-hazardous' domain of spaceflight was a logic consequence.

The term 'liability' in the wider context of international space law, and in the specific context of the Liability Convention, refers to exclusive state liability, i.e. liability of one or more state actors; second, it refers in a large part to '*sine delicto* liability',[22] i.e. the absence of *necessitas delictum*;[23] third, it refers to third party liability, i.e. liability towards an 'innocent bystander' in the absence of a contractual legal relation.[24]

4.2 *The Early Resolutions*

Although being dealt with early on, liability was not among the first principles included in the 1961 United Nations General Assembly (UNGA) Resolution 1721 (XVI) 'International Co-operation in the Peaceful Uses of Outer Space'.[25] Nevertheless, a year later, in 1962, the UNGA stressed "the necessity of the progressive development of international law pertaining to (…) liability for space vehicle accidents"[26] and made reference to a draft proposal on the matter having had been brought forward by the United States.[27]

21 See Article I, Outer Space Treaty.

22 I.e. liability even in the absence of fault or negligence.

23 Julio Barboza, 'Draft Principles Relating to Liability and Compensation for Damages arising from the Transboundary Movement of Hazardous Wastes' in Najeeb Al Nauimi and Richard Meese (eds), *International Legal Issues Arising under the United Nations Decade of International Law* (Nijhoff Publishers 1995) 235.

24 On contractual liability in spaceflight, see 5.1.

25 International Co-operation in the Peaceful Uses of Outer Space, UNGA Res 1721 (XVI) (20 December 1961), focuses on three main elements: (i) the applicability of international law to outer space; (ii) the freedom of exploration and use of outer space; (iii) the non-appropriation principle.

26 International Co-operation in the Peaceful Uses of Outer Space, UNGA Res 1802 (XVII) (14 December 1962), preambular paragraph 3.

27 Ibid, section I.4.

Another year on, in the 1963 'Legal Principles Declaration',[28] a formula for international liability was established. It differed in nuances to what would later become Article VII Outer Space Treaty. Yet, it already contained the elements that ever since are understood to constitute the basis for liability for damage caused by space objects:

> Each State which launches or procures the launching of an object into outer space, and each State from whose territory or facility an object is launched, is internationally liable for damage to a foreign State or to its natural or juridical persons by such object or its component parts on the Earth, in air space, or in outer space.[29]

4.3 *Article VII Outer Space Treaty*

In 1967, at the height of the Space Race, the Outer Space Treaty entered into force. Manfred Lachs described the conclusion of the Outer Space Treaty as, "a serious commitment, an international commitment of historic dimensions",[30] and even six decades later this treaty remains central to space law.

The Outer Space Treaty establishes a series of general legal principles for the conduct of space activities. In Article VII, it deals with liability for damage caused by space objects as follows:

> Each State Party to the Treaty that launches or procures the launching of an object into outer space, including the Moon and other celestial bodies, and each State Party from whose territory or facility an object is launched, is internationally liable for damage to another State Party to the Treaty or to its natural or juridical persons by such object or its component parts on the Earth, in air space or in outer space, including the Moon and other celestial bodies.

Article VII Outer Space Treaty establishes a concept that the Liability Convention later defines as 'the launching state', and links it with the principle of 'international liability for damage caused by space objects'.[31] Both are, therefore, conditional upon one another: there is no launching state without

28 Declaration of Legal Principles Governing the Activities of States in the Exploration and Use of Outer Space, UNGA Res1962 (XVIII) (13 December 1963).

29 Ibid, section 8.

30 Manfred Lachs, 'Foreword' in Nandasiri Jasentuliyana (ed), *Space Law: Development and Scope, International Institute of Space* Law (Praeger 1992) x.

31 Both will be described and elaborated further below.

international liability, and no international liability without being the launching state in relation to a space object having caused damage.[32]

Unlike the Liability Convention, the Outer Space Treaty makes no difference between damage caused on Earth or elsewhere, and consequently no difference between strict and fault-based liability; in absence thereof, liability under Article VII Outer Space Treaty is generally presumed to be strict, or absolute.[33]

Moreover, under the Outer Space Treaty, liability for damage caused by space objects is a treaty-based and, consequently, a treaty-limited principle that can only bind state parties. Although the Outer Space Treaty establishes some rights *erga omnes*,[34] Article VII limits international liability to damage that is caused "to another State Party to the Treaty or to its natural or juridical persons". This has not prevented scholars from asserting, over time, that the principle of international liability for damage caused by space objects may have transcended, together with other principles of the treaty, into the realm of customary international law.[35]

The absence of a requirement of fault, and the limitation of damage to other state parties, lead to the question of the Outer Space Treaty's relation with the Liability Convention, for, in the latter, both aspects are dealt with in a different way.[36] Notwithstanding the tenet of *lex specialis derogat legi generali*, Article VII Outer Space Treaty retains "a separate, on occasion, even residual role"[37] – both in terms of scope and applicability.

4.4 *The Liability Convention*

States did not view the Outer Space Treaty as a single, solitary constitution of space law, although there were different senses of urgency for the development of additional norms.[38] While the United States and the USSR were

32 At least not on the grounds of the Outer Space Treaty or the Liability Convention; subsidiarly, other liability norms may be applicable.

33 See Lesley J Smith and Armel Kerrest, 'Article III' in Stephan Hobe, Bernhard Schmidt-Tedd and Kai-Uwe Schrogl (eds), *Cologne Commentary on Space Law*, vol II (Carl Heymanns Verlag 2013) 132: "In contrast to Art. III LIAB, the basis of liability under the Declaration [of 1963] and the OST is generally presumed to be absolute."

34 See Article I, Outer Space Treaty.

35 For an overview of the discussion on possible customary value of the Outer Space Treaty, see for example Alexander Soucek, *Space Law Essentials* (Linde Verlag 2015) 27.

36 Notably, fault-based liability (Article III, Liability Convention) and no limitation to state parties.

37 Lesley J Smith and Armel Kerrest, 'Article VII' in Stephan Hobe, Bernhard Schmidt-Tedd and Kai-Uwe Schrogl (eds), *Cologne Commentary on Space Law*, vol I (Carl Heymanns Verlag 2009) 142.

38 Vladmir Kopal, 'Evolution of the Doctrine of Space Law' in Nandasiri Jasentuliyana (ed), *Space Law: Development and Scope, International Institute of Space* Law (Praeger

primarily interested in further regulating the rescue of astronauts and the return of space objects,[39] the detailing of *liability* was the concern of many other states as they witnessed achievements and accidents at the side-line of history. Eventually, both the Astronaut Rescue and Return Agreement (1968)[40] and the Liability Convention (1972) saw the light of day, in this order.

The Liability Convention is an international treaty in its own right.[41] It details the regulation of international liability for damage caused by space objects, including a catalogue of terms defined, more differentiated material norms and a detailed claims procedure.[42] Most notably, Articles II and III Liability Convention establish *two different liability regimes* depending on the geographical occurrence of the damage:

a) *Damage caused by a space object on the surface of Earth (or to aircraft in flight)*

Under Article II Liability Convention, a launching state is absolutely liable to pay compensation, i.e. regardless of fault: "[a] launching State shall be absolutely liable to pay compensation for damage caused by its space object on the surface of the earth or to aircraft flight."[43]

The mere occurrence of damage, causally inflicted by a space object, leads to liability of the launching state, i.e. the obligation of compensation. A state whose space object causes damage on Earth will have to pay compensation for that damage independently of fault, or of any non-faulty breach of obligation. The absence of a requirement of fault, and consequently of the proof of fault, is crucial from the victim's perspective: in spaceflight, proof of fault by an outside party, possibly a non-spacefaring state, would be virtually impossible.[44]

1992) 17–32. See also UNGA Res 1472 (XIV) (12 December 1959) section 1(b) containing the continuing mandate of the UN Committee on the Peaceful Uses of Outer Space (UNCOPUOS) "to study the nature of legal problems which may arise from the exploration of outer space".

39 Not unexpectedly, as human spaceflight advanced towards the climax of the 'space race'.

40 Agreement on the Rescue of Astronauts, the Return of Astronauts and the Return of Objects Launched into Outer Space (adopted 22 April 1968, entered into force 3 December 1968) 672 UNTS 119 (Rescue Agreement).

41 This means it is independent from the Outer Space Treaty insofar as state parties to the Liability Convention do not have to be state parties of the Outer Space Treaty.

42 For a detailed overview and discussion of the Liability Convention, see for example Stephan Hobe, Bernhard Schmidt-Tedd and Kai-Uwe Schrogl (eds), *Cologne Commentary on Space Law*, vol II (Carl Heymanns Verlag 2013) 83–222.

43 Article II, Liability Convention.

44 See Frederick E Goldie, 'Liability for Damage and the Progressive Development of International Law' (1965) 14 The International and Comparative Law Quarterly 1189–1264: "[t]he basis for strict liability is said to lie in the limitations of science and engineering in many fields. (…) Owing to the difficulty of proving what kind of conduct is

The Liability Convention thus grants particular protection to those (states) suffering damage on Earth and not involved in that space activity. While several international conventions address liability for hazardous activities, e.g. in the fields of aviation[45] and nuclear power,[46] the express regulation of strict state liability in the Liability Convention "is the only clear example of its kind"[47] in international law.

b) *Damage Caused by a Space Object Elsewhere Than on the Surface of the Earth*

In case of damage caused by a space object to a space object of another launching state (or to persons or property on board thereof) while in outer space, the Liability Convention refers to fault-based liability:

> In the event of damage being caused elsewhere than on the surface of the Earth to a space object of one launching State or to persons or property on board such a space object by a space object of another launching State, the latter shall be liable only if the damage is due to its fault or the fault of persons for whom it is responsible.[48]

---

negligent, as well as the difficulty of presenting facts necessary to establish negligence, merely to impose the standards of fault liability may well be equivalent to exempting from obligations to compensate harmed individuals the very undertakings which are most likely to expose the public to risk. For how may negligence be established?" 1203.

45 For third party liability, see the Convention on Damage Caused by Foreign Aircraft to Third Parties on the Surface (adopted 7 October 1952, entered into force 4 February 1958) 4493 UNTS 310 (Rome Convention); for contractual liability, see the Convention for the Unification of Certain Rules for International Carriage by Air (adopted 28 May 1999, entered into force 4 November 2003) 2242 UNTS 309.

46 For example, the Vienna Convention on Civil Liability for Nuclear Damage (adopted 21 May 1963, entered into force 12 November 1977) 1063 UNTS 265; the Convention on Third Party Liability in the Field of Nuclear Energy (adopted 29 July 1960, entered into force 1 April 1968) 956 UNTS 251, as amended by the Additional Protocol of 28 January 1964 and by the Protocol of 16 November 1982. Both provide for strict liability of the operators whereby state liability is subsidiary to the civil liability of the operator. See Julio Barboza, 'Draft Principles Relating to Liability and Compensation for Damages arising from the Transboundary Movement of Hazardous Wastes' in Najeeb Al Nauimi and Richard Meese (eds), *International Legal Issues Arising under the United Nations Decade of International Law* (Nijhoff Publishers 1995) 235. Other cases concern oil pollution: International Convention for Civil Liability for Oil Pollution Damages (adopted 29 November 1969, entered into force 19 June 1975), 973 UNTS 3; or the International Convention On The Establishment of an International Fund for Compensation for Oil Pollution Damage (adopted 18 December 1971, entered into force 30 May 2006) 1110 UNTS 57.

47 Malcolm N Shaw, *International Law* (7th edn, Cambridge University Press 2010) 888.

48 Article III, Liability Convention.

The Liability Convention does, therefore, not grant absolute protection between space-faring states, but only relative protection to the extent that the damage was caused by fault.

4.5 *Space Law Liability: Innovation and Practice*

The regulation of liability in space law represents a comparatively detailed and innovative liability regime based on the understanding that spaceflight is an ultra-hazardous undertaking, the freedom of which comes at the price of accepting to compensate others for resulting damage.[49] Appreciating this background is relevant in the context of planetary defence which, even by the measure of contemporary spaceflight, may necessitate using novel technologies and undertaking even more hazardous action.[50]

Beyond the space law treaties, general international law may provide a basis for claims for reparation of damage suffered. However, as long as the specific perspective of space activities is to be considered, the regulation of liability under international space law is applicable and, in principle, overrides other international legal norms regulating aspects of liability.

So far, the probability for damage caused in outer space as well as for damage caused to human life or property on the surface of Earth has been statistically low.[51] Despite some dramatic accidents involving space objects,[52] the Liability Convention has been rarely applied,[53] and its claims procedure was never tested in practice. Yet, it would be imprudent to measure the importance of a legal institute solely by the amount of times it has been triggered. As risk is the combined result of likelihood and severity of an undesired consequence, space activities do not become less risky because the risk has not often materialised yet. Moreover, as will be shown, the regulation of liability in

49 Alexander Soucek, *Space Law Essentials* (Linde Verlag 2015) 33.

50 See chapters 1–8 in this book.

51 Due to the burning-up of spacecraft during atmospheric re-entry (friction heat), their comparatively small size, the predominant water coverage of the Earth's surface and, on land, the relative scarcity of human settlements, the probability of a spacecraft, or fragment thereof, hitting a person is even smaller ('on-ground casulaty risk').

52 Severe accidents such as the explosion of Space Shuttle Challenger (1986), the defragmentation of Space Shuttle Columbia (2003) or the fatal incident of Soyuz 11 (1971) had mostly national dimension and did, therefore, not include problems of international law. Also the comparatively few on-orbit collisions of space objects did not trigger major international legal problems so far.

53 The only often-cited case is the crash of the Soviet Cosmos 954 satellite over Canada in 1978.

international space law may have had its positive imprint on the development of spaceflight altogether: a self-fulfilling prophecy of prudence.

5 Other Forms of Regulating Liability in Spaceflight

5.1 *Contractual Liability in Spaceflight*

Third party liability must be distinguished from contractual, or agreed, liability. Contractual liability distributes the burden and benefit of liability in an *ex-ante* agreed form between cooperative partners. It plays an important role in international space cooperation, where, over time, a rich body of state practice has developed. States use different methods to regulate liability *inter-se*, including hold harmless clauses and cross-waivers of liability.

An example is the International Space Station (ISS) Intergovernmental Agreement of 1998, a treaty ratified by fifteen governments[54] that enabled the most complex international space cooperation to date. The ISS partners established a cross-waiver of liability for 'Protected Space Operations', i.e. for "all launch vehicle activities, Space Station activities, and payload activities on Earth, in outer space, or in transit between Earth and outer space",[55] as follows:

> Each Partner State agrees to a cross-waiver of liability pursuant to which each Partner State waives all claims against any of the entities or persons listed (…) below based on damage arising out of Protected Space Operations.[56]

In contrast to directly agreed forms of liability, or its exclusion, between two or more subjects of international law, third party liability refers to liability vis-à-vis an outside subject, i.e. towards an 'innocent by-stander'. The third party is a 'party' only in the tortious relation to the one causing damage. To underline this notion, it is sometimes referred to as the 'victim'.

Strictly speaking, the liability regime of international space law represents an agreed form of liability, too, for it is rooted in treaty norms established and accepted by states. In absence of a vertical legal order in international law, it

54 United States, Russian Federation, Canada, Japan and 11 European States.

55 Article 16(2)(f) Agreement Among the Government of Canada, the Governments of Member States of the European Space Agency, the Government of Japan, the Government of the Russian Federation, and the Government of the United States Concerning Cooperation on the Civil International Space Station (entered into force 27 March 2001).

56 Article 16(3)(a), first sentence, IGA.

is the states parties themselves which devised a liability regime by which they accepted to be bound by virtue of them being contracting parties. However, as will be described below, the 'independence' of the 'third party' is not measured in relation to the treaty regime itself (i.e. it is not directed to third states outside the liability regime), but in relation to a given space activity that caused a damage (i.e. it is related to states not involved in the injuring space activity).

Consequently, third party liability in international space law can be considered a law-making regime rather than a cooperative mechanism of damage compensation in a concrete undertaking.

5.2 *Liability at the Level of National Space Law*

As states are liable under international law for damage caused by space objects even when the latter are carried out by non-governmental actors, they may flow down their liability to the actual operator, or owner, of the space object by means of national space legislation. As a result, international liability transcends into national law. The regulation for the liability of non-governmental entities has become a key element of national space law.[57]

6 The Dividing Line between Launching States and Third Parties in Planetary Defence

6.1 *The Concept of the Launching State as a Prerequisite to Attributing Liability*

It has been shown that liability is a burden for the actor (potentially held liable) and a protection for the victim of action (potentially compensated). But who is who, and how are both identified? This question is at the origin of the concept of the 'launching state'.

Under international space law, the launching state is the primary legal focal point in relation to a space object, more than the actual spacecraft operator.[58] Legal attributions, particularly the one of liability for damagecaused by a space object, are made in relation to the respective launching state. Tying such attributions to the circumstances of the launch inevitably introduces a historic, i.e. time-bound, connotation that might not be representative of the factual circumstances at the moment of occurrence of a damage. However, this is also

---

57 See Recommendations on National Legislation Relevant to the Peaceful Exploration and Use of Outer Space, UNGA Res 68/74 (11 December 2013).

58 In contrast, owner and/or operator remain important focal points in various national space laws.

not the prime concern of international law. In a victim-oriented approach, the main objective is to facilitate and stabilise the attribution of liability to an identifiable actor.

The qualification of a state as 'launching state' depends on the objective fulfilment[59] of at least one of the four criteria established by Article VII Outer Space Treaty and Article 1(c) Liability Convention, respectively. Under the Liability Convention, where two or more states fulfil those criteria in relation to the same space object, they will be jointly and severally liable for any damage caused.[60] Once established, the status of 'launching state' remains with the respective state(s) for the duration of the space object's existence;[61] neither foregoing or subsequent legal transactions[62] nor factual occurrences[63] can alter this status.

Often, a launching state may not have direct physical control over a space object or its operator; yet, it will be the one bearing liability for damage caused by the object:

> On the international plane it is almost always the launching State being held liable for damage caused by a space object, even though in practical terms the damage may have been caused by a private operator. While a government may recover from such private operator part of the compensation paid to a third party, it can never pass on its liability under international law to the operator altogether.[64]

Although the concept of the 'launching state' is fundamental to space law, its suitability for depicting the multifaceted realities of modern-day spaceflight is frequently challenged. Planetary defence is but one example that shows the

59 See SMPAG LWG Report 51: "The quality of 'launching State' thus arises from factual circumstances and their legal interpretation, not from an act accepting such status".

60 Article V(1), Liability Convention.

61 This means that the liable actor is 'frozen' in time, allowing easy identification and attribution even long after the launch of a space object, and regardless of legal arrangements and transactions involving the space object, such as an in-orbit transfer of ownership.

62 For example, launch of a foreign payload; on-orbit transfer of ownership of a space object; bancruptcy of an operator, etc. However, a launching State is free to make necessary international arrangements with other States, for example for being held harmless horizontally in case of damage caused by the space object when operated by another entity outside the launching State's jurisdiction.

63 For example, a space mission's End Of Life (EOL); fragmentation; change of orbit; atmopsheric re-entry, etc.

64 SMPAG LWG Report 51.

limits of a concept developed at a time when spaceflight was considerably less complex than it is today, or will be tomorrow.

6.2 *The Concept of the Launching State in the Context of Planetary Defence*

Considering the amount of required resources, it is probable that a planetary defence mission will be a cooperative undertaking between a group of states.[65] Even more likely, it will be undertaken in the interest of an even wider group of states. The impact of a Near-Earth Object (NEO) on Earth will, in all probability, not be an event of only local concern; even if so, it is probable that those states threatened or affected will not be those capable of taking planetary defence action alone.[66] Either way, planetary defence "may raise the somewhat novel situation of a State that requests, supports or endorses a respective mission, but does not participate in it."[67]

This leads to a distinction of at least three groups of states, separated by the degree of their relative relation to the planetary defence activity:

a) *Launching States in a Narrow Sense*

The circle of actual launching states of a planetary defence mission will be those states which, in the meaning of Article I(c) Liability Convention, have cumulatively launched or procured the launching of the space object, and from whose territory or facility the space object has been launched. In other words, this group will consist of the states carrying out the planetary defence activity. This will include the state that provides the launch service.[68]

One state among the circle of launching states will register the spacecraft and consequently obtain (the recognition of) jurisdiction and control over it.[69] However, this has no legal bearing on the question of liability for damage-caused by the space object.

---

65 See chapters 1–8 in this book.

66 Technical and operational know-how, especially when it comes to planetary defence, is limited, and from today's perspective, only few countries would have, or be able to develop in short time, the necessary capabilities.

67 SMPAG LWG Report 50.

68 Like for other more complex space mission, the relations of contributing entities and responsible governments may be intricate, however. The establishment of the launching states is not always a straight-forward exercise.

69 As provided for in the Convention on Registration of Objects Launched into Outer Space (adopted 12 November 1974, entered into force 15 September 1976) 1023 UNTS 15 (Registration Convention), the Outer Space Treaty, or UNGA Res 1721 (XVI) (20 December 1961).

b) Launching States in a Wider Sense

A second group are states requesting planetary defence action, being interested in it or directly benefitting from it. Those states will neither launch nor directly procure the launch of the spacecraft, nor will it be their territories or facilities from which the space object is launched. But are they third parties – 'innocent by-standers' – or rather second-degree launching states?

Neither the Outer Space Treaty nor the Liability Convention distinguish between different degrees, or types, of launching states. The 'launching state' is a merely a legal formula. Its purpose is to identify those state actors which may be held liable for damage caused by a space object, not those exercising control over the object, or being interested in its mission. However, a state requesting planetary defence action may be regarded as a state *procuring* a launch in a wider sense.[70] The term 'procure' in Article VII Outer Space Treaty and Article I(b) Liability Convention is far from unequivocal and has given rise to discussion in space law literature:

> It was clear that the expression 'procure' leaves room for different interpretation. (…) Taking the ordinary meaning of the word, this allows an interpretation in the sense of a State placing an order for a launch.[71]

Interpreting a request, an endorsement or even just an appeal as 'procurement' would amount to an extensive, perhaps too extensive, interpretation, but it is not inconceivable. Such qualification would inverse role and relation: instead of being entitled, as a third party, to compensation for damagecaused, the requesting state would, as a launching state, incur liability for damage.

Alternative to assessing whether requesting states could fall under the definition of 'launching state' – based on an extensive interpretation of the term 'procure' – it could be questioned whether those states should benefit from third party liability. Arguably, states requesting or endorsing a planetary defence action, or directly benefitting from it, might not be regarded as third parties in relation to the action, as they have an interest in the action being carried out. It is thus questionable whether they would, or should, profit from the full protection granted by the Liability Convention.[72]

---

70 See SMPAG LWG Report 55.

71 Lesley J Smith and Armel Kerrest, 'Article III' in Stephan Hobe, Bernhard Schmidt-Tedd and Kai-Uwe Schrogl (eds), *Cologne Commentary on Space Law,* vol II (Carl Heymanns Verlag 2013) 114.

72 However, mere interest in an action should not be sufficient to exclude protection against damage suffered from that action.

c) *States Not Affected, but Supportive of a Mission*
There is one more group: states which are neither directly involved in carrying out the mission nor directly affected by the NEO threat (and thereby dependant on the success of the mission), but still supporting a planetary defence action at international level, for example as part of a Security Council resolution.[73] Again, the question must be raised whether or not those states could be qualified as classic third parties entitled to full protection under the space law liability regimes.

7 Damage, Object and Causation Examined in the Context of Planetary Defence

Damage and causationare the principal elements of liability. Without damage, there is no need – and no room – for liability. Causality is the condition for the *attribution* of liability.[74] Finally, the damage must have been caused by a space object.[75]

All three elements are inescapably tied together. If any one of them is absent, the link is broken and liability precluded. Evidently, establishing all three is not only a question of facts but one of legal interpretation, qualification, and attribution. While this is valid for any space activity, the particular circumstances of planetary defence – most notably: *the intervening element of a celestial body* – require a closer look that will be given in the following.

7.1 *'Damage'*

Damage is the first required element in the liability equation. Where there is no damage, no liability can occur – for there is nothing to compensate. Although the very goal of planetary defence is to prevent, or divert, damage,[76] it could eventually result in damage itself, i.e. damage caused through, and as the result of, the intervening action.

The Liability Convention[77] defines 'damage' as "loss of life, personal injury or other impairment of health; or loss of or damage to property of States or of

73 See for example chapter 22 'International Bodies and Procedures for Decision-Making Regarding Planetary Defence Actions' in this book.

74 Alexander Soucek, *Space Law Essentials* (Linde Verlag 2015) 33.

75 While the launching State carries the burden of liability, i.e. the obligation for the compensation of damage, it is not (necessarily) the actor directly causing the damage.

76 Namely damage by a celestial body that would materialise if no intervening action were taken.

77 The Outer Space Treaty does not include a definition of damage.

persons, natural or juridical, or property of international intergovernmental organizations".[78] While various damage scenarios are plausible, not all would be covered by the Liability Convention based on that definition.

The first scenario is for the interceptor spacecraft to cause damage independently from its interaction with the NEO, for example by colliding with another satellite, by exploding and causing a debris cloud or re-entering the Earth's atmosphere. From the perspective of space law, this scenario represents a standard case. It is independent from the NEO-specific circumstances. As long as no interaction with the NEO has taken place, an interceptor mission is a space mission like any other and to be legally treated accordingly.[79]

The second scenario is that the mission fails by falling short of its objective to intercept a NEO. As a result, the NEO will cause the predicted damage. This scenario would inverse the notion of liability: not compensation for damage caused by a space object, but compensation for damage not prevented by a space object. This scenario falls outside the scope of the Liability Convention and its object and purpose. It might however play a role in a contractual or other legal arrangement between involved parties.

The third scenario is that the NEO, once diverted or destroyed by the interceptor spacecraft, causes damage different to the damage originally predicted.[80] Here, the intervention will be the root cause for alternative damage, although it was successful in preventing the original damage from happening. The legal qualification of this scenario depends on a variety of elements. For example, an intervention deliberately done to divert the NEO impact from one state's territory to another state's territory would inevitably raise questions of international responsibility.

The fourth scenario is damage on, or of, the NEO, for example its destruction by the planetary defence action taken.[81] Damage of a celestial body falls outside the definition of the Liability Convention and will not be recoverable thereunder, most importantly because there is no injured party that would be entitled to compensation. However, interfering in such way with a celestial object may raise issues of planetary protection.[82]

---

78 Article 1(a), Liability Convention.

79 Depending on the circumstances, additional risk or rules may apply, for example in case of a interceptor spacecraft carrying nucelar explosive devices on board. See chapter 3 'Planetary Defence Technologies' and chapter 15 'Legal Aspects of the Use of Nuclear Explosive Devices in Planetary Defence' in this book.

80 For example on the territory of a third state, or to satellites in outer space.

81 This could be, for example, a nuclear explosion.

82 See chapter 17 'Understanding the Social Aspects of an Asteroid Impact Threat from Socio-Anthropological Lessons Learned in Natural Disaster Management' in this book.

Finally, there are various scenarios that would inhibit planetary defence action (that could have been possible otherwise) from being taken, or cause it to be taken too late, or in the wrong manner.[83] Again, those circumstances fall outside the scope of the Liability Convention which focuses on damage caused by space objects. Terrestrial telescopes, mathematical models or political decisions are neither space objects nor space activities.[84] However, such scenarios may give rise to international responsibility or liability on other grounds.

7.2 *'Space Object'*

To be recoverable under the Liability Convention, the damage must have been caused by a space object. The Liability Convention establishes a definition of the term 'space object' that has been called "more a clarification than a legal definition",[85] a description "for the sake of clarity".[86] Prevailing opinion considers the term to refer to an artificial, i.e. human-made, and material object.[87]

A celestial body is no 'space object' in the meaning of the Liability Convention.[88] Superficially, it may therefore seem that damage directly caused by a celestial body, e.g. upon impact, would not fulfil the condition "by a space object". But this interpretation ignores the possibility of indirect or consequential damage. The question therefore is: Does 'damage' that is physically caused by an asteroid equal 'damage' that is legally caused by an intercepting spacecraft?

---

83 Examples include: information not being relayed or published too late, the NEO not having been detected despite the possibility to do so; planetary defence action refused or delayed, etc.

84 Alexander Soucek, *Space Law Essentials* (Linde Verlag 2015) 115.

85 Lesley J Smith and Armel Kerrest, 'Article III' in Stephan Hobe, Bernhard Schmidt-Tedd and Kai-Uwe Schrogl (eds), *Cologne Commentary on Space Law,* vol II (Carl Heymanns Verlag 2013) 115.

86 Francis Lyall and Paul B Larsen, *Space Law: A Treatise* (2nd edn, Routledge 2018) 107.

87 For example: Bernhard Schmidt-Tedd, 'Article I' in Stephan Hobe, Bernhard Schmidt-Tedd and Kai-Uwe Schrogl (eds), *Cologne Commentary on Space Law,* vol II (Carl Heymanns Verlag 2013) 247: "Even if the term 'space object' as such is not defined, there is a common understanding that space object means any man-made object which is launched or intended to be launched into outer space." For further discussion, see also: Frans G von der Dunk, 'International Space Law' in Frans G von der Dunk and Fabio Tronchetti (eds), *Handbook of Space Law* (Edward Elgar Publishing 2015) 86–87.

88 Space law uses but does not define the term 'celestial body'. The International Astronomical Union (IAU) defines some celestial bodies like 'planet', 'asteroid' and 'comet'. Those scientific definitions are useful anchors but not legally accepted definitions of international law, despite being occasionally used in space law literature.

7.3 *Causation*

Damage must be caused by a space object for it to be recoverable from the launching state(s), both under the Outer Space Treaty (Article VII)[89] and the Liability Convention (Articles II and III). Causation is, therefore, "the sine qua non or causal nexus for liability".[90]

Causation has been described as an evidentiary challenge.[91] The link between cause and effect must be demonstrated, not only in the case of fault liability, but equally in the case of strict liability, where, despite absence of need of proof of fault, it must still be established that the damage was actually caused by a particular space object.[92]

In case of damage directly inflicted by a space object, for example through collision with another spacecraft, causation "should not present a legal problem"[93] (but will still have to be evidenced). The more problematic, and legally challenging, scenario is damage caused by a celestial body as a result of a planetary defence intervention. The damage would not have materialised had the celestial body not been affected by a spacecraft. But can it still be attributed to the launching state?

The Liability Convention does not require direct, neither immediate cause and effect: "Damage may be the result of a chain of events, stemming from the original incident caused by the space object (...) it may only appear after the lapse of time".[94] However, the chain of events from the space object's intervention to the damage must be uninterrupted: "Where the causal chain or nexus is interrupted or broken, the damage is no longer the consequence of the space object".[95] An intervening element (*causa interveniens*) or an unrelated event (*causa nova*) may therefore preclude liability: "For the condition

---

89 Instead of "caused by", Article VII Outer Space Treaty speaks of "damage (...) by such object".

90 Lesley J Smith and Armel Kerrest, 'Article VII' in Stephan Hobe, Bernhard Schmidt-Tedd and Kai-Uwe Schrogl (eds), *Cologne Commentary on Space Law,* vol I (Carl Heymanns Verlag 2009) 141.

91 Jutta Brunnée, 'Of Sense and Sensibility: Reflections on International Liability Regimes as Tools for Environmental Protection' (2004) 53 The International and Comparative Law Quarterly 354.

92 In the case of damage caused on the surface of Earth or to aircraft in flight, the establishment of causationis therefore of central importance, as there is no further requirement, i.e. faulty behaviour, to proof.

93 SMPAG LWG Report 52.

94 Lesley J Smith and Armel Kerrest, 'Article VII' in Stephan Hobe, Bernhard Schmidt-Tedd and Kai-Uwe Schrogl (eds), *Cologne Commentary on Space Law,* vol I (Carl Heymanns Verlag 2009) 142.

95 Ibid.

of causality to be satisfied, the damage must be attributable to the incident caused by the space object, foreseeable, perhaps reasonably foreseeable, and not too remote".[96]

Additional difficulties in establishing causation may be the unambiguous identification of the incidental source (i.e. the actual root cause), the attribution of particular damage to a particular source, and potential cumulative effects during the chain of events unfolding.[97] Those aspects may result in complex causation issues.[98]

8 Strict vs Fault-based Liability in the Context of Planetary Defence

The distinction between strict and fault-based liability under the Liability Convention is based on an exclusively geographical criterion. Damage caused in outer space requires the subjective element of fault on the side of the launching state for the latter to be held liable.

8.1 *Strict Liability and the Notion of 'Ultra-hazardous Activities'*

The regulation of liability for space activities is intrinsically linked to the associated risks, a relation recognised by the preamble of the Liability Convention:

> Taking into consideration that, notwithstanding the precautionary measures to be taken by States and international intergovernmental organizations involved in the launching of space objects, damage may on occasion be caused by such objects (…).[99]

By comparison with other domains, space activities have been characterised as ultra-hazardous. The notion of 'ultra-hazardous activities' has early on been discussed in international law.[100] There is no accepted legal definition of the

96 SMPAG LWG Report 52.

97 Jutta Brunnée, 'Of Sense and Sensibility: Reflections on International Liability Regimes as Tools for Environmental Protection' (2004) 53 The International and Comparative Law Quarterly 354–355.

98 Ibid.

99 Liability Convention, 3rd preambular paragraph.

100 "Early on" refers to the age of technology unfolding after the second world war. See for example Wilfred C Jenks, 'Liability for Ultra-Hazardous Activities in International Law'(1966) 117 Collected Courses of The Hague Academy of International Law; Jenks states, at 106, that "the question is not whether international law can or should recognize ultra-hazardous liability but how far it recognizes such liability, whether such liability exists only in specific cases for which special provision has been made or whether it rests

term. It aims at the potential of injurious damage rather than at the probability of accident, as already observed by Wilfred C Jenks:

> The expression ultra-hazardous activities is not a term of art (...). It does not imply that the activity is ultra-hazardous in the sense that there is a high degree of probability that the hazard will materialize, but rather that the consequences in the exceptional and perhaps quite improbable event of the hazard materializing may be so far-reaching that special rules concerning the liability for such consequences are necessary if serious injustice and hardship are to be avoided.[101]

Similarly, Malcom Shaw observes:

> The definition of what constitutes such activity (...) is somewhat uncertain, but the characterisation can be taken to revolve around the serious consequences that are likely to flow down from any damage that results, rather than upon the likelihood of pollution occurring from the activity in question. The focus therefore is upon significant or exceptional risk of severe transnational damage.[102]

In spite of its focus on consequence rather than probability, the notion of 'ultra-hazardous activities' is fluid and may evolve over time.[103] It is of special interest in the context of planetary defence, which, even by standards of modern-day spaceflight, represents an undertaking of extraordinary complexity and risk.

---

on some more general principle which we may expect to have a widening range of new applications, whether the liability is 'absolute', 'strict', or 'without proof of fault', or constitutes some other variant of these possibilities, and how the elements of civil and international liability are related to each other".

101 Ibid, 107.

102 Malcolm N Shaw, *International Law* (7th edn, Cambridge University Press 2010) 887, quoting Gunther Handl, 'State Liability for Accidental Transnational Environmental Damage by Private Persons' (1980) 74 American Journal of International Law 554.

103 In his work 'Liability for Ultra-Hazardous Activities in International Law' published in 1966, Wilfred C Jenks listed aviation hazards, nuclear hazards, space hazards, probing and drilling hazards; furthermore 'environmental changes', 'electronics and cybernetics' and 'biological experiments'; on the other hand, he did not include maritime hazards, even though single ship catastrophes have often caused far more loss of life than single aviation accidents; today, neither modern ship traffic nor aviation may be regarded as an ultra-hazardous activity any more, for a variety of reasons. See Wilfred C Jenks, 'Liability for Ultra-Hazardous Activities in International Law'(1966) 117 Collected Courses of The Hague Academy of International Law 169.

At first glance, the degree of risk of a space activity may seem irrelevant as it is no element for establishing liability. However, this falls short of two considerations: first, the ultra-hazardous nature of spaceflight is the very rational of the strict liability regime for damagecaused on Earth; second, there is an intrinsic link to the assessment of fault, as will be shown in the following section: the more dangerous a space activity, the higher will the requirements for precaution be, thus having a bearing on the measurement and qualification of subjective behaviour.

8.2 *The Constituents of 'Fault'*

In the context of planetary defence, the danger of damage caused on Earth may be of greater concern for two reasons: on the victim's side, its potential to affect life and property at a large scale, and, on the actor's side, the absolute liability of the launching state(s). In contrast, damage caused to other space objects in outer space[104] may "be less likely or of a lesser size or impact than on Earth".[105] While damage on Earth triggers liability regardless of the subjective behaviour of the launching state, the latter can be held liable for damage to other space objects (including persons and property on board) only "if the damage is due to its fault or the fault of persons for whom it is responsible".[106]

The notion of fault "is not common in international law; international law generally refers to violation of a legal obligation and not to fault".[107] The Liability Convention does not define the term 'fault', and there is neither detailed regulation nor state practice on the constitution of fault when it comes to space activities.[108] This problem has been extensively discussed in space law literature.[109] The assessment and establishment of 'fault', or of the absence thereof, would become central to triggering liability for damagecaused to space objects in outer space. In general, the notion of 'fault' "denotes the failure to adhere

104 Most probably to satellites in orbit around Earth; however, there is also the future possibility that another celestial body carrying human-made infrastructure may be hit (for example the Moon with lunar bases thereon), or that debris clouds might hinder access to certain parts of outer space.

105 SMPAG LWG Report 53.

106 Article III, Liability Convention.

107 Lesley J Smith and Armel Kerrest, 'Article III' in Stephan Hobe, Bernhard Schmidt-Tedd and Kai-Uwe Schrogl (eds), *Cologne Commentary on Space Law*, vol II (Carl Heymanns Verlag 2013) 133.

108 SMPAG LWG Report 53.

109 On the notion of fault, see for example Lesley J Smith and Armel Kerrest, 'Article III' in Stephan Hobe, Bernhard Schmidt-Tedd and Kai-Uwe Schrogl (eds), *Cologne Commentary on Space Law*, vol II (Carl Heymanns Verlag 2013) 132–134.

to, or breach of, an obligation imposed by law".[110] Consequently, fault liability "connotes the attachment of liability to an actor who causes the harm intentionally or negligently (...) in breach of a duty to take care".[111]

As fault includes both an objective and a subjective component, it will have to be measured by reference to a variety of norms, both legally binding and non-legally binding, including best practices,[112] operational standards of safety and due care, and more general by reference to state conduct in the carrying-out of ultra-hazardous activities.

In the context of planetary defence, an important factor will be, initially, the novelty and, generally speaking, the rarity of any such mission, coupled with the elevated risk and the absence of standards of behaviour. This makes it difficult to benchmark such behaviour and renders it necessary to consider several elements at once, such as mission planning, choice of methods, procedures, or international cooperation and coordination.[113] However, while those "may be indicators of what is to be considered desirable, reasonable and responsible behaviour in the conduct of planetary defence activities",[114] none of these indicators has yet been sufficiently developed to allow assessing the degree of diligence or negligence of the launching state. In the absence of tailored norms and practice, 'fault' remains, for the time being, a largely unknown variable in the context of planetary defence.

9 A Last-Minute Addition to Address Large-Scale Danger to Human Life

Often overlooked and rarely commented,[115] Article XXI Liability Convention provides for the possibility of assistance if a space object causes damage at large scale:

> If the damage caused by a space object presents a large-scale danger to human life or seriously interferes with the living conditions of the

110 Ibid, 132.

111 Frederick E Goldie, 'Liability for Damage and the Progressive Development of International Law' (1965) 14 The International and Comparative Law Quarterly 1189, 1196.

112 Alexander Soucek, *Space Law Essentials* (Linde Verlag 2015) 33.

113 SMPAG LWG Report 53.

114 Ibid.

115 See for example Fabio Tronchetti, Lesley J Smith and Armel Kerrest, 'Article XXI' in Stephan Hobe, Bernhard Schmidt-Tedd and Kai-Uwe Schrogl (eds), *Cologne Commentary on Space Law*, vol II (Carl Heymanns Verlag 2013) 200–201.

> population or the functioning of vital centres, the States Parties, and in particular the launching State, shall examine the possibility of rendering appropriate and rapid assistance to the State which has suffered the damage, when it so requests.[116]

Article XXI Liability Convention was included at the eleventh hour of the negotiation process, in June 1971, shortly before the adoption of the final draft text.[117] The circle of norm addressees in this Article goes beyond the launching states; it includes all states parties of the Liability Convention. However, it does not affect their obligations under the Convention and represents no supplementary regulation of liability. Instead, states parties shall evaluate options for appropriate and rapid assistance upon request of a state which suffered damage, whatever those "rather vague"[118] types of measures may be. It also remains open which type of large-scale danger is referred to, but the formulation "[serious interference] with the living conditions of the population or the functioning of vital centres" suggests addressing veritable catastrophes and not only mere accidents.[119]

Planetary defence activities have the potential to cause such serious interference. What can be deducted from this Article is the recognition of the need for a circle of states as large as possible to render assistance when large-scale danger emerges. This correlates with the recommendation for broad international cooperation and coordination in planetary defence.[120]

10 Managing Liability: A Question of Circumstances

A final observation shall shed light on the surrounding circumstances of planetary defence, and their relation to the management of liability.

Although third party liability is a consequence at the end of a chain of events that have to first materialise and then be established and recognised, it can be figured in already during the planning and development phases of

---

116 Article XXI, Liability Convention, first sentence.

117 Fabio Tronchetti, Lesley J Smith and Armel Kerrest, 'Article XXI' in Stephan Hobe, Bernhard Schmidt-Tedd and Kai-Uwe Schrogl (eds), *Cologne Commentary on Space Law*, vol II (Carl Heymanns Verlag 2013) 201.

118 Ibid.

119 Some authors proposed a connection to nuclear accidents involving space objects; see for example Francis Lyall and Paul B Larsen, *Space Law: A Treatise* (2nd edn, Routledge 2018) 113.

120 SMPAG LWG Report 57–58.

a space activity, in order to define anticipatory measures of risk mitigation and management. Classic space project management tools will form part of the measures to manage liability for a planetary defence mission, but not all will work.[121] One focus to manage liability risks, besides technical, financial and other measures, will therefore be on international cooperation and coordination.[122]

It is probable that a state, prior to taking planetary defence action, will seek cooperation with partners, and coordination with the international community. It is unlikely that it will act in splendid isolation to undertake an ultrahazardous activity with the potential to severely and negatively affect others, or, in case of success, benefit and protect others. Somehow or other, there will be an international dimension to such activity. This will facilitate addressing questions of risk distribution and liability, and may result in some sort of arrangement prior to carrying out a planetary defence mission, for example an international mandate, an international agreement or waivers of liability between launching states and third parties.[123]

The actual circumstances will play a significant role, particularly the motivation to act and the role allocation between the states acting and those bystanding. It will make a difference whether a single state takes action to divert a NEO impact from its own territory, or an international effort is organised to safe humanity from a potentially global catastrophe. Should the launching state(s) take action on behalf of third parties, either on their explicit request or for their direct or collateral benefit, exoneration from liability under the Outer Space Treaty and Liability Convention could be contemplated: relief in return for action.[124]

Ultimately, addressing those questions, and handling those potentialities, may further the development of international and national space law, of non-legally binding instruments or of international coordination mechanisms for planetary defence. The on-going work of the SMPAG is an example for intergovernmental coordination in this regard.

---

121 For example, it is improbable that a private insurer would cover liability risks from planetary defence.

122 SMPAG LWG Report 57–58.

123 Ibid, 56.

124 Ibid.

11 Concluding Remarks

International space law is applicable to planetary defence activities. From the perspective of the Liability Convention, a NEO interceptor spacecraft is no different than a satellite in Earth orbit, or a scientific space probe on an interplanetary trajectory. The launching state(s) will be strictly liable for damage on Earth, whether directly caused by the spacecraft or indirectly by the deflected NEO. However, as has been shown, planetary defence raises questions that may not be sufficiently answered by reverting to textbook solutions. It is unlikely that a single state or group of states would engage in carrying out a NEO deflection mission without appropriate risk mitigation measures – including the risk of being held liable.

Liability is not only benefit and burden, but also an encouragement to plan ahead, to exchange and cooperate, and to act responsibly within the limit of what is rightful or permissible under international law.[125] This 'by-product' of liability has accompanied the development of spaceflight throughout the decades and will continue doing so, just as spaceflight remains hazardous by nature. It could be perceived as an irony that planetary defence activities, because of their sheer dimension and complexity, could eventually endanger the greater goods they are meant to protect. More than being a remedy for when it is too late, liability should therefore facilitate international solutions early on, making society better prepared for planetary defence when the day has come to take action.

125 See Julio Barboza, *The Environment, Risk and Liability in International Law* (Martinus Nijhoff 2011) 29: "Compensation (…) is not the single goal of a legal regime intending to cope with risk. Equally important is the minimization of risk in order to lower exposure to significant harm – in other words: prevention for the sake of people and the environment. Some measure of prevention flows as a by-product of liability, since its exercise tends to reduce the number of accidents and, consequently, lower the cost of compensations."

CHAPTER 19

Critical Issues and Future Perspectives on Liability in the Context of Planetary Defence

Henry Hertzfeld

1 Introduction

International liability for space objects under the current space law treaty regime attaches to a launching state and is unlimited in amount and in time. All space activities are inherently high risk. Liability, therefore, can be a serious deterrent to a space mission that has never been done before. Such missions may be undertaken by either a nation or a group of nations to protect the Earth and its peoples from harm. Significant harm may be predicted from a Near-Earth Object (NEO) hitting the Earth. The humanitarian benefits may outweigh the risks involved in undertaking the mission if a technology-driven space project has a reasonable expectation of preventing a catastrophe. A systematic approach at an international level needs to be established to enable and insure that appropriate responses to existing legal space law obligations are used at key times during the mission to both uphold existing law and provide relief from excessive liability claims. This chapter will show that the current liability regime is flexible and includes provisions and precedents that can successfully address this problem. Consequently a nation should be able to organise or join others in a planetary defence mission without triggering future massive liabilities. The tools exist; the hurdles are essentially two-fold: first to implement a near-term international agreement on a process to address future liability issues for planetary defence in a structured manner, and second is to overcome society's unwillingness to act when a potential threat is acknowledged but no immediate danger or loss is imminent. Said in another way, societies are reluctant to commit funds today to a recognised danger that has a low probability of occurring but if it does occur, may have a very high cost to undefined people or nations in the indefinite future.

 | DOI:10.1163/9789004467606_021

2 General Aspects of Liability for Damage Caused by Space Objects

Liability only attaches if something goes wrong. The space treaty regime specifically is oriented toward third party liability, that is, a payment or other compensation to an injured party that is an 'innocent victim'. That is, one that is not a participant in the space activity in question. The current space legal regime is based on liability attaching to a launching state (or states) and applies specifically to space objects that are launched into outer space.[1] A space object is not clearly defined in either the Liability Convention, the Registration Convention, or in Article VII of the Outer Space Treaty. The Outer Space Treaty simply makes states parties liable for their actions in space. The Liability Convention adopts two different regimes. The first is for damage from a space object to the Earth or airplanes in flight where absolute liability attaches, while damage elsewhere than on the surface of the Earth to other space objects or people and property on board a space object is based on a finding of fault.[2]

It should also be noted that the space treaty liability regime focuses only on one state doing harm to another state's property or persons. It does not directly provide for claims that involve harm to the space environment itself. Thus, debris, pollution, waste, and other human created things in outer space are only subject to liability claims when and if they damage or adversely affect the space object(s) of another nation. There is no time limit on this potential liability and it is well established that objects in outer space may remain there for a very long time.[3]

The treaties, drafted during the 1960s and 1970s were clearly oriented to compensation to innocent victims from nations engaging in activities deemed to be ultra-hazardous.[4] Launching a satellite from the Earth involves very toxic

1 Treaty on Principles Governing the Activities of States in the Exploration and Use of Outer Space, including the Moon and other Celestial Bodies (adopted 19 December 1966, entered into force 10 October 1967) 610 UNTS 205 (Outer Space Treaty), Article VII; Convention on International Liability for Damage Caused by Space Objects (adopted 29 November 1971, entered into force 1 September 1972) 961 UNTS 187 (Liability Convention), Articles I and XII. With respect to the definition of the launching state, see also the Convention on Registration of Objects Launched into Outer Space (adopted 12 November 1974, entered into force 15 September 1976) 1023 UNTS 15 (Registration Convention).

2 Articles II and III, Liability Convention.

3 Article IX of the Outer Space Treaty does recognise the potential for harmful contamination to outer space and calls for nations to adopt appropriate measures. However, there are no penalties or enforcement mechanisms in Article IX and it calls for consultations among nations if the activities of one nation might adversely affect those of another nation in outer space.

4 Ultra-hazardous activities have been defined in tort law as an activity or process that presents an unavoidable risk of serious harm to the other people or others' property, for which

chemicals and has always been considered ultra-hazardous or, in more recent terms abnormally dangerous.

Most intentional activities occurring once a space object is in outer space are not immediately hazardous to people or property on the Earth, but only might be if and when the object is returned to Earth. It is arguable that a Near-Earth Object (NEO) whose position in outer space is changed by a space object is not itself a space object.[5] That would bring into question whether liability for a NEO mission that ended in a failure (i.e. impact with the Earth) attributable to it being misdirected in space would be legally considered under the absolute liability regime of the Liability Convention, under the fault liability for objects in space, or under general international law.

Space is a unique non-sovereign location. The law of outer space is also a unique regime in that it is governed by a series of treaties that obligates states to be both responsible and liable for all of their national activities in space and also ultimately responsible and liable for the activities of their private citizens and companies.[6] No other economic activity is treated this way, although there are analogies to aviation, the high seas, and nuclear energy and other activities that operate in non-sovereign regions and involve potentially very hazardous materials. In some ways the problems facing space and NEO operations can also be considered as analogous to international climate change agreements in that both are as much political as legal.[7]

---

the actor may be held strictly liable for the harm, even if the actor has exercised reasonable care to prevent that harm. (Restatement (Second) of Torts, § 520).

5 The definition of a space object in Article I of the Liability Convention is limited to objects launched into orbit. The human intervention to the orbit or composition of a natural object in space such as an asteroid would not be considered a "space object" under the treaties. However, some nations such as the United States consider things manufactured in space by US equipment as being the property and responsibility of the United States or its citizens (35 U.S. Code § 105, Pub. L. 101–580, § 1(a), Nov. 15, 1990, 104 Stat. 2863) This would include objects manufactured using resources obtained in space. Also, more recent UN Resolutions on space debris mitigation guidelines, UNGA Res A/62/20 (5 December 2007), and state practice define human created debris in space as the responsibility of the launching state, even though it might not necessarily be a space object under the definitions in the Liability Convention and Convention on Registration of Objects Launched into Outer Space (adopted 12 November 1974, entered into force 15 September 1976) 1023 UNTS 15 (Registration Convention).

6 Articles II, VI, and VII, Outer Space Treaty.

7 Joshua B Horton, Andrew Parker and David Keith, 'Liability for Solar Geoengineering: Historical Precedents, Contemporary Innovations, and Governance Possibilities' (2015) 22 NYU Environmental Law Journal 225–273. The authors argue that international agreements for space law and climate change law involve governments as ultimately liable as distinguished from other hazardous activities such as oil platforms and tankers where the liability is attributed to private owners and operators.

There will never be any guarantees about eliminating future liability from decisions to conduct a planetary defence mission, but there are many precedents that could protect such reasonable national and international space activities from facing devastating liability payments.

To insure that these legal remedies are available, an international step-wise systematic process needs to be agreed upon now, before any specific NEO threat requires a planetary defence activity or mission to be initiated. Such steps, as described below, are based on both open scientific information and international notification communication precedents.

Liability law has a complex history and this chapter will summarise various conclusions and not attempt to document in detail the development and stages of liability in all related fields or present all relevant arguments on the issues.[8] It will, however suggest workable solutions with existing precedents to waivers, reduction, or exoneration of participating states from liability in analogous situations.

Finally, space law is inherently political since the international treaty regime attaches both international responsibility and international liability directly to states. In turn, states are ultimately responsible and liable for the actions of their citizens and companies in space activities. States may choose methods to either transfer or absorb all or part of that liability for private entities operating under their national laws or authorisations.

3 Background

The basic humanitarian principle underlying these future space endeavours is a desire to protect the Earth (or regions of the Earth) and human civilisation from catastrophic damage. In this case that damage would occur from a NEO that has been identified as clear threat to collide with the Earth. It is analogous to many other potentially catastrophic natural events such as hurricanes, tornados, volcanic eruptions and earthquakes, and even climate change. They all represent challenges that in one way or another are unpredictable by even the best current scientific endeavours. Governments, companies and individuals spend uncountable funds in prediction, prevention, mitigation, insurance, and many other ways to deal with these uncertainties as best they can. Legal

8 For a discussion of the development of international liability, see: ILC, 'Survey on liability regimes relevant to the topic: International liability for injurious consequences arising out of acts not prohibited by international law: study prepared by the Secretariat, Extract from the Yearbook of the International Law Commission, vol II' (23 June 1995), UN Doc A/CN.4/471.

systems in all nations not only allow, but also encourage, these activities to protect their citizens. Such legal protections with appropriate caveats can also serve to balance unreasonable risk-taking in the protection from a NEO impact on the Earth.

The legal system should encourage responsible NEO missions. Liability should not be a deterring factor in national and international decisions to undertake reasonable measures for planetary defence. At the same time, just as it is in current space law, national and international actions that are grossly negligent or that may be performed with willful intent to harm other nations will and should face liabilities.[9]

Any agreed upon international system or process for planetary defence can be negotiated within the existing space treaty regime and incorporate the principles outlined in the Outer Space Treaty. However, where necessary, some of the ambiguities of that Treaty along with the other space treaties, may need further formal clarification.[10]

Finally, because elements of planetary defence missions may use technologies that have other future uses in the exploration and use of outer space, liability concerns for those other activities are not addressed in detail in this chapter. For example, undertaking a satellite servicing mission or conducting the exploration of asteroids for resource use will involve rendezvous and proximity operations that are likely quite similar to those that might be used in a planetary defence mission. This chapter assumes that the law regarding those liabilities will remain as it currently is and the exceptions noted below are limited to planetary defence missions.[11]

In order to clearly discuss this proposed system for planetary defence, this analysis will focus on one general scenario for planetary defence and rely on some simplifying assumptions.

---

9 Article III, Liability Convention.

10 The other space treaties are: The Agreement on the Rescue of Astronauts, the Return of Astronauts and the Return of Objects Launched into Outer Space (adopted 19 December 1967, entered into force 3 December 1968) 672 UNTS 119 (Rescue Agreement); and finally, The Agreement Governing the Activities of States on the Moon and Other Celestial Bodies (adopted 5 December 1979, entered into force 11 July 1984) 1363 UNTS 3 (Moon Agreement).

11 The scope and logic of developing new liability protocols for these other in-space activities is beyond the subject addressed in this chapter. However, given that the current space liability system is oriented toward launch and re-entry space activities, it will be appropriate and perhaps necessary for the space community to consider changes to the current international space liability regime to accommodate both new technologies and the growth of non-governmental ownership of many space assets.

- First, the threat from a NEO must be identified well in advance of a possible collision with the Earth.
- Second, the scenario applies mainly to NEOs that are large enough to seriously threaten a part of the Earth.
- Third, technologies that will be applied to the space mission must encompass best practices and be executed as expertly as possible.
- Fourth, the specific location of impact won't be precisely predictable in advance.[12]

Given our current knowledge of NEOs, this scenario may be today's most realistic and most probable one that nations will face and for which there is enough advance time to execute a successful mission to deflect the NEO with a reasonable probability of success.

The Final Report of the SMPAG Ad-hoc Working Group on Legal Issues addresses some of the specific legal issues that will be discussed in this chapter.[13] Below are a few relevant excerpts from that document that develop a foundation for the remainder of this chapter.

1. Concerning asteroid warning and avoidance:
   Article XI Outer Space Treaty (copied below) may provide a legal basis for an obligation to share the scientific results of a space activity when those results demonstrate that an asteroid or comet could collide with the Earth to the greatest extent feasible and practicable.[14]
2. Concerning the observation that overall benefits to humanity may outweigh the social and political aspects of imposing liability on mission to protect the Earth and people on the Earth:
   Moreover, the human right to life could present a basis for a duty to act in case of a NEO threat scenario. While it creates primarily a 'negative' obligation of states not to interfere, it also contains a 'positive' obligation

12 Other scenarios such as the discovery of a very large NEO that may hit the Earth in a very short period of time and do catastrophic damage to all humanity are likely to present different legal and technical solutions and are discussed in other chapters of this book.

13 Ad-Hoc Working Group on Legal Issues to SMPAG, 'Planetary Defence Legal Overview and Assessment' (SMPAG-RP-004, 8 April 2020).

14 Ibid, 19. Article XI Outer Space Treaty reads: "In order to promote international cooperation in the peaceful exploration and use of outer space, States Parties to the Treaty conducting activities in outer space, including the Moon and other celestial bodies, agree to inform the Secretary-General of the United Nations as well as the public and the international scientific community, to the greatest extent feasible and practicable, of the nature, conduct, locations and results of such activities. On receiving the said information, the Secretary-General of the United Nations should be prepared to disseminate it immediately and effectively."

of states to ensure the right to life of those under their jurisdiction, which includes the duty to take appropriate steps to safeguard human lives. With respect to disasters more specifically, the International Law Commission (ILC) in its Articles on the Protection of Persons in the Event of Disasters highlights that the protection of the right to life "entails a positive obligation on states to take the necessary and appropriate measures to prevent harm from impending disasters". An important legal foundation for this obligation is also the widespread practice of states reflecting their commitment to reduce the risk of disasters.[15]

The case law of the International Court of Justice (ICJ) adds another element to the discussion on the duty of states to inform, namely 'elementary consideration of humanity'. In the *Corfu Channel Case*, the ICJ found that Albania was under the obligation to inform foreign vessels about the existence of a minefield in its territorial waters. This obligation was, according to the Court, based on "general and well-recognised principles, namely: elementary considerations of humanity". In this case, the failure to notify foreign ships led to the death or injury of over 80 persons. Since "nothing was attempted by the Albanian authorities to prevent the disaster", the Court found that Albania was responsible under international law for the damage and loss of human life which resulted from the explosion of the minefield and that there was a duty upon Albania to pay compensation. While the case does not address the specific situation of a NEO impact threat, it can nevertheless support the argument that elementary considerations of humanity can form the basis of a duty to share information in order to avoid the loss of human lives.[16]

3. Concerning benefits to all nations:

A planetary defence action may ultimately serve to protect states beyond those carrying out the action. Planetary defence could thus be viewed as a space activity based on the capacities of a few, but for the benefit of many. Nevertheless, applicable liability regimes should be duly considered as they may be triggered regardless of good intention or overall benefit of a planetary defence mission. As will be shown in this chapter, the consequences of liability could be mitigated or contained primarily through the establishment of an appropriate international understanding by means of legal and / or political instruments. The likelihood of

15 Ibid, 23 (footnotes omitted).

16 Ibid, 20 (footnotes omitted).

achieving this will ultimately be linked to the degree to which balance and coordination of interests can be reached.[17]

4. Concerning waivers of liability:

   The legal basis for a particular mission could include waivers of liability in order to create incentives for states to conduct planetary defence missions. At the same time, it would also be advisable to include safeguards against negligent or intentionally destructive actions and to ensure compensation of victims on the ground as well as assistance by the international community to states that suffered damage. It is by achieving a clear and adequate balance of interests that the likelihood of later disputes can be reduced.[18]

4 A Suggested Process for a Legal Approach to Liability for Planetary Defence

The table depicted further below (Table 19.1) outlines a number of discrete time elements for a future planetary defence mission. Note that it is designed for illustrative purposes only. It is oriented to important questions concerning legal liability and at this point in time cannot cover all scenarios or possibilities. Each mission will likely involve different types of NEOs and very different technologies and time frames. Also, over time some of the liability issues may change due to legal and political space-related issues that may address similar space operational technologies and capabilities in a different context.

The objective of this chapter is to address legal mechanisms to reduce the risk of liability for nations undertaking a planetary defence mission to the point where potential liability will not preclude the efforts to initiate a planetary defence mission. Since there are numerous analogues to current practices in space law, it should be possible to adopt elements of those within the scope of the existing space law regime and international law.

5 Legal/Liability Related Questions and Issues at Each Stage

At every stage outlined in Table 19.1 there are a number of important issues that need clarity and that will affect the approach to legal liability for a state's actions.

17 Ibid, 46.
18 Ibid, 57.

TABLE 19.1 Potential system for planetary defence

Stage	Current Liability Regime	Primary Legal Reference	Possible Adjustments for Planetary Defence	Current Legal Authority/Source of Analogy or State Practice
Monitoring Space for NEOS	– No state liability for scientific and other measurements and observation of space and space objects – Observation and monitoring satellites operate under treaty liability obligations and national laws	– OST, Art. I (freedom of access and freedom of scientific investigation) – Registration and Liability Conventions for satellites – National laws on Earth observation and remote sensing	– None needed for liability concerns – All space objects and equipment in orbit should be registered in UNOOSA Register (Adherence to this international obligation is weak and needs strengthening) – Expand open data systems now in existence to insure all possible information is available to all nations	– OST, Art. VIII (registration), Art. XI (open notification of scientific information), Registration Convention Art. I and Art. II – UNOOSA or other international agency could establish a registry of information about the properties and trajectory of NEOS – Expand the UNGA Resolution on Remote Sensing to include deep space observations; interpretation of Principles IX, X, and XI refer to benefits from remote sensing concerning Earth's natural environment and natural disasters

TABLE 19.1 Potential system for planetary defence (*cont.*)

Stage	Current Liability Regime	Primary Legal Reference	Possible Adjustments for Planetary Defence	Current Legal Authority/Source of Analogy or State Practice
Issue Notice and Warnings of Potential NEO Impacts	– None – states can interpret the information as they see fit – Potential liability for intentional misinformation	– OST, Art. I and Art. XI – Liability Convention, Art. IV[a] – General international law[b]	– Establish a new international reporting/warning system, or – Base a warning system on existing international notification systems such as UNOOSA posting of space object registry – Model could parallel the Hague Code of Conduct on Ballistic Missiles	– OST, Art. XI reporting to UN on scientific information – (Might require a protocol to expand the use of Art. XI specifically for Planetary Defence purposes) – OST, Art. IX requires nations to show due regard for their activities that may affect other nations; it also calls for consultations if damage to another nation's space activities is possible – Establish a new notification system using analogies to other existing warning systems such as the Hague Code of Conduct on Ballistic Missiles

Stage	Current Liability Regime	Primary Legal Reference	Possible Adjustments for Planetary Defence	Current Legal Authority/Source of Analogy or State Practice
National and International Actions	– National terrestrial liability regimes for manufacture of equipment and product liability – Treaty regime for accidents related to launches and space operations	– National law – OST, Art. VI and Art. VIII (ownership) – Liability Convention, Arts. II, III, IV, and V	– Exoneration of liability for in-space operations to encourage nations/international organisations to undertake planetary defence mission – Possibly establish a limit on liability amounts for this purpose only – No waiver for intentional actions or gross negligence in mission	– Liability Convention, Art. XXIII agreements among nations – Potentially helpful analogies currently in force: – ISS Cross-Waiver liability regime – Disaster Charter limiting liability on imagery provided – Maritime analogies limiting liability – Private sector insurance or government insurance/ indemnification fund – Other risk-management techniques
Results of Planetary Defence Mission	– Same as above	– Same as above	– Success or failure of mission determines liability or partial liability exposure	– If failure of mission creates damages, agreed upon prior waivers may be invoked – Diplomatic negotiations or agreements after the fact

TABLE 19.1 Potential system for planetary defence (*cont.*)

Stage	Current Liability Regime	Primary Legal Reference	Possible Adjustments for Planetary Defence	Current Legal Authority/Source of Analogy or State Practice
Secondary long-term outcomes	– Unknown and undefined	Not applicable – unknown in advance	– Would vary by nature of incident	– Same as above; may be unpredictable

[a] Liability in space is primarily focused on compensation for damages to innocent victims (third party liability) and not for actions between two parties participating in space activities. Article IV of the Liability Convention provides also for liability to attach to a nation that has shown gross negligence or that does intentional harm to another nation. For damage on the Earth resulting from gross negligence in space, there is no additional liability because that type of extreme negligence would also involve a finding of fault. Intentional and wilful bad conduct is another matter. And, it is not clear that misinformation of the type addressed in this table would be the same as the drafter's vision of gross negligence in the Liability Convention. However, such an interpretation may not be too great an extension of the simple meaning of the words in Article IV to develop a reasonable threshold for purposes of planetary defence.

[b] The Liability Convention itself allows for invoking general international law (Article III). The *Corfu Channel Case* that awarded compensation to Great Britain for the destruction of ships by Albania clearly focuses on the fact that Albania withheld the knowledge and information it had about the location of mines it had placed in the Chanel. Those mines caused damage to people and property, *Corfu Channel Case* (*UK v Albania*) (Merits) [1949] ICJ Rep 4; also, the *Trail Smelter Arbitration* established a general rule that a nation has the responsibility to protect other states against harmful acts by individuals from within its jurisdiction at all times, *Trail Smelter Arbitration* (*United States v. Canada*) [1941] 3 RIAA 1905.

Note that not all liability issues raise problems to the level that they might become deterrents to proceed with a planetary defence mission. However, if a mission fails and errors can be traced to mistakes at an early stage, a legal argument involving the degree those errors created the proximate cause of a chain of events leading to a failure could be advanced. Whether that would involve significant monetary penalties is unknown but remains a risk. It is a risk that is unlikely to deter a nation to plan and carry out a planetary defence mission since information gathering, issuing warnings about possible space incidents, and other monitoring of space is an integral part of all space faring nation's space programmes. As mentioned above, the current initiatives related to information about space debris tracking and warnings is expanding rapidly and involves both government and private sector companies working together on space safety issues. Liability concerns exist but are not deterring any government or company from advancing these services. Similar approaches and even using these tools for monitoring NEOs will become standard practice. There could be future liability issues, particularly for private companies performing these services, but it appears that in the future, the liability related to this information service is manageable.

6 Precedents and Analogies: Waivers of Liability for Space Activities

The following are examples of adjustments to liability laws and systems that nations have agreed on in the past. They have been developed to deal with special situations and industries that deal with both natural events that have the potential for large scale damage on the Earth and with technologies that are also capable of major damage but where that damage might be preventable through warning systems and other interventions. Both situations are related to the liabilities that could face a planetary defence mission and the examples provided establish the precedent for discussing future mechanisms that could lessen the risks and liability for nations and companies engaging in a planetary defence initiative.

6.1 *Disasters*

One example from the space domain emanates from the UN General Assembly Resolution on Remote Sensing.[19] Principles VI through IX, in particular call for international cooperation and assistance in case of disasters. The subsequent

19 Principles Relating to Remote Sensing of the Earth from Outer Space, UNGA Res 41/65 (3 December 1986).

Disaster Charter is one such agreement among government agencies that enables nations to obtain remote sensing data from other nations free of charge for mitigating damage from disasters.[20] Section 5.4 of that Charter further protects the state(s) providing data from liability:

> [States] confirm that no legal action will be taken against the parties in the event of bodily injury, damage or financial loss arising from the execution or non-execution of activities, services or supplies arising out of the Charter.[21]

In other words, information is provided and those receiving it cannot hold the provider responsible for inaccuracies or misuse of the data. It should also be noted that those receiving data are obligated to use it for humanitarian purposes and not to sell or profit from those data.

To date, there have been many organisations, conferences, and international attempts to systematically address the humanitarian and legal aspects of issuing warnings about potential disasters. In spite of the recognised need and the available technology to provide such warnings in a timely fashion, and to do it without incurring liability for errors in the warnings, there is still no recognised international agreement on this topic. Nations or international organisations that issue such warnings may face claims for the damages. To date, none of these claims has ever been legally recognised and no monetary compensation has been paid.[22]

6.2 *Technological Risks*

The International Space Station (ISS) Agreement includes a cross-waiver provision that establishes a cross-waiver regime among the partner states.[23] This cross-waiver does not protect the nations from third party liability. But it does illustrate how nations can contractually agree on specific liability issues when undertaking joint space projects. If a nation were to proceed to organise an international planetary defence initiative that involved the construction and

20 Charter on Cooperation to Achieve the Coordinated Use of Space Facilities in the Event of Natural or Technological Disasters, UN Doc Rev.3 (25 April 2000).

21 Ibid § 5.4.

22 An example of these types of claims is discussed in: David P Fidler, 'The Indian Ocean and International Law' (2005) 9 ASIL 3.

23 Article 16, Agreement Among the Government of Canada, the Governments of Member States of the European Space Agency, the Government of Japan, the Government of the Russian Federation, and the Government of the United States Concerning Cooperation on the Civil International Space Station (entered into force 27 March 2001); see also

use of equipment in outer space, it would be imperative that these nations agreed in writing to potential liability issues arising from the interaction and actions of the technical contributions to that project. This undertaking would have analogies to both the space station and to the currently planned US led Gateway/Artemis Moon programme. The Space Station Agreement liability clauses are and likely will continue to be the starting point for precedents waiving liability among the partners as well as possibly waiving or limiting other liability concerns.[24]

6.3 *Missile Launches*

The launching of guided missiles for testing and national security measures creates a risk that a launch could be misjudged for an armed attack. To lessen the risks involved, after the serious close call of the 1962 Cuban missile crisis a secure telephone connection between the United States and the Soviet Union was negotiated and put into place to prevent a potentially catastrophic miscalculation between those two superpowers. In 2002 the Hague Code of Conduct against Ballistic Missile Proliferation was formally adopted.[25] Civil space rocket launches were included in this agreement and nations agreed to provide at least 24 hours notice to all other nations for planned space launches as well as for ballistic missile launches. This agreement is yet another example of nations exchanging timely information to prevent a situation that could result in large scale damage.

6.4 *Debris Mitigation*

The space environment itself is now threatened by a number of events. Historically, space faring nations have left a significant amount of debris in orbit. The debris consists of many things including defunct satellites, third-stage rocket bodies, nuts, bolts and other waste from the separation of launch rocket stages, the remains of several satellite collisions, and even tools dropped by astronauts on space walks. As the number of very small satellites placed

---

UNCOPUOS, 'Report of the Committee on the Peaceful Uses of Outer Space in its fifty-second session' (16 April 2013) UN Doc A/AC.105/C.2/2013/CRP.24.

24 The Liability Convention itself enables such agreements through Article XXIII (2), which states "[n]o provision of this Convention shall prevent States from concluding international agreements reaffirming, supplementing, or extending its provisions."

25 Hague Code of Conduct against Ballistic Missile Proliferation (HCOC) (adopted on 25 November 2002). HCOC is a politically-binding agreement. The number of signatories has increased from 93 to 143, see 'List of HCoC Subscribing States' (*Hague Code of Conduct*) <www.hcoc.at/?tab=subscribing_states&page=subscribing_states> accessed 30 January 2021.

into orbit grows exponentially, near-term risks to the sustainability of at least some of the valuable orbits in space have emerged.

There are a number of important international responses developing to mitigate these risks. These include the 2007 UNCOPUOS Space Debris Mitigation Guidelines based on the IADC Debris Mitigation Guidelines,[26] the 2019 UNCOPUOS guidelines on Long-Term Sustainability,[27] and many national laws and guidelines.[28] In the future it can be expected that similar additional rules and regulations will be enabled, primarily at national levels but also possibly under international agreements as part of initiatives commonly called Space Traffic Management (STM). Liability for damage as a result of interference with debris in space is a major concern and these rules and regulations will vary in their strength and enforcement mechanisms. However, even if they cannot be easily enforced in international legal forums, they will help to develop norms, standards, and definitions that will be useful in slowing down the proliferation of debris and in developing legal tests and precedents in dealing with on-orbit issues.

6.5 *Rebuilding and Reparations Following a Possible Failed Planetary Defence Mission*

Although planetary defence missions do not fall within the general area of armed attacks or the law *ad bellum* or *in bello*, the issue of state responsibility and liability under Article VI and VII of the Outer Space Treaty coupled with Article 51 of the UN Charter do address some analogous issues. The term planetary defence itself suggests that nations undertaking the mission are engaging in a space activity that will defend either the Earth or a region of the Earth from a NEO. This clearly is not warfare in the traditional sense, but if the actions during such a planetary defence mission involved damage to a different part of the Earth than the planned mission (for example, an accidental error in the calculations), there might be claims made by the damaged nation toward the nation or nations involved in the failed mission.

---

26 Space Debris Mitigation Guidelines of the Committee on Peaceful Uses of Outer Space, UNGA Res 62/20 (5 December 2007).

27 Guidelines for the Long-term Sustainability of Outer Space Activities of the Committee on the Peaceful Uses of Outer Space, UNGA Res A/74/20 (20 August 2019), para 163 and Annex II.

28 UNOOSA, 'Compendium of Space Debris Mitigation Standards Adopted by States and International Organisations' (*United Nations Office for Outer Space Affairs*) <www.unoosa.org/oosa/en/ourwork/topics/space-debris/compendium.html> accessed 30 January 2021.

A full discussion of state responsibility for transnational harm is beyond the purview of this chapter, but many of the principles developed in the 2001 Articles on State Responsibility[29] are considered customary international law (CIL) and, on the surface, are directly analogous to liability issues if a state action in a planetary defence mission creates serious damage to people or property of another state.

However, there are significant differences in the use of this analogy. Crawford addresses these issues directly and writes about state responsibility in three categories: 1) reparations, 2) criminal activity, and 3) payment penalties aimed at preventing state actors from bad actions (i.e. ignoring rules and CIL regarding trade issues).[30] None of these categories is directly related to states acting with all the best intentions to protect themselves and other states from catastrophic damage directly related to natural and unpredictable events.

The closest category for planetary defence missions is in reparations, or making one whole after damage has been done. Both the Outer Space Treaty[31] and the Liability Convention[32] are oriented toward the objective of absolute liability and unlimited compensation for damage on the Earth from a space object under the premise that nations launching space objects are automatically engaging in ultra-hazardous activities.

Although that assumption of ultra-hazardous activity is clearly recognised in launch activities it is not so obvious for actions in outer space where fault must be found to impose liability on nations that are involved in those space activities. Fault is hard to prove in outer space because gathering clear evidence is more difficult than for incidents terrestrially. Those difficulties range from a lack of precise information about the location and trajectory of many space objects to the reality than many satellites and objects in space use proprietary or classified equipment and procedures. Operations in space always incur a high level of risk. But it is an open and unresolved legal question whether these

---

29 ILC, Articles on the International Responsibility of States for Internationally Wrongful Acts, with Commentaries, 'Report of the International Law Commission on the Work of its 53rd Session' (23 April–1 June and 2 July–10 August 2001) UN Doc A/56/10.

30 James R Crawford, 'State Responsibility' in Rüdiger Wolfrum (ed), *Max Planck Encyclopedia of Public International Law* (Oxford University Press 2012) vol IX 517, paras 1–2. See in more detail chapter 20 'The International Responsibility of States for Planetary Defence Activities' in this book.

31 Article VII, Outer Space Treaty.

32 Article I (a) of the Liability Convention defines damage as the loss of life, personal injury, or other impairment of health, or loss of or damage to property for States or of persons, natural or juridical, or property of international intergovernmental organisations. Article XII specifically deals with monetary compensation and reparations and directs that "the

risks rise to the level of being ultra-hazardous. Further, damage in outer space may not just be to the property (i.e. spacecraft or assets) of another nation since there can also be environmental damage. Finding significant monetary values for these damages may be very difficult and cleanup may physically be impossible.[33] These difficulties, coupled with the humanitarian purpose of planetary defence missions, may strongly support a practical legal argument that unlimited liability would not apply in cases of planetary defence missions not being successful, assuming all nations involved have acted responsibly and with due regard for the property of other nations. The other two responsibility issues discussed by Crawford, criminal activities and payments to prevent future bad acts, are not directly applicable to planetary defence missions.

6.6 *Oil Spills and Civil Nuclear Accidents*

Damages caused by accidents involving private companies involved in high technology and inherently risky endeavours present different legal issues. Examples are oil spills and nuclear power accidents. Internationally, there are treaties among a relatively small number of nations dealing with these types of incidents.[34] These treaties essentially limit the maximum liability and involve national interests in the resolution of the liability and payment for damages. These international agreements demonstrate that, to a limited extent, agreements can be reached to incentivise and encourage the use of advanced technologies that have become economically important in world production and commerce.

It should also be noted that the International Convention on Civil Liability for Oil Pollution was ratified by only 33 nations but also includes a long list of nations declaring reservations on many of its clauses. The Vienna Convention on Civil Liability for Nuclear Damage has been ratified by only 13 nations, with

damage as will restore the person, natural or juridical, State or international organisation on whose behalf the claim is represented to the condition which would have existed if the damage had not occurred."

33 It should be noted that accidents in space have occurred, but as of the writing of this chapter, there have been no accidents that have incurred enough economic damage to warrant a lawsuit. Thus, there are no judicial opinions that have addressed these issues. This will be one area of space law which is likely to remain open for debate and discussion in the future.

34 See, for example, International Convention on Civil Liability for Oil Pollution Damage (adopted 29 November 1969, entered into force 19 June 1975) 973 UNTS 3 replaced by 1992 Protocol (adopted 27 November 1992, entered into force: 30 May 1996); Vienna Convention on Civil Liability for Nuclear Damage (adopted 21 May 1963, entered into force on 12 November 1977) 1063 UNTS 265 amended by a 1997 protocol (entered into force 4 October 2003).

another 40 nation acceding to it. It is notable that, in comparison, the Outer Space Treaty and the Liability Convention have been ratified or signed by 133 and 117 nations, respectively, of the 193 members in the United Nations including all of the current space faring nations.

These statistics suggest a serious divergence between the space faring nations which through existing treaties dealing with space matters have acknowledged their collective international responsibilities and, as described below, other major high-technology activities where states have not assumed ultimate liability for their national activities. However, the application of those state responsibilities when and if there were a very major international incident involving space assets may be questioned. Will nations uphold their commitments if faced with large liabilities from space activities and how will the legal obligations be balanced or overturned by political realities? In essence, it may hinge on two issues: 1) whether a definitive finding of fault can be made, and 2) whether states can agree beforehand on a different approach to liability in a planetary defence mission. The former is a technical and fact-finding problem that may be very difficult from a practical perspective, and the latter would be a political issue at the time the mission is anticipated and organised. There is a strong possibility that given the difficulties in agreeing on liability in other industries, that it may also be difficult in space.

However, there are significant differences between outer space and terrestrial industry and environments. In particular, oil and civil nuclear equipment are often corporate in nature, may involve insurance claims, and can more easily be settled in national courts or in international arbitration rather than through diplomatic means. As private sector initiatives in outer space expand, similar legal analogies may be applied. As explained below, the space environment is unique since it is defined as a non-sovereign area where nations are ultimately responsible and liable for their non-governmental entities operating in space in just the same way they are for their own national assets and operations in space. There is no other industry that has the same liability shield.

Outer space activities are still primarily government managed and funded operations. As such, they are more political than corporate. Horton, Parker, and Keith make a very interesting analogy of Geoengineering (managing climate change) to the law of outer space where they argue that there are similar political issues that make legal agreements on liability and other issues very difficult.[35]

35 Joshua B Horton, Andrew Parker and David Keith, 'Liability for Solar Geoengineering: Historical Precedents, Contemporary Innovations, and Governance Possibilities' (2015) 22 NYU Environmental Law Journal 225–273.

Planetary defence liability issues will likely also be more political than private, even if private companies develop programmes and missions to 'save the Earth'. Any company launching into space needs a license from a government, will use or rely on government technology for guidance systems and other technical assistance, and will also likely need some government funding as these missions are inherently risky and expensive. In essence, all such missions, at least in the near-term future will likely be partnerships between governments and companies and the contractual relationships between the two will include negotiated clauses specifically dealing with the sharing of risk and therefore also liability.

6.7 *Antarctica*

The Antarctic Treaty was negotiated a few years earlier but during the same era as the Outer Space Treaty.[36] It contains similar philosophical principles and essentially, by mutual agreement of the nations ratifying the Treaty, makes the continent of Antarctica a non-sovereign area reserved primarily for scientific research.[37] Over time there have been research operations and facilities there and more recently even some private operations and tourism. The treaty has no specific language on liability but subsequent protocols do address threats to environmental emergencies.

In 2005 there was a proposed Annex (Annex VI) to the Protocol on Environmental Protection to the Antarctic Treaty on 'Liability Arising from Environmental Emergencies'.[38] It contains some relevant clauses that may foreshadow the future liability issues relevant to outer space and to planetary defence.

For example, Article 4 establishes a process for contingency plans that includes notification, resource mobilisation, response plans, etc. Article 6

36 The 1959 Antarctic Treaty (adopted 1 December 1959, entered into force 23 June 1961) 402 UNTS 71.

37 Unlike the Outer Space Treaty, Article IV(1) of the Antarctic Treaty preserved prior national claims through the following language: 1. Nothing contained in the present Treaty shall be interpreted as: (a) a renunciation by any Contracting Party of previously asserted rights of or claims to territorial sovereignty in Antarctica; (b) a renunciation or diminution by any Contracting Party of any basis of claim to territorial sovereignty in Antarctica which it may have whether as a result of its activities or those of its nationals in Antarctica, or otherwise; (c) prejudicing the position of any Contracting Party as regards its recognition or non-recognition of any other State's right of or claim or basis of claim to territorial sovereignty in Antarctica.

38 Secretariat of the Antarctic Treaty, Measure 1 (2005) – ATCM XXVIII – CEP VIII. Annex VI has not yet achieved the required ratification by all Consultative Parties for entering into force.

addresses liability and focuses on the duty to respond to an emergency and monetary compensation for the cost of that response that should have been undertaken. It provides for strict liability but does not specifically define it and does not provide for compensation from direct environmental damage. Article 10 deals with state liability and provides an exclusion for the failure of a non-state operator if the state took appropriate measures within its competence. Article 11 directs states to require operators to provide insurance or financial security to cover liability.

The proposed Annex VI is not in force, again highlighting the difficult and time consuming process of an international agreement on liability for a catastrophe or event that is anticipatory and has not as yet occurred.

7 Additional Issues

The treaties that established international space law are basically a set of international principles, leaving many details of their implementation to interpretation through national laws and to future circumstances. The last two of the ratified treaties recognise the need to review their provisions in the future.[39] But that has never formally been done for any of the treaties. Given that space technology has dramatically changed over the years, as have international alignments in policy and economics affecting space activities, it will become essential to review and re-evaluate a number of lacunae and even provisions in space law. The issues of planetary defence will necessarily be of concern and affected by these future provisions. It is not the objective of this chapter to make those decisions or fully interpret or suggest the changes that will occur, but only to highlight the major topics that will need to be reviewed with respect to liability.

Important issues, as have been mentioned above, include:

- A refinement or clarification of what a 'space object' is under definitions in the Liability Convention and Registration Conventions.
  - A NEO today would not be a space object since it is not something launched. But, if a NEO were moved or destroyed by the space object of a nation and if it caused damage to other nations, either in space or on the Earth, some evaluation of liability for that damage should

39 Article X, Registration Convention, Article 18, Moon Agreement, both recommending a review 10 years after they were in force.

  be assigned to the nation that caused the damage. The question of a waiver of liability is different.
- A clarification or better process for nations to agree on which states are 'launching states' under the Liability and Registration Conventions.
  - If damage occurs in outer space, all launching states are potentially liable, jointly and severally. In a situation where there are multiple launching states, this could include nations that do not have operational control over the spacecraft and have no direct connection with any operation or manoeuvre in space, and thus may have no direct bearing on any negligence or fault finding.
  - Associated with this (and with the definition of space object as well) is the process of registration of space objects. The obligation to register all space objects has never been well enforced, either with respect to time of registration or even of exactly what to register. It will become more important with the proliferation of human created objects in space to refine this process and coordinate it with ownership, control, and responsibility of nations for their space activities.
- Issues of secondary damage
  - If a space object does damage to other space objects of the same nation or on that nation's territory on the Earth, it is a matter of national, not international law and therefore can be handled legally internally within that nation.
  - However, if a nation incurs direct damage and that damage creates environmental or other secondary damage outside of its borders as a result of a NEO, can that nation be held liable for the resultant damage? Is there a time limit on secondary damage?
- Liability could attach for either a successful planetary defence mission or an unsuccessful one. If, for example, the mission was successful in diverting a NEO from the Earth, but it unintentionally damaged an asset in outer space, technically there is potential for liability for the space object damaged. Is this an outcome that should fall under the current liability regime or not?
- Issues of Enforcement
  - The current space treaties represent agreements among governments. If there is a dispute among nations, the Outer Space Treaty suggests that nations negotiate the resolution through diplomatic channels. On issues of liability, the Liability Convention (Article IX) calls for states to present claims by negotiating solutions through diplomatic channels. (Article XI also allows claims to be brought

to national courts.) The Convention, in Articles XV through XX also provides for dispute settlement method through establishing a non-binding Claims Commission. The latter has never been invoked and states have been able to solve the very few liability issues that have occurred diplomatically.[40]

– If a planetary defence mission triggered a catastrophic accident terrestrially on the sovereign territory of a nation not involved in the mission, it might have a valid legal claim against the nation(s) undertaking the mission under the absolute liability provision in Article II of the Liability Convention. However, as mentioned above, if the object striking the nation were a NEO, and not the space object of the other nations, it is technically not a claim under the Liability Convention but rather one under general international law. Thus, the recovery for damages might rest on a variety of other arguments and not be an automatic recovery for unlimited amounts as suggested in the Liability Convention. Predicting the outcomes and arguments would be incident-specific and thus outside the scope of this chapter. The point for now is that the dagger of a catastrophic payment under the theory of absolute liability for damage on Earth from a space object might not be the appropriate liability measure in such an instance.

8 Conclusion

Planetary defence missions should pose no major future issues or involve any radical changes to the current space law liability regime.

What is important is the ability of nations today to adequately plan ahead to face the unique liability issues that a planetary defence mission might involve and that will distinguish it from other developing space activities and capabilities. To address these situations it will be important in space law to clearly define and develop an international agreement that establishes a formal

40 The Cosmos 954 incident in 1978 where a Soviet reconnaissance satellite crashed into Canadian territory and involved an expensive clean-up of nuclear material was settled by negotiations between those two nations and resulted in an agreed upon payment for damages by the Soviet Union to Canada. In 2009 when a US military satellite was intentionally deorbited with hazardous chemicals onboard, and the landing site not predictable, the US Department of State made sure that any affected nation would be compensated for potential damage. Fortunately, it deorbited in the Pacific Ocean and there was no terrestrial damage to any nation.

process to address potential legal and liability problems at all stages of a planetary defence initiative and to be prepared to invoke precedents to limit or waive liability as nations have done for other high technology/high risk critical activities.

This proposed agreement would not directly address specific liability solutions since they may vary with the type of planetary defence mission, but be limited to establishing a system for approaching and finding solutions to these problems. Such solutions could range from establishing specific limits to specific potential liabilities, dedicated funded insurance (either public or private) reserves, or even a formula for after-the-fact taxation on the participating states. Alternatively, appropriate wording of *force majeure* clauses could be considered.[41]

No nation can afford to pay for catastrophic global damage from a NEO, whether it occurs naturally or from an unsuccessful attempt to 'save' the planet. Even a large regional occurrence resulting from a 'mistake' in calculations might be so large that no nation alone could pay to restore that property and other damage.

Looking ahead to a legal system that does not penalise a nation with the technical skills and equipment to prevent a major NEO collision with the Earth will require legal agreements that grant waivers from liability regardless of whether the mission is successful or if it fails.[42] If no nation had the technical capability to possibly prevent the collision, the damage to Earth would legally be no different than a major natural event such as a volcanic eruption, hurricane, tsunami, or earthquake. It would be a force majeure or an 'act of God', exonerating a party from the obligation to compensate anyone for the damage. Insurance might or might not be available depending on the willingness of an insurer to write a policy and the specifics of what that policy would cover (most insurance policies have *force majeure* clauses and will not pay such claims).

41 During the current Covid-19 pandemic, the wording of various contracts and agreements that include clauses waiving damage compensation from 'acts of God' have stimulated new attention to the potential liability of companies for their responses to the pandemic. Analogies to waivers for a NEO mission planetary defence may also need to be clarified, given the unknowns involved and the reason for the mission is to prevent such an 'act of God' to damage the Earth.

42 For simplicity, this chapter equates private companies and non-governmental organisations with nations, given that through Article VI of the Outer Space Treaty requires nations to authorise and continuously supervise their activities. Ultimately nations are responsible for their national activities in space, which may also impose primary liability on those nations.

Of course there are humanitarian considerations. If possible, help, aid, and money for rebuilding from such an event would likely be supplied, either from the government of the nation that was affected or from donations and international voluntary sources.

The question faced in this chapter addresses the legal requirements that might be forthcoming to shield a nation or group of nations from liability in the attempt to prevent a known and identified NEO from hitting the Earth. Under the best of conditions this shield would be created only if the actors operated in good faith, gave adequate notice to other nations, used the best-known technology to the best of their abilities and made no tactical or operational errors.

The techniques that will be used in a planetary defence mission may mirror other new capabilities and activities now being perfected in outer space by the most advanced space nations, such as rendezvous and proximity operations and in-situ use of resources. The types of changes to the future space liability regime are suggested here only for planetary protection missions. Whether they might also apply to other similar technologies is a complex issue that will need to be addressed differently and in different forums.

In summary, liability issues are present at all stages of any planned space mission. Most liabilities, even for damage in outer space to space objects, are within the boundaries of current risks that space faring nations as well as private companies have routinely absorbed. This chapter has argued that the liability for a space project on a humanitarian mission to prevent a catastrophic loss from a NEO impact with the Earth should not deter any nation from undertaking such a mission. If successful, the mission would represent an unprecedented intervention in preserving life on Earth. Many other scenarios are possible, ranging from the NEO being undisturbed in its trajectory to the NEO being shifted and either doing damage in outer space to space objects or to hitting the Earth in a different location. If that happened, liability issues will arise. These liability risks can be clearly handled through adequate planning and invoking analogies to existing legal options.

CHAPTER 20

The International Responsibility of States for Planetary Defence Activities

Sergio Marchisio

1 Introduction

Since 1995, the United Nations have adopted several recommendations warning the international community on the potential threat from Near-Earth Objects (NEOs). The 1999 Vienna Declaration on Space and Human Development declared, in the context of the Third United Nations Conference on the Exploration and Peaceful Uses of Outer Space (UNISPACE III), the need to improve international coordination of activities related to NEOs and to develop a common strategy to face such threats. While the probability of a large object impacting Earth is small, it could have catastrophic consequences of a global scale. In recent years, space agencies have increased their efforts in the detection and appraisal of hazardous NEOs and the development of strategies to prevent and mitigate potential impacts.

At the international level, upon recommendation of the United Nations Committee on the Peaceful Uses of Outer Space (UNCOPUOS) the International Asteroid Warning Network (IAWN) and the Space Mission Planning Advisory Group (SMPAG) were established to maintain an international clearing house for the receipt, acknowledgment and processing of NEO observations and to lay out a framework, timeline and options for NEO threat response activities.[1] IAWN and SMPAG were created in 2014, and a SMPAG Ad-Hoc Working Group on Legal Issues was established in 2016 for the identification and assessment of legal issues related to NEO response actions.[2]

1 See UNCOPUOS, 'Report of the Scientific and Technical Subcommittee on its fiftieth session' (7 March 2013) UN Doc A/AC.105/1038 <www.unoosa.org/pdf/reports/ac105/AC105_1038E.pdf> accessed 25 February 2021 and the website of the United Nations Office for Outer Space Affairs: <https://www.unoosa.org/oosa/en/ourwork/topics/neos/index.html> accessed 25 February 2021. See also chapter 4 'International Cooperation in Planetary Defence – UNCOPUOS, IAWN and SMPAG' in this book.

2 Ad-Hoc Working Group on Legal Issues to SMPAG, 'Planetary Defence Legal Overview and Assessment' (SMPAG-RP-004, 8 April 2020). See also chapter 11 'The SMPAG Ad-hoc Working Group on Legal Issues' in this book.

 | DOI:10.1163/9789004467606_022

Among the legal issues raised by space missions related to NEOs, this chapter focuses on the international responsibility of states for planetary defence activities, describing the particularities of responsibility under international space law and analysing its application to planetary defence. It also refers to the difference between responsibility and liability, which has been dealt with in two previous chapters and addresses the applicability of circumstances precluding wrongfulness to planetary defence missions. The topic of the involvement of private actors, which is discussed in the next chapter, is mentioned here only as far as it regards the attribution of conducts of individuals to a state as source of international responsibility. From a general standpoint, the topic is treated with the aim of analysing whether the international responsibility of states for planetary defence activities presents any peculiarities with regard to the international responsibility of states under international law at large and under international space law as a part of international law.[3]

The international responsibility of states is a situation which results from the breach of any international obligation. State responsibility is a fundamental principle of international law, which provides that whenever one state commits an internationally unlawful act, international responsibility is established. Shortly, the law of state responsibility is concerned with the incidence and consequences of illegal acts, as the International Court of Justice (ICJ) held in its advisory opinion on the Interpretation of Peace Treaties with Bulgaria, Hungary and Romania (Second Phase): "refusal to fulfil a treaty obligation" involves international responsibility.[4]

2 Primary Norms of International Law on Planetary Defence Activities

This kind of 'responsibility' for wrongful conducts is regulated by norms of international law qualified as 'secondary', inasmuch as they are concerned with determining the legal consequences of the failure to fulfil obligations established by the substantive rules, which, in one or another sector of interstate relations, impose specific obligations on states, and may be termed as 'primary'.[5] It is outside the scope of this chapter to address the primary norms

3 Stephan Hobe, *Space Law* (Nomos 2019) 53–57.

4 *Interpretation of Peace Treaties with Bulgaria, Hungary and Romania (Second Phase)* (Advisory Opinion) [1950] ICJ Rep 1950, 228.

5 This distinction was made by the International Law Commission in 1973, when Roberto Ago took over the task of Special Rapporteur for the topic of International Responsibility of States

of international law regulating planetary defence whose breach entails the responsibility of states for internationally wrongful acts. This topic is covered in other chapters of this book, where state obligations in the matter of planetary defence activities are discussed.

In general, international law, including international space law, does not contain specific norms on planetary defence operations yet. There is no definite, broadly accepted source of international law which spells out legal standards, procedures, rights and duties pertaining specifically to planetary defence activities.

There are of course principles and norms of international law and space law which, even without dealing expressly with planetary defence, are applicable to these activities. However, due to the different dimensions of possible threats posed by NEOs, the applicable norms and the legal implications can vary substantially.

The preliminary assumption is that planetary defence operations are outer space activities as all other human activities in outer space, on the Moon and on other celestial bodies carried on by states and intergovernmental organisations or by private entities under the jurisdiction of the state that authorised the activity. Thus, the main UN space treaties apply also to planetary defence operations. Mitigation is used as including measures to prevent, predict, prepare for, respond to, monitor and/or mitigate the impact of, disasters, as defined by Article 1(7) of the Tampere Convention on the Provision of Telecommunication Resources for Disaster Mitigation and Relief Operations of 18 June 1998.[6]

Several provisions of the 1967 Outer Space Treaty are obviously relevant as they provide the basic framework for all outer space activities.[7] In this sense, operations of planetary defence shall be in conformity with Article I of the Outer Space Treaty, stating that exploration and use of outer space shall be carried out for the benefit and in the interests of all countries, and Article II, which prohibits any claim of sovereignty over outer space and celestial bodies. Article III of the Outer Space Treaty highlights that international law,

---

for wrongful acts. See, ILC, 'Yearbook of the International Law Commission, vol II' (1973) UN Doc A/9010/Rev. 1, para 40.

6 Tampere Convention on the Provision of Telecommunication Resources for Disaster Mitigation and Relief Operations (adopted 18 June 1998, entered into force 8 January 2005) 2296 UNTS 5.

7 Treaty on Principles Governing the Activities of States in the Exploration and Use of Outer Space, including the Moon and other Celestial Bodies (adopted 19 December 1966, entered into force 10 October 1967) 610 UNTS 205.

including the UN Charter, applies to state activities in the exploration and use of outer space in the interest of maintaining international peace and security and promoting international cooperation. Moreover, Article IV prohibits the placement of objects carrying nuclear weapons or any other kinds of weapons of mass destruction in Earth orbit, the installation of such weapons on celestial bodies and their stationing in outer space, as well as the establishment of military bases, installations and fortifications, the testing of any type of weapons and the conduct of military manoeuvres on celestial bodies. In addition, other arms control and non-proliferation treaties contain restrictions regarding the use of nuclear explosive devices in outer space, in particular the Limited Test Ban Treaty[8] and the Nuclear Non-Proliferation Treaty.[9]

Article IX of the Outer Space Treaty declares that the principle of cooperation and mutual assistance shall guide states in their activities in outer space, with due regard to the corresponding interests of all other states.[10] Article XI of the Outer Space Treaty comes into play when considering the sharing of information dealing with threats posed by NEOs[11] as well as other international instruments of a non-legally binding nature, such as Principle XI of the 1986 UN Principles relating to Remote Sensing adopted in 1986[12] and Principles 18

8 Treaty Banning Nuclear Weapon Tests in the Atmosphere, in Outer Space and Under Water (adopted 5 August 1963, entered into force 10 October 1963) 480 UNTS 43. The treaty commits states parties to undertake to prohibit, to prevent, and not to carry out any nuclear weapon test explosion or any other nuclear explosion in the atmosphere, in outer space or under water. The same obligation is contained in two other legal instruments: the 1996 Comprehensive Nuclear-Test-Ban Treaty, which is not yet in force but applied provisionally and bans all nuclear explosions, for both civilian and military purposes, 'at any place', and the 2017 Treaty on the Prohibition of Nuclear Weapons, also not yet in force, where states parties, undertake 'never under any circumstances' to develop, test, produce, possess, stockpile, transfer, receive or use nuclear explosive devices.

9 Treaty on the Non-Proliferation of Nuclear Weapons (adopted 1 July 1968, entered into force 5 March 1970) 729 UNTS 169.

10 Sergio Marchisio, 'Article IX' in Stephan Hobe, Bernhard Schmidt-Tedd and Kai-Uwe Schrogl (eds), *Cologne Commentary on Space Law,* vol I (Carl Heymanns Verlag 2009) 169–182.

11 Thus, the scope of this provision is quite clear: if a State discovers information regarding a significant NEO impact threat to Earth as a result of its space activities, such information should be made available to the "greatest extent feasible and practicable".

12 Principles Relating to Remote Sensing of the Earth from Outer Space (hereafter UN Principles on Remote Sensing), UNGA Res 41/65 (3 December 1986) UN Doc A/AC.105/572/Rev.1. Principle XI of the same instrument concerns the protection of humankind from natural disasters, and commits States participating in remote sensing activities that have identified processed data and analysed information in their possession that may be useful to States affected by natural disasters, or likely to be affected by impending natural disasters, to transmit such data and information to the States concerned as promptly as

and 19 of the 1992 Rio Declaration on Environment and Development.[13] On early warning as a major element of disaster risk reduction and prevention of loss of life, already the ICJ, in the *Corfu Channel Case*, found that Albania was under the obligation to warn foreign vessels about the existence of a minefield in its territorial waters, mentioning "elementary considerations of humanity".[14]

In addition, international disaster law is another area of international law which has given a certain contribution to the development of early warning systems which could also be relevant in the context of planetary defence operations.[15] From this perspective at the international level IAWN and SMPAG are actively working, as already noticed, to set up a first framework for international coordination. Another legal issue relates to the 'duty to act' in order to prevent or avoid catastrophic consequences of a collision between an asteroid and the Earth, as well as other obligations such as to execute deflection or disruption missions for states that have the capability to carry on such missions.

3 Secondary Norms of International Law on State Responsibility

On the secondary norms side, the task is easier because the International Law Commission (ILC) Articles on State Responsibility, adopted in 2001, reflect customary international law.[16] The general rules on the international responsibility of states for internationally wrongful acts govern all the new legal relationships, which may follow from an internationally wrongful act of a state, regardless of the field of law to which the rule violated by the act may belong.

---

possible (Cf. Sergio Marchisio, 'The 1986 United Nations Principles on Remote Sensing: A Critical Assessment' in Gaetano Arangio-Ruiz (ed), *Studi di diritto internazionale in onore di Gaetano Arangio-Ruiz* (Editoriale Scientifica 2004) 1311–1340.

13 1992 Rio Declaration on Environment and Development (adopted 16 June 1992) UN Doc. A/CONF.151/26 (vol. I), 31 ILM 874, provides respectively that States "shall immediately notify other States of any natural disasters or other emergencies that are likely to produce sudden harmful effects on the environment of those States. Every effort shall be made by the international community to help afflicted States", and that "States shall provide prior and timely notification and relevant information to potentially affected States on activities that may have a significant adverse transboundary environmental effect and shall consult with those States at an early stage and in good faith".

14 *Corfu Channel Case* (*UK v Albania*) (Merits) [1949] ICJ Rep 4, 4, 22.

15 ILC, Draft Articles on the Protection of Persons in the Event of Disasters, with Commentaries, 'Report of the International Law Commission on the Work of its 68th Session' (2 May–10 June and 4 July–12 August 2016) UN Doc A/71/10.

16 See ibid. See also Robert Kolb, *The International Law of State Responsibility: An Introduction* (Edward Elgar Publishing 2017).

There are two main groups of secondary norms: the first group determines on the basis of which facts and in which circumstances there exists on the part of a state an internationally wrongful act which, as such, is the source of international responsibility. The second group determines the consequences attached by international law to an internationally wrongful act in the various cases, in order to derive therefrom a definition of the content, form and degree of the international responsibility.

The fundamental principle attaches responsibility to every internationally wrongful act of a state and needs to be applied to planetary defence missions since any violation of an international obligation in the course of such activities leads to the accountability of the involved state(s) and may provide the basis for claims for compensation. According to Article 2 of the ILC Articles on State Responsibility, an internationally unlawful act of a state occurs when conduct consisting of an action or omission is attributable to the state in terms of international law and is a breach of an international obligation of the state.

This notion of international wrongful act was used by the ICJ in the decision in the *Tehran Hostage Case*, where it asserted the presence of both elements and, therefore, attributed to Iran the responsibility for breaching multiple obligations of international law, primarily those related to the treatment of diplomatic missions and their personnel.[17]

To speak of imputation to a state, therefore, indicates that the international legal order must be able to regard the action or omission concerned as an act of the state, if it is to be allowed further to assume the creation of those new subjective legal situations which are covered by the overall, synthetic expression 'international responsibility of states'. And since the state, as a legal entity, is not physically capable of conduct, it is obvious that all that can be imputed to a state is the act or omission of an individual or of a group of individuals.[18] This is where the general principles of international law apply in terms of attributing to the state the conduct of individuals with the quality of organs, even de facto ones (that is, determined not only with regard to the domestic legal system and legal structure of the state, but also, where appropriate, to its factual organisation).[19]

---

17 *United States Diplomatic and Consular Staff in Tehran* (*United States of America v Iran*) (Judgment) [1980] ICJ Rep 3, 68, 74.

18 "States can act only by and through their agents and representatives". See *Certain questions relating to settlers of German origin in the territory ceded by Germany to Poland* (Advisory Opinion) [1923] PCIJ Rep Series B No 6, para 22.

19 In this sense, the following may constitute an international wrongful act of the state: a) the conduct of an individual who, for the internal order of the state, possesses the quality of organ of that state and has acted within the limits of the competence attributed to him;

As regards the attribution to the state of behaviours of individuals who do not have the quality of organs, Articles 5 – 7 of the ILC Articles on State Responsibility take into account the imputation to the state of the conduct of persons or entities that are not organs of the state under internal law, but exercise elements of government authority (e.g. cases of state bodies privatised but that retain certain public functions). In such cases, the reference is to the actual organisation of the state, to which, therefore, such behaviours are attributed. From Article 7, however, it is clear that the competence of the organs is not relevant for the attribution of wrongful acts, because what matters is the quality of the organs: in the case of *ultra vires* acts, which are carried out outside the competence attributed or in contravention to the instructions received, the misconduct is nevertheless attributed to the state.[20]

A further problem is that of the degree of control that must be exercised by the state over individuals and groups of individuals not to be considered as organs of the state but acting on behalf of the state so that their conduct is attributed to the latter. According to Article 8 of the ILC Articles on State Responsibility, the conduct of individuals or groups acting according to instructions and under the direction and control of the state must be attributed to the latter. On those aspects, the reference to various international judicial decisions shows that there are different opinions on what criterion should be used in order to attribute the conducts of those subjects to the state. Firstly, there is the criterion of the 'effective control', inferred from the judgments of the ICJ of 27 June 1986 on the *Nicaragua Case*, and of 11 July 1996 on the case of the *Genocide Case*.[21] The second criterion of the 'overall control' was referred to by the Appeal Chamber of the International Criminal Tribunal for the former Yugoslavia in the 1999 *Tadic Case*: in attributing to the Yugoslav Republic the actions of irregular armed forces, the judges stated that 'the degree of control' varies according to the different circumstances (in this case serious human rights violations).[22]

---

b) in certain circumstances, the conduct of an individual who has acted beyond these limits or who does not have the status of a state organ for the internal order of the state.

20 Article 91, First Additional Protocol to the 1949 Geneva Conventions (adopted 9 June 1977, entered into force 7 December 1978) 1125 UNTS 3 says that: "[a] Party to the conflict (…) shall be responsible for all acts by people forming part of its armed forces". This provision clearly covers acts committed in contravention of the orders received.

21 *Military and Paramilitary Activities in and against Nicaragua* (*Nicaragua v United States of America*) (Jurisdiction and Admissibility) [1984] ICJ Rep 392, 80, 110–115; *Application of the Convention on the Prevention and Punishment of the Crime of Genocide* (*Bosnia and Herzegovina v Serbia and Montenegro*), (Merits) [2007] ICJ Rep 43, 400–415.

22 *Tadic Case* (Judgment) ICTY-94-1 (26 January 2000) paras 137–145. The first, more restrictive approach appears more convincing and in line with international practice.

By contrast, the conduct of mere individuals who have acted as such is not attributable to the state under general international law. However, there could be circumstances in which the existence of an internationally wrongful act by the state can nevertheless be contemplated in connexion with certain conducts of private individuals. These alleged cases of state responsibility for the acts of individuals are really cases of responsibility of the state for omissions by its organs: the state is responsible for having failed to take appropriate measures to prevent or punish the individual's act.

4 The Special Regime of International Space Law

If this is the current situation under general international law regarding international responsibility for wrongful acts, as noted above, planetary defence activities fall also under the scope of the Outer Space Treaty, including in particular its Article VI.[23] This norm encompasses under the title of 'international responsibility' all the legal consequences of national activities of a state in outer space, such as the obligation of reparation in case of wrongful acts or omissions by public or private entities; the obligation of the appropriate state to authorise and continuously supervise the activities of non-governmental entities in outer space, including the Moon and other celestial bodies; the obligation of supervision and control, for assuring that national activities in outer space are carried out in conformity with the provisions of the Outer Space Treaty; and the obligation to compensate damage in case of liability under Article VII of the Treaty. The elements to be considered by states when enacting a national regulatory framework for space activities aimed at implementing the obligations set forth by Article VI of the Outer Space Treaty are spelled out in Resolution 68/74 on 'Recommendations on national space legislation relevant to the peaceful exploration and use of outer space', adopted by the UN General Assembly on 11 December 2013.[24]

23 On the question whether Article VI constitutes a deviation or not from the rule of general international law on the attribution to the state of the conducts of private persons see, Luigi Condorelli, 'L'imputation à l'Etat d'un fait Internationalement Illicite: Solutions Classiques et Nouvelles tendances' (1984) 189 Recueil des Cours de l'Académie de Droit International de La Haye 120–121; Gaetano Arangio-Ruiz, 'State Responsibility Revisited. The Factual Nature of the Attribution of Conduct to the State' (2017) 11 Quaderni della Rivista di Diritto Internazionale 123–126.

24 UNGA Res 68/74 (16 December 2013). A dedicated Working Group was set up within the UNCOPUOS LSC in 2008, based on a multi-year programme of work. See, Irmgard Marboe, 'National Space Legislation' in Frans von der Dunk (ed), *Handbook of Space Law*

In other words, 'international responsibility' under Article VI means general accountability and involves not only a general duty of diligence by the appropriate state, but also – and this is the most relevant point – the direct attribution of the conducts of private entities to that state.[25] This is of significance in case of private entities involved in planetary defence activities and means that a breach of international law committed by private actors in outer space shall be directly attributed to the appropriate state. While Article VI does not define the 'appropriate state', there is a growing understanding that, in principle, it should be the state which has jurisdiction over the space activity which ultimately leads to the launching state or the state of registry.[26] In case the mission is conducted by an international organisation, responsibility for compliance with the Outer Space Treaty is borne both by the international organisation and by the states parties to the Outer Space Treaty participating in such organisation.

5 The Consequences of International Responsibility for Planetary Defence Activities

In case of international responsibility deriving from breaches of international obligations attributable to a state in the context of planetary defence operations, the legal consequences are the same as in case of responsibility for violations of obligations in force in other sectors of international law.

(Edward Elgar Publishing 2015) 127 ff.; Frans G von der Dunk, 'Scoping National Space Law: the True Meaning of "National Activities in Outer Space" of Article VI of the Outer Space Treaty' in IISL (ed), *Proceedings of the IISL Colloquium on the Law of Outer Space* (International Astronautical Federation 2019) 214–226.

25 The two regimes (international responsibility for wrongful acts and liability for damages) are not alternatives, but rather complementary and can coexist. In fact, there can be absolute or fault-based liability without or with international responsibility for wrongful acts. The space law treaties do not affect states' rights to invoke state responsibility according to general international law and vice versa. On the relation between the Outer Space Treaty and the Liability Convention, see Olivier Ribbelink, 'Article III' in Stephan Hobe, Bernard Schmidt-Tedd, Kai-Uwe Schrogl (eds), *Cologne Commentary on Space Law,* vol I (Carl Heymanns Verlag 2009) 64–69. The case of the claims of Canada against Soviet Union for the Cosmos 954 accident is very instructive in this sense. See Olga A Volynskaya, 'Landmark Space-Related Accidents and the Progress of Space Law' (2012) 61 Zeitschrift fur Luft- und Weltraumrecht 220–228.

26 See Michael Gerhard, 'Article VI', in Stephan Hobe, Bernard Schmidt-Tedd, Kai-Uwe Schrogl (eds), *Cologne Commentary on Space Law,* vol I (Carl Heymanns Verlag 2009) 112–114.

Firstly, the responsible state must cease the wrongful conduct and pledge not to repeat it; then, it is requested to make reparation, which can assume different forms depending on the content of the violated obligation (satisfaction, restitution, compensation).

Furthermore, a state could be required to pay compensation even if there is no issue of a violation of international obligations, in cases where its liability as launching state is at stake because the planetary defence activities produced damage according to Article VII of the Outer Space Treaty and the 1972 Liability Convention.[27] Liability under this convention focuses exclusively on compensation of damage under two different legal regimes, depending on the place where the damage occurs: absolute liability for damage caused on the surface of the Earth or to aircraft in flight; fault-based liability for damage caused elsewhere. 'Damage' means "loss of life, personal injury or other impairment of health; or loss of or damage to property of States or of persons, natural or juridical, or property of international intergovernmental organizations".[28]

From the perspective of a launching state carrying out a planetary defence mission, the regime of absolute/objective liability represents a risk that, in the case of intervention on behalf of another state or of the whole international community, could be very burdensome. In this sense, special agreements aimed at including ad hoc waivers for the mitigation of liability risks would be highly advisable.

In conclusion, while the general principles on responsibility under current international law and space law treaties are applicable to missions and their wrongful consequences, it would be better for the subjects concerned to frame them through specific agreements/contracts. Other possible solutions include an international mandate for a planetary defence mission given through a resolution adopted by the UN Security Council under Chapter VII of the Charter.[29]

6 Circumstances Precluding Wrongfulness

International law recognises the existence in given cases of a circumstance precluding the wrongfulness of an otherwise prohibited action. In the case of planetary defence activities, the circumstances self-defence, consent, distress

27 Convention on International Liability for Damage Caused by Space Objects (adopted 29 November 1971, entered into force 1 September 1972) 961 UNTS 187 (Liability Convention).

28 Article I(a), Liability Convention.

29 See on this point, chapter 22 'International Bodies and Procedures for Decision-Making Regarding Planetary Defence Actions' in this book.

and necessity could be relevant to justify actions that are not in compliance with international obligations.

Article 21 of the ILC Articles on State Responsibility states: "The wrongfulness of an act of a State is precluded if the act constitutes a lawful measure of self-defence taken in conformity with the Charter of the United Nations".[30] The question of 'self-defence' could be particularly relevant in determining whether nuclear explosions for deflecting or destroying an asteroid which is seriously threatening the Earth could be admitted in view of safeguarding the survival of humanity or of a large part of it. The ICJ in its advisory opinion on the *Legality of the Threat or Use of Nuclear Weapons* concluded that "in view of the current state of international law, and of the elements of fact at its disposal, the Court cannot conclude definitively whether the threat or use of nuclear weapons would be lawful or unlawful in an extreme circumstance of self-defence, in which the very survival of a State would be at stake".[31] However, planetary defence operations do not involve the use of force in the sense of Article 2(4) of the UN Charter, because the use of force by one or more states against the independence and the territorial integrity of another state is not at stake. Referring to 'self-defence' would thus not serve the purpose of justifying planetary defence activities.[32]

'Consent', however, may play a more relevant role in this context. It precludes the wrongfulness of an act of a state, when a state validly gives its consent to the commission by another state of a specific act not in conformity with an obligation of the latter state towards the former state. It precludes the wrongfulness of the act in relation to that state to the extent that the act remains within the limits of the consent.[33] Consistent with current international law, a deflection mission to protect another country from a NEO impact could be subject to the prior consultation and agreement of the concerned state.[34] However, if the mission is necessary for the sake of a vital interest of the totality of the other subjects or of the international community as a whole (a concept used in the context of Article 53 of the 1969 Vienna Convention on the law of treaties), the consent of all states would be more easily collected

30 Article 21, Articles on the International Responsibility of States for Internationally Wrongful Acts, UNGA Res 56/83, Annex (12 December 2001) (ILC Articles on State Responsibility).

31 *Legality of the Threat or Use of Nuclear Weapons* (Advisory Opinion) [1996] ICJ Rep 1996, 226.

32 See in more detail the discussion on the 'use of force' in chapter 14 'The Use of Force in Planetary Defence' in this book.

33 Article 20, ILC Articles on State Responsibility.

34 See also chapter 14 'The Use of Force in Planetary Defence' in this book.

within the framework of an existing international institution like the United Nations. Moreover, the threat to humanity posed by the potential impact of an asteroid could be considered equivalent to a threat to peace and security in terms of the UN Charter Chapter VII. The latter endows the Council with the power to decide measures to maintain peace, including authorising member states to use all necessary means to eliminate a threat to peace through actions taken by groups and coalitions of willing member states. In order the mechanism of the Security Council to respond to a NEO threat properly function, it would be highly desirable the adoption within the UN of a code of conduct for planetary defence, whereby the relevant cases are clearly defined as well as a veto restraint proposal.[35] Finally, we cannot exclude an action by a more restricted coalition of willing states, having the technological capabilities to act for the sake of humanity. These actions, if carried out without the consent of all other states, could be approved or endorsed after by the Security Council. In this line, the best solution would be to set up a collective system providing for the conditions, modalities and financing of deflection missions in case of emergency, through a multilateral treaty, in analogy with models in force in the field of the prevention of some major environmental emergencies (oil pollution, transport of nuclear materials).

'Distress', which represents another circumstance precluding wrongfulness, is when the author of the act has no other reasonable way, in a situation of distress, of saving the author's life or the lives of other persons entrusted to the author's care.[36] The interest concerned is the immediate one of saving people's lives, irrespective of their nationality.

Nevertheless, the most appropriate circumstance seems to be 'necessity', which is a situation clearly distinguishable from other concepts. It differs from consent by the fact that, in the case of consent, the existence of a prior conduct is the *sine qua non* whereby the act of the state is rid of its wrongfulness. The conduct in question is represented by the expression of consent to the commission by the latter state of an act not in conformity with an obligation binding it to the 'consenting state'. In determining whether the wrongfulness

35 The intervention by the Security Council seems to be the best response to deal with the emergency on an "expeditious, global basis", see David A Koplow, 'Exoatmospheric Plowshares: Using a Nuclear Explosive Device for Planetary Defence Against an Incoming Asteroid' (2019) 23 Journal of International Law & Foreign Affairs 76–158. A less efficient option could be to ask the General Assembly to express its consent to the mission under the 377 (V) resolution procedure 'Uniting for Peace'.

36 Article 24, ILC Articles on State Responsibility.

is precluded by necessity, there is no need to ascertain whether the state in question had consented to an internationally wrongful act.

A feature common to 'necessity' and 'distress' is that the state must have been induced by an external factor to adopt a conduct that is not in conformity with an international obligation.

In the case of necessity, the deliberate nature and intentional aspect of the failure to conform with an international obligation are not only undeniable, but in some sense logically inherent in the justification alleged; invoking necessity implies perfect awareness of having deliberately chosen to act in a manner not in conformity with an international obligation.

Article 25 of the ILC Articles on State Responsibility is particularly cautious and uses a negative language: 'necessity' may not be invoked by a state as a ground for precluding the wrongfulness of an act not in conformity with an international obligation of that state unless the act is the only way for the state to safeguard an essential interest against a grave and imminent peril, and does not seriously impair an essential interest of the state or states towards which the obligation exists, or of the international community as a whole. The situation of extreme peril alleged by the state consists in a grave danger to the existence of the state itself, to its survival, the maintenance of conditions in which its essential services can function, the survival of part of its population, the ecological preservation of all or some of its territory, and so on. The restrictive approach has been confirmed by international case law, especially by the ICJ and the International Tribunal for the Law of the Sea.[37]

Thus, the concept of necessity accepted in international legal relations is very restrictive. It is restrictive as regards the determination of the essential importance of the interest of the state which must be in jeopardy in order for the plea to be effective; it is also restrictive as regards the requirement that the conduct not in conformity with an international obligation of the state must really be, in the case in question, the only means of safeguarding the essential interest which is threatened.

The fact that abuses are feared – abuses which are avoidable if detailed and carefully worded provisions are adopted – is no reason to bar the legitimate operation of a ground for precluding the wrongfulness of conduct by a state in cases in which the utility of this ground is generally acknowledged.

---

37 *Gabčíkovo–Nagymaros Project (Hungary/Slovakia)* (Merits) [1997] ICJ Rep 7, 42, 54; *Legal Consequences of the Construction of a Wall in the Occupied Palestinian Territory* (Advisory Opinion) [2004] ICJ Rep 136, 140–142; *M/V 'Saiga' (No 2) (Saint Vincent and the Grenadines v Guinea)* (Judgement, 1 July 1999) ITLOS Reports 1999, paras 128–133.

The circumstance of necessity encompasses exceptional cases where the only way for a state to safeguard an essential interest of its own, or of a group of states, or of the international community threatened by a grave and imminent peril is not to perform other international obligations of lesser urgency. In addition to being grave, the peril must be imminent in the sense of proximate. However, as the Court said in the *Gabčíkovo-Nagymaros Case*:

> That does not exclude (…) that a peril appearing in the long term might be held to be imminent as soon as it is established, at the relevant point in time, that the realisation of that peril, however far off it might be, is not thereby any less certain and inevitable.[38]

Considering that the peril must be objectively established, the involvement of an international mechanism seems to be appropriate in order to avoid any concern and abuse. In case of decisions relating to planetary defence involving nuclear explosions, the risks of arbitrariness, inconsistencies and conflict involved in deciding on the existence of a serious threat and in subsequently implementing the consequences will be particularly high.

However, the restrictive approach accompanying the necessity as a circumstance precluding wrongfulness opens another critical issue about how this circumstance would work in scenarios where the risk may be for a mission only partly successful, which results in merely 'shifting the hit' as opposed to really precluding any hit to the Earth. In this case, when a deflection mission carried on by a state affected by a situation of extreme peril is only partially successful and the impact of a NEO on Earth is not completely avoided, but only shifted, it would be difficult to justify the action under necessity. According to the Article 25(1)(b), the plea of necessity would be effective only as long as the conduct does not seriously impair an essential interest of "the State or States towards which the obligation exists, or of the international community as a whole." In this case it would be extremely difficult to outweigh the interest of the acting state with all other considerations. The key element would be the involvement of the state(s) whose territory would be hit in the decision concerning the deflection mission, the acquisition of its (their) consent(s) and possibly the conclusion of an agreement dealing with all relevant issues. We can say that in this case the circumstance precluding wrongfulness would be the consent of the targeted state(s), in accordance with Article 20 of the ILC Articles.

38 *Gabčíkovo–Nagymaros Project* (*Hungary/Slovakia*) (Merits) [1997] ICJ Rep 7, 42, 54.

On the contrary, the intrusion of a deflected NEO into the territory of one state would constitute an illegitimate violation of its sovereignty if the action to shift the hit from one state or group of states to another state or group of states was intentional. This would amount to the application of the primitive rule on the fight for life, *mors tua vita mea*, which certainly has no foundation in international law.

Furthermore, the assessment of the legality of the case is different when the shifting would be the result of an unintended action, occurred even though all precautionary measures were adopted. In this case, considering the possible destructive outcome for the countervailing interest of the other state(s) concerned, it would be very difficult for the acting state(s) to rely on other circumstances precluding wrongfulness, like force majeure or distress. Thus, the most adequate course of action for the acting state(s) would be to comply with the standard of absolute liability for space activities, considering the damage caused by an asteroid deflected by a planetary defence mission equivalent to that caused by the space object(s) used for the mission. Such a conclusion is valid, in our mind, even if the acting state(s) rely on a circumstance precluding wrongfulness. In fact, we should acknowledge that Article 27 of the ILC Articles establishes that the invocation of such a circumstance does not affect the question of compensation for any material loss caused by the action. A state relying on a circumstance precluding wrongfulness should nonetheless be expected at least to contribute to repair the damage suffered by any state directly affected.

7 Conclusions

Without an institutional framework to channel issues concerning responsibility of states, the mere fact of having rules of international law applicable to planetary defence is a weak shield. There is need for an international mandate, a waiver from non-launching states, an exoneration from or sharing of responsibility and liability.

This is more important if we think that, in case of violation of the multilateral treaties on the prohibition of nuclear explosions in outer space, we are certainly faced with legal instruments containing obligations *erga omnes partes*, which are owed to the group of states parties to the treaties. These are not obligations which, although part of the multilateral context, are essentially bilateral in the sense that each recipient is required to fulfil a certain obligation to each other without creating a collective interdependence of subjective legal situations. In the mentioned treaties, each state party is required to keep the conduct corresponding to those obligations to all other parties to the same treaty. Without an authorisation of the Security Council, the breach of these obligations can therefore be invoked by each of the parties against the perpetrator of the wrongful conduct.

Finally, it should be borne in mind that no provision on the circumstances excluding wrongfulness precludes the illegality of an act of a state that does not comply with an obligation arising from a peremptory norm of international law.

CHAPTER 21

The Involvement of Private Actors in Planetary Defence Missions

Peter Stubbe

1 Introduction

The role of private entities in space activities has changed over time. At the beginning, space activities were the exclusive domain of the public sector, not least due to the military and strategic significance of space. These dimensions are equally important today. In addition, there is a growing relevance of the private sector in space activities – a phenomenon that has been observed for many years.[1] Today, this development is described as the *'new space'* dynamic which is characterised by novel ways by which the private sector is involved in space activities.

Against this background, the present chapter discusses what role private entities could assume in regard to planetary defence. It will, first, look into the changing role of the private sector in general and into its role in planetary defence in particular. On that basis, the relevant legal questions will be identified and further scrutinised. In the legal analysis, particular attention will be paid to the specific provisions on the responsibility for private activities in space. Finally, the discussion will be summarised and put into future perspectives.

2 Increasing Role of Private Space Activities

2.1 *Early Developments*

Despite the initially predominant strategic relevance for military and security purposes,[2] the consideration of private activities in outer space is not a recent phenomenon. In fact, one of the discussions in the early years of space law development focused on whether or not non-governmental activities in

1 See Christophe Venet, 'The Economic Dimension' in Christian Brünner and Alexander Soucek (eds), *Outer Space in Society, Politics and Law* (Springer 2011) 55, 56.

2 See ibid, 55.

 | DOI:10.1163/9789004467606_023

outer space should be allowed at all. Eventually, the view prevailed that space is open to private activities – establishing at the same time a strong legal bond between such non-governmental conduct and the corresponding state.[3]

While the legal ground was prepared for the private activities to evolve, space remained a largely publicly dominated domain. Nevertheless, there were some private activities already from the outset of the space age as private companies were involved in building early Mars and human spaceflight systems; the INTELSAT consortium included governmental as well as commercial partners.[4] The role of industry was to develop technology and act as a contractor of the public agencies. In the 1980ies, private companies began developing space-related markets. Arianespace was founded early in the decade and entrusted with the exploitation of ESA developed launchers, thus providing as a private entity European launch services.[5] As regards satellite telecommunications, significant progress in the commercialisation occurred when the formerly state-dominated telecommunication sector was liberalised. This had its bearing also on the space sector where opportunities for telecommunication products and services were opened up. The intergovernmental satellite telecommunication organisations INTELSAT, EUTELSAT and INMARSAT were transformed into private companies.[6] This sector largely remained the most viable commercial space business model.[7]

To some extent, the trend also extended to Earth observation as, for example, the previously public US Landsat program was transferred to a private entity to provide services for a number of different applications.[8] Commercialisation in the area of remote sensing was primarily driven by an increasing resolution and quality of Earth observation data which, in turn, increased their commercial value. In addition, public-private partnerships emerged for building and

---

3 The legal basis is Art VI Outer Space Treaty which will be further elaborated below. The discussion on the role of private actors in space is highlighted in Michael Gerhard, 'Article VI OST' in Stephan Hobe, Bernhard Schmidt-Tedd and Kai-Uwe Schrogl (eds), *Cologne Commentary on Space Law,* vol I (Carl Heymanns Verlag 2009) 105–106. The USA and the Western states favoured a liberal approach allowing for private activities, whereas the Soviet Union was against any non-governmental activities. See ibid.

4 Commercial partners only joined the Consortium at a rather late stage, though, and they were from the USA only.

5 See Peter van Fenema, 'Legal aspects of launch services and space transportation' in Frans G von der Dunk and Fabio Tronchetti (eds), *Handbook of Space Law* (Edward Elgar 2015) 391.

6 See Francis Lyall and Paul B Larsen, *Space Law: A Treatise* (Ashgate 2009) 319–358.

7 See Ram S Jakhu and Joseph N Pelton, *Global Space Governance: An International Study* (Springer 2017) 113–114.

8 See Jerry J Sellers, *Understanding Space: An Introduction to Astronautics* (3rd edn, McGraw Hill Companies 2005) 399.

operating remote sensing satellites.[9] Presently, the processing, value-adding and dissemination of application-specific imagery products and services constitutes a dynamically developing space business.[10]

2.2 *New Space*

Since a couple of years, there is additional dynamic as new business cases emerge and new private actors enter the market. *New space* describes a number of simultaneous developments that are intertwined with each other. The number of private actors in the space sector is significantly increasing – this ranges from start-ups to companies that are backed by billionaires.[11] This development is part of a broader trend which is characterised by a growth in actors also on the governmental side as more and more states recognise the economic and strategic significance of space. This trend is at the same time coupled with a diversification of space activities as new types emerge, such as on-orbit servicing, the increasing use of small satellites, or the deployment of large-scale satellite constellations.[12]

The broadening of the activities through private actors is also driven by a decline in costs. The use of components from other areas ('commercial off-the-shelf') – such as the automotive sector – and the large-scale production of satellites and components – which is particularly associated with the use of small satellites – facilitate a cheaper production of space systems. In addition, the application of new and more cost-effective industrial processes in terms of development and production furthermore contributes to lower the costs.[13]

---

9 See for example the German TerraSAR-X high-resolution radar satellite. In order to facilitate the commercialization of remote sensing data, Germany introduced a dedicated national law that sets conditions for the dissemination of high-resolution remote sensing data. See Satellite Data Security Act (Satellitendatensicherheitsgesetz) of 23 November 2007 (BGBL I 2590), as amended (BGBL I 626).

10 On the different phases of remote sensing activities, including their commercialization, see Fabio Tronchetti, 'Legal aspects of satellite remote sensing' in Frans G von der Dunk and Fabio Tronchetti (eds), *Handbook of Space Law* (Edward Elgar 2015) 505–513.

11 See Ram S Jakhu and Joseph N Pelton, *Global Space Governance: An International Study* (Springer 2017) 114.

12 This goes along with challenges to the sustainability, safety and security of space activities. There is a lack of regulation when it comes to organizing the increased space traffic resulting from the additional actors and activities. See European Space Policy Institute (ed), 'ESPI Report 71 – Towards a European Approach to Space Traffic Management' (ESPI 2020) 10.

13 See Matteo Tugnoli and Leyton Wells (eds), 'ESPI Report 70 – Evolution of the Role of Space Agencies' (ESPI 2019) 32–34; Norbert Frischauf and others, 'New Space: Geschäftsmodelle an der Schnittstelle von Raumfahrt und digitaler Gesellschaft' (SpaceTec Partners and BHO Legal 2016) 20.

In addition, access to financing of space activities has changed significantly. In recent years, a rise of investments in space companies has occurred driven in particular by venture capital and angel investors.[14] Novel instruments such as the UNIDROIT Space Assets Protocol, which would enable asset-based financing also in the space sector, could additionally increase the availability of space financing by reducing the costs of borrowing money.[15] The Protocol has not attained much support and did not enter into force yet.[16] In the context of the *new space* development, however, there is generally an increased interest in novel financing instruments[17] which may also help the Protocol attracting further signatories.

Lowering costs for space systems and space financing has a direct bearing on the development of businesses: It reduces the barrier to enter the market which benefits especially newcomers to bring their innovative products and services to the market. New upstream solutions as well as new applications are being developed, thus making space activities economically more viable.[18]

Changes on the public side are also part of the current trend towards an increasing role of the private sector in particular with regard to public procurement. Beyond the traditional role of space agencies as public procurement bodies for research and development, there are new forms of cooperation between the public and the private sector. Such cooperation can take many different forms of public private partnerships, while all of them are characterised by a long-term relationship between the public and the private sector with some risk-sharing and an increased decisional role of the private side.[19]

---

14 See European Investment Bank, 'The future of the European space sector: How to leverage Europe's technological leadership and boost investments for space ventures' (2019) 20–21.

15 See Mark J Sundahl, 'Financing space ventures' in Frans G von der Dunk and Fabio Tronchetti (eds), *Handbook of Space Law* (Edward Elgar 2015) 887–888; Hans-Georg Bollweg and Simon Schultheiß, 'Das Berliner Weltraumprotokoll: Zur Verabschiedung des Weltraumausrüstungsprotokolls zum Kapstadt Übereinkommen über Internationale Sicherungsrechte an beweglicher Ausrüstung in Berlin, am 9. März 2012' (2012) 61 Zeitschrift für Luft-und Weltraumrecht 389.

16 See UNIDROIT, 'Status: UNIDROIT Protocol to the Convention on International Interests in Mobile Equipment on Matters Specific to Space Assets' (Berlin, 2012) <www.unidroit.org/status-2012-space> accessed 25 February 2021.

17 See European Investment Bank, 'The Future of the European Space Sector: How to Leverage Europe's Technological Leadership and Boost Investments for Space Ventures' (2019) 116.

18 See Matteo Tugnoli and Leyton Wells (eds), 'ESPI Report 70 – Evolution of the Role of Space Agencies' (ESPI 2019) 32–33.

19 See ibid, 22–26.

The different types encompass solutions where, for example, the design, construction, deployment and operation are taken over by the private entity.[20] In addition, *new space* marks the shift towards governmental purchase of products and services offered by private companies.[21] Such partnerships are often driven by pre-defined public needs for a particular regular service.[22] A well-known example is the procurement of cargo delivery services to the International Space Station (ISS) through the US 'Commercial Orbital Transportation Services' programme, later followed by a similar model for crewed missions to the ISS.[23]

In this way, the involvement of private actors even extends to areas – such as space exploration, resource exploitation, and space transportation/launchers – that were traditionally considered exclusively as public domains. It is important to note that the changes described in terms of public procurement are at least partially different from other *new space* elements,[24] in that the demand or need that is to be covered by a particular service remains public – irrespective of whether that service is implemented by a private entity or a public space agency.[25] Nevertheless, such public private partnership models may not only serve to satisfy a public demand, but also to develop a corresponding commercial market.

3 The Role of Non-governmental Entities in Planetary Defence

Generally, there are many different roles that the non-state sector can assume in addressing the risks associated with NEOs. The scientific community creates the knowledge about the nature of these risks, i.e. the quantity, characteristics,

---

20 See ibid, 24.

21 See Ram S Jakhu and Joseph N Pelton, *Global Space Governance: An International Study* (Springer 2017) 114.

22 Such as the provision of cargo to the ISS by privately owned and operated space transportation systems. See NASA, 'Commercial Orbital Transportation *Services* (*COTS*)' (*NASA*) <www.nasa.gov/commercial-orbital-transportation-services-cots> accessed 25 February 2021.

23 See Matteo Tugnoli and Leyton Wells (eds), 'ESPI Report 70 – Evolution of the Role of Space Agencies' (ESPI 2019) 41–44; see also Norbert Frischauf and others, 'New Space: Geschäftsmodelle an der Schnittstelle von Raumfahrt und digitaler Gesellschaft' (SpaceTec Partners and BHO Legal 2016) 63.

24 Even though some of them are linked to the novel procurement approaches: Increased space investments are, for example, a prerequisite for realizing large-scale projects based on corresponding government needs.

25 It is, therefore, better described with the term 'privatisation' rather than 'commercialisation'.

and trajectories of these bodies. This information is the starting point for assessing the risks for humans on Earth and the subsequent development of appropriate solutions for addressing them – i.e. potentially NEO deflection missions. Non-governmental organisations may also act as advocacy groups raising the awareness of the problem, or as expert groups providing advice on NEO-related issues. Non-governmental actors may moreover contribute to civil protection measures in the prevention of and response to a NEO impact, as well as in subsequent reconstruction efforts.

When it comes to the involvement of non-governmental entities in the implementation of planetary defence, the space industry could have its role in developing the systems which may extend to the provision of the spacecraft, ground systems, launcher or components thereof.

Beyond that, the private sector may directly engage in a deflection mission. A company could itself carry out individual elements of the space mission or even the full NEO mitigation mission. Different models of public-private partnerships may be applied to that effect. Which elements of a mission may be taken over by a private actor very much depends on the set-up of the mission itself (kinetic impactor, gravity tractor etc.).[26]

In the case of planetary defence, related space missions can be held to have a rather singular character (one-off technology demonstration or actual deflection mission). *Prima facie*, the absence of regular demand for a standardised service may make it less likely for a private entity to invest own financial means. Planetary defence *per se* appears to be less suitable for commercialisation as there is no private market for a corresponding full mitigation mission. It is instead an activity that is driven by humanitarian concerns, aiming to minimise the loss of life and destruction of property and the human livelihood that would result from a NEO impact on Earth.[27] Nevertheless, there may be (standardised) space solutions offered by the private sector that could be relied upon in a planetary defence mission. This could be solutions that would either need to be specifically developed, or which are available on the commercial market. Examples are the provision of launch services (for transporting the space systems required for the mission into Earth orbit or beyond), or cargo delivery services to space stations orbiting the Earth or the Moon, or the investigation and determination of NEOs.[28]

26 See Frans G von der Dunk and others, 'Legal Aspects of NEO Threat Response and Related Institutional Issues' (February 2010) 33.

27 See ibid, 34.

28 See ibid.

That being said, it cannot be excluded that a planetary defence mission is carried out by a private company in its entirety. The commercial success of such mission alone may not be the only motivation for its full realisation by a private entity.[29] In fact, some billionaire-backed endeavours seem to be motivated by other than purely direct commercial concerns: Elon Musk's SpaceX aims to facilitate colonising Mars,[30] Jeff Bezos of Amazon announced to set-up a multi-billion dollar fund for fighting climate change,[31] Bill Gates warns of pandemic diseases and gives money to fight them.[32] It should against this background not be ruled out that also protecting the Earth from destruction by a NEO would receive the same level of attention and engagement.

The relevance of private conduct for planetary defence is also considered in the context of space resources exploitation activities: there may be commercially motivated resource mining activities on NEOs (several ambitious projects have been announced by private companies).[33] Once such activities are being pursued, due consideration would have to be given to potential situations in which a commercially interesting NEO turns into a threat for the Earth and thus a target for planetary defence.[34]

---

29 For a large-scale business structure comprising many business branches, a highly visible space mission that – in the case of planetary defence – serves a high public purpose, could be seen as an attractive endeavour for reasons of publicity and positive spill-over effects to the other business branches.

30 See Jeff Foust, 'SpaceX's Mars Plans Call for Massive 42-engine Reusable Rocket' (*Space News*, 27 September 2016) <https://spacenews.com/spacex-unveils-mars-mission-plans> accessed 25 February 2021.

31 He links the objective to preserve the Earth with BlueOrigin's objective to get people living and working in outer space. See Mike Wall, 'Jeff Bezos Putting $10 billion toward Climate-change Fight' (*Space.com*, 19 February 2020) <www.space.com/jeff-bezos-blue-origin-climate-change-fight.html> accessed 25 February 2021.

32 See Holly Secon, 'The Gates Foundation is Spending $ 100 million to Fight the Coronavirus Outbreak. Bill Gates Has Warned about a Pandemic for Years' (*Business Insider*, 6 February 2020) <www.businessinsider.de/international/gates-foundation-10-million-to-fight-wuhan-coronavirus-2020-1/?r=US&IR=T> accessed 25 February 2021.

33 While the issue continues attracting much attention, some companies have already re-oriented their business interest: Jeff Foust, 'The Asteroid Mining Bubble Has Burst' (*The Space Review*, 7 January 2019) <www.thespacereview.com/article/3633/1> accessed 25 February 2021.

34 It was also discussed whether the exploitation of resources of a NEO (in the frame of an international regime yet to be established) that results in the body's complete 'consumption' would be an option to eliminate a NEO threat. See Frans G von der Dunk and others, 'Legal Aspects of NEO Threat Response and Related Institutional Issues' (February 2010) 35.

4 Legal Aspects Relevant to the Involvement of Private Entities in Planetary Defence

As private entities may very well play a role in planetary defence missions, there are a number of legal questions as different issues are at stake. Some of them are primarily subject to national law; some are of an international character. Still others relate to particular fields outside the space sector, such as disaster response and civil protection.[35] Of particular relevance is the special status of private/non-governmental activities in space under international law, the question of how to address space resources exploitation (an area where private companies have a particular interest) in the context of planetary defence and some contractual considerations. They will be addressed in the following.

4.1 *Contract Law*

As regards the involvement of privates in a NEO deflection mission, contract law is applicable to the procurement of particular works in the government-to-industry relation. Different types of contracts exist, depending on the product or service industry is providing to the public side and the roles of both sides (for example through public private partnerships).[36]

Such contractual arrangements may become very complex, in particular if a planetary defence mission is realised in international cooperation. In fact, the Space Mission Planning Advisory Group (SMPAG), a body mainly composed of space agencies with relevant planetary defence-related activities,[37] has as one of its tasks the planning of cooperative NEO threat mitigation activities.[38] Given the status of NEOs as a *res communis*[39] and – according to the Moon

---

35 The latter shall not be considered in this chapter.

36 See Laurence Ravillon, 'Typology of Contracts in the Space Sector' in Lesley J Smith and Ingo Baumann (eds), *Contracting for Space: Contract Practice in the European Space* Sector (Ashgate 2011) 161–163.

37 Other governmental or inter-governmental entities, or entities designated by a government can become members. See Article 4, SMPAG, 'Terms of Reference V2.0' (13 September 2019) <www.cosmos.esa.int/web/smpag/terms_of_reference_v2> accessed 25 February 2021 (hereafter referred to as 'SMAPG ToR').

38 See Article 3(4) SMPAG ToR. The mandate acts on the assumption that more than one government would coordinate and fund planetary defence missions, see Article 3(4)(c) SMPAG ToR.

39 Outer space itself is a global common. See Jutta Brunnée, 'Common Areas, Common Heritage, and Common Concern', in Daniel Bodansky, Jutta Brunnée and Ellen Hey (eds), *The Oxford Handbook of International Environmental Law* (Oxford University Press 2007) 557.

Agreement – a common heritage of mankind,[40] and considering that a NEO impact potentially affects more than one world region, NEO mitigation efforts should generally be regarded as an international endeavour, requiring international collaboration.[41]

Generally, such collaborative missions are more complex to implement in terms of their contractual design because they rely on agency cooperation which is – other than purely commercial relations – subject to political considerations. In addition, issues such as export control, risk mitigation and different approaches to industrial policy – including in terms of procurement law – need to be taken into consideration.[42] They are regularly handled by the public side as well as by industry and would also have to be addressed in a collaborative planetary defence mission.

4.2 *Article VI of the Outer Space Treaty*

The private involvement in a NEO deflection mission is of particular interest in its quality as a space activity. Such private conduct in space may be the launch of a space object into Earth orbit or beyond and the operation of a mission-related spacecraft in Earth orbit or the trajectory to or around the targeted NEO. Article VI of the Outer Space Treaty is the central provision relevant to private conduct in outer space, including for NEO deflection missions and shall be further analysed in the following. Non-governmental entities are explicitly mentioned in the provision:

> States Parties to the Treaty shall bear international responsibility for national activities in outer space, including the Moon and other celestial bodies, whether such activities are carried on by governmental agencies or by *non-governmental entities*, and for assuring that national activities are carried out in conformity with the provisions set forth in the present Treaty. The activities of *non-governmental entities* in outer space, including the Moon and other celestial bodies, shall require authorization

40 The Moon Agreement, which is applicable to all celestial bodies, thus also for NEOs, stipulates that such bodies are the common heritage of mankind. See Article 1(1) and Article 11(1). The Moon Agreement itself has not yet attracted a high number of ratifications (18) and signatures (4). See Status of International Agreements relating to activities in outer space as of 1 January 2019, UN Doc A/AC.105/C.2/2019/CRP.3, 10.

41 See chapter 22 'International Bodies and Procedures for Decision-Making Regarding Planetary Defence Actions' in this book.

42 See Cristian Bank, 'The Complexities of International Space Industry Contracts' in Lesley J Smith and Ingo Baumann (eds), *Contracting for Space: Contract Practice in the European Space Sector* (Ashgate 2011) 133.

and continuing supervision by the appropriate State Party to the Treaty. (emphasis added).

4.2.1 Direct Attribution in the Context of State Responsibility Law

Article VI Outer Space Treaty is relevant in different ways. First of all, it has a significant bearing on state responsibility law. The secondary rules of international law are embodied in the International Law Commission's (ILC) Articles on State Responsibility[43] – which, to a large extent, reflect customary international law – and address 'internationally wrongful acts' of a state. Such an internationally wrongful act of a state is defined as a "conduct consisting of an action or omission [that]: (*a*) is attributable to the State under international law; and (*b*) constitutes a breach of an international obligation of the State".[44] State responsibility law thus applies to the situation when a state has violated an international legal norm (a primary rule of international law) and sets out the conditions and consequences of responsibility, the rules for its invocation etc. This secondary law is *mutatis mutandis* largely applicable also to the conduct of international organisations, for which the ILC has developed a specific set of rules.[45]

The first sentence of Article VI Outer Space Treaty is relevant to responsibility law because it establishes a space-specific attribution rule. It has an effect on the relationship between a state and a private actor. According to Article 2 ILC Articles on State Responsibility, an internationally wrongful act consists of two elements: the norm violation and the attribution of such (non-) action to a state. With regard to the first element, the conduct of a state has to be examined *vis-à-vis* the content of a primary norm of international law in order to establish whether there is a violation. If the state does not comply with the objectively required conduct or omission, the respective norm has been breached. What amounts to the breach of an international legal obligation depends on the content of the primary norm.[46] Potentially relevant law may be norms from general international law as well as the various norms that are applicable to NEO deflection missions discussed in previous chapters.[47]

---

43 Articles on the International Responsibility of States for Internationally Wrongful Acts, UNGA Res 56/83, Annex (12 December 2001).

44 Article 2, ILC Articles on State Responsibility.

45 See International Law Commission, Draft Articles on the Responsibility of International Organizations, 'Report of the International Law Commission on the Work of its 63rd Session' (26 April–3 June and 4 July–12 August 2011) UN Doc A/66/10, para 87.

46 See James Crawford, 'The System of International Responsibility' in James Crawford and others (eds), *The Law of International Responsibility* (Oxford University Press 2010) 20.

47 See for example chapter 13 'Rules of International Law Regarding an Obligation of States to Undertake Planetary Defence Activities'.

The second element demands that the conduct in question must be attributable (i.e. it must be imputed or connected) to a state in order for it being internationally responsible. The secondary rules determine how the conduct is attributed (Articles 4–11 ILC Articles on State Responsibility). Should a particular conduct be carried out by an organ of a state, or should a state control the conduct in questions, these actions are attributable to that state.[48]

The conduct of private entities is, as a general principle, not attributable to a state under international law. Here is where Article VI Outer Space Treaty introduces a space-specific, additional attribution rule. According to this rule, states are in any event internationally responsible for national activities (i.e. provided that there was a breach of an international legal obligation in the course of these activities) irrespective of whether the conduct in question is carried out by governmental agencies or non-governmental entities. There is thus a direct attribution of private conduct to the respective state. This constitutes a space-specific alteration of broader responsibility law.[49] The state shall be responsible for 'national activities' which means – in the case of private entities – activities of its nationals. This could be natural or juridical persons, including, most importantly, private companies. Moreover, also those activities carried out from a state's territory, including those carried out by non-governmental entities, are to be regarded as 'national activities' which are to be attributed directly to that state.[50] In addition to that, the ordinary attribution

48 For a general discussion of state responsibility see Alain Pellet, 'The definition of responsibility in international law' in James Crawford and others (eds), *The Law of International Responsibility* (Oxford University Press 2010) 3–16.

49 See Luigi Condorelli and Claus Kress, 'The Rules of Attribution: General Considerations' in James Crawford and others (eds), *The Law of International Responsibility* (Oxford University Press 2010) 227. Article VI, Outer Space Treaty can therefore be regarded as a 'special rule' of international law that take precedence over the general rules of state responsibility law as set forth in Article 55, ILC Articles on State Responsibility. However, one may also understand this (only) as the responsibility to assure that non-governmental activities 'are carried out in conformity' with the Outer Space Treaty. See Michael Gerhard, 'Article VI OST' in Stephan Hobe, Bernhard Schmidt-Tedd and Kai-Uwe Schrogl (eds), *Cologne Commentary on Space Law*, vol I (Carl Heymanns Verlag 2009) 116.

50 This finding corresponds to the practice in national space legislation as those national acts establish that space activities of a state's nationals and space activities carried out from a state's territory are subject to authorisation and continuing supervision according to Article VI, Outer Space Treaty. In fact, the UN General Assembly, when considering the practice of national space legislation, recommended to assert jurisdiction over space activities carried out from its territory. See UNGA 'Recommendations on national legislation relevant to the peaceful exploration and use of outer space' UNGA Res 68/74 (1 December 2013) UN Doc A/RES/68/74, 2.

rules remain applicable. If a state, for example, exercises control over a particular private activity, it is imputed to that state.[51]

This system of attribution is applicable to space activities which include planetary defence missions. If the conduct of a private company in the course of such a mission amounts to a breach of an international legal provision, this violation would be directly attributable to the corresponding state,[52] thus entailing its international responsibility for the conduct of the private entity.

The attribution rule of Article VI Outer Space Treaty is not only relevant in the context of responsibility law itself. Also when it comes to liability for damage caused by space objects – which may be relevant to a planetary defence mission[53] – questions of how to impute a certain conduct may arise as well. This relates to the status of a 'launching state' which is the state that is liable for damage under international law.[54] The definitions provided in space law[55] only refer to states, while in practice also private entities launch and procure the launching of satellites into orbit and even operate launch facilities.[56] By way of Article VI Outer Space Treaty, the launching activities are directly attributed to a state, when, for example, one of its nationals engages in such activities.[57] As discussed above, a private company may be involved in a planetary defence mission by providing the launch services for the mission. The direct attribution in terms of the launching state status corresponds to the attribution of the fault by private persons to a launching state[58] in the context of fault liability.[59]

---

51 The basis is Article 8 ILC Articles on State Responsibility addressing conduct directed or controlled by a state.

52 See chapter 20 'The International Responsibility of States for Planetary Defence Activities' in this book.

53 In space law, a particular liability regime has been established under the Convention on International Liability for Damage Caused by Space Objects (adopted 29 November 1971, entered into force 1 September 1972) 961 UNTS 187 (Liability Convention). See also chapter 18 'The Current International Space Law Regime on Liability and Its Application to Planetary Defence' in this book.

54 See Article II-III, Liability Convention.

55 See Article I(c), Liability Convention; Article I(a), Registration Convention.

56 See Peter van Fenema, 'Legal Aspects of Launch Services and Space Transportation' in Frans G von der Dunk and Fabio Tronchetti (eds), *Handbook of Space Law* (Edward Elgar 2015) 384.

57 See Bin Cheng, *Studies in International Space Law* (Clarendon Press 2004) 613–14, 637–38. However, when it comes to the practice under national space laws, there is no uniform picture. Some states do not seem to accept such direct attribution given that launching activities carried out elsewhere (outside that state's territory) are not made subject to authorization.

58 See Article III, Liability Convention.

59 See Lesley J Smith and Armel Kerrest, 'Article III LIAB', in Stephan Hobe, Bernhard Schmidt-Tedd and Kai-Uwe Schrogl (eds), *Cologne Commentary on Space Law*, vol II (Carl Heymanns Verlag 2013) 135.

4.2.2 Authorisation and Continuing Supervision on the Basis of National Space Legislation

As a corollary of the direct attribution rule, states are obligated under the second sentence of Article VI Outer Space Treaty to authorise and continuously supervise the space activities of non-governmental entities. In view of its international accountability, it is in the state's own interest to closely involve itself in the activity by monitoring the conduct of non-governmental entities. States are also bound to assure the compliance of the conduct of any space activities, including those of non-governmental entities, with international law according to Article VI Outer Space Treaty.

Authorisation and continuing supervision are usually implemented through national space legislation. There is an abundance of national space laws for this purpose.[60] They are meant to fulfil the international obligations of a state, but also to facilitate and support private space activities by providing a predictable, stable and enabling regulatory environment. Most of these space laws include the requirement of private entities to seek prior authorisation as well as the continuous monitoring of private activities in outer space.[61]

In a dedicated working group of the Legal Subcommittee of the United Nations Committee on the Peaceful Uses of Outer Space (UNCOPUOS), the Subcommittee has worked to identify the ways in which states regulate governmental and non-governmental space activities. As a result of this work, the United Nations General Assembly adopted a resolution on national space legislation,[62] in which it recommended states to consider certain elements when enacting national space laws. Authorisation and continuing supervision counted among these elements.[63] Apart from ensuring the implementation of the international obligations of the authorising/supervising state, the recommendations also emphasise the function of national space law in ensuring the

---

60 An overview on existing national space legislation is provided on the websites of the United Nations Office for Outer Space Affairs (UNOOSA). See UNOOSA, 'National Space Law Collection' (*United Nations Office for Outer Space Affairs*) <www.unoosa.org/oosa/en/ourwork/spacelaw/nationalspacelaw/index.html> accessed 25 February 2021.

61 UNOOSA also offers a database highlighting the different regulatory categories of national space laws, the latest version dating from 2014: UNCOPUOS, 'Schematic overview of national regulatory frameworks for space activities' (17 March 2014) UN Doc A/AC.105/C.2/2015/CRP.5.

62 See Recommendations on national space legislation relevant to the peaceful exploration and use of outer space, UNGA Res 68/74 (16 December 2016) UN Doc A/RES/68/74.

63 See in particular ibid, para 2–5.

safety of space operations by implementing safety standards and provision, for example those related to the mitigation of space debris.[64]

As for NEO deflection missions, it is clear that private space activities contributing to those missions must be made subject to national space legislation, i.e. to authorisation and continuing supervision by the appropriate state. In this way, the monitoring state would assure that the private activities carried out are consistent with the international obligations of that state. It would also guarantee a safe implementation of the mission by making applicable respective safety standards – to the extent they exist – in order to reduce the risk of mission failure and ensuing damage to the maximum extent possible.

4.2.3 Legal Regime for Space Resource Exploitation

Another aspect needs to be taken into account from a public international law perspective: it needs to be considered how a potential regime for the exploitation of space resources, including possible exploitation rights granted to private companies under such a regime, interacts with the planning and implementation of a planetary defence mission. No exploitation regime governing resources exploitation has been elaborated yet. The Moon Agreement provides that it is to be established "as such exploitation is about to become feasible".[65]

Whether the regime for exploitation of space resources as foreseen under the Moon Agreement will be implemented is largely an open question. While asteroid mining has long been regarded as a distant project, at best, the question of the legal basis for resources exploitation reappeared when a number of private companies announced plans for asteroid mining activities that would be market-driven and based on commercial demand for space resources. The USA,[66] Luxembourg[67] and the United Arab Emirates[68] reacted by enacting national space legislation for asteroid mining (dedicated specifically to that topic or addressing it in the scope of a wider piece of legislation) allowing private entities to own and sell space resources. In the meantime, though, it became clear the prospects of the business cases did not live up to the initial

64 See ibid, para 4.

65 See Article 11(5), Moon Agreement.

66 See US Commercial Space Launch Competitiveness Act, Public Law 114-90, 25 November 2015.

67 See Loi du 20 juillet 2017 sur l'exploration et l'utilisation des ressources de l'espace, Mémorial A674.

68 See Federal Law No. (12) of 2019 on the regulation of the space sector, issued on 19 December 2019.

expectations.[69] The discussion about space resources, nevertheless, recently re-emerged in the context of public exploration programmes. The US Artemis programme aims at returning to the Moon with a human presence. NASA plans to purchase, from private companies, resources for the purpose of implementing the programme (propellant, construction of habitats etc.).[70]

In order to further the programme, the USA currently promotes the so-called 'Artemis Accords' concluded on a bilateral basis, addressing a number of issues such as the utilisation of resources, dissemination of information etc.[71] The Accords establish principles, guidelines and best practices for the civil exploration and use of outer space with the objective to promote the Artemis programme. They are meant specifically to "(…) provide for operational implementation of important obligations contained in the Outer Space Treaty and other instruments."[72] The Accords represent a notable departure from space law governance as their parties, a limited number of states, prejudge international deliberations on universally accepted understandings on the application of existing space law and its further development by defining among themselves rules and practices.[73] This pertains, for example, to the discussion on space resources: while the Artemis Accords "(…) affirm that the extraction of space resources does not inherently constitute national appropriation under Article II of the Outer Space Treaty", the ongoing discussions in UNCOPUOS indicate that there is currently no such consensus.[74] In fact, the

69 See Jeff Foust, 'The Asteriod Mining Bubble Has Burst' (*The Space Review*, 7 January 2019) <www.thespacereview.com/article/3633/1> accessed 25 February 2021.

70 See NASA, 'Artemis Plan: NASA's Lunar Exploration Program Overview' (September 2020) 28–29.

71 NASA, 'The Artemis Accords, Principles for Cooperation in the Civil Exploration and Use of the Moon, Mars, Comets, and Asteroids for Peaceful Purposes' (*NASA*, 13 October 2020) <www.nasa.gov/specials/artemis-accords/img/Artemis-Accords-signed-13Oct2020.pdf > accessed 25 February 2021.

72 See Section 1 subpara 1, Artemis Accords.

73 This is the statutory role of UNCOPUOS that has developed not only the basic treaties of international space law, but also subsequently worked on clarifying the notion of certain concepts and ways of their implementing, for example with regard to the launching state, registration practice and national space legislation. On the ongoing discussion on exploration, exploitation and utilization of space resources see UNCOPUOS, 'Report of the Committee on the Peaceful Uses of Outer Space on its sixty-second session' (12–21 June 2019) UN Doc A/74/20, paras 250–259.

74 Precisely because of this, there are ongoing discussions on that subject in UNCOPUOS, including through the establishment of a dedicated working group.

US government denies the status of outer space as a global common.[75] The Artemis Accords have a strong focus on delineating ('deconflicting') spheres of influence that the parties can establish as so-called 'safety zones'. Such zones are set up to encourage, among others, the exploitation of space resources. They are established on a first-come, first-served basis and the parties maintaining safety zones "(…) should do in a manner that protects public and private personnel, equipment, and operations from harmful interference."[76] Since the Artemis Accords are established to apply also to asteroids,[77] and given that asteroids can be very small celestial objects (with only a few hundred meters of diameter), the setting up a safety zone may amount to a full claim over the entire asteroid.

Planetary defence is not directly addressed in the Artemis Accords, but their provisions may, nevertheless, become relevant for NEO threat mitigation. The right to establish safety zones on an asteroid and protect operations, personnel and equipment carried out therein may conflict with a NEO mitigation mission that targets that same NEO. The interest in protecting asteroid operations may, thus, prevent effective threat reduction measures carried out in the global public interest. In addition, the commitment of the parties to openly sharing scientific data is explicitly excluded from applying to private companies. The discovery of a potential NEO threat through a private company may, thus, not be made public for commercial interest, while at the same time delaying or even preventing timely NEO mitigation measures.

In any event, any regime governing space resources exploitation should foresee procedures, which ensure the consideration of planetary defence objectives. Under no circumstances should exploitation activities or other commercial interests pose an obstacle to take appropriate measures against a NEO threat. The interest of protecting the Earth from a NEO impact should in any event prevail.[78]

---

75 See The White House, 'Executive Order on Encouraging International Support for the Recovery and Use of Space Resources' (6 April 2020) <www.federalregister.gov/documents/2020/04/10/2020-07800/encouraging-international-support-for-the-recovery-and-use-of-space-resources> accessed 25 February 2021.

76 Section 11(9), Artemis Accords.

77 See Section 1 subpara 2, Artemis Accords.

78 See Frans G von der Dunk and others, 'Legal Aspects of NEO Threat Response and Related Institutional Issues' (February 2010) 33.

5 Conclusion

Private actors have come a long way from being initially reduced to their role in developing and supplying space technology to a broader involvement in space through completely commercially motivated space activities and participation in public private partnerships. They continue to assume an increasingly important role in the space sector. This may also benefit future NEO deflection missions. While planetary defence is driven by humanitarian concerns, private companies can nevertheless play their role in NEO deflection missions: industry may carry out parts of NEO deflection missions and it is also not excluded that they implement such mission in its entirety. It will be interesting to see how the *new space* dynamic will affect the future involvement of private companies in planetary defence and the corresponding contractual arrangements in this respect.

In this regard, private involvement in NEO activities is not different from private involvement in other types of space activities from the point of view of international space law. Also in the NEO context, non-compliance with international law would be directly attributable to the state behind the private entity. In addition, states would need to authorise and continuously supervise private space activities.

Non-governmental entities' involvement in NEO deflection missions therefore needs to fully reflect the specific rules that international space law embodies for non-governmental entities in general. To a large extent, they pertain to state responsibility and therefore cannot be discussed without reference to the primary obligations of states relevant to NEOs and corresponding deflection missions. The various rules that have been addressed in other chapters are therefore also important for non-governmental entities. Beyond the *status quo*, any further legal development related to the requirements for planetary defence, including the possible development of (safety) standards, would have to be taken into account by states authorising and supervising private contributions to NEO deflection missions.

The establishment of a regime for space resource exploitation was found to be a further legal development that will directly become relevant to planetary defence. Given that NEOs are a potential target for mining companies, a future regime must give due account the humanitarian concerns of planetary defence.

CHAPTER 22

International Bodies and Procedures for Decision-Making Regarding Planetary Defence Actions

Olavo de Oliveira Bittencourt Neto

1 Introduction

This chapter discusses the role that various international multilateral bodies can play in planetary defence. Relevant entities include the United Nations General Assembly, the United Nations Security Council, and the United Nations Committee on the Peaceful Uses of Outer Space (UNCOPUOS), which reports to the General Assembly. Additionally, international expert groups such as the Space Mission Planning Advisory Group (SMPAG) and the International Asteroid Warning Network (IAWN)[1] are taken into consideration, as well as possible *ad hoc* alternatives. Issues of representation, working methods and procedures of these multilateral bodies are discussed, and some topics for discussion, coordination, and decision-making are highlighted.

It will be argued that the necessary steps should be undertaken as soon as practical. Timely action is warranted to prevent wasting time with uncoordinated actions when and if an actual threat by a Near-Earth Object (NEO) is detected and actions will have to be executed without delay or misstep. A number of relevant and complex legal and policy issues are related to asteroid threat planning and response. By having these issues discussed and agreed upon by the international community *before* a NEO threat becomes a reality, many obstacles to clear, decisive, and successful international action can be resolved beforehand.

When the day comes when a NEO threat is real, collective and coordinated response will be needed, rather than an uncoordinated impromptu response. This insight is highlighted by the SMPAG Ad-hoc Working Group on Legal Issues in its report "Planetary Defence – Legal Overview and Assessment", finalised in early 2020.[2] Consequently, this chapter takes findings from this

1 On these international initiatives see chapter 4 'International Cooperation in Planetary Defence – UNCOPUOS, IAWN and SMPAG' in this book.

2 Ad-Hoc Working Group on Legal Issues to SMPAG, 'Planetary Defence Legal Overview and Assessment Report' (SMPAG-RP-004, 8 April 2020).

 | DOI:10.1163/9789004467606_024

report and operationalises them as topics for discussion and agreement among the international community.

In times of grave danger, states may occasionally lean towards unilateral actions to safeguard their national interests. Thus, a potential NEO threat could trigger initiatives by states capable of executing independent planetary defence activities without open discussions on methods or international repercussions. States willing to take matters in their own hands would then bear the costs and responsibilities emerging from such unilateral actions.[3] Such a unilateral course of action could expedite procedures but would lack global legitimacy. Furthermore, lack of coordination may hamper effective results.

Cosmic threats do not respect borders. Therefore, a multilateral approach is advised.[4] Multilateralism[5] allows states to reduce coordination costs and, combined with greater international legitimacy, serves to support effective global governance. As explained by John Ruggie, multilateralism is characterised by three major components:[6] 1) common principles as the basis for coordination among states; 2) indivisible principles, applied to all without distinction; and, 3) diffuse reciprocity of obligations, i.e. ongoing (potentially indefinite) series of exchanges of concessions and/or obligations amongst a group of partners, rather than only mutual exchanges.[7] Since planetary defence relates to emergencies of widespread relevance capable of severely affecting international peace and security, open debate and cooperation are important to secure international legitimacy and optimum results.

A relevant number of multilateral bodies could be considered for planetary defence actions. Different factors must be taken into account, including functions, structures and powers, in order to identify particular advantages and disadvantages. One of the most strategic features to be considered is the applicable decision-making procedure. By assessing the circumstances of a cosmic

3 Marco Pedrazzi, 'Outer Space, Liability for Damage', in Rüdiger Wolfrum (ed), *Max Planck Encyclopedia of Public International Law* (Oxford University Press 2012) vol VII 1109, para 1–2.

4 Romana Kofler, Daniel Garcia Yarnoz, and Martin Staško, 'Near-Earth Objects and the United Nations' in Nikola Schmidt (ed), *Planetary Defense: Global Collaboration for Defending Earth from Asteroids and Comets* (Springer 2018) 139–140.

5 "Multilateralism can be defined as the practice of co-ordinating national policies in groups of three or more states, through ad hoc arrangements or by means of institutions". Robert Keohane, 'Multilateralism: an Agenda for Research' (1990) 45 International Journal 731.

6 John Ruggie, *Winning the Peace: America and World Order in the New Era* (Columbia University Press 1998) 48.

7 See the characterisation by James Scott, 'Multilateralism' *Encyclopedia Britannica* (2015), <www.britannica.com/topic/multilateralism> accessed 25 February 2021.

threat, states may choose one or multiple bodies for planetary defence, possibly acting in coordination.

A limited coalition of states wiling to conduct planetary defence could expedite decision-making procedures. However, membership would most likely be reserved to members deemed capable of effectively addressing the issue. Examples already exist in relation to different space-related activities and issues, such as the Inter-Agency Space Debris Coordination Committee (IADC), which serves as coordination body between national space agencies in their efforts to mitigate human-made and natural space debris.[8] On the other hand, instances of 'minilateralism'[9] (often conducted behind closed doors) favour action in detriment of universal representation. In view of a common global threat, such a level of exclusiveness may be regarded as unsound.

To create an *ad hoc* international body with broad representation from scratch to deal with a planetary defence situation can, as a matter of fact, prove to be unrealistic. Indeed, the economic and political costs involved with constituting a new structure must be realised by all relevant parties. Such an option would also require a timeframe perhaps unavailable or unwarranted in case of impending threats, delaying effective international decision-making.

Therefore, existing international bodies should be considered as pragmatic and practical options. International expert groups on planetary defence as well as structures within the United Nations system should deserve special attention, whether acting alone or in conjunction with other specialised international bodies. By accessing their features and decision-making procedures, the alternative best suited for any given planetary defence may be properly identified.

2 Planetary Defence Decision-Making Options at the United Nations General Assembly

As the plenary organ of the United Nations[10] the General Assembly may be considered as one of the prime international bodies to discuss actions related

8 The Inter-Agency Space Debris Coordination Committee (IADC) is an international forum for worldwide coordination of activities related to space debris. It is not institutionalised and does not have a political mandate. See <www.iadc-home.org/what_iadc> accessed 25 February 2021.

9 *International Encyclopedia of Political Science* (2011) vol I 1635.

10 Charter of the United Nations (adopted 26 June 1945, entered into force 24 October 1945) 1 UNTS 16 (UN Charter).

to planetary defence, even in times of urgency. The representation of all United Nations member states arguably fosters international legitimacy and facilitates public debate on global issues.[11] Nevertheless, particular challenges towards expedited and effective decision-making for planetary defence within the General Assembly must be acknowledged.

2.1 *Competences*

The General Assembly has a comprehensive mandate and may discuss any issue within the scope of the United Nations Charter or relating to the powers and functions of any organ, in accordance with Article 10 of the Charter.[12]

As provided in Article 11(1) of the Charter, the General Assembly may consider, at its discretion, general principles of cooperation whenever the maintenance of international peace and security is at stake. Among these principles, those governing disarmament and the regulation of armaments are expressly mentioned. The General Assembly is entitled to make recommendations to member states and the Security Council.[13]

The important role that the United Nations and its organs can play in the prevention and removal of international threats which may lead to international friction or give rise to an international dispute was acknowledged by the UN General Assembly Resolution 43/51 of 1988. Indeed, as emphasised

---

11 In the General Assembly all UN Member States are represented. The criteria for membership are provided in Chapter II of the UN Charter. Article 3 of the Charter refers to the participants of the United Nations Conference on International Organization at San Francisco, in 1945 as original Members, while Article 4 opens UN membership to "all other peace-loving states which accept the obligations contained in the present Charter and, in the judgment of the Organization, are able and willing to carry out these obligations." See also Ulrich Fastenrath, 'Ch.II Membership, Article 3' in Bruno Simma and others (eds), *The Charter of the United Nations: A Commentary* (3rd edn, Oxford University Press 2012) vol I 341.

12 "Article 10 vests the GA with a general power of discussion and recommendation regarding any questions which comes within the scope of the Charter (the 'comprehensive jurisdiction' of the GA)." Eckart Klein and Stefanie Schmahl, 'Ch.IV The General Assembly, Functions and Powers, Article 10' in Bruno Simma and others (eds), *The Charter of the United Nations: A Commentary* (3rd edn, Oxford University Press 2012) vol I 464.

13 See, however, the limits set by Article 12 of the Charter. According to this provision, the General Assembly shall not make any recommendation with regard to a dispute or a situation in respect to which the Security Councilis exercising its functions. Yet, in practice Article 12 has not hindered the General Assembly to make recommendations concerning situations that were also on the agenda of the Security Council. See Eckart Klein and Stefanie Schmahl, 'Ch.IV The General Assembly, Functions and Powers, Article 12' in Bruno Simma and others (eds), *The Charter of the United Nations: A Commentary* (3rd edn, Oxford University Press 2012) vol I 507–508.

by Manuel Diez de Velasco, the fundamental goal of the United Nations, as a whole, is to sustain peace and international security.[14] Therefore, due to its broad mandate, the General Assembly may in fact address issues related to the maintenance of international peace and security, provided that the primary – but not *exclusive* – competency of the Security Council in that regard is respected.[15]

A NEO impact threat, due to its potentially devastating global effects, may represent a threat to international peace and security.[16] International planetary defence initiatives could therefore be considered by the United Nations. The vast political, economic, and environmental impacts potentially deriving from a possible NEO impact must not be underestimated.[17] Thus, the General Assembly, endowed with comprehensive functions and powers, could pay particular attention to various NEO impact threat scenarios and consider military, economic, as well as social aspects.

Studies and recommendations may be developed by the General Assembly for the purpose of promoting international cooperation not only in the political field, but also involving an ample spectrum of relevant areas (Article 13 UN

14 Manuel Diez de Velasco, *Las Organizaciones Internacionales* (16th edn, Tecnos 2010) 226–228.

15 "Article 12 has a special position insofar as it undertakes expressly to delimit the powers of the GA and the SC, even though this only applies with regard to disputes and other situations that threaten the peace. There are no corresponding provisions clarifying the relationship between the GA or the SC and other UN organs, nor the interrelations of those other organs. Thus, for instance, the fact that the SC is dealing with a dispute between member States does not prevent the ICJ from taking action on the same issue. The Charter usually confines itself to defining the competences of the individual organs and leaves any further determination to them, at least temporarily. Shortcomings that may appear can thus only be overcome if the organs concerned are ready to cooperate in good faith in effectively accomplishing the purposes of the UN." Eckart Klein and Stefanie Schmahl, 'Ch.IV The General Assembly, Functions and Powers, Article 12' in Bruno Simma and others (eds), *The Charter of the United Nations: A Commentary* (3rd edn, Oxford University Press 2012) vol I 509.

16 Similarly, the terrorist attacks on the World Trade Center in 2001 led to a Security Councilresolution referring to international terrorism "as a threat to international peace and security", see UN SC Res 1368 (12 September 2001) UN Doc S/RES/1368. See also UNSC Res 2177 (18 September 2014) UN Doc S/RES/2177, where the Security Council decided that the "unprecedented extent of the Ebola outbreak in Africa constitutes a threat to international peace and security".

17 David P S Dearborn and Paul L Miller state that a "Terrestrial impact by an asteroid or comet represents a rare but potentially catastrophic hazard", in Joseph N Pelton and Firooz Allahdadi (eds), *Handbook of Cosmic Hazards and Planetary Defence* (Springer 2015) 733–736.

Charter).[18] In order to speed up deliberations and incorporate technical input to the decision-making procedure, a subsidiary body of *ad hoc* nature may be created by the General Assembly devoted exclusively to address planetary defence matters, as per Article 7(2)[19] and Article 22 of the Charter.[20] Moreover, the General Assembly may consider collaboration with and input from international expert groups devoted to planetary defence, such as SMPAG, to provide know-how and expertise for a proper appraisal of scenarios.

2.2 *Uniting for Peace*

General Assembly Resolution 377 A (V), of 3 November 1950, known as the 'Uniting for Peace' Resolution, may be relevant in dealing with NEO threats. The resolution states that, if the Security Council, due to a lack of unanimity amongst its permanent members, fails to exercise its primary responsibility for the maintenance of international peace and security, "the General Assembly shall consider the matter immediately with a view of making appropriate recommendations to Members for collective actions."[21] This resolution, which included and approved amendments to the General Assembly's rules of procedure, establishes that, if the General Assembly is not in session in any given situation, an Emergency Special Session may be organised within twenty-four hours of the request thereof. Such Emergency Special Sessions shall be called if requested by the Security Council on the vote of any seven members, or by a majority of the members of the United Nations.[22] Therefore, the General Assembly may be called upon in case of planetary defence emergencies not solved by the Security Councilby reason of deadlock.

---

18 "Codification and progressive development under the auspices of the GA cater to the practical needs of the community of States and the products of these processes, as well as the processes themselves, therefore also have diplomatic features in their nature and content." Carl-August Fleischhauer and Bruno Simma, 'Ch.IV The General Assembly, Functions and Powers, Article 13' in Bruno Simma and others (eds), *The Charter of the United Nations: A Commentary* (3rd edn, Oxford University Press 2012) vol I 525.

19 "It is generally accepted that organs may create subsidiary organs. Thus, for example, the General Assembly has created such subsidiary organs as UNCTAD; under the Charter, the authority for doing so derives from Article 7, para. 2, which provides that 'such subsidiary organs as may be found necessary may be established in accordance with the present Charter'." Jan Klabbers, *An Introduction to International Institutional Law* (2nd edn, Cambridge University Press 2009) 163.

20 Article 22, UN Charter. See Chittharanjan F Amerasinghe, *Principles of the Institutional Law of International Organizations* (2nd edn, Cambridge University Press 2005) 132–137.

21 UNGA Res 377(V) A (3 November 1950) UN Doc A/RES/377.

22 Ibid.

In the *Certain Expenses Case* before the International Court of Justice in 1962, the functions of United Nations bodies were examined.[23] The Court considered that, while the responsibility for the maintenance of international peace and security is conferred primarily to the Security Council, this fact does not preclude the General Assembly from acting on matters affecting international peace and security. The Advisory Opinion concludes that "the Charter makes it abundantly clear, however, that the General Assembly is also to be concerned with international peace and security."[24] Consequently, two primary organs of the United Nations (the General Assembly and the International Court of Justice) have determined that the General Assembly is capable of making decisions and taking actions regarding threats to international peace and security, such as those represented by NEOs.

2.3 *Voting*

Based on the principle of sovereign equality of states, the UN Charter grants one vote to each member at the General Assembly irrespective of any political, economic, or geographical disparities.[25] Article 18 of the Charter specifically provides that decisions shall be made by a two-thirds majority of the members present and voting in relation to "important questions" – including recommendations with respect to the maintenance of international peace and security.[26] Other questions may be decided by a simple majority, such as those involving occasional procedural concerns.[27] Reviewing recent voting records in the General Assembly, Rüdiger Wolfrum noted that

> the vast majority of the GA's more recent decisions have been adopted without a vote, others have been adopted by an affirmative vote by two-thirds or more of its members. In very few cases a decision was approved unanimously. However, the number of cases where only a few delegates voted against a resolution is almost equally low. In the majority of cases, the application or interpretation of the provisions of Art. 18 has not raised much discussion. Most decisions do not indicate whether the members were aware that the voting procedure for "important questions" applied.

---

23 *Certain Expenses of the United Nations* (Advisory Opinion) [1962] ICJ Rep 151, 167–68.

24 Ibid.

25 Rüdiger Wolfrum, 'Ch.IV The General Assembly, Voting, Article 18' in Bruno Simma and others (eds), *The Charter of the United Nations: A Commentary* (3rd edn, Oxford University Press 2012) vol I 624.

26 Article 18 (2), UN Charter.

27 Article 18 (3), UN Charter.

> Only in a few cases was reference made to the application of the rule regarding "important questions" during deliberations.[28]

Ordinary sessions of the General Assembly are regularly arranged once a year, starting on the third Tuesday of September, but member states may be convened in special sessions called for by the Secretary General by request of the Security Council, or by a majority of UN members.[29] However, the practical difficulties of assembling all member states on short notice to address complex space-related emergencies such as planetary defence should not be minimised.

Irrespective of its almost universal representation and its broad mandate, the General Assembly must not be confused with a 'world legislature', since – in accordance with the UN Charter – decisions by the General Assembly are generally recommendatory, as highlighted by Malcolm Shaw.[30] In the face of a NEO threat, the international community must realise that while enjoying wide representation and competency the General Assembly is limited in relation to decisions necessary to initiate international action to mitigate NEO impact threats. Consequently, appropriate alternatives should also be taken into account.

2.4 *The United Nations Committee on the Peaceful Uses of Outer Space*

To support its activities, the General Assembly may establish subsidiary organs.[31] The United Nations Committee on the Peaceful Uses of Outer Space (UNCOPUOS) was created to consider international aspects on the exploration

---

28 Rüdiger Wolfrum, 'Ch.IV The General Assembly, Voting, Article 18' in Bruno Simma and others (eds), *The Charter of the United Nations: A Commentary* (3rd edn, Oxford University Press 2012) vol I 628.

29 Article 20, UN Charter; see also Christopher Eick, 'Ch.IV The General Assembly, Procedure, Article 20' in Bruno Simma and others (eds), *The Charter of the United Nations: A Commentary* (3rd edn, Oxford University Press 2012) vol I 659–660. Reference should be made to the Uniting For Peace-Resolution mentioned earlier, which establishes that, if the General Assembly is not in session in any given situation, an Emergency Special Session may be organised within twenty-four hours of the request thereof.

30 "Except for certain internal matters, such as the budget, the Assembly cannot bind its members. It is not a legislature in that sense, and its resolutions are purely recommendatory. Such resolutions, of course, may be binding if they reflect rules of customary international law and they are significant as instances of state practice that may lead to the formation of a new customary rule, but Assembly resolutions in themselves cannot establish binding legal obligations for member states." Malcolm N Shaw, *International Law* (8th edn, Cambridge University Press 2017) 929–930.

31 Article 7 and Article 22, UN Charter. See already above, section 2.1 in this chapter. See also Chittharanjan F Amerasinghe, *Principles of the Institutional Law of International Organizations* (2nd edn, Cambridge University Press 2005) 132–137.

and use of outer space for the benefit of all mankind, as well as to execute programmes and studying legal problems arising from the exploration of outer space.[32] Constituted as a committee contributing to the work of the General Assembly, the legal nature of UNCOPUOS deserves particular attention. Sergio Marchisio observed that

> UNCOPUOS was intended to be more of a political organ devoted to strengthening international cooperation among spacefaring Nations with their national space programmes, rather than as a technical organization with the competency to realize direct operational activities in space.[33]

Consequently, the General Assembly retains relevant influence over UNCOPUOS' composition and agenda. The diplomatic negotiations which led to the creation of UNCOPUOS are reflected in its structure and procedures, including its decision-making mechanisms, which reveal the political context of the Cold War. The reasons behind the creation of a specific committee dedicated to outer space activities within the United Nations were appraised by Peter Jankowitsch, who observed that the global reach of such activities required, right from the onset, "a high degree of international cooperation that, by its nature, could only be found and practised in a universal organization like the United Nations."[34]

The proposal to establish a distinct body within the United Nations tasked with addressing the exploration and use of outer space independent from disarmament negotiations was made during the first few years of the space race. In that context, the United States of America advanced the respective proposal, which was accepted by the other superpower of the period, the Soviet Union.[35] Based on bilateral negotiations between both nations, General

---

32 UNGA Res 1472 (XIV) (12 December 1959) UN Doc A/RES/1472; see also above, chapter 4 'International Cooperation in Planetary Defence – UNCOPUOS, IAWN and SMPAG' in this book, and Nathan C Goldman, 'UNCOPUOS is the World's de facto Space Legislature – Debating, Drafting, and Negotiating International Law for Outer Space' in *Space Policy: An Introduction* (Iowa State University Press 1992); Francis Lyall and Paul B Larsen, *Space Law–A Treatise* (2nd edn, Routledge 2017) 13.

33 Sergio Marchisio, 'The Evolutionary Stages of the Legal Subcommittee of the United Nations Committee on the Peaceful Uses of Outer Space (COPUOS)' (2005) 31 Journal of Space Law 219, 221.

34 Peter Jankowitsch, 'The Background and History of Space Law' in Frans G von der Dunk (ed), *Handbook of Space Law* (Edward Elgar Publishing 2015) 1, 10.

35 Bin Cheng, *Studies on International Space Law* (Oxford University Press 1998) 162–163.

Assembly Resolution 1348 (XIII) of 1958 created an *ad hoc* Committee on the Peaceful Uses of Outer Space. This body was originally comprised of only eighteen member states. Conflicts emerged in relation to the *ad hoc* Committee's composition and procedures, but soon afterwards the creation of UNCOPUOS as a permanent committee followed with General Assembly Resolution 1472 (XIV) of 1959.[36]

Two standing subcommittees were created in 1961, the Scientific and Technical Subcommittee (STSC), devoted to scientific and technical aspects of space activities, and the Legal Subcommittee (LSC), where legal questions regarding the use and exploration of outer space would be considered and developed.[37] Both subcommittees meet once per year and provide input for the UNCOPUOS plenary meeting, also organised yearly.[38] Reports from this UNCOPUOS plenary session are then submitted to the General Assembly's Fourth Committee (Special Political and Decolonization Committee), which is responsible for preparing an annual resolution on international cooperation on the peaceful uses of outer space.[39]

The decision-making mechanisms and procedures were subject to major debates during the early sessions of UNCOPUOS.[40] General Assembly Resolution 1721 (XVI) of 1961 settled this matter with the adoption of the consensus rule, meaning the absence of objection by any member state.[41] As explained by Nathan Goldman, consensus at the Committee means that, "silence is approval, and just one objection vetoes a provision".[42] Such a mechanism, besides favouring joint work and confidence building among members, requires support, at least implicitly, by the major space faring nations.[43]

36 UNGA Res 1472 (XIV) (12 December 1959) UN Doc A/RES/1472; For a history of UNCOPUOS, see Manfred Lachs, *The Law of Outer Space: an Experience in Contemporary Law-Making* (Brill 2010, originally published 1972) 27–39.

37 'Committee on the Peaceful Uses of Outer Space' (*United Nations Office for Outer Space Affairs*) <www.unoosa.org/oosa/en/ourwork/copuos/current.html> accessed 16 February 2021; see also Christian Brünner and Alexander Soucek (eds), *Outer Space in Society, Politics and Law* (Springer 2011) 224–226.

38 Fabio Tronchetti, *Fundamentals of Space Law and Policy* (Springer 2013) 38.

39 Tanja Masson-Zwaan and Mahulena Hoffman, *Introduction to Space Law* (4th edn, Wolters Kluwer 2019) 10.

40 Eilene Galloway, 'Consensus Decisionmaking by the United Nations Committee on the Peaceful Uses of Outer Space' (1979) 7 J. Space L. 3.

41 UNGA Res 1721 (XVII) (21 December 1961) UN Doc A/RES/1721.

42 Nathan C Goldman, *Space Policy: An Introduction* (Iowa State University Press 1992) 23.

43 "The UN Committee on the Peaceful Uses of Outer Space was the first UN standing body to use this procedure [consensus] in its purest form. The fact that all the space law agreements drafted in its Legal Sub-Committee were therefore adopted by consensus, although this methodology sometimes slowed down negotiations, provided them with broad

Christopher Joyner clarifies that, under the consensus rule, the approval of treaties or international principles is settled by general agreement, without vote, but not necessarily unanimity. Therefore, "abstentions and unilateral interpretations of a provision do not qualify as dissent in this process, and consent during the deliberations does not obligate a State to become a party to the treaty".[44]

Although originally considered reasonable by member states, the decision-making process at UNCOPUOS has proved to be cumbersome.[45] Indeed, in face of a rising number of members and complex issues being included in the agenda, consensus has increasingly become difficult to be built, especially in the Legal Subcommittee.[46]

Nonetheless, the legacy of UNCOPUOS should not be underestimated since this body was important for fostering the peaceful uses of outer space during the Cold War. The Committee continues to serve as an important open forum for space faring and non-space faring nations to discuss relevant aspects of space activities, most recently with the completion of 21 Guidelines for the Long-term Sustainability of Outer Space Activities.[47] Additionally, it must be acknowledged that UNCOPUOS has been instrumental to the advancement of space law, conceiving some of its most important international instruments, including the Outer Space Treaty of 1967.

With a total of 95 Member States in 2020, UNCOPUOS has recently experienced a remarkable expansion both in participation and agenda items, manifesting the relevance of international cooperation in space activities. Nevertheless, the difficulty of building consensus at the Committee, together with the lack of universal representation and of the possibility to take binding decisions, may hinder effective measures in times of pressure. When analysing the current dynamics at UNCOPUOS, Xu Yu noticed that recent sessions

---

international acceptance, particularly from the major space powers, who could thus identify with the compromise solutions found in the Committee. The fact that today – with one exception – the majority of outer space treaties are accepted by a large number of states also testifies to this." Peter Jankowitsch, 'The Background and History of Space Law' in Frans G von der Dunk (ed), *Handbook of Space Law* (Edward Elgar Publishing 2015) 1, 12.

44 Christopher C Joyner, *The United Nations and International Law* (The American Society of International Law and Cambridge University Press 1997) 340.

45 Xu Yu, 'UNCOPUOS 50 Years On: Assessing Current Dynamics and Exploring its Future Role' (2012) 28 Space Policy 146–148.

46 Kai-Uwe Schrogl, 'The New Debate on the Working Methods of the UNCOPUOS Legal Subcommittee' (2014) Acta Astronautica 101–108.

47 UNCOPUOS, 'Report of the Committee on the Peaceful Uses of Outer Space' (12–21 June 2019) UN Doc A/74/20, Annex II.

proved to be "busier, but less accomplished."[48] As more members enjoy international debates on complex issues such as planetary defence, governance may in fact be hindered without proper acknowledgement of key features and perspectives.[49]

3 Planetary Defence Decision Making at the United Nations Security Council

3.1 *Competence*

Conceived as the executive organ of the United Nations, the Security Council holds the "primary responsibility for the maintenance of international peace and security", as solemnly stated in Article 24 of the UN Charter. Anne Peters explains:

> Because the primary responsibility implies a primary competence, too, the phrase in Art. 24 contains a guideline for the resolution of conflicts of competences among the organs. In the *Wall* Advisory Opinion, the ICJ emphasized 'that Article 24 refers to a primary, but not necessarily exclusive, competence'. Because it is not exclusive, a space for responsibilities of other organs remains, and there can be overlap. This raises the question of the distribution of the responsibilities between the Security Council and General Assembly on the one hand, and of the former's relation to the International Court of Justice (ICJ) on the other, in the area of overlap. Generally speaking, the different organs must observe the institutional balance and must pay each other mutual due respect.[50]

Unlike the General Assembly, the Security Council functions permanently and continuously, and was designed to address international crises, especially those requiring urgent consideration. Within the Security Council's competence lies

---

48 "Although delighted by the increase in the agenda items and membership of the Committee, some are worried about a lack of progress in certain fields and duplication of efforts between the Committee and other initiatives." Xu Yu, 'UNCOPUOS 50 Years On: Assessing Current Dynamics and Exploring its Future Role' (2012) 28 Space Policy 146–148.

49 Kai-Uwe Schrogl, 'The New Debate on the Working Methods of the UNCOPUOS Legal Subcommittee' (2014) Acta Astronautica 105.

50 Anne Peters, 'Ch.v The Security Council, Functions and Powers, Article 24' in Bruno Simma and others (eds), *The Charter of the United Nations: A Commentary* (3rd edn, Oxford University Press 2012) vol I 767.

the collective security mechanism conceived by the Charter,[51] that is, "effective collective measures for the prevention and removal of threats to the peace, and for the suppression of acts of aggression or other breaches of the peace".[52]

3.2 *Representation and Decision Making*

Originally consisting of eleven members, the composition of the Security Council was broadened to fifteen members in 1963, of which ten members are non-permanent, while five members are permanent members.[53] The permanent members are China, France, Russian Federation, United Kingdom of Great Britain and Northern Ireland, and the United States of America. These permanent five can be said to enjoyed a special status which "embodies an exemption to the principle of sovereign equality", as explained by Rudolf Geiger.[54] Indeed, while each member of the Security Council is entitled to one vote, each of the permanent members has the power to block a decision.[55]

Article 27(3) of the UN Charter provides that the decisions of the Security Council on all non-procedural issues shall be made by an affirmative vote of nine members, including the concurring votes of the permanent members. Subsequent practice at the United Nations has interpreted and applied Article 27(3) of the UN Charter in an interesting fashion.[56] Even though a first read of its text may lead to the conclusion that the five permanent members must provide a concurring affirmative vote, the practice of the Council as early as 1946 was to interpret concurring as merely meaning not objecting.[57] Therefore, if a permanent member wishes to block a decision, it is not enough for it to abstain, or even be absent; rather, it must cast a negative vote (known as "the veto").

This interpretation was confirmed by the International Court of Justice in the *Namibia Case* in 1971, according to which abstentions by any permanent member in non-procedural matters are not to be considered as vetoes. The Court held that "by abstaining, a member does not signify its objection to the

51 Thomas M Franck, 'Collective Security and UN Reform: Between the Necessary and the Possible' (2006) 6 Chicago Journal of International Law 7.

52 Article 1, UN Charter.

53 Alejandro Rodiles, 'Non-Permanent Members of the United Nations Security Council and the Promotion of the International Rule of Law' (2013) 5 Goettingen Journal of International Law 333–373.

54 Rudolf Geiger, 'Ch.v The Security Council, Composition, Article 23' in Bruno Simma and others (eds), *The Charter of the United Nations: A Commentary* (3rd edn, Oxford University Press 2012) vol I 753.

55 Malcolm N Shaw, *International Law* (8th edn, Cambridge University Press 2017) 926.

56 Manuel Diez de Velasco, *Las Organizaciones Internacionales* (16th edn, Tecnos 2010) 213.

57 Anthony Aust, *Modern Treaty Law and Practice* (Cambridge University Press, 2000) 194–195.

approval of what is being proposed; in order to prevent the adoption of a resolution requiring unanimity of the permanent members, a permanent member has only to cast a negative vote."[58]

The decision-making process at the Security Council has been subject to scrutiny by scholars and governments, as well as international jurisprudence.[59] By arguably granting a different status to permanent members of the Security Council, the veto power may be considered as *prima facie* contradicting Article 2(1) of the Charter, which praises the principle of sovereign equality of all its members, a principle upon which the organisation is said to be built.[60] The composition of the Security Council itself is occasionally regarded as outdated and as leading to an executive organ not fully representative of the current United Nations.[61]

Therefore, whenever answering global threats, such as those justifying planetary defence actions, the Security Council should open its doors to any UN member states considered to be particularly affected, or even invite states to provide information considered relevant to address the situation. Such a possibility is covered by Article 31 of the Charter, which provides that any UN member, irrespective of its membership in the Security Council, may participate in discussions therein whenever the latter considers the interests of the state in question are particularly affected. A caveat, nevertheless, must be acknowledged: in those circumstances, non-members of the Security Council do not have the right to vote.[62]

Additionally, states which are not a member of the Security Council may channel their considerations through international alliances, including within its Regional Group, represented by holders of non-permanent seats.[63] Although not specifically provided by Article 23 of the Charter, in practice the geographic

---

58 *Legal Consequences for States of the Continued Presence of South Africa in Namibia (South West Africa) notwithstanding Security Council Resolution 276* (Advisory Opinion) 1970 ICJ Rep 1971, 20–22.

59 Loraine Sievers and Sam Daws, *The Procedure of the UN Security Council* (4th edn, Oxford University Press 2014).

60 Simon Chesterman, Ian Johnstone and David M Malone, *Law and Practice of the United Nations – Documents and Commentary* (2nd ed, Oxford University Press 2016) 7.

61 Jan Klabbers, *An Introduction to International Institutional Law* (2nd edn, Cambridge University Press 2009) 87–88.

62 Rudolf Dolzer and Charlotte Kreuter-Kirchhof, 'Ch.v The Security Council, Procedure, Article 31', in Bruno Simma and others (eds), *The Charter of the United Nations: A Commentary* (3rd edn, Oxford University Press 2012) vol I 1052.

63 Edith Drieskens, 'Beyond Chapter VIII: Limits and Opportunities for Regional Representation at the UN Security Council' (2010) 7 International Organisation Law Review 156.

distribution concept has been adopted to non-permanent seats at the Security Council for the term of two years to secure proportional representation. As such, of the ten available positions, three are reserved to the African Group, two to the Asia-Pacific Group, one to the Eastern European Group, two to the Latin American and Caribbean Group, and the final two to Western European and Others Group.[64]

Non-permanent members of the Security Council, considered by Alejandro Rodiles as, "key players for incrementally improving the Council's adherence to the rule of law",[65] may hold positions to express concerns and perspectives of the nations of its Regional Group. Through those diplomatic channels it could be assured that the voices of states which are not members of the Security Council are heard, whenever needed.

While the composition of the Security Council is often criticised for lack of equitable representation,[66] this composition may eventually prove to be instrumental for planetary defence. All permanent members are major space-faring nations with significant technical prowess to carry out or at least contribute meaningfully to any related mission. Also, as some of the few recognised nuclear powers, the permanent members would have the capability to deploy Nuclear Explosive Devices (NEDs) whenever accorded necessary for a planetary defence mission.[67] It seems reasonable to assume that these states would be crucially involved in the decision-making process on planetary defence in one way or another.

As will be discussed further below, technical assistance and advice from experts on planetary defence may also be requested by the Security Council, in order to ensure responsible and informed decision-making. In fact, coordination with other relevant international bodies is key to improve awareness and appreciation of the issue at hand, as proved by Security Council practice.

---

64 Rudolf Geiger, 'Ch.v The Security Council, Composition, Article 23' in Bruno Simma and others (eds), *The Charter of the United Nations: A Commentary* (3rd edn, Oxford University Press 2012) vol I 753.

65 Alejandro Rodiles, 'Non-Permanent Members of the United Nations Security Council and the Promotion of the International Rule of Law'(2013) 5 Goettingen Journal of International Law 371.

66 Sabine Hassler, *Reforming the UN Security Council Membership: The Illusion of Representativeness* (Routledge 2013) 195–200.

67 For further consideration of Nuclear Explosive Devices (NEDs) as far as planetary defence is concerned, see chapter 15 'Legal Aspects of the Use of Nuclear Explosive Devices in Planetary Defence' and chapter 16 'Nuclear Non-Proliferation and Planetary Defence: Competing Potential Disaster' in this book.

Enjoying vast competences on matters relating to international security, one may conclude that the Security Council is capable of prompting and organising major spacefaring nations towards effective measures against cosmic threats, especially when not much time is available and relatively quick decision-making is essential.

3.3 *Binding Force*

The primary responsibility for the maintenance of international peace and security is conferred to the Security Council by the member states, who "agree that in carrying out its duties under this responsibility the Security Council acts on their behalf" (Article 24 UN Charter). Indeed, Article 25 of the Charter obliges UN members to accept and carry out the Security Council's binding decisions – including decisions focused on the peaceful settlement of disputes and measures of collective security.

Chapter VII of the Charter provides (in Article 39) that measures of collective security may be decided by the Security Council whenever it determines the existence of "any threat to the peace, breach of peace, or act of aggression." Those measures could be provisional in nature, in order to prevent the aggravation of the situation (Article 40). Additionally, measures taken may or may not involve the use of armed forces, in accordance with Security Council evaluation (Articles 41 and 42).[68]

As mentioned above, due to their potentially devastating global effects, NEOs could be regarded as relevant threats to international peace and security.[69] Consequently, planetary defence missions can be regarded as 'measures of collective security' and under the Security Council's purview. The Security Council may therefore authorise specific measures to be conducted in response to a dangerous asteroid or comet, and in accordance with the Charter, the decisions implementing such measures shall be followed by all members of the United Nations.

---

68 Nico Krisch, 'Ch.VII Action with Respect to Threats to the Peace, Breaches of the Peace, and Acts of Aggression, Article 41' in Bruno Simma and others (eds), *The Charter of the United Nations: A Commentary* (3rd edn, Oxford University Press 2012) vol I 1305.

69 See also chapter 15 'Legal Aspects of the Use of Nuclear Explosive Devices in Planetary Defence' in this book.

3.1.1 The Legality of Nuclear Explosive Devices[70]

One area that might be explored is the legality of Nuclear Explosive Devices (NEDs) in the context of planetary defence. In principle, the use of a nuclear device in outer space would be contrary to the Limited Test Ban Treaty of 1963[71] and may be problematic with respect to the Non-Proliferation Treaty of 1968.[72] If placed in orbit, a nuclear device would also violate Article IV Outer Space Treaty.[73] However, Article 103 of the UN Charter clarifies:

> In the event of a conflict between the obligations of the Members of the United Nations under the present Charter and their obligations under any other international agreement, their obligations under the present Charter shall prevail.

The priority of obligations under the UN Charter over conflicting other international obligations as stipulated in Article 103 extends to binding decisions of the Security Council.[74] The last decades have shown an increased legislative activity of the Security Council.[75] Article 103 provides some legal certainty for states confronted with the risk of violating conflicting obligations.[76]

However, the Security Council's latitude conferred by the Charter is not limitless. It is bound by the Charter itself as well as by fundamental principles of

70 See in more detail chapter 15 'Legal Aspects of the Use of Nuclear Explosive Devices in Planetary Defence' and chapter 16 'Nuclear Non-Proliferation and Planetary Defence: Competing Potential Disaster' in this book.

71 Treaty Banning Nuclear Weapon Tests in the Atmosphere, in Outer Space and Under Water (adopted 5 August 1963, entered into force 10 October 1963) 480 UNTS 43.

72 Treaty on the Non-Proliferation of Nuclear Weapons (adopted 1 July 1968, entered into force 5 March 1970) 729 UNTS 161. See in more detail chapters 15 and 16 in this book.

73 Article IV, "States Parties to the Treaty undertake not to place in orbit around the Earth any objects carrying nuclear weapons or any other kinds of weapons of mass destruction, install such weapons on celestial bodies, or station such weapons in outer space in any other manner." See also Fabio Tronchetti, *Fundamentals of Space Law and Policy* (Springer 2013) 9.

74 *Questions of Interpretation and Application of the 1971 Montreal Convention Arising from the Aerial Incident at Lockerbie* (*Libyan Arab Jamahiriya v United Kingdom and United States*) (Provisional Measures) [1992] ICJ Rep 3, 114; see also Karl Zemanek, 'The Legal Foundations of the International System' (1977) 266 Recueil des Cours 230.

75 Stefan Talmon, 'The Security Council as World Legislature' (2005) 99 AJIL 177–179.

76 Johann Ruben Leiæ and Andreas Paulus, 'Ch.XVI Miscellaneous Provisions, Article 103' in Bruno Simma and others (eds), *The Charter of the United Nations: A Commentary* (Oxford University Press 2012) vol II 2123.

international law.[77] In the exercise of its legislative capacity it should primarily relate to the maintenance of international peace and security.[78] As observed by James Green in the context of planetary defence:

> The Council cannot authorize states to violate any norm of international law that it wishes. It is widely agreed, for example, that it cannot act or authorize states to act in a manner that would be contrary to norms that have acquired the status of *jus cogens*.[79]

Ius cogens are peremptory norms under international law accepted and recognised by the international community as norms from which no derogation is permitted and which can be modified only by subsequent norms of general international law having the same character.[80] Similarly, a binding decision conflicting with an obligation *erga omnes,* i.e. a norm of international law that is owed to the international community as a whole so that all states have a legal interest in their protection, would become inapplicable.[81] The old adage that 'the king can do no wrong' is therefore not applicable to the Security Council, as far as international law is concerned, and this means that its powers should not be construed as unconditional and absolute.[82]

Consequently, when adopting resolutions, the Security Council is not operating in a legal vacuum as "neither the text nor the spirit of the Charter conceives of the Security Council as legibus solutus (unbound by law)."[83] The main purpose of Article 103 of the Charter is to maintain the coherence and the unity of the international legal system under the umbrella of the Charter.[84] Furthermore, the principle of systematic integration pursuant to

---

77 Anne Peters, 'Ch.v The Security Council, Functions and Powers, Article 24' in Bruno Simma and others (eds), *The Charter of the United Nations: A Commentary* (3rd edn, Oxford University Press 2012) vol I 766–768.

78 Paul C Szasz, 'The Security Council Starts Legislating' (2002) 96 Am J Int'l L 904.

79 James A Green, 'Planetary Defense: Near-Earth Objects, Nuclear Weapons, and International Law' (2019) 42 Hastings International & Comparative Law Review 1 60.

80 Article 53, Vienna Convention on the Law of Treaties (adopted 23 May 1969, entered in to force 27 January 1980) 1115 UNTS 331 (VCLT).

81 See *Barcelona Traction Case (Belgium v Spain)* (Merits) [1970] ICJ Rep 3; see also ILC, 'Report of the Study Group of the International Law Commission', Fifty-eighth session (1 May–9 June and 3 July–11 August 2006) UN Doc A/CN.4/L.682, 324 ff.

82 Malcolm N Shaw, *International Law* (8th edn, Cambridge University Press 2017) 523–566.

83 *Prosecutor v Tadic* (Appeal on Jurisdiction) (1996) 35 ILM 32.

84 Johann Ruben Leiæ and Andreas Paulus, 'Ch.XVI Miscellaneous Provisions, Article 103' in Bruno Simma and others (eds), *The Charter of the United Nations: A Commentary* (Oxford University Press 2012) vol II 2136.

Article 31(3)(c) of the Vienna Convention on the Law of Treaties[85] and the presumption of compatibility need to be taken into consideration to avoid a conflict in the first place.[86]

Finally, the text of Article 103 of the Charter should be understood as 'last resort' if all other efforts for interpreting conflicting binding provisions fail.[87]

It follows from the above that discussions and decisions concerning the use of NEDs for planetary defence could meaningfully take place in this framework. A decision taken by the Security Council in this context would not be impeded by the prohibitions contained in the Limited Test Ban Treaty and Article IV of the Outer Space Treaty, subject to the condition of being in conformity with the rules of the UN Charter, as well as *ius cogens* and *erga omnes* obligations. It could also alleviate existing concerns with respect to the Non-Proliferation Treaty. Such a decision could and should contain conditions and limitations in order to keep the scope of the exception from the respective prohibitions as narrow as possible. Consequently, Article 103 of the Charter paves the way to ensure that the use of NEDs for the purpose of planetary defence could be in accordance with international law.

Whether the veto power of the permanent members will make such a decision unlikely, is a political question. It could be addressed beforehand by the formulation of agreed principles and criteria related to potential future planetary defence activities to which the permanent members abide. An *ad hoc* agreement would also be possible but bears the risk of uncertainty. Despite the frequent differences in opinion among the permanent members on issues of international peace and security on Earth, the threat posed to the entire planet by an approaching NEO represents a common concern for all humanity against which concerted action would be in the interest of all countries. This insight could be sufficiently convincing to ensure the required consent by the permanent Security Council members.

---

85 Article 31 (3)(c) VCLT prescribes that, in the interpretation of a treaty, any relevant rules of international law applicable in the relations between the parties, shall be taken into account, together with the context of the treaty.

86 Johann Ruben Leiæ and Andreas Paulus, 'Ch.XVI Miscellaneous Provisions, Article 103' in Bruno Simma and others (eds), *The Charter of the United Nations: A Commentary* (Oxford University Press 2012) vol II 2119.

87 Johann Ruben Leiæ and Andreas Paulus, 'Ch.XVI Miscellaneous Provisions, Article 103' in Bruno Simma and others (eds), *The Charter of the United Nations: A Commentary* (Oxford University Press 2012) vol II 2114.

3.1.2 Possible Waiver of Liability

Another issue that could be solved with reference to Article 103 of the Charter is the question of liability. Under the principles of international space law, launching states are liable for any damage caused by their space objects.[88] States therefore run the risk of being liable as launching states for damage caused on Earth or in outer space in the course of their planetary defence operations. This heavy burden could prevent states from getting involved in the respective space operations. A waiver of liability in the context of planetary defence activities would therefore be in the interest of potential launching states, but also in the interest of other states which may face a NEO impact on their territory but do not have the relevant capability in space technology to do anything against it.

With respect to Article 103 of the Charter, the Security Council could take the decision to waive the liability of the launching states that are involved in a planetary defence activity and define criteria and conditions for such a waiver. Within the limits mentioned above, the Security Council may take a decision in contradiction of existing treaty law when it considers it necessary to preserve international peace and security. The Liability Convention of 1972, which establishes international liability of launching states for damage caused by their space objects,[89] could eventually be subject to a Security Council resolution designed to support emergency action in the face of a NEO threat. The same instrument could also relieve states from other international obligations imposing on them heavy burdens, which they should not carry when they are acting in a planetary defence scenario for the benefit of humankind.

3.1.3 Measures of Collective Security

The Security Council could also be instrumental in permitting the use of military force by states, individually or collectively, to face a NEO impact threat. It could authorise or even oblige states to support planetary defence missions by appropriate means, including permissions to use their territories, territorial waters, and/or air spaces. Eventually, other capable international bodies such as NATO could be asked to assist in operations, when deemed appropriate.[90]

---

88 See in more detail chapter 18 'The Current International Space Law Regime on Liability and Its Application to Planetary Defence' in this book.

89 Tanja Masson-Zwaan and Mahulena Hoffman, *Introduction to Space Law* (4th edn, Wolters Kluwer 2019), 26–30.

90 Thilo Marauhn, 'North Atlantic Treaty Organization', *Max Planck Encyclopedia of Public International Law* (Oxford University Press 2016) para 1.

Irrespective of shortcomings and idiosyncrasies, the binding nature of its decisions, as well as its permanent operation, favours the Security Council whenever the international community faces planetary defence emergencies, requiring urgent concerted action with sufficient legal certainty. The Security Council may authorise or even oblige member states to use all necessary means for tackling threats from outer space. Binding resolutions prevail over conflicting treaty obligations and allow a deviation from them, as long as they remain within the boundaries of Article 103 of the Charter and serve the principles and purposes of the United Nations including, most importantly, the protection of international peace and security.

4 International Expert Groups

The United Nations organs and bodies discussed above are characterised by representation of governments and can therefore legitimately take decisions on planetary defence activities. However, they may lack the specific expertise necessary to make an informed decision and to balance the respective risks. In order to fill this gap the respective organs and bodies could require assistance from other entities with the required technical expertise and knowhow. Ideally, the necessary input should be provided not by individual scientists, but by a larger international group of experts. In the following, potential candidates for providing expert advice will be examined.

4.1 *The Space Mission Planning Advisory Group*

The Space Mission Planning Advisory Group (SMPAG), as discussed in more detail in chapter 3, is the entity with the most direct and singular focus on preparing an international response to a NEO impact threat and mitigation activities.[91] The purpose of SMPAG is to "prepare for an international response to a NEO impact threat through the exchange of information, development of options for collaborative research and mission opportunities, and NEO threat mitigation planning activities."[92] Endorsed by UNGA Resolution 68/75 in 2013,[93] SMPAG is comprised of eighteen national and regional space

91 See in more detail chapter 11 'The SMPAG Ad-hoc Working Group on Legal Issues' in this book.

92 SMPAG, 'Terms of Reference for the Near-Earth Object Threat Mitigation Space Mission Planning Advisory Group – Version 2.0' (13 September 2019) <www.cosmos.esa.int/web/smpag/terms_of_reference_v2> accessed 25 February 2021.

93 UNGA Res 68/75 (13 December 2013) UN Doc A/RES/68/75.

agencies and some space-related institutions as observers.[94] Additionally, a number of observer organisations also contribute to the work of SMPAG.[95] The International Asteroid Warning Network (IAWN), with the corresponding role of NEO detection, cataloguing, and characterisation, was created at the same time and provides important scientific input to the work of SMPAG.[96]

4.1.1 SMPAG Scope of Work

According to its statement of purpose, SMPAG will neither execute an actual NEO-response mission, nor would it take the decision to conduct such a mission. Rather, SMPAG's role is to *prepare for a response* to NEO threats through information exchange, research option development, and planning activities.[97] SMPAG is not a space agency, or even a space actor *per se.* Nevertheless, SMPAG planning activities will be fundamental in any actual planetary defence space mission. According to its Terms of Reference, SMPAG's scope of work is limited to a few certain activities:

1. reference missions, technology roadmaps and collaborative research;
2. communication and exchange of information;
3. legal and policy aspects; and
4. mitigation planning activities.[98]

---

94 Austria (Austrian Research Promotion Agency – FFG), Belgium (BELSPO), China (CSA), Czechia, the European Space Agency (ESA), France (CNES), Germany (DLR), Israel (ISA), Italy (ASI), Japan (JAXA), Korea (KASI), Mexico (AEM), Pakistan (SUPARCO), Romania (ROSA), the Russian Federation (ROSCOSMOS), Ukraine (SSAU), the United Kingdom (UK Space Agency), and the United States of America (NASA). See List of SMPAG Members as of 18 October 2018, <www.cosmos.esa.int/web/smpag/smpag_members> accessed 25 February 2021.

95 The Association of Space Explorers (ASE), the Committee on Space Research (COSPAR), the European Southern Observatory (ESO), the International Academy of Astronautics (IAA), the International Astronomical Union (IAU), and the United Nations Office for Outer Space Affairs (UNOOSA) are granted observer status to SMPAG.

96 See in more detail chapter 4 'International Cooperation in Planetary Defence – UNCOPUOS, IAWN and SMPAG'; see also Romana Kofler, Gerhard Drolshagen, Line Drube, Alissa Haddaji, Lindley Johnson, Detlef Koschny and Rob Landis, 'International coordination on planetary defence: The work of the IAWN and the SMPAG' (2019) 156 Acta Astronautica 409–415.

97 Alan Harris, Line Drube and Lindley Johnson, 'SMPAG- Roadmap to relevant Research for Planetary Defense' (SMPAG/ESA Workplan Document 2019) 3–34.

98 SMPAG, 'Terms of Reference for the Near-Earth Object Threat Mitigation Space Mission Planning Advisory Group – Version 2.0' (13 September 2019) <www.cosmos.esa.int/web/smpag/terms_of_reference_v2> accessed 25 February 2021; see in more detail chapter 4 'International Cooperation in Planetary Defence – UNCOPUOS, IAWN and SMPAG' in this book.

As such, SMPAG may serve as a non-politicised, science and evidence-driven forum for the discussion of legal and policy issues in a more abstracted form, and before taking them into more politicised forums. Thus, SMPAG appears to be an appropriate venue for the voicing and discussion of many of the issues and topics of concern examined throughout this book.

Any specific cooperative activities endorsed by SMPAG could be implemented through arrangements negotiated among members, pursuant to their applicable legal requirements and instruments. Members are encouraged to exchange data resulting from their planetary defence programs, also as appropriate and consistent with their applicable legal requirements and instruments. Here, operational responsibilities and specific cooperative activities are contemplated. In the event of an actual and credible NEO threat, SMPAG will recommend "viable concepts for a possible mitigation campaign."[99]

4.1.2 SMPAG Procedures and Decision-Making

Even with its broad scope and ambitious mandate, SMPAG's structure and decision-making processes are quite modest. In terms of membership, SMPAG members include national space agencies, governmental or inter-governmental entities, and UN member state appointed space-related entities.[100] New SMPAG members are included upon consensus of the current SMPAG members.[101]

The organisational structure of SMPAG is a plenary group of delegates, along with a Steering Committee.[102] There also exists the possibility of the Steering Committee to establish working groups, as needed.[103] The SMPAG Steering Committee is permitted to organise SMPAG activities, revise the SMPAG Terms of Reference, establish and coordinate working group activities, define new areas of SMPAG activity, represent SMPAG at other organisations, and determine appropriate public release of SMPAG data, findings, and reports.[104]

Decisions by the SMPAG Steering Committee, other than the confirmation of the chair, are made on the basis of consensus.[105] Minority positions, if offered

99 See above ibid 3(4)(c) Mitigation planning activities.

100 Ibid 4, Membership, sentences 1–2.

101 Ibid 4, Membership, sentence 3.

102 Ibid 5, Organizational Structure.

103 Ibid.

104 Ibid 6, Steering Committee.

105 Romana Kofler, Gerhard Drolshagen, Line Drube, Alissa Haddaji, Lindley Johnson, Detlef Koschny and Rob Landis, 'International coordination on planetary defence: The work of the IAWN and the SMPAG' (2019) 156 Acta Astronautica 412.

in writing, are to be documented.[106] Consequently, it appears that SMPAG takes steps based on the decisions of its Steering Committee, and operates in all respects (except for determining who will chair the Steering Committee) by a process of consensus. Consensus is also the decision-making method of various other bodies to be considered in this chapter. While it means that any member can object to decisions, and thereby break consensus, it allows some smooth planning and execution of tasks, so long as there is a general will of the constituents, and perhaps pre-coordination amongst members. Additionally, because there are presently only eighteen members of SMPAG, consensus will be easier to achieve as compared to larger bodies.[107]

Balanced against this operation by consensus is a *caveat* contained in the SMPAG Terms and Conditions section of its Terms of Reference. It states:

> These ToR demonstrate the mutual interest of the Members of the SMPAG to exchange information on planetary defence and to develop recommended responses. These ToR do not establish any obligation or legal requirement to do so, nor do they establish any obligation to conduct any particular cooperative activity. Each Member shall provide its own funding and resources for its activities. These ToR may be modified or terminated by consensus of the Steering Committee.[108]

As such, while SMPAG may take a wide range of decisions and perform a wide variety of actions according to its purpose and scope of work, these actions in and of themselves do not establish any binding obligations or legal requirements on SMPAG members, or upon SMPAG itself. SMPAG serves as a platform or clearing-house for information-sharing, coordination, and mutual planning, but no more. However, this alone certainly fosters successive unilateral, bilateral, or multilateral arrangements and plans by SMPAG members to actually conduct NEO threat mitigation missions.

106 SMPAG, 'Terms of Reference for the Near-Earth Object Threat Mitigation Space Mission Planning Advisory Group – Version 2.0' (13 September 2019) <www.cosmos.esa.int/web/smpag/terms_of_reference_v2> accessed 25 February 2021.

107 One might compare the size of UNCOPUOS during the drafting and negotiations of the UN treaties on outer space, during the 1960s and 1970s, with its current size of close to 100 Member States.

108 See SMPAG, 'Terms of Reference for the Near-Earth Object Threat Mitigation Space Mission Planning Advisory Group V2.0' (13 September 2019) <https://www.cosmos.esa.int/web/smpag/terms-of-reference-v0, 9. Terms and Conditions> accessed 25 February 2021.

4.1.3 SMPAG Reference Missions – an Avenue to Address Law and Policy Issues?

According to its Terms of Reference, SMPAG can look at law and policy aspects of NEO threat responses.[109] Additionally, looking at both SMPAG's scope of work as including a desire to develop reference missions,[110] as well as mitigation planning activities,[111] there may be an avenue for SMPAG itself to begin to solve a variety of law and policy aspects of NEO threats. In developing both reference missions and mitigation planning activities, this work will of course consider and evaluate various technical aspects of NEO threat response, such as which technical paths to pursue.

However, and importantly, no reference mission or response plan is complete without considering the legal rights and responsibilities of its partners, including their obligations and risks. Consequently, any good reference mission developed by SMPAG will consider these aspects, and include proposed solutions (such as which state bears which risk, and how responsibility and liability should be apportioned if the mission fails to be executed according to plan) as a fundamental part of any NEO threat response scenario that it develops.

4.2 *Other Potential Advisory Groups*

As mentioned in chapter 4, the discussions and recommendations leading to the creation of SMPAG and IAWN also included additional recommendations which were not adopted or implemented. The report recommending their creation also suggested an impact disaster planning group to "link together existing national and international disaster response agencies to prepare coordinated response activities in case of both predicted and unexpected NEO impact disasters."[112] According to these recommendations, such a planning group could

a) Review lessons learned from earthquake, tsunami and other large-scale natural disasters to develop recommendations on how nations should

109 Ibid 3, Scope, at 3. Legal and policy aspects.

110 Ibid 3, Scope, at 1. Reference missions, technology roadmaps and collaborative research, especially "b. Develop and agree to a set of reference missions addressing a variety of potential NEO impact scenarios and deflection/disruption possibilities, including evaluations of various scenarios. These reference missions will facilitate realistic technical and resources and resource planning."

111 Ibid 3, Scope, at 4. Mitigation planning activities, especially "a. Recommend operational responsibilities for a space-based NEO mitigation campaign."

112 UNCOPUOS, 'Near Earth Objects, 2011–2012 – Recommendations of the Action Team on Near-Earth Objects for an international response to the near-Earth object impact threat' (21 December 2012), A/AC.105/C.1/L.329, 11 para. 49.

coordinate multination disaster response activities for both unexpected and predicted NEO impact disasters;

b) Identify research opportunities to enhance understanding of immediate and long-term effects of NEO impacts on humans, weather, environment, infrastructure and economies;

c) Sponsor, with the advice of IAWN, periodic exercises to build and test national and international responses to disasters that might result from asteroid impacts;

d) Develop recommendations, timelines and procedures for evacuating areas that would be affected by an impact.

However, at the time it was felt that these roles and responsibilities were already present in other United Nations groups, and this NEO impact planning group was not established. It is worth revisiting this decision and assessing whether the underlying assumptions behind it still hold, or whether a specific advisory group for these impact planning purposes ought to be established.

While this potential impact coordination advisory group would be focusing its work on the results of a potential NEO impact here on Earth, another advisory group could be looking upward and determining the mechanisms for deciding when and how to act upon NEO threats. A group with this type of mandate was also discussed in the early planning phases that lead to the creation of IAWN and SMPAG. Such a Mission Authorization and Oversight Group (MAOG) would determine thresholds for action and other issues, including

a) Determination of criteria and thresholds for action (for example, notification of a significant impact risk, initiation of observation and/or mitigation campaign);

b) Development of decision and event timelines for mitigation campaign analysis;

c) Distribution of coordinated actions for mitigation campaign operational responsibilities;

d) Identification of methods to engage designated national and international disaster response entities and utilize existing functions and infrastructures;

e) Development of detailed agreements on the implementation of a mitigation campaign to include NEO deflection disaster response activities;

f) Communication of the agreements to the international community through the relevant United Nations organizations[113]

113 Ibid, para 53.

This proposed Mission Authorization and Oversight Group was possibly seen as premature. However, in light of greater participation in the IAWN and SMPAG, it stands to reason that the international community revisit the possibility of these two groups, especially in light of the findings of the SMPAG Ad-hoc Working Group on Legal Issues.

5 Conclusion

The present chapter addressed international bodies necessary for any internationally-cooperative planetary defence initiatives and considered their applicable competencies and mandates. After having discussed various organs and sub-organs of the United Nations, it can be concluded that the UN Security Council may have a particularly important role in this context.

The Security Council, as the executive organ of the United Nations, has preeminent capacity to assure prompt and effective action, whenever facing threats to international peace and security. Interpreting the UN Charter one may conclude that the Security Council is not limited to exercise its powers in relation to violation of international law by a state,[114] enjoying quite some discretion when considering the existence of a threat to peace. A cosmic threat as significant as a NEO impact could produce significant hazard to the international order as a whole, with profound political, economic, and environmental consequences.

Member states shall, in accordance with the UN Charter, carry out the decisions of the Security Council. This could include cases of planetary defence actions. In view of Article 103 of the UN Charter binding decisions of the Security Council prevail over conflicting obligations under other international agreements, providing sufficient latitude to emergency actions, not only in relation to means of engagement but also with respect to the legal consequences. This could pave the way for decisions to authorise the use of NED in planetary defence and to waive the liability of launching states. Nevertheless, the power of the Security Council is not limitless, and the decision-making process may lead to complicated stalemates whenever facing sensitive issues.

In those cases, a resolution of the UN General Assembly may in fact prove to be an interesting alternative. Possibly based on discussions at UNCOPUOS, such a resolution (although not binding) could reflect a common understanding in

---

114 Erika de Wet, *The Chapter VII Powers of the United Nations Security Council* (Hart Publishing 2004) 183–184.

relation to planetary defence actions, authorising coordinated efforts. The consensus required at UNCOPUOS may represent an obstacle to decision making. However, at the General Assembly, a two thirds majority vote would be sufficient. Nevertheless, the General Assembly does not have the power to issue decisions countervailing provisions in other international treaties, in contrast to the Security Council under Article 103 of the Charter. It could thus not allow the use of NEDs or waive the liability of launching states.

The IAWN and SMPAG groups were discussed, and while these bodies might not have significant technical capacity themselves, they at least offer the opportunity for fostering and coordinating the significant technical capacity of their member organisations. As SMPAG operates by consensus and is specifically focused on NEO threat scenarios, it makes it a natural first forum for beginning and developing many of these conversations.

One benefit of discussions within SMPAG is that they regularly deal with concrete NEO threat scenarios. In that context, many issues – including obligations to warn, responsibility for precautions taken by others, thresholds for action, risks accepted and waived by undertaking NEO threat missions, and the desirability and legality of various technologies – are addressed and considered at both technical and policy/legal levels.

In closing, this chapter has stressed the idea that discussions and decisions in preparation for a NEO threat are warranted at an early stage, and that various international forums exist to carry them out, whether individually or in conjunction with others. Alternative courses of action shall be evaluated based not only on the applicable procedures, but also taking into account the international legitimacy and effectiveness of the respective body. Multilateral cooperation is key to develop actions capable of addressing cosmic threats in an effective manner. Due to its powers and strategic representation, the UN Security Council should be regarded as a prime instance for planetary defence initiatives. On the other hand, input from expert groups and working in consonance with other United Nations bodies would also be highly advisable.

Conclusions and Considerations on the Way Forward

Irmgard Marboe

1 Introduction

The previous 22 chapters of this book have dealt with a large range of issues, which have to be considered in the context of analysing the legal aspects of planetary defence. They help to get a better understanding of the interaction of scientific expertise and legal aspects, which is essential for preparing against potential NEO impacts. The collection of scientific data about asteroids and comets threatening the Earth is taking place in various parts of the world and represents an important starting point. However, the questions of what should be done with this information and how to proceed are not yet answered. Most importantly, it is not yet clear how future missions to deflect a NEO in order to avoid an impact on the Earth shall be planned and organised. The next steps on the way forward raise a number of legal and policy questions, which – based on the insights gained in this book – will be addressed in the following.

At the outset it will be highlighted that early international coordination and cooperation is required. While this is mandated from the technical perspective, it is also essential for addressing legal and policy questions. They need equally much time for coordination and agreement, in particular as this should take place at the international level. Many authors of this book have explicitly pointed out that an advance agreement on the terms and conditions of a future planetary defence mission would be highly desirable. Such an agreement should be made between states, as they are in the position to provide the necessary means – through their space agencies – and are responsible for activities carried in outer space and on celestial bodies under international law. The possible contents of such an advance agreement will be discussed in consideration of the choice of methods, responsibility, liability, and the involvement of private actors. The last part of the chapter will be dedicated to procedural question and aims at outlining suitable international instruments, which could fulfil this purpose.

 | DOI:10.1163/9789004467606_025

2 Early International Coordination and Cooperation Required

One of the recurring themes in the present book is that early international coordination and cooperation is essential. Planetary defence requires considerable expertise and multifaceted efforts, which can hardly be provided by one state alone. And they need time.[1] This is particularly true, when it comes to the preparation of a NEO deflection mission. Forces must be joined to address numerous technical and financial challenges, but also legal and policy risks. When a NEO impact threat becomes imminent, information-sharing and cooperation at the international level may even rise to an international obligation,[2] which early coordination would facilitate to implement.

Various countries have started activities for the detection of NEOs, the collection of information, and research on technologies suitable for potential future deflection missions.[3] International information exchange on these issues has developed within IAWN and SMPAG under the auspices of the United Nations since 2014.[4]

However, international coordination so far is primarily concerned with scientific and technical aspects. Legal and policy issues have hardly been discussed. It is not a coincidence that IAWN and SMPAG work under the auspices of the Scientific and Technical Subcommittee (STSC) of UNCOPUOS and not – as proposed by an expert report in 2010[5] – under the auspices of the Legal Subcommittee (LSC) of UNCOPUOS. The SMPAG Ad-hoc Working Group on Legal Issues (SMPAG Legal WG) was a first attempt to address this lacuna. The final report of 2020 represents a valuable first result of the discussion on legal and policy issues.[6] It also highlights the need for advance planning.

The obstacle to early coordination and cooperation in legal and policy terms is the lack of awareness of the problem. Why should one care about an event that may or may not occur in the future? Even if it might have catastrophic

1 See chapter 2 'What is Planetary Defence?' in this book.

2 See chapter 12 'International Law Rules Related to the Sharing of Information about Potential NEO Threats' and chapter 13 'Rules of International Law Regarding an Obligation of States to Undertake Planetary Defence Activities' in this book.

3 See, in particular, chapter 6 'The United States Planetary Defence Programme: NASA and the Planetary Defense Coordination Office', chapter 7 'ESA Activities in Planetary Defence', and chapter 8 'Planetary Defence Activities Beyond NASA and ESA' in this book.

4 See chapter 4 'International Cooperation in Planetary Defence – UNCOPUOS, IAWN and SMPAG' in this book.

5 See chapter 10 'The 2010 Report on Legal Aspects of NEO Threat Response and Related Institutional Issues' in this book.

6 See chapter 11 'The SMPAG Ad-hoc Working Group on Legal Issues' in this book.

consequences? The psychological attitude of mental blocking is described in this book as scotomisation or 'comprehension denial'.[7] Societies as a whole are rather unwilling to act when a potential threat is acknowledged, but no concrete danger or loss is imminent.[8] Specifically, they are reluctant to commit funds today to a recognised danger that has a low probability of occurring, but if it does occur, may have a very high cost to undefined people or nations in the indefinite future.[9]

This attitude represents the first hurdle that needs to be overcome. The Association of Space Explorers (ASE), consisting of former astronauts and cosmonauts, was the first to address the need to raise awareness of asteroid hazards and to develop the technical possibilities to mitigate them.[10] It initiated the 'Asteroid Day' on 30 June, which was proclaimed by the United Nations General Assembly in 2016. It aims at promoting events across the world to generate public interest in ongoing campaigns to detect potentially hazardous asteroids[11] and create public pressure on governments to support them. This may also prepare the ground for more difficult and politically sensitive discussions on how then to handle any actual threat.[12]

The good news is that – unlike scientific research on NEO detection and deflection techniques – coordination and cooperation on legal and policy aspects requires relatively small amounts of money. Sophisticated scientific hardware is not required, but merely meetings and communication of people with a mandate to discuss and prepare solutions for decision makers. As there are already existing fora where the competent people meet, in particular at the occasion of the sessions of UNCOPUOS and its two Subcommittees, it should not be an unsurmountable obstacle to devote some time for the discussion of international coordination and cooperation of a possible future NEO deflection mission.

7 See chapter 17 'Understanding the Social Aspects of an Asteroid Impact Threat from Socio-Anthropological Lessons Learned in Natural Disaster Management' in this book.

8 See also chapter 19 'Critical Issues and Future Perspectives on Liability in the Context of Planetary Defence' in this book.

9 Ibid.

10 See chapter 5 'Enhancing Public Awareness: The Establishment of "Asteroid Day"' in this book.

11 With respect to the definition of hazardous asteroids, comets, and NEOs, see chapter 1 'Near-Earth Objects – Basic Terms and Characteristics' in this book.

12 See chapter 5 'Enhancing Public Awareness: The Establishment of "Asteroid Day"' in this book.

3 Scope of an Advance Agreement between States

In order to diminish political concerns and to increase international acceptance for a planetary defence mission, the SMPAG Legal WG highlighted, in its report of 2020, that additional steps could be taken by states in advance.[13] It proposed a draft agreement by the state(s) willing to conduct the planetary defence mission and the potentially affected state(s). Such an advance agreementbetween states could lay down common procedures and elements of a mandate to undertake the mission, as well as liability considerations and modalities for the compensation of victims on the ground. In addition, the SMPAG Legal WG highlighted the need for the development of criteria and standards, such as for the selection of planetary defence methods.[14]

The present book has dealt in more detail with issues that should be agreed on beforehand between states in order to address legal uncertainties. It contains a number of suggestions about the possible contents of an advance agreement between states, which shall be summarised and considered in the following.

3.1 *Choice of NEO Deflection Method*

The choice of the NEO deflection method, in technical terms, is primarily determined by the available time.[15] When an asteroid threat is detected early, a range of different techniques is available. The common idea of most NEO impact mitigation technologies is the deflection of the asteroid or comet.[16]

The technologies to move a NEO from its original orbit discussed in the present book include slow push/pull methods and impulsive techniques.[17] In all cases some 'force' is used to achieve the envisaged result. However, such 'force' is not equivalent to the 'use of force' as it is defined and prohibited under Article 2(4) of the United Nations Charter.[18] The main reason is that the force applied – even by use of military technology including explosive devices – is not directed against the integrity and political independence of any state. This includes the effects of the force applied on the object. Consequently, even in the unfortunate event that the deflection mission is not (entirely) successful and the asteroid hits the Earth (at a different place), the effects will legally not

13 See chapter 11 'The SMPAG Ad-hoc Working Group on Legal Issues' in this book.
14 Ibid.
15 See chapter 3 'Planetary Defence Technologies' in this book.
16 Ibid.
17 Ibid.
18 See chapter 14 'The Use of Force and Planetary Defence' in this book.

be considered as resulting from the 'use of force' under the UN Charter and general international law. It would legally be regarded as 'damage' caused on the surface of the Earth, which is regulated under international space law.[19]

From the legal perspective, not only the slow push-pull technologies but also kinetic impactors used for planetary defence are not considered as 'weapons' under international law.[20] The so-called 'purpose'-test is applied which is based on the distinction between devices that are used as a weapon and those that are not. There is only one exception, namely nuclear explosive devices (NEDs). During the negotiations of the Limited Test Ban Treaty (1963) and the Nuclear Non-Proliferation Treaty (1968) it was discussed whether a nuclear explosion could be used for 'peaceful purposes', for example for civil engineering.[21] In both cases the result was that nuclear explosions are qualitatively different from all other explosive devices, because they are not only much more powerful but also much more threatening to global peace and security. In addition, devices used for peaceful nuclear explosions would be largely indistinguishable from nuclear weapons.[22] It follows that the 'purpose'-test, which is applied for the definition of a 'weapon' in general, is not applicable. NEDs are 'inherently' weapons. They are therefore not only prohibited by the two treaties mentioned above but also under Article IV of the Outer Space Treaty which prohibits the placing in orbit around the Earth any objects carrying nuclear weapons, install such weapons on celestial bodies, or station such weapons in outer space in any other manner.

Only if the time available is too short, a NED may be the only option because of the strong forces it can emit. Generally, it will not be used to blow up the asteroid but to deflect it from its path towards the Earth.[23] But even if that method were applied, the legal problems will remain. They could be avoided by early detection, preparation, and decision making in favour of other and legally unproblematic deflection techniques.

In the advance agreement between states the different techniques could be described and their thresholds established. Efforts in this respect are already

---

19 Ibid. On the relationship between general international law, including the UN Charter, and international space law, see chapter 9 'Overview of Current International Space Law in the Context of Planetary Defence' in this book.

20 Ibid. See also chapter 15 'Legal Aspects of the Use of Nuclear Explosive Devices in Planetary Defence' in this book.

21 See chapter 15 'Legal Aspects of the Use of Nuclear Explosive Devices in Planetary Defence' and chapter 16 on 'Nuclear Non-Proliferation and Planetary Defence: Competing Potential Disasters' in this book.

22 Ibid.

23 See chapter 3 'Planetary Defence Technologies' in this book.

undertaken within IAWN and SMPAG.[24] With the exception of NEDs, none of these would create legal problems radically different from traditional human activities in outer space. As the use of NEDs is entirely different from a legal point of view it should not be included in the list of available tools in the advance planning of NEO impact threat scenarios. It needs completely separate considerations, which will be addressed in more detail further below. For all other techniques, a variety of different legal issues could be considered in an advance agreement between states as will be discussed in the following.

3.2 *Liability*

Essentially, an advance agreement between states will be dedicated to risk management, most importantly the risk of liability.[25] Legal risks involve the question who will eventually be liable if something goes wrong. This is a question of utmost importance, because uncertainties about it may deter states and private operators from participating in or consenting to any NEO deflection mission.[26]

The challenge of legal risk management in the context of future planetary defence missions lies in the fact that they will entail a greater degree of uncertainty than traditional space activities.[27] Pertinent experience is likely to be missing to a large extent. Foreseeability will be diminished, and the potential consequences of failure or only partial success may be catastrophic. However, failure to act may also have catastrophic consequences. The question of causation will therefore play a central role in delineating liability.

3.2.1 The Concept of the 'Launching State'

Under current international space law, liability for damage caused by space objects on the surface of Earth or to aircraft in flight is unlimited in time and in financial terms. The burden has to be carried by the 'launching state', which is defined under international space law as a state which launches or procures the launching of an object into outer space, and each state from whose territory or facility an object is launched.[28] This broad definition, in particular by

24 See chapter 4 'International Cooperation in Planetary Defence – UNCOPUOS, IAWN and SMPAG' in this book.

25 See chapter 18 'The Current International Space Law Regime on Liability and Its Application to Planetary Defence' in this book.

26 Ibid. See also chapter 19 'Critical Issues and Future Perspectives on Liability in the Context of Planetary Defence' in this book.

27 See chapter 18 'The Current International Space Law Regime on Liability and Its Application to Planetary Defence' in this book.

28 Article VII, Outer Space Treaty. The same definition is also contained in Article I, Liability Convention and Article I, Registration Convention.

the term 'procure', shall ensure that up to four launching states may be jointly and severally liable for the damage caused by a space object to a third party.[29] This victim-oriented approach is based on the understanding that the freedom of states to carry out space activities shall not be to the detriment of others.[30]

However, planetary defence activities are not entirely fitting to the classical distinction between benefits and burdens of the liability regime.[31] They are ultimately carried out for the benefit of the international community at large. In a planetary defence scenario it is therefore not so clear who is the 'launching state' – and thus burden-bearer – and who is a 'third party' – and thus the protected victim.

The SMPAG Legal WG report of 2020 outlined some ideas of how the dichotomy between 'launching state' and 'third party' could be addressed in an advance agreement between states. It suggested that, in addition to the states directly carrying out a planetary defence mission, states which are threatened by a NEO impact and ask for, or agree to, conducting a planetary defence mission may also be regarded as states 'procuring' the launch. This result could be achieved by an expansive interpretation of the term 'to procure', which would include the meaning of 'to prompt' or 'to trigger'.[32]

Such an expansive interpretation of the term 'procure' would reverse the role of the requesting state from a 'third party' to a 'launching state', which not only does not receive compensation for damage, but even incurs liability for damage. If this interpretation is conceived as too far-reaching, it still could be suggested that a requesting state should not be regarded as a 'third party' either and not benefit from the full protection of the space law liability regime.[33]

A third group of states needs to be considered in an advance agreement, namely states which are neither directly involved in carrying out the mission nor directly affected by the NEO threat, but still generally supporting and potentially benefitting from a successful planetary defence mission. The question should be addressed whether these states should be qualified or not as classical 'third parties' entitled to full compensation for damage if the mission is not (entirely) successful.[34]

---

29 Article V, Liability Convention.

30 See chapter 18 'The Current International Space Law Regime on Liability and Its Application to Planetary Defence' in this book.

31 See chapter 18 'The Current International Space Law Regime on Liability and Its Application to Planetary Defence' in this book.

32 See SMPAG LWG Report 55.

33 Ibid. See also chapter 18 'The Current International Space Law Regime on Liability and Its Application to Planetary Defence' in this book.

34 See ibid.

In order to implement the above suggestions to enlarge the concept of the 'launching state' and to reduce the circle of 'third parties' of the current space law liability regime, an international binding agreement between states would be the optimal solution to avoid uncertainties. If this cannot be achieved, an alternative way of expressing international support for this solution could be a resolution of the UN General Assembly or the UN Security Council. The former would only represent a 'recommendation', but could nevertheless provide guidance for states in the interpretation and application of the space treaties.[35] The latter would create more legal certainty as it could override the exiting liability regime.[36]

3.2.2 The Concept of 'Damage'

The current space law liability regime is based on the occurrence of 'damage'. The question for legal risk management would be to envisage which kind of damage may occur in the course of a planetary defence mission and which one requires advance regulation.

Various scenarios have been outlined in the present book: (1) the planetary defence spacecraft causes damage before it reaches its target, for example by colliding with another space object, by exploding and causing a debris cloud or by impacting the Earth; (2) the mission fails and the NEO causes damage on Earth as originally predicted; (3) the mission causes damage on Earth different from the damage originally predicted; (4) the mission causes destruction on or to the NEO creating fragments; and (5) damage caused by the NEO because of the failure to undertake a planetary defence mission (that could have been possible), or because the mission is undertaken too late, or in the wrong manner.[37]

Some of these types of damage are covered under the space law liability regime, others may play a role in a contractual or legal arrangement between involved parties. Others may give rise to international responsibility or liability on other grounds. An advance agreement should identify them and provide solutions on how to address them.

35 A UN General Assembly resolution can even evolve into customary law, when the support by states is strong so that it can be considered as being representative of *opinio iuris*, and when state practice follows.

36 See chapter 22 'International Bodies and Procedures for Decision-Making Regarding Planetary Defence Actions'; see also further below in this chapter on the powers of the UN General Assembly and the UN Security Council.

37 See chapter 18 'The Current International Space Law Regime on Liability and Its Application to Planetary Defence' in this book.

3.2.3 The Question of 'Causation'

The duty to compensate for damage under the existing space law liability regime depends on the demonstration that the damage results from a given human-made space object.[38] Damage caused by a NEO – without any human intervention and absent any other agreement between states – does not trigger liability. However, if a NEO causes damage as the result of an intervention by a human-made space object, the situation becomes more complex. It raises the question to what extent the damage was 'caused by a space object'. The interaction of natural forces and human action may present considerable evidentiary challenges. These are not alleviated by the existing strict liability regime (for damage caused on Earth), which does not require 'fault'. It is still necessary to establish that the damage was actually caused by a particular space object.

In an advance agreement it could be regulated how data and information should be collected to gain the respective evidence for establishing causation. It could also be addressed how the identification of the incidental source, the attribution of particular damage to a particular source, and potential cumulative effects during the chain of events could be analysed.[39]

3.2.4 The Question of 'Fault'

'Fault' under the current space law liability regime is only relevant, if damage is caused to *other space objects in outer space*. Liability of the launching state is triggered when such damage is caused by a planetary defence mission or the deflected NEO, if the damage is due to the fault of the launching state or the fault of persons for whom it is responsible. In the absence of detailed regulation and practice, it remains to be clarified what constitutes 'fault' in this context. The SMPAG Legal WG suggests to develop a general understanding of what may constitute fault in terms of (1) planetary defence space mission planning and implementation (execution); (2) choice of planetary defence methods; (3) planetary defence standards, procedures and requirements; and (4) international coordination and information sharing.[40]

An important factor in this context will be the novelty and the rarity of any planetary defence mission, coupled with the elevated risk.[41] The respective benchmarks could help to clarify the notion of fault in the future. An

---

38 SMPAG LWG Report 52.

39 See chapter 18 'The Current International Space Law Regime on Liability and Its Application to Planetary Defence' in this book.

40 SMPAG LWG Report 53.

41 See chapter 18 'The Current International Space Law Regime on Liability and Its Application to Planetary Defence' in this book.

international understanding on them may protect both those carrying out planetary defence activities and those suffering damage from such activities.[42]

3.2.5 Compensation without Liability

Even though alleviating the burden of liability from potential launching states will be an important aim of an advance coordination and cooperation of states, provision should nevertheless also be made for the compensation of victims. Ultimately, the consent of states to a mission as envisaged above would amount to a renunciation of their liability claims they would have otherwise and leave potential victims without protection. This should be avoided, not the least to receive the consent of states for planetary defence missions in the first place. There needs to be an alternative protection of victims.

This book has addressed alternative ways of dealing with liability for hazards. The proposed advance agreementwould probably not directly address specific liability solutions since they may vary with the type of planetary defence mission. Nevertheless, it could envisage principles and approaches for solving the problem of compensation for victims. Such solutions could range from establishing specific limits to potential liabilities of participating states, dedicated funded insurance (either public or private) reserves, or a formula for after-the-fact taxation on the participating states.[43]

3.3 *Responsibility*

Any possible violation of international law in the course of a planetary defence mission may trigger responsibility of the state to which it is attributable. The SMPAG Legal WG report explained the difference between liability and responsibility as follows:

> [A] State may be held internationally responsible for a wrongful act although there is no material damage; a State may be held internationally liable for damage caused although it did not act wrongfully.[44]

The potential violations of international law during a planetary defence mission are numerous. They include, in particular, obligations of states concerning non-intervention, self-determination, human rights, and environmental

42 SMPAG LWG Report 54.

43 See chapter 19 'Critical Issues and Future Perspectives on Liability in the Context of Planetary Defence' in this book.

44 SMPAG LWG Report 37.

law. In addition, provisions of the Outer Space Treaty, mainly those contained in Articles I, II, IV, IX, and XI, are relevant.[45]

A special feature of international space law – as opposed to general international law – is the 'international responsibility' of states for national activities in outer space carried out by 'non-governmental entities' under Article VI of the Outer Space Treaty. This is significant when private actors are involved in planetary defence activities, because the breach of international law committed by private actors in outer space shall be directly attributed to the appropriate state.[46]

On the other hand, the law of state responsibility recognises that there may be circumstances in which compliance with international law is not feasible.[47] The so-called 'circumstances precluding wrongfulness' are instances that are expected to occur only rarely, but can excuse the violation of an international obligation.[48] However, utmost care should be applied in resorting to the invocation of circumstances precluding wrongfulness in order to limit their operation to exceptional cases in the interest of maintaining the full validity of international law.[49]

'Consent' and 'necessity' have been identified as the most appropriate circumstances precluding wrongfulness in the context of planetary defence in the present book.[50] In order to avoid uncertainty, any concern and abuse, an international agreement or mandate is highly recommended.[51] This means that an advance agreement between states should aim at defining as clearly as possible, which prerequisites must be fulfilled that the states potentially injured by a planetary defence mission could be assumed to have 'consented', and which conditions of 'necessity' would justify a deviation from international obligations that otherwise would need to be respected. The latter conditions would have to reflect the criteria established under general international law, namely to encompass exceptional cases where the only way to safeguard

45 See chapter 20 'The International Responsibility of States for Planetary Defence Activities' in this book.

46 Ibid.

47 Articles 21 to 27, Articles on the International Responsibility of States for Internationally Wrongful Acts, UNGA Res 56/83, Annex (12 December 2001) (ILC Articles on State Responsibility).

48 See chapter 20 'The International Responsibility of States for Planetary Defence Activities' in this book.

49 SMPAG LWG Report 37.

50 See chapter 20 'The International Responsibility of States for Planetary Defence Activities' in this book.

51 Ibid.

an essential interest of the state(s) in question or of the international community as a whole threatened by a grave and imminent peril is not to perform other international obligations of lesser urgency.[52]

3.4 *Private Actors*

Private actors may assume important roles in planetary defence. Starting from awareness raising, data collection and knowledge creation about the location and nature of hazardous asteroids, the contribution to civil protection measures in the prevention of and response to a NEO impact as well as potential reconstruction efforts, until active participation in NEO deflection missions.[53] Due to the significant input of private actors their active participation in the planning and preparation of planetary defence activities should be considered at an early stage.[54]

If private actors are involved in planetary defence missions, they must be made subject to governmental oversight and comply with applicable national space legislation (in particular by authorisation and continuing supervision by the appropriate state in accordance with Article VI of the Outer Space Treaty).[55] In this way, the responsible state would ensure that the private activities are carried out in compliance with the international obligations of that state.

The involvement of private actors in NEO deflection missions needs to reflect the specific rules that international space law embodies for non-governmental entities in general. Essentially, they pertain to state responsibility and therefore are closely related to the primary obligations of states relevant to NEOs and corresponding deflection missions addressed in this book.[56] Beyond the *status quo*, any further legal development related to the requirements for planetary defence, including the possible development of safety standards, would have to be taken into account for considerations of state responsibility as well as for the involvement and of private actors.[57]

---

52 Ibid.

53 See chapter 21 'The Involvement of Private Actors in Planetary Defence Missions' in this book. See also chapter 5 'Enhancing Public Awareness: The Establishment of "Asteroid Day"' and chapter 17 'Understanding the Social Aspects of an Asteroid Impact Threat from Socio-Anthropological Lessons Learned in Natural Disaster Management' in this book.

54 See, in particular, chapter 17 'Understanding the Social Aspects of an Asteroid Impact Threat from Socio-Anthropological Lessons Learned in Natural Disaster Management' in this book.

55 SMPAG LWG Report 44.

56 See chapter 21 'The Involvement of Private Actors in Planetary Defence Missions' in this book.

57 Ibid. See also SMPAG LWG Report 45.

4 Appropriate Form and Forum

An in-depth discussion on the appropriate form and forum for decision-making took place in the framework of a research project which was presented to UNCOPUOS in 2010.[58] The report of the project recommended to soon start discussions within the framework and the present structure of the United Nations, taking into consideration the roles of the Security Council and the General Assembly, as to whether and how to develop an international decision-making framework.[59] It recommended, in particular, to institute a working group by UNCOPUOS, notably by the Legal Subcommittee in close consultation with the Scientific and Technical Subcommittee, to further investigate, discuss, and develop the various options available.[60]

Within the United Nations, a process had already started in 1995 and eventually led to the establishment of the International Asteroid Warning Network (IAWN) and the Space Mission Planning Advisory Group (SMPAG) in 2013.[61] However, these groups do not operate under the auspices of the Legal Subcommittee, but report to the Scientific and Technical Subcommittee of UNCOPUOS. This shows the emphasis on scientific and technical matters of planetary defence rather than on the legal and policy ones.

However, there are elements in the mandate of SMPAG,which point into the pertinent direction. As per its Terms of Reference SMPAG shall develop cooperative activities among its members and build consensus on recommendations for planetary defence measure, including on 'Legal and Policy Issues':

> Identify for possible detailed review within appropriate forums any legal and policy issues (e.g., liabilities) that may arise in undertaking NEO mitigation actions or selecting any likely mitigation options.[62]

SMPAG therefore could develop a proposal for an advance agreement between states on planetary defence measure, which could contain the most important elements for consideration and include suggestions on solutions. In the

58 See chapter 10 'The 2010 Report on Legal Aspects of NEO Threat Response and Related Institutional Issues' in this book.

59 Ibid.

60 Ibid.

61 See chapter 4 'International Cooperation in Planetary Defence – UNCOPUOS, IAWN and SMPAG' in this book.

62 Ibid.

following it will be discussed, how SMPAG could advance such a proposal and which further steps on the way forward can be envisaged.

4.1 *The Role of SMPAG, STSC, and UNCOPUOS*

Under the current working methods and mandates, SMPAG could present its proposal for an advance agreement among states to the Scientific and Technical Subcommittee and to UNCOPUOS.[63] A discussion could follow, whether the establishment of a dedicated working group would be feasible and useful. It could also be considered to involve the Legal Subcommittee, in addition to the Scientific and Technical Subcommittee. Arguments in favour of a working group would include the traditional practice to establish working groups in similarly important projects, which need deeper considerations of a topic.[64] Furthermore, representation of UN members is broader in UNCOPUOS with its 95 members,[65] while SMPAG only consists of eighteen national and regional space agencies as members and some space-related organisations as observers.[66]

In any event, the discussion in UNCOPUOS and its Subcommittees, including a possible working group, would need specific expertise and experience both in technical and legal terms. Most probably, they would recur to the expert knowledge represented in IAWN and SMPAG instead of looking for expertise outside. Eventually, a text for a proposal for an advance agreementbetween states would be discussed by the main committee of UNCOPUOS, which operates on the basis of consensus.[67] The 95 UNCOPUOS members, which

63 See chapter 4 'International Cooperation in Planetary Defence – UNCOPUOS, IAWN and SMPAG' in this book.

64 See, for example, the establishment of the Working Group on the Long-term Sustainability of Outer Space Activities in 2010. UNCOPUOS, 'Report of the Scientific and Technical Subcommittee on its forty-seventh session' (8–19 February 2010) UN Doc. A/AC.105/958, para 181.

65 'Members of the Committee on the Peaceful Uses of Outer Space' (*United Nations Office for Outer Space Affairs*) <https://www.unoosa.org/oosa/en/members/index.html> accessed 17 March 2021.

66 SMPAG members are AEM (Mexico), ASI (Italy), FFG (Austria), Belspo (Belgium), CNES (France), CNSA (China), Czech Republic, DLR (Germany), ESA, ISA (Israel), JAXA (Japan), KASI (Republic of Korea), NASA (USA), ROSA (Romania), ROSCOSMOS (Russian Federation), SSAU (Ukraine), SUPARCO (Pakistan), UKSA (UK) and IAWN (ex officio). SMPAG observers include the Association of Space Explorers (ASE), European Southern Observatory (ESO), International Academy of Astronautics (IAA), International Astronomical Union (IAU), and the United Nations Office for Outer Space Affairs (UNOOSA). See 'SMPAG' (*United Nations Office for Outer Space Affairs*) <https://www.unoosa.org/oosa/en/ourwork/topics/neos/smpag.html> accessed 17 March 2021.

67 See chapter 22 'International Bodies and Procedures for Decision-Making Regarding Planetary Defence Actions' in this book.

participate in the discussion, represent those states that have so far shown an interest in international coordination and cooperation of space activities in the framework of the United Nations. This forum therefore seems to be suitable to discuss in depth the legal and policy considerations with respect to the proposed advance agreement.

UNCOPUOS would also decide in which format a proposed advance agreement would be put in front of the General Assembly. This could be done as a proposal for a dedicated stand-alone General Assembly resolution. The alternative, to add it to the annual resolution on International Cooperation in the Peaceful Uses of Outer Space[68] as an annex, would also be possible.

Even though a resolution of the General Assembly will not have a legally binding effect, it would still be the result of a joint effort of the international community represented in the United Nations, with the inclusion of expert advice from IAWN and SMAPG. It could provide a coordinated multilateral basis for the further planning and preparing of future activities in the area of planetary defence, as opposed to uncoordinated unilateral actions taken by one state or only a small group of states.

4.2 *Legal Value of a UN General Assembly Resolution*

A General Assembly resolution would be regarded as a 'recommendation' in accordance with Articles 10, 11, 12, or 13 of the United Nations Charter.[69] Whatever legal basis is chosen, a resolution by the General Assembly will not have a legally binding effect and not create international obligations for states. It is not binding upon them but expresses an exhortation, a desire.[70] Despite the lack of legally binding effect, a General Assembly resolution is not only a political statement but has also some legal value. This is why it is sometimes denoted as a 'soft law'-instrument.[71]

First, as it is outlined in numerous books and articles on international law,[72] a General Assembly resolution may serve as the starting point for the

---

68 See, for example, International Cooperation in the Peaceful Uses of Outer Space, UNGA Resolution 74/82 (13 December 2019) UN Doc A/Res/74/82.

69 See chapter 22 'International Bodies and Procedures for Decision-Making Regarding Planetary Defence Actions' in this book.

70 See Eckart Klein and Stefanie Schmahl, 'Ch.IV The General Assembly, Functions and Powers, Article 10' in Bruno Simma and others (eds), *The Charter of the United Nations: A Commentary* (3rd edn, Oxford University Press 2012) vol I 463, 480.

71 Frans von der Dunk, '*Contradictio in terminis* or Realpolitik? A Qualified Plea for a Role of "Soft Law" in the Development of International Space Law' in Irmgard Marboe (ed), *Soft Law in Outer Space* (Böhlau 2012) 31, 48–56.

72 For example, Malcolm N Shaw, *International Law* (8th edn, Cambridge University Press 2017) 84–86; Anthea Roberts and Sandesh Sivakumarani, 'The Theory and Reality of the

development of an international treaty. Once agreement is achieved among states on the formulation of certain pieces of texts, it is not any more excluded that the states can also agree on a binding instrument, which they are ready to observe. The most prominent examples include the Universal Declaration on Human Rights, which paved the way for the subsequent two Covenants on Human Rights,[73] and, indeed, the Declaration on Legal Principles Governing the Activities of States in the Exploration and Use of Outer Space of 1963, which prepared the ground for the Outer Space Treaty of 1967 with almost identical text.[74] However, at the moment the political will of states to conclude treaties on matters relating to the use of outer space is rather limited.[75] Nevertheless, it cannot be excluded that this situation may change in the future, and perhaps it is possible in view of the risk of a NEO impact threat. When states are becoming more aware of this risk, they may gratefully turn to the text of the General Assembly resolution and not only regard it as valuable guidance, but also find merit in formally accepting its provisions as binding obligations under international law by concluding a treaty with identical or similar text. This would certainly serve legal security and clarify particular issues which would involve a new interpretation or even deviation from existing international law, for example as regards absolute liability of the launching state(s) for damage caused on Earth or to aircraft in flight.

Secondly, General Assembly resolutions can be representative of *opinio iuris*, which denotes the legal opinion of states that provisions contained in the text represent legally binding obligations under international law (as opposed to only recommendations). Such a conviction has to be reflected in 'state practice', the other element in the creation of customary international law.[76] The intensity required of state practice varies depending on the circumstances. According to the ICJ, state practice of the state 'whose interests are specifically

Sources of International Law' in Malcom D Evans (ed) *International Law* (5th edn, Oxford University Press 2018) 102–103; Christopher C Joyner, 'U.N. General Assembly Resolutions and International Law: Rethinking the Contemporary Dynamics of Norm-Creation' (1981) 11 California Western International Law Journal 469; Steven Freeland, 'For Better or for Worse? The Use of 'Soft Law' in the International Legal Regulation of Outer Space'(2011) XXXVI Annals of Air and Space Law 437.

73 Bertrand G Ramcharan, 'The Foundations' in Carla Ferstman and others (eds) *Contemporary Human Rights Challenges: The Universal Declaration of Human Rights and its Continuing Relevance* (Routledge 2019) 9.

74 See in more detail chapter 9 'Overview of Current International Space Law in the Context of Planetary Defence' in this book.

75 See ibid.

76 See Article 38(1)(b), Statute of the International Court of Justice (18 April 1946) 33 UNTS 993.

affected' or of the state 'concerned' is a decisive element.[77] In the context of planetary defence this could mean that the practice of those states that are actively involved in the planning and preparation of NEO deflection missions is decisive. They must not only follow the respective practice, but do so because they consider it to be their duty and not merely for altruistic motives on a voluntary basis. Whether the future General Assembly resolution on an advance agreement on planetary defence will meet the criteria of being susceptible of representing *opinio iuris* depends to a large extent on the wording of the resolution. If the provisions are more strictly formulated and frequently contain the word 'shall', this is more likely than if the resolution emphasises the 'voluntary' nature of its provisions.

Thirdly, the legal value of a recommendation by the General Assembly also includes that a state which takes action in accordance with it is presumed to act lawfully.[78] This presumption of lawfulness is a valuable aspect for any state in situations of uncertainty. If a situation is not yet regulated under international law and the state is not certain how its intended behaviour will be judged by others, the state is well advised to base its action on a General Assembly resolution, if available. This has the legal effect of shifting the burden of proof. As a consequence, any state wanting to challenge the lawfulness of the state's action must prove the unlawfulness. This may provide a certain amount of comfort for states willing to engage in risky and uncertain NEO deflection missions. The same holds true for states, which need to decide to cooperate in or to approve such missions. It follows that states are relatively safe as regards the lawfulness of their behaviour as long as they remain within the limits of a recommendation by the General Assembly in a resolution.

Fourthly, an advance agreement on planetary defence endorsed by the General Assembly may be regarded as 'consent' for the purposes of state responsibility. As pointed out in this book, 'consent' may play a relevant role, because it precludes the wrongfulness of an act of a state.[79] When a state validly

---

77 *North-Sea Continental Shelf Cases* (*Germany v Denmark/ Germany v Netherlands*) (Merits) [1969] ICJ Rep 1969, 74, para 77: "The States concerned must therefore feel that they are conforming to what amounts to a legal obligation." Alex G Oude Elferink, 'North Sea Continental Shelf Cases', *Max Planck Encyclopaedia of Public International Law* (Oxford University Press 2013) para 9.

78 See James Crawford, *Brownlie's Principles of Public International Law* (Oxford University Press 2019) 40.

79 See Article 20 of the Articles on the International Responsibility of States for Internationally Wrongful Acts, UNGA Res 56/83, Annex (12 December 2001). See also chapter 20 'The International Responsibility of States for Planetary Defence Activities' in this book.

gives its consent to the commission by another state of a specific act not in conformity with an obligation of the latter state towards the former state, the wrongfulness of the act in relation to that state is precluded to the extent that the act remains within the limits of the consent. This means that a NEO deflection mission which follows the recommendations of the General Assembly resolution would be covered by the consent given by the respective states in their voting behaviour. The limits to the consent given therefore depend on (a) the terms of the resolution, the (b) actual support by states (adoption by consensus or vote), and (c) objective criteria for valid consent under international law, which exclude, for example, consent to the violation of *ius cogens* obligations.[80]

Fifthly, the terms of a General Assembly resolution may be relevant for the determination of criteria of 'necessity', which constitutes another circumstance precluding wrongfulness under the international law of state responsibility.[81] The circumstance of necessity refers to exceptional cases where the only way for a state to safeguard an essential interest of its own from a grave and imminent peril is not to perform the respective obligation, provided that this does not seriously impair an essential interest of other states or the international community as a whole. Considering that the peril must be objectively established, the involvement of an international mechanism seems to be appropriate in order to avoid any concern and abuse.[82]

Despite these legal aspects or consequences of General Assembly resolutions it must be kept in mind that they cannot create international law. Most importantly, a General Assembly resolution cannot change existing treaty obligations, which will require a resolution by the Security Council. In the context of planetary defence this is primarily relevant, when – because of lack of time – the use of NEDs is considered as the only technology capable of deflecting a NEO approaching the Earth. In this scenario it is noteworthy that the

80 *Ius cogens* or peremtory norms of general international law are norms accepted and recognized by the international community of states as a whole as norms from which no derogation is permitted and which can be modified only by subsequent norms of general international law having the same character. See Article 53, Vienna Convention on the Law of Treaties (adopted 23 May 1969, entered in to force 27 January 1980) 1115 UNTS 331.

81 See chapter 20 'The International Responsibility of States for Planetary Defence Activities' in this book.

82 Ibid.

General Assembly may make recommendations not only to the member states but also to the Security Council.[83]

4.3 *The Role of the United Nations Security Council*

The Security Council has the power to take decisions, which are binding upon the members of the United Nations.[84] It has been argued in the present book that a potential NEO impact may represent a threat to international peace and security.[85] This would be especially the case, if relatively little time is available and actions need to be taken quickly. The Security Council has considerable discretion in its determination what constitutes a threat to international peace and security,[86] so that also early action is possible if its attention is raised and the geopolitical situation is favourable.

Even in the absence of an imminent NEO impact threat, the Security Council could take a decision on legal and policy aspects of planetary defence. Based on the considerations above with respect to a possible resolution by the General Assembly it could decide on a general legal framework for planetary defence activities in advance. Such a framework could be based on or complement a respective previous General Assembly resolution. It would have the advantage of being binding upon all states and therefore create legal certainty about issues which are specific to planetary defence and arguably not appropriately regulated under general international law or international space law. The Security Council decisions would even prevail over conflicting obligations in other treaties, such as the Outer Space Treaty and the Liability Convention, in accordance with Article 103 of the United Nations Charter.[87]

Furthermore, the Security Council could also limit itself to the authorisation of specific measures in response to a dangerous asteroid or comet, in

83 See Articles 10 and 11, UN Charter. Eckart Klein and Stefanie Schmahl, 'Ch.IV The General Assembly, Functions and Powers, Article 10' in Bruno Simma and others (eds), *The Charter of the United Nations: A Commentary* (3rd edn, Oxford University Press 2012) vol I 463, 480; Eckart Klein and Stefanie Schmahl, 'Ch.IV The General Assembly, Functions and Powers, Article 11' in Bruno Simma and others (eds), *The Charter of the United Nations: A Commentary* (3rd edn, Oxford University Press 2012) vol I 491, 492–493.

84 Article 25, UN Charter. See chapter 22 'International Bodies and Procedures for Decision-Making Regarding Planetary Defence Actions' in this book.

85 See chapter 15 'Legal Aspects of the Use of Nuclear Explosive Devices in Planetary Defence', Chapter 16 'Nuclear Non-Proliferation and Planetary Defence: Competing Potential Disasters', and chapter 22 'International Bodies and Procedures for Decision-Making Regarding Planetary Defence Actions' in this book.

86 See chapter 22 'International Bodies and Procedures for Decision-Making Regarding Planetary Defence Actions' in this book.

87 Ibid.

particular when time is short. This brings in the situation where the use of NEDs as a means for deflecting a NEO from its orbit may be the only realistic method available in the very unlikely event of the late discovery of a relatively large hazardous object.[88] The authorisation to the use NEDs for an explosion in outer space would, however, be in conflict with the Limited Test Ban Treaty of 1963[89] and highly problematic with respect to the Non-Proliferation Treaty of 1968.[90]

While the Security Council is a political organ, its discretion in decision-making is not unlimited. In particular, in conflicts with existing treaty obligations the exercise of its powers under Article 103 should be understood as 'last resort' if all other efforts for interpreting conflicting binding provisions fail.[91] The aim of Article 103 of the Charter is to maintain the coherence and the unity of the international legal system under the umbrella of the Charter.[92] In the context of a potential use of NEDs the Security Council must balance the competing risks caused to humanity by an imminent NEO impact threat and the threat to international peace and security emanating from the proliferation of nuclear weapons.[93] Most importantly, it needs to be considered that the international system of nuclear non-proliferation under the Non-Proliferation Treaty rests on the distinction of nuclear weapon states and non-nuclear-weapon states.[94] It is therefore important that this distinction is not blurred by a Security Council resolution. Non-nuclear weapon states should not be indirectly authorised to participate in the respective planetary defence activity.

From the system of nuclear non-proliferation under the Non-Proliferation Treaty follows that the authorisation by the Security Council to use NEDs in planetary defence cannot be given in advance. Before the NEO impact threat is imminent the ensuing dangers and threats to international peace and security are not known. The competing threats cannot be balanced. In addition, it is

88 See chapter 3 'Planetary Defence Technologies' in this book.

89 See chapter 15 'Legal Aspects of the Use of Nuclear Explosive Devices in Planetary Defence' in this book.

90 See chapter 16 'Nuclear Non-Proliferation and Planetary Defence: Competing Potential Disasters' in this book.

91 See Johann Ruben Leiæ and Andreas Paulus, 'Ch.XVI Miscellaneous Provisions, Article 103' in Bruno Simma and others (eds), *The Charter of the United Nations: A Commentary* (Oxford University Press 2012) vol II 2114. See also chapter 22 'International Bodies and Procedures for Decision-Making Regarding Planetary Defence Actions' in this book.

92 Ibid.

93 See chapter 16 'Nuclear Non-Proliferation and Planetary Defence: Competing Potential Disasters' in this book.

94 Ibid.

entirely uncertain whether the Security Council would take such a decision for unrelated geopolitical reasons. The right to veto by any of the five permanent members may forestall a decision in this respect at any time.

The use of NEDs for deflecting or disrupting a NEO approaching the Earth is therefore the technology least likely to be lawfully applied. It is unpredictable whether the Security Council will ultimately come to the conclusion that this would constitute an appropriate technology to achieve the planned objective or whether for a variety of other reasons it would refrain from an authorisation, even if it could do so under Article 24 of the Charter.

On the other hand, the role of the Security Council in helping to create, in advance, a legal framework for planetary defence activities using other technologies could be further explored. Whether or not instigated by a prior resolution of the General Assembly, a Security Council resolution could provide legal certainty on several issues described in this book and remove concerns by states, even before a NEO threat becomes imminent.

5 Conclusion

This last chapter of the book has summarised the main findings contained in the different chapters and attempted to draw conclusions on the way forward. While scientific and technical progress is advancing, the solution of legal and policy questions becomes ever more pressing. The book has shown that some ground has been prepared in the framework of the United Nations, but further actions are required. The activities of IAWN and SMPAG need to be complemented by legal and policy evaluations to allow swifter progress in the development of a proposal for an advance agreement between states, as it has been advocated by many authors in this book. For this purpose, the work of the SMPAG Ad-hoc Working Group on Legal Issues could be useful. However, it would also be important that UNCOPUOS and its two Subcommittees, the long-established and experienced fora within the United Nations, give this topic higher priority on their agenda and create the necessary dynamics for the development of an appropriate international instrument to provide the legal and policy framework which would oust uncertainties and alleviate concerns in the planning and coordination of planetary defence activities.

Index

www.ingramcontent.com/pod-product-compliance
Lightning Source LLC
LaVergne TN
LVHW020631300926
849161LV00004B/667
9789004467590